POLICE USE OF FORCE UNDER INTERNATIONAL LAW

Policing is commonly thought to be governed by domestic legal systems and not international law. However, various international legal standards are shown to have an impact in situations where police use force. *Police Use of Force under International Law* explores this tension in detail for the first time. It critically reviews the use of force by law enforcement agencies in a range of scenarios: against detainees, during protests, in counter-terrorism and counterpiracy operations, as well as during everyday policing. Key trends, such as the growing use of private security services, are also considered. This book provides a human rights framework for police weaponry and protection of at-risk groups based on critical jurisprudence from the last twenty years. With pertinent case law and case studies to illustrate the key principles of the use of force, this book is essential reading for anyone interested in policing, human rights, state use of force or criminology.

STUART CASEY-MASLEN is Honorary Professor at the Faculty of Law of the University of Pretoria. He holds a doctorate in international humanitarian law, a master's degree in international human rights law, and a master's degree in forensic ballistics. He was formerly Head of Research at the Geneva Academy of International Humanitarian Law and Human Rights and is Editor of the *Mine Action Review*, an assessment of the implementation of international disarmament law.

SEAN CONNOLLY is an expert on policy development and implementation across the public sector, especially in reducing inequality and promoting community safety and involvement. He has particular experience in programme management of neighbourhood-based regeneration programmes. Most recently he was Intelligence & Analysis Manager at Birmingham City Council, managing a partnership approach to shared intelligence across the police, the council, and the National Health Service with a view to supporting families with multiple needs.

POLICE USE OF FORCE UNDER INTERNATIONAL LAW

STUART CASEY-MASLEN
University of Pretoria

SEAN CONNOLLY
Intelligence & Analysis Expert

CAMBRIDGE
UNIVERSITY PRESS

CAMBRIDGE
UNIVERSITY PRESS

University Printing House, Cambridge CB2 8BS, United Kingdom

One Liberty Plaza, 20th Floor, New York, NY 10006, USA

477 Williamstown Road, Port Melbourne, VIC 3207, Australia

4843/24, 2nd Floor, Ansari Road, Daryaganj, Delhi – 110002, India

79 Anson Road, #06–04/06, Singapore 079906

Cambridge University Press is part of the University of Cambridge.

It furthers the University's mission by disseminating knowledge in the pursuit of education, learning, and research at the highest international levels of excellence.

www.cambridge.org
Information on this title: www.cambridge.org/9781316510025
DOI: 10.1017/9781108186575

First published 2017

Printed in the United Kingdom by Clays, St Ives plc

A catalogue record for this publication is available from the British Library.

Library of Congress Cataloging-in-Publication Data
Names: Casey-Maslen, Stuart, author. | Connolly, Sean, 1967- author.
Title: Police use of force under international law / Stuart Casey-Maslen, University of Pretoria; Sean Connolly, Intelligence & Analysis Expert.
Description: Cambridge, United Kingdom; New York, NY, USA : Cambridge University Press, 2017. | Includes bibliographical references and index.
Identifiers: LCCN 2017006891 | ISBN 9781316510025 (hardback)
Subjects: LCSH: Police. | Law enforcement. | International and municipal law. | International law and human rights.
Classification: LCC K3465 .C37 2017 | DDC 344.05/2–dc23
LC record available at https://lccn.loc.gov/2017006891

ISBN 978-1-316-51002-5 Hardback

CONTENTS

ACKNOWLEDGEMENTS

The authors would like to thank Professor Christof Heyns, Director of the Institute for International and Comparative Law in Africa at the University of Pretoria; Dr Colin Roberts, Operations Manager for the Universities Police Science Institute (UPSI) at the University of Cardiff; and Dr Abi Dymond, Lecturer at the University of Exeter for their comments on earlier drafts of this book. Of course, the views expressed herein are those of the authors alone.

ABBREVIATIONS AND ACRONYMS

ACLU	American Civil Liberties Union
ACmnHPR	African Commission on Human and Peoples' Rights
ACPO	Association of Chief Police Officers
ATF	Bureau of Alcohol, Tobacco and Firearms
BAME	Black, Asian and minority ethnic
BJS	Bureau of Justice Statistics (US)
BPD	Baltimore City Police Department
BRI	Research and Intervention Brigade (French Police)
CCTV	Closed circuit television
CED	Conducted energy device
CEW	Conducted energy weapon
CONTEST	Counterterrorism Strategy (UK)
CPT	European Committee for the Prevention of Torture
CRS	Republican Security Companies (France)
DCAF	Geneva Centre for the Democratic Control of Armed Forces
DCS	Department of Correctional Services
DOJ	United States Department of Justice
DWB	'Driving while black'
ECHR	1950 European Convention on Human Rights and Fundamental Freedoms
ECtHR	European Court of Human Rights
ECW	Electronic control weapons
EEZ	Exclusive economic zone
EST	Emergency Security Team
EU	European Union
EU NAVFOR	European Union Naval Force
FBI	Federal Bureau of Investigation
FPD	Ferguson Police Department (Missouri)
GDELT	Global Database of Events, Language, and Tone
HMIC	Her Majesty's Inspectors of Constabulary
IACtHR	Inter-American Court of Human Rights
ICCPR	International Covenant on Civil and Political Rights (1966)

ICoC	International Code of Conduct for Private Security Service Providers
IMB	International Maritime Bureau
IMO	International Maritime Organization
IPCC	Independent Police Complaints Commission
IPID	Independent Police Investigations Directorate (South Africa)
IRA	Irish Republican Army
IS	Islamic State
ITLOS	International Tribunal for the Law of the Sea
LAPD	Los Angeles Police Department
LOAC	Law of armed conflict
LOLE	Law of law enforcement
LRAD	Long Range Acoustic Device
LTTE	Tamil Tiger rebels
MPS	Metropolitan Police Service
NATO	North Atlantic Treaty Organization
NYPD	New York Police Department
OAS	Organization of American States
OC	Oleoresin capsicum
OCLP	Occupy Central with Love and Peace
ODIHR	Office for Democratic Institutions and Human Rights
OEFF	One Earth Future Foundation
OHCHR	Office of the UN High Commissioner for Human Rights
OSCE	Organization for Security and Co-operation in Europe
PCA	Permanent Court of Arbitration
PERF	Police Executive Research Forum
PIM	Post Incident Manager
PLAN	Proportionality, Legality, Accountability, and Necessity
PNP	Philippines National Police
POP	Problem-oriented Policing
PPE	Personal protective equipment
PSNI	Police Service of Northern Ireland
RUC	Royal Ulster Constabulary
SAPS	South African Police Service
SARA	Scanning, Analysis, Response, and Assessment
SAS	Special Air Service
SCSL	Special Court for Sierra Leone
SFPD	San Francisco Police Department
SIA	Security Industry Authority
SOLAS	International Convention for the Safety of Life at Sea (1974)
SPG	Special Patrol Group
TRT	Tactical Response Team (South African Police Service)

UK	United Kingdom
UN	United Nations
UNCLOS	UN Convention on the Law of the Sea (1982)
UNMISS	UN Mission in the Republic of South Sudan
UNODC	UN Office on Drugs and Crime
US	United States
VPD	Vessel protection detachment
WGYCF	Walnut Grove Correctional Facility
WTO	World Trade Organization

Introduction

> In sum, the frequently heard talk about the lawful use of force by the police is practically meaningless and, because no one knows what is meant by it, so is the talk about the use of minimum force. Whatever vestigial significance attaches to the term 'lawful' use of force is confined to the obvious and unnecessary rule that police officers may not commit crimes of violence.
>
> Egon Bittner, 1970[1]

Force and Law Enforcement

For as long as there has been law – loosely defined as a set of binding rules governing the behaviour of the members of a nation or community – there has been a need for ways and means to enforce that law. As Echols wrote in 1958, 'Wherever there is organised government, there is law; and wherever there is law, there is inevitably an agency for the enforcement of that law, for Man has yet to devise a system of government which is able to dispense with the services of an adequate body of police.'[2] For as a consequence of humankind's propensity for violence counterbalanced by a widespread desire for social and public order, the police, *a public or private body authorised by the state for law enforcement*,[3] need to have the power to arrest and detain criminal suspects or to prevent crime, and to have the option and ability to use force where it is needed to achieve those aims.

[1] E. Bittner, *The Functions of the Police in Modern Society*, National Institute of Mental Health, Maryland, 1970, p. 38, at: www.ncjrs.gov/pdffiles1/Digitization/147822NCJRS.pdf.

[2] E. Echols, 'The Roman City Police: Origin and Development', *Classical Journal*, Vol. 53 (1958), 377–85, at 377.

[3] The police was defined in the 1960s as 'a specialized armed force used partially or wholly for norm enforcement'. R. D. Schwartz and J. C. Miller, 'Legal Evolution and Societal Complexity', *American Journal of Sociology*, Vol. 7, No. 1 (1964), 159–69, at p. 161; see R. Reiner, *The Politics of the Police*, 4th Edn, Oxford University Press, Oxford, 2010, p. 6.

Traditionally called constabulary powers in the United Kingdom (UK) and policing powers elsewhere today the discipline exercised by police officers is generally known as law enforcement. And although the term 'police force' is increasingly eschewed in favour of 'police service', and while the nature and form of law enforcement have varied markedly, both over time and across and within societies, throughout history there has been one constant, inherent in the notion of law enforcement: the implicit or explicit use or threat of use of force,[4] that is to say, *coercion backed by the use or threat of violent action.*[5]

Most often force seeking to ensure respect for the law has been meted out by a formally constituted body, such as the police or the army. Regularly too, though, force has manifested itself individually or collectively as 'citizen's justice'. Frequently this has been brutal in nature or arbitrary in dispensation, though on many occasions it has been restrained. Whatever the legality or morality of the use of force, each year police around the world employ it hundreds of millions of times and in a myriad of different ways. Most often the physical consequences of any use of force are minimal, but sometimes they are serious; they may even be fatal.

Until the modern era that followed the devastation of the Second World War, regulation of police use of force was exercised almost exclusively by reference to domestic rules and regulations. Since then, however, the development of international human rights law and criminal justice standards has brought law enforcement, and especially associated use of force, within the purview of international law and its implementing mechanisms and institutions. As a consequence, today it is possible to talk of an 'international law of law enforcement': a framework of general and dedicated principles and norms under international law.[6] In articulating that framework this book seeks to tackle two

[4] Although, as Reiner correctly observes, this 'does not imply that all policing is about the use of force. On the contrary, "good" policing has often been seen as the craft of handling trouble without resort to coercion, usually by skilful verbal tactics.' Reiner, *The Politics of the Police*, p. 8 and citations.

[5] The definition is taken from the *Collins Pocket Deluxe English Dictionary*. According to the Geneva Centre for the Democratic Control of Armed Forces (DCAF), use of force 'is generally understood as any physical constraint, ranging from physical restraint by hand or with a restraining device, to the use of firearms or weapons.' *Legislative Guidance Tool for States to Regulate Private Military and Security Companies*, DCAF, Geneva, 2016, p. iv, at: http://dcaf.ch/News/Legislative-Guidance-Tool-for-States-to-Regulate-Private-Military-and-Security-Companies-is-published.

[6] This body of international law, which is outlined in Chapter 3, is defined by reference to the three primary sources of international law (treaty, custom, and general principles of

overarching themes: how states use force to prompt respect for their laws and to ensure order, and to what extent police use of force complies with the international law of law enforcement.

It should be acknowledged from the outset that the data we have on police use of force globally is, in general, desperately poor. Researchers always crave more and better data, and lament its absence. But it is remarkable how little we know about how often law enforcement personnel use force around the world, especially potentially lethal force. In a speech to Georgetown University in February 2015, the director of the United States (US) Federal Bureau of Investigation, James Comey, remarked:

> Not long after riots broke out in Ferguson late last summer, I asked my staff to tell me how many people shot by police were African-American in this country. I wanted to see trends. I wanted to see information. They couldn't give it to me, and it wasn't their fault. Demographic data regarding officer-involved shootings is not consistently reported to us through our Uniform Crime Reporting Program. Because reporting is voluntary, our data is incomplete and therefore, in the aggregate, unreliable.
>
> I recently listened to a thoughtful big-city police chief express his frustration with that lack of reliable data. He said he didn't know whether the Ferguson police shot one person a week, one a year, or one a century, and that in the absence of good data, "all we get are ideological thunderbolts, when what we need are ideological agnostics who use information to try to solve problems." He's right.
>
> The first step to understanding what is really going on in our communities and in our country is to gather more and better data related to those we arrest, those we confront for breaking the law and jeopardizing public safety, and those who confront us. "Data" seems a dry and boring word but, without it, we cannot understand our world and make it better.
>
> How can we address concerns about "use of force," how can we address concerns about officer-involved shootings if we do not have a reliable grasp on the demographics and circumstances of those incidents? We simply must improve the way we collect and analyze data to see the true nature of what's happening in all of our communities.[7]

law) and the two subsidiary sources (judicial decisions and the writings of leading public international lawyers). As is explained, important elements of the law governing law enforcement also originated in soft (non-binding) legal instruments, notably a 1979 Code of Conduct and a set of Basic Principles adopted in 1990.

[7] Speech of James B. Comey, Director, FBI, Georgetown University, Washington, DC, 12 February 2015, at: www.fbi.gov/news/speeches/hard-truths-law-enforcement-and-race.

In October 2016, the Obama administration announced an ambitious set of plans to collect comprehensive national data on fatal police encounters, as well as to attempt to collect records of non-lethal use of force incidents. The FBI pilot scheme was due to begin in 2017 and to include around 178,557 officers in some of the nation's largest police departments, as well as some federal and state law enforcement agencies. Every month, agencies will be asked to report each incident in which force caused death or serious bodily injury as well as every time officers fire a gun 'at or in the direction of' a person.[8]

Certain individual police departments were also engaging in dedicated efforts to reform their use of force and promote better accountability. In October 2015, the New York Police Department (the largest in the United States, with more than 35,000 officers) announced that, 'for the first time in its modern history', it was establishing explicit guidelines, underpinned by a new tracking system, for using and documenting force below discharge of a firearm. Police officers will have to detail virtually every instance when force is used, not only in an arrest but also in other encounters with the public, including 'the sort of brief, violent detention and release that occurs routinely on the street'. Officers will face formal discipline, up to and including dismissal, not only if they fail to step in or report excessive force but also if they also fail to seek medical assistance for someone who requests it.[9]

Several European nations, including, for example, Germany and the United Kingdom, already collect and publish robust data on fatal shootings by their law enforcement personnel. But all states need to take seriously the need to gather, analyse, and publish data on all potentially lethal use of force. Ensuring accountability, the subject discussed in Chapter 11 of this book, is predicated on accurate information, which in turn must encompass such data.

It should be stressed from the outset that this book is not in any way anti-police or anti-policing. These functions are critical to any society. The authors are, however, unashamedly in favour of good police and good policing, both of which require the threat or use of necessary and proportionate force. As George Orwell famously wrote, 'People sleep

[8] O. Laughland and C. McCarthy, 'FBI to Begin Collecting Self-Reported Data on Fatal Police Encounters in 2017', *The Guardian*, 13 October 2016, at: www.theguardian.com/us-news/2016/oct/13/fbi-police-use-of-force-data-obama-administration.

[9] A. Baker and J. D. Goodman, 'New York Police Will Document Virtually All Instances of Force', *New York Times*, 1 October 2015.

peaceably in their beds at night only because rough men stand ready to do violence on their behalf.'

We hope, therefore, that this book will help to demonstrate that the late Egon Bittner's earlier claim that 'talk about the lawful use of force by the police is practically meaningless' was one assertion that this thoughtful man did not get right. For excessive or wild violence, or force that is used as a means purely of maintaining a regime in power, or which is applied in a discriminatory manner against individuals because of the colour of their skin or their chosen lifestyle, is unlawful and must be repressed.

Thus, as a service to society, the police must reflect diversity in society and show discipline, integrity, and restraint. Dostoevsky's assertion that 'you can judge a society by how well it treats its prisoners' is often cited by sociologists. We would broaden that maxim slightly. If you want to judge a society, look too at how its police service is viewed by the public and how its police officers behave on the streets. Or even, as Lord Dunsany wrote in a 1933 novel, reflect on how they are armed.[10] Appropriate defensive and offensive policing equipment, when backed up by realistic training and measured accountability, will ensure that police can truly serve the public good.

The Layout of the Book

The first part of the book puts policing in its economic, historical, legal, and social context. Chapter 1 describes the historical development of law enforcement, reviewing a range of mechanisms and institutions by which selected societies have sought to promote compliance with their laws from time immemorial. Although Robert Peel's London 'bobbies' are traditionally cited as the world's first true police force, evidence supports the view that policing as an action, and even the police force as an institution, are forms of law enforcement that date back to antiquity. Brief mention in this regard is made of Mesopotamia and the ancient Egyptian, Greek, and Roman empires. Greater consideration is given over to law enforcement as it has developed in the modern world, particularly across England and Wales, France, and the United States.

[10] 'It has always struck me that one of the readiest ways of estimating a country's regard for law is to notice what arms the officers of the law are carrying: in England it is little batons, in France swords, in many countries revolvers, and in Russia the police used to have artillery.' Lord Dunsany, *The Curse of the Wise Woman*, Valancourt Books, London, 1933.

In Chapter 2, Sean situates policing and law enforcement policy in social and economic context, looking at the rationale and justification for policing and its costs. Arguably, a general – and fundamental – shift is occurring in the nature of law enforcement, away from policing as prevention to policing as a response to detection of crime. The demise of the police officer's 'beat', lamented by some,[11] welcomed by others, is characteristic of this shift, partly a reaction to austerity, and partly an acceptance that societal changes demand different approaches. And when Reiner refers to 'police fetishism', by which he means 'the ideological assumption that the police are a functional prerequisite of social order so that without a police force chaos would ensue',[12] does he exaggerate for rhetorical effect or lay bare an inconvenient truth? Or are the police truly the 'thin blue line' holding 'the line between chaos and order in society'?[13]

Chapter 3 offers an overview of the law of law enforcement and its core principles governing the use of force. This body of international law is composed of three main elements: international human rights law, especially the rights to life, liberty, humane treatment, and to protest peacefully; customary international law, derived especially from criminal justice standards, particularly the 1979 Code of Conduct for Law Enforcement Officials, the 1990 Basic Principles on the Use of Force and Firearms by Law Enforcement Officials, and the 2015 Nelson Mandela Rules;[14] and general principles of law, which reflect core principles of national criminal law across democratic nations. Foremost among those principles are necessity for, and proportionality of, use of force.

The second part of the book goes into detail about the use of particular types of force and the use of force in specific settings or contexts. Chapter 4 addresses use of firearms, for which specific rules exist under customary international law. Shooting 'to stop' is generally only permissible where a threat of death or serious injury is imminent; threats of damage to property alone do not suffice. Stricter requirements operate where a law enforcement official is shooting with the intent to kill: under international law this may only occur where such intentional lethal use of force is

[11] Ed Conlon, for instance, claimed: 'They call it the beat for what it does, not what it is – it beats you down . . .' E. Conlon, *Blue Blood*, Ebury Press, London, 2011, p. 95.

[12] Reiner, *The Politics of the Police*, p. 3. In Reiner's view, 'Altogether the police are marginal to the control of crime and the maintenance of order and always have been.' *Ibid.*, 19.

[13] L. A. Steverson, *Policing in America*, ABC CLIO, Santa Barbara, CA, 2008, p. 1.

[14] The revised Standard Minimum Rules for the Treatment of Prisoners, adopted by the UN General Assembly in December 2015, are discussed in Chapter 6.

strictly unavoidable to protect life. The chapter also briefly discusses the boundaries between the military and the police as criticism mounts in some quarters of an alleged 'militarisation' of policing. At the same time, use of expanding ammunition – prohibited as a method of warfare during armed conflict – is becoming generally accepted in law enforcement as a means to reduce the risk of innocent bystanders being hurt when the police open fire on a dangerous suspect.

Chapter 5 considers how 'less-lethal' weapons can prevent or at least minimise loss of life by replacing firearms in certain scenarios. But in many instances, such weapons (batons, pepper spray, and conducted energy weapons, among many others) are instead used as compliance tools or, just gratuitously, to inflict pain. Over the past few years, the lack of specific international regulation, apart from brief mention in the 1990 Basic Principles, has been noted and regretted by human rights bodies, most notably the UN Human Rights Council.

Chapter 6 looks at the role of law enforcement agencies in facilitating peaceful protest and ensuring crowd safety during assemblies. Here some of the specific provisions of the 1990 Basic Principles on the Use of Force and Firearms have been overtaken by evolution in human rights law. This means that a decision by the authorities to disperse a peaceful protest will rarely be lawful. Often people assemble to protest against the regime in power; this may include specific protests against the police. Thus, for example, 2015 (and to a lesser extent 2016) can be seen as a year of protests against excessive use of police force in the United States (US) as a catalogue of incidents involving death or serious injury among African Americans at the hands of US law enforcement personnel brought many onto the streets.

Chapter 7 looks at how force may be, and is being, used in custodial settings, including in light of the 2015 Nelson Mandela Rules adopted by the UN General Assembly. Detainees face an especial risk of excessive violence being inflicted by their warders or other custodial officials, as well as from fellow inmates. Although protection of the rights of prisoners is not always well received in some sections of the general public, it is clear and right that prisoners do not forgo their fundamental rights as they pass through the prison gate. This chapter also considers the use of force during police interviews.

Chapter 8 considers the use of force in counterterrorism. It distinguishes, as does international law, between use of force in law enforcement and in the conduct of hostilities in armed conflict. This distinction is sometimes contentious. In addition to assessing the human rights framework, it assesses use of force that proved fatal in specific counter-terrorism operations: by the United Kingdom against members of the Irish Republican Army on Gibraltar in 1988 and against a suspected Islamist terrorist in 2005 (who was in fact a Brazilian electrician); by the Russian security forces in relieving a major hostage situation in a Moscow theatre in 2002; against al-Shabaab militants who attacked a shopping centre in downtown Nairobi in 2013; and the terror attacks in Paris in November 2015.

Private security service providers are being increasingly used for law enforcement, as Chapter 9 explores. A decade ago, annual spending on private security in the United States had been estimated at US$90 billion, compared to $40 billion a year for public law enforcement.[15] Even the US government was said to be spending more on private security than on hiring public police.[16] In 2012, expenditure on private-sector security was said to total more than $281 billion, of which expenditure devoted to operational security amounted to about $200 billion, with information technology contributing another $80 billion of costs.[17] While their ability to use force lawfully is generally more constrained than law enforcement officials with state-endowed police powers to arrest and detain, private security service personnel are using force on a daily basis. For some, private security is the future of law enforcement, a potential that has concomitant challenges for international law.

Chapter 10 reflects on counterpiracy operations at sea, especially off the coast of Africa where much of the world's commercial shipping passes. While state warships are explicitly authorised under the international law of the sea to board suspected pirate vessels and detain suspected pirates (with the implicit right to use force where necessary and proportionate), vessel protection detachments (VPDs) or private security personnel are assuredly not. Thus, such defensive functions mean that private security personnel and even military personnel in

[15] M. J. Palmiotto, *Policing: Concepts, Strategies, and Current Issues in American Police Forces*, 3rd Edn, CreateSpace Independent Publishing Platform, United States, 2013, p. 64.

[16] Ibid., citing B. Minnis, Technology Asset Protection Association (URL no longer available).

[17] *The United States Security Industry: Size and Scope, Insights, Trends, and Data*, Executive Summary, ASIS International and Institute of Finance and Management, 2013, United States, p. 2, at: www.asisonline.org/Documents/ASIS%20IOFM%20Executive%20Summary%208.23.13.%20final.pdf.

VPDs are restricted in their lawful ability to use force only in self-defence or in defence of others.

The final part of the book describes how the principle of accountability is critical to ensuring that international law of law enforcement rules are respected in practice. Chapter 11 outlines the duty to investigate, the forms that a requisite investigation may take, the duty to prosecute, and the ways in which accountability mechanisms can influence better policies on use of force consonant with the duty of precaution under international human rights law.

1

A History of Law Enforcement

> 'Let it once become the duty of one body of men to charge themselves with the execution of the Laws for the prevention of crimes and the detection of offences – let them be armed with proper and apposite powers for that purpose, and the state of Society will speedily become ameliorated and improved; a greater degree of security will be extended to the peaceful subject, and the blessings of civil liberty will be enlarged.'
>
> Patrick Colquhoun (1806)[1]

Most contemporary societies are 'policed' by a force answerable, in some form, to the state, meaning that a group of public officials are mandated and entrusted to investigate crimes and arrest and detain suspects. As Stead has observed, the ethnic, political, social, and economic nature of the state is what determines the nature of the police.[2] Hence, the nature of the police has typically differed very widely from country to country, and continues to do so.

For many centuries, a key law enforcement task was the collection of taxes for the sovereign. Sustaining the sovereign in power and enabling his rule to perpetuate took precedence over concern for the rights of individual 'citizens' to protection from harm. Today, policing's use of force for taxation purposes tends to manifest itself only in the form of bribes demanded by individual officers in certain countries, enabling them unlawfully to supplement a meagre salary paid (often only in theory) by the government of the day. Far more time and effort is generally dedicated to preserving law and order on the streets, though sometimes, even in ostensibly democratic societies in which government is supposed to be determined by the people,

[1] P. Colquhoun, *A Treatise on the Police of the Metropolis*, 7th Edn, Bye and Law, London, 1806, p. 562.

[2] P. J. Stead (ed.), *Pioneers in Policing*, Patterson Smith, Montclair, NJ, 1977, p. 3.

the police are also used to seek to maintain the existing regime in power or to defend unpopular policies.

Policing in Antiquity

Available evidence in antiquity – admittedly extremely limited for many early societies – points to the fact that when law enforcement was conducted for the benefit of the general public it generally demanded 'a much higher degree of personal initiative'.[3] In part, this state of affairs may owe itself to a far narrower delineation of criminal offences deemed to have been committed against the state (or empire) than is the case in the modern world.[4] Underlying the reality of the times, though, was a pervasive lack of interest among sovereigns to repress infractions of such law as did exist, at least when these did not directly imperil either their own status or personal security. Nonetheless, the notion of crime certainly existed within ancient societies. The Code of Hammurabi, an eighteenth century BC ruler of Mesopotamia, stipulated some 280 ordinary crimes, including assault, robbery, the non-payment of debts, and sexual offences; penalties were fixed for each, some of which could be extremely harsh.[5]

Policing in Ancient Egypt

A national police force as such does not appear to have existed in pharaonic times in Egypt, although a force of river patrols – what could be considered the first formalised police force – was watching over the Nile beginning in 1340 BC.[6] On land, the *Medjay*, a nomadic people from the Nubian eastern desert, were employed to patrol towns, desert regions, and borders (as well as to serve as royal bodyguards and to protect state assets). But papyri from later Ptolemaic Egypt – the Hellenistic dynasty that followed the death of Alexander the Great in 323 BC and which ended with the Roman conquest of 30 BC – indicate that a range of bodies were given considerable latitude to conduct core law enforcement

[3] J. Bauschatz, *Law and Enforcement in Ptolemaic Egypt*, Cambridge University Press, New York, 2013, p. 1; *cf* also p. 31.

[4] Ibid., p. 1 note 2.

[5] Ibid., p. 9. Often oversimplified in modern descriptions of the Code as 'an eye for an eye', in fact the penalty for most of the offences was a fine.

[6] L. A. Steverson, *Policing in America*, ABC CLIO, Santa Barbara, CA, 2008, p. 4.

tasks, particularly at village level.[7] Thus, Fuhrmann argues that when the Romans seized Egypt, 'they absorbed a country with its own deep tradition of institutional policing, perhaps stretching all the way back to the Old Kingdom' (c. 2600–2150 BC).[8]

Of all the law enforcement officials that existed in Ptolemaic Egypt, the *phylakitai* are said to have most closely resembled a modern police force. These officials whose jurisdiction covered the Egyptian countryside ('professional police officers' in the words of a leading authority) had the power to arrest, transport, and detain suspects, and to carry out investigations at crime scenes, but they were also charged with protecting ordinary citizens. Among others, their duties included assuring safety along the Nile in efforts akin to modern counterpiracy operations.[9]

The *phylakitai* were supervised by the *epistatēs*, another professional body, and one that performed some of the same functions as the *phylakitai* but whose members were considered as an officer corps, perhaps constituting one of policing's oldest accountability mechanisms.[10] In addition to acting to repress crimes between citizens, force was used to extract tax revenue for the authorities from an occasionally unwilling populace. These actions were '[p]erhaps the most coercive function performed by the Ptolemaic police'.[11] Nonetheless, while 'rough handling' was sometimes tolerated, excessive or arbitrary use of force could result in sanction that could be 'fast and stern'.[12]

Policing in Classical Athens

Despite the etymology of the word police, which comes ultimately from the ancient Greek word for a city state (*Πολις*), in classical Athens professional agents were not engaged to police the city, although a number of officials and slaves were empowered to enforce a limited degree of law and order.[13] Three hundred Scythian slaves known as *toxotai* (archers) assisted a group of magistrates responsible for penal issues (called the Eleven) by acting as security guards in public

[7] Bauschatz, *Law and Enforcement in Ptolemaic Egypt*, pp. 4, 15, 17, 36, and 37. In border zones, and during riots and violent uprisings, the army was generally responsible for security. Ibid., p. 284.

[8] C. J. Fuhrmann, *Policing the Roman Empire*, Oxford University Press, New York, 2012, p. 75.

[9] Bauschatz, *Law and Enforcement in Ptolemaic Egypt*, pp. 45, 53, 97, 286, and 311.

[10] Ibid., pp. 101, 102. [11] Ibid., pp. 282, 283, 311. [12] Ibid., p. 34.

[13] Ibid., p. 18, and citations in note 63.

assemblies, 'arresting, torturing, and executing offenders', and 'pursuing escaped prisoners'. While they carried out many police functions, the *toxotai* did not have the authority to investigate crimes.[14] According to Wiedemann,

> There were several reasons why slaves were thought particularly suitable for responsible jobs involving supervision over the activities of citizens. Not only does policing involve unsocial hours and inevitably result in friction and misunderstandings with the population at large, making it highly unpopular, there is also the danger that normal social obligations towards particular individuals will threaten the objectivity of the police and perhaps result in corruption. These problems were solved by giving the responsibility for law and order to slaves whose only loyalty was to their owner.[15]

In what would become a recurrent theme throughout the ages, for the police have often been ridiculed, this urban force was the butt of many jokes, in particular during Aristophanes' comedies.[16]

Policing in the Roman Empire

As Fuhrmann describes, in the early days of the Roman Empire, a range of officials were empowered to physically subdue, arrest, imprison, fine, and even execute ordinary offenders:[17] 'Variety is the keyword. A wide spectrum of civilian and military groups policed the Roman Empire, from the municipal slave serving as prison guard to the praetorian guardsman outposted to a North African military station.'[18] Fuhrmann also points to the 'striking' absence of police 'in many episodes of disorder in the Roman Empire'. Accordingly, 'self-help', whereby citizens were called on to tackle criminal behaviour without recourse to state institutions, 'was vital in every era of Roman civilization and evident in every phase of Rome's history'.[19] Moreover, even where active police forces did exist, rivalry as to

[14] Ibid., pp. 18, 19.

[15] T. Wiedemann, *Greek & Roman Slavery*, 2005 Digital Print Edn, Routledge, London/New York, 1981, p. 155.

[16] See, e.g., M. Trundle, 'Light Troops in Classical Athens', ch. 5 in D. M. Pritchard (ed.), *War, Democracy and Culture in Classical Athens*, Cambridge University Press, 2010, p. 149.

[17] Bauschatz, *Law and Enforcement in Ptolemaic Egypt*, p. 25.

[18] Fuhrmann, *Policing the Roman Empire*, p. 7.

[19] Ibid., pp. 5, 49.

jurisdiction or a lack of cooperation between them could result in a lack of effective action – to the probable benefit of the offender.

Law enforcement was performed by both civilian and military personnel throughout the history of the Roman Empire. As time went on, an expansion of military policing led to heightened abuse of civilians as well as significant (negative) social impact, showing policing in the ancient world 'at its best and at its worst'.[20] Indeed, by the late fourth and early fifth centuries, emperors were even permitting civilians to kill soldiers who were trespassing or committing highway robbery. It is therefore an understatement to observe that Roman soldiers 'were obviously an imperfect instrument of law enforcement'.[21]

Perhaps the closest to a local police force in most western communities of the Roman Empire were the town magistrates and their attendants, the *apparitores*.[22] Challenges to their authority included, on one occasion, fighting between supporters of Pompeii and Nuceria at a gladiatorial show, not unlike modern-day enmity between supporters of rival football teams. But what began as insults and taunting soon escalated to stone-throwing and then into sword fighting. With the dead littering the arena, the games were banned for ten years as a punishment.[23]

In Rome itself, the *tresviri capitales*, a board of three men concerned with capital crimes, organised night-time fire-brigades composed of slaves (the *vigiles*), while also leading patrols to search for fugitive slaves.[24] Indeed, the recovery of slaves in flight was a major preoccupation in ancient Rome, just as it would become, many centuries later, in pre-Civil War America.[25] Professional fugitive slave hunters existed – the *fugitivarii* – but these olden-day bounty hunters were notoriously corrupt.[26]

In the Roman provinces, nominally only the governor had the power to impose the death penalty, a right known as *ius gladii*.[27] In the eastern provinces of Asia Minor, *eirenarchs* (peace officers, a title that brings to mind, among others, contemporary French police officers, referred to as *gardiens de la paix*) were involved in targeted arrests and judicial process. The *paraphylakes* seem to have maintained their responsibility for

[20] Ibid., p. 11. [21] Ibid., p. 237. [22] Ibid., p. 58. [23] Ibid., p. 83.

[24] Ibid., p. 25; *cf* also Fuhrmann, *Policing the Roman Empire*, p. 57.

[25] Fuhrmann (ibid., p. 22) cites the observation of American historians that white slave owners probably invested more resources in the recovery of fugitive slaves than in any other aspect of slavery.

[26] Ibid., p. 23. [27] Ibid., p. 171.

patrolling outlying areas.[28] Yet, much of the time of both the *eirenarchs* and the *paraphylakes* seems to have been spent, as it was in Ptolemaic times, in ensuring taxation was paid to the authorities. In Mitchell's words, 'The old euphemism that a police force exists to maintain law and order rarely appears more hollow than in the communities of Roman Asia Minor.'[29]

As had occurred within the Egyptian Empire that predated it, the Roman Empire was constrained to tackle a significant piratical threat. A young Julius Caesar was kidnapped and ransomed by pirates in the Aegean in the first century BC (he subsequently hunted down his kidnappers and killed them). In the late republic, Emperor Augustus famously boasted that he had 'not only brought peace to the provinces' but also 'freed the sea of pirates'.[30]

In fact, Augustus' law enforcement challenge was considerable. The last century of the Roman Republic (133–31 BC) had seen a steady deterioration in law and order, with the Senate often passing laws to instil what was, in effect, martial law.[31] As a consequence of widespread insecurity, including in Rome itself, Augustus introduced a number of significant police reforms during his reign, notably, in 27 BC, establishing the Praetorian Guard. Nine cohorts, each composed of five hundred men, were responsible directly to him. But while their primary function was as imperial guards, they were also deployed to keep order at games and other public events, as well as to guard prisoners.

The use of such paramilitary units was controversial, however. In a sensitivity that would be echoed centuries later in nineteenth-century England and beyond, Romans had not forgotten Pompey's use of legions to quell 'mob warfare' in Rome in 52 BC, a role that had generated 'considerable disquiet, even among his ardent supporters'.[32] To mitigate public concern, the Praetorian Guard were quartered in private or lodging houses rather than military-style barracks, and wore togas, not uniforms, under which their swords were normally concealed.[33]

After a series of failed attempts to create a quasi-civilian force in the capital, in AD 6, Augustus reconstituted the *vigiles* (translated as 'the

[28] Ibid., p. 71.

[29] S. Mitchell, *Anatolia: Land, Men, and Gods in Asia Minor*, 2 vols., Oxford University Press, Oxford, 1993, p. 104, cited by Fuhrmann, *Policing the Roman Empire*, p. 74.

[30] Fuhrmann, ibid., p. 95.

[31] R. W. Davies, 'Augustus Caesar, A Police System in the Ancient World', ch. 1 in Stead, *Pioneers in Policing*, p. 12.

[32] Ibid., p. 13. [33] Ibid., p. 14.

night watch') into seven cohorts of one thousand men each, who not only patrolled the streets extinguishing fires[34] but also dealt with burglary, assault, and other petty crimes, along with interrogating and imprisoning suspects.[35] Only in the last years of his reign did the emperor finally dare to create a dedicated metropolitan police force, the fifteen-hundred-strong Urban Cohorts (*cohortes urbanae*). 'The very idea of a regular police force was still repugnant to many citizens, no doubt accounting for Augustus's long delay in introducing it and the smallness of the force.'[36]

Writing in the 1970s, Stead noted that features of the two main components of Roman policing, at least from later imperial times – a semi-civil watch force and a body of élite troops – are found in many contemporary police systems:

> Modern Italy is policed by civilian forces on the one hand – chiefly the Pubblica Sicurezza, a national force, and municipal police forces, the Vigili Urbani – and on the other by military police, the Carabinieri. France, too, has a dual system, the Police Nationale, civilian police, and the military police of the Gendarmerie Nationale.[37]

The combined Roman policing bodies were great in size. One conservative estimate holds that by 6 AD, Augustus had nearly 10,000 security personnel policing Rome, a city whose total population numbered only one million (of whom several hundred thousand were slaves). This ratio of 1 to 100 compares to 1 to 285 in 1890s Paris, and 1 to 435 in late nineteenth-century London and Vienna. Yet, despite this significant law enforcement presence, Rome remained a dangerous place, especially at night.[38] By the third century BC, the number of military law enforcement officials had climbed dramatically so that there was now one military police officer for every forty-two residents of the city.[39] As Echols recalled, 'kings, consuls and emperors alike had at all times an agency for law enforcement on duty in the streets of Rome'.[40]

[34] Fires were a perpetual concern in Rome; where one occurred due to the negligence of a resident, he could expect to receive a salutary beating or flogging. Ibid., pp. 19, 20.

[35] Bauschatz, *Law and Enforcement in Ptolemaic Egypt*, p. 25; and Davies, 'Augustus Caesar, A Police System in the Ancient World', p. 15.

[36] Davies, ibid., p. 16.

[37] Stead, *Pioneers in Policing*, p. 3. While the nomenclature has since changed in Italy, the fundamental structure remains the same.

[38] Fuhrmann *Policing the Roman Empire*, pp. 117, 118, and 119.

[39] Ibid., p. 130.

[40] E. Echols, 'The Roman City Police: Origin and Development', *Classical Journal*, Vol. 53 (1958), p. 377.

Policing in England and Wales

When the Western Roman Empire was overrun by the 'barbarians' of Northern Europe, England was introduced to community law enforcement: 'a police of the neighbourhood, as opposed to a police of the prince'.[41] Central to this system became the office of parish constable.[42] King Alfred had divided the country into shires into which he placed a reeve (a Saxon word for a steward or administrator); over the years the name shire reeve became shortened to sheriff.[43] At village level, however, the primary law enforcement official was a 'Tithingman', a man elected to serve by his own community. After 1066, the Norman conquerors gave this post the name of constable, originally a high office (the chief of the stables, the keeper of the horses).[44] By the time of Henry III's reign (1216–72 AD), each village was required to have one or two constables; the position was formalised by legislation in 1328 and 1330 under Edward III.[45] After Henry VII became king, the parish constables were ordered to 'favour, help and assist' tax collectors within their townships[46] – a law enforcement task harking back, as we have seen, to antiquity.

Traditionally parish constables were recruited from householders, often by rotation from house to house. They kept their usual job and took fees for their police duties.[47] While this 'parochial system worked well enough in a static, agricultural society in which people knew each other', with the growth of urban areas it became increasingly ineffective. Even if a thief were caught, the victim had to fund his own claim through the courts, for no state body was yet responsible for criminal prosecution.[48] In the middle of the seventeenth century, Oliver Cromwell had made a short-lived and unsuccessful attempt to transfer local control of

41 Stead, *Pioneers in Policing*, p. 4.

42 Watchmen also played an important role. Shakespeare's character of Dogberry in *Much Ado About Nothing* is a less than flattering portrayal of a watchman.

43 R. Cowley, *A History of the British Police*, The History Press, Stroud, 2011, p. 9.

44 Ibid., p. 10.

45 H. Smith, 'The Parish Constable in Georgian Times', *Barwicker*, No. 59 (September 2000), at: www.barwickinelmethistoricalsociety.com/5950.html.

46 Ibid.

47 Open University and Metropolitan Police Authority, 'Origins of the Metropolitan Police', International Centre for History of Crime, Policing and Justice, 2009, at: www.open.ac.uk/Arts/history-from-police-archives/Met6Kt/MetHistory/mhParishPol.html.

48 Cowley, *A History of the British Police*, p. 14.

'policing' to the army.[49] By the end of the seventeenth century, 'life and property were seriously imperilled by crime; in the eighteenth century the situation was aggravated by mob violence'.[50]

In the mid-eighteenth century, London in particular was plagued by a series of highway robberies. Henry Fielding, a magistrate at Bow Street in Westminster and a lawyer by vocation (but with experience in journalism and as a playwright), selected a number of parish constables 'of proven honesty and mettle' to disrupt the gangs. Having achieved this within only a year, he was then tasked by the government to tackle a series of gang murders, and allocated the sum of six hundred pounds for the work (equating to more than £110,000 today). He accomplished this within a month whereupon he dedicated the remaining funds, only one-third of which had been spent, to maintaining an armed force of 'pursuers', who became known as the Bow Street Runners.[51] This body of men would be used not only in London but also throughout the rest of England.[52] As Emsley explains, an early use of forensic science techniques saw one of the Runners, Harry Adkins, match a mark on a bullet that had killed a Staffordshire farmer with a bullet mould used by the killer.[53]

Subsequently, Fielding proposed that a troop of army cavalry be assigned to pursue robbers. This, though, was a step too far for the government of the day, evoking memories of Cromwell's major-generals and James II's efforts to create an army to do his bidding,[54] and heightened by Londoners' fears of continental Europe's 'notoriously' despotic practices.[55] Thus, when in 1785 William Pitt the Younger presented a bill to Parliament calling for the creation of a police force in London, his proposal met with instant opposition. Many argued that such a force would be like the *Gendarmerie* in Paris, a force said to be full of spies and informants who reported to the nobility and who, in turn, placed thousands of people in prisons such as the Bastille. Few wished to

[49] C. Reith, *A New Study of Police History*, 1st Edn, Oliver & Boyd, Edinburgh, 1956, p. 125.

[50] Stead, *Pioneers in Policing*, p. 4.

[51] In rural districts, they carried cutlasses and subsequently some also bore pistols, confronted as they often were with armed poachers. W. R. Miller, *Cops and Bobbies: Police Authority in New York and London, 1830–1870*, University of Chicago Press, 1977, p. 49.

[52] J. B. Rubinstein, 'Henry and John Fielding, Police Philosophy and Police Technique', ch. 2 in Stead, *Pioneers in Policing*, p. 41.

[53] C. Emsley, *The Great British Bobby*, Quercus, London, 2010, p. 22.

[54] Ibid., p. 33.

[55] Rubinstein, 'Henry and John Fielding', pp. 41–42. People called London's New Police 'Jenny Darbies' (after the French gendarmes) as well as other more uncomplimentary names. See, e.g., Miller, *Cops and Bobbies*, p. 105.

give greater power to what was already considered to be a very centralist authoritarian government, and in the face of such disapproval, Pitt's bill was withdrawn.[56]

Eighteenth-century London did, though, see the creation of one dedicated police force: the Marine Police. Patrick Colquhoun, a Scottish businessman and later justice of the peace, whose contribution to preventive policing is said to have been 'singularly neglected' by police historians, advocated the establishment of a force to counter what he termed the 'river pirates'. They, along with other malfeasants, were committing 'acts of peculation, fraud, embezzlement, pillage and depredation' on the Thames, imperilling the lucrative economy and taxation that resulted from the trade that passed up and down the river.[57] Colquhoun estimated that, in a single twelve-month period through to early January 1798, half a million pounds' worth of goods (equivalent to about £55 million today) were plundered in the port of London.[58]

The authorities were swift to implement Colquhoun's recommendations, with the Marine Police (probably the first use of the term police in its modern, narrow sense),[59] already operational by June 1798. Personnel included 'ship constables' who were paid by the shipowners themselves, as a replacement for the 'inefficient and corrupt old watchmen'.

> The success was spectacular. The river pirates vanished within a year; and the systematic vigilance of the police, patrolling in boats on the river itself, where no police boat had previously existed, and standing guard on the ships, on the quays, and on the warehouses, eliminated opportunity for the kinds of thief who had flourished in the absence of any methodical prevention. Theft of West India goods fell in the first eight months by over 95%.[60]

But not everyone was delighted by this achievement. In one incident, a mob of coal-heavers attacked a police court in Wapping. Colquhoun, who had been appointed the superintending magistrate for the marine police force, stood alongside its resident magistrate to face down the mob armed with pistols. After a court officer was killed in the fighting, one of

[56] 'A History of Policing', accessed on 27 February 2015 at: www.klis.com/allsaints/pnotes.htm.

[57] Stead, 'Patrick Colquhoun, Preventive Police', in *Pioneers in Policing*, pp. 48, 55, 56.

[58] Ibid., p. 57; see also P. Colquhoun, *A Treatise on the Commerce and Police of the River Thames*, H. Baldwin and Son, London, 1800.

[59] *Oxford English Dictionary* online, accessed on 27 February 2015 at: www.oed.com.

[60] Stead, *Pioneers in Policing*, pp. 58–59.

the ring leaders was arrested, tried, and condemned to death. To his credit, Colquhoun felt the example would suffice; 'no witch hunt' ensued.[61] Today, the Marine Policing Unit is a Central Operations branch of London's Metropolitan Police Service, responsible for policing 47 miles of the River Thames between Dartford and Hampton Court; its base remains in Wapping High Street.[62] One of the Unit's boats is still named the *Patrick Colquhoun*.

The Creation of the Metropolitan Police

London's Metropolitan Police was arguably the brainchild of three men, all with links to Ireland, although Sir Robert Peel is most often given the credit for its establishment. Peel was a politician who became the 'virtual ruler' of Ireland at the age of twenty-four; Charles Rowan was an Irish soldier who fought at the Battle of Waterloo; while Richard Mayne, the son of an Irish judge, was a barrister.[63] Each contributed his own expertise and experience to the creation and operation of the Metropolitan Police:

> Peel brought the political thrust, and the ability to carry Parliament with him in creating the minimum statutory base for the force. Mayne brought a trained lawyer's mind to establish a code of legal practice on which the police could operate. Rowan was able to apply a soldier's knowledge of military organization and discipline to mould the body of men into the hybrid between a force and a service that has always been the outstanding characteristic of the British police.[64]

In eighteenth-century London, rioting was 'the only effective avenue of protest for the working classes, which the ruling elite learned to live with as a hazard of political life'.[65] As a consequence, as Reith notes, 'Throughout the eighteenth century and later, authority and people in England believed almost unanimously that the only means by which order in the community could be maintained was to repress crime with violence and brutality.'[66]

The Gordon Riots of 1780, which began as an anti-Catholic protest in London against the 1778 Papists Act, a measure intended to reduce

[61] *Ibid.*, p. 59. [62] http://content.met.police.uk/Site/marineaboutus.

[63] T. A. Critchley, 'Peel, Rowan, and Mayne, The British Model of Urban Police', ch. 5 in Stead, *Pioneers in Policing*, pp. 82–83.

[64] Ibid., p. 83. [65] Miller, *Cops and Bobbies*, p. 7.

[66] Reith, *A New Study of Police History*, p. 24.

discrimination against British Catholics, descended into violence and led to a march on parliament by up to 60,000 people. The Prime Minister of the day, Lord North, had forgotten to issue an order mobilising the small number of constables in the area and a detachment of soldiers had to be summoned; for once, dispersal of the crowd was achieved without recourse to violence. But deploying the military to the streets of London on a regular basis was never a realistic option, as events outside the capital would clearly demonstrate. Yet, England was still not ready for a civilian police force, and a Police Bill, drafted for Peel by Patrick Colquhoun in 1785, was not presented to Parliament.[67]

In 1812, 12,000 regular troops were sent to the Midlands and the north of the country to suppress the activities of the Luddites.[68] Following show trials, public hangings administered by the troops eventually put an end to the uprising, but at huge social and political cost.[69] On 16 August 1819, in St Peter's Field in Manchester, cavalry charged with sabres drawn into a crowd of up to 80,000 who had gathered to demand reform of parliamentary representation. Fifteen people were killed and up to seven hundred others were injured. The massacre was given the name Peterloo by a Manchester newspaper editor in an ironic reference to the Battle of Waterloo, which had taken place four years earlier. The organisers of the protest were jailed and a crackdown mounted on journalists who had covered the event. A 'test case' was brought against four members of the Manchester Yeomanry in April 1822 but all were acquitted, with the court ruling their actions to disperse an illegal gathering were justified. The defendants' legal costs were met by the government.[70]

Despite the widespread repression that ensued, the tragic events at St Peter's Field had clearly demonstrated the unsuitability of military personnel for policing crowds and demonstrations. During much of the early nineteenth century, England was teetering on the edge of rebellion, with appalling social conditions a result of the industrial revolution that had enriched the few and impoverished the many. In tandem, crime on the country's roads and canals was increasing at an alarming rate and the local system of part-time parish constables and ineffective and corrupt

[67] Ibid., p. 124. [68] Critchley, 'Peel, Rowan, and Mayne', p. 83.

[69] The public hanging of fourteen men at York Castle in a single day in January 2013 was York's largest ever hanging; five were condemned for riot, six for burglary, and three for robbery, having been convicted under the Frame Breaking Act that came into force the previous year. 'York Castle Prisons', at: www.capitalpunishmentuk.org/york.html.

[70] R. Reid, *The Peterloo Massacre*, William Heinemann, London, 1989, p. 204. The yeomanry corps was, however, disbanded on 9 June 1824.

watchmen was unable to stem the tide. This was despite a legal system in which the penalty for 233 crimes, including the theft of a pocket handkerchief, was death by hanging.[71] In 1823, the Duke of Wellington advocated a civilian-controlled police 'to preserve the lives and properties of His Majesty's subjects against domestic insurrection and disturbance'.[72]

Sir Robert Peel too believed that reform was urgently needed in the way the country was policed, but public opinion and his political instincts counselled caution. Indeed, his first calls for a centralised police force were opposed by elements of rich and poor alike. The rich thought they would have to pay for the force financially, while the poor feared they would pay physically, 'fed by reports of excesses committed by the French and Prussian state police'.[73] In 1822, seeking to advocate for the establishment of a police force in London, Peel was told by a parliamentary select committee that: 'It is difficult to reconcile an effective system of police with that perfect freedom of action and exemption from interference which are the great privileges and blessings of society in this country.'[74]

But in 1829, in a move said by some to be applying ideas developed by Edwin Chadwick, a student of the utilitarian philosopher Jeremy Bentham, who was arguing that prevention of crime rather than its punishment should be the governing principle of policing, Peel presented the Metropolitan Police Bill to Parliament.[75] The Bill passed with little debate – Peel had proposed to include the City of London within the scope of the police force purely as a bargaining chip[76] – and the headquarters of the 'new police' was soon fixed at 4 Whitehall Place, better known as Scotland Yard (as the building had previously been used as a residence for royalty from Scotland).[77]

[71] Reith, *A New Study of Police History*, p. 123.
[72] Miller, *Cops and Bobbies*, p. 7.
[73] Critchley, 'Peel, Rowan, and Mayne', p. 85.
[74] Cited by Reith, *A New Study of Police History*, p. 28.
[75] Critchley, 'Peel, Rowan, and Mayne', pp. 85–86. Reith argues strongly that in fact it was General Sir John Moore who had much earlier pushed and practiced the prevention of crime (among the military who served under him), making the repression by use of force unnecessary. His principles were later adopted and adapted to the police by Charles Rowan. Reith, *A New Study of Police History*, pp. 28, 199, 261. Reith contrasts Moore's approach with Wellington's, who, in Reith's words, believed that the 'moral degradation of the British soldier was a disease that was incurable, and controllable in its severe manifestations, only by flogging and hanging . . .' Ibid., and see also p. 112.
[76] Ibid., p. 124.
[77] Critchley, 'Peel, Rowan, and Mayne', pp. 20, 23; Steverson, *Policing in America*, p. 9.

The 1829 Metropolitan Police Act stipulated that the members of the new police force would be sworn in as constables, a nominally low rank of service but with the highly significant power of arrest and a concomitant authority to use force.[78] Even today, British officials sometimes still refer to 'constabulary powers' rather than police or law enforcement powers. Charles Rowan, one of the two original Metropolitan Police Commissioners, gave clear instructions to each new constable on how his powers should be exercised:

> He will be civil and obliging to all people of every rank and class ... He must be particularly cautious not to interfere idly or unnecessarily in order to make a display of his authority; when required to act, he will do so with decision and boldness; on all occasions he may expect to receive the fullest support in the proper exercise of his authority. He must remember that there is no qualification so indispensable to a police officer as a perfect command of temper, never suffering himself to be moved in the slightest degree by any language or threats that may be used; if he do his duty in a quiet and determined manner, such conduct will probably excite the well-disposed of the bystanders to assist him, if he requires them.[79]

The new 'Bobbies' wore a blue uniform (red being considered too evocative of the military)[80] and a leather top hat, the crown of which contained supports to enable the constable to peer over walls.[81] To enable identification of the individual police officer, a letter and number was worn on the collar of the coat. Rowan and Mayne limited the constable's weaponry to the truncheon, which, until 1863, each officer was supposed to carry concealed. Its use was as a last resort and 'not to be used in response to insulting language or actions which did not endanger the policeman.'[82]

Only on dangerous assignments[83] or beats might certain officers be allowed to carry a pistol or cutlass, since '[d]enial of lethal force emphasized the bobby's moral authority and his role as an agent of the law;

[78] As noted above, the word comes from *comes stabuli*, a Late Latin phrase meaning 'count of the stable' with its origins in the fifth century AD.

[79] Quoted in Critchley, 'Peel, Rowan, and Mayne', p. 53.

[80] Reith argues that it was not only the excessive force used by the army that was the cause of their hatred among the general public; ordinary citizens were recruited into the military through force, guile, or fraud by 'crimps' who were paid a fixed price per head. Reith, *A New Study of Police History*, p. 17.

[81] Miller, *Cops and Bobbies*, p. 33. [82] Ibid., p. 49.

[83] This did not include riot control. Reith, *A New Study of Police History*, p. 155.

punishment was left to the judiciary'.[84] Any constable who drew his sword on duty 'had to report the circumstances to his sergeant and to the desk officer when he returned to the station house'.[85] Each 'use', which included the mere drawing of a weapon (as it would do, more than a century later, with respect to a firearm or a Taser),[86] was thus 'closely scrutinized'.[87] When, in 1863, a constable seeking to arrest a man stealing fowl hit him over the head with his cutlass three times injuring the suspect so severely that he was unable to appear in court, the poor man's lawyer said that the officer's behaviour was such that he thought 'would never be permitted in England'.[88]

The Metropolitan Police constables were not, though, at least in their early days, 'thief-takers'; their primary role was as a deterrent. Indeed, it had little role in detection: the forerunner to the Criminal Investigation Department was only established in 1842; it comprised two inspectors and six sergeants.[89] The prevention of crime was to be achieved by regular patrolling of a beat,[90] supported by the intimate knowledge of the people and places along the route, and by the constable's extensive legal authority. This regimental approach to policing was not hugely attractive; a chief constable of Birmingham in the 1830s even required his officers to walk the beat at exactly two and a half miles an hour.[91] As Emsley observes, 'prevention of crime by regular patrolling was neither cerebral nor skilled'.[92] Perhaps not surprisingly, therefore, when allied to relatively poor pay, constables were not always the brightest and the best, with drunkenness a considerable problem, to the extent that it was the main reason for dismissal from the force in its early years.[93]

[84] Miller, *Cops and Bobbies*, p. 48. Miller cites the words of a detective in an 1860s melodrama, who says, 'I always feel ashamed to burn powder. Any fool can blow a man's brains out.' Ibid., p. 50.

[85] Miller, *Cops and Bobbies*, p. 50.

[86] See, for detail, the introductions to Chapters 4 and 5.

[87] R. Reiner, *The Politics of the Police*, 4th Edn, Oxford University Press, Oxford, 2010, pp. 72–73.

[88] Emsley, *The Great British Bobby*, p. 86.

[89] Reith, *A New Study of Police History*, p. 221.

[90] The precise etymology of the term is not known, although a number of suggestions have been made over the years. Cowley, *A History of the British Police*, p. 24.

[91] Emsley, *The Great British Bobby*, p. 80.

[92] Ibid., pp. 108, 109.

[93] Ibid., p. 43. Of the 2,800 constables serving in the force in 1830, only 562 remained four years later.

The temptation to overstep or misuse one's authority as a police constable was considerable. In 1854, one of the satirical magazine Punch's *Maxims for the Police* was:

> Necessity is the mother of invention; so when you find it necessary to make a charge against somebody you locked up, invent one.[94]

Indeed, in 1863, Mayne felt constrained to warn his constables against arbitrary arrests.[95]

There are many reports of policemen in the early years being attacked. These included one constable being held down while a horse-drawn cab was driven over him. Nine months after the Metropolitan Police's operational launch, the force suffered its first fatality. PC Joseph Grantham died from a brain haemorrhage after being kicked in the head when he intervened to try to separate two drunken Irishmen fighting over a woman. Sadly, there was little public sympathy for the officer. In 1869–72, a total of almost 16,000 attacks were reported against the London police, meaning an officer could expect, on average, to be attacked once every two years.[96] In 1829–99, a total of 165 Metropolitan Police officers lost their lives, 52 as a result of assaults while on duty.[97] The police were even attacked by British soldiers.[98] In Gilbert and Sullivan's 1879 comic opera, *The Pirates of Penzance*, a policeman famously utters the following verse:

> Our feelings we with difficulty smother,
> When constabulary's duty to be done.
> Ah, taking one consideration with another,
> A policeman's lot is not a happy one.

Writing in 2011, Richard Cowley noted that nearly 4,000 police and other law enforcement officers were recorded to have died in the course of duty in England and Wales.[99]

Serious concerns continue to be engaged by the use of police in undercover operations and even as *agents provocateurs*. In recent years, police officers have been accused of inciting and encouraging illegal behaviour after infiltrating groups, such as those of radical animal rights campaigners.[100]

[94] Cited by Miller, *Cops and Bobbies*, p. 62. [95] Ibid., p. 117.
[96] Cowley, *A History of the British Police*, p. 31. [97] Ibid., p. 35.
[98] Reith, *A New Study of Police History*, p. 149.
[99] Cowley, *A History of the British Police*, p. 215. See: www.policememorial.org.uk/.
[100] See, e.g., R. Evans, 'Undercover Police Spy Accused of Encouraging Activist to Crime', *The Guardian*, 4 December 2014, at: www.theguardian.com/uk-news/2014/dec/04/undercover-met-spy-animal-rights-overturn-conviction-appeal.

What is less well known is that this tactic dates back to the early days of policing. In the 1830s, Police Sergeant William Popay successfully infiltrated the radical National Political Union in London but went considerably beyond the intended role of 'listen and report' to actively encouraging extremist actions through his violent anti-police rants.[101]

Outside London, policing remained largely ad hoc while crime was rampant. A three-year Commission rendered its report in 1839, recommending the creation of a single police force for the entire country, organised along the lines of the Metropolitan Police and operating ostensibly under its control. The force, which would be funded one quarter by Great Britain's Exchequer with the remainder coming from county rates, was a political non-starter. Law enforcement outside the capital was under the control of county magistrates, and they had no interest, much less any inclination, to hand over such power to Londoners. Cowley found the Commission's ignorance of human nature and misreading of the times 'astonishing'.[102] In 1856, the County and Borough Police Act made police forces obligatory for every such area; local not national accountability, however, was the only realistic way to achieve this step forward.[103]

The 1856 Act also established Her Majesty's Inspectors of Constabulary, a body that would determine whether each local police force was 'efficient', thereby entitling it to receive funding from central government. This body, which is independent of the government and the police, endures today, its remit to independently assess police forces and policing in England and Wales and to report on their efficiency and effectiveness to Parliament.[104]

Among many challenges to effective policing stand riot control and crowd management. In 1961, the Special Patrol Group (SPG) was set up as a unit of the Metropolitan Police, providing a centrally-based mobile capability for combating serious public disorder and crime akin to the French CRS (see below).[105] Widely criticised for excessive and indiscriminate use of force, allegedly including the killing of Blair Peach, a 33-year-old special-needs teacher from New Zealand and anti-fascist

[101] Emsley, *The Great British Bobby*, pp. 56–58.
[102] Cowley, *A History of the British Police*, p. 49.
[103] Until the 1938 Fire Brigade Act, the police had also been responsible for fire-fighting, as had occurred with the vigiles in Roman times. The 1947 Fire Service Act formally abolished police fire brigades, handing the responsibility to local authorities.
[104] www.justiceinspectorates.gov.uk/hmic/about-us/.
[105] Emsley, *The Great British Bobby*, p. 255.

protester, during a 1979 demonstration against the National Front in Southall, West London,[106] the SPG was replaced in 1987 by the Territorial Support Group (TSG or CO20), a Central Operations unit of the Met.

In the West Midlands Police Force, the Serious Crimes Squad was set up in 1974. But by the mid-1980s, allegations were swirling of serious criminal behaviour by its officers, which included targeting of Blacks and Asians, and torturing suspects into confessions by putting plastic bags over their heads. One officer was reported to have claimed that his fist was 'a truth drug'.[107] Some disciplinary charges were brought against individual officers but none was ever prosecuted.

The idea of an independent body to oversee and investigate complaints against the British police had already been under consideration for decades. Lord Scarman's inquiry into the Brixton riots in 1981 (see Chapter 11) and the Stephen Lawrence inquiry in 1999 had both called for the establishment of an independent mechanism to improve police accountability. Prior to the setting up of the Independent Police Complaints Commission (IPCC) in 2002, grievances about police conduct were handled first by a Police Complaints Board, set up by the 1976 Police (Complaints) Act),[108] and later by the Police Complaints Authority, created under the authority of the 1984 Police and Criminal Evidence Act (as later amended by the 1996 Police Act).

In April 2000, the non-governmental human rights organisation, Liberty, issued a study called *An Independent Police Complaints Commission*. Subsequent government consultations on a new complaints system culminated in the 2002 Police Reform Act that established the IPCC; this

[106] P. Lewis, 'Blair Peach Killed by Police at 1979 Protest, Met Report Finds', *The Guardian*, 27 April 2010, at: www.theguardian.com/uk/2010/apr/27/blair-peach-killed-police-met-report. The nature of Peach's injuries led at least one pathologist to conclude his skull had been crushed with an unauthorised weapon, such as a lead-weighted cosh or police radio. Commander John Cass, who ran the Met's internal complaints bureau and who led the investigation into Peach's death, raided lockers at the SPG's headquarters, finding a stash of unauthorised weapons, including illegal truncheons, knives, two crowbars, a whip, a three-foot-long wooden stave, and a lead-weighted leather stick. One officer was caught trying to hide a metal cosh, although it was not the weapon that killed Peach. Another officer was found with a collection of Nazi regalia. In his report, Cass said the arsenal of weapons caused him 'grave concern', but claimed there was insufficient evidence to prosecute the officers involved.

[107] Emsley, *The Great British Bobby*, p. 279.

[108] Critchley wrote in 1978 that 'few sections of police opinion, least of all the Police Federation, shared the Home Secretary's enthusiasm for it' and cautioned that 'the price in terms of police morale may well be high'. T. A. Critchley, *History of Police in England and Wales*, 2nd Rev'd Edn, Constable, London, 1978, pp. 325–26.

new body became operational in April 2004. In 2012, however, the Labour Party's Shadow Home Secretary pledged to abolish the misfiring accountability mechanism, should it be elected to government, and to replace it with a far more robust Police Standards Authority to restore public trust. In January 2014, then Conservative Prime Minister David Cameron was said to be considering reforms to the IPCC[109] following police misconduct in the Andrew Mitchell 'plebgate' scandal[110] and errors in the police investigation that culminated in the shooting to death of Mark Duggan by an armed officer.[111] Adopted at the end of January 2017, the Policing and Crime Act renamed the IPCC as the Independent Office for Police Conduct.[112]

Along with accountability, the lack of representativeness of the police was a recurring theme. Women police officers were a creation during the First World War.[113] Edith Watson was probably the first to appear in uniform, in September 1914, as one of the Women Police Volunteers.[114] In December 1918, one hundred women were recruited and trained to be fully empowered police constables, taking up their duties in February 1919 as the first Metropolitan policewomen.[115] During the Second World War, the number of 'attested' women police officers increased from 282 in 1940 to 418 in 1945.[116]

Writing about her experiences as a WPC (women police constable) in 1950s Yorkshire, Pamela Dixon noted that she was given a whistle but not a truncheon and was not provided with handcuffs, even though she had the nominal power of arrest. She left the service upon her betrothal (to another officer); only much later was the ludicrous requirement that women be single (or resign from the police force upon getting married) finally dropped.[117] Yet problems persisted. One woman police officer said that when she joined the force in 1972, a woman recruit was 'either a nymphomaniac or a dyke, you couldn't be normal'.[118] In 1978, Detective

109 R. Mason, 'David Cameron Considers IPCC Reforms', *The Guardian*, 15 January 2014, at: www.theguardian.com/politics/2014/jan/15/david-cameron-ipcc-reforms-police.

110 See, e.g., '"Plebgate" Row: Timeline', BBC, 27 November 2014, at: www.bbc.co.uk/news/uk-24548645.

111 See, e.g., V. Dodd, 'Mark Duggan's Death: Two Shots Fired and Two Conflicting Stories', *The Guardian*, 8 January 2014, at: www.theguardian.com/uk-news/2014/jan/08/mark-duggan-death-london-riots.

112 S. 33, Policing and Crime Act (2017), at: www.legislation.gov.uk/ukpga/2017/3/section/33/enacted.

113 Emsley, *The Great British Bobby*, p. 178.

114 Cowley, *A History of the British Police*, p. 145.

115 Ibid., p. 146.

116 Emsley, *The Great British Bobby*, p. 245.

117 Ibid.

118 Ibid., p. 271.

Sergeant Frederick Connor, Chairman of the Scottish Police Federation, offered his 'expert' opinion that:

> I am not saying there is no place for women in the police service ... but they have their limitations. God made us differently and an Act of Parliament cannot change that.[119]

In June 1995, the first woman chief constable, Pauline Clare, was appointed to head Lancashire's police service.[120] By 2012, more than one in four police officers were female.[121]

A black police officer had been appointed in Carlisle during Queen Victoria's reign, but as late as 1966, the year Norwell Roberts became the first black police officer in London, ethnic minority officers were almost unheard of. By the end of the 1970s, there were more than 100 police officers from ethnic minorities in the Met, but this was in a force of some 25,000.[122] As at 31 March 2013, of almost 130,000 police officers in the 43 police forces of England and Wales, more than 6,500 were from ethnic minorities. This represents 5 per cent of the total, the same percentage as on 31 March 2012.[123] In one force, West Midlands Police, which covers one of the United Kingdom's most ethnically diverse cities, Birmingham,[124] the force's Police and Crime Commissioner revealed in April 2015 that from among 162 new recruits just one black constable had received a warrant card that year.[125]

119 A. Hamilton, 'Recruitment of Women no Answer to Fall in Police Manpower', *The Times*, 27 April 1978, cited by K. Segrave, *Policewomen, A History*, 2nd Edn, McFarland, Jefferson, North Carolina, 2014, p. 286.

120 Segrave, ibid., p. 314.

121 Data from UN Office on Drugs and Crime, at: Data available at: https://data.unodc.org/#state:1.

122 Emsley, *The Great British Bobby*, p. 263–65.

123 Home Office, 'Police Workforce, England and Wales, 31 March 2013', 18 July 2013, at: www.gov.uk/government/publications/police-workforce-england-and-wales-31-march-2013/police-workforce-england-and-wales-31-march-2013.

124 According to the 2011 national census, some 42 per cent of residents were from an ethnic group other than white.

125 N. McCarthy, 'West Midlands Police Recruit One Black Officer in 160-Strong Intake', *Birmingham Post*, 9 April 2015 (as updated on 10 April 2015), at: www.birminghampost.co.uk/news/local-news/west-midlands-police-recruit-one-9012117. Later in 2015, however, West Midlands Police was nominated for a diversity award. N. McCarthy, 'Force which Recruited 15 Black or Asian Officers out of 162 Trainees Shortlisted for Diversity Award', *Birmingham Post*, 15 September 2015, at: www.birminghammail.co.uk/news/midlands-news/force-recruited-15-black-asian-10051931?ptnr_rid=41704&icid=EM_BirminghamMail_Nletter_News_Home_largeteaser_Text_Story2.

Fear of the politicisation of the police predated the creation of the Metropolitan Police[126] and continues to this day. Some argue that the police are inherently a tool of class warfare, conceived of as a means for the rich to preserve their property and possessions and oppress the poor. With a view to allying such fears, especially among the working class,[127] on its creation the 1829 Metropolitan Police Act had denied to 'bobbies' the right to vote. In the 1860s, a journalist opined that: 'One great merit in the police is that they know nothing of politics; the man in blue always preserves his neutral tint.'[128] One hundred and twenty years later, this view of the police would be severely tested by their actions during the 1984–85 miners' strike.[129]

The most notorious incident in this bitter industrial dispute occurred in South Yorkshire on 18 June 1984. The so-called Battle of Orgreave resulted in 51 miners and 72 police officers being injured and 93 people arrested.[130] The Prime Minister at the time, Margaret Thatcher, had already termed the striking miners 'the enemy within', while MI5, the United Kingdom's domestic counterintelligence and security agency, had reportedly infiltrated the miners. At the Orgreave coking plant, 10,000 striking miners clashed with 5,000 waiting police officers. Those arrested at Orgreave were held for a variety of offences, with several put on trial for rioting. However, the trial collapsed after 16 weeks when it became

[126] Although nominally under the control of the Home Secretary, the Metropolitan Police was cast 'rather as a service than a force', with its constitutional position more than a little obscure. Critchley, 'Peel, Rowan, and Mayne', p. 87. After 1945 and until 1989, however, its official title was the Metropolitan Police Force. On the recommendation of corporate identity consultants, Wolff Olins, and following their report entitled 'A Force for Change: Report on the Corporate Identity of the Metropolitan Police' the title was formally changed to the Metropolitan Police Service. Today, the MPS is still commonly known as the Met (among other names, some markedly less favourable).

[127] Miller notes that many workers 'must have felt that the "strong arm of the law"' was 'exceedingly powerful against the weak but extremely weak against the powerful'. Miller, *Cops and Bobbies*, p. 124.

[128] Cited in ibid., p. 13.

[129] Cabinet documents are said to show how Margaret Thatcher was frustrated at being told by Leon Brittan, the home secretary, that he had gone to 'the limit of what [he] could do while respecting the constitutional independence of police forces' and urged him to 'stiffen the resolve' of chief constables to adopt 'the more vigorous interpretation of their duties which was being sought'. D. Macintyre, 'How the Miners' Strike of 1984–85 Changed Britain For Ever', *New Statesman*, 16 June 2014, at: www.newstatesman.com/politics/2014/06/how-miners-strike-1984-85-changed-britain-ever.

[130] 'Arthur Scargill Calls for 1984 Orgreave Arrest Probe', BBC, 22 November 2013, at: www.bbc.co.uk/news/uk-england-south-yorkshire-25053844.

clear that police evidence was unreliable.[131] In 1991, South Yorkshire Police paid out £500,000 to 39 miners arrested during the policing operation at Orgreave.[132]

In October 2012, a BBC documentary into what happened at Orgreave reported evidence that South Yorkshire Police had deliberately sought to coordinate arrest statements in order to charge the miners with riot. Following the programme, South Yorkshire Police referred itself to the IPCC; the referral contained allegations of assault, perjury, perverting the course of justice, and misconduct in a public office.[133] In June 2015, the IPCC announced its decision not to conduct an investigation into South Yorkshire Police's handling of events. This was done on the basis that the passage of time meant that allegations of assault and of misconduct could not be pursued; that some matters were subject to complaints and civil proceedings at the time; and detailed analysis had not revealed other issues in relation to individual officers which could be investigated.[134] In response, Yvette Cooper, Labour's then shadow Home Secretary, said the decision 'lets down' the Orgreave miners' families, and she questioned the IPCC's fitness to handle police misconduct allegations. Ms Cooper called for an independent inquiry, saying of the IPCC: 'If they are too limited to do the job, then someone else needs to. For too long there have been serious allegations about the way the miners were treated at Orgreave, but we have never had the truth.'[135] In October 2016, Secretary of State for Home Affairs, Amber Rudd, announced there would not be a public inquiry into policing tactics used at Orgreave.[136]

131 N. Tarver, '"Battle of Orgreave": Miners and Police Remember', BBC, 14 November 2013, at: www.bbc.co.uk/news/uk-england-24941194.

132 See, e.g., D. Conn, 'Tell Us the Truth about the Battle of Orgreave', *The Guardian*, 24 November 2014, at: www.theguardian.com/commentisfree/2014/nov/14/battle-orgreave-policing-1984–85-miners-strike-britain-ipcc.

133 IPCC, 'IPCC Receives Orgreave Referral from South Yorkshire Police', 16 November 2012, at: www.ipcc.gov.uk/news/ipcc-receives-orgreave-referral-south-yorkshire-police.

134 IPCC, 'IPCC Announces Decision Following Orgreave Scoping Exercise', 12 June 2015, at: www.ipcc.gov.uk/news/ipcc-announces-decision-following-orgreave-scoping-exercise#sthash.Ny6PdBw5.dpuf.

135 D. Conn, 'IPCC will not Investigate Orgreave Police Action during Miners' Strike', *The Guardian*, 12 June 2015, at: www.theguardian.com/politics/2015/jun/12/ipcc-will-not-investigate-orgreave-police-action-during-miners-strike.

136 A. Travis, 'Government rules out Orgreave inquiry', *The Guardian*, 31 October 2016, at: https://www.theguardian.com/politics/2016/oct/31/government-rules-out-orgreave-inquiry.

British Colonial Policing

Policing in Ireland

Mawby suggested it was 'perhaps unsurprising' that the first paid police was established in Ireland, given that by the eighteenth century 'a number of baronial police forces ... enabled the Protestant minority to maintain control over the Catholic peasantry'.[137] Ireland had had a police force of salaried sub-constables since 1784, but this system was swept away by the 1822 Constabulary Act that saw the creation of the Royal Irish Constabulary (RIC).[138]

Peel had asserted '[t]he Irishman's predilection for outrage and a lawless life which I believe nothing can control'.[139] Notwithstanding this view, he had (perhaps naively) hoped that his Metropolitan Police model would function equally well in Ireland. Despite certain commonalities, however,

> whereas the Metropolitan Police was an unarmed civil police, the Royal Irish Constabulary was a semi-militarized force, a *gendarmerie*, which always had at the forefront of its mind the maintenance of law and order amongst a population large elements of which were often actively or passively opposed to the whole system of law which the force sought to uphold.[140]

Thus, training given to RIC cadets 'comprised extensive musketry training, including the use of rifle and bayonet, military and physical drill, and equitation'.[141] In the fighting that led to the creation of the Irish Free State in 1922, many casualties were suffered among RIC officers. Between 1919 and 1922, it is estimated by one authority that 588 were killed and a further 700 or so were injured; this from a total force of only 16,000.[142] Following the partition of the island, a new force, the Royal Ulster Constabulary (RUC), was created in the North,

[137] R. I. Mawby, 'Variations on a Theme: The Development of Professional Police in the British Isles and North America', ch. 3 in R. I. Mawby (ed.), *Policing Across the World. Issues for the Twenty-First Century*, Routledge, London, 1999, p. 31.

[138] J. J. Tobias, 'The British Colonial Police, An Alternative Police Style', ch. 14 in Stead, *Pioneers in Policing*, pp. 243–44, 245.

[139] G. Ellison and J. Smyth, *The Crowned Harp: Policing Northern Ireland*, Pluto Press, London, 2000, p. 9.

[140] Tobias, 'The British Colonial Police', pp. 242–43; *cf* also Miller, *Cops and Bobbies*, p. 1.

[141] G. Sinclair, *At the End of the Line. Colonial Policing and the Imperial Endgame, 1945–80*, Manchester University Press, Manchester, 2010, p. 17.

[142] Emsley, *The Great British Bobby*, p. 199.

initially numbering 3,000. Its membership was supposed to be one-third Catholic and two-thirds Protestant, but Catholics never exceeded 22 per cent and were said to be about 10 per cent of the total by the 1960s.[143] The institution manifested itself as an agency of state control.[144]

'The Troubles', as the sectarian violence between Catholics and Protestants in Northern Ireland and Britain's armed response to it is widely known, began in 1968 and continued for thirty years, during which more than 3,600 people were killed and many thousands more were injured.[145] The RUC was in the firing line for much of that period, though the British Army also played a significant frontline role. According to Ellison and Smyth, the refusal of the British state 'to address, or even acknowledge, the grievances of the [Catholic] minority made it inevitable that when street protest began in the summer of 1968 the first line of confrontation would be with the RUC'.[146] During one of the first civil rights marches in Derry in October 1969 in which some 400 people participated, one commentator reported that the RUC 'punched, batoned and pursued civil rights demonstrators in a brutal display of concerted violence'.[147]

Increasingly, though, the British army was taking over responsibility for policing. Initial efforts to remain – and be seen as – impartial in this role were quickly swept away, with the events in Londonderry/Derry on 'Bloody Sunday' on 30 January 1972 undermining claims that Catholics in the north were being protected. During a protest march against internment organised by the Northern Ireland Civil Rights Association, British soldiers from the 1st Battalion of the Parachute Regiment shot twenty-six unarmed civilians, many while fleeing and some while trying to help the wounded. Fourteen died, thirteen on the scene. Two protesters were also injured when they were run over by army vehicles.

143 Mawby, 'Variations on a Theme: The Development of Professional Police in the British Isles and North America', p. 35.

144 Ibid., citing J. D. Brewer, A. Guelke, I. Hume, E. Moxon-Browne, and R. Wilford, *The Police, Public Order and the State*, Macmillan, London, 1988.

145 At: www.bbc.co.uk/history/troubles. A. M. Wilson (*Policing Ireland's Twisted History*, iUniverse, Bloomington, Indiana, p. xiv) points out that this fatality rate equates to one in five hundred citizens in the province.

146 Ellison and Smyth, *The Crowned Harp*, p. 56.

147 N. O. Dochartaigh, *From Civil Rights to Armalites*, Cork University Press, Cork, 1997, p. 5, cited by ibid., p. 57.

In the days leading up to Bloody Sunday, Major-General Robert Ford, Commander of Land Forces in Northern Ireland, wrote to his army superior in confidence in the following terms:

> I am coming to the conclusion that the minimum force necessary to achieve a restoration of law and order is to shoot selected ring leaders ... In other words, we would be reverting to the methods of IS [internal security] found successful on many occasions overseas.[148]

In the immediate aftermath, though, Ford claimed that the paratroopers had only fired after having been fired upon.[149]

Two investigations into the killings were held. The Widgery Tribunal, convened soon afterwards, described the soldiers' shooting as 'bordering on the reckless' but largely absolved them and the authorities of responsibility. In 1998, the Saville Inquiry was tasked with reinvestigating the incident. Following a twelve-year inquiry that cost almost £200 million, its report was made public in 2010, concluding that all of those who had been shot were unarmed, and that the killings were both 'unjustified and unjustifiable'. The then UK Prime Minister, David Cameron, made a formal apology on behalf of the state.

In December 2012, senior commanders from the Police Service of Northern Ireland, which replaced the discredited RUC,[150] announced that a murder inquiry into the killings would begin in 2013; it recommenced in January 2015.[151] In August 2015, the chief constable of the Police Service of Northern Ireland said it was 'unacceptable' that some families of those killed on Bloody Sunday had not heard from the investigation in more than a year.[152] In December of that year, a former Parachute Regiment soldier was arrested.[153] In August 2016, it was reported that as many as twenty former soldiers had been questioned

[148] Cited by Ellison and Smyth, ibid., p. 129.

[149] At: www.bbc.co.uk/programmes/p00nm4k6.

[150] The future of policing was a key element in the peace talks in Northern Ireland in the late 1990s. In 2001, the RUC was replaced by the Police Service of Northern Ireland (PSNI).

[151] 'Bloody Sunday Murder Investigation to Recommence', *TheJournal.ie*, 8 January 2015, at: www.thejournal.ie/bloody-sunday-murder-investigation-recommence-1871266-Jan2015/.

[152] BBC, 'PSNI Chief Constable Says Bloody Sunday Families' wait "Unacceptable"', 27 August 2015, at: www.bbc.co.uk/news/uk-northern-ireland-34071197.

[153] O. Bowcott, 'Bitter Legacy of Bloody Sunday Rumbles on as Former Soldier Arrested', *The Guardian*, 10 November 2015, at: www.theguardian.com/uk-news/2015/nov/10/bitter-legacy-bloody-sunday-rumbles-former-soldier-arrested.

by police over the Bloody Sunday shootings. Detectives said they had finished their interviews and were drawing up a report for prosecutors.[154]

British Colonial Police forces

The 'success' of the Irish model, at least in British eyes, led to its export to India and Ceylon (modern-day Sri Lanka).[155] The Indian Police Service was predominantly military: 'The training of the force was almost entirely in the use of arms, and most of its work consisted of armed guard, escort and patrol duties.'[156] The Palestine Police in the 1920s was a direct export of the RIC.[157] According to one line of argument, the French 'transported their policing model lock, stock and barrel to their colonies. The British allegedly created a brand new model . . . Yet, in both instances, policing relied more heavily on coercion than on consent.'[158]

At its height, several dozen British Colonial Police forces were deployed in British colonies, protectorates, and trust territories. The forces often differed from those in England and Wales as some were armed and controlled by the central government.[159] Termed the Colonial Police Service from 1 October 1936, it primarily served the interests of the British nation. In Larnaca, Cyprus, during disturbances in 1955, the Deputy Commissioner of the Cyprus Police wrote that 'demonstrations were very quickly dispersed by baton parties and I am glad to report that a few heads were broken'. Use of force was, though, supposed to be minimal not maximal, and to extend to firearms only in extreme circumstances. Proposals from London for the use of tear gas met with scepticism from many colonial policemen. One officer suggested that Africa, with its 'open spaces and warm still air', did not lend itself to the use of such a weapon.[160]

154 B. Farmer, 'Bloody Sunday Police Finish Quizzing Soldiers for Possible Prosecutions', *Daily Telegraph*, 19 August 2016, at: www.telegraph.co.uk/news/2016/08/19/bloody-sunday-police-finish-quizzing-soldiers-for-possible-prose/.

155 Tobias, 'The British Colonial Police', p. 250.

156 Ibid., p. 252, citing C. J. Jeffries, *The Colonial Police*, M. Parrish, London, 1952, p. 36.

157 Sinclair, *At the End of the Line*, p. 11.

158 Ibid., p. 223, citing R. I. Mawby 'Models of Policing', in T. Newburn (ed.), *Handbook of Policing*, Willan, Cullompton, 2005, p. 22.

159 Cowley, *A History of the British Police*, p. 172. Cowley cites a figure of thirty-seven; Sinclair claims forty-three separate police forces in the Colonial Police Service in 1948. Sinclair, *At the End of the Line*, p. 56.

160 Sinclair, *At the End of the Line*, pp. 68–69.

In 1956, the Home Office was challenging the Colonial Office, maintaining that

> the important point is that without an independent and impartial police force which is respected by the community and which can rely on citizens for information and help no democratic system can work efficiently. The police ought not to be used as soldiers or soldiers as police.[161]

But as the British Empire faded, former colonies established their own police forces. The last force regularly to take British police officers was the Royal Hong Kong Police; this persisted until the return of the province to China in 1999.[162]

Policing in France

Despite claims that the Metropolitan Police was the world's first modern police force, on the continent, full-time, paid police forces had existed for far longer. Indeed, although implicitly derided by Peel in 1822 as 'a system of espionage',[163] the police of France 'have probably [existed] as a professional body longer than any other police in Europe'.[164] As Stead further explains,

> In France, the *maréchaussée*, the provost police of the marshals of France, had policed the highways and rural areas of the country since the end of the Middle Ages, incarnating the royal authority throughout the land, and under its post-Revolutionary title of the Gendarmerie Nationale it is still one of the two mainstays of the French police system.[165]

Reminiscent in many ways of the Roman Praetorian Guard, the *gens d'armes* ('people under arms') were originally the bodyguards of the kings of France. These professional soldiers stood around the royal standard during the battles of Crécy and Azincourt; later they were entrusted with the additional tasks of policing the highways and countryside during the Middle Ages.[166] Briefly dissolved during the French Revolution, a 1791 law renamed the corps the Gendarmerie Nationale

161 Home Office Minute of 19 April 1956, cited by Sinclair, ibid., p. 56.
162 Cowley, *A History of the British Police*, p. 174.
163 C. Emsley, *Crime, Police, & Penal Policy: European Experiences 1750–1940*, Oxford University Press, Oxford, 2007, p. 107.
164 P. J. Stead, *The Police of France*, Macmillan, New York, 1983, p. 158.
165 Stead, *Pioneers in Policing*, p. 5; see also Stead, 'Joseph Fouché, The Napoleonic Model of Police', ch. 4 in ibid., p. 65.
166 Stead, 'Joseph Fouché, The Napoleonic Model of Police', p. 65.

and required that all *gendarmes* be literate, be at least 25 years of age, and have served in the army.[167] Among other tasks, the Gendarmerie were required to patrol, arrest thieves and killers, disperse revolts and seditious assemblages, report on fires, and to be available for large gatherings.[168] The Republican Guard, formed in 1848, and which today is a part of the Gendarmerie, exists to provide security in the Paris area and serves to protect, among others, the French president.

A separate force, though, was needed for policing the streets of Paris on a daily basis. Even before the Metropolitan Police was formally created, Paris had put into uniform one hundred *sergents de ville*, a public post in would later become the Police Nationale.[169] In Emsley's view, the *sergents* had been created partly as a public relations exercise and partly to try and improve the behaviour of police officers through better control. Thus, the etymology of the word *sergent* is from the Latin *serviens*, meaning in this case a public servant rather than a soldier,[170] and its distant semantic origins seemingly predate those of the military rank of sergeant. Like their American equivalents, initially they were armed only with a baton during the day and a sabre at night.[171] The *sergent* was touchingly described in 1856 as 'the guardian angel of peaceful citizens, and the terror of criminals'.[172]

A Ministry of General Police was created in January 1796, but in three years nine ministers came and went; the tenth was Joseph Fouché, a religious man and a freemason, but one associated in the public mind with the Revolutionary Reign of Terror.[173] Fouché left the policing of what he thoughtfully termed 'the whores, the thieves, and the street lamps' to his subordinates; he was more concerned with easing the path to power of Napoleon Bonaparte in a *coup d'état*. Yet his revolutionary and anti-republican background notwithstanding, Fouché also promoted

[167] It is famously said that a gendarme is a soldier, but a soldier is not a gendarme. Stead, *The Police of France*, p. 140.

[168] Stead, 'Joseph Fouché, The Napoleonic Model of Police', p. 65.

[169] Stead, *Pioneers in Policing*, p. 5. From 1944 to 1966, the force was known as the Sûreté nationale.

[170] Stead, *The Police of France*, p. 17.

[171] Emsley, *Crime, Police, & Penal Policy*, p. 111.

[172] A. Wynter, 'The Police and the Thieves', *Quarterly Review*, Vol. 99 (1856), London, cited by ibid., p. 163.

[173] Stead, *The Police of France*, pp. 70–71. Along with a colleague, Fouché ensured the Revolutionary Tribunal in Lyon sentenced 1,667 people to death. As even the guillotine could not cope with this level of killing, the executions were carried out by cannon fire. Ibid., p. 38.

good policing practice. In a famous circular to prefects of police in 1799 he wrote:

> Police are reproached for harassing the innocent, justice for being unable to prevent or arrest crime. Because it was in the king's hands, police has generally passed for an instrument of despotism . . .
>
> Never forget how dangerous it is to make arrests on mere suspicion; reflect that your actions, even when they are in error, will be a primary presumption against those whom you take before justice; and meditate in the quick of your conscience upon the history of so many innocent people who were sent by justice to the scaffold only because they were taken before justice in error.[174]

Today the Police Nationale has primary jurisdiction in cities and large towns whereas the Gendarmerie's primary jurisdiction covers smaller towns and rural and border areas. All routinely carry arms. A specialised unit within the force set up in 1945, the ever-controversial Republican Security Companies (known 'popularly, or rather, unpopularly' as the CRS),[175] is responsible for riot control. In February 2016, for instance, a section of Chelsea football fans were targeted with tear gas by the CRS riot squad during a Champions League game in Paris.[176] A similar unit exists within the Gendarmerie; following the deaths of demonstrators in the 1930s, research was carried out into alternative methods of crowd control, specifically tear gas, plastic bullets, and coloured dye that could be shot from fire hoses.[177]

Women have only been accepted as regular appointments to the French police since the 1970s. Not until 1978 were women allowed to perform frontline roles as officers; fifty-one were initially accepted into the Police Nationale from a thousand candidates.[178] In 1987, Isabelle Guion de Méritens became the first woman officer in the Gendarmerie Nationale; in 2013, she became the first woman to be appointed a general in the force.[179] Ethnic minority enrolment in the police appears to be

174 Ministerial Circular of 21 November 1799, cited by ibid., p. 75.

175 Stead, *The Police of France*, p. 6.

176 J. de Menezes, 'Chelsea Fans Sprayed with Tear Gas as Police Force Supporters to Leave Seats during PSG Defeat', *Independent*, 17 February 2016, at: www.independent.co.uk/sport/football/european/chelsea-fans-targeted-with-cs-gas-as-police-spray-supporters-during-psg-defeat-a6878611.html.

177 Emsley, *Crime, Police, & Penal Policy*, p. 253.

178 Stead, *The Police of France*, pp. 111, 112.

179 'Première femme nommée général de gendarmerie', *Le Figaro*, 28 March 2013, at: www.lefigaro.fr/actualite-france/2013/03/28/01016–20130328ARTFIG00562-premiere-femme-nommee-general-de-gendarmerie.php. In Germany it was 1978 before women

extremely low, but because it is prohibited to publish data on the ethnic breakdown of the police, no one knows for sure what the numbers or percentages are.

Policing in the United States

Indigenous American tribes used 'an array of methods of social control'.[180] The nomadic Cheyennes of the West were said to have six different military groups that also served as a form of police.[181] When the settlers arrived in America, beginning in the early seventeenth century, they instituted the law enforcement mechanisms with which they were familiar: the sheriff, the constable, and the watch. The first night watch was created in Boston in February 1636, staffed by citizens appointed by the town government.[182] But this early law enforcement system was 'ineffective and inefficient. Some watchmen slept on duty, while some citizens paid substitutes to serve for them. At times, service as a watchman was a sentence of punishment. Fees were paid to constables and sheriffs for testifying in court, serving papers, and other tasks. As in England, unscrupulous officials became entrepreneurs.'[183]

In Frank Morn's view, the modern police department came late to America, a fact he ascribes to a widespread fear of a standing army and of the costs of 'big' government.[184] Law enforcement remained for a long time an amateurish affair in the cities, with the ancient constable and night-watch system the mainstay, making it cheap but largely ineffective. But as American cities experienced a huge expansion in the first half of the nineteenth century – between 1820 and 1860 the urban population grew eightfold – the old system buckled under the social pressures. In Chicago, private companies, notably the Chicago Detecting and Collecting Police Agency and the Pinkerton Protective Patrol (see below),

were admitted into the regular uniformed police service, and even then initially this only applied to the capital, Berlin. The last state in federal Germany to admit women – Bavaria – only did so in 1990. B. Frevel and P. Kuschewski, 'Police Organization and Police Reform in Germany: The Case of North Rhine-Westphalia', *German Policy Studies*, Vol. 5, No. 2 (2009), p. 66, at: www.spaef.com/file.php?id=1136.

180 Steverson, *Policing in America*, p. 10. 181 Ibid.

182 M. J. Palmiotto, *Policing: Concepts, Strategies, and Current Issues in American Police Forces*, 3rd Edn, CreateSpace Independent Publishing Platform, United States, 2013, p. 16.

183 Ibid.

184 F. T. Morn, 'Allan Pinkerton, Private Police Influence on Police Development', ch. 6 in Stead, *Pioneers in Policing*, p. 102.

moved swiftly to fill the gap in public service; by 1860, these two agencies 'more closely resembled a modern police department than the Chicago police force itself'.[185]

In 1845, the Municipal Police Act established in New York 'the first police force modelled on London's precedent outside of the British Empire'.[186] Known as 'cop' or 'copper' owing to the metal badge each of the 100 officers wore,[187] during the day, they carried a cane; by night, a sabre.[188] In 1853, the Commissioner refused to hire any officers who would not wear a uniform; some felt, though, that it would make them more visible to thieves, or that it was 'un-American', or even that it undermined their masculinity.[189] Others 'felt it represented a militaristic and undemocratic type of organization'.[190] The police force, as with its counterpart in London, also had to overcome public apprehension of a police force as equating to, in Miller's words, 'a standing army susceptible to the political machinations of an ambitious despot'.[191]

In ethnic riots in mid-nineteenth-century New York, 'the physical force of military and police weaponry had to compensate for the police's lack of numerical strength and moral force. Many riots became battles in which no quarter was asked or given on either side.'[192] The Astor Riot of 1849, which arose between supporters of rival American and British actors, was so violent that the mayor of the day called in militia troops to support the police. The troops fired over the heads of the rioters, hitting many innocent spectators behind them. Miller cites a contemporary writer who held that:

> We cannot in this consummation recognize any triumph of the laws, nor find any cause to congratulate the friends of order that the arm of the law has been sufficient for the emergency. The bayonet and cartridge are not elements in the administration of the American laws.[193]

But the economics that had arguably been at the heart of efforts to establish London's police force were just as persuasive across the Atlantic.

[185] Ibid., pp. 103–7. [186] Miller, *Cops and Bobbies*, pp. 2–3.

[187] Emsley, *The Great British Bobby*, p. 4. [188] Stead, *The Police of France*, p. 54.

[189] Palmiotto, *Policing: Concepts, Strategies, and Current Issues in American Police Forces*, p. 17.

[190] Steverson, *Policing in America*, p. 15. [191] Miller, *Cops and Bobbies*, p. 4.

[192] Ibid., p. 22. Miller suggests elsewhere that 'the Irish background of both policemen and offenders may have encouraged rather than dampened violence'. In London, Mayne was reluctant to recruit the Irish as policemen. Ibid., p. 155, 170.

[193] Miller, *Cops and Bobbies*, p. 22.

In the words of one anonymous New Yorker following the passing of the Act who Miller cites, 'Men will go with reluctance to make money in a city where pestilence of violence renders life unsafe.'[194] Effective policing 'contributed to the city's economic health',[195] an issue to which we return in Chapter 2.

In the early days of New York policing, the political impartiality that characterised London's 'New Police' was not, though, reflected across the Atlantic. 'Before 1853, patrolmen looked to local politicians for appointment and promotion. Consequently they were less amenable to their superior officers' orders and friction developed ... Policemen participated in political clubs, often resigning to work for re-election of their aldermen, who left the positions vacant until they won the election and could reappoint the loyal patrolmen.'[196] In 1860, to improve police performance, the rank of inspector was introduced to monitor their behaviour, a measure said by a contemporary to have made the force 'attentive and efficient, as if by magic'.[197]

Until 1857, New York police officers were armed only with a truncheon, like their counterparts in London. In response to several riots that year, however, commissioners quietly permitted the use of revolvers; by July, 'pretty much all the men' were armed. In the words of one superintendent that year,

> The mere exhibition of firearms in the hands of those who can legally use them produces a most instantaneous revulsion in the courage of the blustering violators of the law. Its efficiency has been tested, and its further application I trust will be proved.[198]

In 1874, the Texas Rangers, whose origins date back to 1823, were formally constituted as a police constabulary by the Texas state legislature; they are the oldest state-level law enforcement body in the United States (though, as Steverson observes, in the 1820s Texas was still a republic).[199] Their antecedents were farmers and small businessmen who had banded together using their own horses, weapons, and rations to fend off native American Indian attacks; this tradition was carried forward into the Rangers. The tactics they employed were largely dedicated to use of brute force; legislators in the state capital, Austin,

[194] Ibid., p. 8. [195] Ibid. [196] Ibid., p. 43. [197] Ibid., p. 44.

[198] Ibid., p. 52, citing Superintendent Frederick A. Tallmadge writing in *The Herald*, 6 November 1857, p. 2.

[199] Steverson, *Policing in America*, p. 19.

accorded the new constabulary 'free rein to dispense violence as needed in order to extend white hegemony' in the state.[200]

The Rangers were said to be 'ruthless in their dealings with certain groups, especially African slaves and Mexicans'.[201] On one occasion in January 1881, a squad of twenty-one Rangers attacked a band of Apache raiders they had been tracking for almost two weeks. They opened fire on the Apaches as they were eating breakfast, killing six, including two women, and injuring several others, including a number of young children. The Rangers' Captain wrote in his report on the ambush that he did not think the Indians 'will sit down to eat breakfast again without looking to see if the Rangers are in sight'.[202] More creditably, the Texas Rangers helped to prevent the assassination of President William Howard Taft in El Paso, a famed town in Texas, and performed with distinction in some of the best-known criminal cases in the history of the Old West, such as the outlaws Bonnie and Clyde. Today, the Texas Rangers Division is the state's chief investigative agency.[203]

After public denunciation of brutal 'third degree' interrogations by local police forces in the late 1920s and early 1930s, the US Supreme Court began to restrict the admissibility of evidence in court proceedings that had been obtained under physical duress.[204] In the 1960s, the famous case of *Miranda* v. *Arizona* clarified the duty to inform a detained suspect of his right to remain silent under police interrogation. The Court argued that 'without proper safeguards the process of in-custody interrogation of persons suspected or accused of crime contains inherently compelling pressures which work to undermine the individual's will to resist and to compel him to speak where he would otherwise do so freely.' Therefore, in a 5-4 majority holding, the Court ruled a defendant

> must be warned prior to any questioning that he has the right to remain silent, that anything he says can be used against him in a court of law, that he has the right to the presence of an attorney, and that if

[200] A. R. Graybill, *Policing the Great Plains, Rangers, Mounties, and the North American Frontier, 1875–1910*, University of Nebraska Press, Lincoln, 2007, pp. 12, 13, 14, and 15.

[201] Steverson, *Policing in America*, p. 19.

[202] Graybill, *Policing the Great Plains*, p. 23. Thus, the Lone Ranger, a fictional character who first appeared on a Detroit radio show in 1933, can be seen as a rather more than stylised representation of the Texas Rangers insofar as the hero, when forced to use guns, never shot to kill but only sought to disarm his opponent as painlessly as possible.

[203] Ibid., p. 201. [204] Miller, *Cops and Bobbies*, p. 46.

> he cannot afford an attorney one will be appointed for him prior to any questioning if he so desires.[205]

Women were admitted in US police forces considerably earlier than they were in England and Wales,[206] though not until 1910 could a female be hired and officially bestowed with the title of policewoman.[207] In 1895, Lily Thomson, a 23-year-old from Charleston, formally applied to join the Washington, DC police force. In her application she argued that 'more can be accomplished while making arrest by the use of moral suasion than by the use of club, pistols and brute force. The experiment of female police officers is worth trying.'[208] It was only in 1910, however, that Alice Stebbins Wells seemingly made history by being the first to be officially hired by a police agency as a policewoman, in Los Angeles.[209] She started on an annual salary of $75; the patrolman's salary was $102.[210]

The initial motivation to include women in law enforcement agencies was to improve the protection of female detainees in the criminal justice system against rape and other forms of sexual assault; the move was strongly resisted 'by much of the male police establishment'.[211] But opposition was not only from men. In 1911, in response to a Boston police commissioner's stated willingness to employ policewomen, a well-known journalist of the day, Nixola Greeley-Smith, asked what woman 'of normal sympathies would want to use the only efficient force possible to her – that of firearms? A group of small boys shooting craps would laugh at the attempts of a woman police officer to break up their game, and laugh not only at her, but at every principle of government she might feebly endeavour to represent.'[212]

205 US Courts, 'Miranda v. Arizona and Criminal Defense, Facts and Case Summary', undated but accessed on 2 March 2015 at: www.uscourts.gov/educational-resources/get-involved/constitution-activities/fifth-amendment/miranda-criminal-defense/facts-case-summary.aspx. The Miranda warning is derived from the Fifth Amendment to the US Constitution, which was adopted in 1791.

206 Germany's first policewoman was said to have been hired 1903. Segrave, *Policewomen, A History*, p. 116.

207 Ibid., p. 33.

208 Ibid., p. 38.

209 www.lapdonline.org/history_of_the_lapd/content_basic_view/833. Lola Baldwin was employed by the Portland Police Department in 1905. Steverson, *Policing in America*, p. 54. In its latest strategic plan, the LAPD records that Georgia Robinson became, in 1919, the nation's first *African-American* policewoman when she was hired as a jail matron. LAPD, *Strategic Plan 2020*, p. 9, at: http://assets.lapdonline.org/assets/pdf/LAPD%20Strategic%20Plan.pdf.

210 Segrave, *Policewomen, A History*, pp. 52, 59.

211 Ibid., p. 3.

212 N. Greeley-Smith, 'Holds the Mirror Up to Women', *The Evening World*, New York, 4 May 1911, cited by Segrave, *Policewomen, A History*, p. 65.

More progressive opinions were, though, expressed in certain sections of the media. In 1912, the *Chicago Daily News* observed that the appointment of policewomen in the 'Windy City' marked the end of the idea 'that any officer of the law must be a heavy-footed and more or less slow-witted male person armed with a formidable club and a revolver.'[213] As Segrave points out, '[t]he user of excessive force is almost always a policeman not a policewoman.' In the United States, civil litigation for excessive use of force by the police costs cities tens of millions of dollars each year.[214]

More and more policewomen were hired in law enforcement agencies across the United States over the decades that followed women's first entry into the police, though they typically encountered hostility and prejudice from their peers, sometimes rising to sexual harassment, sexual assault, and even rape. In 1971, Los Angeles' Chief of Police told an audience of 100 policewomen that they did not belong in cars and could not be trusted with guns 'during that time of the month'.[215] Black policewomen faced additional abuse. In 1991, Constance Barron, an agent in training at the Bureau of Alcohol, Tobacco and Firearms (ATF), regularly heard her white colleagues use the word 'nigger' in her presence. A class action suit by black ATF agents in 1993 led to the agency being supervised by a federal judge for five years.[216]

The Christopher Commission that conducted the inquiry into the Los Angeles Police Department (LAPD) after the Rodney King assault[217] and the violence that followed the police officers' subsequent acquittal at trial found 'a significant number of officers in the LAPD who repetitively use excessive force against the public and persistently ignore the written guidelines of the department regarding force.'[218] The Commission's report called for women to be increased to 44% of the police force, from the 16% strength at the time.[219] Women were entirely absent from the elite SWAT team. But even these days, the LAPD has struggled to meet its own 20% target; it was 19.2% in November 2012.[220] Representation of women at high ranks remains a small percentage, while across the United States policewomen amount to only 14% of total police strength.[221]

[213] Cited in Segrave, *Policewomen, A History*, p. 85. [214] Ibid., p. 5. [215] Ibid., p. 210.

[216] Ibid., pp. 255, 256. [217] See, e.g., www.rodneykingvideo.com.ar/.

[218] Christopher Commission report, 1991, pp. iii and 31.

[219] Segrave, *Policewomen, A History*, p. 239.

[220] R. Palta, 'LAPD still trying to attract more women officers', *Southern California Public Radio*, 13 November 2012, at: www.scpr.org/blogs/news/2012/11/13/11059/lapd-still-chasing-more-women-officers/.

[221] Segrave, *Policewomen, A History*, p. 5.

Also significantly underrepresented in US police forces are ethnic minorities; in the late 1970s of the 3,400-strong New York state police only 31 were black men, 25 were Hispanic men, there was 1 Asian American man, and 7 American Indian men. Of the 15 women on the force 1 was black while the other 14 were white.[222]

A series of police shootings and killings of black men by forces across the United States in 2014–16 shocked the nation. In November 2014, in Ferguson, Missouri, rioting and looting followed a jury's decision not to bring charges over the killing of a black teenager. Michael Brown was shot dead by a white police officer, Darren Wilson, on 9 August, sparking protests.[223] An investigation by the US Department of Justice concluded there was 'a pattern or practice of unlawful conduct' within the Ferguson Police Department (FPD) that violated the US Constitution and US federal law (see further Chapter 11).[224] The report found that the

> FPD engages in a pattern of excessive force in violation of the Fourth Amendment [which prohibits unreasonable searches and arbitrary arrests by the government]. Many officers are quick to escalate encounters with subjects they perceive to be disobeying their orders or resisting arrest ... Some incidents of excessive force result from stops or arrests that have no basis in law. Others are punitive and retaliatory ... Furthermore, ... Ferguson's pattern of using excessive force disproportionately harms African-American members of the community. The overwhelming majority of force — almost 90% — is used against African Americans.[225]

US Attorney General Eric Holder said the Department's investigation revealed racially discriminatory practices that have 'severely undermined the public trust' and used law enforcement 'not as a means for protecting public safety, but as a way to generate revenue'.[226] Following the publication of the report, the FPD Police Chief, Thomas Jackson, resigned. The police force had only three black officers, despite the fact that the city of 21,000 people was predominately black.[227]

222 Ibid., p. 228.

223 'Ferguson Riots: Ruling Sparks Night of Violence', BBC, 25 November 2014, at: www.bbc.co.uk/news/world-us-canada-30190224.

224 US Department of Justice, 'Investigation of the Ferguson Police Department', Civil Rights Division, 4 March 2015, p. 1, at: www.justice.gov/sites/default/files/opa/press-releases/attachments/2015/03/04/ferguson_police_department_report.pdf.

225 Ibid., p. 28.

226 'U.S. Justice Department Finds Ferguson Police and Courts Targeted African Americans', Equal Justice Initiative, 9 March 2015, at: www.eji.org/node/1048.

227 'Ferguson Police Chief Tom Jackson Quits', BBC, 11 March 2015, at: www.bbc.co.uk/news/world-us-canada-31843626.

At a rally to mark the fiftieth anniversary of America's 'Bloody Sunday' (7 March 1965), which took its name from the beating that some 600 peaceful civil rights activists in Selma, Alabama, sustained at the hands of white state troopers and police who attacked them with batons and sprayed them with tear gas,[228] US President Barack Obama noted that what happened in Ferguson is no longer 'sanctioned by law and custom'. But neither is racism banished, he said:

> We don't need the Ferguson report to know that's not true. We just need to open our eyes, and ears, and hearts, to know that this nation's racial history still casts its long shadow upon us.[229]

The FBI

Today, there are six levels of law enforcement agency in the United States: federal, state, county, city, rural, and 'special district'. At federal level, perhaps the best known among some 50 law enforcement agencies[230] is the Federal Bureau of Investigation (FBI). As its name suggests, the FBI is a federal agency that investigates federal crimes, i.e. those deemed to be against the United States as a nation. Such crimes were said to number 3,300 in 2001;[231] this figure has since increased.

The agency's origins are traced back to 1871 when the US Department of Justice borrowed detectives from the Secret Service (established by President Lincoln to prevent counterfeiting) to penetrate and destroy the Ku Klux Klan.[232] Efforts to use the army to achieve this aim had failed.[233] The FBI itself gives its founding date as 26 July 1908, when the US Attorney-General issued an order stating that Department of Justice investigations would henceforth be conducted by the Department's own staff. This order followed the failure of President Roosevelt to secure

[228] T. Chappelle, 'Thousands March on Selma, Alabama Bridge to Mark "Bloody Sunday"', *Reuters*, 8 March 2015, at: www.reuters.com/article/2015/03/08/us-usa-civil-rights-selma-idUSKBN0M40TK20150308.

[229] 'In Selma, President Obama Calls for Criminal Justice Reform', Equal Justice Initiative, 9 March 2015, at: www.eji.org/node/1049.

[230] Mawby, 'Variations on a Theme: The Development of Professional Police in the British Isles and North America', p. 49.

[231] R. Jeffreys-Jones, *The FBI, A History*, Yale University Press, New Haven, 2007, p. 2.

[232] The Ku Klux Klan was initially set up in Pulaski, Tennessee, in 1866; similar initiatives followed in other former Confederate states. Jeffreys-Jones, *The FBI, A History*, p. 21.

[233] Ibid., p. 3.

Congressional approval for the new agency, which was named the Bureau of Investigation in 1909.[234]

In its early days, agents' powers were limited: they had no authority to arrest, were not permitted to carry firearms, and were not supposed to be involved in political work.[235] Over time, though, their powers were considerably expanded; by 1918, one estimate holds that about half of the Bureau's investigations were into political dissent.[236] In 1936, the FBI's manual noted that agents had access to Thompson sub-machine guns.[237]

Few law enforcement figures are as controversial, or as contradictory, as the FBI's erstwhile director John Edgar Hoover. He headed the FBI for 38 years from 1924 to 1972, turning the FBI into a 'model criminal investigation agency'. He actively sought out lawyers and accountants to serve as special agents, set up a national training agency, and, already in 1932, its 'superb' forensic science laboratory was operational. He also laid down policies to limit the use of weapons by FBI personnel to acts of self-defence.[238] Indeed, Hoover was an advocate of broader gun control, famously declaring in 1933, 'What excuse can there possibly be for permitting the sale of machine guns?'[239] He will also, though, be remembered for the FBI's generally unfavourable dealings with the civil rights movement and mass dissent over the Vietnam War; his hatred of Dr Martin Luther King was legendary.[240]

The FBI was reformed in the 1930s; Hoover contributed to the new Attorney-General's avowed 'war on crime' by creating the FBI's 'Public Enemy Number One'. In 1934, the former military prison on Alcatraz in San Francisco Bay was converted into a prison fortress to house the captured Public Enemies.[241] In 1947, President Truman enacted the National Security Act; this law prohibited the FBI from operating abroad (it had been very active in Latin America), creating for that purpose the Central Intelligence Agency (CIA). Intense rivalry ensued between the two agencies, to the obvious detriment of national security.[242] For decades, the FBI engaged in an anti-communist witch hunt,

[234] Ibid., p. 51. [235] Ibid., p. 56. [236] Ibid., p. 71. [237] Ibid., p. 91.

[238] P. V. Murphy, 'John Edgar Hoover, The Federal Influence in American Policing', in Stead, *Pioneers in Policing*, p. 263. He also sought summary dismissal for any agent caught drinking. Jeffreys-Jones, *The FBI, A History*, p. 85.

[239] During an address by to the International Association of Chiefs of Police in Chicago.

[240] At a press conference in November 1964, for instance, Hoover famously asserted that King was the 'most notorious liar in the country'.

[241] Jeffreys-Jones, *The FBI, A History*, p. 91. [242] Ibid., p. 11.

also persecuting homosexuals; only in December 1993, during a class action suit, was the Bureau's ban on gays serving as agents lifted.[243]

The year 1993 is also infamous for the deaths of more than 70 people, almost a third of whom were children, at the compound of a Christian sect, the Branch Davidians, in Waco, Texas. The group had been suspected of weapons violations, and a search and arrest warrant was obtained by the ATF, a federal law enforcement organisation relocated after 9/11 to the US Department of Justice (and renamed the Bureau of Alcohol, Tobacco, Firearms and Explosives).[244] Four ATF agents and six Davidians were killed during an initial two-hour firefight at Waco, both sides claiming the other had fired first. After seven weeks laying siege to the compound, the FBI's Hostage Rescue Team fired tear gas inside and the Davidians responded with gunfire. A fire raged out of control, killing most of those inside the compound.

Six years after the deaths, a ten-month investigation was later conducted by a special counsel, former Republican senator John C. Danforth, to re-examine the attack to determine how the fire started and whether there was a cover-up of information implicating law enforcement officials or the Justice Department. Danforth concluded in his report[245] that an FBI agent fired three pyrotechnic tear gas rounds at a concrete pit some 20 metres from the living quarters in the compound. Although these rounds did not start the fire, government officials did not admit their use until August 1999. Danforth found that this negligence was at best a mishandling of evidence, and at worst a criminal attempt to conceal the truth from investigators.[246]

According to Jeffreys-Jones, this and other incidents 'suggested a need to have some women on the FBI's over-macho crisis negotiation teams'.[247] Patience is also a virtue in law enforcement. Thus, in February 2016, a peaceful outcome to the standoff in Oregon after armed militia members occupied the Malheur National Wildlife Refuge near Burns was achieved after 41 days. 'It took 25 days before the FBI and state police

243 Ibid., pp. 149, 217.

244 The transfer was mandated under the 2002 Homeland Security Act.

245 J. C. Danforth, Interim Report of the Attorney General Special Counsel to the Deputy Attorney General Concerning the 1993 Confrontation at the Mt. Carmel Complex, Waco, Texas, Pursuant to Order No. 2256–99, 21 July 2000, at: www.cesnur.org/testi/DanforthRpt.pdf.

246 PBS, 'Chronology: Waco – The Inside Story', Frontline, accessed 27 February 2015 at: www.pbs.org/wgbh/pages/frontline/waco/timeline.html; see Danforth, ibid., p. 5.

247 Jeffreys-Jones, *The FBI, A History*, p. 227.

moved to arrest several leaders of the occupation and to barricade the refuge. It took another 15 days before the last of the final occupiers walked out.'[248] According to the *Washington Post*, 'mindful of the severe backlash' after the siege at Waco, and a subsequent siege at Ruby Ridge, Idaho, which turned bloody, also in the 1990s, the FBI 'did not send its elite Hostage Rescue Team to the refuge to avoid the perception that authorities were using disproportionate force'.[249]

Other complaints against the FBI have related to the ethnic make-up of its special agents. In 2000, only 21 of more than 10,000 agents could speak Arabic and in 2003, of its 11,500 agents only six were Muslims. This had doubled, to twelve, by 2007 and still only thirty-three agents were fluent in Arabic! Yet somewhere between 1.3 million and 3.9 million Arab Americans were living in the Unites States in the early 2000s.[250] As of the end of September 2012, the FBI had a total of 36,074 employees, of whom 15,649 were women, 8,762 were minorities, and 1,281 were persons with disabilities.[251] According to the Census Bureau's estimate for 2012, however, 50.4 per cent of American children under the age of 1 belonged to minority groups.[252] Among special agents, less than one of every twenty was black/African American,[253] while more than 12 per cent of the population (roughly one in eight people) is African American.

Outlook

This has, by necessity, been a cursory and selective history of law enforcement. But it has sought to offer snapshots of some of the milestones in policing across history, both good and bad. Today, diversity

248 D. A. Graham, 'Patience: The FBI's Strategy to End the Oregon Standoff and Nab Cliven Bundy: The bureau successfully played the long game in both cases', *Atlantic*, 12 February 2016, at: www.theatlantic.com/national/archive/2016/02/fbi-patience-cliven-bundy-oregon-malheur-arrests/462525/.

249 C. Wolf, M. Berman, and K. Sullivan, 'Oregon Wildlife Refuge Standoff Ends as Last Four Occupiers Surrender to FBI', *Washington Post*, 11 February 2016, at: www.washingtonpost.com/national/oregon-wildlife-refuge-stand-off-ends-as-last-four-occupiers-surrender-to-fbi/2016/02/11/eb330550-c782-11e5-8965-0607e0e265ce_story.html.

250 Jeffreys-Jones, *The FBI, A History*, pp. 230, 243.

251 US Department of Justice, *Today's FBI: Facts and Figures, 2013–2014*, p. 51, at: www.fbi.gov/stats-services/publications/todays-fbi-facts-figures/facts-and-figures-031413.pdf.

252 C. Morello and T. Mellnik, 'Census: Minority Babies Are Now Majority in United States', *Washington Post*, 17 May 2012.

253 US Department of Justice, *Today's FBI: Facts and Figures, 2013–2014*, p. 51.

prevails across the Westphalian state structures that still, more or less, predominate in the world in which we live. As Bayley explains, with respect to policing, 'countries vary enormously in national structures, mechanisms for achieving accountability, weapons and the use of force, role of women, organization and training for crowd-control, dependence on technology, development of operational personnel, standards of recruitment, nature and length of training, levels of remuneration, public regard, acceptance of the rule of law, separation from the military, styles of management, relations among ranks, and morale'.[254]

But many of the key features of these different policing systems today can be traced back to past experience. To a remarkable extent, Harry Truman's oft-cited aphorism that 'There is nothing new in the world except the history you do not know' is reflected in the history of law enforcement. And whoever conducts policing (in the narrow sense of the term), as Reiner predicts, an 'escalation of controversy about police use of force is likely. In addition to the continuing risk of terrorist incidents, the economic collapse will fan the political conflicts already presaged by the anti-globalization protests.'[255] Further, instances of excessive or mistaken use of force will attract instant publicity owing to the proliferation of video recording devices.[256] This remains true whether you are an advocate of forceful or consensus policing.

[254] D. H. Bayley, 'Policing the World Stage, ch. 1 in Mawby, *Policing Across the World*, pp. 6–7.

[255] Reiner, *The Politics of the Police*, p. 102.

[256] Ibid.

2

Policing and Social and Economic Policy

> Police fetishism: 'The ideological assumption that the police are a functional prerequisite of social order so that without a police force chaos would ensue.'
>
> Robert Reiner[1]

Introduction

Chapter 1 set out the path to today's policing but left key questions unanswered about what constitutes modern policing; its links to government, legitimacy, and public perceptions; and ultimately about how the use of force by police forces is influenced. Accordingly, this chapter considers how contemporary societies perceive of and conduct policing and how such policing fits into their social and economic structures.

Is policing fundamentally preventive or reactive? As Bayley asks, what effect does policing have on society, and what effect does society have on the police?[2] What impact can economic analysis have on our understanding of crime and the role of the police? Does sovereignty demand a police force of public servants, or can policing be contracted out effectively to the private sector in a similar manner to other public services? Is a police force cost-effective or merely an exercise in public relations? Does police use of force vary across the world, and if so, why? And to what extent is Reiner's claim of police fetishism a valid critique of modern society?

In 1974, Egon Bittner, a sociologist whose best work described and analysed the function of the police in modern society, neatly summarised many of the key issues involved in considering the role of social

[1] R. Reiner, *The Politics of the Police*, 4th Edn, Oxford University Press, Oxford, 2010, p. 3. In Reiner's view, 'Altogether the police are marginal to the control of crime and the maintenance of order and always have been.' *Ibid.*, p. 19.

[2] D. Bayley, 'Policing the World Stage', in R. I. Mawby (ed.), *Policing Across the World: Issues for the Twenty-First Century*, Routledge, London, 1999, p. 8.

and economic policy in relation to policing. He drew attention both to the extraordinary breadth of functions and responsibilities that constitute modern policing and to the inescapable role of government and of public perceptions in framing the way that police forces operate:

> The unifying feature of the tasks that come to be seen as police work is not that they are aspects of a particular social function, whether it be crime control, social service, order maintenance or political repression. Rather it is that they all involve 'something that ought not to be happening and about which someone had better do something now'.[3]

A useful starting point is to summarise thinking about what the terms 'police' and 'policing' mean. Both Wright[4] and Reiner[5] distinguish between the two, considering the police a rather narrow concept. Other authorities claim that the police officer is a peacekeeper rather than an enforcer, spending far more time keeping public order than enforcing domestic criminal law.[6] While clearly accepting the complexity of the range of functions that constitute policing, Wright argues that 'we can now define policing as an activity which a number of agencies, groups or individuals (including the public police) may deliver'. He describes policing in terms of its functions or 'modes of practice', which he summarises as being fourfold:

- peace keeping,
- crime investigation,
- risk management, and
- promotion of community justice.

Reiner goes further with his view that policing is 'an aspect of *social control processes* which occurs universally in all social situations in which there is at least the potential for conflict, deviance or disorder'. Certainly, few (whether within or outside the police) would unreservedly refute his view that 'the sources of order lie outside the ambit of the police, in the political economy and culture of a society'.

[3] E. Bittner, 'Florence Nightingale in Pursuit of Willie Sutton: A Theory of the Police', in H. Jacob (ed.), *The Potential for Reform of Criminal Justice*, Sage, California, 1974, p. 30; see Reiner, *The Politics of the Police*, p. 7.

[4] A. Wright, *Policing: An Introduction to Concepts and Practice*, Willan, Cullompton, 2002, pp. 25ff.

[5] Reiner, *The Politics of the Police*, pp. 15*ff.*

[6] T. Newburn, *Criminology*, 2nd Edn, Routledge, London, 2013, p. 616.

Forms of Policing

Policing by Consent

The origin and tenets of modern policing, at least insofar as the Metropolitan Police Service is concerned, are firmly preventive in nature. Termed 'policing by consent', according to the United Kingdom Home Office, this notion views the power of the police as coming from 'the common consent of the public, as opposed to the power of the state'. It does not mean, of course, the consent of any given individual.[7] Essentially, as Reith affirmed in 1956 in his fascinating *New Study of Police History*, it was a philosophy of policing 'unique in history and throughout the world because it derived not from fear but almost exclusively from public co-operation with the police, induced by them designedly by behaviour which secures and maintains for them the approval, respect and affection of the public'.[8]

Policing by consent is defined by reference to a long-standing philosophy of British policing, known as Robert Peel's *Nine Principles of Policing*. According to the Home Office, though, no evidence exists of any link to Robert Peel and it is more likely that they were devised by the first Metropolitan Police Commissioners (Charles Rowan and Richard Mayne).[9] The nine principles were set out in the 'General Instructions' issued to every new police officer from 1829, and read as follows:

1. To prevent crime and disorder, as an alternative to their repression by military force and severity of legal punishment.
2. To recognise always that the power of the police to fulfil their functions and duties is dependent on public approval of their existence, actions, and behaviour and on their ability to secure and maintain public respect.
3. To recognise always that to secure and maintain the respect and approval of the public means also to secure the willing cooperation of the public in the task of securing observance of laws.
4. To recognise always that the extent to which the cooperation of the public can be secured diminishes proportionately to the necessity of

[7] Home Office, 'Definition of Policing by Consent', Freedom of Information release, Published 10 December 2012, at: www.gov.uk/government/publications/policing-by-consent/definition-of-policing-by-consent.

[8] C. Reith, *A New Study of Police History*, 1st Edn, Oliver & Boyd, Edinburgh, 1956.

[9] Home Office, 'Definition of Policing by Consent', 2012.

the use of physical force and compulsion for achieving police objectives.

5. To seek and preserve public favour, not by pandering to public opinion, but by constantly demonstrating absolutely impartial service to law, in complete independence of policy, and without regard to the justice or injustice of the substance of individual laws; by ready offering of individual service and friendship to all members of the public without regard to their wealth or social standing; by ready exercise of courtesy and friendly good humour; and by ready offering of individual sacrifice in protecting and preserving life.
6. To use physical force only when the exercise of persuasion, advice, and warning is found to be insufficient to obtain public cooperation to an extent necessary to secure observance of law or to restore order, and to use only the minimum degree of physical force which is necessary on any particular occasion for achieving a police objective.
7. To maintain at all times a relationship with the public that gives reality to the historic tradition that the police are the public and that the public are the police, the police being only members of the public who are paid to give full-time attention to duties which are incumbent on every citizen in the interests of community welfare and existence.
8. To recognise always the need for strict adherence to police executive functions, and to refrain from even seeming to usurp the powers of the judiciary of avenging individuals or the State, and of authoritatively judging guilt and punishing the guilty.
9. To recognise always that the test of police efficiency is the absence of crime and disorder, and not the visible evidence of police action in dealing with them.

It is safe to say, though, that policing by consent in the United Kingdom is under pressure as never before. One reason, as discussed below, is reduced funding. But at the same time as austerity bites, critics note the huge underrepresentation of Black, Asian, and minority ethnic (BAME) in the police: according to a report in January 2016, in London, a public that is 40.2% BAME is represented by 11.7% of the members of the Metropolitan Police Service.[10] In Hopkinson's view,

[10] F. Hopkinson, '"Policing by Consent" in Contemporary Britain', *Cherwell*, 6 January 2016, at: www.cherwell.org/comment/opinion/2016/01/06/policing-by-consent-in-contemporary-britain.

> When communities begin to be cut off from the police in these ways, opportunities for dialogue break down. A lack of BAME representation in our police forces is a problem for all of us because it represents a severed link between these communities and the people that are meant to be working for them.[11]

Clearly, a public perception of 'them' (the police) and 'us' (the economically oppressed who are targeted by policing) helps to undermine the notion of policing by consent, while making the use of force more likely in any interaction between the police and the public.

Reactive Policing

According to Reiner, 'Altogether the police are marginal to the control of crime and the maintenance of order and always have been.'[12] His controversial view of policing is that it is – or should be – almost exclusively reactive in nature. 'Tank' Waddington had argued in 1983: 'The police are the social equivalent of the AA or RAC patrolmen, who intervene when things go unpredictably wrong and secure a provisional solution.'[13] On this basis, Reiner concludes that 'to think of policing as capable of achieving the grand functions of order and security is a dangerous category error', though he acknowledges that the police 'can bring balm to desperate suffering'.

This appears to be the current trend, at least in the United Kingdom. In July 2015, Rick Muir, the director of an independent think tank, The Police Foundation, claimed that policing in the United Kingdom 'could go back to the fire brigade model . . . where officers are just turning up in cars responding to incidents. You haven't got those established relationships with the public in the first place which is a key driver in public confidence'.[14] Furthermore, as discussed below and also in Chapter 9, financial restrictions – and arguably, to a certain extent, technology – are pushing law enforcement in many countries towards a more reactive approach to policing.

But policing as reaction almost necessarily brings the police into contact – and often conflict – with certain socio-economic, ethnic, and gender groups or categories. As Reiner observes, 'Groups that are low in

[11] Ibid. [12] Reiner, *The Politics of the Police*, p. 19.

[13] P. A. J. Waddington, 'Beware the Community Trap', *Police*, March 1983, p. 34.

[14] 'Neighbourhood Policing Cuts Put Policing by Consent at Risk', *Police*, July 2015, at: www.policemag.co.uk/editions/July2015_Neighbourhood_policing_cuts.aspx.

power and status, such as the poor and unemployed, ethnic minorities, young men (and underclass young women), gays and lesbians become "police property",[15] disproportionately likely to be treated as suspects at each stage of the criminal justice process: stop-search, arrest, detention, charge and prosecution.'[16] Analysis of police use of force strongly suggests that those suffering from mental health issues should also be added to this list.

Few would dispute that issues of police use of force are often linked to and influenced by race, even though the relationship between the two is both complex and subject to change. Given the disproportionate scale of the number of victims from BAME communities of police use of force in many countries, including deaths at the hands of law enforcement personnel, no analysis of police use of force can ignore this issue. In the United States, relations between law enforcement and African Americans continue to be extremely fraught. Thus, for instance, the practice of targeting motorists for police stops because of their colour has been ironically termed DWB ('driving while black').[17]

And this fraught problem of perception cuts both ways. While most of the analysis considered in this chapter is drawn from traditional academic research and evidence, the rapidly changing picture of race and police use of force suggests that more anecdotal or experiential insight could also play a valuable role in developing policy. An excellent example of how such issues translate into current practice in the United States was provided by the public radio programme, *This American Life*, in 2015. Drawing on a number of recent incidents of police use of force, the programme directly addresses police bias and prejudice, highlighting examples of where these issues have been handled well or badly.

Starting from the premise that 'cops see things differently', the programme shows what happened when the programme producer (Robyn Semien) watched a video of the arrest and death of Eric Garner with a friend who is a serving police officer in the New York City Police Department (NYPD).[18] Eric Garner was an unarmed black man who died when a group of NYPD officers sought to arrest him for selling loose

[15] J. A. Lee, 'Some Structural Aspects of Police Deviance in Relations with Minority Groups', in C. Shearing (ed.), *Organizational Police Deviance*, Butterworth, Toronto, 1981, pp. 53–54.

[16] Reiner, *The Politics of the Police*, p. 25.

[17] L. A. Steverson, *Policing in America*, ABC CLIO, Santa Barbara, CA, 2008, p. 53.

[18] At: www.thisamericanlife.org/radio-archives/episode/548/cops-see-it-differently-part-two.

cigarettes ('loosies') on the street in July 2014.[19] Robyn wanted to understand what a police officer sees as they watch the incident unfold.

Robyn is black, female, and not a police officer. Her friend is a white police officer, also female. Ira Glass is the presenter of the programme. The following is a transcript:

Robyn Semien Is this good policing, bad policing? Where does this go wrong? What does Eric Garner do right? What does he do wrong? . . .

Ira Glass Robyn and her friend sat down in front of a computer, and they basically just walked through the video, stopping and starting and talking. Her friend told her that at every step, right from the start, Eric Garner seems to be resisting arrest. He is not compliant. He does not produce an ID. He keeps talking and stalling. Even once he's on the ground, there's this five or six seconds where he's lying on his right side. Police go to cuff his left hand. Meanwhile, his right arm is extended on the concrete, his right palm facing up. His fingers are apart.

Robyn Semien Just watch his right hand. It's face up.

Friend Put your hand behind your back.

Robyn Semien Put your hand behind your back, they say. OK, and it's right at this moment where there's five police officers on him. His hands are spread. She's saying, why isn't he put – she says to me over and over, why isn't he putting his hand behind his back? See, he's resisting. At that moment, five officers on him, he's on the ground – yeah, like, I don't see how he could put his hand behind his back if he wanted to ... he's down on the ground. He's crawling. His arm is pinned. His right arm is pinned, and then they all pull his arm around and handcuff him. We watched it over and over. She only saw it as him not complying, basically, wrestling and refusing to be arrested. And I can only ever see it, I mean, as the opposite. I can only ever see it as, like, a person who seems thoroughly detained. Like, I'm thinking at this point, it's under control.

Ira Glass Why keep applying force?

Robyn Semien And she's like, it's clearly not under control and there is more force to be applied.

Ira Glass When Eric Garner says over and over, I can't breathe, Robyn sees a man who's dying. Her friend does not. She tells Robyn people say that all the time when they're being arrested. They can't breathe. You're hurting them. It happens all the time. The officer totally understood why the police on the scene did not pay any attention to it.

Ira Glass And does she understand why you see it the way you do?

Robyn Semien No.

Ira Glass She thinks that when you look at it, you should see it the way she sees it.

[19] See also Chapter 6 on protests for a brief discussion of the case.

Robyn Semien Yeah.

Ira Glass And did it make her mad that you couldn't see it?

Robyn Semien Yeah. Yeah, it did.

Ira Glass Because to her it's obvious.

Robyn Semien Yeah, and that's a very weird feeling to be sitting next to someone – anyone, let alone a friend – and to be watching a video and saying, like, don't you see this person is in pain, struggling to communicate? What's odd to me is that now, even after the fact, we know that he really couldn't breathe. And she kind of wouldn't even totally cop to the fact that he was probably telling the truth as we watched the video.

Ira Glass Robyn went into this conversation figuring they would have at least some common ground. But they talked for four hours, and the longer they talked, the more they both realised there was just nothing, just none. Robyn's friend said she did understand why people saw this as a racial incident, but she definitely did not.

What this programme illustrates is how strongly our perceptions and our understanding of facts are influenced by our background and our experience, and how sharply they may differ from someone else's. In social psychology, social perception is the study of how people form impressions of other people. A report published in 2014 by a Washington, DC-based national non-profit organisation engaged in research and advocacy on criminal justice issues laid part of the blame for a bias against minorities (among the public at large as well as the police) at the door of the media.[20] The report also recorded that implicit bias tests show that the public 'holds negative associations of blacks and Latinos, and suspects them of criminality. These biases have also been documented among police officers and judges, and are believed to reach all corners of the criminal justice system.'[21]

This plays out to some extent as one might expect both in real policing as well as in simulated use-of-force cases. Thus, in video-simulated shooter studies, subjects are asked to quickly identify and shoot armed suspects, but not to shoot unarmed suspects. The report cites one such study which found that 'non-black participants more quickly and accurately decided to shoot an armed target when the target was African American, but more quickly and accurately did not shoot when an unarmed target was white'.[22]

[20] N. Ghandnoosh, *Race and Punishment: Racial Perceptions of Crime and Support for Punitive Policies*, The Sentencing Project, 2014, at: http://sentencingproject.org/wp-content/uploads/2015/11/Race-and-Punishment.pdf.

[21] Ibid., p. 15.

[22] Ibid., citing J. Correll, B. Park, C. M. Judd, and B. Wittenbrink, 'The Police Officer's Dilemma: Using Ethnicity to Disambiguate Potentially Threatening Individuals', *Journal of Personality and Social Psychology*, Vol. 83, No. 6 (2002), pp. 1314–29.

Of particular note, however, is the fact that when researchers conducted a study with a predominantly white group of Denver-based police officers, they found that the officers were *less likely* than the general public to mistakenly shoot at unarmed black suspects.[23] In contrast, the officers shot at *armed* black suspects more quickly than they did at armed white suspects. The researchers concluded that while these officers exhibited bias in their speed to shoot, their training reduced bias in their decision to shoot. Training may thus succeed in reducing fatalities and serious injuries.

The 2002 article that conducted and described the results of the video-simulated shooter studies among members of the public began by summarising a real-life case of police use of force. In February 1999, around midnight, four plain-clothes NYPD officers were searching a Bronx neighbourhood for a rape suspect. They saw Amadou Diallo, a 22-year-old West African immigrant, standing in the doorway of his apartment building. According to the police, Diallo resembled the suspect they were tracking. When they ordered him to 'freeze', Diallo reached into his trouser pocket. Believing he was going for a gun, the police fired a total of 41 shots, 19 of which hit and killed Mr Diallo. He was in fact unarmed. All four officers were later acquitted of any wrongdoing.

As the authors observe, the police could not have known that Diallo was harmless. In the dark, they had ordered a potentially dangerous man not to move, and that man reached for something. If Diallo had been armed, their decision to open fire would never have been questioned. But, they postulate, the decision to shoot a black man who later proved to be unarmed raised one fundamental question in particular: would the police have responded differently if Diallo had been white? They wonder aloud whether he would have been given the benefit of the doubt; or perhaps the order to freeze would have been repeated; or perhaps a slight delay in the decision to fire could have given the officers the time to see that he was not reaching for a gun.[24]

Community Policing

A counterview to 'policing as reaction' is that policing needs to be conducted at community level and on a largely preventive basis. The

[23] J. Correll, B. Park, C. M. Judd, B. Wittenbrink, M. S. Sadler, and T. Keesee, 'Across the Thin Blue Line: Police Officers and Racial Bias in the Decision to Shoot', *Journal of Personality and Social Psychology*, Vol. 92, No. 6 (2007), pp. 1006–23.

[24] Correll *et al.*, 'The Police Officer's Dilemma', p. 1314.

primary strategies of this approach, which incorporates important elements of 'policing by consent', are the police officer's beat (to build relationships) and broader community engagement from the police to discuss their approach to policing local communities. In community policing, use of force is firmly set in the background, while 'good' policing is seen as the craft of handling trouble without resort to coercion, usually by skilful verbal tactics.[25]

Views differ widely as to the virtue of 'the beat', as noted in both the introduction to the book and the Chapter 1. In the 1950s, Reith was arguing forcefully that while detection is a necessary function of police, it and other associated functions must be 'in service to the principle of prevention'.[26] In an unwitting nod to the future, though, he concludes that, 'Where there are not enough police to prevent crime and disorder effectively, it follows inevitably that the existing numbers will tend to become employed exclusively in detection.'[27] For others, the deployment of police on patrol is almost purely for show. Sara Thornton, for instance, the Chair of the UK National Police Chiefs' Council which brings together senior British police officers to coordinate national operational policing, said patrols did not prevent crime or even make people feel safer: 'The evidence would say a random police patrol doesn't prevent crime, doesn't solve crime, it doesn't make people feel safer.'[28]

But what exactly is meant by the term 'community policing'? There are widely differing understandings, but Brogden and Nijhar suggest that it is best defined in the negative:

> It is not military-style policing with a central bureaucracy obedient to directive legislation which minimises discretion. It is not policing that is autonomous of public consent and accountability. It is not policing that is committed primarily to reactive crime-fighting strategies. It is not policing that is measured by output in terms of professional efficiency. Rather it is policing which is determined by strategies, tactics and outcomes based on community consent.

[25] Reiner, *The Politics of the Police*, p. 8.

[26] Reith, *A New Study of Police History*, pp. 223–24. [27] Ibid., p. 224.

[28] A. Martin, 'We Can't Afford Bobbies on the Beat, Claims the Police Chief Paid £250,000 a Year: Top Officer Says Patrols Do Not Help to Cut Crime or Make People Feel Safer', *Daily Mail Online*, 29 October 2015, at: www.dailymail.co.uk/news/article-3294419/We-t-afford-bobbies-beat-claims-police-chief-paid-250-000-year-Officer-says-patrols-not-help-cut-crime-make-people-feel-safer.html.

Skogan concurs with this definition but develops it by suggesting that what police do when they are 'doing community policing' *should* vary a great deal. Communities with different problems – and different resources to bring to bear to tackle them – should try a range of approaches. Projects and tactics should come and go as conditions change. Adopting community policing involves changing the structure of organisations and their decision-making processes so that they manage this flexibility effectively.

Accepting that 'finding a concept of universal applicability' might prove impossible, Brogden and Nijhar set out five key propositions:

- Neighbourhoods or small communities serve as primary foci of police organisation and operations.
- Communities have unique and distinctive policing problems that conventional police organisations have not traditionally addressed.
- Community consensus and structures should guide police response to the community's crime and security problems.
- Policing should be both locally accountable and transparent.
- Police discretion is a fact and should be used positively to maximise community confidence in the police.

A 1994 monograph published by the US Department of Justice (DOJ) asserted that community policing is 'in essence, a collaboration between the police and the community that identifies and solves community problems. With the police no longer the sole guardians of law and order, all members of the community become active allies in the effort to enhance the safety and quality of neighborhoods.'[29] The monograph notes that the foundations of any successful community policing strategy are 'the close, mutually beneficial ties between police and community members'.[30] It explains that community policing consists of two complementary core components – community partnership and problem-solving:

> To develop community partnership, police must develop positive relationships with the community, must involve the community in the quest for better crime control and prevention, and must pool their resources with those of the community to address the most urgent concerns of

[29] Preface to: Bureau of Justice Assistance, *Understanding Community Policing: A Framework for Action*, DOJ Office of Justice Programs, 1984, at: www.ncjrs.gov/pdffiles/commp.pdf.

[30] Ibid., p. 13.

> community members. Problem solving is the process through which the specific concerns of communities are identified and through which the most appropriate remedies to abate these problems are found.[31]

It is also noted, though, that community policing 'does not imply that police are no longer in authority or that the primary duty of preserving law and order is subordinated'.[32] Table 1 summarises broad-brush differences between reactive and preventive 'community' policing.

While these clarifications help to define community policing, they fail to explain adequately the notion of 'community'. Arguably one of the most overused and ill-defined terms in public policy-making, 'community' sometimes seems to be a synonym for 'everybody'. A more nuanced view is needed. As Reiner argues,

> For policing to be accepted as legitimate, it is not necessary that all groups or individuals in a society agree with the substantive content or direction of specific police operations. It means at minimum only that the broad mass of the population, and possibly even some of those who are policed against, accept the authority, the lawful right, of the police to act as they do, even if disagreeing with or regretting some specific actions.

Or, as 'Tank' Waddington summarised it, 'community policing is an oxymoron, for if the police could serve the *whole* community there would be little point in having a police at all'.

Intuitively, these distinctions have a degree of plausibility about them, if we consider, for example, the significant shifts in police practice over the last generation or so in the United Kingdom and the United States in relation to BAME communities. As the proportion of BAME populace has grown compared to majority white populations, police forces have been compelled to adapt their practices and ways of working (albeit not as rapidly or significantly as many would have wished).

While two principles of Peelian policing, namely 'policing by consent' and 'local community contact', form key components of these definitions of community policing, the term in its modern form can probably be traced back to the United States in the early 1970s. The increasingly pervasive view that policing was 'failing' after the city riots of the 1960s, combined with rising crime rates and widespread social disorder, led academics, researchers, and policy-makers to look to different models of policing to address these concerns.

[31] Ibid. [32] Ibid.

Table 1. *Traditional versus community policing*

Traditional Policing	Community Policing
Reactive to incidents	Proactive in solving community-related problems
Roles of police officers limited to incident response	Roles of officers broadened to include identification and solving of problems
Focus on internal resources	Leverage on community resources
Limited linkages with the community	Extensive links with the community
Random patrols in cars to respond to crime	Visible patrols to interact with the community
Information from the community is limited	Information from the community comes from many sources
Organisation control-oriented; authoritative style or command and control	Decentralisation of authority and autonomy to front-line officers
Rewards based on solving cases	Performance evaluation rewards service activities, crime prevention, satisfaction, and a sense of safety of the community

'Broken Window' Theory

One such model was the 'broken window' theory. This controversial criminological theory that originated in the early 1980s holds that in urban environments, acting swiftly to prevent minor offences such as petty vandalism, loitering, littering, and drinking in public generates an atmosphere of order and lawfulness, preventing more serious crimes. The theory is credited to a 1982 article by social scientists James Q. Wilson and George L. Kelling.[33] In words that could equally have been written today, they observed that

> the police forces of America are losing, not gaining, members. Some cities have suffered substantial cuts in the number of officers available for duty. These cuts are not likely to be reversed in the near future. Therefore, each department must assign its existing officers with great care. Some neighborhoods are so demoralized and crime-ridden as to make foot patrol

[33] J. Q. Wilson and G. L. Kelling, 'Broken Windows: The Police and Neighborhood Safety', *The Atlantic*, 1982, available at: www.manhattan-institute.org/pdf/_atlantic_monthly-broken_windows.pdf.

> useless; the best the police can do with limited resources is respond to the enormous number of calls for service. Other neighborhoods are so stable and serene as to make foot patrol unnecessary.[34]

The solution they proffered was to focus social intervention not on areas that were deemed to be already lost, but those where law and order were losing ground. In the words of Wilson and Kelling, 'The key is to identify neighborhoods at the tipping point – where the public order is deteriorating but not unreclaimable, where the streets are used frequently but by apprehensive people, where a window is likely to be broken at any time, and must quickly be fixed if all are not to be shattered.'[35] Above all, they argue,

> we must return to our long-abandoned view that the police ought to protect communities as well as individuals. Our crime statistics and victimization surveys measure individual losses, but they do not measure communal losses. Just as physicians now recognize the importance of fostering health rather than simply treating illness, so the police — and the rest of us — ought to recognize the importance of maintaining, intact, communities without broken windows.[36]

Policing as 'community protection' and broken-window theory has since been advanced as justification for major reforms in criminal policy, including mass use of 'stop and frisk' by the NYPD. Once again, the negative impact on the marginalised and the disenfranchised is readily discerned, with the potential for discriminatory policing placed front and centre.

In October 2015, Professor Robert Friedmann of Georgia State University, a leading advocate of broken-window theory, discussed – and rejected – criticism of the theory.[37] Most of the criticism concerning 'Broken Windows', as he asserts, focuses on

> rejecting its premise that disorder leads to crime. At best, argue the critics, Broken Windows confuses association with causality. Namely, disorder and crime may appear together, but that is not to say that disorder causes crime. Some even go as far as suggesting that Broken Windows is racist because of the negative impact this approach may have on minority communities where individuals often face a higher risk of arrest.[38]

[34] Ibid., p. 9. [35] Ibid. [36] Ibid., p. 10.

[37] R. R. Friedmann, 'Broken Windows and Policing', *Police Chief*, Vol. 82 (October 2015), pp. 60–65, at: www.policechiefmagazine.org/magazine/index.cfm?fuseaction=display_arch&article_id=3919&issue_id=102015#1.

[38] Ibid., citing G. Stewart, 'Black Codes and Broken Windows: The Legacy of Racial Hegemony in Anti-Gang Civil Injunctions', *Yale Law Journal*, Vol. 107, No. 7 (1998), pp. 2249–79.

He also notes, but similarly rejects, the provocative claim in *Freakonomics* by authors Steven Levitt and Stephen Dubner that what caused the drop in crime in New York was the legalisation of abortion in the 1970s, resulting in a decrease in the birth of would-be juvenile delinquents. He does, though, acknowledge, that 'what makes testing Broken Windows difficult is that there may be other factors at play that are not easy to identify, isolate, and control. For example, unemployment dropped in New York by almost 40% in less than 10 years (1992–99) during the Broken Windows original implementation. At the same time, felony arrests increased by 50–70%, which reduced the criminal population in the city.'[39] According to Eugene O'Donnell, Professor of Police Studies at John Jay College of Criminal Justice, however, echoing Reiner's sentiments, 'The idea that the NYPD has a huge impact on crime was always a very dubious claim.'[40] Indeed, a report in March 2016 by the NYPD's independent Inspector General concluded that focusing on offences such as urinating in public and riding bikes on sidewalks had no influence on felony crime rates. It also accused the 36,000-officer department, the nation's largest, of unfairly singling out communities of colour for quality-of-life enforcement at a time when Mayor Bill de Blasio was emphasising the protection of civil rights.[41]

Edward Conlon, however, an NYPD cop for 16 years until his retirement in 2011, writes positively about stop and frisk, at least from the perspective of reducing gun violence. Arguing that Mayor Rudy Giuliani and NYPD Commissioner William Bratton's 'zero-tolerance policing'[42] had brought 'a new vigour' to the Department, he affirmed that stop and frisk 'encounters'

> changed the culture of how criminals carried their weapons: in the 1980s and early '90s, many dealers would carry guns in their waistbands, and the decision to shoot someone – because he crossed into their territory, or he said something about their mother, or he looked at them funny, or just because – was a three-second decision. After Bratton, the dealers still had guns, but they were hidden under their beds or on rooftops, and the delay from impulse to act took five minutes or ten, allowing people to move and tempers to cool.[43]

[39] Friedmann, 'Broken Windows and Policing'.

[40] T. Hays, 'NYPD's Champion of "Broken Windows" Policing Retires', *Forensic Magazine*, 16 September 2016, at: www.forensicmag.com/news/2016/09/nypds-champion-broken-windows-policing-retires.

[41] Ibid. [42] Newburn, *Criminology*, p. 635.

[43] E. Conlon, *Blue Blood*, Ebury Press, London, 2011, p. 13.

Research, according to Brogden and Nijhar, offers evidence that, at least in general:

- Doing more of the same does not have a measurable effect on crime levels.
- Car patrols have little effect on crime or on arrests.
- Most calls for police assistance are unrelated to crime; perhaps quality-of-life issues rather than crime should be the new rationale for policing.
- The police already deliver a range of necessary social services.
- Police crime-fighting (already) depends upon public support for information.
- A concern with fear of crime may often be more of a problem than crime itself.
- Foot patrols have the particular virtue not just of ensuring contact and cooperation from the public but also in reassuring the people and enhancing their quality of life, though such patrols may have little direct impact on crime and on arresting offenders.
- Dealing with crime is an inter-agency problem rather than simply the prerogative of the police.
- Local knowledge was a neglected resource in policing.[44]

Problem-Oriented and Intelligence-Led Policing

Given these realities, alternative models of policing that draw on some aspects of community policing but which focus on gathering and analysing information have been gaining currency in recent years. Problem-oriented policing, or POP, attributed to the US policing academic Herman Goldstein, calls for analysis by the police of the problems that confront them. This reposes on a proactive approach that seeks patterns and commonalities, such as in crime hotspots, prolific offenders, or particular classes of victim.[45] A central component of POP is the SARA process: Scanning, Analysis, Response, and Assessment. Scanning means obtaining information from a range of sources, such as surveys or community complaints. Analysis means examination of the information with a view to identifying underlying causes. Response should involve 'all

[44] M. Brogden and P. Nijhar, *Community Policing (B)*, 1st Edn, Willan, Cullompton, 2005.
[45] Newburn, *Criminology*, p. 626.

available resources'. Finally, Assessment seeks to evaluate whether the measures taken have had the desired effect.[46]

In a similar vein, intelligence-led policing is being promoted by some in the United Kingdom, though it is 'very much in its infancy' and is struggling to overcome an innate bias in favour of reactive models.[47] According to Steverson, '"Intelligence" does not mean simple information; the term refers to information that has been collected and analyzed. Sometimes the information is gathered from and analyzed within the police agency itself, and in other cases, the information is gathered from an outside party, then analyzed to determine where police resources may be best utilized.'[48] In the United States, criminal justice practitioners distinguish strategic intelligence, tactical intelligence, evidential intelligence, and operational intelligence.[49]

Cope describes the five-stage process of intelligence-led policing. The first is acquisition and storage of information. The second is analysis that converts raw information to actionable intelligence by identifying patterns in the data. The third stage involves prioritising crimes that should be addressed first. The fourth involves the development of an action plan. In the fifth and final stage, actions taken are assessed for their effectiveness.[50]

The Economics of Crime and Criminal Justice

The Costs of Crime

No one knows exactly how much crime costs globally, though partial estimates exist. For sure, the total, whatever it is, is staggering. Cybercrime alone was estimated in 2014 to cost the global economy US$445 billion, damaging trade between nations, competitiveness, innovation, and global economic growth. Cyber espionage and stealing individuals' personal information are believed to have affected more than 800 million people during 2013, while financial losses from cyber theft could cause as many as 150,000 Europeans to lose their jobs, according to a report conducted by internet security company McAfee.[51]

[46] See Steverson, *Policing in America*, p. 59 and quoted source.

[47] Newburn, *Criminology*, 626–27. [48] Steverson, *Policing in America*, p. 63.

[49] Ibid., p. 64.

[50] N. Cope, 'Intelligence Led Policing or Policing Led Intelligence: Integrating Volume Crime Analysis into Policing', *British Journal of Criminology*, Vol. 44, No. 2 (2004), pp. 188–203; see Steverson, *Policing in America*, p. 65.

[51] Cited in R. Williams, 'Cyber Crime Costs Global Economy $445 Bn Annually', *Daily Telegraph*, 9 June 2014, at: www.telegraph.co.uk/technology/internet-security/10886640/Cyber-crime-costs-global-economy-445-bn-annually.html.

A year previously, a study by the Institute for Economics and Peace of the situation in the United Kingdom had concluded that, for 2012, violent crime cost the economy more than £124 billion a year, equivalent to £4,700 for every household. The figure, which equated to 7.7 per cent of gross domestic product (GDP) at the time, included the cost of police investigations, courts, and prison expenditure as well as a vast amount in lost productivity. Murder was thought to have cost the economy £1.3 billion, while other violent crimes were thought to have cost as much as £45 billion. This was said to be the first time an overall figure had been put on the cost of violent crime.[52] Meanwhile, in the Caribbean, the World Bank calculated that Haiti and Jamaica could boost economic growth per capita by 5.4 per cent annually if they were to bring their homicide rates down to the levels of Costa Rica.[53]

Criminal Justice and Policing Costs

In 2013, for 132 nations reporting, UN Office on Drugs and Crime data indicated that they employed more than 7.265 million police officers, of whom 1.7 million were in India alone.[54] Of the overall total, some 808,000 were female (just over 11 per cent).[55]

In December 2003, Shaw, van Dijk, and Rhomberg published an article assessing trends in global crime and justice on the basis of UN data. They reported that, on average, there are just over 400 inhabitants for every police officer across the globe. Africa had the highest number of citizens per police officer across all its regions, with East Africa showing almost 1,000 inhabitants per police officer. Various sub-regions in Asia also appear to have comparatively small numbers of police officers per head of population. European, North American, and Latin American jurisdictions all record higher numbers of police officers (360–380), with the Caribbean displaying the smallest number of inhabitants (200) per police officer.[56]

[52] M. Evans, 'Violent Crime Costs the UK Economy £124 Billion, Report Suggests', *Daily Telegraph*, 24 April 2013, at: www.telegraph.co.uk/news/10013830/Violent-crime-costs-the-UK-economy-124-billion-report-suggests.html.

[53] The World Bank, 'Socioeconomic Costs of Crime', at: http://siteresources.worldbank.org/INTHAITI/Resources/CaribbeanC&VChapter4.pdf.

[54] Data available at: https://data.unodc.org/#state:1. [55] Ibid.

[56] M. Shaw, J. van Dijk, and W. Rhomberg, 'Determining Trends in Global Crime and Justice: An Overview of Results from the United Nations Surveys of Crime Trends and Operations of Criminal Justice Systems', *Forum on Crime and Society*, Vol. 3, Nos. 1 and 2 (December 2003), p. 55, at: www.unodc.org/pdf/crime/forum/forum3_Art2.pdf.

On average, calculated for the period 1998–2000, nations spent just under 1 per cent of their GDP on policing, though some spent significantly more, while most European countries appeared to spend less.[57] The largest recorded spend was in Bahrain, where 4.4% of GDP was devoted to policing, by some distance the highest. Dominica, Jamaica, and St. Vincent and the Grenadines all spent 2% of above on policing.[58] The United States spent just over 0.6% on policing, while France allocated some 0.7%.[59]

The article notes that when the number of homicides for every 1,000 police officers is calculated, the global average is 35, whereas the comparative figures for Colombia and South Africa are in the region of 200. 'For these reasons, the fact that comparative expenditure on criminal justice does not provide a measure of crime control capacity is widely acknowledged.'[60]

Economics and Crime

As we have seen above, there is a long tradition of applying elements of social sciences to our understanding of crime. Sociology and criminology – the study of the development, structure, and functioning of human society; and the more focused scientific study of crime and criminals – were for a significant period (stretching back nearly a century) the dominant disciplines, but for the last fifty years or so, economics has also begun to be applied to our understanding of crime.

Economics can broadly be defined as the study of how individuals, governments, firms, and nations make *choices* about the allocation of scarce resources to satisfy their unlimited wants. As a result, it clearly offers only a partial insight into improving our understanding of crime and specifically police use of force, but it is nevertheless a helpful addition towards our broad appreciation of the issues. Professor Gary Becker was the first academic to apply economic principles to crime.

But as Cook, Machin, Mastrobuoni, and Marie argue in *Lessons from the Economics of Crime*, Becker chose to bypass, rather than engage with sociology and criminology: their light-hearted reference to his 'disciplinary imperialism' asserted that 'a useful theory of criminal behaviour can dispense with special theories of anomie, psychological inadequacies, or inheritance of special traits and simply extend the economist's analysis of

[57] Ibid., pp. 55–56. [58] Ibid., p. 58. [59] Ibid. [60] Ibid., p. 59.

choice'.[61] In other words, Becker argued that a useful model for understanding crime should see potential criminals rationally consider the expected costs and benefits of committing a specific crime: if the probability of being caught or the level of fine imposed is too low, then the expected costs are likely to outweigh the benefits. In these circumstances, the argument goes, perpetrating a criminal act may well be a rational choice and crime might indeed pay.

Becker launched economics into the criminology arena by 'using economic analysis to develop optimal public and private policies to combat illegal behaviour'. In his seminal 1950 work, 'Crime and Punishment: An Economic Approach', Becker sought to answer the question, 'how many resources and how much punishment should be used to enforce different kinds of legislation?' He concluded that two key variables needed to be examined – namely *p*: the probability that an offence is discovered and the offender convicted and punished (representing the potential criminal's rational weighing of the chances of getting away with the crime); and *f*: the size and form of the punishment that flows from each type of offence. He argued that the optimal values of *p* and *f* could be chosen by policy-makers, subject to the constraints imposed by three behavioural relations: first, the damage caused by a given number of illegal actions; second, the cost of achieving a given level of *p*; and finally, the effect of changes in *p* and *f* on the actual crime rate.[62]

This leads Becker to conclude that setting financial penalties and assessing the optimal spend on crime prevention and criminal justice interventions (such as prison sentences) would be a preferable way to consider social policy decisions in relation to crime. 'If the costs of apprehending, convicting and punishing offenders were nil and if each offence caused more external harm than private gain the social loss from offences would be minimised by setting punishments high enough to eliminate all offences.'

This approach to crime, which to many people may appear stark, can easily be dismissed. It might shed light on criminal behaviour, but to seek to measure the harm that crime does to its victims in financial and numerical terms would lead many people to view the approach as

[61] P. J. Cook, S. Machin, G. Mastrobuoni, and O. Marie, *Lessons from the Economics of Crime*, MIT, United States, 2013.

[62] G. Becker, 'Crime and Punishment: An Economic Approach', in G. Becker and W. Landes (eds.), *Essays in the Economics of Crime and Punishment*, NBER, Cambridge, MA, 1974.

misplaced at best and hopelessly out of touch at best. Becker counters this view by stating clearly that his is *a* model for seeking to understand crime and how best society might respond to it. (And certainly at the time, it would be true to say that it was an entirely new framework for considering these issues.)

Becker does seek to anticipate some criticisms of the applicability of an economic approach: 'Another argument made against fines is that certain crimes, like murder or rape, are so heinous that no amount of money could compensate for the harm inflicted. This argument has obvious merit and is a special case of the more general principle that fines cannot be relied on exclusively whenever the harm exceeds the resources of offenders. For then victims could not be fully compensated by offenders, and fines would have to be supplemented with prison terms or other punishments in order to discourage offences optimally.'[63]

While it seems unlikely that such acknowledgement would satisfy the general conclusion that Becker's application of economic principles to the field of public policy and crime management is wholly appropriate ('the incentive-based model of crime left out too much for some tastes'[64]), it does go some way to establishing the boundaries and limits that this type of analysis provides. Becker concluded that his approach sought to 'demonstrate that optimal policies to combat illegal behaviour are part of an optimal allocation of resources. Since economics has been developed to handle resource allocation, an "economic" framework becomes applicable to, and helps enrich, the analysis of illegal behaviour'.[65]

Three decades after Becker published his work, Richard Freeman sought to re-evaluate the contribution economic analysis has brought to criminal justice. In his 1999 essay, 'The Economics of Crime',[66] he summarised the impact of economics in areas that include participation, 'earnings', rates of offending, whether crime 'pays', and crime prevention. He argued that while the underpinning scientific basis of the impact of crime reduction interventions tends to be 'weak' (i.e. without random assignment or a well-specified control group, without sufficient sample size to detect modest effects with any confidence, or without serious

63 Becker, 'Crime and Punishment: An Economic Approach'.

64 R. B. Freeman, 'The Economics of Crime', in O. Ashenfelter and D. Card (eds.), *Handbook of Labor Economics*, Vol. 3c, Elsevier, 1999, p. 3562.

65 Becker, 'Crime and Punishment: An Economic Approach'.

66 Freeman, 'The Economics of Crime'.

consideration of attrition of the treatment/control sample), there is sufficient evidence to draw some helpful conclusions. Meta-analysis (the statistical technique of combining the findings from *y* different independent studies) of juvenile delinquency programmes and experiences from various rehabilitation programmes find that 'the typical programme has modest crime-reducing effects'. This, he believes, has 'shifted the view of many social scientists from the 1970s that "nothing works" to the current belief that "most things work a bit"'.[67]

Freeman also cites the 1996–97 University of Maryland review of crime prevention programmes. The review covered more than 500 initiatives, ranging from school programmes to family interventions to job training to policing strategies. It scored studies by their 'scientific rigour' and tried to assess 'what works, what doesn't, what's promising'. Overall, the review found that most (though not all) inexpensive short programmes were ineffective in reducing crime. This includes such well-publicised programmes as Scared Straight (taking young at-risk youths to prisons to see what awaits them if they commit crimes), correctional boot camps, police visits to homes where there is domestic violence, random patrols (see the section below on the privatisation of police activity) and rapid response by police to 999 calls (911 in the United States), Neighbourhood Watch reports, and Midnight Basketball initiatives, among others.

Conversely, longer-term and more expensive interventions were more positively evaluated, including 'intensive residential training programmes for at-risk youths ... long-term frequent home visitation to at-risk youths and their parents, intensive supervision of probated or paroled criminals (and) additional police patrols at hot spots of crime'. Freeman concludes that 'contrasting the efficacy per dollar spent on the relevant alternatives, rather than studying a single programme in isolation' should be the way forward.

Freeman also revisits the thorny issue raised by Becker of applying monetary values to the costs of crime. Citing the US National Crime Victimisation Survey, which asks victims to estimate losses from theft or damage, medical expenses, and pay and loss due to injury, he notes that the (1992) estimate was that 'the average burglary cost US$834, the average car theft $3,990, and the average robbery $555'. While this evidence takes us closer to understanding the costs of largely

[67] Freeman, 'The Economics of Crime', p. 3557, citing M. W. Lipsey and D. B. Wilson, 'The Efficacy of Psychological, Educational, and Behavioural Treatment: Confirmation from Meta-Analysis', in *American Psychologist*, Vol. 48 (1993), pp. 1181–209.

property-related crime, it also attests to the limitations of an economic approach to more serious person-to-person crime.

Freeman also touched on the issue of privatisation of criminal justice activities (of which more later). He cites Benson's 1998 study of the role of the private sector in criminal justice, which includes

> the growing number of private prisons, San Francisco's long-standing use of "Private Special Police" to patrol neighbourhoods [see further Chapter 9], police outsourcing of some services, local government contracting police services from private firms, Federal Bureau of Prisons contracting all of its halfway houses to the private sector, university use of private campus policing, company preferences for resolving some criminal acts by employees (and) diverse forms of mediation, liaisons between the police and private security forces.

He concludes that 'whatever one's views of where the public/private divide should be in criminal justice activities, [it is] clear that there is much action on the private side that merits analytic attention'.

On the contribution that economics can and is making to our understanding of crime, Freeman concludes that: it is

> heartening for an economist to see the great stress ethnographers put on economic rewards in the behaviour of youth gangs and the way young at-risk youths view working legally versus working illegally as options that fit the basic economic calculus. It must be heartening for the non-economists to see that economic researchers have come to stress social interactions and other non-market factors in crime as well. My (biased economist's) assessment is that economics has made a major positive contribution to our knowledge of crime, and that economic ideas and professional economists will play a larger role in research on crime in the future.

Contracting Out Policing to the Private Sector

Does it really matter who exercises the functions of the police? Does privatisation have a role in policing and what issues does that raise for police use of force? Bayley and Shearing argued in 1996 that modern societies 'have reached an evolution in the evolution of their system of crime control and law enforcement' and affirmed that 'future generations will look back on our era as a time when one system of policing and another took its place'.[68]

[68] D. Bayley and C. Shearing, 'The Future of Policing', in T. Newburn (ed.), *Key Readings in Criminology*, Willan, Cullompton, 1996, p. 585. Newburn justly contests their Weberian-

Actually, as discussed further in Chapter 9, while it is not difficult to find individuals and organisations that promote the desirability of police privatisation and extol its potential benefits, it would be inaccurate to suggest that this view represents the thinking of even a significant minority of commentators (or indeed members of the public). A far more widely held perspective, however, is that benefits might accrue from 'contracting out' specific elements of police functions – such as information technology (IT), call handling, or transport. This process has become an increasingly common feature of public-sector provision over the last 30 or 40 years, with examples to be found in health and social care, education, and other local and national government functions. Thus, as Adam White of the University of York suggests, 'Privatisation is probably the wrong word for what the Police have been doing since it implies a far greater degree of market penetration than is actually happening. Outsourcing is a much better word.'[69]

Of course, many economists argue that there is a fundamental obstacle to promoting private provision of policing functions – the existence of 'externalities' and 'free riders'. If we take a simple example of street patrols and imagine that you are required to pay directly for them to be carried out: the police officer (paid for by you) passing down a street does not benefit your house alone, he or she benefits every house in the street. Potential criminals will not know that it is your house that is being protected, and therefore if they are deterred from committing a crime on your house, they are just as likely to be deterred from committing a crime on your neighbours' houses. As a result, the patrols have not only generated *private or internal* benefits (for you); they have also created *external* ones (for your neighbours).[70] And, of course, if your neighbours know that they are benefitting from your provision of police patrols, they might very well decide not to pay for any themselves – they will take a 'free ride'. It seems reasonable to conclude, therefore, that creating an efficiently functioning market even for such a

like assertion, often repeated, of the police holding a monopoly of violence. Newburn, *Criminology*, p. 646. See also Reiner, *The Politics of the Police*, p. 6.

[69] A. White, 'Five Reasons Why It Is Difficult to Privatise the Police', LSE British Politics and Policy Blog, 29 October 2014, at: http://blogs.lse.ac.uk/politicsandpolicy/five-reasons-why-its-difficult-to-privatise-the-police/; and see also A. White, 'Post-Crisis Policing and Public–Private Partnerships', *British Journal of Criminology*, Oxford University Press, 2014, available at: http://bjc.oxfordjournals.org/content/early/2014/09/16/bjc.azu063.short?rss=1.

[70] J. Le Grand and R. Robinson, *The Economics of Social Problems: The Market versus the State*, 2nd Edn, Macmillan, London, 1984.

narrow slice of criminal justice interventions such as for street patrols is fraught with difficulties, and that funding police forces by government from taxed income is unlikely to change.

But government – as opposed to private individual – funding of the police is only one aspect of the term privatisation. Leaving aside the critical issue of legitimacy, very potent *practical* reasons help to explain why private provision of police services has not been widely pursued. (It would of course be easy to cite a wide range of examples of private security provision – in shopping centres or outdoor entertainment events, for instance – but arguably these are not examples of core functions of a police service.)

White goes on to cite five reasons why it is difficult to achieve this in practice, at least in the United Kingdom.[71]

First, **media scaremongering**. White argues that the way that the media tends to frame the debate about the delivery of police services is heavily driven by their desire to sell newspapers and that by using the term 'privatisation', it is more likely to raise the fears of the public – 'a more nuanced commentary on police outsourcing does not have the same fear-inducing effect'.

Second, **public fear**. Closely linked to the first reason, White argues that scaremongering has been so effective precisely because 'many members of the public are truly fearful of what might happen if police forces are over-exposed to the market'. If we accept Reiner's analysis of groups of citizens who have become 'public property', this position is entirely understandable.

Furthermore, high-profile examples of fraud and mismanagement have highlighted the dangers of private-sector companies being awarded contracts for criminal justice work. In 2015, *The Guardian* newspaper reported that in the United Kingdom in relation to a 'tagging' contract, companies, including Serco and G4S, 'billed the state until they had a document telling them not to, even if the subjects had died, disappeared or were no longer wearing a tag . . .. When the anomalies came to light in 2013 they showed that the companies had invoiced the taxpayer for millions of pounds' worth of non-existent work'.[72] 'You are charging us for people who are dead', one cabinet official is quoted as saying.

[71] White, 'Five Reasons Why It Is Difficult to Privatise the Police'.

[72] S. Knight, 'Can Winston Churchill's Grandson Save Serco?', *The Guardian*, 2 July 2015, at: www.theguardian.com/business/2015/jul/02/serco-rupert-soames-outsourcing-privatisation.

Third, **scepticism in senior ranks**. White believes that 'many senior police officers are simply not comfortable with – or are actively hostile towards – a greater role for the private sector', providing a further block or barrier towards outsourcing. As these senior employees are central to pursuing the contracting out of police functions, 'this means that in some forces outsourcing never enters onto the agenda as a matter of principle'.

Fourth, **inexperience in the mechanics of contracting out**. There are significant technical and legal barriers to overcome if a service is to be tendered on the open market. Understandably, police forces tend not to see outsourcing as one of their core competencies, historically have had very few staff with significant experience of its complexity, and, at least until recently, have not tended to think in terms of business processes and unit costs for the services that they provide. 'They think in terms of victims and criminals, evidence and arrests', says White. Despite ambitious plans announced by the UK government to outsource more than £1.5 billion worth of police services (including investigating crimes, detaining suspects, and managing intelligence), the proposals have never reached the point of implementation and, at least for now, appear to have been stopped. (While technical barriers have clearly contributed to the current hiatus, it is also probably true that political opposition from certain Police and Crime Commissioners has also been a factor in these decisions.)

Fifth, **staffing the contract**. As White argues, even if a police force were prepared to put to one side the media scaremongering, the perceived public fear and opposition, and resistance from police staff, and believed it were possible to employ staff with sufficient experience of the technical skills required to offer services to the open market, the result might not actually look that different. He cites the example of Lincolnshire Police, which in 2011 outsourced some of their services to G4S. Due to UK legal requirements (known as TUPE), any service which is contracted out must offer those jobs to the individuals previously employed to carry them out – albeit while transferring their employment to G4S – meaning, in many instances, that the staff simply transfer to a new employer. While this is not necessarily a barrier to outsourcing (although it can make winning contracts a less attractive proposition), it certainly contributes to the conclusion that 'privatisation' of the police is not quite the sea change that the media phrase implies.

Despite these arguments and barriers against privatisation and even 'contracting out', it would be wrong to conclude that private provision of some elements of police work (starting with backroom services) is not making any impact at all. In November 2015, G4S were claiming that they were helping to make significant savings to police budgets through their (UK) Lincolnshire contract, and with continuing pressures on public finances intensifying, there will continue to be impetus for other forces to follow their approach. But there are important caveats to this conclusion. In May 2016, *The Guardian* reported that five G4S control room staff working for Lincolnshire Police were suspended after allegations that they were making hundreds of emergency 999 calls at quiet times to improve their perceived performance. The suspended officers were all former Lincolnshire Police employees who transferred to G4S in 2012 when the private security company took over a £200 million contract – the largest ever – to run the force's back-office services. G4S had previously claimed that the contract saves the force £6 million a year and hailed it as a potential model for the rest of British policing.[73]

Why Does Police Use of Force Vary So Significantly across Nations?

These contrasting approaches, which contribute to the complexity of defining policing because of the variety of roles and approaches that are thrust upon them, combined with the wider social and political forces which necessarily impact the police, begin to provide a platform to help understand the important societal influences that frame use of force by the police.

There can be no doubt that police use of force varies significantly in nature and extent as well as in fundamental approach across nations (and arguably also within them). Maguire, writing in *Police Use of Force: A Global Perspective*, a fascinating compilation of experiences of policing across different countries, begins his analysis of this question by citing two starkly contrasting examples.[74] The first, which occurred in Hong Kong, involved police officers investing a burglary encountering two men

[73] A. Travis, 'G4S Police Control Room Staff Suspended over Claims of Bogus 999 Calls', *The Guardian*, 23 May 2016, at: www.theguardian.com/uk-news/2016/may/23/g4s-police-control-room-staff-suspended-claims-bogus-999-calls-lincolnshire-force.

[74] E. R. Maguire, 'Conclusion: A Journey through the World of Police Use of Force', in J. B. Kuhns and J. Knutsson (eds.), *Police Use of Force: A Global Perspective*, Praeger, Westport, CT, 2010, p. 199ff.

loitering in a nearby alley. 'When one of the men ran away, a 23-year-old police constable chased after him and fired three shots during the pursuit. All three shots missed the man and he was arrested at the conclusion of the chase.' The review after the incident concluded that 'no disciplinary action against the constable was warranted for shooting at the man, because the constable was acting on the knowledge that a serious crime (the burglary) had been committed'.[75]

The second incident happened in Canada. Two police officers responded to a call requesting the removal of an intoxicated male. 'The suspect had a lengthy criminal record and a propensity for violence. When the police arrived he armed himself with a concealed knife. When the officers tried to arrest him (one officer) sustained knife wounds to his head and back ... the officers succeeded in subduing the offender and arresting him ... (and) both officers were issued with a commendation for bravery.'[76]

Maguire's examples highlight two very different responses by police officers: the first involved purely a property-related crime with no obvious imminent threat, yet the officer shot at the suspect (which violates international law, as Chapters 3 and 4 explain); in the second, the suspect was armed and presented a clear threat to life, but the officers showed commendable restraint in choosing not to shoot.[77] These two incidents happened in different countries, but as Maguire asks, 'if theories that purport to explain police use of force are robust, shouldn't they be able to explain police use of force across its full range of variation across the globe?'[78]

[75] Ibid., p. 199. [76] Ibid.

[77] In September 2016, a West Virginia police officer was fired for failing to open fire on a man brandishing an unloaded gun, on the basis that he put fellow officers in danger. Officer Stephen Mader told *The Pittsburgh Post-Gazette* that he was dispatched to a domestic dispute and found Ronald Williams, 21, armed with a handgun. When Officer Mader told him to put down the gun, Mr Williams said: 'Just shoot me.' And I told him, 'I'm not going to shoot you brother.' Mader thought he could talk to him and de-escalate the situation. 'I knew it was a "suicide-by-cop" situation.' When two other officers arrived on the scene, however, they shot Mr Williams dead as he walked towards them. A police investigation concluded that the killing was justified despite the gun being unloaded. 'Police Officer Sacked for Not Shooting Black Man Holding an Unloaded Gun', *Independent*, 13 September 2016, at: www.independent.co.uk/news/police-officer-sacked-not-shooting-black-man-virginia-stephen-mader-ronald-williams-a7245681.html.

[78] Maguire, 'Conclusion: A Journey through the World of Police Use of Force', p. 200.

3

Core Principles Governing Use of Force for Law Enforcement

> 'We take one great principle of the common law to be, that . . . the use of force to prevent crimes to preserve the public peace and to bring offenders to justice . . . is subject to the restriction that the force used is necessary; that is, that the mischief sought to be prevented could not be prevented by less violent means; and that the mischief done by or which might reasonably be anticipated from the force used is not disproportionate to the injury or mischief, which it is intended to prevent.'
>
> 1879 Royal Commission of Great Britain[1]

Introduction

While international human rights law provides the overarching framework for the international law of law enforcement (LOLE), much of the detail of that body of law, at least insofar as it regulates police use of force, is found in a combination of customary rules and two general principles of law:[2] necessity and proportionality. A third general principle of law enforcement has emerged in recent decades – the principle of precaution requires that states ensure that law enforcement operations are planned and conducted so as to minimise the risk of injury. Many, though not all of the relevant rules were first articulated in two soft-law instruments[3] adopted under United Nations (UN) auspices: the 1979 Code of Conduct for Law Enforcement

[1] 1879 Royal Commission appointed to consider the law relating to indictable offences, *House of Lords Papers*, Vol. 36 (1879), p. 167.

[2] The primary and secondary sources of international law are set out in Art. 38(1)(b) and (c) of the 1945 Statute of the International Court of Justice. Customary law and general principles of law are both primary sources of law, along with treaties.

[3] Soft-law instruments do not have the same normative value as a treaty since they are hortatory rather than legally binding.

Officials[4] and the 1990 Basic Principles on the Use of Force and Firearms by Law Enforcement Officials.[5]

The 1990 Basic Principles elaborate in greater detail on the norms on use of force set out in Article 3 of the 1979 Code of Conduct, which stipulates that law enforcement officials 'may use force only when strictly necessary and to the extent required for the performance of their duty'. Further detail is included in the associated official commentary on Article 3, which provides, among other things, that 'every effort should be made to exclude the use of firearms'. Although the provisions of the two instruments were not incorporated within the confines of an international treaty,[6] many of the key norms they espouse are widely regarded today as constituting more generally binding international law. Both the European Court of Human Rights and the Inter-American Court of Human Rights have cited the 1990 Basic Principles as authoritative statements of international rules governing use of force in law enforcement.[7]

[4] The 1979 Code of Conduct for Law Enforcement Officials was adopted by UN General Assembly Resolution 34/169 of 17 December 1979. The Assembly decided to 'transmit it to Governments with the recommendation that favourable consideration be given to its use within the framework of national legislation or practice as a body of principles for observance by law enforcement officials'. Resolution 34/169, §1.

[5] The Basic Principles were adopted by the Eighth UN Congress on the Prevention of Crime and the Treatment of Offenders, Havana, Cuba, 27 August to 7 September 1990. The UN General Assembly in its Resolution 45/166, adopted without a vote on 18 December 1990, welcomed the Basic Principles and invited governments to respect them (§4).

[6] Under international law, a treaty is defined as 'an international agreement concluded between States in written form and governed by international law, whether embodied in a single instrument or in two or more related instruments and whatever its particular designation'. Art. 2(1)(a), 1969 Vienna Convention on the Law of Treaties.

[7] See, e.g., European Court of Human Rights (ECtHR), *Benzer* v. *Turkey*, Judgment (Former Second Section), 12 November 2013, as rendered final on 24 March 2014, §90; Inter-American Court of Human Rights (IAmCtHR), *Cruz Sánchez and Others* v. *Peru*, Judgment (Preliminary Objections, Merits, Reparation, and Costs), 17 April 2015, §264. The Court refers to the 1979 Code of Conduct in the same paragraph. In its draft general comment on the right to life (not yet finalised as of writing), the Human Rights Committee states as follows: 'In particular, all operations of law enforcement agents should comply with relevant international standards, including the Code of Conduct for Law Enforcement Officials ... and the Basic Principles on the Use of Force and Firearms by Law Enforcement Officials (1990), and law enforcement agents should undergo appropriate training designed to inculcate these standards so as to ensure, in all circumstances, the fullest respect for the right to life'. Human Rights Committee, 'Draft General Comment No. 36 (Article 6: Right to Life)', Draft prepared by Yuval Shany and Nigel Rodley, Rapporteurs, UN doc. CCPR/C/GC/R.36/Rev.2, 7 September 2015, §19.

The Basic Principles and the Code of Conduct apply explicitly to the acts of any organs of the state when using force for the purpose of law enforcement. Thus, LOLE rules govern not only the police but also any other law enforcement agency, state security force, paramilitary force (such as a *gendarmerie*), or the military, whenever it is engaged in acts of law enforcement.[8]

The rules similarly apply to a private security company to which the state or one of its organs has delegated police powers. When such a company operates under a private contract, at a minimum the two general principles of necessity and proportionality should restrict any use of force by its personnel (in addition, of course, to domestic law provisions).[9] As the UN Special Rapporteur on extrajudicial, summary, and arbitrary executions wrote in 2016, 'states must adopt a clear legislative framework for the use of force by law enforcement or other individuals that complies with international standards, including the principles of necessity and proportionality'.[10] But the Special Rapporteur has gone

[8] As the 1990 Basic Principles state: 'In accordance with the commentary to Article 1 of the Code of Conduct for Law Enforcement Officials, the term "law enforcement officials" includes all officers of the law, whether appointed or elected, who exercise police powers, especially the powers of arrest or detention. In countries where police powers are exercised by military authorities, whether uniformed or not, or by State security forces, the definition of law enforcement officials shall be regarded as including officers of such services.' 1990 Basic Principles, n1. LOLE rules do not apply to the conduct of hostilities during a situation of armed conflict, but they do apply to acts of law enforcement amid armed conflict.

[9] See further Chapter 9. These principles may apply directly as a matter of international law. According to the African Commission on Human and Peoples' Rights (ACmnHPR), 'Given the widespread violations perpetrated by the Government of Nigeria and by private actors (be it following its clear blessing or not), the most fundamental of all human rights, the right to life has been violated. The Security Forces were given the green light to decisively deal with the Ogonis, which was illustrated by the widespread terrorisations and killings.' ACmnHPR, *Social and Economic Rights Action Centre and the Centre for Economic and Social Rights* v. *Nigeria*, 2001, §67. See also F. Viljoen, *International Human Rights Law in Africa*, 2nd Edn, Oxford University Press, Oxford, 2012, p. 216. In May 2016, Christof Heyns, the Special Rapporteur on extrajudicial, summary, or arbitrary executions, affirmed in his report to the UN Human Rights Council that states 'must adopt a clear legislative framework for the use of force by law enforcement or other individuals that complies with international standards, including the principles of necessity and proportionality'. 'Report of the Special Rapporteur on Extrajudicial, Summary or Arbitrary Executions on the Right to Life and the Use of Force by Private Security Providers in Law Enforcement Contexts', UN doc. A/HRC/32/39, 6 May 2016, §75.

[10] 'Report of the Special Rapporteur on Extrajudicial, Summary or Arbitrary Executions on the Right to Life and the Use of Force by Private Security Providers in Law Enforcement Contexts', §75.

further, arguing that 'before and during any use of force by private security personnel, all reasonable precautionary steps to protect life and prevent excessive violence must be taken, including the provision of appropriate equipment and training, the proscription of inappropriate weapons, and careful planning of individual operations.'[11]

Necessity and Proportionality

The two fundamental principles governing any use of force under LOLE are necessity and proportionality. Any force used must be only the minimum necessary in the circumstances (the principle of necessity). In addition, the force used must be proportionate to the threat (the principle of proportionality). Law enforcement officials must comply with both principles: failure to respect either will usually mean that the victim's human rights have been violated by the state. And as the European Court of Human Rights affirmed in *Douet* v. *France*, 'it is normally for the Government to provide relevant evidence that the use of force was both proportionate and necessary'.[12]

The Principle of Necessity

As noted above, Article 3 of the 1979 Code of Conduct stipulates that law enforcement officials may use force 'only when strictly necessary'. The accompanying official commentary 'emphasises' that any use of force by law enforcement officials 'should be exceptional'. Accordingly, in many circumstances no force at all will be permitted under LOLE. As the 2015 report by the United States (US) Department of Justice (DOJ) on the Ferguson Police Department (FPD) recalls, for instance, 'the ability of a police officer to bring calm to a situation is a core policing skill'.[13]

The principle of necessity encompasses three integral legal duties: to use non-violent means wherever possible; to use force only for a legitimate law enforcement purpose; and to use only the minimum necessary force that is reasonable in the prevailing circumstances. These are discussed in turn.

[11] Ibid.

[12] ECtHR, *Douet* v. *France*, Judgment (Fifth Section), 3 October 2013 (rendered final on 3 January 2014), §30 (author's translation).

[13] US DOJ, *Investigation of the Ferguson Police Department*, 4 March 2015, p. 26.

The Duty to Use Non-Violent Means

Wherever possible, therefore, police should use non-violent means to achieve a legitimate law enforcement objective before resorting to physical force. This default position is explicitly affirmed in 1990 Basic Principle 4:

> Law enforcement officials, in carrying out their duty, shall, as far as possible, apply non-violent means before resorting to the use of force and firearms. They may use force and firearms only if other means remain ineffective or without any promise of achieving the intended result.[14]

As part of a widely used use-of-force continuum, several steps do not involve use of physical force. Palmiotto, for example, describes three categories of action: controlled confrontation (e.g. the symbolic influence of the police authority, presence, their uniform, or the police car); body language (e.g. a body shift toward the offender or intensified eye contact with the individual); and verbal persuasion (e.g. pointing out the futility of resistance, providing reassurance, or making time for more assistance to arrive).[15] These are not just theoretical steps. Edward Conlon, a New York Police Department (NYPD) officer for 16 years, writing about his experiences on the job, noted that

> what you say and how you say it comes into play far more often than anything you do with your stick or gun, and can prevent the need for them. If you talk a good game, you're halfway there. A talker can do things, or undo them. I know cops who have talked would-be suicides from rooftops, and who have convinced raving gunmen to release child hostages. More often, you talk people into talking, only talking, instead of screaming and waving a knife.[16]

Similarly, there may be merit in stepping back and waiting for appropriate resources to arrive, for instance in seeking to effect an arrest. A 2014 case before the European Court of Human Rights concerned a Russian citizen who was suffering from mental illness that required institutional treatment. Mr Kirill Shchiborshch feared that anyone entering his apartment was a burglar and the police had been informed of this fact. They

[14] Such non-violent means include the powers of persuasion, negotiation, and mediation backed by the authority that comes from being a law enforcement official of the state with the authority to use force when strictly necessary.

[15] M. J. Palmiotto, *Policing: Concepts, Strategies, and Current Issues in American Police Forces*, 3rd Edn, CreateSpace Independent Publishing Platform, United States, 2013, p. 245.

[16] E. Conlon, *Blue Blood*, Ebury Press, London, 2011, p. 19.

chose to enter forcibly, and following a struggle Mr Shchiborshch was taken to hospital with multiple wounds and in a coma. He died without regaining consciousness, having sustained cranio-cerebral trauma, brain oedema, concussion, and slash wounds to the head, body, and extremities, several fractured ribs, and a ruptured jugular vein.[17]

Under the relevant domestic legislation in force in Russia, police officers have to assist medical personnel in carrying out an involuntary hospitalisation and ensure safe access to the person concerned and his or her examination.[18] The Court observed that dealing with individuals with serious mental health issues 'clearly requires special training, the absence of which is likely to render futile any attempted negotiations with a person with a mental disorder as grave as that of Mr Shchiborshch'. The Russian authorities did not explain why the police had taken 'actions aimed at securing Mr Shchiborshch's involuntary hospitalisation without being accompanied by qualified medical personnel'.[19] The Court further regretted that the police used force as if they were dealing with any armed offender and without regard to Mr Shchiborshch's delirious state or to the fact that he did not pose an immediate danger to either himself or others. The Russian police chose to storm the kitchen in which Mr Shchiborshch had barricaded himself, in the course of which he sustained injuries that proved lethal. This decision, which was not subject to any preliminary planning and assessment, was hastily taken at the scene without their being any necessity for urgent action.[20]

A need for the police to use force may also be obviated, or at least minimised, by their appropriate equipping with 'self-defensive equipment such as shields, helmets, bullet-proof vests and bullet-proof means of transportation'.[21] Failure to provide its law enforcement agencies with appropriate defensive equipment may mean that a state has violated the principle of precaution, for instance when it leads inexorably to excessive force being used.[22] A police officer who suffers injury, or worse, in the

[17] ECtHR, *Shchiborshch and Kuzmina* v. *Russia*, Judgment (First Section), 16 January 2014 (as rendered final on 2 June 2014), §§6–10.

[18] Law on Psychiatric Assistance and Citizens' Rights in this Respect of 2 July 1992 (as amended on 21 July 1998, 25 July 2002, 10 January 2003, and 29 July 2004), s. 30(3).

[19] ECtHR, *Shchiborshch and Kuzmina* v. *Russia*, Judgment, §233. [20] Ibid., §240.

[21] 1990 Basic Principle 3.

[22] In January 2016, the US Police Executive Research Forum (PERF) published a set of valuable guidelines on use of force. One of the guiding principles noted that: 'Personal protection shields may support de-escalation efforts during critical incidents, including situations involving persons with knives, baseball bats, or other improvised weapons that

performance of his/her duties could also have a legitimate claim against the state since, of course, the police are also entitled to enjoy protection of their fundamental human rights to life and to bodily integrity.[23]

Force Must Be Used for a Legitimate Law Enforcement Purpose

A second element of the principle of necessity is that each use of force, whatever its nature and extent, must be for a legitimate purpose. As Article 3 of the 1979 Code of Conduct stipulates, law enforcement officials may use force only 'to the extent required for the performance of their duty'. The accompanying official commentary clarifies that law enforcement officials may use such force, and no more, 'as is reasonably necessary under the circumstances' to prevent crime or to effect or assist in the lawful arrest of offenders or suspected offenders. The 2001 European Code of Police Ethics similarly stipulates that the police may use force 'only when strictly necessary and only to the extent required to obtain a legitimate objective'.[24]

Accordingly, force must never be used vindictively or as a form of extrajudicial punishment; meted out in a discriminatory manner; or applied against an individual offering no resistance. In any event, force must cease to be applied when the need for further violent action has passed (for example, when a suspect is safely and lawfully detained). Unlawful arrest or detention do not amount to legitimate law enforcement purposes.[25]

are not firearms.' PERF, *Use of Force: Taking Policing to a Higher Standard. 30 Guiding Principles*, Critical Issues in Policing Series, 29 January 2016, Guiding Principle 28 (bold emphasis removed). The Guidelines further call for officers with access to personal protection shields to be 'adequately trained' in their use, 'both individually and as part of a team operation'.

[23] PERF recommends that agencies acquire personal protection shields for use by patrol officers and others in managing some critical incidents. Ibid.

[24] European Code of Police Ethics, adopted by the Committee of Ministers of the Council of Europe on 19 September 2001, §37, available at: http://polis.osce.org/library/f/2687/500/CoE-FRA-RPT-2687-EN-500.

[25] Thus, for example, as the 2016 DOJ report on the Baltimore City Police Department (BPD) found, in violation of domestic US law officers frequently made 'investigative stops without reasonable suspicion of people who are lawfully present on Baltimore streets. During stops, officers commonly conduct weapons frisks – or more invasive searches – despite lacking reasonable suspicion that the subject of the search is armed. These practices escalate street encounters and contribute to officers making arrests without probable cause . . . Indeed, BPD's own supervisors at Central Booking and prosecutors in the State's Attorney's Office declined to charge more than 11,000 arrests made by BPD

Discriminatory practices, such as those executed against minorities, are clearly unlawful under international law, and, in many countries, also national law. Thus, for example, a DOJ investigation in 2014–15 found that the practices of the FPD 'disproportionately harm African Americans', uncovering 'substantial evidence that this harm stems in part from intentional discrimination in violation of the Constitution'. This included use of force against African Americans 'at disproportionately high rates, accounting for 88% of all cases from 2010 to August 2014 in which an FPD officer reported using force'. In all fourteen uses of force involving a police dog bite for which the DOJ had information about the race of the person, the person was African American.[26]

Force Used Must Be the Minimum Necessary in the Circumstances

A third, critical element of the principle of necessity is that when force is necessary, it must be only the minimum reasonably necessary in the circumstances and no more.[27] This requires, for example, that even potentially violent suspects should be arrested, not killed, whenever it is reasonably possible to do so,[28] and that force used 'must be in keeping with the level of resistance offered'.[29] In the case of *Bouyid* v. *Belgium*, adjudged by the European Court of Human Rights in 2015 on appeal from the Court's Fifth Section, the Grand Chamber reiterated that 'in respect of a person who is ... confronted with law-enforcement officers, any recourse to physical force which has not been made strictly necessary by his own conduct diminishes human dignity and is, in principle, an infringement' of the right

officers since 2010.' US DOJ, *Investigation of the Baltimore City Police Department*, 10 August 2016, p. 24, at: www.justice.gov/opa/file/883366/download.

[26] Ibid., p. 62.

[27] See Commentary (a) on Art. 3, 1979 Code of Conduct; and 'Report of the Special Rapporteur on Extrajudicial, Summary or Arbitrary Executions, Christof Heyns', UN doc. A/HRC/26/36, 1 April 2014, §59.

[28] N. S. Rodley, 'Integrity of the Person', in D. Moeckli *et al.* (eds.), *International Human Rights Law*, Oxford University Press, Oxford, 2010, p. 223. Sir Nigel cited the 1982 Human Rights Committee case of *Guerrero v. Colombia* in which the state shot suspected terrorists instead of arresting them as they could certainly have done in the circumstances.

[29] IAmCtHR, *Nadege Dorzema and Others* v. *Dominican Republic*, Judgment (Merits, reparations and costs), 24 October 2012, §85(iii). See also N. S. Rodley with M. Pollard, *The Treatment of Prisoners under International Law*, 3rd Edn, Oxford University Press, Oxford, 2011, p. 499.

to freedom from torture and inhuman or degrading treatment (inscribed in Article 3 of the 1950 European Convention on Human Rights).[30]

Controversially, however, the 2011 judgment of the European Court in the *Finogenov* case suggests that a 'margin of appreciation' might be allowed to the state for use of force in exceptional circumstances (the case in question related to a major terrorist incident).[31] This would seem to imply that acts that would otherwise be considered to amount to excessive or indiscriminate use of force to be not unlawful in similarly 'exceptional' circumstances. However, the decision was issued not by the Grand Chamber but only a section of the Court, weakening its broader normative effects. What is more, one expert has suggested that had the decision been appealed to the Grand Chamber, this latitude would not have remained.[32] In any event, it is doubtful that extant international law allows a state an additional margin of appreciation for use of force beyond that inherent in the principles of necessity and proportionality as they apply to a particular incident.[33]

A margin of discretion may, though, legitimately be granted to individual police officers. At domestic level, the US Supreme Court held in *Graham* v. *Connor* that: 'The calculus of reasonableness must embody allowance for the fact that police officers are often forced to make split-second judgments in circumstances that are tense, uncertain, and rapidly evolving – about the amount of force that is necessary in a particular situation.'[34] A police officer

[30] ECtHR, *Bouyid* v. *Belgium*, Judgment (Grand Chamber), 28 September 2015, §§88, 100.

[31] ECtHR, *Finogenov and Others* v. *Russia*, Judgment (First Section), 20 December 2011 (as rendered final on 4 June 2012), §213, at: http://hudoc.echr.coe.int/sites/eng/pages/search.aspx?i=001-108231. Contrast the notion of a margin of appreciation for use of potentially lethal force regarding compliance with Art. 2 of the 1950 European Convention on Human Rights (ECHR) with that granted to states parties to the ECHR with respect to other rights. See Council of Europe and The Lisbon Network, 'The Margin of Appreciation', undated but accessed 19 August 2015 at: www.coe.int/t/dghl/cooperation/lisbonnetwork/themis/echr/paper2_en.asp.

[32] Remarks (author's notes) citing conversation with the Deputy Registrar of the European Court of Human Rights, Michael O'Boyle, at 'Lethal Force, Policing and the ECHR: *McCann and Others v UK* at Twenty', Event organised by the University of Exeter's Centre for European Legal Studies and Doughty Street Chambers, Doughty Street Chambers, London, 25 March 2015.

[33] More broadly, the notion of a margin of appreciation could be considered inconsistent with 1990 Basic Principle 8 whereby: 'Exceptional circumstances such as internal political instability or any other public emergency may not be invoked to justify any departure from these basic principles.' Though see ECtHR, *Tagayeva and others* v. *Russia*, Judgment (First Section), 13 April 2017, §492.

[34] US Supreme Court, *Graham* v. *Connor*, 490 US 386 (1989), Decided 15 May 1989, at 396–97.

may make an honest mistake and not be held criminally liable, unless that mistake was manifestly unreasonable in the circumstances. In the *McCann* case, the Grand Chamber of the European Court of Human Rights stated that use of force by agents of the State may be justified

> where it is based on an honest belief which is perceived, for good reasons, to be valid at the time but which subsequently turns out to be mistaken. To hold otherwise would be to impose an unrealistic burden on the State and its law-enforcement personnel in the execution of their duty, perhaps to the detriment of their lives and those of others.[35]

Nonetheless, in general, each use of force will need justification.[36] This is especially important when firearms or other forms of force that may result in death are being employed.[37] And when the necessity for force ends, so too must the use of force.

Moreover, law enforcement officials are expected to seek to calm, not inflame any situation, much less deliberately provoke violence. The DOJ's 2015 report on the FPD, referred to above, contains the following assessment of use of force by Ferguson police officers:

> Many officers are quick to escalate encounters with subjects they perceive to be disobeying their orders or resisting arrest. They have come to rely on ECWs [electronic control weapons], specifically Tasers®, where less force – or no force at all – would do. They also release canines on

[35] ECtHR, *McCann and Others* v. *UK*, Judgment (Grand Chamber), 27 September 1995, §200; approved, inter alia, in *Armani da Silva* v. *UK*, Judgment (Grand Chamber), 30 March 2016, §§244ff.

[36] Thus, for example, in *Meyers* v. *Baltimore County*, the US Court of Appeals for the Fourth Circuit (covering Maryland, Virginia, West Virginia, North Carolina, and South Carolina) a defendant-officer's discharging of a Taser was adjudged based on the level of resistance the arrestee was offering – and the danger that resistance posed to the officers – when each shock was administered. See US Court of Appeals (Fourth Circuit), *Meyers* v. *Baltimore County*, 713 F.3d 723 (2013), pp. 733–34. The 'first three deployments of [the] taser did not amount to an unreasonable or excessive use of force[] [because the arrestee] was acting erratically, was holding a baseball bat that he did not relinquish until after he received the second shock, and was advancing toward the officers . . .' Ibid., p. 733. But seven later deployments of the taser did amount to excessive force: 'It is an excessive and unreasonable use of force for a police officer repeatedly to administer electrical shocks with a taser on an individual who no longer is armed, has been brought to the ground, has been restrained physically by several other officers, and no longer is actively resisting arrest.' Ibid., p. 734.

[37] See, e.g., Amnesty International, *Use of Force: Guidelines for Implementation of the UN Basic Principles on the Use of Force and Firearms by Law Enforcement Officials*, AI Dutch Section, Police and Human Rights Programme, 2015, p. 121.

> unarmed subjects unreasonably and before attempting to use force less likely to cause injury.[38]

In a similar vein, in 2016 the DOJ criticised the Baltimore City Police Department for its training of officers 'to be aggressive, inculcating an adversarial mindset in its recruits and teaching them to, for example, point a weapon at unarmed and innocent civilians to control a scene. Tactics such as these unnecessarily escalate encounters, increase tensions and lead to unnecessary force.'[39] The DOJ further found that BPD officers 'approach incidents involving mere quality of life violations in a confrontational manner and fail to use basic conflict resolution skills, creating conflict where it did not exist before'.[40]

Differentiated and Progressive Use of Force?

Arguably, but not certainly, LOLE rules demand that force be applied progressively by law enforcement officials. According to Basic Principle 5, 'Whenever the lawful use of force and firearms is unavoidable, law enforcement officials shall . . . [e]xercise restraint in such use and . . . [m]inimize damage and injury . . .'[41] That is a clear statement of the law as it stands. But in interpreting this principle, the Inter-American Court of Human Rights has asserted that law enforcement agents 'must apply the criteria of differentiated *and progressive* use of force, determining the degree of cooperation, resistance or violence of the subject against whom the intervention is intended and, on this basis, employ negotiating tactics, control or use of force, as required'.[42] Similarly, in the view of the UN Special Rapporteur on extrajudicial, summary, or arbitrary executions, 'Where non-violent means prove ineffective or without promise of achieving the intended result, necessity requires that the level of force used should be escalated as gradually as possible.'[43]

Although not everyone supports the use-of-force continuum, a series of alternatives are available to police officers before a potentially lethal

[38] US DOJ, *Investigation of the Ferguson Police Department*, 4 March 2015, p. 28.

[39] US DOJ, *Investigation of the Baltimore City Police Department*, 10 August 2016, p. 75.

[40] Ibid. [41] 1990 Basic Principle 5(a) and (b).

[42] IAmCtHR, *Nadege Dorzema and Others* v. *Dominican Republic*, Judgment (Merits, Reparations, and Costs), 24 October 2012, §85(iii) [added emphasis]. See also Rodley with Pollard, *The Treatment of Prisoners Under International Law*, p. 499.

[43] 'Report of the Special Rapporteur on Extrajudicial, Summary or Arbitrary Executions, Christof Heyns', §61.

course of action is considered and engaged. One such model is described as follows:

> **Contact Controls** — a reluctant individual can be brought into compliance with the placement of "hands-on" and the assumption of an arrest posture. Generally the officer assumes control of the subject's arm while positioning himself to the rear/side of the subject. This contact allows potential flexibility if resistance is continued and in many cases adds a degree of futility to further subdue aggression.
>
> **Joint Restraint** — a mildly resistant subject can be placed into a controlled posture with a leverage domination technique. Usually the wrist or elbow is the focus of a variety of restraint tactics which can grow in tension or pain reciprocal to subsequent resistance.
>
> **Nerve Centre Controls** — aggressively resistant subjects may necessitate additional pain compliance concentrated upon nerve centres throughout the body until an effective threshold of pain is experienced, done along with another simultaneous control tactic.[44]

Certain US officials and practitioners, though, contest whether graduated increase in use of force represents good law enforcement practice. Ken Wallentine, for example, the Chief of Law Enforcement for the Utah Attorney General in the United States, argues that 'rigid application of a force continuum is just as unsuitable to a street encounter between an officer and a violent suspect as are the Marquess of Queensbury rules'.[45] In his view, '[p]erhaps the most frightening tactical defect of force continua is the inherent tendency for hesitation when, not seconds, but fractions of seconds may determine whether an officer lives or dies.'[46] Securing a suspect rapidly may obviate the need for deadly force to be used later.[47] According to others, 'setting an example' may also prevent an escalation in a potentially volatile situation.[48]

[44] Palmiotto, *Policing: Concepts, Strategies, and Current Issues in American Police Forces*, pp. 245–46, citing G. Connor, 'Use of Force Continuum', *Law and Order*, Vol. 34, No. 1 (1986), p. 19.

[45] K. Wallentine, 'The Risky Continuum: Abandoning the Use of Force Continuum to Enhance Risk Management', *International Municipal Lawyers Association Articles*, July 2009, p. 2, available at: www.ecdlaw.info/outlines/Wallentine-continua.pdf.

[46] Ibid., p. 5. [47] Ibid., p. 6.

[48] In a comment posted by DaveinCanada, responding to a blog post on a use-of-force continuum model, it was claimed that: 'The major flaw I can see with the model is that it encourages constant (re)analysis rather than action. In your scenario the only relevant bit is that you're faced with a drunken man armed with a lump of wood, the fact that you don't have his date of birth, his home address or his missing medication is irrelevant, if

Widespread opposition in the United States, in particular, led one academic to claim in 2008 that the use-of-force continuum 'is dying a slow death'.[49]

In defence of the continuum model, Fridell *et al.* have argued that sound continua 'highlight the importance of the totality of the circumstances and allow for needed flexibility based on subject factors, officer factors, and other factors'.[50] The authors assert that 'a good expert can educate juries as to the nuances of the continuum, including the flexibility they accord officers and the fact that officers need not "climb the stairs one at a time".'[51]

For sure, if non-violent or minimal use of physical force proves ineffective, or if there is a significant threat of harm, officers will need to consider more forceful alternatives in pursuit of a legitimate law enforcement objective. These include the following, according to the 1986 model cited above (each of which, as discussed in the following chapters, can have fatal consequences):

> **Chemical Irritants** — individual aero-canisters containing a tear-gas formulation can be used to subdue an aggressively non-compliant subject.
>
> **Electrical Devices** — a type of mechanism effective on physically agitated individuals is the electrically based weapon. Via high voltage and low amperage, these devices override the body's nervous system and cause muscle dysfunction allowing for submission until control is assumed.
>
> **Extending Impact Weapons** — an extremely violent subject makes close proximity techniques very dangerous. Therefore strikes or thrusts can best be made by weapons under the generic heading of batons or nightsticks. With the distancing these allow, the officer has the ability to control the subject's violent actions with a minimized risk.
>
> **Weaponless Techniques with Debilitating Potential** — extremely violent subjects must be immediately subdued to minimize risks. These techniques attack vital centres of the body and, therefore, allow for total

the wood in question is baseball-bat sized, you're going to have to shoot him, and if running away from that (sorry "tactical withdrawal") is a serious "tactical option" the people in charge need to have a serious word with themselves.' Post on blog post by Police Geek, 'Use of Force – Decision Making', 31 July 2012, at: https://policegeek.wordpress.com/2012/07/31/use-of-force-decision-making/.

49 J. Shults, 'Contextual Compliance Tool Kit', *The Police Perspective* (Blog), 13 October 2013, at: http://joelshults.blogspot.co.uk/2013/10/contextual-compliance-took-kit.html.

50 L. Fridell, S. Ijames, and M. Berkow, 'Taking the Straw Man to the Ground: Arguments in Support of the Linear Use-of-Force Continuum', *The Police Chief*, Vol. 78 (December 2011), pp. 20–25.

51 Ibid.

control. Perhaps the most widely used technique is the lateral vascular neck restraint. Once initiated, it results in unconsciousness within several seconds, or possible death if tension is continued.

Weapon Technique with Debilitating Potential — again, if distance is essential, a powerful baton strike to the knee joint can cause joint dislocation and prevent further movement.

Firearm — where necessity requires control of deadly, aggressive behaviour, the use of the firearm in combination with centre-mass targeting of the perpetrator, may be the most acceptable alternative.[52]

Special care is obviously needed where any weapon with potentially lethal consequences (e.g. firearms or electroshock weapons such as Tasers®) is discharged or a similarly violent technique used. There is also the duty to comply with the principle of proportionality, whose normative content is now discussed.

The Principle of Proportionality

The principle of proportionality as it applies to use of force for law enforcement is much misunderstood. Despite views to the contrary, proportionality does not mean that force must be used by a law enforcement official in strict accord with any use-of-force continuum as described above, or as a 'tit-for-tat' response to violence from a criminal suspect. Instead, it sets a ceiling on what amounts to lawful use of force, in accord with the threat posed by an individual or group of individuals and the offence that has been or is about to be committed. According to the commentary on Article 3 of the 1979 Code of Conduct,

> National law ordinarily restricts the use of force by law enforcement officials in accordance with a principle of proportionality. It is to be understood that such national principles of proportionality are to be respected in the interpretation of this provision. In no case should this provision be interpreted to authorize the use of force which is disproportionate to the legitimate objective to be achieved.[53]

Similarly, according to 1990 Basic Principle 5, 'Whenever the lawful use of force and firearms is unavoidable, law enforcement officers shall ...

[52] Palmiotto, *Policing: Concepts, Strategies, and Current Issues in American Police Forces*, p. 246, citing Connor, 'Use of Force Continuum', p. 19.
[53] Commentary (b) on Art. 3, 1979 Code of Conduct.

act in proportion to the seriousness of the offence and legitimate objective to be achieved.'

It is important to bear in mind that proportionality need only be assessed when the use of force is already necessary and when the force that is actually used is no more than the minimum necessary to achieve a legitimate law enforcement objective (meaning that the principle of necessity is being respected). Proportionality may act to render such necessary force unlawful. Classic examples to illustrate its practical application are the pub brawl or the common theft from a shop. To effectively break up a pub brawl or to stop an escaping thief might be taken to require, in the prevailing circumstances, that a firearm weapon be discharged. But the principle of proportionality will intervene to prevent such use even where it unquestionably amounts to the minimum necessary force in any particular situation. As the European Court of Human Rights has held in the *Nachova* case, an escaping suspect (at least when he or she does not pose a grave threat to life) may not be shot 'even if a failure to use lethal force may result in the opportunity to arrest the fugitive being lost'.[54]

Thus, proportionality holds that the threat an individual poses, whether to a law enforcement official or to the general public, as well as the seriousness of the offence an individual is suspected of committing (or is about to commit), will determine the *maximum* level of force that may lawfully be used.[55] This is particularly important when force that may have lethal consequences is being contemplated.[56] That the principle of proportionality has particular implications for any use of firearms is clear. The specific rules to be applied where recourse to firearms is envisaged are summarised below and then discussed in detail in Chapter 4.

[54] ECtHR, *Nachova* v. *Bulgaria*, Judgment (Grand Chamber), 6 July 2005, §95.

[55] The January 2016 PERF guidelines on use of force state, in relation to proportionality, that: 'In assessing whether a response is proportional, officers must ask themselves, "How would the general public view the action we took? Would they think it was appropriate to the entire situation and to the severity of the threat posed to me or to the public?"' PERF, *Use of Force: Taking Policing to a Higher Standard. 30 Guiding Principles*, Critical Issues in Policing Series, 29 January 2016, Guiding Principle 3.

[56] As the European Court of Human Rights has stated: 'the legitimate aim of effecting a lawful arrest can only justify putting human life at risk in circumstances of absolute necessity. The Court considers that in principle there can be no such necessity where it is known that the person to be arrested poses no threat to life or limb and is not suspected of having committed a violent offence …' ECtHR, *Nachova* v. *Bulgaria*, Judgment (Grand Chamber), 6 July 2005, §95.

Is It Necessary to PLAN?

Some commentators like to use the acronym PLAN to summarise the boundaries of lawful use of force. PLAN stands for Proportionality, Legality, Accountability, and Necessity. In England and Wales, a second 'L' is sometimes added, meaning that the force used should be the 'least intrusive' among a set of viable options. This is not required by international law, though it may be a valid policy for law enforcement operations.

The principle of legality means that force must not be exercised arbitrarily (in the narrow sense of not according to law).[57] As 1990 Basic Principle 1 instructs, 'Governments and law enforcement agencies shall adopt and implement rules and regulations on the use of force and firearms against persons by law enforcement officials.' The principle of accountability means the actual user of force (and, where appropriate, his or her commanders), the law enforcement agency as a legal person, and ultimately the state must be held responsible for any unlawful use of force.[58]

While a useful moniker in certain respects, ultimately the acronym PLAN is confusing and therefore, in our view, unhelpful. It mixes the order of the two fundamental principles governing use of force: as we have seen, proportionality ordinarily comes into play only if and when the principle of necessity has been met. Second, the notions of legality and accountability underpin the fundamental rules, they do not supplant them, nor do they act as primary rules to determine what level of force is lawful. In fact, as we will see later in this book, they are critical elements that serve to help ensure effective domestic implementation of the core LOLE rules on police use of force.

[57] According to General Comment No. 3 on Article 4 of the African Charter on Human and Peoples' Rights (the right to life), 'States must adopt a clear legislative framework for the use of force by law-enforcement and other actors that complies with international standards, including the principles of necessity and proportionality.' ACmnHPR, 'General Comment No. 3 on the African Charter on Human and Peoples' Rights: Article 4, the Right to Life', adopted in November 2015, §27, at: www.achpr.org/files/instruments/general-comments-right-to-life/generalcommentno.3_eng.pdf. With respect to arbitrary deprivation of life, the Inter-American Court stated that this would occur when the use of force is illegitimate, excessive or disproportionate. IAmCtHR, *Cruz Sánchez and Others* v. *Peru*, Judgment (Preliminary Objections, Merits, Reparation, and Costs), 17 April 2015, §261. In original Spanish: 'no cualquier privación de la vida será reputada como contraria a la Convención, sino solo aquella que se hubiera producido *de manera arbitraria*, por ejemplo por ser producto de la utilización de la fuerza de forma ilegítima, excesiva o desproporcionada'. [added emphasis]

[58] See 1990 Basic Principles 22 to 26.

The Principle of Precaution

Acting as a precursor to the principles of necessity and proportionality is the duty on the authorities to plan law enforcement operations in a manner that minimises the risk of the police having recourse to a potentially lethal weapon and thereby to curtail the risk of death or serious injury to any member of the public or law enforcement official. As noted above, according to 1990 Basic Principle 5(b), whenever lawful use of force and firearms is unavoidable, law enforcement officials must 'minimize damage and injury' and 'respect and preserve human life'. But as the UN Special Rapporteur on extrajudicial, summary or arbitrary executions has written,

> Once a situation arises where the use of force is considered, it is often too late to rescue the situation. Instead, in order to save lives, all possible measures should be taken 'upstream' to avoid situations where the decision on whether to pull the trigger arises, or to ensure that all the possible steps have been taken to ensure that if that happens, the damage is contained as much as is possible.[59]

The precautionary principle was first enunciated by the European Court of Human Rights in its landmark 1995 judgment in the *McCann* case: 'the Court must carefully scrutinise ... not only whether the force used by the soldiers was strictly proportionate to the aim of protecting persons against unlawful violence but also whether the anti-terrorist operation was planned and controlled by the authorities so as to minimise, to the greatest extent possible, recourse to lethal force.'[60] In a similar vein, the Inter-American Court of Human Rights has held that proportionality

> is also related to the planning of preventive measures, since it involves an assessment of the reasonableness of the use of force. Thus, it is useful to analyze the facts rigorously to determine ... whether the violations could have been avoided with the implementation of less harmful measures ...[61]

In an earlier case brought against Venezuela, the Inter-American Court had declared that 'use of force by the security forces must be exceptional, and must be planned and restricted by the authorities on the basis of proportionality.'[62]

[59] 'Report of the Special Rapporteur on Extrajudicial, Summary or Arbitrary Executions, Christof Heyns', §63.

[60] ECtHR, *McCann and Others* v. UK, Judgment (Grand Chamber), 27 September 1995, §194. See also ECtHR, *Tagayeva and Others* v. *Russia*, Judgment (First Section), 13 April 2017, §574.

[61] IAmCtHR, *Nadege Dorzema and Others* v. *Dominican Republic*, Judgment (Merits, Reparations, and Costs), 24 October 2012, §87.

[62] IAmCtHR, *Montero-Aranguren and Others (Detention Centre of Catia)* v. *Venezuela*, Judgment (Preliminary Objection, Merits, Reparations, and Costs), 5 July 2006, §67.

In addition, with a view to preserving life, law enforcement officials must also ensure that 'assistance and medical aid are rendered to any injured or affected persons at the earliest possible moment'.[63] This must equally be part of the planning process for law enforcement operations. In the *Finogenov* case, the European Court examined whether the rescue operation was planned and implemented in compliance with the authorities' positive obligations under the right to life (Article 2 of the European Convention), 'namely whether the authorities took all necessary precautions to minimise the effects of the gas on the hostages, to evacuate them quickly and to provide them with necessary medical assistance.'[64] The duty to assist applies even if the injured person is a suspected offender.

Controversially (though not illegally under international law), following the November 2015 terror attacks in Paris, British firearms officers called to tackle terrorist gunmen have been ordered to ignore the injured and dying in the event of an attack in the United Kingdom and instead race towards the threat to try to minimise the total number of casualties. Pat Gallan, Metropolitan Police Service (MPS) assistant commissioner for special crime and operations, said that

> In asking them to go forward we are asking them not to give first aid to people injured and it might be their colleagues ... The most important thing is to actually get to the threat and stop them killing additional people, and that is why we've got to keep going forward and not tend to those that are injured at the time.[65]

Use of Firearms

In addition to the general principles of necessity and proportionality, which apply to any use of force, specific provisions in both the 1979 Code of Conduct and the 1990 Basic Principles cover the use of firearms.[66]

Author's translation, the official translation being of a rather poor standard. In the original Spanish, the phrase was as follows: 'El uso de la fuerza por parte de los cuerpos de seguridad estatales debe estar definido por la excepcionalidad, y debe ser planeado y limitado proporcionalmente por las autoridades.'

63 1990 Basic Principle 5(c).

64 ECtHR, *Finogenov and Others* v. *Russia*, Judgment (First Section), 20 December 2011 (as rendered final on 4 June 2012), §237.

65 V. Dodd, 'UK Armed Police Told to Race to Stop Terrorists and Ignore the Dying, *The Guardian*, 2 December 2015, at: www.theguardian.com/uk-news/2015/dec/02/uk-counter-terror-plans-revised-to-ensure-police-tackle-gunmen-as-priority.

66 It would seem that, as in UK law, the use of firearms means, in addition to discharge, brandishing a firearm. Evidence to support this assertion is found in the 1990 Basic Principles, Principle 11 of which stipulates that rules and regulations on the use of

These are widely misunderstood, or at least subject to materially differing interpretation.

Shooting 'to Stop'

The commentary on Article 3 of the 1979 Code of Conduct provides, in part, that 'Every effort should be made to exclude the use of firearms, especially against children. In general, firearms should not be used except when a suspected offender offers armed resistance or otherwise jeopardizes the lives of others and less extreme measures are not sufficient to restrain or apprehend the suspected offender.' These guiding principles are elaborated in the 1990 Basic Principles, with the critical Principle 9 providing, in part, that:

> Law enforcement officials shall not use firearms against persons except in self-defence or defence of others against the imminent threat of death or serious injury, to prevent the perpetration of a particularly serious crime involving grave threat to life, to arrest a person presenting such a danger and resisting their authority, or to prevent his or her escape, and only when less extreme means are insufficient to achieve these objectives.[67]

This means that four scenarios may allow recourse to use of firearms, though in each, such use is only lawful when less extreme means are insufficient:

1. In defence against imminent threat of death or serious injury.
2. To prevent a particularly serious crime involving grave threat to life.
3. To enable a person resisting arrest to be arrested if he or she is about to commit a particularly serious crime that involves grave threat to life.
4. To prevent a person resisting arrest from escaping where he or she is about to commit a particularly serious crime that involves grave threat to life.

These four scenarios each apply when firearms are not brandished or discharged with the intention of killing but only stopping the suspect

firearms by law enforcement officials should include guidelines that: '(b) Ensure that firearms are used only in appropriate circumstances and in a manner likely to decrease the risk of unnecessary harm' and '(e) Provide for warnings to be given, if appropriate, when firearms are to be *discharged*'. [added emphasis]

[67] For Sir Nigel Rodley, Principle 9 'impose[s] a principle of proportionality'. Rodley with Pollard, *The Treatment of Prisoners Under International Law*, p. 499.

('shooting to stop'). In none is it possible to use firearms merely to protect property. This standard is not, though, accepted or respected in every state.

The default situation is where there is an imminent threat of death or serious injury, whether to a law enforcement official or member of the public. The threat posed by the suspect does not need to come from the wielding of a firearm; a knife, iron bar, a car being driven at someone, a potentially lethal chokehold, or even a baseball bat could be sufficient, depending on the situation. In general, though, serious injury should be construed narrowly to mean potentially fatal injuries.[68] The US Border Customs Police define a serious physical injury as one 'which creates a substantial risk of death or which causes serious disfigurement, serious impairment of health or serious loss or impairment of the function of any bodily organ or structure or involves serious concussive impact to the head'.[69]

According to the UN Special Rapporteur on extrajudicial, summary, or arbitrary executions, 'an imminent or immediate threat' should be considered 'a matter of seconds, not hours'.[70] It may well be the case that imminence under LOLE should be construed as being limited to a second or even a split second.[71]

Scenarios two to four as set out in Basic Principle 9 concern a grave threat to life only (i.e. not also a threat of serious injury) and where use of firearms is necessary but where the threat is not necessarily imminent. Some argue that imminence is implicit or should be read into the caveat 'only when less extreme means are insufficient to achieve these objectives', but this overstretches the interpretation grammatically, making the sentence rather nonsensical.[72]

Evidence is lacking that, today, imminence is an element of every single scenario where a discharge of firearms may be lawful. Examples could be a serial killer escaping from a high-security prison or an individual driving through a roadblock when a terrorist attack is feared. Such examples are

[68] See further on this issue Chapter 4.

[69] US Customs and Border Protection, *Use of Force Policy, Guidelines and Procedures Handbook*, Office of Training and Development, HB 4500-01C, May 2014, p. 3, s. D(3)(a), at: www.cbp.gov/sites/default/files/documents/UseofForcePolicyHandbook.pdf.

[70] 'Report of the Special Rapporteur on Extrajudicial, Summary or Arbitrary Executions, Christof Heyns', §59, citing UN docs. A/68/382 (§§33–37) and A/HRC/14/24.

[71] Thus, imminence under LOLE should be distinguished from the notion of imminence under *jus ad bellum*: the law governing inter-state use of force.

[72] What is more, that could even be exploited to weaken the notion of imminence, which, as we saw, should be defined as a matter of seconds or even a split second.

truly exceptional and the test is stringent, as discussed further in Chapter 4 on use of firearms. This is not a 'get-out-of-jail-free' card that allows suspects to be shot in the back, or firearms to be used when the threat is actually to property alone. The UN Special Rapporteur on extrajudicial, summary, or arbitrary executions has stated in a report on Nigeria that the risk of escape by an alleged violent criminal, 'who presents no direct threat to the lives of others, cannot justify shooting to kill'.[73]

The exception does not authorise shooting to kill, as discussed below, and there must be no feasible alternative to using a firearm in order to stop an individual where the threat to life is not imminent. Thus, for example, in *M. D.* v. *Turkey*, the erstwhile European Commission on Human Rights considered the shooting of an escaping terrorist bombing suspect to fall within the exception set out in Article 2(2)(b) of the ECHR, namely 'to prevent the escape of a person lawfully detained'.[74]

Shooting 'to Kill'

An additional, heightened standard applies to intentional lethal use of firearms,[75] which, according to the final sentence of Basic Principle 9, 'may only be made when strictly unavoidable in order to protect life'. The UN Special Rapporteur on extrajudicial, summary, or arbitrary executions has termed this the 'protect life' principle, whereby 'a life may be taken intentionally only to save another life'. This he describes as 'the guiding star of the protection of the right to life'.[76] Although there is an obvious reluctance on the part of authorities to accept the term, it is clear that in certain instances death is the deliberate intention. An example would be to stop a suicide bomber or a hostage-taker from killing others; this is sometimes called in Germany 'the last resort shot'.[77]

[73] 'Report of the Special Rapporteur on Extrajudicial, Summary or Arbitrary Executions, Philip Alston: Mission to Nigeria', UN doc. E/CN.4/2006/53/Add.4 (2006), §47.

[74] European Commission on Human Rights, *M. D.* v. *Turkey*, Decision, 30 June 1997.

[75] Use of the terms 'lethal force' or 'deadly force' is not generally to be recommended as they are open to a range of interpretations. Some use either term to mean a use of force that *proves* fatal; others use it to describe force that is *likely* to prove fatal (or at least to cause serious injury) or as a synonym for the use of firearms; while still others use it to describe force that is *intended* to be fatal.

[76] 'Report of the Special Rapporteur on Extrajudicial, Summary or Arbitrary Executions, Christof Heyns', §70.

[77] See, e.g., B. Frevel and P. Kuschewski, 'Police Organization and Police Reform in Germany: The Case of North Rhine-Westphalia', *German Policy Studies*, Vol. 5, No. 2 (2009), p. 53, at: www.spaef.com/file.php?id=1136.

In this heightened standard, imminence is an integral part of the test of lawful use of force. If a suspect is not honestly believed to be about to pull the trigger of a firearm aimed at a hostage's head, or to detonate a bomb, intentional lethal use of force cannot be said to be strictly unavoidable to protect life. The intentional lethal use of firearms is given further consideration in Chapter 8 in the context of counterterrorism operations.

Use of 'Less-Lethal' Weapons

The 1990 Basic Principles refer specifically to 'non-lethal incapacitating weapons' in two of the twenty-six principles. While the notion, discussed here, is important, that particular term is unfortunate, for two reasons. First, the weapons foreseen by this nomenclature are not non-lethal in practice – they can, and do, kill; indeed, almost every 'non-lethal' weapon has killed or seriously injured a number of suspects as well as innocent bystanders. For this reason, the term 'less-lethal' is widely preferred, including in this work.

Second, the reference to 'incapacitating' could tend to be confused with chemical incapacitants, such as the anaesthetic used by Russia in the Moscow theatre siege. It appears that a fentanyl derivative was pumped into the theatre before it was stormed by Russian Special Forces,[78] resulting in the death of all the hostage-takers (many of whom were shot while unconscious) as well as 129 of the 1,000 or so hostages.[79] Fentanyl is a toxic chemical whose use for other than peaceful purposes is prohibited under the 1992 Chemical Weapons Convention.[80]

The term 'less-lethal' designates a wide array of weapons, ranging from the traditional police baton to encompass pepper spray, tear gas, electroshock weapons such as Tasers®, flash-bang grenades, rubber and plastic bullets, water cannon, acoustic weapons, and malodorants. Dogs and horses are also used as 'less-lethal' weapons in certain circumstances. As Colin Roberts has observed, the intention of law enforcement officials should be to incapacitate not kill, even though death may be the likely or indeed almost certain outcome of certain acts.[81]

[78] ECtHR, *Finogenov and Others* v. *Russia*, Judgment (First Section), 20 December 2011 (as rendered final on 4 June 2012), §101.

[79] The exact number is not known as some hostages did not report to the Russian authorities after release. See Ibid., §24.

[80] See generally M. Crowley, *Chemical Control*, Palgrave Macmillan, United Kingdom, 2015.

[81] Email to the author on 14 March 2016.

The 1990 Basic Principle 2 calls on governments and law enforcement agencies to 'develop a range of means as broad as possible and equip law enforcement officials with various types of weapons and ammunition that would allow for a differentiated use of force and firearms.' Among others, this should include 'non-lethal incapacitating weapons for use in appropriate situations', with the aim of 'increasingly restraining the application of means capable of causing death or injury to persons'. Thus, the rationale for less-lethal weaponry is not only to effectively replace firearms but also to reduce the number of injuries inflicted during other instances of use of force by law enforcement officials.

While the 1990 Basic Principles may seem unequivocally to endorse use of less-lethal weaponry, this is not the case. Principle 3 states that: 'The development and deployment of non-lethal incapacitating weapons should be carefully evaluated in order to minimize the risk of endangering uninvolved persons, and the use of such weapons should be carefully controlled.' The focus of concern is thus on the potential lack of discrimination, though the reference to careful control over the use of less-lethal weapons must be interpreted more broadly to encompass also the risk of death and injury to intended targets

Use of Force and At-Risk Groups

According to Article 2 of the 1979 Code of Conduct, 'In the performance of their duty, law enforcement officials shall respect and protect human dignity and maintain and uphold the human rights of all persons.' The official commentary on this provision notes that relevant international instruments include the 1966 International Covenant on Civil and Political Rights and the 1965 International Convention on the Elimination of All Forms of Racial Discrimination.[82] Otherwise, surprisingly little attention is paid in both the 1979 Code of Conduct and the 1990 Basic Principles to the duty to respect and protect especially vulnerable individuals and at-risk groups, such as members of ethnic minorities, women, children, and persons with disabilities. Yet, as noted in Chapter 2, minorities or those with mental health problems are especially likely to come into contact with the police, and perceptions and fears (on both sides) will increase the risk that such encounters lead to use of force or even violence.

[82] Commentary (a) to Art. 2, 1979 Code of Conduct.

The Role of Discriminatory 'Stop and Search'

Discriminatory police use of force against minorities has been a persistent problem in many countries and across many law enforcement agencies. In its report on the Baltimore City Police Department, for example, the Department of Justice found that officers 'disproportionately use force – including constitutionally excessive force – against African-American subjects. Nearly 90 percent of the excessive force incidents identified by the Justice Department review involve force used against African Americans.'[83]

Discriminatory searches stir up ill will against the police, putting colleagues at risk and increasing the likelihood of violence. The DOJ found that African Americans accounted for some 88 per cent of the subjects of non-deadly force used by BPD officers in a random sample of more than 800 cases it reviewed. 'This trend is consistent across different types of non-deadly force, including tasers, the most common weapon used by BPD officers.'[84]

In August 2013, a US federal judge ruled that the American equivalent of stop and search, known as stop and frisk, was, at least in its usage by the NYPD, a violation of the constitutional rights of minorities in the city.[85] Although use of police stops was widely claimed to have significantly reduced murders and major crimes, and to have saved the lives of thousands of young black and Hispanic men by removing thousands of guns from the streets, the judge in the case, Shira A. Scheindlin, found that the NYPD resorted to a 'policy of indirect racial profiling' as it increased the number of stops in minority communities. That led to officers' routinely stopping 'blacks and Hispanics who would not have been stopped if they were white'.[86]

Judge Scheindlin called for a federal monitor to oversee broad reforms, including the use of body-worn cameras for some patrol officers, though she was 'not ordering an end to the practice of stop-and-frisk.'[87] In February 2016, however, the federal monitor, Peter Zimroth, reported to a federal court in Manhattan that even though the NYPD had reduced

[83] US DOJ, *Investigation of the Baltimore City Police Department*, 10 August 2016, p. 47.

[84] Ibid. [85] *Floyd* v. *City of New York*, 959 F. Supp. 2d 540 (2013).

[86] J. Goldstein 'Judge Rejects New York's Stop-and-Frisk Policy', *New York Times*, 12 August 2013, at: www.nytimes.com/2013/08/13/nyregion/stop-and-frisk-practice-violated-rights-judge-rules.html.

[87] Ibid.

its use of stop and frisk, unconstitutional stops persisted because police officers did not know about reforms:

> Many police officers, including supervisors, are not well informed as yet about the changes underway or the reasons for them and, therefore, have yet to internalize them … Many appear not to understand what is expected of them.[88]

Analysis by the New York Civil Liberties Union had revealed that 'innocent New Yorkers have been subjected to police stops and street interrogations more than 4 million times since 2002', and that 'black and Latino communities continue to be the overwhelming target of these tactics'.[89]

In the United Kingdom in April 2014, Theresa May, then Secretary of State for Home Affairs (now Prime Minister), announced reforms to police stop-and-search powers declaring that: 'Nobody wins when stop and search is misapplied. It is a waste of police time. It is unfair, especially to young black men. It is bad for public confidence in the police'.[90] Stop and search powers have been repeatedly cited as contributory factors in inquiries into disorder such as the Brixton, Broadwater Farm, and 2011 riots across England and Wales.[91]

Yet figures for 2013–14 showed that more than one quarter of all stop and searches by officers of the MPS were still of self-styled black (or black British) individuals.[92] In August 2015, it was reported that Northamptonshire Police in England[93] were stripping individual officers of their right to stop and search suspects 'if they are deemed to have abused the controversial law-enforcement tactic'. Adam Simmonds, the Police and Crime Commissioner for Northamptonshire,

[88] Cited in V. Bekiempis, 'Some NYPD Officers Continue Unconstitutional Stop-and-Frisks because They're Unaware of Reforms', *New York Daily News*, 16 February 2016, at: www.nydailynews.com/new-york/stop-and-frisk-continues-cops-don-reforms-article-1.2533429.

[89] NYCLU, 'Stop-and-Frisk Campaign: About the Issue', at: www.nyclu.org/issues/racial-justice/stop-and-frisk-practices.

[90] Home Office, 'Stop and Search: Theresa May Announces Reform of Police Stop and Search', 30 April 2014, at: www.gov.uk/government/news/stop-and-search-theresa-may-announces-reform-of-police-stop-and-search.

[91] J. Simpson, 'New Training to Cut Police Bias in Stop and Search', *The Times*, 27 October 2016, at: www.thetimes.co.uk/article/af3084bc-9bb5-11e6-af4a-15a7db50bae8 (subscription required).

[92] Data.Police.UK, 'Stop and Search Data', available at: https://data.police.uk/data/stop-and-search/.

[93] Police forces in the United Kingdom continue to be organised on a sub-national basis, a legacy of historical fear of abuse of policing powers.

said officers would have their stop-and-search powers removed if they had conducted searches that were deemed inappropriate on three occasions.

> If someone is stopped for no reason or inappropriately then that person is a victim. I want the restorative justice approach for cops. I want a cop to say sorry ... This will make the police more accountable and give the public confidence in the police. It's a good opportunity for cops to step up their game.[94]

In October 2016, it was announced that police forces in England and Wales would further reduce use of stop and search under new training designed to address controversy around officers' 'unconscious bias'. The College of Policing has introduced guidance for forces in England and Wales Garth Stinson, the college's stop-and-search spokesman, said: 'There's a massive step between, "I've got a gut instinct he's a wrong'un" through to, "That gives me the evidence to get in their pockets."'[95] Sir Bernard Hogan-Howe, the Metropolitan Police Commissioner, had previously warned that a reduction in the use of the powers was linked to increases in knife crime.[96]

Respecting Persons with Disabilities

The 2006 Convention on the Rights of Persons with Disabilities requires states parties to 'take, in accordance with their obligations under international law, including international humanitarian law and international human rights law, all necessary measures to ensure the protection and safety of persons with disabilities in situations of risk ...'[97] However, those with disabilities are especially at risk of being subjected to use of force by the police. In Canada, for instance, Toronto police figures for 1987 to 1997 indicate that people who had previously been diagnosed

[94] J. Grierson, 'Police Force Bans Stop and Search by Officers who Abuse Their Powers', *The Guardian*, 18 August 2015, at: www.theguardian.com/law/2015/aug/18/police-force-bans-stop-and-search-officers-who-abuse-powers-adam-simmonds?CMP=Share_iOSApp_Other. Of eight officers whose powers had been removed since October 2014, six had seen their powers reinstated after completing additional training, while two remained unable to conduct searches.

[95] Simpson, 'New Training to Cut Police Bias in Stop and Search'.

[96] Ibid., and see, e.g., D. Barrett, 'Scotland Yard Chief Defies Theresa May Over Stop and Search', *Daily Telegraph*, 2015, at: www.telegraph.co.uk/news/uknews/crime/11954934/Scotland-Yard-chief-defies-Theresa-May-over-stop-and-search.html.

[97] Article 11, 2006 Convention on the Rights of Persons with Disabilities.

with a mental illness made up the third-largest category of people who were shot, preceded only by those suspected of involvement in robberies and drugs.[98]

In the United Kingdom, a study on police use of force, and specifically of complaints to the Independent Police Complaints Commission (IPCC), the IPCC found that those who experienced 'multiple incidents of force were twice more likely to have a mental health concern and be fatally injured than those who experienced one incident. They were also more likely to be under the influence of alcohol and/or drugs.'[99] The mental health issues included 'depression, schizophrenia, personality disorders, bi-polarity, known threats of or previous attempts of self-harm or suicide, and paranoia'.[100] The IPCC recommended that the National Police Chiefs' Council (NPCC) review authorised professional practice and relevant guidance to ensure that 'sufficient emphasis is placed on the needs of vulnerable people when officers are considering using any type of force'.[101]

The Washington Post reported in July 2015 that a pervasive problem in the United States is lack of training for police officers confronting the mentally ill, a situation that often escalates into violent confrontation.[102] In its August 2016 report on the BPD, the Department of Justice found that officers often use excessive force against individuals with mental health disabilities or in crisis:

[98] K. Cenzura and M. Federico, 'Use of Force Committee, Final report', Detective Support Command, Toronto Police, May 1998, p. 9: see Urban Alliance on Race Relations, 'Saving Lives: Alternatives to the Use of Lethal Force by Police', Report on a Conference on 23–24 June 2000, Toronto, 2002, p. 2, at: https://urbanalliance.files.wordpress.com/2012/05/savinglivesreport.pdf. Conlon suggests that, with respect to New York, 'if you got rid of narcotics, you could send half of the cops in this city home.' E. Conlon, *Blue Blood*, Ebury Press, London, 2011, p. 175. In the early 1990s, the murder rate in New York annual homicide rate had passed two thousand, half of which were believed to be drug-related. Ibid., p. 174.

[99] IPCC, *Police Use of Force: Evidence from Complaints, Investigations and Public Perception*, London, March 2016, p. 41.

[100] Ibid., p. 43. [101] Ibid.

[102] See: J. Wihbey and L. W. Kille, 'Excessive or Reasonable Force by Police? Research on Law Enforcement and Racial Conflict', *Journalist's Resource*, 1 July 2015, at: http://journalistsresource.org/studies/government/criminal-justice/police-reasonable-force-brutality-race-research-review-statistics#sthash.eL5jD7df.dpuf, citing W. Lowery, K. Kindy, and K. L. Alexander, 'Distraught People, Deadly Results; Officers Often Lack the Training to Approach the Mentally Unstable, Experts Say', *The Washington Post*, 30 June 2015, at: www.washingtonpost.com/sf/investigative/2015/06/30/distraught-people-deadly-results/.

> When families in Baltimore confront a family member experiencing a mental health issue, they often call 911 to request an officer to safely escort their family member to a hospital for a mental health evaluation and, if necessary, commitment. In too many of these calls, officers arrive at the homes of families, knowing they are being called to assist with a mental health incident, without a plan to account for the mental health issue. Because of their lack of planning and proper tactics, they end up in violent confrontations with individuals with mental health disabilities or in crisis and use force, sometimes deadly, against these vulnerable individuals.[103]

In one case, on 9 March 2015, a police officer in Atlanta, Georgia, shot and killed Anthony Hill, a US Air Force veteran who had returned from service in Afghanistan and had been diagnosed with bipolar disorder. Officer Robert Olsen of DeKalb County was responding to a 911 call. Witnesses said that Mr. Hill, an African American, approached the officer, who was white, with his hands either up or at his sides and naked, but that he did not heed the policeman's order to stop. Officer Olsen fired.[104] DeKalb police officials said Officer Olsen had a Taser with him at the time of the shooting. They also said the officer had undergone training in dealing with the mentally ill.

Two weeks later, the department announced it would increase its training requirements for 'critical incidents', which include encounters with the mentally ill, a decision said to be unrelated to the shooting.[105] In January 2016, prosecutors announced they would be seeking grand jury indictments against Officer Olsen for felony murder, aggravated assault, violation of oath of office, and making a false statement.[106] In June 2016, Mr Olsen, who had since left the force, pleaded not guilty to the charges against him.[107]

Issued in January 2016, the US Police Executive Research Forum (PERF) guidelines on use of force provide the following valuable guidance in relation to mental health issues:

> Mental Illness: Implement a comprehensive agency training programme on dealing with people with mental health issues. Officers must be trained

[103] US DOJ, *Investigation of the Baltimore City Police Department*, 10 August 2016, p. 75.

[104] R. Fausset, 'Police Shooting Victim in Georgia Tried to Follow "Sensible" Path', *New York Times*, 24 March 2015, at: www.nytimes.com/2015/03/25/us/atlanta-police-shooting-victim-tried-to-live-a-life-that-mattered.html?smid=tw-nytimes&_r=3.

[105] Ibid.

[106] A. Blinder, 'Georgia Prosecutors Seek Indictment of Officer Who Shot Unarmed Man', *New York Times*, 7 January 2016, at: www.nytimes.com/2016/01/08/us/anthony-hill-officer-robert-olsen-grand-jury.html.

[107] L. Harris, 'Dekalb Officer Robert Olsen Pleads Not Guilty', *CBS Atlanta*, 6 June 2016, at: http://atlanta.cbslocal.com/2016/06/06/dekalb-officer-robert-olsen-pleads-not-guilty/.

in how to recognize people with mental health issues and deal with them in a safe and humane manner ... [M]any agencies already provide some form of crisis intervention training as a key element of de-escalation, but crisis intervention policies and training must be merged with a new focus on tactics that officers can use to de-escalate situations. At a minimum, agencies should seek to:

- Provide all officers with awareness and recognition of mental health and substance abuse issues, as well as basic techniques for communicating with people with these problems ...
- Crisis Intervention Teams, made up of police officers and mental health workers, can be the most effective option. These teams are called to respond to all incidents involving mental illness or similar issues, and thus develop expertise, as well as familiarity with individuals who generate multiple calls for service over time. In some cases, Crisis Intervention Teams also work to solve underlying problems by helping persons with mental illness to obtain treatment.
- For all of their mental health training, agencies should coordinate with local mental health professionals on content and delivery.[108]

[108] PERF, *Use of Force: Taking Policing to a Higher Standard. 30 Guiding Principles*, Guiding Principle 19.

4

Use of Firearms

'I can make it clear that we do not have a shoot to kill policy. The law says that the police can use reasonable force, firstly to stop a crime, and secondly, to arrest someone who is putting someone else in danger . . . If someone's life is as risk, a police officer can intervene. If they are armed or otherwise so dangerous, we can stop them . . . So we work within the law – we make sure that those on the other side – the terrorists – know that whilst we are as determined as they are, as ruthless as they are, there is a difference between us. We work within the law.'

Metropolitan Police Commissioner Sir Bernard Hogan-Howe,
17 November 2015[1]

Introduction

As we saw in Chapter 3, use of firearms is subject to specific regulation under the law of law enforcement (LOLE) both in the 1979 Code of Conduct for Law Enforcement Officials and in the 1990 Basic Principles on the Use of Force and Firearms by Law Enforcement Officials. This regulation incorporates the general principles of necessity and proportionality, and reflects extant international law applicable to all states.

The 1990 Basic Principles do not define firearms, though they are defined in the 2001 Firearms Protocol[2] as 'any portable barrelled weapon that expels, is designed to expel or may be readily converted to expel a

[1] 'Commissioner's Appearance on LBC', 17 November 2015, at: http://news.met.police.uk/news/commissioner-s-appearance-on-lbc-138161.

[2] The formal title is the Protocol Against the Illicit Manufacturing of and Trafficking in Firearms, Their Parts and Components and Ammunition, Supplementing The United Nations Convention Against Transnational Organized Crime. As of writing, a total of 113 states and also the European Union were party to the Protocol. (Regional economic integration organisations are permitted to sign and ratify or accede to the Protocol by virtue of its Article 17(2)–(4).) France, Germany, the United Kingdom (UK), and the United States (US) are not states parties.

shot, bullet or projectile by the action of an explosive, excluding antique firearms or their replicas.'[3] This broad definition encompasses all conventional handguns,[4] shotguns,[5] rifles,[6] submachine guns/machine pistols,[7] and machine guns.[8] The inclusion of the word 'portable' restricts the scope of the term, excluding heavy artillery pieces, but potentially extending to cover light artillery and other light weapons that can be carried and used by up to three persons.[9] The Firearms Protocol

[3] Art. 3(a), 2001 Firearms Protocol. This provision further clarifies that 'Antique firearms and their replicas shall be defined in accordance with domestic law. In no case, however, shall antique firearms include firearms manufactured after 1899.'

[4] So called as they are designed to be capable of firing with one hand (even though standard training advises use of both hands for stability, and therefore accuracy, of firing).

[5] A shotgun typically has a smooth bore, and fires cartridges containing pellets. Used primarily for hunting (among other things); when used against a person at close range, the wounds can be devastating. The United States (US) defines a shotgun as 'a weapon designed or redesigned, made or remade, and intended to be fired from the shoulder and designed or redesigned and made or remade to use the energy of an explosive to fire through a smooth bore either a number of ball shot or a single projectile for each single pull of the trigger'. 18 US Code §921 (Definitions), (a)(5).

[6] As its name suggests, a rifle has a rifled barrel to spin the bullet as it exits the gun. It normally requires two hands to operate a rifle. The United States defines a rifle as 'a weapon designed or redesigned, made or remade, and intended to be fired from the shoulder and designed or redesigned and made or remade to use the energy of an explosive to fire only a single projectile through a rifled bore for each single pull of the trigger.' 18 US Code §921 (Definitions), (a)(7).

[7] These weapons normally fire handgun ammunition (e.g. 9mm Luger rounds) but exit the gun at higher muzzle velocities.

[8] A machine gun fires rifle-calibre ammunition in fully automatic mode, meaning the gun keeps firing once the trigger is pulled until either the trigger is released or the magazine is empty. The United States defines a machine gun as 'any weapon which shoots, is designed to shoot, or can be readily restored to shoot, automatically more than one shot, without manual reloading, by a single function of the trigger. The term shall also include the frame or receiver of any such weapon, any part designed and intended solely and exclusively, or combination of parts designed and intended, for use in converting a weapon into a machinegun, and any combination of parts from which a machinegun can be assembled if such parts are in the possession or under the control of a person.' 26 US Code §5845 (Definitions), (b).

[9] The 2005 International Tracing Instrument (ITI), a soft-law instrument, defines light weapons as those 'designed for use by two or three persons serving as a crew, although some may be carried and used by a single person. They include, inter alia, heavy machine guns, hand-held under-barrel and mounted grenade launchers, portable anti-aircraft guns, portable anti-tank guns, recoilless rifles, portable launchers of anti-tank missile and rocket systems, portable launchers of anti-aircraft missile systems, and mortars of a calibre of less than 100 millimetres'. International Instrument to Enable States to Identify and Trace, in a Timely and Reliable Manner, Illicit Small Arms and Light Weapons, UN doc. A/CONF.192/15, adopted on 8 December 2005 within the policy framework established by the 2001 Programme of Action on Small Arms s. 4(b).

definition also does not cover certain potentially lethal portable weapons such as, for example, electroshock weapons (e.g. Tasers), because the barbs through which the current passes into the body are expelled by means of gas propulsion, not explosive.[10]

The term *use* could be construed narrowly to refer only to the actual discharge of a firearm but in fact it extends to threat of use, as it does in a number of national jurisdictions. In the United Kingdom (UK), for example, a police officer pulling his or her handgun out of its holster and aiming it at a person would be 'using' the weapon, even if no round was fired, and the act would be recorded as such.[11] In Denmark, police use of a firearm includes not only aiming the gun and discharging a round but also firing a warning shot, or drawing a firearm and threatening someone, with the purpose of ensuring that a given order is followed.[12] A broader definition of the use of firearms appears to reflect its understanding in the 1990 Basic Principles.[13]

In its 1995 judgment in *Bailey* v. *United States*, the United States (US) Supreme Court defined 'use' of a firearm (albeit in relation to drug trafficking for the purpose of the federal criminal code,[14] not by the

[10] In the United States, a Taser® or other conducted electrical device is not considered a firearm and can be legally owned in 45 of the nation's 50 states. See Taser Laws, accessed on 16 September 2015 at: www.defenseproducts101.com/statestatutesummary_page2.html. Under the law in force in England and Wales, such electroshock weapons are 'prohibited weapons' under s. 5(1)(b) of the 1968 Firearms Act as amended ('any weapon of whatever description designed or adapted for the discharge of any noxious liquid, gas or other thing') but are also not defined as firearms.

[11] According to the UK College of Policing (the professional body for policing), a police officer will be deemed to have used a firearm or a less-lethal weapon when 'it is pointed or aimed at another person', 'fired at another person', or 'discharged in any other operational circumstances, including an unintentional discharge'. College of Policing, 'Armed Policing: Use of Force, Firearms and Less Lethal Weapons', Webpage last modified on 23 October 2013, §2, at: www.app.college.police.uk/app-content/armed-policing/use-of-force-firearms-and-less-lethal-weapons/.

[12] F. Z. Olsen, 'The Use of Police Firearms in Denmark', Copenhagen, 2008, p. 2, at: www.politi.dk/NR/rdonlyres/20DE43AF-33F4-48C5-A710-6A58457E35D2/0/Engelskresum%C3%A9afendeligrapport.pdf.

[13] The 1990 Basic Principle 11 stipulates that rules and regulations on the use of firearms by law enforcement officials should include guidelines that: '(b) Ensure that firearms are used only in appropriate circumstances and in a manner likely to decrease the risk of unnecessary harm' and '(e) Provide for warnings to be given, if appropriate, when firearms are to be *discharged*'. [added emphasis]

[14] The origin of the federal statutory provisions was the 1968 Gun Control Act. See, e.g., A. M. Gilbert, 'Defining Use of a Firearm', *Journal of Criminal Law & Criminology*, Vol. 87 (1996–97), 842–63, at p. 843, available at: http://scholarlycommons.law.northwestern.edu/cgi/viewcontent.cgi?article=6923&context=jclc.

police) as 'active employment'. The Court said that such active employment 'certainly includes brandishing, displaying, bartering, striking with, and, most obviously, firing or attempting to fire a firearm'.[15] In 2016, the US Department of Justice's (DOJ) report on the Baltimore City Police Department implies at one point that officers pointing of a weapon 'at unarmed and innocent civilians to control a scene'[16] amounts to use of force. The DOJ further observes that:

> Pointing a gun at an individual for general control is an inappropriate use of a firearm and is a threat of deadly force where the underlying offense, if any, does not justify deadly force being used.[17]

In sum, for the purpose of international law, police use of a firearm encompasses, in addition to any discharge, whether intentional or not, aiming or brandishing the weapon.

The Human Rights Framework

The human rights most relevant to the use of firearms are the rights to life and to humane treatment. Article 6(1) of the 1966 International Covenant on Civil and Political Rights stipulates that 'No one shall be arbitrarily deprived of his life', while Article 7 provides that: 'No one shall be subjected to torture or to cruel, inhuman or degrading treatment'. According to the Human Rights Committee's 2015 draft General Comment on the right to life,

> A deprivation of life may be authorized by domestic law and still be arbitrary. The notion of "arbitrariness" is not to be equated with "against the law", but must be interpreted more broadly to include elements of inappropriateness, injustice, lack of predictability, and due process of law as well as elements of reasonableness, necessity, and proportionality. For example, in order not to be qualified as arbitrary, the application of lethal force in self-defense must be reasonable and necessary in view of the threat posed by the attacker; it must represent a method of last resort after non-lethal alternatives, including warnings, have been exhausted or deemed inadequate; the amount of force applied cannot exceed the amount strictly needed for responding to the threat; the force applied must be carefully directed, as far as possible, only against the attacker; and the threat responded to must be extreme, involving

[15] US Supreme Court, *Bailey* v. *United States*, 516 US 137 (1995), at 148.

[16] US DOJ, *Investigation of the Baltimore City Police Department*, 10 August 2016, p. 75, at: www.justice.gov/opa/file/883366/download.

[17] Ibid., p. 79.

> imminent death or serious injury. The deliberate use of lethal force for law enforcement purposes which is intended to address less extreme threats, such as protecting private property or preventing the escape from custody of a suspected criminal or a convict who does not pose a serious and imminent threat to the lives or bodily integrity of others, cannot be regarded as a proportionate use of force.[18]

When the discharge of a firearm by a law enforcement official in violation of international law results in the death of the victim, this is likely to amount to a violation of the right to life. When the result of unlawful use is injury rather than death, a violation of the right to humane treatment is more likely.[19] In a situation where the victim of a police shooting survives, a violation of the right to life may, though, still be found if it is held that the state either intended to kill but failed to do so, or if it recklessly endangered life. Both the European and Inter-American Courts of Human Rights have so held, albeit in a very small number of cases and on an exceptional basis.

As the European Court's Grand Chamber stated in *Ilhan* v. *Turkey*: 'In almost all cases where a person is assaulted or ill-treated by the police or soldiers [and survives], their complaints will fall to be examined rather under Article 3 of the Convention.'[20] In the *Acar* case, a chamber of the European Court had to determine whether the right to life of two of the applicants had been violated. They had been wounded during a mass shooting of villagers by village guards (acting as agents of the state) in Mardin province, south-east Turkey, in April 1992. The Court approved the finding in *Ilhan* that 'it is only in exceptional circumstances that physical ill-treatment by State officials which does not result in death may disclose a breach of Article 2 of the [European] Convention' [which protects the right to life].[21] Nonetheless, the Court held that

[18] Human Rights Committee, 'Draft General Comment No. 36 (Article 6: Right to Life)', Draft prepared by Yuval Shany and Nigel Rodley, Rapporteurs, UN doc. CCPR/C/GC/R.36/Rev.2, 7 September 2015, §18.

[19] The European Court has made it clear that although the wording of Art. 2, 1950 European Convention on Human Rights (ECHR) could be inferred as only referring to intentional lethal use of force ('No one shall be deprived of his life intentionally', according to Art. 2 (1)), in fact it encompasses also 'force which may result, as an unintended outcome, in the deprivation of life'. European Court of Human Rights (ECtHR), *Andronicou and Constantinou* v. *Cyprus*, Judgment (Chamber), 9 October 1997, §171.

[20] ECtHR, *Ilhan* v. *Turkey*, Judgment (Grand Chamber), 27 June 2000, §76. Under Art. 3, ECHR: 'No one shall be subjected to torture or to inhuman or degrading treatment or punishment.'

[21] ECtHR, *Ilhan* v. *Turkey*, Judgment, §76, approved in *Acar and Others* v. *Turkey*, Judgment (Fourth Section), 24 May 2005 (rendered final on 12 October 2005), §77.

> the two applicants were wounded in the course of a sustained and lethal attack with firearms which resulted in the death of eight of their fellow villagers. In these circumstances, and in particular the degree and type of force used, the Court concludes that, the applicants were the victims of conduct which, by its very nature, put their lives at grave risk, even though, in the event, they survived. Article 2 of the Convention is thus applicable in the instant case to the applicants.[22]

The *Makaratzis* case concerned an applicant who had driven through a red traffic light in the centre of Athens. He was chased by several police officers in cars and on motorcycles. After the applicant had broken through five police roadblocks set up to stop him, police officers started firing at his car. Eventually, the applicant stopped at a petrol station, but did not get out. The police officers continued firing.[23] The Court accepted the government's claim that the police did not intend to kill Mr Makaratzis, but observed that the fact that he was not killed was 'fortuitous':

> According to the findings of the ballistic report, there were sixteen holes in the car caused by bullets following a horizontal or an upward trajectory to the car driver's level. There were three holes and a mark on the car's front windscreen caused by bullets which came through the rear window; the latter was broken and had fallen in. In the end, the applicant was injured on the right arm, the right foot, the left buttock and the right side of the chest and was hospitalised for nine days.[24]

In the light of the circumstances, 'and in particular the degree and type of force used', the Court concluded that, 'irrespective of whether or not the police actually intended to kill him, the applicant was the victim of conduct which, by its very nature, put his life at risk, even though, in the event, he survived.' Furthermore, 'given the context in which his life was put at risk and the nature of the impugned conduct of the State agents concerned', the Court was 'satisfied' that the facts called to be examined under Article 2 of the European Convention.[25]

In *Trévalec* v. *Belgium*, the Court was asked to judge whether the Belgian state had violated the Convention when two police officers shot

[22] ECtHR, *Acar and Others* v. *Turkey*, §79.

[23] ECtHR, *Makaratzis* v. *Greece*, Judgment (Grand Chamber), 20 December 2004, §§11 and 12.

[24] Ibid., §54. [25] Ibid., §55.

a reporter, seriously injuring but not killing him, while he was filming the operations of an anti-gang squad in the Belgian police. He had been granted authorisation for the filming by the authorities. While the actions of the officers, who were unaware of his presence and role during the specific operation, was adjudged not unlawful, the failure to properly supervise the applicant was found to be attributable to the authorities, and their lack of due vigilance meant that the potentially lethal force used had not been absolutely necessary 'in defence of any person from unlawful violence', within the meaning of Article 2(2)(a) of the European Convention.[26]

In the *Rochela Massacre* case, the Inter-American Court of Human Rights cited the European Court's judgment in *Acar* in support of its findings of 'extraordinary circumstances that lay a foundation for a violation of Article 4 of the [Inter-American] Convention and its analysis with regard to the three survivors of the massacre, taking into account the force employed, the intent and objective of the use of this force, and the situation in which the victims found themselves.'[27] Article 4 of the 1969 American Convention on Human Rights stipulates: 'Every person has the right to have his life respected.'

As of writing, the African Court of Human and Peoples' Rights had not yet pronounced on the issue, though in November 2015 the African Commission on Human and Peoples' Rights issued a General Comment on the right to life (Article 4 in the 1981 African Charter on Human and Peoples' Rights). In this General Comment, the Commission stated that:

> Where a State or its agent has attempted unlawfully to kill a person, but that person survives, or threatens the life of someone, or where it has conducted an enforced disappearance, in addition to other rights violations, a violation of the right to life may have occurred.[28]

[26] ECtHR, *Trévalec* v. *Belgium*, Judgment (Second Section), 14 June 2011.

[27] Inter-American Court of Human Rights (IAmCtHR), *Rochela Massacre* v. *Colombia*, Judgment (Merits, Reparations, and Costs), 11 May 2007, §§123–25. According to Article 4 of the 1969 American Convention on Human Rights, 'Every person has the right to have his life respected. This right shall be protected by law and, in general, from the moment of conception. No one shall be arbitrarily deprived of his life.'

[28] African Commission on Human and Peoples' Rights, 'General Comment No. 3 on the African Charter on Human and Peoples' Rights: Article 4, The Right to Life', adopted in November 2015, §8, at: www.achpr.org/files/instruments/general-comments-right-to-life/generalcommentno.3_eng.pdf.

Scenarios Where Use of Firearms May Be Lawful under the Law of Law Enforcement

Shooting 'to Stop'

As discussed in Chapter 3, in addition to the general principles of necessity and proportionality that apply to any use of force, provisions in both the 1979 Code of Conduct and the 1990 Basic Principles specifically regulate the use of firearms. These are widely misunderstood, while also being subject to varying interpretation.

The commentary on Article 3 of the 1979 Code of Conduct provides, in part, that: 'Every effort should be made to exclude the use of firearms, especially against children. In general, firearms should not be used except when a suspected offender offers armed resistance or otherwise jeopardizes the lives of others and less extreme measures are not sufficient to restrain or apprehend the suspected offender.' These guiding principles, which are general in nature and rather vague, indicate more of a policy statement than a rule of law. The rationale underpinning them is, though, supplemented and given specificity in the 1990 Basic Principles, with Principle 9 providing, in part, that:

> Law enforcement officials shall not use firearms against persons except in self-defence or defence of others against the imminent threat of death or serious injury, to prevent the perpetration of a particularly serious crime involving grave threat to life, to arrest a person presenting such a danger and resisting their authority, or to prevent his or her escape, and only when less extreme means are insufficient to achieve these objectives.

These rules are fully reflected in customary international law. The provision means that four scenarios may allow recourse to use of firearms, though in each such case use can only be lawful when less extreme means are insufficient (meaning that the use of firearms is necessary in the circumstances):

1. In self-defence or defence of others against imminent threat of death or serious injury to one or more persons.
2. To prevent a particularly serious crime that involves grave threat to life.
3. To stop a person resisting arrest from committing a particularly serious crime that involves grave threat to life.
4. To prevent a person who is resisting arrest from escaping when he or she is intending to commit a particularly serious crime that involves grave threat to life.

This represents customary international law, regulating when a police officer or other law enforcement official may lawfully have recourse to a firearm, and especially when he or she actually discharges the weapon. In no case is it lawful to use a firearm merely to protect property, whether movable or immovable. If there is no direct or indirect threat to the life or limb of a person, the use of firearms is excluded under the law of law enforcement.

It is also important to note that death is by no means the inevitable result of a police officer opening fire and hitting a person. It is therefore a misconception that use of firearms automatically equates to an intention to kill. As a *ballpark overall figure*, if a person is hit by a bullet in the main body mass in a Western nation, he or she has at least a 50-50 chance of survival. Of course, the type of bullet, where it hits, the speed and quality of emergency medical assistance, and the strength of the victim, among other factors, will all affect survivability. Further bullet wounds are likely to reduce these odds significantly.

Survivability has increased in many countries in recent decades. In the United States, for instance, over the last 20 years, the chances that a person will survive a critical gunshot wound have increased substantially, perhaps by around 30–40 per cent according to Dr. Thomas Scalea, professor of surgery at the University of Maryland Medical Center's Shock Trauma Center. Within major organs such as the heart or liver, some injuries are more serious than others because they cause more bleeding. For example, being shot in the left side of the heart generally causes more bleeding than being shot in right side of the heart, because the right side has lower blood pressure. An injury to more than one of the heart's four chambers causes more bleeding than an injury to only one chamber, and a wound that goes through the septum – which separates the heart's left and right sides – is worse than an injury that does not go through the septum.[29]

A 2014 study from the Perelman School of Medicine at the University of Pennsylvania found no significant difference in adjusted overall survival rates between gunshot and stabbing victims in Philadelphia whether they were transported to the emergency department by the police department or the emergency medical services (EMS) division of the fire department. The study examined 4,122 patients taken to eight adult

[29] R. Rettner, 'Colorado Survivors: How Do People Survive Gunshot Wounds?', *Live Science*, 23 July 2012, at: www.livescience.com/21774-bullet-gunshot-wound-survive .html#sthash.xJSjbGcN.tgpLilzu.dpuf.

trauma centres in Philadelphia between 1 January 2003 and 31 December 2007. Of these, 2,961 were transported by EMS and 1,161 by the police. The overall mortality rate was 27.4 per cent. Just over three-quarters (77.9 per cent) of the victims suffered gunshot wounds, and just under a quarter (22.1 per cent) suffered stab wounds. The majority of patients in both groups (84.1 per cent) had signs of life on delivery to the hospital. A third of patients with gunshot wounds (33.0 per cent) died compared with 7.7 per cent of patients with stab wounds.[30]

A study published in 1989 found that within a 12-year period ending in March 1984, 1,109 patients with penetrating thoracic injuries were treated at King-Drew Medical Center located in south-central Los Angeles. The average age of the patients was 28.1 years. There were 607 stab wounds and 502 gunshot wounds. The mortality rate of gunshot wounding of the heart was 24.5 per cent and that of stab wound of the heart was 11.5 per cent. The mortality rate in non-cardiac thoracic injuries is very low compared with that of cardiac injury. Because of the complexity of the injury, gunshot wound of the heart has the highest mortality rate.[31]

A study published in 1993 of 119 patients with penetrating cardiac trauma over a 15-year period (59 had gunshot wounds, 49 had stab wounds, and 11 had shotgun wounds) found survival rates of 46% for gunshot wounds, 78% for stab wounds, and 36% for shotgun wounds.[32] In the wake of the 2012 Aurora, Colorado shooting, 58 people survived gunshot wounds while 12 were killed. Survivors suffered gunshot wounds to the neck, abdomen, brain, throat, and legs.[33]

In 1993–98, an estimated average of 115,000 firearm-related injuries (including 35,200 fatal and 79,400 non-fatal injuries) occurred annually in the United States. Males were seven times more likely to die or be treated in a hospital emergency department for a gunshot wound than females. The proportion of firearm-related injuries that resulted in death increased from younger to older age groups. Approximately 68% of

[30] R. A. Band, 'Severity-Adjusted Mortality in Trauma Patients Transported by Police', *Annals of Emergency Medicine*, Vol. 63, No. 5 (May 2014), p. 608ff.

[31] A. K. Mandal and S. S. Oparah, 'Unusually Low Mortality of Penetrating Wounds of the Chest. Twelve Years' Experience', *Thoracic Cardiovascular Surgery*, Vol. 97, No. 1 (January 1989), pp. 119–25.

[32] M. E. Mitchell, F. F. Muakkassa, G. V. Poole, R. S. Rhodes, and J. A. Griswold, 'Surgical Approach of Choice for Penetrating Cardiac Wounds', *Journal of Trauma*, Vol. 34, No. 1 (January 1993), pp. 17–20.

[33] Rettner, 'Colorado Survivors: How Do People Survive Gunshot Wounds?'

firearm-related injuries for teenagers and young adults aged 15–24 years were from interpersonal violence, and 78% of firearm-related injuries among older persons aged >65 years were from intentionally self-inflicted gunshot wounds.

Black males aged 20–24 years had the highest average annual fatal (166.7/100,000 population) and non-fatal (689.4/100,000 population) firearm-related injury rates during the six-year period. Although 51.4% of intentionally self-inflicted non-fatal wounds were to the head or neck, 71.8% of unintentional and 45.8% of assault-related non-fatal wounds were to the extremities. During the six-year period, estimates are that quarterly fatal firearm-related injury rates declined 29.3%, and quarterly non-fatal firearm-related injury rates declined 46.9%. Firearm-related injury rates declined for intentionally self-inflicted, assault, and unintentional causes.[34]

In Defence against Imminent Threat of Death or Serious Injury

The foremost, and by far the most prevalent scenario potentially permitting recourse to firearms is where such use is necessary in self-defence or defence of others to prevent death or serious injury where the threat is imminent. This exists whether the threat is to a law enforcement official or to a member of the public. According to the UN Special Rapporteur on extrajudicial, summary or arbitrary executions, 'an imminent or immediate threat' should be considered 'a matter of seconds, not hours'.[35] It may even be the case that the specific notion of imminence should be limited to a second or even a split second.

Serious injury should be construed narrowly to mean potentially fatal injuries. As examples of national state practice, the 1861 Offences Against the Person Act in force in England and Wales proscribes 'grievous bodily harm', which according to the Crown Prosecution Service (CPS) means, in general terms, 'really serious' bodily harm. It is for the jury to decide whether harm in any case before the courts is really

[34] K. E. Gotsch, J. L. Annest, J. A. Mercy, and G. W. Ryan, 'Surveillance for Fatal and Nonfatal Firearm-Related Injuries – United States, 1993–1998', *Morbidity and Mortality Weekly Report*, Centers for Disease Control and Prevention, United States, 13 April 2001, at: www.cdc.gov/mmwr/preview/mmwrhtml/ss5002a1.htm.

[35] 'Report of the Special Rapporteur on Extrajudicial, Summary or Arbitrary Executions, Christof Heyns', UN doc. A/HRC/26/36, 1 April 2014, §59, citing UN docs. A/68/382 (§§33–37), and A/HRC/14/24.

serious, but the following examples indicate what would usually amount to such a level of harm:

- Injury resulting in permanent disability, loss of sensory function, or visible disfigurement
- Broken or displaced limbs or bones, including fractured skull, compound fractures, broken cheek bone, jaw, ribs
- Injuries which cause substantial loss of blood, usually necessitating a transfusion or result in lengthy treatment or incapacity
- Serious psychiatric injury.[36]

Arguably, the term 'serious injury' in Basic Principle 9 would extend beyond serious bodily harm to encompass rape. The New York state penal code, for instance, specifically defines serious injury justifying use of lethal force to include forcible rape.[37] However, the reasonably envisageable circumstances in which a law enforcement official – as opposed to a potential victim – could lawfully fire a gun to prevent a rape occurring are limited because of the necessity requirement for the use of force as well as potentially the risk to the victim him- or herself.[38]

In the United States, there has been considerable controversy surrounding an alleged 21-foot rule (the distance it is said to take a

[36] CPS, 'Offences Against the Person, Incorporating the Charging Standard', undated but accessed 18 August 2015, at: www.cps.gov.uk/legal/l_to_o/offences_against_the_person/#a15.

[37] New York State Penal Law, Part I, Title C, Art. 35, at: http://ypdcrime.com/penal.law/article35.htm: 'A person may not use deadly physical force upon another person … unless: … (b) He or she reasonably believes that such other person is committing or attempting to commit a kidnapping, forcible rape, forcible criminal sexual act or robbery …' The reference to forcible rape would distinguish it from statutory rape where sexual relations involve someone below the age of consent who cannot legally consent to having sex, but who engages in sexual relations without the use or threat of force being involved.

[38] In an undated incident, a Wheeling, West Virginia Sunday school teacher was said to be walking after church when he and his fiancée were surrounded by a group of nine men who began making threats. Chris Harris and Ms Roxby said they were frightened for their lives. 'It was one of the most scariest [*sic*] experiences I have ever been through,' Ms Roxby told WTOV Television. Mr Harris added, 'They surrounded me saying … they were going to rape my wife in front of me, cut me.' Even after Mr Roxby called 911, the aggression continued. Finally, Harris pulled his gun and fired a warning shot, prompting the men to flee. Police arrived and handcuffed Harris and charged him with wanton endangerment for firing a gun in a public place. 'Why You Should Never, EVER Fire a Warning Shot — Even If 9 Men Are Threatening to Rape Your Fiancée', *The Right to Bear Arms* website, Undated but accessed on 23 February 2016 at: http://therighttobear.com/man-arrested-after-he-fires-warning-shot-at-9-men-threatening-to-rape-his-fiance/.

dangerous suspect armed with a knife to reach a police officer before the officer can draw his firearm and shoot twice).[39] In practice, this has been used by many law enforcement agencies to guide its officers in when they may use a firearm. In January 2016, the US Police Executive Research Forum (PERF) published a set of guidelines on use of force. This included the following:

> **Use Distance, Cover, and Time to replace outdated concepts such as the "21-foot rule" and "drawing a line in the sand."**
>
> Agencies should train their officers on the principles of using distance, cover, and time when approaching and managing certain critical incidents. In many situations, a better outcome can result if officers can buy more time to assess the situation and their options, bring additional resources to the scene, and develop a plan for resolving the incident without use of force.
>
> Agencies should eliminate from their policies and training all references to the so-called "21-foot rule" regarding officers who are confronted with a subject armed with an edged weapon. Instead, officers should be trained to use distance and cover to create a "reaction gap" between themselves and the individual, and to consider all options for responding.[40]

In late February 2016, serious disorder broke out in Salt Lake City after a police officer shot a teenage male wielding a hollow metal mop handle. Detective Ken Hansen of the Unified Police Department, which was investigating the shooting, said that two officers were called to break up a fight in the evening near a homeless shelter. When the officers arrived, they found that a young man in the street had been hitting another person with the mop handle. The officers opened fire as the youth advanced slowly towards the other individual again, hitting him in the upper and lower torso. He was seriously injured but survived.[41] Salt Lake City police detective Greg Wilking said two police officers were on administrative leave as a result of the shooting.[42]

[39] See, e.g., E. Conlon, *Blue Blood*, Ebury Press, London, 2011, p. 268.

[40] PERF, *Use of Force: Taking Policing to a Higher Standard. 30 Guiding Principles*, Critical Issues in Policing Series, 29 January 2016, Guiding Principle 16 (original emphasis).

[41] R. Boyd, 'Citizen Review Board: Officers Who Shot Teen at Rio Grande "Not Within" Policy', *Fox13*, Salt Lake City, 2 September 2016, at: http://fox13now.com/2016/09/02/investigation-report-reveals-details-after-officers-shoot-abdi-mohamed-at-rio-grande/.

[42] Associated Press, 'Utah Police Battle Angry Crowd after Officer Shoots Male Wielding Broomstick', *The Guardian*, 28 February 2016, at: www.theguardian.com/us-news/2016/feb/28/utah-police-shooting-male-holding-broomstick-unrest?CMP=Share_iOSApp_Other.

In September 2016, a Salt Lake County Police Civilian Review Board led by the Sheriff's Office reported the view of the Panel that the shooting was 'not within department policy'.[43] This policy stipulates that 'deadly force' may 'only be exercised when all reasonable alternatives have been exhausted or appear impractical'.[44] A formal investigation was launched by the Unified Police Department, although the Salt Lake County District Attorney concluded in August 2016 that the shooting was justified. Among other issues, an investigation consonant with international law would need to determine whether the principle of necessity for use of a firearm was met in the case at hand.

To Prevent a Serious Crime Involving Grave Threat to Life

Scenarios two to four as set out in Basic Principle 9 concern a grave threat to life and where use of firearms is necessary in the circumstances, but where the threat to life is not imminent. As argued in Chapter 3, reading imminence into the caveat 'only when less extreme means are insufficient to achieve these objectives' would render the sentence rather nonsensical. Evidence is lacking that imminence is today an essential element of every scenario where use of firearms may be lawful under LOLE, though this is certainly a view held by some.[45]

We saw in Chapter 3 how the principle of proportionality acts to render what could be deemed to amount to minimum necessary force involving use of firearms unlawful in certain circumstances, such as to break up a pub brawl, stop an escaping thief, or enable (re-)capture of a fugitive from justice. As the Grand Chamber of the European Court of Human Rights held in the *Nachova* case, an escaping suspect not believed to have committed a serious offence may not be shot 'even if a failure to use lethal force may result in the opportunity to arrest the

[43] Police Civilian Review Board, Report (Internal Affairs Case No. S2016-0016), Salt Lake City, 19 August 2016, p. 16, available at: www.slcdocs.com/civreview/PCF/S2016-0016.pdf.

[44] Ibid., p. 15.

[45] As cited above, the draft new General Comment on the right to life by the Human Rights Committee affirms that the 'deliberate use of lethal force for law enforcement purposes which is intended to . . . prevent . . . the escape from custody of a suspected criminal or a convict who does not pose a serious and imminent threat to the lives or bodily integrity of others, cannot be regarded as a proportionate use of force.' See UN doc. CCPR/C/GC/R.36/Rev.2, 7 September 2015, §18.

fugitive being lost'.[46] Nowhere in its judgment, which concerned use of firearms against army deserters, does the European Court say imminence is an integral element in assessing whether any and all use of firearms is lawful; rather, it was a question of whether or not the suspects were themselves armed and whether they were being arrested for a serious offence (the link potentially to the 'grave threat to life' criterion in Principle 9). The Inter-American Court of Human Rights similarly 'considers that, even when abstaining from the use of force would have allowed the individuals that were the subject of the State's action to escape, the agents should not have used lethal force against people who did not represent a threat or a real *or* imminent danger to the agents or third parties'.[47]

This exceptional circumstance of a 'grave threat to life', where imminence is not formally part of the test for determining the legality of use of firearms, is especially tightly drawn, however. As noted in Chapter 3, it could potentially cover an escaping serial killer that posed a proximate risk or an individual failing to stop at a roadblock set up in the aftermath of a terrorist attack.[48] But it would not allow suspects not manifestly posing a grave threat to life to be shot in the back, or firearms to be used when a threat is to property alone. The UN Special Rapporteur on extrajudicial, summary, or arbitrary executions has stated in a report on Nigeria that the risk of escape by an alleged violent criminal 'who presents no direct threat to the lives of others, cannot justify shooting to kill.'[49]

Case Examples

The exception does not authorise shooting to kill, which, as discussed below, is subject to a heightened restriction under international law. But there may be circumstances in which it is not unlawful to shoot to stop an individual, even where the threat to life is not perceived to be imminent. For example, in December 2015, a *gendarme* in Paris fired

[46] ECtHR, *Nachova v. Bulgaria*, Judgment (Grand Chamber), 6 July 2005, §95. See also *Putintseva* v. *Russia*, Judgment (First Section), 10 May 2012 (as rendered final on 10 August 2012), §§44–46.

[47] IAmCtHR, *Nadege Dorzema and Others* v. *Dominican Republic*, Judgment (Merits, Reparations, and Costs), 24 October 2012, §85(ii) [added emphasis].

[48] Thus, the example can be distinguished from the European Court's judgment in the *Makaratzis* case: ECtHR, *Makaratzis* v. *Greece*, Judgment (Grand Chamber), 20 December 2004.

[49] 'Report of the Special Rapporteur on Extrajudicial, Summary or Arbitrary Executions, Philip Alston: Mission to Nigeria', UN doc. E/CN.4/2006/53/Add.4 (2006), §47.

around ten shots when a driver refused to stop and then forced his way through the one of the main entrances of Les Invalides on Rue Grenelle in the French capital. The incident took place at the complex where a remembrance ceremony had recently been held for the 130 people killed in the 13 November Islamist attacks across Paris.[50] The decision to open fire at that instant might not infringe international law.[51]

More difficult cases are where a terrorist suspect is escaping actual or possible arrest. In 1997, in the case of *M. D.* v. *Turkey*, the erstwhile European Commission on Human Rights considered that the shooting of an escaping terrorist bombing suspect fell within the exception set out in Article 2(2)(b) of the ECHR, namely 'to prevent the escape of a person lawfully detained'.[52] This meant that the Commission did not sustain the applicant's claim of a violation of the right to life. In March 2016, in Brussels, Salah Abdeslam, a prime suspect for the November 2015 Paris terror attacks, was shot by armed police in the leg as he left a building that was surrounded by police officers. No evidence has been proffered that he was suspected to have been armed at the time.[53] Indeed, Belgian state prosecutor Eric Van der Sypt was reported in the press as admitting that Mr Abdeslam was not armed, but stated that he was shot when he did not immediately obey orders when confronted by police.[54] Amnesty International has argued that:

[50] Associated Press, 'Police Open Fire on Car after Driver Tries to Ram Barrier at Paris's Invalides Monument', *Daily Telegraph*, 16 December 2015, at: www.telegraph.co.uk/news/worldnews/europe/france/12053493/Police-open-fire-on-car-after-driver-tries-to-ram-barrier-at-Pariss-Invalides-monument.html.

[51] One might, though, enquire as to why a spike strip was not available to prevent a car from breaking through the roadblock, thereby potentially obviating the necessity for recourse to firearms. See (despite the favourable decision to the law enforcement officer who fired despite use of a spike strip by other officers), US Supreme Court, *Chadrin Lee Mullenix* v. *Beatrice Luna*, Petition for Writ of Certiorari to the US Court of Appeals for the Fifth Circuit, Decision (Case No. 14–1143), 9 November 2015, 577 US __ (2015) 1. It is noted that spike strips are 'often ineffective', and that officers operating them 'are vulnerable to gunfire from passing cars'. Ibid., p. 4.

[52] European Commission on Human Rights, *M. D.* v. *Turkey*, Decision, 30 June 1997.

[53] See, e.g., 'Salah Abdeslam: Video of Paris Attacks Suspect Being Shot by Police Marksmen During Raid', *Independent*, 22 March 2016, at: www.independent.co.uk/news/world/europe/salah-abdeslam-video-of-paris-attacks-suspect-being-shot-by-police-marksmen-during-raid-a6944341.html.

[54] J. Curtis and T. Wyke, 'Terror Mastermind Salah Abdeslam Escaped Police by Hiding in a Wardrobe Then Walked the Streets of Brussels Freely for Weeks before He was Captured in Sting Triggered by a PIZZA Delivery', *Daily Mail Online*, 20 March 2016, at: www.dailymail.co.uk/news/article-3500011/Hollande-vows-arrests-follow-world-s-wanted-terrorist-Paris-massacre-shot-captured-Brussels-trying-flee-hideout.html.

'The mere fact a person flees from arrest or escapes from custody does not justify the use of a firearm, unless this person presents an ongoing grave threat to the life of another person that can be realized at any time.'[55] In 2005, the then UN Special Rapporteur on Torture, Manfred Nowak, affirmed that 'for the purpose of arresting a person suspected of having committed murder or a terrorist attack, the police may, of course, use firearms if other less intrusive methods prove ineffective'.[56]

Of course even in a case where discharge of firearms may be justified, the force used must not be excessive in the circumstances. For the risks to other members of the public of opening fire must always be a paramount consideration in any law enforcement operation.[57] In *Burton* v. *Waller*, the US Court of Appeals for the Fifth Circuit (covering Louisiana, Mississippi, and Texas) held in 1974 that use of massive firepower in response to a suspected shot by a sniper during a civil disturbance was excessive and therefore unlawful use of force.[58] In the case, forty-three officers from the Mississippi Highway Safety Patrol and five officers from the Jackson Police Department admitted firing their weapons. Despite orders to cease fire, firing continued for another 20 seconds and totalled some 150 rounds of ammunition. By the end of the volleys of shots two people were dead and another twelve were injured. The Court found that the fire was 'excessive in volume and in intensity, and the size of the area subjected to fire was beyond the physical limits of justifiable response'.[59]

Although today police shootings in the United States are far lower than in Brazil, for instance (a country discussed below), their

[55] Amnesty International, *Use of Force: Guidelines for Implementation of the UN Basic Principles on the Use of Force and Firearms by Law Enforcement Officials*, AI Dutch Section, Police and Human Rights Programme, 2015, p. 31, Guideline 2.

[56] 'Torture and Other Cruel, Inhuman or Degrading Treatment, Report of the Special Rapporteur on the Question of Torture, Manfred Nowak', E/CN.4/2006/6, 23 December 2005, note 2.

[57] Thus, for example, Amnesty International cites a 1992 law on policing from Germany's state of Baden-Württemberg: 'The use of a firearm is prohibited if this creates a serious risk for clearly uninvolved persons . . . This is not applicable if the use of the firearm is the only means of defence against a grave threat to life.' 1992 Police Law, Baden-Württemberg, Art. 53(2).

[58] US Court of Appeals (Fifth Circuit), *Burton* v. *Waller*, 502 F.2d 1261 (1974) certiorari denied US 964, rehearing denied 421 US 39.

[59] Ibid., §56.

number is still very high, particularly when compared with European nations. (This is despite the fact that, as the director of the Federal Bureau of Investigation affirmed in February 2015, there is no authoritative annual count of the number of people shot to death by US law enforcement personnel.)[60] The Counted, *The Guardian* newspaper's database of people killed by police in the United States, recorded that the figure totalled 1,138 in 2015. Of this total, 223 were reportedly unarmed at the time.[61] *The Washington Post* reported a lower figure: 965 had been shot and killed by US police during the same time period, including nine killed between 24 and 26 December.[62] In contrast, in Germany only two people were reportedly killed by police all year: one man in Bavaria in March and another in September in Berlin.[63] For the United Kingdom, the total was three in 2015 (the highest since 2008), one in 2014, while for 2013 it was none.[64]

The US Supreme Court in its landmark 1989 judgment in *Tennessee* v. *Garner* held that: 'This case requires us to determine the constitutionality of the use of deadly force to prevent the escape of an apparently unarmed suspected felon. We conclude that such force may not be used unless it is necessary to prevent the escape and the officer has probable cause to believe that the suspect poses a significant threat of death or serious physical injury to the officer or others.'[65] This is a rather lower threshold than the international standard, which, as we have discussed, does not concede lawful use of firearms other than in a grave threat to life unless the threat is imminent.

[60] Speech of James B. Comey, Director, FBI, Georgetown University, Washington, DC, 12 February 2015, at: www.fbi.gov/news/speeches/hard-truths-law-enforcement-and-race.

[61] The Counted, accessed 18 January 2016 at: www.theguardian.com/us-news/ng-interactive/2015/jun/01/the-counted-police-killings-us-database#.

[62] See 'A Year of Reckoning: Police Fatally Shoot Nearly 1,000', *Washington Post*, accessed 18 January 2016 at: www.washingtonpost.com/sf/investigative/2015/12/26/a-year-of-reckoning-police-fatally-shoot-nearly-1000/.

[63] See CounterCurrent News, 'Police in America Have Killed More Since Christmas Than German Cops Have All Year', 27 December 2015, at: http://countercurrentnews.com/2015/12/police-in-america-have-more-since-christmas-than-german-cops-have-all-year/#.

[64] Inquest, 'Fatal Police Shootings', at: www.inquest.org.uk/statistics/fatal-police-shootings.

[65] US Supreme Court, *Tennessee* v. *Garner*, 471 US 1 (1985), Decided on 27 March 1985.

Shooting 'to Kill'

A distinct and considerably stricter international legal standard applies when law enforcement officials 'shoot to kill', e.g. where they continue firing until the target is dead or where they seek to kill an individual. Despite an obvious reluctance on the part of authorities to accept the term, it is clear that in certain instances death is the deliberate intention of law enforcement officials. According to the final sentence of Basic Principle 9,

> In any event, intentional lethal use of firearms may only be made when strictly unavoidable in order to protect life.[66]

The UN Special Rapporteur on extrajudicial, summary or arbitrary executions has termed this the 'protect life' principle, whereby 'a life may be taken intentionally only to save another life'. This he describes as 'the guiding star of the protection of the right to life':[67]

> The 'protect life' principle demands that lethal force may not be used intentionally merely to protect law and order or to serve other similar interests (for example, it may not be used only to disperse protests, to arrest a suspected criminal, or to safeguard other interests such as property). The primary aim must be to save life. In practice, this means that only the protection of life can meet the proportionality requirement where lethal force is used intentionally, and the protection of life can be the only legitimate objective for the use of such force.[68]

Such intentional lethal use of force may be strictly necessary to save the life of a hostage or to stop a suicide bomber detonating explosives or to stop an ongoing terrorist attack (see further Chapter 8). In contrast to the standard above relating to a grave threat to life, imminence is an integral part of the standard applying to intentional lethal use of force.

Jan Hessbruegge has discussed whether, under the strict standard, a sniper would have to 'stand by' if a hostage-taker 'merely' chopped off a

[66] Note that the Spanish version of the Basic Principles mistranslates this provision. The Spanish version 'sólo se podrá hacer uso intencional de armas letales cuando sea estrictamente inevitable para proteger una vida' translates as 'intentional use of lethal weapons may only be made when strictly unavoidable in order to protect life', a very different meaning to the one intended. The French version correctly translates the meaning of the English version: 'ils ne recourront intentionnellement à l'usage meurtrier d'armes à feu que si cela est absolument inévitable pour protéger des vies humaines.'

[67] 'Report of the Special Rapporteur on Extrajudicial, Summary or Arbitrary Executions', 1 April 2014, §70.

[68] *Ibid.*, §72.

hostage's fingers or ears in order to lend weight to his/her demands.[69] But once a hostage taker starts to mutilate his or her victim, opening fire – if it is reasonably safe to do so – would not be unlawful. In contrast, in *Wasilewska and Kałucka* v. *Poland*, a chamber of the European Court noted reports that within a very short period of time,

> five police officers fired between five and eleven shots each, or a series of shots from automatic guns, aiming at the car in which the two men were trying to escape. At that time it cannot be said that the suspects still posed a threat to the police officer . . . The car was moving, according to an expert, no faster than 20kph towards a swimming pool from which there was no way out.[70]

The Court, in finding a violation of the right to life by Poland, also observed that most of the shots were fired at the escaping vehicle once it had passed a police officer who had been allegedly hit by it. 'At that moment there had been no direct danger to the police officer and the only intention of the police officers had been to prevent the escape of the suspects.'[71]

The Special Rapporteur has affirmed that: 'A common sense understanding of the scope of application of Principle 9 suggests that all weapons that are designed and are likely to be lethal should be covered, including heavy weapons such as bombs and (drone) missiles, the use of which constitutes an intentional lethal use of force.'[72] Thus, any use of armed drones or piloted aircraft in law enforcement falls to be judged by the higher 'protect life'

[69] J. Hessbruegge, *Human Rights and Personal Self-Defence in International Law*, Oxford University Press, New York, 2017, p. 174, citing K. Doehring, 'Zum "Recht auf Leben" aus nationaler und internationaler Sicht', in R. Bernhardt (ed.), *Völkerrecht als Rechtsordnung, internationale Gerichtsbarkeit, Menschenrechte: Festschrift für Hermann Mosler*, Springer, Berlin, 1983, p. 152.

[70] ECtHR, *Wasilewska and Kałucka* v. *Poland*, Judgment (Fourth Section), 23 February 2010 (as rendered final on 23 May 2010), §53(i).

[71] Ibid., §53.

[72] *Ibid.*, §71. See also, e.g., *Esmukhambetov and Others* v. *Russia*, Judgment (First Section), 29 March 2011 (as rendered final on 15 September 2011). Of note, US domestic legislation considers the term 'firearm' to extend to a 'destructive device', which is stipulated to mean 'any explosive, incendiary, or poison gas—

(i) bomb,
(ii) grenade,
(iii) rocket having a propellant charge of more than four ounces,
(iv) missile having an explosive or incendiary charge of more than one-quarter ounce,
(v) mine, or
(vi) device similar to any of the devices described in the preceding clauses." 18 US Code §921 (Definitions), (a)(3) and (4)(A).

standard, at least insofar as the aircraft is armed with bombs or missiles. Landmines should also be considered as intentional lethal use of force according to jurisprudence before the European Court of Human Rights.[73]

'Death Squads'

It is a serious violation of international law for the authorities to instruct police officers to summarily execute suspected criminals and, *a fortiori*, for the state to employ or even tolerate so-called death squads (which may amount to crimes against humanity). Concern that law enforcement officials in a democratic nation, the Philippines, were engaging in such practices was raised in 2016 after the election to the presidency at the end of June of Rodrigo Duterte. In late September, President Duterte, after citing Hitler and the Holocaust, said he would happily 'slaughter' three million drug addicts. This followed testimony at an ongoing senate inquiry where a self-confessed assassin testified that Mr Duterte, when mayor of the city of Davao, had ordered the killing of criminals and his opponents, and that in one instance personally 'finished off' an employee from the justice department with a submachine gun.[74] *The Guardian* newspaper cited an interview with one senior officer in the Philippines National Police (PNP) who claimed to be a member of a death squad that had killed eighty-seven people in only one month:

> The officer claims he is part of one of 10 newly formed and highly secretive police special operations teams, each with 16 members . . . He claims the teams are coordinated to execute a list of targets: suspected drug users, dealers and criminals . . .
>
> The killings mostly take place at night, he says, with the officers hooded and dressed in all black. They set their watches, giving themselves one minute or two to extract target individuals from their houses and kill on the spot – swift, precise, no witnesses . . . He claims they then dump the

[73] In *Alkin* v. *Turkey*, the European Court of Human Rights affirmed that injury resulting from landmines is a violation of Art. 2 of the 1950 European Convention on Human Rights because the very nature of the weapon makes their use unlawful: 'the Court considers that the laying of such indiscriminate and inhumane weapons as anti-personnel landmines, which affect the lives of a disproportionate number of civilians and children, amounts to intentional use of lethal force.' ECtHR, *Alkin* v. *Turkey*, Judgment (Second Section), 13 October 2009, §30.

[74] K. Lamb, 'Philippines Secret Death Squads: Officer Claims Police Teams Behind Wave of Killings', *The Guardian*, 4 October 2016, at: www.theguardian.com/world/2016/oct/04/philippines-secret-death-squads-police-officer-teams-behind-killings.

> bodies – in the next town or under a bridge – or they plaster masking tape around the head of the corpse and place a cardboard sign on the body that reads "drug lord" or "pusher".
>
> 'We put placards in order for the media, in order for those investigating [the] bodies to redirect their investigation,' he explains, leading them to think: 'Why should I investigate this guy, he is a drug pusher, he is a rapist, never mind with that one, I will just investigate the others. It's a good thing for him that happened to him.'
>
> In the Philippines they have a term for it: 'salvage' victim. Someone killed and dumped in the street or thrown in the river. A corpse that is later salvaged.[75]

Until the recent events in the Philippines, Brazil was often cited as an example of some of the worst policing in the modern world. It has been estimated that on-duty Brazilian police, especially the uniformed militarised police, are responsible for up to 70 per cent of all civilian murders in Brazil, and such figures may even underestimate the extent of lethal violence by off-duty Brazilian police.[76] In one notorious instance available on *YouTube*, in 2012 a helicopter pursued a suspected drug dealer (known as the Mathematician) driving through the narrow streets of São Paulo at night, firing .50 calibre ammunition from machine guns at him until they killed him.[77]

As a point of comparison, at an average rate from the 1990s at which Washington, DC and New York City police kill citizens, it would take approximately fifty years for Washington police and twenty-five years for New York police to kill as many citizens as São Paulo police did in just 1999.[78] To counter claims by Brazilian police that civilian deaths result from resistance to police during a citizen-initiated 'shoot-out', academics have developed a formula for exploring this claim. A police shooting is thus considered an execution when:

1. After immobilising an alleged criminal, police continue to shoot ('immobilisation/over-kill ratio').
2. Police kill more people than they injure ('lethality ratio').
3. More civilians are killed than police ('citizen–police death ratio').

[75] Ibid.

[76] M. K. Huggins, 'Systemic Police Violence in Brazil', in J. B. Kuhns and J. Knutsson (eds.), *Police Use of Force: A Global Perspective*, Praeger, Santa Barbara, CA, 2010, p. 73.

[77] Available at: www.youtube.com/watch?v=skomhYqOqjM.

[78] Huggins, 'Systemic Police Violence in Brazil', p. 80.

4. The civilians killed are largely despised 'others': a recognisable underclass ('representational lethality index').[79]

Belur similarly describes the existence of police 'encounters'[80] in Mumbai, India, which involve 'a spontaneous, unplanned shoot-out between the police and alleged criminals, where the criminal is usually killed with few or no police injuries'.[81] In the 1990s, a proliferation in shootings, extortion cases, and kidnappings for ransom cases was accompanied by a rise in the number of 'encounters'. Between 1993 and 2003, the Crime Branch Statistics of the Mumbai Police recorded a total of 453 such 'encounters' in which 589 alleged criminals were killed, with the numbers of the dead reaching a peak in 2001 and tapering off thereafter.[82] Distinctions are, however, made – by police officers themselves – between 'fake' and 'genuine' encounters. It was acknowledged that certain such 'fake' encounters:

- involved a person with no criminal history
- resulted from a mistaken identification of the person killed
- employed blatantly excessive use of force
- emerged from a 'catch-and-kill' policy (where a person under surveillance is detained, questioned, and then taken to a lonely spot at night where he is executed), and
- either resulted from bad faith or malice on the part of the officer concerned (e.g. corruption, the taking of money to execute members of rival gangs, or from a personal grudge), or led to personal gain for the officer through medals, promotions,[83] or enhanced status within the department.[84]

The Legality of an Honest but Mistaken Belief in the Need to Open Fire

What is the situation under international law if a police officer fires at a suspect in the honest but mistaken belief that he is legally entitled to do

[79] Ibid.

[80] She notes that the term 'encounter' is not just police jargon, but is part of everyday discourse in India, used also by the media and the general public to refer to police use of deadly force.

[81] J. Belur, 'Police "Encounters" in Mumbai, India', in Kuhns and Knutsson, *Police Use of Force: A Global Perspective*, p. 52.

[82] Ibid., p. 154.

[83] Some state police forces in India are said to operate on the basis of a one encounter = one rank promotion.

[84] Belur, 'Police "Encounters" in Mumbai, India', p. 59.

so, such as in self-defence or defence of others against an imminent threat of death or serious injury?

The issue of the legality of an honest but mistaken belief has come before the European Court of Human Rights in a number of cases. The Grand Chamber of the Court expounded its position on this issue in the *McCann* case, which concerned the shooting to death by British soldiers of three members of the Irish Republican Army on Gibraltar in 1988:

> The Court accepts that the soldiers honestly believed, in the light of the information that they had been given, . . . that it was necessary to shoot the suspects in order to prevent them from detonating a bomb and causing serious loss of life . . . The actions which they took, in obedience to superior orders, were thus perceived by them as absolutely necessary in order to safeguard innocent lives.
>
> It considers that the use of force by agents of the State in pursuit of one of the aims delineated in [Article 2(2)] of the Convention may be justified under this provision . . . where it is based on an honest belief which is perceived, for good reasons, to be valid at the time but which subsequently turns out to be mistaken. To hold otherwise would be to impose an unrealistic burden on the State and its law-enforcement personnel in the execution of their duty, perhaps to the detriment of their lives and those of others.[85]

The position of the Court on this issue was subsequently upheld in a number of its judgments, such as in the *Makaratzis* case, cited above.[86] It was explicitly contested in the *da Silva* case, which concerned the shooting to death of Jean-Charles de Menezes in 2007 by firearms officers of London's Metropolitan Police Service (MPS).[87] Mr de Menezes, a Brazilian electrician, was mistakenly believed to be a suicide bomber about to detonate explosives on a tube train in the British capital. According to the applicant, the definition of self-defence under the law in force in England and Wales is flawed, since the officers who shot de Menezes only had to show that they had an honest belief – as opposed to an honest and objectively reasonable belief – that the use of force was absolutely necessary.[88] In the view of the United Kingdom, an honest belief did not need

[85] ECtHR, *McCann and Others* v. *UK*, Judgment (Grand Chamber), 27 September 1995, §200.

[86] *Makaratzis* v. *Greece*, §66. See also *Andronicou and Constantinou* v. *Cyprus*, Judgment, 9 October 1997.

[87] *Armani da Silva* v. *UK* (App. No. 5878/08), application lodged on 21 January 2008.

[88] *Armani da Silva* v. *UK*, Judgment (Grand Chamber), 30 March 2016, §192. See also Registrar of the ECtHR, ECHR Press Release 190 (2015), 10 June 2015, available at: www.statewatch.org/news/2015/jun/echr-menezes-grand-chamber-hearing-Armani-Da-

'to be shown to be reasonable by reference to objectively established facts, although the objective reasonableness of the belief would nevertheless be relevant in determining whether or not it was genuinely held'.[89]

At the end of March 2016, the Court's Grand Chamber handed down its judgment in the case, declining to hold the United Kingdom responsible for a violation of Article 2 of the ECHR (which protects the right to life). The Grand Chamber affirmed it was 'apparent both from the application of the stated test to the particular facts in *McCann and Others* itself and from the Court's post-*McCann and Others* case-law that the existence of "good reasons" should be determined subjectively'.[90] It further stated that

> the principal question to be addressed is whether the person had an honest and genuine belief that the use of force was necessary. In addressing this question, the Court will have to consider whether the belief was subjectively reasonable, having full regard to the circumstances that pertained at the relevant time. If the belief was not subjectively reasonable (that is, it was not based on subjective good reasons), it is likely that the Court would have difficulty accepting that it was honestly and genuinely held.[91]

This accurately describes the state of the law both as it is and indeed as it should be in order for law enforcement officials to be able to protect the public. However, as the Grand Chamber's judgment in the *McCann* case shows, the duty of precaution requires that the process leading up to the imminent threat that caused a law enforcement official to shoot be carefully examined. It is surprising that Ms da Silva's lawyers did not focus on this issue in her application to the Court.[92]

Silva-v-United-Kingdom%20.pdf; see also O. Bowcott, 'Jean Charles de Menezes Arguments Heard in Strasbourg', *The Guardian*, 10 June 2015, at: www.theguardian.com/uk-news/2015/jun/10/jean-charles-de-menezes-arguments-strasbourg. The Coroner in the inquest into Mr de Menezes' death set out the law for the jury as follows: 'Did the officer honestly and genuinely believe that it was necessary for him to use force in defence of himself and/or others? This is a question of subjective belief. Even if the belief was mistaken, and even if the mistake was unreasonable, the defence can still run. The reasonableness of the belief is only relevant in helping the jury to decide whether the belief was honestly held.' See *Armani da Silva* v. *UK* (App. No. 5878/08), Statement of Facts (Fourth Section), 28 September 2010, §55, available at: http://hudoc.echr.coe.int.

89 Ibid., §208.

90 *Armani da Silva* v. *UK*, Judgment (Grand Chamber), 30 March 2016, §§245, 246.

91 Ibid, §248.

92 See ibid., Joint Dissenting Opinion of Judges Karakaş, Wojtyczek and Dedov, §§3, 7. However, in what is in other respects a somewhat bizarre judicial opinion, the three dissenting judges also assert that: 'Force used in putative self-defence is never absolutely

In practice, where a mistake is made and there is insufficient evidence to support the police officer's claim that the mistake was an honest one, serious consequences may ensue, both for the officer concerned and for his or her police department. In the United States, a fatal shooting by a police officer in 1999 resulted in an $18 million award of compensation to the victim's family. LaTanya Haggerty, a 26-year-old black woman, was fatally shot on 4 June 1999 by Officer Serena Daniels as Ms Haggerty sat in a friend's car talking on her mobile phone. She was a passenger in a car that had been pursued for 31 blocks by Officer Daniels and three other officers after the driver had driven off at speed after being stopped by the police. Officer Daniels claimed she feared for her life and shot Ms Haggerty after mistaking a silver padlock for a gun that was being aimed at her.[93] The Chicago Police Board discharged Officer Daniels from the force, a decision that was upheld on appeal to the Illinois Court of Appeal:

> The Board remarked that police expert James Marsh testified that use of deadly force might be justified if the officer thought the suspect had a weapon and the suspect made a furtive movement toward the officer. However, Marsh stated that this was only warranted if the suspect made the furtive movement after refusing to obey warnings from the officer to drop the weapon or 'don't move or I'll shoot.' Here, Daniels admits that she gave no such warnings. The Board also noted Marsh's opinion that, in the entire context of what occurred during the Haggerty shooting, Daniels did not have a reasonable basis for using deadly force. The record reflects Marsh's view that no extreme conditions existed at 64th Street that justified the shooting because Daniels had no basis for her belief that Haggerty was armed given that nothing in the previous stops or chase indicated that either Smith or Haggerty were armed; no weapon was pointed at Daniels; Daniels issued no warnings to Haggerty to drop the weapon; Daniels was not in front of Haggerty but rather was to the rear and side of the car and could have shielded her position; and, although a suspect turning toward an officer with what could be a weapon might justify shooting, here the alleged weapon was merely being raised rather than pointed at anyone and the shooting was premature.[94]

necessary' (and therefore violates ECHR Article 2). This is an incorrect statement of international law.

93 T. Lighty and G. Washburn, 'City to Pay Haggertys $18 Million, Deal Makes Daley Meet with Family', *Chicago Tribune*, 8 May 2001, at: http://articles.chicagotribune.com/2001-05-08/news/0105080231_1_settlement-latanya-haggerty-mayor-richard-daley.

94 Court of Appeals for the First District (Fourth Division), *Daniels* v. *Police Board of City of Chicago*, Judgment (Cases nos. 1-01-2419, 1-01-2495), 1 May 2003.

Two high-profile shootings of suspected criminals in London, one of Azelle Rodney in 2005 and the other of Mark Duggan in 2011, tested the application of the criminal law in force in England and Wales. In both cases, intelligence and prior briefings had led to a perception that the danger of use of firearms was greater than was in fact the case. Inadequate or inaccurate briefings may engage the state's responsibility under international human rights law, but they may also exonerate a police officer who genuinely believed that he or she needed to open fire at a given moment when in fact this was not the case.

Mr Azelle Rodney was shot to death in Edgware, north London, in April 2005, after police forced a car he was travelling in to stop. Officers had intelligence that Mr Rodney was part of a gang, possibly armed with automatic weapons, on its way to attack a Colombian drugs gang with the intent of robbing them. The marksman, referred to publicly at the time as E7, shot Mr Rodney, a 24-year-old black man, six times without warning. A judicial inquiry that published its conclusions in 2013 found the officer had 'no lawful justification' for opening fire. Sir Christopher Holland, the retired high court judge who led the inquiry, said he did not find that E7 was deliberately lying to him, but found 'E7's accounts of what he saw are not to be accepted'.[95] A year later, Mr Anthony Long (Officer E7) was charged with murder. His subsequent trial in June 2015 resulted in his acquittal by the jury's majority verdict. During the trial, the judge, Mr Justice Sweeney ruled, correctly, that Long was entitled to rely on police intelligence, whether it was right or wrong.[96]

Mark Duggan, an alleged member of the Tottenham Man Dem gang, was shot twice on 4 August 2011 in Tottenham, an area of north London, after 11 MPS firearms officers stopped the minicab in which he was travelling on suspicion that he had an illegal firearm. While no gun was found on him, a handgun in a sock was discovered on grassland about four metres from his body. His death sparked the worst riots for decades across cities and towns in England.[97]

[95] V. Dodd, 'Azelle Rodney Death: Unlawful Killing Verdict for Met Marksman', *The Guardian*, 5 July 2013, at: www.theguardian.com/uk-news/2013/jul/05/unlawful-killing-met-marksman-azelle-rodney.

[96] V. Dodd, 'Azelle Rodney Shooting: Police Marksman Cleared of Murder', *The Guardian*, 3 July 2015, at: www.theguardian.com/uk-news/2015/jul/03/police-marksman-anthony-long-cleared-azelle-rodney-murder.

[97] C. Davies and D. Taylor, 'Mark Duggan Shooting: Armed Officers Cleared of Wrongdoing', *The Guardian*, 25 March 2015, at: www.theguardian.com/uk-news/2015/mar/25/armed-police-cleared-wrongdoing-fatal-shooting-mark-duggan-tottenham.

The jury of the inquest into his death unanimously concluded that insufficient intelligence had been gathered prior to the police operation, suggesting that an application to the European Court of Human Rights for a violation of the right to life by the United Kingdom based on the actions of the MPS might be successful.[98] The jury also concluded, by majority, that Mr Rodney did not have a gun in his hand at the time he was shot, but concluded by majority decision, based on the 'honest belief' test, that the decision to fire was lawful.[99]

In March 2015, the Independent Police Complaints Commission (IPCC), which oversees the actions of the police in England and Wales, cleared armed officers of wrongdoing in the killing of Mr Duggan, asserting it was likely that he was in the process of throwing away a handgun (in a sock) when he was shot. However, in its 500-page report, the IPCC called for consideration of the feasibility of recording all radio communications taking place during covert firearms operations and of fitting audio/visual recording devices in covert armed response vehicles (to be active throughout an armed operation), and called for covert armed response vehicles to be fitted with in-car data-recording systems (otherwise known as 'Incident Data Recorders').[100]

The 'Militarisation' of Policing

Certain commentators have referred to increasing militarisation (or 'paramilitarisation', in the words of Peter Squires and Peter Kennison)[101] of policing. Already in the late 1990s it was suggested that policing in the United States 'is very much like going to war'.[102] The term

98 As the *McCann* case has made clear, while the decision to open fire may not be unlawful, the failure of the authorities, including law enforcement authorities, to plan so as to minimise the risk of recourse to the use of lethal force (i.e. the principle of precaution) may amount to a violation of the right to life. *McCann and Others* v. *UK*, §§194, 201–14.

99 Inquest Touching Upon the Death of Mark Duggan, Form 2: Record of an inquest, 8 January 2014, at: http://dugganinquest.independent.gov.uk/docs/Jurys_Determination_and_Conclusion(1).pdf.

100 IPCC, 'The Fatal Police Shooting of Mr Mark Duggan on 4 August 2011', Independent Investigation Final Report, IPCC Ref. 2011/013399, Recommendations 2, 4, and 3, p. 510, at: www.ipcc.gov.uk/sites/default/files/Documents/investigation_commissioner_reports/IPCC-investigation-report-fatal-shooting-of-MD.pdf.

101 P. Squires and P. Kennison, *Shooting to Kill?: Policing, Firearms and Armed Response*, Wiley-Blackwell, London, 2010, p. 1.

102 D. H. Bayley and J. H. Skolnick, *The New Blue Line: Police Innovation in Six American Cities*, Simon and Schuster, New York, 1998; see M. Punch, *Shoot to Kill*, Policy Press, Bristol, 2011, p. 82.

militarisation is, though, used to describe a number of different issues as they pertain both to mindset as well as to weaponry. Squires and Kennison contrast the 'restraint paradigm' of everyday policing with

> a more military paradigm which is characterised by low discretion, hierarchical chains of command, 'risk management' or overwhelming superiority of firepower and target incapacitation (arguably, 'shooting to kill') to eliminate the danger.[103]

The Small Arms Survey, a non-governmental research institute based in Geneva, has tended to focus more on the weaponry. In 2011, the Survey even referred to an 'arms race of US law enforcement' with respect to handguns and semi-automatic rifles.[104]

Use of Assault Rifles and Firing Modes

International law does not prohibit the use of submachine gunes, assault rifles, or 'specialist' rifles (as used by snipers) for law enforcement. For instance, in the MPS firearms officers may be equipped with, among other weapons, Heckler & Koch G36 assault rifles or MP5 submachine guns. Similar situations exist in many other European law enforcement jurisdictions.

Given the need for necessity and proportionality to be strictly observed in the case of use of firearms, however, such weaponry should never be fired in fully automatic mode[105] (where the gun keeps firing once the trigger is pulled until either the trigger is released or the magazine is empty). Every shot fired should be justifiable, and therefore only semi-automatic mode should be considered lawful for firearms used in law enforcement.

In South Africa, a country badly marred by gun crime, one of the most notorious incidents of recent years was the shooting to death of 34 striking miners by officers belonging to the South African Police Service (SAPS) and the injury of more than 70 others at Marikana during a single day in August 2012.[106] The Commission of Inquiry that was

[103] Ibid., pp. 1–2.

[104] P. Gobinet, 'Procurement and Policy: Police Use of Emerging Weapons Technology', ch. 3 in *Small Arms Survey 2011: States of Security*, Cambridge University Press, Cambridge, 2011, p. 74.

[105] In its 2010 judgment in *Wasilewska and Kałucka* v. *Poland*, the ECtHR did not specifically address the use by police of automatic weapons fired in automatic mode.

[106] See Marikana Commission of Inquiry, *op. cit.*

established in the aftermath of the killings stated that it was 'mindful of the dangers inherent in the situation when Public Order Policing members are faced with a crowd armed with sharp weapons and where non-lethal force is ineffective. However the use of R5[107] or any automatic rifle is clearly untenable, not only because of the Constitutional imperatives, but also because the effects seen at Marikana are just too disturbing and devastating for South Africa even to contemplate any recurrence.'[108] According to the Commission's 2015 report,

> Several of the TRT [South African Police Service Tactical Response Team] members who fired … admitted in the statements they made that their rifles were on automatic fire … Lieutenant Colonel Classen confirmed that in his view this was grossly negligent … and Mr Cees de Rover, the policing expert called by the SAPS, said that in his view automatic rifle fire has no place in law enforcement. "You still at every pull of the trigger need to prove the existence of an imminent threat to life or serious injury".[109]

Firearm Ammunition Types

The Need to Penetrate Body Armour

It is often claimed that members of drug gangs, bank robbers, and other criminals are commonly bedecked in Kevlar©. In Alberta, Canada, for instance, the Justice and Solicitor General has claimed that gang members 'often wear bullet resistant vests (body armour) when they engage in various forms of criminal activity, including drug trafficking and drive-by shootings. Some will even wear body armour while in public, which can be intimidating.'[110]

[107] The R5 assault rifle is based on the Israeli Galil, which was inspired by the AK-47. It was introduced into service with the South African police in the late 1980s, at the height of police oppression during apartheid. K. Moeti, 'Time to Say Goodbye to Police's R5 Assault Rifles', Blog post on 23 February 2015, *Mail & Guardian*, at: http://thoughtleader.co.za/koketsomoeti/2015/02/23/time-to-say-goodbye-to-polices-r5-assault-rifles/.

[108] Marikana Commission of Inquiry, pp. 548–49.

[109] Marikana Commission of Inquiry: Report on Matters of Public, National and International Concern Arising Out of the Tragic Incidents at the Lonmin Mine in Marikana, in the North West Province, 31 March 2015, p. 258, available at: http://107.6.66.171/Full%20Report%20of%20the%20Marikana%20Commision%20of%20Inquiry.pdf.

[110] Justice and Solicitor General, Alberta, 'Body Armour Control', 2015, at: www.solgps.alberta.ca/programs_and_services/public_security/BACAct/Pages/default.aspx.

While there is certainly truth to some of the claims, media reports have also on numerous occasions exaggerated or misrepresented the situation. For instance, James Holmes, who was found guilty in July 2015 of murdering twelve people and wounding seventy others in a cinema in Aurora, Colorado, in 2012, was said in the press at the time (and later) to have been wearing (Kevlar) body armour, when in fact he was wearing a non-protective tactical vest that enabled him to carry more ammunition.[111]

The Heckler & Koch MP7 fires 4.6 x 30mm calibre rounds, which are designed to penetrate body armour. Although the weapon is of questionable effectiveness, the round it fires is claimed to be capable of penetrating a 1.6mm titanium plate and 20 layers of Kevlar® body armour[112] at 200 metres.[113] The 4.6mm-calibre bullets were intended to replace 9 x 19mm rounds.[114] In the United States, reference is often made to a famous shoot-out in the North Hollywood district of Los Angeles in February 1997 when two bank robbers, one wearing level III-A body-armour,[115] fought off law enforcement personnel (many firing 9 x 19mm bullets) for 44 minutes, firing 1,100 rounds in the process. (The police and other law enforcement personnel are said to have fired 650 rounds at the bank robbers.)[116]

[111] See, e.g., S. J. Evans, S. Malm, and S. Farberov, 'Posing With a Gun and Wearing BLACK Contact Lenses', *Daily Mail Online*, 27 April 2015, at: www.dailymail.co.uk/news/article-3057030/Long-odds-insanity-defense-theater-shooting-trial.html#ixzz3gEPOjpyo.

[112] According to the manufacturer, DuPont™, 'statistics show' that body armour made with Kevlar® aramid fibre 'reduces the chance of bodily injury or death caused by physical, ballistic, stab, and slash attacks'. DuPont, 'Body Armor', at: www.dupont.com/products-and-services/personal-protective-equipment/body-armor.html.

[113] F. C. Barnes, *Cartridges of the World*, 14th Edn, Gun Digest Books, Iola, WI, 2014, p. 84.

[114] Named after their inventor, Georg Luger. They are often referred to as parabellum rounds in the United States, derived from the Latin phrase, *Si vis pacem, para bellum* ('If you want peace, prepare for war'), the slogan of the German arms manufacturer Deutsche Waffen- und Munitionsfabriken, which first made the 9mm round for their Luger semi-automatic pistol in 1902.

[115] This is the highest blunt-trauma protection rating in soft body armour, intended to resist 9mm Luger rounds fired at submachinegun velocity. 'Bullet Proof ME Body Armor', at: www.bulletproofme.com/Ballistic_Protection_Levels.shtml.

[116] See, e.g., R. Orlov, 'North Hollywood Shootout, 15 Years Later', *Los Angeles Daily News*, 27 February 2012, at: www.dailynews.com/general-news/20120227/north-hollywood-shootout-15-years-later.

Use of Expanding Ammunition

It is not a violation of international law to use expanding ammunition for law enforcement operations. In 2005, the International Committee of the Red Cross asserted that, in general, law enforcement officials only use handguns to fire expanding ammunition:

> [E]xpanding bullets commonly used by police in situations other than armed conflict are fired from a pistol and therefore deposit much less energy than a normal rifle bullet or a rifle bullet which expands or flattens easily. Police forces therefore do not normally use the type of expanding bullet that is prohibited for military rifles.[117]

This is not a representative statement of today's law enforcement realities.

It could, though, be considered incongruous that expanding bullets,[118] ammunition that is designed to expand in the human body, depositing greater kinetic energy and potentially causing more serious wounds than their full-metal-jacketed equivalents, are permissible for law enforcement operations. After all, use of expanding bullets by armed forces in the conduct of hostilities is not only a serious violation of the law of armed conflict; it is also potentially, when it occurs with the requisite *mens rea*, a war crime.[119] So, under international law, a soldier of one state may not use expanding bullets against a soldier of another state, but a police officer may lawfully use such expanding ammunition against one of his state's own citizens.

117 ICRC Study of Customary International Humanitarian Law, Rule 77, at: www.icrc.org/customary-ihl/eng/docs/v1_rul_rule77.

118 Expanding bullets are defined, under the law of armed conflict, as 'bullets which expand or flatten easily in the human body, such as bullets with a hard envelope which does not entirely cover the core or is pierced with incisions'. They are colloquially known as 'dum-dum' bullets, following their manufacture by the British in their arsenal at Dum Dum in India in the 1890s. Such bullets are generally agreed to include both hollow-point (where an opening is drilled into the nose) and soft-point rounds (where the nose is filed down to expose the bullet's lead core).

119 The 1998 Rome Statute of the International Criminal Court gave the ICC possible jurisdiction over the war crime, in international armed conflict, of '[e]mploying bullets which expand or flatten easily in the human body, such as bullets with a hard envelope which does not entirely cover the core or is pierced with incisions'. Art. 8(2)(b)(xix), 1998 Rome Statute. An amendment to the Rome Statute adopted by states parties in 2010 extends the court's jurisdiction to cover use of expanding bullets in non-international armed conflicts (that is, a situation in which one or more states is/are engaged in regular and intense armed violence against an organised armed group). Art. 8 (2)(e)(xv), Rome Statute.

There is, though, a certain degree of logic behind the paradox. Given that law enforcement operations are often conducted in public places, and that expanding ammunition is believed to significantly reduce the risk of overpenetration and possibly also of ricochet, the danger of innocent bystanders being harmed when police officers open fire must be reduced to a minimum. Already in 1998, the New York City Police Department (NYPD) decided to equip its entire force with hollow-point bullets, making it 'almost the last' US law enforcement agency to change from full-metal-jacket rounds.[120] According to NYPD statistics, 15 innocent bystanders were struck by police officers using full-metal-jacket bullets in 1995 and 1996: eight were hit directly, five were hit by bullets that had passed through other people, and two were hit by bullets that had passed through objects.[121] Police Commissioner Howard Safir said (arguably incorrectly, at least at that time), 'It is the standard around the world in law enforcement to use hollow points.'[122]

In May 2011, the MPS announced that hollow-point 9 x 19mm rounds were to be standard issue for its Glock handgun and Heckler & Koch MP5 carbine with soft-point 5.56 x 45mm rounds for its H&K G36 assault rifles.[123] From 2005 to 2011, only Specialist Firearms Officers from the MPS had access to hollow-point 9 x 19mm rounds, and only in particular circumstances. Hollow-point ammunition was used on 22 July 2005 to kill Jean Charles de Menezes, the Brazilian electrician mistaken for a terrorist.[124]

In 2009, the Independent Police Complaints Commission (IPCC) had raised concern that police use of conventional ammunition may endanger innocent bystanders. The warning followed the police shooting of David Sycamore outside Guilford Cathedral in November 2009; Mr Sycamore was shot and killed with G36 rifles using full-metal-jacket bullets when he went to the cathedral armed with a replica gun and refused to put it down. One of the two bullets which hit him then 'went

[120] M. Ayoob, 'The Dangers of Over-Penetrating Bullets', *Gun Digest*, 19 April 2012, at: www.gundigest.com/tactical-gear/tactical-military-arms-blog/massad-ayoob-the-dangers-of-over-penetrating-bullets.

[121] M. Cooper, 'New York Police Will Start Using Deadlier Bullets', *New York Times*, 9 July 1998, at: www.nytimes.com/1998/07/09/nyregion/new-york-police-will-start-using-dead lier-bullets.html.

[122] Ibid.

[123] Response by the MPS to a Freedom of Information request, September 2012, at: www.met.police.uk/foi/pdfs/disclosure_2012/september_2012/2012070003365.pdf.

[124] I. Overton, *Gun Baby Gun*, Canongate, Edinburgh, 2015.

through a window, hit a wall, went through another window and came to rest within the cathedral'.[125]

Within Western Europe, expanding bullets are used by police forces in, among others, Austria, Belgium, Denmark, Finland, France, Germany, the Netherlands, Spain, Sweden, Switzerland, and the United Kingdom.[126] For several years now France has been equipping its police, gendarmerie, customs, and penal law-enforcement officials with expanding ammunition ('munitions à expansion contrôlée'),[127] following a series of incidents of overpenetration and of ricochet.[128] In June 2014, Norway announced plans to equip its police forces with expanding ammunition. This followed the terror attacks of 22 July 2011 for which Anders Behring Breivik reportedly used expanding ammunition during the shootings on Utøya island in which he murdered 68 people in cold blood.[129]

In 2012, a case against Sweden for, inter alia, using expanding ammunition, was judged inadmissible by the European Court of Human Rights. In 2005, 22-year-old Daniel Franklert Murne was shot dead by police in his parents' home in Lindesberg, Sweden, using hollow-point

[125] J. Davenport, 'Met Police Say New "Dumdum" Bullets Will Help Stop Injuries to Bystanders', *Evening Standard*, 11 May 2011, at: www.standard.co.uk/news/met-police-say-new-dumdum-bullets-will-help-stop-injuries-to-bystanders-6400473.html. See also IPCC, 'Commissioner's Report Following the IPCC Independent Investigation into the Shooting of David Sycamore by Surrey Police on Sunday 30 November 2008', at: www.ipcc.gov.uk/sites/default/files/Documents/investigation_commissioner_reports/sycamore_report_1.pdf.

[126] In South Africa, it is not permitted for law enforcement officials to use expanding bullets but private citizens may purchase them for self-defence. Oscar Pistorius reportedly killed Ms Reeva Steenkamp using Ranger T series expanding bullets, manufactured by Winchester that had produced the controversial Black Talon rounds on which they were based. S. Wiley, 'Black Talon and Today's Best Self-Defense Ammo', *Ammunition* (website), 12 October 2014, available at: http://blog.cheaperthandirt.com/black-talon-todays-self-defense-ammo/ ; P. Ross, 'What Are Expanding Bullets? "Dum-Dums" Used by Oscar Pistorius to Shoot Reeva Steenkamp Cause More Damage than Regular Bullets', *International Business Times*, 11 March, 2014, at: www.ibtimes.com/what-are-expanding-bullets-dum-dums-used-oscar-pistorius-shoot-reeva-steenkamp-cause-more-damage.

[127] Email to author from Capt. Erwan Roche, Military Advisor, Permanent Mission of France to the United Nations in Geneva, 22 January 2015.

[128] See B. Kemmet, 'Jugées "trop dangereuses", la police change de munitions', *France Soir*, 13 September 2010, at: http://archive.francesoir.fr/actualite/societe/jugees-trop-dangereuses-police-change-munitions-56850.html.

[129] 'Police Seek to Use Expanding Bullets', *Newsinenglish.no*, 5 June 2014, at: www.newsinenglish.no/2014/06/05/police-seek-to-use-expanding-bullets/.

ammunition. Mr Murne had suffered from a psychosis and needed medical care.[130]

It appears that no application has yet been brought to a human rights court or other human rights mechanism by an innocent bystander hit by a police full-metal-jacket bullet that overpenetrated through the target. Were such a case to arise, an applicant might have an arguable case for a violation of his or her right to life.

Use of Warning Shots

The use of warning shots before opening fire is controversial and there is no settled position under international law given contradictory state practice. Some states (e.g. Denmark)[131] generally require that a warning shot be fired before opening fire at a suspect; others, such as the United States, generally prohibit warning shots altogether, at least as a matter of policy. The case of *Bakan* v. *Turkey* concerned the use of warning shots by a gendarme against a fleeing suspect that missed and ricocheted, killing an innocent bystander. Turkish law required warning shots and then shooting at the legs, before 'free' shooting was permissible.[132] A chamber of the European Court of Human Rights noted that the killing was accidental and that the gendarme had not used his assault rifle in automatic mode.[133] The 2001 European Code of Police Ethics seems to endorse the use of warning shots.[134]

As one member of the public in the United States has noted, albeit in relation to use of firearms by ordinary citizens not by law enforcement officials,

> Warning shots are always a bad idea, if not always explicitly illegal. In the past they might have gotten away with it, but not now. The problem with warning shots, apart from the obvious possibility of accidentally injuring/killing a bystander, is that it calls into question the necessity of using a

[130] Civil Rights Defenders, 'Case on Police Shooting Judged Inadmissible by the European Court', Press release, 4 July 2012, at: www.civilrightsdefenders.org/news/svenska-daniels-familj-nekas-provning-av-europadomstolen/.

[131] Act on Police Activities, 2004, s. 17(2).

[132] ECtHR, *Bakan* v. *Turkey*, Judgment (Second Section), 12 June 2007 (as rendered final on 12 September 2007), §34.

[133] Ibid., §§54–55.

[134] According to the official commentary on §37, 'if lethal weapons are deemed necessary, they should not be used beyond what is considered strictly necessary – shoot to warn before shoot to wound and do not wound more than is strictly necessary'.

> firearm in the first place. If the situation was not dire enough that shooting the suspect was justified, then it was not dire enough for a shot to be fired at all. There is nothing that can be accomplished with a warning shot that can't also be accomplished with a verbal warning.[135]

Indeed, in Denmark the prevailing legislation refers to the need for verbal warnings before any warning shot is countenanced.

In Northern Ireland, in an incident on 26 January 2010, police ombudsman Mr Al Hutchinson concluded that a police officer was justified in discharging three warning shots when he and a colleague came under a sustained and dangerous attack in the County Down village of Carrowdore. The incident happened when the officers were attacked by four men throwing stones. The men confronted the officers when they knocked at the door of a house in connection with a report that a vehicle had been involved in an earlier incident. The officers were forced to withdraw under a barrage of stones. They used CS spray in an attempt to defend themselves but this proved ineffective.[136]

One of the officers then lost his footing and fell to the ground. A warning shot was fired towards a field as the men bore down on him. He later told Police Ombudsman investigators that he believed his life was in danger. The men kept coming towards him and the officer again tried using his CS spray, and again it had no effect. Finally, he discharged a further two warning shots, also aimed towards adjacent fields. The four men went back indoors.[137] Unlike the rest of the United Kingdom, the police officers of the Police Service of Northern Ireland are routinely armed.

In 1998, an article in a US journal, *Law and Order*, examined the danger, value, and legality of police use of warning shots 'to gain compliance from a suspect'.[138] It noted that many police departments had had a policy against warning shots for years, due to concern that a warning shot may be misplaced and result in unintended injury or death to a suspect or bystander. On the other hand, the authors argued that there is

[135] Remarks by Chris Bast, a 'long-time gun owner', on 'Do Police Fire Warning Shots?', Quora, 23 May 2014, at: www.quora.com/Do-police-fire-warning-shots.

[136] Police Ombudsman for Northern Ireland, 'Police Justified in Firing Warning Shots During Attack on Police at Carrowdore', at: www.policeombudsman.org/Investigation-Reports/Police-justified-in-firing-warning-shots-during-at.

[137] Ibid.

[138] D. E. Mulroy and J. Santiago, 'Warning Shots Revisited', *Law and Order*, Vol. 46, No. 4 (April 1998), pp. 96–99.

'evidence that a safely placed warning shot can shock a suspect into compliant behaviour that precludes shooting the suspect'.[139]

In reviewing dozens of cases in which officers or civilians fired a warning shot, they found the shots were effective in the vast majority of cases, and no further shots were fired. In the cases where warning shots were fired, the arrests remained valid, and the courts were not concerned about the use of warning shots. The authors argued that if an officer's option 'is to fire a safely placed warning shot or shoot to kill or incapacitate a suspect, the option of the warning shot is less likely to lead to a civil action against the department'.[140] They concluded that it was perhaps time to look at the possibility of warning shots in cases in which they would serve as an alternative to injury or death.[141]

In January 2017, the 'National Consensus Policy on Use of Force', [142] a policy supported by 11 professional law enforcement bodies in the United States, was published. While acknowledging that warning shots are 'inherently dangerous', the Policy proposes that they be permitted only when they have 'a defined target'; 'the use of deadly force is justified'; the warning shot 'will not pose a substantial risk of injury or death to the officer or others'; and 'the officer reasonably believes that the warning shot will reduce the possibility that deadly force will have to be used'.

Post-Shooting Procedures

The United Kingdom has clear and strict procedures to follow in the immediate aftermath of a police shooting of any person; these can be seen as a model for accountability for use of firearms. According to the Police Firearms Officers Association,[143] at the scene, officers are required to give immediate first aid to the person who has been shot and the scene must be cordoned off while the officers involved in the shooting 'will be removed from the scene as soon as possible'. A situation report is given to the tactical firearms commander.

Officers are required to return to a designated 'suite' where post-incident procedures take place. A Post Incident Manager or PIM (usually an Inspector or above) is called out while a Police Federation Representative is summoned to support the officer or officers involved. The host Force Professional Standards Department is also called and the IPCC is to be informed.

139 Ibid. 140 Ibid. 141 Ibid., p. 99.

142 National Consensus Policy on Use of Force, January 2017, p. 4, at: http://www.theiacp.org/Portals/0/documents/pdfs/National_Consensus_Policy_On_Use_Of_Force.pdf.

143 This section is based on PFOA, 'Post Shooting Procedures', 2016, at: www.pfoa.co.uk/211/post-shooting-procedures.

Those officers that have discharged their firearms will have their weapons forensically examined and will thus hand their weapons to an exhibits officer in a controlled forensic environment. The investigators may also take clothing as it may contain potential evidence. Police officers involved in a shooting incident are not required in law to provide blood samples.

The PIM ensures that a police witness at the scene gives a written account clarifying who were present, what their roles were, and who fired shots. A solicitor will be called to represent officers that have discharged their firearms as well as to any others who request advice given their role in the incident (e.g. tactical or strategic commanders). Officers involved in the shooting will consult with their lawyer privately. All officers involved will see a doctor to ascertain if they have any injuries. Officers will make a phone call to their families to let them know they are ok.

The Senior Investigating Officer will then introduce him- or herself to the relevant officers and the issue of evidential notes will be discussed. How this is addressed depends on what is known about what has happened. Officers that have witnessed events but did not discharge their firearms normally make a written statement about the incident.

Officers then make 'personal initial accounts': a brief account detailing their role and their honestly held belief at why they discharged their firearms. Officers who are legally represented will write notes, subject to any legal or medical advice to the contrary. Personal initial accounts would be followed by lengthy formal statements forty-eight hours later. (This delay is to allow memory to be reconstituted more accurately following any personal shock at what has occurred.) Detailed statements containing a full account of events, including the 'absolute necessity' for use of force, have to be submitted to the IPCC within seven days of the incident.

When the investigators are happy with the information and evidence they have, officers will go home. Officers involved in a shooting are removed from operational duty until such time as the investigators along with the officers' senior commanders make a decision for them to return to duty.

The officers will meet up again about forty-eight hours later. They have to undertake a hearing test if they have been exposed to gunshots without hearing protection. Officers that are legally represented meet up with their lawyer and prepare detailed statements for the investigators. All other officers will write statements and hand them directly to the investigators. When the officers write their notes they are allowed to confer. This conferring consists of 'times, locations, routes, etc.' The officers do not confer about their honestly held belief at the time they fired their weapons. This is 'strictly adhered to'.

There will later be an inquest if the shooting has resulted in a death.

5

Use of 'Less-Lethal' Weapons

> If we can put a man on the moon and return him safely to earth, should we not be able to put a man on the ground and take him safely to jail or to an appropriate facility?
>
> Captain Greg Meyer, Los Angeles Police Department, 2000[1]

Introduction

Depending on the weapon and the context, 'less-lethal' weapons are used to facilitate safe arrest of a dangerous suspect, to disarm or prevent an armed individual firing or using a weapon, to dissuade violence, or to disperse violent protesters. There is no agreed definition under international law of less-lethal (or 'non-lethal') weapons. The North Atlantic Treaty Organization (NATO) defines non-lethal weapons as 'weapons which are explicitly designed and developed to incapacitate or repel personnel, with a low probability of fatality or permanent injury, or to disable equipment with minimal undesired damage or impact on the environment'.[2]

[1] Urban Alliance on Race Relations, 'Saving Lives: Alternatives to the Use of Lethal Force by Police', Report on a Conference on 23–24 June 2000, Toronto, 2002, p. 33, at: https://urbanalliance.files.wordpress.com/2012/05/savinglivesreport.pdf.

[2] See, e.g., NATO, 'Non-Lethal Weapons Effectiveness Assessment Development and Verification Study', RTO Technical Report, Doc. RTO-TR-SAS-060, ch. 1, p. 1-1. France has argued that this definition is very broad and suggests a narrower one: 'Less-lethal weapons are devices specifically conceived and developed to render hors de combat or repel persons, and which, in the ordinary course of their intended use, have a low risk of causing death, serious wounds, or permanent injuries.' Author's translation from 'Concept for Use of Less Lethal Weapons', PIA No. 03-100, Doc. 098/DEF/EMA/EMP.1/NP, 27 January 2005, §1.3: 'Les armes à létalité réduite sont des équipements spécifiquement conçus et mis au point pour mettre hors de combat ou repousser les personnes, et qui, dans les conditions normales prévues pour leur emploi, présentent une faible probabilité de provoquer une issue fatale, des blessures graves ou des lésions permanentes.'

The authors propose the following working definition of less-lethal weapons when used in law enforcement:

> 'Less-lethal' weapons are those that have a low risk of killing or causing serious injury as a result of ordinary or reasonably predictable use. The term does not encompass firearms charged with metal-jacketed rounds or cyber weapons.

Thus, in practice the term encompasses a wide array of weapons and associated ammunition, ranging from the traditional police baton to electroshock weapons such as Tasers®, flash-bang grenades, rubber and plastic bullets, tear gas, water cannon, acoustic weapons, and malodorants (among others). Police dogs and horses are also used as weapons in certain circumstances.

The development, deployment, and use of less-lethal weapons under the law of law enforcement (LOLE) are specifically addressed in the 1990 Basic Principles on the Use of Force and Firearms by Law Enforcement Officials (1990 Basic Principles).[3] Indeed, two of the twenty-six principles concern directly 'non-lethal incapacitating weapons'. But while the notion of a class of weapons below firearms is important, this particular term is unfortunate, for two reasons. First, the weapons foreseen by the term are not non-lethal in practice – they can, and do, kill. Indeed, almost every 'non-lethal' weapon has resulted in the death or serious injury of a number of suspects as well as innocent bystanders. For this reason, the term 'less-lethal' (an implicit comparison to firearms) is widely preferred, including in this work.

Second, the reference to 'incapacitating' could tend towards confusion with chemical incapacitants,[4] such as the anaesthetic used by Russia in its

[3] The Basic Principles were adopted by the Eighth United Nations (UN) Congress on the Prevention of Crime and the Treatment of Offenders, Havana, Cuba, 27 August to 7 September 1990, and welcomed by the UN General Assembly in Resolution 45/166, adopted without a vote on 18 December 1990 (§4). In its 2015 draft new General Comment on the right to life (not yet finalised as of writing), the Human Rights Committee states as follows: 'In particular, all operations of law enforcement agents should comply with relevant international standards, including the Code of Conduct for Law Enforcement Officials … and the Basic Principles on the Use of Force and Firearms by Law Enforcement Officials (1990), and law enforcement agents should undergo appropriate training designed to inculcate these standards so as to ensure, in all circumstances, the fullest respect for the right to life.' Human Rights Committee, 'Draft General Comment No. 36 (Article 6: Right to life)', Draft prepared by Yuval Shany and Nigel Rodley, Rapporteurs, UN doc. CCPR/C/GC/R.36/Rev.2, 7 September 2015, §19. The 1979 Code of Conduct does not specifically address less-lethal weapons.

[4] Michael Crowley describes incapacitants as 'substances whose purported intended purpose is to cause prolonged but non-permanent disability; they include centrally acting agents producing loss of consciousness, sedation, hallucination, incoherence, paralysis,

violent resolution of the 2002 Moscow theatre siege. It appears that a derivative of fentanyl – a powerful opiate used as an anaesthetic or analgesic – was pumped into the theatre before it was stormed by Russian Special Forces,[5] leading to the death of all the hostage-takers (Chechen fighters, many of whom were shot while lying unconscious from the effects of the drug) as well as 129 of the approximately 1,000 hostages.[6] Fentanyl is a toxic chemical whose use for other than peaceful purposes is generally prohibited under the 1992 Chemical Weapons Convention.[7]

The Human Rights Framework

The human rights most at risk of being violated by indiscriminate or excessive use of less-lethal weapons are the rights to life and to humane treatment. Enjoyment of the (umbrella) right to protest, which combines the rights to freedom of peaceful assembly, association, and of opinion, among others, is also potentially imperilled, as discussed in greater detail in Chapter 6. This is not to deny the interest and value of less-lethal weapons to law enforcement. Indeed, in seeking to respect and protect the right to life, states are expected to ensure that their police forces and other law enforcement agencies are equipped with, and effectively trained in, the use of appropriate less-lethal weapons.

The Duty to Equip and Train Police with Less-Lethal Weapons

The 1990 Basic Principle 2 calls on governments and law enforcement agencies to 'develop a range of means as broad as possible and equip law enforcement officials with various types of weapons and ammunition that would allow for a differentiated use of force and firearms'. Among others, this should include 'non-lethal incapacitating weapons for use in appropriate situations', with the aim of 'increasingly restraining the

disorientation or other such effects'. He contrast these with riot control agents 'which act mostly on the peripheral nervous system to produce rapid sensory irritation of the eyes, mucus membranes and skin, and whose effects disappear shortly after termination of exposure'. M. Crowley, *Chemical Control*, Palgrave, London, 2015, pp. 10–11.

5 ECtHR, *Finogenov and Others* v. *Russia*, Judgment (First Section), 20 December 2011 (as rendered final on 4 June 2012), §101.

6 Many died outside the theatre after chocking on their own vomit. The exact number of hostages is not known, as some did not report to the Russian authorities after release. See Ibid., §24.

7 See Crowley, *Chemical Control*, *esp.* pp. 15–16, 126–30, and 169–71.

application of means capable of causing death or injury to persons'. Thus, the rationale for less-lethal weaponry is not only to effectively replace firearms in certain circumstances but also more generally to reduce the number and extent of injuries inflicted during use of force for law enforcement purposes. When used in a professional manner, such weapons can and do save lives, while not unduly risking the safety of law enforcement personnel or the maintenance of public order.

The Right to Life

The right to life, for instance as set out in Article 6(1) of the 1966 International Covenant on Civil and Political Rights (ICCPR),[8] implicitly requires that states parties equip their law enforcement officials with, and train them in the use of, less-lethal weapons.[9] The use of less-lethal weapons is in line with the precautionary obligation on states under the right to life, which requires, among other things, that states minimise the risk of death from the actions of law enforcement officials, including recourse to firearms by their agents. The duty of precaution[10] is reflected in jurisprudence before the European Court of Human Rights and the Inter-American Court of Human Rights.

In the *Dorzema* case, the Inter-American Court reiterated, in relation to the means used, that states 'have an obligation to plan the actions taken by their agents adequately in order to minimize the use of force and the fatalities that may result from it'.[11] In its 2007 judgment in the *Zambrano Vélez* case, the Court found 'no evidence demonstrating that agents of the armed forces who participated in the operation attempted to use less lethal means of intervention in the specific case of the alleged

[8] According to Art. 6(1) of the ICCPR, 'Every human being has the inherent right to life. This right shall be protected by law. No one shall be arbitrarily deprived of his life.'

[9] While not legally binding, in its 2015 draft General Comment No. 36 on the right to life under the ICCPR (not yet finalised as of writing), the Human Rights Committee stated as follows: 'States parties are expected to take reasonable long-term measures intended to prevent arbitrary deprivations of life by their law-enforcement organs, such as police training, mandatory reporting of lethal incidents, and the equipping of police forces responsible for crowd control with effective non-lethal means.' Human Rights Committee, 'Draft General Comment No. 36', *op. cit.*, §19. Although the draft text privileges the equipping of police responsible for crowd control, the obligation to ensure appropriate less-lethal weapons are available must be understood to extend generally to all law enforcement personnel and all law enforcement scenarios.

[10] 'Report of the Special Rapporteur on Extrajudicial, Summary or Arbitrary Executions, Christof Heyns', UN doc. A/HRC/26/36, 1 April 2014, §63.

[11] Inter-American Court of Human Rights (IACtHR), *Nadege Dorzema and Others* v. *Dominican Republic*, Judgment (Merits, reparations and costs), 24 October 2012, §88.

victims', and concluded that Ecuador had not proved that the action of its security forces 'was necessary and proportional in relation to the exigencies of the situation'.[12] The Court held that Ecuador had violated the right to life of the applicants – suspected drug dealers – who were killed during an operation by the Ecuadorian armed forces and national police.[13]

In its 1998 judgment in the case of *Güleç* v. *Turkey*, which concerned Turkish security forces firing metal jacketed ammunition into groups of protesters, some of whom were engaged in serious acts of violence, a chamber of the European Court deemed the lack of availability of an alternative to firearms 'unacceptable'. It further noted that

> a balance must be struck between the aim pursued and the means employed to achieve it. The gendarmes used a very powerful weapon because they apparently did not have truncheons, riot shields, water cannon, rubber bullets or tear gas. The lack of such equipment is all the more incomprehensible and unacceptable because the province of Sirnak, as the Government pointed out, is in a region in which a state of emergency has been declared, where at the material time disorder could have been expected.[14]

In 2005, in its judgment in *Şimşek*, a case that also involved protests in Turkey, the European Court held that 'it was the responsibility of the Security Forces, who had been aware of the tense situation in both districts, to provide the necessary equipment, such as tear gas, plastic bullets, water cannons, etc., to disperse the crowd'. The Court again held that the lack of such equipment was 'unacceptable'.[15] The Court concluded that the force used to disperse the demonstrators, which caused the death of seventeen people, was more than absolutely necessary within the meaning of Article 2 of the 1950 European Convention on Human Rights (ECHR).[16] The article explicitly provides that deprivation of life, when absolutely necessary 'in action lawfully taken for the purpose of quelling a riot', does not constitute a violation of the right to life.[17]

12 IACtHR, *Zambrano Vélez and Others* v. *Ecuador*, Judgment (Merits, Reparations and Costs), 4 July 2007, §108.

13 Ibid., §110.

14 European Court of Human Rights (ECtHR), *Güleç* v. *Turkey*, Judgment (Chamber), 27 July 1998, §71.

15 ECtHR, *Şimşek and Others* v. *Turkey*, Judgment, 26 July 2005 (as rendered final on 26 October 2005), §111.

16 Ibid., §112.

17 Art. 2(2)(c), ECHR.

A similar position exists in Africa. In November 2015, the African Commission on Human and Peoples' Rights (ACHPR) issued a General Comment on the right to life (Article 4 in the 1981 African Charter on Human and Peoples' Rights).[18] In this General Comment, the Commission stated that: 'Particular attention should be paid to ensuring the availability and use of weapons less likely to cause death or serious injury than are firearms.'[19]

The Duty to Control Less-Lethal Weapons

While the 1990 Basic Principles may seem unequivocally to endorse use of less-lethal weaponry, this is not the case. Principle 3 states that: 'The development and deployment of non-lethal incapacitating weapons should be carefully evaluated in order to minimize the risk of endangering uninvolved persons, and the use of such weapons should be carefully controlled.' The focus of concern is thus the lack of discrimination of a weapon (where harm affects bystanders), though the reference to careful control over the use of less-lethal weapons should be interpreted more broadly to comprehend also the risk of death and serious injury to intended targets.

As the name suggests, the 1990 Basic Principles largely give only broad-brush guidance on use of force for law enforcement. The lack of detailed regulation of less-lethal weapons (especially when compared to the rules on use of firearms), some of which were developed and deployed only after the adoption of the Basic Principles in 1990, is recognised in Resolution 25/38 of the United Nations (UN) Human Rights Council. Among other things, this 2014 resolution 'encourages' states to make 'non-lethal weapons available to their officials exercising law enforcement duties, while pursuing international efforts to regulate and establish protocols for the training and use of non-lethal weapons'.[20]

[18] According to Art. 4, 'Human beings are inviolable. Every human being shall be entitled to respect for his life and the integrity of his person. No one may be arbitrarily deprived of this right.'

[19] ACHPR, 'General Comment No. 3 on the African Charter on Human and Peoples' Rights: Article 4, the Right to Life', adopted in November 2015, §30, at: www.achpr.org/files/instruments/general-comments-right-to-life/generalcommentno.3_eng.pdf.

[20] Human Rights Council Resolution 25/38, adopted on 28 March 2014 by 31 votes to 9, with 7 abstentions. Those opposing the resolution were China, Cuba, India, Kenya, Pakistan, Russia, South Africa, Venezuela, and Vietnam.

In 2016, in their joint report to the Council under a mandate given by Resolution 25/38, the UN Special Rapporteurs on the rights to freedom of peaceful assembly and of association (Maina Kiai), and on extrajudicial, summary or arbitrary executions (Christof Heyns) further recommended that states 'work to establish and implement international protocols for the training and use of less-lethal weapons'.[21]

The Right to Life

Of course, as noted above, 'less' lethal does not mean 'non' lethal. As the ACHPR's General Comment on the right to life notes, 'such weapons should not be abused – they can also cause death or serious injury'.[22] Indeed, at a 1986 conference on the issue organised by the United States (US) Department of Justice, an expert remarked that 'excessive use' of such weapons

> may result in no net improvement in rates of fatal injury when compared to lethal weapons practice. If, for example, a less than lethal weapon is one-tenth as lethal as a handgun but is used ten times more frequently, an identical number of subjects will be fatally injured.[23]

Indeed, where excessive or indiscriminate use of a less-lethal weapon is alleged and the victim dies as a result or shortly thereafter, a violation of the right to life may well have occurred.

To reduce the risks of abuse with less-lethal weapons, the ACHPR calls for special training to be provided on their lawful use.[24] Similarly, the Human Rights Committee's 2015 draft new General Comment on the right to life provided that the use of less-lethal weapons (notably Tasers®, rubber bullets, and plastic bullets) 'must be strictly regulated and restricted only to security agents who have undergone the necessary training'.[25] The Committee argues that such less-lethal weapons 'can

[21] 'The Proper Management of Assemblies', Joint report of the Special Rapporteur on the rights to freedom of peaceful assembly and of association, Maina Kiai, and the Special Rapporteur on extrajudicial, summary or arbitrary executions, Christof Heyns, UN doc. A/HRC/31/66, 4 February 2016, §55.

[22] ACHPR, 'General Comment No. 3 on the African Charter on Human and Peoples' Rights: Article 4, the Right to Life', §30.

[23] S. Sweetman, 'Report on the Attorney General's Conference on Less Than Lethal Weapons', National Institute of Justice, Washington, DC, 1987, p. 26.

[24] ACHPR, 'General Comment No. 3 on the African Charter on Human and Peoples' Rights: Article 4, the Right to Life', §30.

[25] Human Rights Committee, 'Draft General Comment No. 36', *op. cit.*, §15.

only be employed in situations of exceptional nature in which other less harmful measures have proven to be, or clearly are inadequate. For example, State parties should not resort to them in routine situations of crowd control and demonstrations'.[26]

The Right to Humane Treatment

In practice, though, a challenge for alleged misuse of less-lethal weapons is more likely to be made in connection with the right to humane treatment than the right to life. According to Article 7 of the ICCPR, 'No one shall be subjected to torture or to cruel, inhuman or degrading treatment or punishment.' In its general comment on the provision, the Human Rights Committee has stated that: 'The Covenant does not contain any definition of the concepts covered by article 7, nor does the Committee consider it necessary to draw up a list of prohibited acts or to establish sharp distinctions between the different kinds of punishment or treatment; the distinctions depend on the nature, purpose and severity of the treatment applied.'[27]

In general terms, however, cruel treatment refers to pain or suffering that is applied wantonly, gratuitously, or sadistically; inhuman treatment is the inflicting of severe pain or suffering; while degrading treatment is intended to humiliate the victim. In contrast, torture is primarily committed when the victim is in the physical power of the perpetrator, whether or not he or she has been formally arrested by a law enforcement official. This is not, though, a hard and fast rule: there may be situations where use of weapons outside a formal custodial context may amount to torture.[28] One example is when a bullet or projectile is fired as a deliberate expression of racial animus.[29] In most cases, though, the actions of a law

[26] Ibid.

[27] Human Rights Committee, 'General Comment 20, Article 7', Forty-fourth session, 1992, §4.

[28] The Elements of Crimes of the International Criminal Court (ICC) for the international crime of torture, when committed as a crime against humanity, stipulate that the elements include that: 'The perpetrator inflicted severe physical or mental pain or suffering upon one or more persons. . . . Such person or persons were in the custody *or under the control of* the perpetrator.' ICC, "Elements of crimes", UN doc. PCNICC/2000/1/Add.2 (2000), p. 7. [added emphasis].

[29] Under the 1984 Convention Against Torture, torture means 'any act by which severe pain or suffering, whether physical or mental, is intentionally inflicted on a person . . . **for any reason based on discrimination of any kind**, when such pain or suffering is inflicted by or at the instigation of or with the consent or acquiescence of a public official or other person acting in an official capacity. It does not include pain or suffering arising only from, inherent in or incidental to lawful sanctions'. Art. 1(1), 1984 Convention and Other

enforcement official firing a weapon without respect for the fundamental principles of necessity and proportionality will fall to be considered as a form of cruel, inhuman, or degrading treatment rather than torture (if, of course, it is not considered a violation of the right to life).[30]

Particular risks exist of torture or other inhumane treatment occurring in the course of detention. These are addressed in detail in Chapter 7. There are also significant risks of an individual being subjected to inhumane treatment while a law enforcement official is seeking to effect an arrest.[31] The European Court of Human Rights has stated in several judgments that 'any recourse to physical force' by a law enforcement official that has not been made 'strictly necessary' by a person's own conduct 'diminishes human dignity and is in principle an infringement' of the prohibition on torture and inhuman or degrading treatment or punishment set out in Article 3 of the ECHR.[32]

These protections apply at all times. In a 2015 judgment, a European Court chamber recalled that it had 'stated on many occasions' that the right to humane treatment in Article 3 'enshrines one of the most fundamental values of democratic societies'.[33] It affirmed that: 'Even in the most difficult circumstances, such as the fight against terrorism and organised crime, the Convention prohibits in absolute terms torture and inhuman and degrading treatment or punishment, irrespective of the victim's conduct.'[34] Similarly, according to the 1979 Code of Conduct for Law Enforcement Officials,

Cruel, Inhuman or Degrading Treatment or Punishment (CAT), adopted by UN General Assembly Resolution 39/46 of 10 December 1984. [added emphasis].

30 Sir Nigel Rodley affirms that the 'extension of the concept of ill-treatment to situations where persons are not already under the physical control of the perpetrators has posed some challenges when it comes to explaining the conceptual or precise legal elements of the concept of cruel, inhuman or degrading treatment'. He argues that 'perhaps' it would have been 'doctrinally simpler and cleaner' to have decided such cases by reference to the right to security of person (as set out in Art. 9(1) of the ICCPR) but he acknowledges that 'this is not how the jurisprudence has developed'. N. Rodley with M. Pollard, *The Treatment of Prisoners Under International Law*, Oxford University Press, Oxford, 2011, p. 134.

31 See, e.g., Rodley and Pollard, *The Treatment of Prisoners Under International Law*, p. 131.

32 ECtHR, *Bouyid* v. *Belgium*, Judgment (Grand Chamber), 28 September 2015, §§88, 100; see also ECtHR, *Ribitsch* v. *Austria*, Judgment (Chamber), 4 December 1995, §38; and J. Murdoch and R. Roche, *The European Convention on Human Rights and Policing*, Council of Europe, Strasbourg, 2013, p. 34, at: www.coe.int/t/dghl/cooperation/capacity building/source/documentation/europeanconventionhandbookforpolice.pdf.

33 ECtHR, *Bobrov* v. *Russia*, Judgment (First Section), 23 October 2014 (as rendered final on 23 January 2015), §31.

34 The absolute nature of this prohibition has been mirrored by jurisprudence in the Inter-American Court on Human Rights. In the *Cantoral-Benavides* case, the Court warned that the fact that a state 'is confronted with terrorism should not lead to restrictions on

> No law enforcement official may inflict, instigate or tolerate any act of torture or other cruel, inhuman or degrading treatment or punishment, nor may any law enforcement official invoke superior orders or exceptional circumstances such as a state of war or a threat of war, a threat to national security, internal political instability or any other public emergency as a justification of torture or other cruel, inhuman or degrading treatment or punishment.[35]

In terms of the burden of proof, while that generally fell to the applicant, the European Court has deemed it 'noteworthy' in one case that while the state in question had acknowledged that the arresting police officers 'used a certain coercion to effect the arrest because the applicant had shown resistance', they did not provide 'any details as to the nature of either the resistance or the coercion in question ... except for referring to the fact that the applicant was at some point handcuffed'.[36] The Court found a violation of Article 3 of the ECHR under its substantive limb.[37]

The Need for Effective Testing of Less-Lethal Weapons

As with the right to life, the right to humane treatment imposes on states a duty to prevent torture, including by their law enforcement officials. According to the Committee against Torture, Article 2(1) of the 1984 Convention against Torture obliges each state party 'to take actions that will reinforce the prohibition against torture through legislative, administrative, judicial, or other actions that must, in the end, be effective in preventing it'.[38] This means, among other things, that states are required to ensure that weapons, including less-lethal weapons, along with any ammunition they fire, be tested prior to procurement and deployment to ensure they comply with human rights law, at the very least the prohibitions on arbitrary deprivation of life, torture, and other inhumane treatment.

More broadly, Human Rights Council Resolution 25/38 underlined 'the importance of thorough, independent and scientific testing of non-lethal weapons prior to deployment to establish their lethality and

the protection of the physical integrity of the person'. IACtHR, *Cantoral-Benavides v. Peru*, Judgment (Merits), 18 August 2000, §96, citing also the *Castillo-Petruzzi and Others* case (Judgment, 30 May 1999, §197); and the *Loayza-Tamayo* case (Judgment, 17 September 1997, §57).

35 Art. 5, 1979 Code of Conduct for Law Enforcement Officials, adopted by UN General Assembly Resolution 34/169 of 17 December 1979. See further Arts. 1 and 2, CAT.

36 Ibid., §40. 37 Ibid., §46.

38 Committee against Torture, 'General Comment No. 2: Implementation of Article 2 by States Parties', UN doc. CAT/C/GC/2, 24 January 2008, §2.

the extent of likely injury, and of monitoring appropriate training and use of such weapons'.[39] Similarly, the Human Rights Committee's 2015 draft of a new General Comment on the right to life stipulates that states parties to the ICCPR 'should also study and monitor the impact on the right to life of less-lethal weapons which are designed for use by law-enforcement agents and soldiers charged with law-enforcement missions, including electro-muscular disruption devices (Tasers), rubber-coated metal bullets, and attenuating energy projectiles'.[40]

Use of Specific Less-Lethal Weapons and Ammunition

This section applies the general international legal rules of LOLE, specifically necessity for and proportionality of force, to use of certain less-lethal weapons by the police: batons and then pepper spray (both close-in weapons); Tasers (close-in or medium distance weapons, depending on the mode used); rubber and plastic bullets and then tear gas (medium- and longer-range police weapons). It also considers their use within the context of the rights to life and to humane treatment. As with any weapons, the risk to especially vulnerable groups (e.g. children, the elderly, or those with disabilities) needs to be considered. Where relevant, case law on specific weapons is cited; in many instances this is from domestic civil and criminal law jurisdictions.

Police Baton

Design and Use of Batons

Also referred to as truncheons, nightsticks, tonfas, coshes, or billy clubs, batons are one of the oldest weapons available to the police.[41] Batons are typically used to force compliance through strikes or holds facilitated by the use of the baton (as well as by the threat of their use). They also serve as a tool for police officers to defend themselves against an assailant.[42]

[39] Human Rights Council Resolution 25/38, §15.

[40] Human Rights Committee, 'Draft General Comment No. 36', *op. cit.*, §15.

[41] Omega Foundation, 'Police Batons', Unpublished document provided by email of 4 August 2014. This sub-section is based on that document a copy of which is held by the author.

[42] The Omega Foundation, an international non-governmental organisation based in the United Kingdom, has described the police baton in the following terms: 'Police batons are most commonly made of wood, metal, rubber, or plastic, and are available in varying lengths. The most common batons are either straight, straight with a side handle, or

In the United Kingdom (UK), police have carried the 'truncheon' since their formation under the legislation introduced in 1829 by Sir Robert Peel (see Chapter 1). Truncheons were issued primarily as a weapon of self-defence; they were chosen over firearms for the relative freedom they gave the officers to strike with the baton with one hand and apprehend the suspect with the other. (Muskets of the time required both hands for firing and thus prevented easy apprehension.[43]) The short wooden club remained in service in the United Kingdom, relatively unchanged, for more than 160 years.[44]

The baton was judged to be an effective tool to control resistant subjects. Use spread worldwide and although products of varying materials, length, and diameter were added to the market, the core design remained fundamentally similar until a new form of baton was marketed in the United States (US) in the 1970s.[45] The PR-24, produced by the Monadnock Corporation, was a side-handle baton designed to enable an officer to gain control of a suspect, while also continuing to serve as a striking and defensive blocking weapon.[46] In the 1980s, again in the United States, the metal collapsible or telescopic baton was introduced to the wider law enforcement community by Kevin Parsons of Armament Systems and Procedures (ASP).[47] Its compact design, which meant that it could easily be kept in a sheath on a patrol belt without the need to remove the baton or the belt while travelling in a patrol car, prompted its swift rise in popularity, and its basic design was soon reproduced by other companies.[48]

Modern-day police forces are, in general, equipped with straight, side-handle, or telescopic batons, or a mixture thereof. Other baton designs

telescopic/collapsible. They are issued to law enforcement officers for use as a defensive blocking weapon, an offensive striking weapon, and to facilitate holds.' Email from Kate Wraith, Research Associate, Omega Foundation, 4 August 2014.

[43] 'A Short History of British Police, Focusing on Truncheon and Armour – Arms in Action', excerpt from the programme *Arms in Action* on the Military History channel on television, uploaded to *YouTube* on 9 June 2010, at: www.youtube.com/watch?v=_MctS6wkAdQ#t=123.

[44] 'Police Arms and Weaponry', *Politics.co.uk* website, undated but accessed on 21 January 2016 at: www.politics.co.uk/reference/police-arms-and-weaponry.

[45] D. Young, 'Where Have All the Batons Gone?', *PoliceOne.com*, 1 April 2005, at: www.policeone.com/police-products/duty-gear/articles/99726-Where-have-all-the-batons-gone/.

[46] Ibid.

[47] AELE Law Enforcement Legal Center, 'Use of Force Tactics and Non-Lethal Weaponry', undated but accessed at: www.aele.org/alert-tactics.html.

[48] Young, 'Where Have All the Batons Gone?', *op. cit.*

were introduced in the 1990s and 2000s, but none has yet attracted the attention or acclaim of the wider law enforcement community as have the straight, side-handle, and telescopic batons. A 2005 European Council Regulation concerning trade in goods that could be used for inhumane treatment prohibits the import and export of 'batons or truncheons made of metal or other material having a shaft with metal spikes' irrespective of the origin of such goods.[49] These are weapons with no legitimate role in law enforcement.[50]

Baton strikes applied to sensitive areas of the body, such as the head, neck and throat, spine, kidneys, and solar plexus, can result in significant injury, including bruising, organ rupture, or serious head injury.[51] Baton strikes to bones and joints can result in dislocations, fractures, and soft-tissue injuries.[52] Groups such as the elderly, pregnant women, children, and those with underlying health issues or injuries are more vulnerable to baton blows. Leverage and control holds, often taught during baton training, also present a high risk of injury.[53] Neck-holds present an especially high risk of death or serious injury as a result of large blood-vessel or airway compression and also risk injury to bodily structures, such as the larynx, trachea, and hyoid bone.[54]

[49] European Commission Council Regulation No. 1236/2005 concerning trade in certain goods which could be used for capital punishment, torture, or other cruel, inhuman, or degrading treatment or punishment (as amended), 27 June 2005, at: http://eur-lex.europa.eu/legal-content/EN/TXT/PDF/?uri=CELEX:02005R1236-20140220&rid=2.

[50] Spiked metal batons, or 'sting' sticks, 'wolf' sticks, or 'wolf-teeth sticks' as they are often marketed, are believed to be manufactured and used only in China.

[51] A 1998 Police Complaints Authority (PCA) report warned that US-style baton training regimes and a lack of refresher training was resulting in an excessive number of injuries in England and Wales. 'Police Arms and Weaponry', Politics.co.uk. The PCA report raised particular concern about the ASP baton, then in use in twelve forces across England and Wales, which had been introduced from the United States with scant changes to the police training manuals. 'One consequence was that officers were trained to stand ready to strike with the baton resting on their shoulder, which risked the suspect being unintentionally struck on the head or another dangerous area.' BBC, 'UK: Police Get Stick Over New Batons', 30 December 1998, at: http://news.bbc.co.uk/2/hi/uk_news/244530.stm.

[52] M. Stark (ed.), *Clinical Forensic Medicine: A Physician's Guide*, 2nd Edn, Humana Press, New York, 2005, p. 198.

[53] See, e.g., Euro Security Products' photo gallery from their training with local police instructors from Georgia in 2013, at: www.euro-security.info/euro-security.info/en/training-courses-esp/photogallery-esp-courses/course-for-instructors-local-police-units-in-georgia.html.

[54] G. M. Vilke, 'Neck Holds' in D. L. Ross and T. C. Chan (eds.), *Forensic Science and Medicine: Sudden Deaths in Custody*, Humana Press, New York, 2006, pp. 15–27.

Human Rights Caselaw

The *Douet* case before the European Court of Human Rights concerned the arrest of Mr Gilbert Douet in 2005 by French *gendarmes* in the course of which officers struck him several times with a telescopic baton.[55] When driving at night on a country road, Mr Douet had made a sudden about-turn upon seeing a police car, which then gave chase. The case concerned his complaint that he had been subjected to unlawful violence when stopped and arrested.

In assessing the legality of the force used against Mr Douet, the European Court cited the April 2009 judgment of the Riom Court of Appeal in France which, while confirming the acquittal of policemen involved in the arrest on charges of having occasioned actual bodily harm, pointed to acts which might amount to 'disproportionate' use of force. This included use of the baton by a gendarme when Douet was already under arrest and had been cuffed on one of his hands, and another gendarme struck him several times while pushing his knee down onto Mr Douet's back. Injuries included a fracture of Douet's elbow and bruising on one arm, as well as an oedema on his elbow and bruises on his back.

The Riom appellate court had also found that the applicant had only shown passive resistance, an element to which the European Court attached particular importance in reaching its decision.[56] The court found a violation of Article 3 of the ECHR (the right to humane treatment) on the basis that France failed to prove that the force used against Mr Douet had been both necessary and proportionate.[57]

Criminal Law Cases

Police batons can be used to kill, or they may have lethal consequences even when death is not the intention. In Uganda, the 2003 conviction and death sentence of prison warder Absolom Omolo Owiny was upheld on appeal in 2008. Mr Owiny was convicted of the murder of Wanok Michael after the appellant 'tortured and beat him up with a baton until he became unconscious. Later the same day, the deceased died from his injuries'.[58]

The 2011 case of *US* v. *Matthew Dean Moore and Melvin Williams* concerned the beating to death of Raymond Robair. Officer Williams was

[55] ECtHR, *Douet* v. *France*, Judgment (Fifth Section), 3 October 2013 (as rendered final on 3 January 2014).

[56] Ibid., §§35–36. [57] Ibid., §§38–39.

[58] *Absolom Omolo Owiny* v. *Uganda*, Criminal Appeal No. 321 of 2003, [2008] UGCA 2, Judgment of 7 April 2008, at: www.ulii.org/ug/judgment/court-appeal/2008/2.

charged with 'unreasonably kicking Robair and striking him with his police baton while acting as a New Orleans Police Department (NOPD) police officer, wilfully depriving Robair of his right to be free from the use of unreasonable force by a law enforcement officer'. The defendants appealed against their convictions and sentence.[59] In February 2013, the US Court of Appeals for the Fifth Circuit (covering Louisiana, Mississippi, and Texas) upheld the decision of the district court.[60]

In 2009, in the United Kingdom, newspaper vendor Mr Ian Tomlinson died after he was struck with a baton and pushed to the ground by Metropolitan Police officer Simon Harwood. Mr Harwood was sacked for gross misconduct after the jury at an inquest rendered a verdict of unlawful killing, concluding that Mr Tomlinson's death had been caused by internal injuries sustained as a result of his unlawful treatment. In 2012, at his subsequent criminal trial on the charge of manslaughter, Mr Harwood claimed that reasonable force included a baton strike to the arm or leg, a push, a kick or punch, CS spray, or handcuffs, and even a 'life-threatening strike'. When asked by the prosecution barrister why he had not recorded the baton strike, Mr Harwood replied: 'It was not significant for me at the time.'[61] At the end of his trial, Mr Harwood was acquitted.[62]

Pepper Spray

Design and Use of Pepper Spray

Pepper spray, also known as OC (oleoresin capsicum) spray, is a lachrymatory agent: a chemical compound that irritates the eyes.[63] The effects

[59] US Court of Appeals (Fifth Circuit), *US* v. *Matthew Dean Moore and Melvin* Williams, Government Brief (Case No. 11–30877), at: www.justice.gov/crt/about/app/briefs/williamsmoorebrief.pdf.

[60] US Court of Appeals (Fifth Circuit), *USA* v. *Matthew Dean Moore and Melvin Williams*, Judgment (Case No. 11–30877), 11 February 2013, at: www.gpo.gov/fdsys/pkg/USCOURTS-ca5-11-30877/pdf/USCOURTS-ca5-11-30877-0.pdf.

[61] P. Walker, 'Simon Harwood Trial: Difficult Testimony and Uncomfortable Viewing', *The Guardian*, 19 July 2012, at: www.theguardian.com/uk/2012/jul/19/simon-harwood-trial-difficult-testimony.

[62] See, e.g., P. Peachy, 'A Payout – and an Apology – to the Family of Ian Tomlinson over Death at Hands of Police at G20 Protest', *Independent*, 5 August 2013, at: www.independent.co.uk/news/uk/crime/a-payout–and-an-apology–to-the-family-of-ian-tomlinson-over-death-at-hands-of-police-at-g20-protest-8746001.html.

[63] See generally Omega Foundation, 'Crowd Control Technologies: An Appraisal of Technologies for Political Control', 2000, at: www.omegaresearchfoundation.org/assets/downloads/publications/19991401a_en.pdf; and Geneva Academy of International Humanitarian Law and Human Rights, 'Riot Control Agents', *Weapons Law*

of pepper spray are said to include dilation of the capillaries and instant closing of the eyes through swelling of the eyelids; immediate respiratory inflammation, including uncontrollable coughing, retching, shortness of breath, and gasping for air with a gagging sensation in the throat; and immediate burning sensations to the mucous membranes, skin, and inside the nose and mouth.[64] The active ingredient in pepper spray is capsaicin, which is not soluble in water, and even large volumes of water will not wash it off. Victims of the spray are encouraged to blink vigorously in order to encourage tears, which will help flush it from their eyes.

OC was developed in 1960 at the University of Georgia by Professor James Jenkins and Dr. Frank Hayes, originally for use as an animal repellent. It is derived from the naturally occurring capsicum species of plant and, as such, its components vary depending on the crop used to manufacture the product. In the late 1980s, following a three-year study, the firearms training unit at the Federal Bureau of Investigation (FBI) Academy in Virginia authorised the use of pepper spray by its special agents and SWAT (Special Weapons and Tactics) teams to 'control unruly subjects without having to resort to a physical confrontation or deadly force'.[65] In 1998, though, it was claimed that pepper spray had been responsible for the deaths of sixty people in the United States.[66]

In US law enforcement, pepper spray is often used in cases where a suspect is resisting arrest.[67] Thus, when a suspect is both under arrest and no longer a threat (for example when handcuffed) pepper spray should no longer be used.[68] A report published by the US Congressional Service noted that, as with the use of Tasers (discussed below), US courts have generally held that an officer's use of pepper spray is not unreasonable when a suspect is actively resisting arrest or, more controversially, fails to

Encyclopedia, undated but accessed on 21 January 2016 at: www.weaponslaw.org/weapons/riot-control-agents.

64 US Court of Appeals (Fourth Circuit), *Park* v. *Shiflett*, 250 F.3d 843, 849 (2001).

65 Safety Gear HQ, 'The History of Pepper Spray', undated but accessed in October 2013 at: www.safetygearhq.com/pepper-spray/pepper-spray-facts.htm#11.

66 T. Romero, 'The Technology of Control', *Tangled Net* 3.08, 4 September 1998.

67 SHouse Law Group, 'Pepper Spray and Police Abuse, California Civil Rights Lawyers', undated but accessed on 21 January 2016 at: www.shouselaw.com/pepperspray.html.

68 Thus, the Los Angeles Police Department (LAPD) came under fire for its officers' use of pepper spray on a homeless man while he was handcuffed in the backseat of a police cruiser. P. McGreevy, 'LAPD Decides No Change to Pepper Spray Policy is Needed', *Los Angeles Times*, 22 November 2006, at: http://articles.latimes.com/2006/nov/22/local/me-pepper22.

heed an officer's direct command.[69] Not every victim of pepper spraying is equally vulnerable. According to one authority, 'tear gas may not be as effective on the insane, drug addicts, intoxicated, or hysterical persons'.[70]

Concerns about police use of pepper spray on children have arisen in several states. Police in Victoria, Australia, were criticised in 2014 by the state's Commissioner for Children and Young People, Bernie Geary, for using pepper spray on children as young as 11. Documents released to a newspaper revealed that 90 children under the age of 15 were sprayed by police between 2011 and August 2014.[71] Mr Geary was critical of using force against children, and urged police to use pepper spray in their interactions with children only as a last resort. Police are trained in the use of OC sprays, but no guidelines or training specific to children were in place.[72]

Police Superintendent David Clayton said growing violence and drug use among youths was prompting a rise in the use of OC sprays.[73] Indeed, in many reported cases children were armed with knives or metal poles, but a number of incidents raised fears that, on occasion, police were also using force against children who just refused to obey orders. In one case, police were alleged to have used pepper spray through a window to subdue a 13-year-old girl who had locked herself in a bathroom for 45 minutes. Affected by the spray, the girl thrashed around the cubicle, hitting her arms and legs against the walls.[74]

Problems continued to be reported in the state in 2015. In February, Victoria Police launched an internal investigation into the actions of two

[69] R. M. Thompson II, *Police Use of Force: Rules, Remedies, and Reforms*, Congressional Research Service, Washington DC, 30 October 2015, p. 12, available at: www.fas.org/sgp/crs/misc/R44256.pdf.

[70] C. E. McGoey, 'Self-Defense: Tear Gas & Pepper Spray', 2015, at: www.crimedoctor.com/self_defense_1.htm. Ed Conlon, for example, describes an arrest where he and a fellow officer fought with the suspect 'and when Gina blasted him with mace, he licked his lips as if it was whipped cream'. E. Conlon, *Blue Blood*, Ebury Press, London, 2011, p. 99.

[71] A. White, 'Police Use Capsicum Spray on "Disobedient" Children', *Herald Sun*, 21 December 2014, at: www.heraldsun.com.au/news/law-order/police-use-capsicum-spray-on-disobedient-children/news-story/9c33fd3ccb55b5647a3eabbd61a53c79.

[72] A study in 1996 by Woodhall Stopford is said to have found a particular risk of pulmonary oedema in children and asthmatics from use of pepper spray. Cited by Environmental Defender's Office (ACT), *The Risks of Use of Capsicum Spray and Pain Compliance Techniques against Public Gatherings, Police Powers of Crowd Control*, Submission to ACT Legislative Assembly Legal Affairs Committee Inquiry, June 2005, at: www.parliament.act.gov.au/__data/assets/pdf_file/0008/380375/LA07_EDOACT_police_powers_01July05_public.pdf, §27.

[73] White, 'Police Use Capsicum Spray on "Disobedient" Children'.

[74] Ibid.

Protective Services Officers,[75] after closed circuit television (CCTV) footage showed two teenage boys being repeatedly sprayed with capsicum foam because one did not have a valid railway ticket. Victoria Police's operational manual on aerosols says pepper spray must only be deployed where the officer believes there is a reasonable threat of violence or serious physical confrontation. It should not be used in situations of 'passive resistance'.[76]

Civil Law Cases

At the end of September 2015, a judgment in a civil action suit in the US state of Alabama included a finding that police officers in Birmingham had used unconstitutional excessive force when they sprayed children who were not resisting arrest or posing a threat to others with a mix of pepper spray and tear gas at school.[77] In one incident, an officer sprayed a 15-year-old pregnant student who was already restrained with handcuffs. She was sprayed because she would not stop crying in the hallway. She was upset because a male student had just cursed at her and called her a derogatory name. After she was sprayed, she vomited.[78]

In contrast, the judge ruled that officers had been justified in using the agent, Freeze+P,[79] where students were either resisting arrest or where they posed a physical threat to those around them. Even in those cases, however, the judge held that officers had violated the students' constitutional rights by failing to decontaminate them and exposing them to fresh air.[80]

[75] These are uniformed protection officers in the Australian Federal Police (AFP).

[76] L. Milligan, 'Victoria Police Launch Internal Investigation into Use of Capsicum Spray on Teenager after Fare Evasion', *ABC News*, 12 February 2015, at: www.abc.net.au/news/2015-02-12/police-investigate-use-of-capsicum-spray-on-teen-fare-evader/6089828.

[77] US District Court for the Northern District of Alabama, Southern Division, *J. W. and Others* v. *Birmingham Board of Education and Others*, Findings of Fact and Conclusions of Law (Civil Action No. 2:10-cv-03314-AKK), at: www.splcenter.org/sites/default/files/documents/findings_of_fact_and_conclusions_of_law.pdf.

[78] E. Brown, 'Judge: Police Can No Longer Pepper-Spray Students for Minor Misbehavior at School', *The Washington Post*, 1 October 2015, at: www.washingtonpost.com/news/education/wp/2015/10/01/judge-police-can-no-longer-pepper-spray-students-for-minor-misbehavior-at-school/.

[79] Freeze+P is described by its manufacturer as 'the most intense incapacitating agent available today'. Aerko International, 'Freeze + P', undated but accessed on 26 January 2016 at: www.aerko.com/freeze-p/.

[80] E. Blad, 'Use of Pepper Spray by School Police Violated Constitution, Judge Rules', 1 October 2015, *Education Week* blog, at: http://blogs.edweek.org/edweek/rulesforengagement/2015/10/use_of_pepper_spray_by_school_police_violated_constitution_judge_rules.html.

US law enforcement agencies also use pepper spray for crowd control in civil disobedience situations. For instance, pepper spray was widely used against protesters at the 1999 World Trade Organization conference in Seattle, allegedly in violation of both manufacturer's recommendations and Seattle Police Department policy and procedure.[81] In *Headwaters Forest Defense* v. *County of Humboldt*,[82] the US Court of Appeals for the Ninth Circuit (covering Alaska and Arizona) held that use of pepper spray against non-violent protestors was an unreasonable use of force inconsistent with the Fourth Amendment to the US Constitution.[83] The case involved a group of protestors who were involved in peaceful environmental demonstrations against the Pacific Lumber Company, locking themselves together using self-releasing lock-down devices known as 'black bears'.[84] The court noted that officers made no attempt to negotiate with the protestors; did not flush out their eyes though the protestors were screaming in pain; and that, with respect to at least some of the protestors, the pepper spray did not cause them to release the lock.[85]

A report published by the US Congressional Service in 2015 cites the judgment of the same year in the case of *Singleton* v. *Darby* in which the Court of Appeals for the Fifth Circuit upheld the use of pepper spray against a group of individuals who were protesting against a pipeline.[86] The court held that the use of pepper spray was not unreasonable because

[81] See, e.g., American Civil Liberties Union of Washington, *Out of Control Seattle's Flawed Response to Protests Against the World Trade Organization*, Special Report, June 2000, pp. 46–47, at: www.aclu-wa.org/sites/default/files/attachments/WTO%20Report%20Web.pdf. The Seattle Police Department's procedures for 'Use of Chemical Agents in Civil Disobedience, Crowd or Riot Situations Involving Unlawful Activity' state: 'The authorized use of chemical agents during civil disobedience, crowd, or riot situations involving unlawful activity shall have as a primary objective one of the following: (1) Prevention of violence. (2) Suppression and dispersal of unlawful assemblies with minimum hazard to the public and law enforcement. (3) To aid in the overcoming of either passive or aggressive resistance to affect arrest. (4) Area or building deprivation to prevent further destruction of property when other means are not practical . . . These devices shall only be deployed subsequent to a verbal dispersal or movement order.' Cited in ibid.

[82] US Court of Appeals (Ninth Circuit), *Headwaters Forest Defense* v. *County of Humboldt*, 240 F.3d 1185 (2000), pp. 1205–06.

[83] According to the Fourth Amendment, 'The right of the people to be secure in their persons, houses, papers, and effects, against unreasonable searches and seizures, shall not be violated . . .'

[84] A 'black bear' is a cylinder with a rod or post welded into the centre.

[85] J. Ryan, 'Pepper Spray', 2006 LLRMI Legal Updates Archive, at: www.llrmi.com/articles/legal_update/pepperspray.shtml#C1.

[86] Thompson, *Police Use of Force: Rules, Remedies, and Reforms*, pp. 12–13.

the state had a significant interest in keeping public roads clear and the police officer faced an 'explosive situation' in which he was greatly outnumbered by the protesters; he provided a warning before using the spray; and pepper spray was likely the least intrusive force available to the officer.[87]

Taser

Design and Use of Conducted Energy Weapons

Many models of Taser® and similar conducted energy weapons (CEWs) use compressed air to fire two darts that trail electric cable back to the weapon's handset. When the darts strike the human body, a 50,000-volt charge is released down the cable, causing the victim's muscles to contract uncontrollably.[88] The weapon causes temporary paralysis.[89] When used in probe-deployment mode,[90] CEWs are designed to temporarily incapacitate a person from a safer distance than some other force options, while reducing the likelihood of death or serious injury.[91] The weapon is considered especially useful in allowing police officers to deal with violent or potentially violent individuals at a safe distance.[92] They are, though, a significant use of force.

[87] US Court of Appeals (Fifth Circuit), *Singleton* v. *Darby*, 609 Fed. Appx. 190 (2015), at p. 195.

[88] Taser runs off 0.0021 amps at average performance.

[89] BBC, 'How the Stun Gun Works', 1 August 2001, at: http://news.bbc.co.uk/2/hi/uk_news/1468188.stm.

[90] In contrast, in drive-stun mode a Taser is discharged without a cartridge in contact with the body rather than fired from a distance. No probes are fired but the Taser causes pain without incapacitating the victim.

[91] 'TASER® Handheld CEW Warnings, Instructions, and Information: Law Enforcement', 1 March 2013, p. 1, at: https://prismic-io.s3.amazonaws.com/tasr%2Fa8e6e721-590b-459b-a741-cd0e6401c340_law-enforcement-warnings.pdf.

[92] See, e.g., Metropolitan Police Service, 'What is Taser?', undated but accessed on 22 January 2016 at: http://content.met.police.uk/Article/What-is-Taser/1400015952958/1400015952958. According to Commander Neil Basu, the national lead on less-lethal weapons, the Taser is an option for use on people who are committing or about to commit extreme violence. In a speech to a conference organised on 18 March 2015 at the Criminal Justice Centre at Queen Mary, University of London by Abi Dymond, then a PhD student at the University of Bristol and the University of Exeter, he affirmed that suspects and police officers are less likely to be injured when a Taser is used, but noted the need for better use of force reporting for both Taser and other weapons. A. Dymond, 'TASER™ Experts Meeting', Notes of the Day, London, 18 March 2015.

CEWs can also be used in drive-stun mode whereby the weapon is placed against a person's body without the cartridge containing the darts/probes and the trigger is pulled causing acute, localised pain (but not incapacitation).[93] As the US Department of Justice (DOJ) has noted: 'The technique also carries a heightened risk of serious harm or injury when used on individuals with mental health disabilities or in crisis.'[94] Indeed, Taser International (since renamed Axon) has issued product warnings to law enforcement about drive-stunning, noting the need for caution and restraint when using the technique on people with mental illnesses:

> Drive-stun use may not be effective on emotionally disturbed persons or others who may not respond to pain due to a mind-body disconnect. Avoid using repeated drive-stuns on such individuals if compliance is not achieved.[95]

The risk of torture or of inflicting other inhumane treatment using a Taser in drive-stun mode is especially severe; there may also be a proportionately higher risk of death, albeit based on limited data.[96]

An important decision on Taser use was handed down by the US Court of Appeals for the Fourth Circuit in January 2016. The Court held that law enforcement officers from the North Carolina village of Pinehurst were entitled to qualified immunity[97] for their actions that led to

[93] A further technique is termed angled drive stun, which 'is achieved when the Taser has been fired towards the intended subject and one probe has missed, or the Taser has been deployed towards the subject and the probes are too close together to incapacitate the subject causing only localised pain, or possibly no reaction at all. In these circumstances if an officer then places the end of the taser in a part of the body away from the probe(s) then it is possible that incapacitation can be achieved'. Association of Chief Police Officers (ACPO) Questions and Answers on Taser, January 2015, at: www.npcc.police.uk/ThePoliceChiefsBlog/201410TaserBlog.aspx.

[94] US DOJ, *Investigation of the Baltimore City Police Department*, 10 August 2016, p. 62, at: www.justice.gov/opa/file/883366/download, citing Police Executive Research Forum & Community Oriented Policing Services, *2011 Electronic Control Weapon Guidelines*, 2001, p. 14.

[95] TASER International, 'TASER® CEW Warnings, Instructions, and Information: Citizen', 15 March 2013, p. 5.

[96] See, e.g., by C. W. Thompson and M. Berman, 'Improper Techniques, Increased Risks: Deaths Have Raised Questions About the Risk of Excessive or Improper Deployment of Tasers', *Washington Post*, 26 November 2015, at: www.washingtonpost.com/sf/investigative/2015/11/26/improper-techniques-increased-risks/.

[97] In US law, qualified immunity 'protects officers who commit constitutional violations but who, in light of clearly established law, could reasonably believe that their actions were lawful'. *Henry* v. *Purnell*, 652 F.3d 524, 531 (4th Cir. 2011).

the death of Ronald Armstrong, an adult male suffering from bipolar disorder and paranoid schizophrenia.[98] They were seeking to re-commit Mr Armstrong involuntarily to an institution consonant with a lawful doctor's order. But the court found that an officer had used unnecessary and disproportionate force by tasering Mr Armstrong five separate times over a period of approximately two minutes in drive stun mode. Indeed, rather than having its desired effect, the tasering increased Armstrong's resistance. In subsequent action by the officers, Armstrong was put in a choke hold and complained he could not breathe. He died shortly thereafter.

In reaching its decision, the Court noted that Mr Armstrong was 'stationary, non-violent, and surrounded by people willing to help return him to the Hospital'.[99] Its finding in a case that involved drive-stun use has broader implications for any taser use. Thus, the Court stated that:

> Immediately tasing a non-criminal, mentally ill individual, who seconds before had been conversational, was not a proportional response . . . Force that imposes serious consequences requires significant circumscription. Our precedent, consequently, makes clear that tasers are proportional force only when deployed in response to a situation in which a reasonable officer would perceive some immediate danger that could be mitigated by using the taser.[100]

As a result of the opinion, the North Carolina Justice Academy, which trains thousands of criminal justice personnel throughout the state, issued a statement to all sheriffs, police chiefs, trainers, school directors, and supervisors in which it affirmed that the Court of Appeals opinion in *Armstrong* v. *Village of Pinehurst*

> dramatically changes the legal landscape governing TASER use by officers. Effective immediately, TASER use as a pain compliance tool against a resisting subject is prohibited by the Fourth Amendment unless the police can articulate "immediate danger" to the officer apart from the fact of resistance alone. This is true whether the TASER is used in probe-deployment or drive-stun mode.[101]

[98] US Court of Appeals (Fourth Circuit), *Estate of Ronald H. Armstrong* v. *Village of Pinehurst and Others* and *Taser International*, Opinion (Case No. 15-1191), 11 January 2016.
[99] Ibid., p. 18. [100] Ibid., pp. 19, 22.
[101] Available at: http://ncja.ncdoj.gov/Armstrong-v-Village-of-Pinehurst.aspx.

Physical Risks from Taser Discharge and Risk Reduction

As with any law enforcement weapon, Taser use may be lawful when it is both necessary and proportionate.[102] This means in practice that a police officer should be confronted with a violent individual or a dangerous suspect, particularly one who is armed, and that the suspected offence should be serious in nature. Other, less hazardous means must be either too hazardous or likely to be ineffective. But while Taser use may be lawful in circumstances where a firearm could not be lawfully used, it is not a mere compliance tool and should never be used gratuitously or in a discriminatory manner. Particular care should be exercised when contemplating discharge against a pregnant woman, the infirm, the elderly, or a child.

The risks from a Taser discharge are both of primary injury from the electricity or the barbs as well as of secondary injury, particularly as a result of falling to the ground without the possibility for the victim to break his/her fall using their hands. Conducted energy weapons should therefore not be used when secondary injuries are likely, for example when the suspect is on a roof, ladder, or wall; could fall on a sharp object or surface; or is restrained or handcuffed.[103] In July 2014, for example, a homeless man with mental health issues was tasered when he was sitting on top of a rooftop billboard in Los Angeles. LAPD officers tried to grab him but he fell to the ground, missing an airbag that had been placed for his protection. He suffered serious head injuries and died later in a nearby medical centre.[104] Taser discharge may also cause flammable

[102] As with firearms, the term *use* refers not only narrowly to actual discharge of a Taser but also to clear threat of use. This includes arcing (where the trigger is squeezed without the cartridge attached and the electric current flows between the two contacts at the end of the weapon) or red-dotting (the laser sighting system allows a police officer to mark the suspect with a red dot). According to the UK Home Office, 'The use of Taser with the most physical impact is "fired" and can result in incapacitation. For the purposes of the police's statistical reporting this is known as the "highest use" of a Taser. When a Taser is "drawn" but not discharged this is known as the "lowest use". The uses "red dot", "arcing" "aimed" and "drawn" are known as "non-discharges" as the Taser does not make contact with the subject.' Home Office, 'Official Statistics: Police use of taser statistics, England and Wales, 2012 to 2013', Published 27 March 2014, at: www.gov.uk/government/publications/police-use-of-taser-statistics-england-and-wales-2012-to-2013/police-use-of-taser-statistics-england-and-wales-2012-to-2013.

[103] Ibid.

[104] 'Skid Row Residents Criticize LAPD after Death of Mentally Ill Man', *Los Angeles Times*, 2 July 2014, at: www.latimes.com/local/lanow/la-me-ln-skid-row-death-20140702-story.html. A subsequent inquiry found that the officer's discharge of his Taser departed from LAPD policy and training, which generally cautions against use against an individual who is danger of falling 'which would likely result in death or serious bodily injury'.

substances to ignite, as a case in the United Kingdom, discussed below, sadly illustrates.

A warning developed for distribution to Taser International's customers notes that 'any use of force, including the use of a CEW, involves risks that a person may get hurt or die due to the effects of the CEW, physical incapacitation, physical exertion, unforeseen circumstances, or individual susceptibilities'.[105] As a consequence, Taser International cautions that law enforcement users should:

- Minimise the number and duration of exposures. (Most human Taser laboratory testing has not exceeded 15 seconds' application, and none has exceeded 45 seconds.)
- Avoid simultaneous Taser exposures.
- Control and restrain the suspect immediately.
- Avoid touching probes or wires during Taser discharge.[106]

According to Taser International, exposure in the chest near the heart 'has a low probability of inducing extra heart beats (cardiac capture). In rare circumstances, cardiac capture could lead to cardiac arrest. When possible, avoid targeting the frontal chest area near the heart to reduce the risk of potential serious injury or death'.[107] Taser International further warns that cardiac capture 'may be more likely in children and thin adults because the heart is usually closer to the . . . discharge . . . Serious complications could also arise in those with impaired heart function or in those with an implanted cardiac pacemaker or defibrillator'.[108]

To reduce the risk of injury, users are recommended to target below the neck for back shots and the lower centre mass (below the chest) for front shots. These 'preferred target areas' increase dart-to-heart distance and reduce cardiac risks.[109] Back shots are considered preferable to front

R. Winton and K. Mather, 'L.A. SWAT Officer Violated Policy in Use of Taser, Police Panel Says', *Los Angeles Times*, 2 May 2015, at: www.latimes.com/local/crime/la-me-taser-fall-20150522-story.html. In October 2015, it was reported that every LAPD officer would be patrolling with a Taser, with a view to restraining use of firearms. F. Stoltze, 'LAPD to Issue Tasers to All Officers', KPCC radio, 5 October 2015, at: www.scpr.org/news/2015/10/05/54819/lapd-to-issue-tasers-to-all-officers/.

105 'TASER® Handheld CEW Warnings, Instructions, and Information: Law Enforcement', 1 March 2013, p. 1; see also www.taser.com/legal.

106 'TASER® Handheld CEW Warnings, Instructions, and Information: Law Enforcement', 1 March 2013, p. 2.

107 Ibid. 108 Ibid. 109 Ibid., p. 3.

shots when practicable. In addition, users should generally avoid targeting sensitive areas of the body such as the face, eyes, head, throat, chest area (area of the heart), breast, groin, genitals, or known pre-existing injury areas.[110] Taser also cautions that use against a pregnant, infirm, elderly, or low body-mass index person, or on a small child could increase the risk of death or serious injury; CEW use 'has not been scientifically tested' on these populations. Taser warns that CEWs should be used on such people 'only if the situation justifies an increased risk'.[111]

National Research and Guidance on Taser Use

Particular problems with Taser use across police services include unnecessary discharge, discharge in violation of the principle of proportionality, or discriminatory use against ethnic minorities, particularly in Canada, the United Kingdom, and the United States.

In its 2015 report on the actions of the Ferguson Police Department (FPD) in Missouri, the DOJ found that the FPD engaged in a pattern of excessive force in violation of the Fourth Amendment to the US Constitution, often using Tasers as compliance tools. 'Many officers are quick to escalate encounters with subjects they perceive to be disobeying their orders or resisting arrest. They have come to rely on ECWs [electronic control weapons], specifically Tasers®, where less force — or no force at all — would do.'[112]

As examples, the DOJ cites the August 2010 incident in which a lieutenant used a Taser in drive-stun mode against an African-American woman in Ferguson City Jail because she had refused to remove her bracelets. The lieutenant resorted to the weapon even though five officers were present and the woman posed no physical threat.[113] In November 2013, a correctional officer fired an ECW at an African-American woman's chest

> because she would not follow his verbal commands to walk toward a cell. The woman, who had been arrested for driving while intoxicated, had yelled an insulting remark at the officer, but her conduct amounted to verbal noncompliance or passive resistance at most. Instead of attempting hand controls or seeking assistance from a state trooper who was also present, the correctional officer deployed the ECW because the woman was "not doing as she was told".[114]

[110] Ibid. [111] Ibid.

[112] US DOJ (Civil Rights Division), *Investigation of the Ferguson Police Department*, Washington DC, 4 March 2015, p. 28.

[113] Ibid., p. 29. [114] Ibid.

This is despite the fact that the FPD had a specific policy on Taser use which describes the weapon as 'designed to overcome active aggression or overt actions of assault'.[115] The policy states that an ECW 'will never be deployed punitively or for purposes of coercion. It is to be used as a way of averting a potentially injurious or dangerous situation'.[116] The DOJ further recalls that guidance produced by its Office of Community Oriented Policing Services, and the Police Executive Research Forum in 2011 warns that ECWs are '"less-lethal" and not "nonlethal weapons"' and 'have the potential to result in a fatal outcome'.[117]

The DOJ concluded that:[118]

> It is in part FPD officers' approach to policing that leads them to violate the Constitution and FPD's own policies. Officers across the country encounter drunkenness, passive defiance, and verbal challenges. But in Ferguson, officers have not been trained or incentivized to use de-escalation techniques to avoid or minimize force in these situations. Instead, they respond with impatience, frustration, and disproportionate force. FPD's weak oversight of officer use of force, described in greater detail below, facilitates this abuse. Officers should be required to view the ECW as one tool among many, and "a weapon of need, not a tool of convenience."[119] Effective policing requires that officers not depend on ECWs, or any type of force, "at the expense of diminishing the fundamental skills of communicating with subjects and de-escalating tense encounters."[120]

Similar problems were recorded by the DOJ in its 2016 report on the Baltimore City Police Department (BPD). The DOJ observed that force was used disproportionately against African Americans by the BPD. This trend was consistent across different types of 'non-deadly' force, including Tasers, 'the most common weapon used by BPD officers'.[121] In one incident cited by the DOJ,

> an officer approached an African-American man walking on a sidewalk in November 2010 in an area the officer stated was "known for violent crime and narcotics distribution." When the officer "attempted to interview him

[115] FPD General Order 499.00. [116] FPD General Order 499.04.

[117] Police Executive Research Forum and US DOJ Office of Community Oriented Policing Services, *2011 Electronic Control Weapon Guidelines*, March 2011, p. 12.

[118] Department of Justice (Civil Rights Division), *Investigation of the Ferguson Police Department*, p. 31.

[119] Ibid., p. 11. [120] Ibid., p. 12.

[121] US DOJ, *Investigation of the Baltimore City Police Department*, 10 August 2016, p. 62.

> about his activities," the man fled. According to the report the officer filed the day of the incident, he chased the man and deployed his taser because the man "refused to comply with my orders to stop." The taser prongs hit the man on the back but failed to stop him. As the chase continued, the officer reloaded his taser cartridge and again fired probes into the fleeing man's back. After catching up with the man, the officer used his taser yet again—this time in drive stun mode—detained the man for investigation, and conducted a weapons frisk. The report provides no reason to believe the man was armed . . . The frisk and investigation found no weapon or other evidence of wrongdoing. The man—after being tased multiple times, taken to the ground, and frisked—was released without charges.[122]

More broadly across the United States, *The Guardian* newspaper reported in November 2015 that in 29 US police departments where a death had occurred after the weapon was deployed during the year, an overwhelming majority did not respect international good practice:

- Twenty police departments do not caution officers not to apply more than three shocks other than in exceptional circumstances
- None of the twenty-nine departments seemingly mandates use-of-force investigations into incidents where an ECW is deployed for more than 15 seconds
- Twenty-two departments do not advise against discharging an ECW if the sole justification is that the suspect is fleeing
- Twenty-five departments do not advise against using an ECW's 'drive stun' mode
- Thirteen departments do not explicitly restrict officers from deploying their ECWs if a suspect is already in handcuffs and does not pose an exceptional threat.[123]

Eight departments do not even explicitly require officers to give a warning, when possible, before the ECW is deployed.

Although far behind the United States in Taser use, these weapons are increasingly being used by authorised police officers in the United Kingdom. In 2009, police forces introduced specially trained Taser units and between 2009 and 2013 Taser use increased by 232 per cent.[124] Since its

[122] Ibid., p. 32.

[123] O. Laughland, J. Lartey, and C. McCarthy, 'Counted: Bolts from the Blue', *The Guardian*, 5 November 2015, at: www.theguardian.com/us-news/2015/nov/05/police-tasers-deaths-the-counted?CMP=Share_iOSApp_Other.

[124] Foreword to Independent Police Complaints Commission (IPCC), 'Learning the Lessons, Bulletin 21: Taser', July 2014, at: www.ipcc.gov.uk/learning-the-lessons.

introduction, the number of operations in which the use of police firearms was authorised decreased every year from 2007–08 to 2012–13.[125] Despite this positive trend, the Independent Police Complaints Commission (IPCC), which investigates complaints against the police, has identified particular concern about the use of Taser in 'drive-stun' mode, Taser use on people with mental health difficulties, the young and other vulnerable people, and Taser use in confined spaces such as a custody cell.[126] The IPCC's study into police use of force in the United Kingdom, published in March 2016, noted claims that blacks were four times as likely as whites to have a Taser used on them.[127]

In October 2015, the IPCC had called for more guidance to be given to officers in the use of Tasers after an inquest jury concluded that the firing of one of the weapons was the most likely cause of a man becoming engulfed in flames and suffering fatal burns. A police constable discharged a Taser at Andrew Pimlott during an incident at his parents' home after he doused himself with petrol. PC Peter Hodgkinson claimed that he fired the stun gun in an attempt to stop Mr Pimlott harming himself because he held a lit match.[128]

In Canada, an inquiry was set up following the death on 14 October 2007 of Robert Dziekański, a 40-year-old Polish immigrant to Canada who was tasered five times by Royal Canadian Mounted Police (RCMP) officers during his arrest at Vancouver Airport. The incident was captured on amateur video, leading to considerable public concern. The Braidwood Inquiry was established by the Provincial Government of British Columbia and headed by a retired Court of Appeal of British Columbia judge, Thomas Braidwood QC, to 'inquire into and report on the use of conducted energy weapons' and to 'inquire into and report on the death of Mr. Dziekański'. An initial report (Phase 1, looking at CEWs in general and Tasers in particular) was issued in June 2009 while the final inquiry report (Phase 2, assessing in detail the circumstances of Mr. Dziekański's death) was published in June 2010. The final report concluded that the RCMP officers were not justified in using a Taser

[125] IPCC, 'IPCC Review of Taser Complaints and Incidents: 2004–2013', 2014, p. 3.

[126] Ibid., p. 12.

[127] IPCC, *Police Use of Force: Evidence from Complaints, Investigations and Public Perception*, IPCC Report, London, March 2016, p. 2.

[128] S. Morris, 'Police Watchdog Calls for Taser Guidance after Inquest into Fire Death', *The Guardian*, 1 October 2015, at: www.theguardian.com/world/2015/oct/01/police-watchdog-calls-for-taser-guidance-after-inquest-into-fireball-death.

against Mr. Dziekański and that the officers later deliberately misrepresented their actions to investigators.[129]

The report noted that Tasers have the capacity to kill in certain situations, and Justice Braidwood recommended they be used only in cases involving bodily harm or the threat of bodily harm. He called for standardised training for police officers, who should be required to file detailed reports whenever a Taser is deployed, and argued any officer carrying a Taser should also be equipped with an automatic defibrillator. The report also stated that Tasers should be subjected to independent testing, warning the government and police departments not to rely on the weapon's manufacturer, Taser International, to decide when and how they should be used. In 2012, Mr Braidwood stated publicly that he was satisfied with the government's response in all of those areas.[130]

Despite the concerns about Tasers, the report affirmed that the weapons are a valuable less-lethal alternative for police. Justice Braidwood stated that someone had said to him, 'We should ban Tasers' to which he replied, 'Well, then we'd just shoot them in the stomach. It's the balance. And I think we've got the balance here.'[131]

Criminal Law Cases

On 10 July 2015, Sandra Bland, an African-American from the Chicago area who had come to Texas for a job at her alma mater, Prairie View A&M University, was arrested after she was stopped while driving a car for failure to signal a lane change. The incident in Prairie View, a town about 50 miles north-west of Houston, was captured on the police dashboard camera. It showed the state trooper, Officer Brian T. Encinia, pulling Ms. Bland over and their encounter escalated into a physical altercation after she refused his order to put out a cigarette. Officer Encinia threatened her with a Taser: 'I will light you up', he said

[129] 'Deep Flaws in Canada's "Braidwood Inquiry" Give Tasers a Bum Rap, Says FSRC', Force Science News No. 130, undated but accessed on 25 January 2016 at: www.forcescience.org/fsnews/130.html; British Columbia Ministry of Public Safety and Solicitor General, 'Province Takes Immediate Action on Taser Report', Press release 2009PSSG0005-000145, 23 July 2009, at: www2.news.gov.bc.ca/news_releases_2009-2013/2009PSSG0005-000145.htm.

[130] Canadian Press, 'Thomas Braidwood, Taser Inquiry Chair, "Very Impressed" With BC's Response', *Huffpost British Columbia*, 16 October 2012, at: www.huffingtonpost.ca/2012/10/16/taser-inquiry-chair-impressed-bc-response_n_1971105.html.

[131] Ibid.

as he pointed the stun gun at her.[132] Neither the brandishing of the ECW nor the confrontation over the cigarette was mentioned in Trooper Encinia's incident report. Ms Bland was found hanging in detention three days later.[133] In March 2016, Mr Encinia was indicted by a grand jury for perjury. In March 2016, Mr Encinia was fired from the state police.[134]

In October 2015, another incident in Prairie View gave rise to concern about ECW use by law enforcement officials. A Texas city councilman, Johnathan Miller, was stunned with a Taser while on his knees, and then arrested outside his Prairie View home. A video of Mr Miller's evening arrest shows him on his knees before being tasered. Prairie View police contended that Mr Miller had pestered them with questions and refused to step back as they questioned his house guests about suspicious activity in the neighbourhood.[135] In January 2016, a grand jury indicted the officer for his use of the Taser for official oppression, a misdemeanour. Official oppression can be a charge filed against a police officer or another public servant on accusations that individual subjected another to mistreatment or arrest he or she knows is unlawful. If convicted, the officer faces up to a year in jail and a fine of up to $4,000.[136]

Civil Law Cases

There has also been considerable civil law jurisprudence in the United States about Taser use.[137] The basic US legal standard for determining legality of any use of force by a law enforcement official is whether his or

[132] D. Montgomery, 'Sandra Bland Was Threatened With Taser, Police Video Shows', *New York Times*, 21 July 2015, at: www.nytimes.com/2015/07/22/us/sandra-bland-was-combative-texas-arrest-report-says.html?_r=0.

[133] Ibid.

[134] Associated Press, 'Texas Trooper Indicted in Sandra Bland Traffic Stop and Arrest is Formally Fired', *The Guardian*, 3 March 2016, at: www.theguardian.com/us-news/2016/mar/02/texas-trooper-fired-sandra-bland-death?CMP=share_btn_link.

[135] N. Hensley, 'Texas Councilman Stunned, Arrested While Defending Friends Being Questioned by Prairie View Police', *New York Daily News*, Updated on 12 October 2015, at: www.nydailynews.com/news/national/texas-councilman-stunned-arrested-defending-friends-article-1.2392950.

[136] Associated Press, 'Officer Indicted for Using Taser on Prairie View City Council Member', *ABC News*, 25 January 2016, at: http://abc13.com/news/officer-indicted-for-using-taser-on-prairie-view-city-council-member/1173392/.

[137] As at 2013, more than 12,000 law enforcement agencies in the United States were reportedly using Tasers. US Department of Justice, Bureau of Justice Statistics, *Local Police Departments, 2013: Equipment and Technology*, 2013, available at: www.bjs.gov/content/pub/pdf/lpd13et.pdf.

her actions were objectively reasonable: the assessment must be made from the perspective of a reasonable officer on the scene, including what the officer knew at the time. This standard was set out in the US Supreme Court decision in *Graham* v. *Connor* in 1989.[138] In June 2015, in *Kingsley* v. *Hendrickson*, the Supreme Court held that the Seventh Circuit's decision in the case that the law required a subjective inquiry into the officers' state of mind (i.e. whether the officers actually intended to violate, or recklessly disregarded, Mr Kingsley's rights) was incorrect. Under the relevant provision in the US code,[139] to prevail on an excessive force claim the applicant had only to show 'that the force purposely or knowingly used against him was objectively unreasonable'.[140]

Mr Michael Kingsley was a pre-trial detainee who was forcibly removed from his cell by recourse to a Taser (among other uses of force). The Court determined that if an officer's Taser goes off by accident, or if an officer unintentionally trips and falls on a detainee, causing him harm, an excessive force claim will not be successful. 'But if the use of force is deliberate — i.e., purposeful or knowing — the pretrial detainee's claim may proceed.'[141] The Court reaffirmed that the assessment of objective reasonableness turns on the 'facts and circumstances of each particular case', as set out in *Graham* v. *Connor*, with the requisite determination to be made 'from the perspective of a reasonable officer on the scene, including what the officer knew at the time, not with the 20/20 vision of hindsight'.[142]

According to the Court of Appeals for the Eighth Circuit (covering Arkansas, Iowa, Minnesota, Missouri, Nebraska, and North Dakota), use of a Taser is unlikely to be lawful when fired against 'nonviolent misdemeanants who do not flee or actively resist arrest and pose little or no threat to the security of the officer'.[143] Whether passive resistance to a law enforcement official's instructions justifies use of a Taser under international law is more debatable. Research for the US Congressional Service affirms, though, that most decisions in the courts permit the use of a Taser against such passive resisters.[144] In *Buckley* v. *Haddock*, for

[138] US Supreme Court, *Graham* v. *Connor*, 490 US 386, 396 (1989). [139] 42 USC §1983.

[140] US Supreme Court, *Kingsley* v. *Hendrickson and Others*, Certiorari to the US Court of Appeals for the Seventh Circuit (Illinois), Case No. 14-6368, 22 June 2015, at: www.supremecourt.gov/opinions/14pdf/14-6368_m6hn.pdf.

[141] Ibid., p. 6. [142] Ibid., pp. 6–7, citing *Graham* v. *Connor*, 396.

[143] US Court of Appeals (Eighth Circuit), *Brown* v. *City of Golden Valley*, 574 F.3d 491, 499 (2009).

[144] Thompson, *Police Use of Force: Rules, Remedies, and Reforms*, p. 10.

example, the Eleventh Circuit (covering Alabama, Florida, and Georgia) upheld the use of a Taser on a man who fell to the ground after being handcuffed and refused to get up after several requests from the officer. After giving the man several warnings, the officer tasered him several times. In rejecting the claim, the court put significant weight on the government's interest, noting that: 'The government has an interest in arrests being completed efficiently and without waste of limited resources: police time and energy that may be needed elsewhere at any moment.'[145]

The report for the US Congressional Service also argues – based on its analysis of US jurisprudence – that use of a Taser against individuals suffering from mental illness is not subject to a heightened standard under US law. It cites a District Court for the Southern District of Ohio holding that a police officer was justified in using a Taser on an elderly suspect suffering from Alzheimer's disease who had 'refused to comply' with the officer's orders. Once the officer decided to engage the suspect, the court accepted that 'he had to continue, and it seems the only way he was able to do this was with a taser'. The age or potential mental illness of a suspect did not require a heightened use-of-force standard.[146] Similarly, in a New York district court decision, the court found that the plaintiff had cited no legal authority in support of the assertion that the use of a Taser against a physically or mentally disabled person is presumptively unreasonable or excessive.[147]

In contrast, in a Texas district court case, the court noted that the Lewisville Police Department's General Order on dealing with the mentally ill counselled officers to approach in a 'low-profile manner'.[148] In a Texas court of appeals case, the court upheld a jury's award of US$3 million in a wrongful death lawsuit after individual was handcuffed and shocked eighteen times with a Taser by law enforcement officials who were attempting to take him to a mental health institution. The appeals court ruled that no reasonable officer could believe that it was legally permissible to use pain compliance measures to stop someone who was

[145] US Court of Appeals (Eleventh Circuit), *Buckley* v. *Haddock*, 292 Fed. Appx. 791, 794 (2008).

[146] Thompson, *Police Use of Force: Rules, Remedies, and Reforms*, pp. 10–11.

[147] US District Court for the Northern District of New York, *Gordon* v. *County of Onondaga*, Case No. #5:09-CV-1182 (2014).

[148] US District Court for the Eastern District of Texas, *Seyfried* v. *City of Lewisville Police Department and Others*, Civil Action No. 4:13cv560, 28 August 2014.

mentally ill from flinching in response to electric shock. The decedent was compliant and also already restrained, so he posed no threat.[149]

Rubber and Plastic Bullets

Design and Use of Rubber and Plastic Bullets

Rubber and plastic bullets are used particularly during riots and should generally only be countenanced when life or serious injury are at serious risk. Rubber bullets, which are technically referred to as baton rounds, are bullets made entirely from rubber or which contain metal (e.g. a steel core). Plastic bullets are hollow cylinders made of plastic, for instance PVC. The concept originated in Singapore in the 1880s, where pieces of wooden broom handle were fired at rioters. Hong Kong police then developed rounds made of teak, but they splintered and caused serious wounds.[150]

The UK Ministry of Defence introduced a rubber bullet in Northern Ireland in July 1970, specifically designed for use outside stone-throwing range.[151] In 1970–75, the UK military fired 55,000 rounds of 15cm rubber bullets there, reportedly killing thirteen people at a lethal rate of 1 per 18,000 rounds and resulting in a severe injury rate of 1 in 800.[152] In 2013, government papers declassified from 1977 revealed that the Ministry of Defence was aware rubber bullets were more dangerous than had been publicly disclosed. The documents contained legal advice to the Ministry to settle a case concerning a child who had been blinded in 1972. The papers revealed that further tests would reveal serious problems with the bullets, including that they were tested 'in a shorter time than was ideal', that they 'could be lethal', and that they 'could and did cause serious injuries'.[153]

Despite subsequent advances in bullet design and technology, autopsy reports of Palestinian civilian fatalities from 1987 to 1993 concluded that rubber bullets fired by the Israeli military had killed at least twenty

[149] US Court of Appeals of Texas, Houston (Fourteenth District), *Harris County, Texas* v. *Nagel*, Case No. #14-09-00780-CV, 349 S.W.3d 769 (2011).

[150] D. Geere, 'How Do Rubber and Plastic Bullets Work?', *Wired*, 9 August 11, at: www.wired.co.uk/news/archive/2011-08/09/rubber-bullets.

[151] Ibid.

[152] C. Conger, 'Can Rubber Bullets Kill You?', *Discovery News*, 15 August 2011, at: http://news.discovery.com/tech/can-rubber-bullets-kill-you-110815.htm.

[153] 'Rubber Bullets: Army Kept Real Dangers in NI Hidden'. BBC, 11 June 2013, at: www.bbc.com/news/uk-northern-ireland-foyle-west-22848421.

people.[154] A study published in *The Lancet* in 2000, which analysed the Israeli military's use of rubber bullets against Palestinians, concluded that: 'Inaccuracy of rubber bullets and improper aiming and range of use resulted in severe injury and death in a substantial number of people. This ammunition should therefore not be considered a safe method of crowd control.'[155] Of 152 casualties, the study highlighted 201 visible injuries inflicted by rubber bullets on the limbs, as well as the head, neck, face, and chest, indicating improper weapon handling since rubber bullets should be aimed at the lower half of a person's body to avoid causing serious harm.[156]

In 1975, rubber bullets were replaced in Northern Ireland by plastic bullets. Over 35 years (1970–2005) a total of about 125,000 rubber and plastic bullets were fired – an average of ten per day.[157] According to the Police Service of Northern Ireland (PSNI), the PSNI do not use baton rounds nor have they purchased or stockpiled any such ammunition in 2009–12. 'The technology used by PSNI since 2005 is referred to as Attenuating Energy Projectile (AEP).'[158] The AEP may also be used on the British mainland. According to the UK's College of Policing, a professional body for policing in the United Kingdom, the AEP forms part of a weapons system approved for use by members of the police service or the armed forces in the United Kingdom. Operational use within the police is limited to authorised officers who have been specifically trained in use of the system. The approved projectile is a 37mm soft-nosed impact bullet, designated the L60A2.[159]

French police have used a particular variant of rubber bullet, the FlashBall, designed by a French ballistics expert as an alternative to conventional firearms. According to Verney-Carron, its FlashBall its 'non-lethal 44mm-gauge weapon' has a 'dissuasive look' is 'ready to be

154 Conger, 'Can Rubber Bullets Kill You?'.

155 A. Mahajna, N. Aboud, I. Harbaji, A. Agbaria, Z. Lankovsky, M. Michaelson, D. Fisher, and M. M. Krausz, 'Blunt and penetrating injuries caused by rubber bullets during the Israeli-Arab conflict in October, 2000: a retrospective study', *The Lancet*, Vol. 359, No. 9320 (2000), pp. 1795–1800.

156 Conger, 'Can Rubber Bullets Kill You?'.

157 A. G. Williams, 'Product Survey: Less Lethal Guns and Ammunition', *Jane's Police Products Review*, October/November 2007.

158 PSNI, 'Baton Rounds', Freedom of Information Request No. F-2012-02259, at: www.psni.police.uk/baton_rounds.pdf.

159 College of Policing, 'Armed Policing: Attenuating Energy Projectile', Last modified on 11 December 2014, at: www.app.college.police.uk/app-content/armed-policing/attenuating-energy-projectiles/.

engaged in an instant' and is 'versatile, adaptable, but always effective'.[160] It was reportedly exported to Canada, Macao (China), Mexico, and Venezuela.[161] In December 2010, a 40-year-old man in Marseilles died after being hit by a FlashBall.[162] In 2013, France's Human Rights Ombudsman published a report calling for the use of the FlashBall to be more tightly restricted.[163] In June 2015, following widespread criticism and falling sales Verner-Carron claimed it was considering withdrawing its product from the market.[164]

In October 2014, rubber bullets were used against Everton football fans who had clashed with French police before the club's match in Lille. A spokesman told the BBC that police had 'missiles thrown at them' after arresting a fan in the city's main square for selling drugs. Officers acted in self-defence, using a stun grenade and rubber bullets to 'drive back the rioters'.[165] One of the reported victims was a 66-year-old grandfather, who was struck on the temple. He was taken to hospital but survived.[166]

Tear Gas

Design and Use of Tear Gas

Tear gas is a generic name for a variety of lachrymatory agents. Tear gas has been used by police forces around the world for many years. Regulations on its use depend on the form in which it is used: either in the form of sprays or grenades shot from a launcher. In contrast to pepper spray,

[160] See: www.verney-carron-security.com/en/.

[161] I. de Foucaud, 'Le fabricant du Flash-Ball défend son produit "made in France"', *Le Figaro*, 29 May 2013, at: www.lefigaro.fr/societes/2013/05/29/20005-20130529ARTFIG00477-le-fabricant-du-flash-ball-defend-son-produit-made-in-france.php.

[162] Agence France-Presse, 'L'homme blessé par un tir de Flash-Ball succombe à ses blessures', *Le Monde*, 13 December 2010, at: www.lemonde.fr/societe/article/2010/12/13/l-homme-blesse-par-un-tir-de-flash-ball-succombe-a-ses-blessures_1452653_3224.html.

[163] C. Cornevin, 'L'utilisation trop fréquente du Taser et du Flash-Ball dénoncée', *Le Figaro*, 28 May 2013, at: www.lefigaro.fr/actualite-france/2013/05/28/01016–20130528ARTFIG00424-l-utilisation-trop-frequente-du-taser-et-le-flash-ball-denoncee.php.

[164] Y. Petiteaux, 'Retrait du Flash-ball: Verney-Carron s'inquiète pour son avenir', *La Tribune*, 24 June 2015, at: http://acteursdeleconomie.latribune.fr/strategie/defense-aeronautique/2015-06-24/retrait-du-flash-ball-verney-carron-s-inquiete-pour-son-avenir.html.

[165] BBC, 'Rubber Bullets Used on Everton "Rioters" in Lille, Say police', 24 October 2014, at: www.bbc.com/news/uk-england-merseyside-29754598.

[166] C. Carter, 'Grandfather Shot in the Head with "Rubber Bullet" During Trouble before Football Match in France', *Daily Mail Online*, 27 October 2014, at: www.dailymail.co.uk/news/article-2809510/Grandfather-shot-head-rubber-bullet-trouble-football-match-France.html#ixzz3yGHeqrx9.

grenades fired from canisters are generally intended for use at a distance of tens or even hundreds of metres, in particular to disperse crowds. In addition to the effects of the gas, if the grenade launcher is improperly used, the grenade can kill or cause serious injuries.[167]

As the European Court of Human Rights has noted, it is 'well-known' that use of tear gas can temporarily cause 'breathing difficulties, nausea, vomiting, irritation of the respiratory tract, irritation of the tear ducts and eyes, spasms, chest pains, dermatitis and allergies. In high doses it can cause necrosis of the tissue in the respiratory tract and the digestive system, pulmonary oedema and internal bleeding (haemorrhaging of the suprarenal glands)'.[168] The most common toxic chemicals reported to be held for riot-control purposes by states parties to the Chemical Weapons Convention have been CS (the most commonly used),[169] CN,[170] and CR[171] (retained by the United Kingdom for counterterrorism purposes).[172] The vomiting agent DM (also known as adamsite), which was previously used as a riot control agent, has been withdrawn from service by most states that held it due to its high level of toxicity.[173] Some states consider malodorants, such as the Skunk, as a riot control agent.[174]

While the Chemical Weapons Convention prohibits the use of riot control agents as a method of warfare,[175] their use for law enforcement, including domestic riot control, is not *a priori* unlawful.[176] Even in such cases, however, their use must comply with the general LOLE principles of necessity and proportionality.[177] Furthermore, there are particular risks associated with certain contexts, such as use in confined spaces,[178] and against certain categories of individual, particularly the very

167 ECtHR, *Abdullah Yaşa and Others* v. *Turkey*, Judgment (Second Section), 16 July 2013 (as rendered final on 16 October 2013), §29.

168 Ibid., §30.

169 [(2-chlorophenyl)-methylene] propanedinitrile.

170 2-chloro-1-phenyl-ethanone.

171 Dibenz-(b,f)1:4-oxazepine.

172 Crowley, *Chemical Control*, p. 42.

173 See, e.g., R. G. Sutherland, 'Chemical and Biochemical Nonlethal Weapons: Political and Technical Aspects', *SIPRI Policy Paper 26*, Stockholm International Peace Research Institute, Stockholm, 2008, p. 15.

174 See Crowley, *Chemical Control*, pp. 44–46.

175 Art. I(5), 1992 Chemical Weapons Convention.

176 Art. II(9), 1992 Chemical Weapons Convention.

177 See, e.g., ECtHR, *Abdullah Yaşa and Others* v. *Turkey*, §50.

178 See Crowley, *Chemical Control*, p. 48. He cites research whereby of 34 people exposed to CS gas in a closed area, 23 had respiratory problems one hour after the end of exposure. In five subjects, problems persisted for ten months afterwards. Y. Karagama, J. Newton, and C. Newbegin, 'Short Term and Long Term Physical Effects of Exposure to CS Spray', *Journal of the Royal Society of Medicine*, Vol. 94, No. 4 (2003), pp. 172–74.

young[179] or elderly or those with breathing difficulties.[180] Michael Crowley also notes concern as to the differing composition, concentrations, and strength of the active chemical agents included in riot-control agents used by law enforcement personnel.[181]

Human Rights Caselaw

As noted above, the dangers from tear gas come not only from the chemical compound itself but also from the canisters themselves. In July 2014, the European Court issued its judgment in the *Ataykaya* case.[182] In March 2006, as he was leaving his place of work, the applicant's son found himself in the middle of a demonstration and was struck in the head by one of several tear-gas canisters fired by the security forces. He died a few minutes later. Administrative and criminal investigations were carried out, but they failed to identify the person who had fired the fatal shot.[183]

At the relevant time, Turkish law had not specifically regulated the use of less-lethal weapons, such as tear-gas canisters, during demonstrations or any guidelines concerning their use. Such a situation, the Court argued, did not provide the level of protection 'by law' of the right to life that was required in modern democratic societies in Europe.[184] With regard to the general measures required of Turkey, the Court stressed the need for strengthened safeguards 'without further delay' to minimise the risks of death and injury associated with the use of tear-gas canisters.[185]

In 2013, the Court had judged a similar case but in which the applicant had survived.[186] Following the deaths of fourteen members of the PKK (the Kurdistan Workers' Party) during an armed clash on 24 March

[179] In October 2015, it was reported that an eight-month-old Palestinian baby died after inhaling teargas in a village near Bethlehem. The baby, Ramadan Mohammad Faisal Thawabta, was said by the Palestinian Ministry of Health to have suffocated inside his family home in Beit Fajjar, a village south of Bethlehem. K. Shuttleworth, 'Baby Dies in West Bank after Inhaling Teargas, Says Palestinian Ministry', *The Guardian*, 30 October 2015, at: www.theguardian.com/world/2015/oct/30/baby-dies-west-bank-inhaling-tear gas-palestinian-ministry-israel?CMP=Share_iOSApp_Other.

[180] See Crowley, *Chemical Control*, p. 46. [181] Ibid.

[182] ECtHR, *Ataykaya* v. *Turkey*, Judgment (Second Section), 22 July 2014, at: http://hudoc .echr.coe.int/eng#{"itemid":["001-145973"]}.

[183] ECtHR, Information Note on the Court's case-law No. 176, July 2014, p. 9, at: www.echr.coe.int/Documents/CLIN_2014_07_176_ENG.pdf.

[184] Ibid., p. 10. [185] Ibid.

[186] ECtHR, *Abdullah Yaşa and Others* v. *Turkey*, Judgment (Second Section), 16 July 2013 (as rendered final on 16 October 2013).

2006, numerous unlawful demonstrations took place in Diyarbakır between 28 and 31 March 2006, during which eleven demonstrators died. In addition to Mr Ataykaya whose case before the European Court is described above, Mr M. Mizrak was killed by a tear-gas grenade in the course of the demonstrations. Abdullah Yaşa, then a 13-year-old boy, was injured in the nose by a tear-gas grenade fired by the police while he was allegedly on his way to his aunt's house. He was taken to the Diyarbakır public hospital the same day. Ten days later he left hospital after undergoing an operation for a maxillo-facial trauma on the day of his arrival, according to the discharge report.[187]

The Court stated its view that 'firing a tear-gas grenade along a direct, flat trajectory by means of a launcher cannot be regarded as an appropriate police action as it could potentially cause serious, or indeed fatal injuries, whereas a high-angle shot would generally constitute the appropriate approach, since it prevents people from being injured or killed in the event of an impact'.[188] It held that it had 'clearly not been established' that the use of force against Mr Yaşa was in the circumstances an appropriate response 'or was proportionate to the aim pursued, namely to disperse a non-peaceful gathering. In fact, the severity of the injuries noted to the applicant's head could not have been commensurate with the strict use by the police officers of the force necessitated by his behaviour.'[189] The Court found a violation of the right to humane treatment protected in Article 3 of the ECHR.[190]

[187] Ibid., §§6–8. [188] Ibid., §48. [189] Ibid., §50. [190] Ibid., §51.

6

Facilitating Peaceful Protest and Ensuring Crowd Safety during Assemblies

'The dogs, the tear gas . . . It haven't gotten no better.'

James Cias, 61, Ferguson, Missouri (2014)[1]

Introduction

The right to engage in peaceful protest is a fundamental human right integral to any democracy and an essential contributor to the prevention of violence. As two United Nations (UN) special rapporteurs wrote in 2016 in relation to peaceful protest, 'The ability to assemble and act collectively is vital to democratic, economic, social, and personal development, to the expression of ideas, and to fostering engaged citizenry.'[2] Assemblies, they affirmed, 'can make a positive contribution to the development of democratic systems, and alongside elections, play a fundamental role in public participation, holding governments accountable and expressing the will of the people as part of the democratic processes'.[3]

An 'assembly', generally understood, is an intentional and temporary gathering in a private or public space for a specific purpose, and could take the form of demonstrations, meetings, strikes, processions, rallies, or sit-ins with the purpose of voicing grievances, aspirations, or celebrations.[4] The notion extends to sporting events and music concerts. And

[1] Cited in A. Nazaryan, 'Words and Images from Ferguson', *Newsweek*, 18 August 2014, at: http://europe.newsweek.com/photos-quotes-ferguson-missouri-265502. Mr Cias grew up in Mississippi during the Civil Rights era.

[2] 'Joint Report of the Special Rapporteur on the Rights to Freedom of Peaceful Assembly and of Association and the Special Rapporteur on Extrajudicial, Summary or Arbitrary Executions on the Proper Management of Assemblies', UN doc. A/HRC/31/66, 4 February 2016, §5 (hereafter, 2016 Joint UN Report on Peaceful Protest).

[3] Ibid.

[4] 'Report of the Special Rapporteur on the Rights to Freedom of Peaceful Assembly and of Association, Maina Kiai', UN doc. A/HRC/20/27, 21 May 2012, §24.

though an assembly is considered to be a 'temporary' gathering, it can include extended sit-ins and 'occupy'-style movements.[5] Although not strictly a form of assembly, analogous protests occur online and especially in social media.

Although protest is only one form of assembly, it is extremely widely exercised. One website that tracks protests based on international media news stories, the Global Database of Events, Language, and Tone (GDELT), found that almost 250 million protests were held around the world between 1979 and mid-2013.[6] The GDELT Event Database seeks to record and geo-reference every riot and protest that occurs.[7] As Article 19, an international non-governmental organisation dedicated to freedom of expression, noted in 2014:

> Throughout history, protests have played a crucial role in overcoming severe repression and demanding democratic and accountable governments – such as the fight against colonialism, labour struggles and strikes, the civil rights movement, anti-apartheid and anti-communism movements, the fall of communism, women challenging patriarchy, anti-war and anti-capitalist mobilisations, protests against "stolen elections" – and often become a default political action of how society seeks to change social, political and economic systems. Protests in the first months of 2014 in Venezuela, Brazil, Mexico, Russia, Ukraine, Bosnia and Herzegovina and Taiwan show this trend is not slowing.[8]

This chapter addresses the policing of protests as follows. The following section summarises the human rights framework applicable to enjoyment of peaceful protest, including the rights to freedom of peaceful assembly and of association. The following section looks at the legality of police use of force during protests, using the three categories employed in the 1990 Basic Principles on the Use of Force and Firearms by Law Enforcement Officials: lawful and peaceful assemblies; unlawful but non-violent assemblies; and 'violent' assemblies.

Separate sections then discuss how the right to protest is exercised in a number of national jurisdictions, notably the United States (US), which

[5] 2016 Joint UN Report on Peaceful Protest, §10.

[6] Results reported in J. D. Stuster, 'From Cairo to Wall Street to the West Bank, Plotting a World of Upheaval', *Foreign Policy*, 23 August 2013, at: http://foreignpolicy.com/2013/08/23/mapped-every-protest-on-the-planet-since-1979/.

[7] See: http://gdeltproject.org/.

[8] Article 19, 'The "Right to Protest": Background Paper', Report, 2015, p. 4, available at: https://right-to-protest.org/wp-content/uploads/2015/06/Right-to-Protest-Background-paper-EN.pdf.

saw widespread protests against excessive use of police force against African Americans in 2015 and the rise of the Black Lives Latter movement. Turning to peaceful protest in repressive regimes, brief consideration is given to protests in Hong Kong, Venezuela, and also in Syria, in the period before the armed conflicts broke out across the country. A final section of the chapter looks at the duty of the police to ensure crowd safety at major sporting events, by considering the case of the 1989 Hillsborough disaster. As of writing, this was the subject of the largest ever investigation into police misconduct in the United Kingdom (UK).

The Human Rights Framework

Under international human rights law, a series of rights co-exist under the umbrella concept of a 'right to protest'. These rights are, most notably, to freedom of peaceful assembly, of association, and of expression, and the right to hold opinions 'without interference'.[9] In all instances – notwithstanding the legality or otherwise of any given protest and its peaceful or violent nature – participants are entitled to respect for their fundamental rights to life, to humane treatment, and to liberty. No one may be arbitrarily deprived of life or liberty, and adverse distinction in respecting and protecting rights, for example on the basis of colour, gender, or social status, may amount to unlawful discrimination. Any form of torture or other inhumane treatment is always prohibited.

As the UN Special Rapporteurs on freedom of assembly and on unlawful killings have observed, states have an obligation not only to refrain from violating the rights of individuals involved in an assembly, but also to ensure the rights of those who participate in, or are affected by an assembly, including by facilitating an enabling environment within which the assembly can proceed peacefully.[10]

The Rights to Freedom of Peaceful Assembly and of Association

The right to freedom of peaceful assembly is assured in Article 21 of the 1966 International Covenant on Civil and Political Rights (ICCPR), among other treaties, while the right to freedom of association is protected in Article 22. In 2010, UN Human Rights Council Resolution 15/21

[9] Arts. 19(1) and (2), 21, and 22, 1966 International Covenant on Civil and Political Rights (ICCPR).

[10] 2016 Joint UN Report on Peaceful Protest, §13.

reaffirmed that 'everyone has the rights to freedom of peaceful assembly and of association' and called on states 'to respect and fully protect the rights of all individuals to assemble peacefully and associate freely, including in the context of elections, and including persons espousing minority or dissenting views or beliefs'.[11]

In March 2016, in responding to the report by the two Special Rapporteurs, by majority vote the Human Rights Council called upon all states to:

> promote a safe and enabling environment for individuals and groups to exercise their rights to freedom of peaceful assembly, of expression and of association, [and] recalls that all States have the responsibility in all circumstances, including in the context of peaceful protests, to promote, respect and protect human rights and to prevent human rights violations, including extrajudicial, summary or arbitrary executions, arbitrary arrest and detention, enforced disappearances, torture and other cruel, inhuman or degrading treatment or punishment, and sexual violence, and calls upon States to avoid the abuse of criminal and civil proceedings or threats of such acts at all times.[12]

ICCPR Article 21 allows certain restrictions to be imposed 'in conformity with the law' on enjoyment of the right to assemble peacefully. Such restrictions may be lawful where they are 'necessary in a democratic society in the interests of national security or public safety, public order . . ., the protection of public health or morals or the protection of the rights and freedoms of others'. Any restrictions, though, should be the exception rather than the norm, and must not impair the essence of the right.[13] They must also respect the principles of necessity and proportionality that govern any restrictions imposed on the enjoyment of rights.

In this respect, Human Rights Council Resolution 15/21 called upon states 'to take all necessary measures to ensure that any restrictions on the free exercise of the rights to freedom of peaceful assembly and of association are in accordance with their obligations under international human rights law'.[14] As the UN Special Rapporteurs on freedom of assembly and unlawful killings have noted: 'To conform to the principle

[11] Human Rights Council Resolution 15/21, adopted without a vote on 30 September 2010, §1.

[12] Human Rights Council Resolution 31/37: 'The Promotion and Protection of Human Rights in the Context of Peaceful Protests', adopted on 24 March 2016 by 31 votes to 5 with 10 abstentions.

[13] Human Rights Committee, General Comment No. 27, UN doc. CCPR/C/21/Rev.1/Add.9, 2 November 1999, §13.

[14] Human Rights Council Resolution 15/21, adopted without a vote on 30 September 2010, §1.

of proportionality, any restriction must be appropriate to achieve its protective function. To meet the necessity requirement it must also be the least intrusive instrument amongst those which might achieve the desired result.'[15] The Special Rapporteurs further affirm that:[16]

> Assemblies are an equally legitimate use of public space as commercial activity or the movement of vehicles and pedestrian traffic.[17] Any use of public space requires some measure of coordination to protect different interests, but they are all legitimate ways in which individuals may use public spaces. A certain level of disruption to ordinary life caused by assemblies, including disruption of traffic, annoyance, and even harm to commercial activities, must be tolerated if the right is not to be deprived of substance.[18]

Not all disruption must, though, be tolerated. In October 2015, the Grand Chamber of the European Court of Human Rights adjudged, on appeal, an alleged violation of the right to peaceful assembly by Lithuania. The original application to the Court concerned farmers who obtained authority to stage a peaceful protest to draw attention to the Lithuanian Government's alleged lack of action in response to agricultural sector problems. The demonstrations were initially held peacefully as per the authorisations. However, negotiations with the government stagnated. To put pressure on the government, the applicants went beyond the authorisations, blocking three major highways for two days and causing significant disruption. The blockage ended when their demands were met. The applicants were subsequently convicted of 'rioting' and sentenced to 60 days' imprisonment, suspended for one year.[19]

The case was on appeal from a chamber of the Court, which, in November 2013, had found a violation by Lithuania of the protection of the right to peaceful assembly in Article 11 of the 1950 European

[15] 2016 Joint UN Report on Peaceful Protest, §30, citing Human Rights Committee, General Comment No. 27, §14.

[16] Ibid., §32.

[17] 'Report of the Special Rapporteur on the Rights to Freedom of Peaceful Assembly and of Association, Maina Kiai', UN doc. A/HRC/20/27, §41; Organization for Security and Co-operation in Europe (OSCE) Office for Democratic Institutions and Human Rights (ODIHR), *Guidelines on Freedom of Peaceful Assembly*, 2010, §20.

[18] European Court of Human Rights (ECtHR), *Kuznetsov* v. *Russia*, Judgment (First Section), 23 October 2008 (as rendered final on 23 January 2009), §44; and Inter-American Commission on Human Rights (IACmnHR), *Report on Citizen Security and Human Rights*, 2009, §197.

[19] ECtHR, *Kudrevičius and Others* v. *Lithuania*, Judgment (Second Section), 26 November 2013.

Convention on Human Rights (ECHR).[20] By majority decision (four votes to three), a chamber of the Court had found that the applicants' conviction for their participation in the gathering amounted to interference with their right to freedom of peaceful assembly.[21] The Court observed that the right to freedom of assembly 'is a fundamental right in a democratic society and, like the right to freedom of expression, is one of the foundations of such a society. Thus, it should not be interpreted restrictively'.[22]

On 14 April 2014, the case was referred to the Grand Chamber at Lithuania's request. The Grand Chamber noted that the applicants' conviction had not been based on involvement in or incitement to violence, but for the breach of public order resulting from the roadblocks. The disruption of traffic was not a side-effect of a meeting held in a public place, but rather the result of intentional action by the farmers. The Court observed that purposely obstructing traffic and the ordinary course of life in order to seriously disrupt the life of others 'was not at the core of freedom of assembly as protected' in the ECHR and that this 'might have implications' for any assessment of 'necessity'.[23]

On the merits, the Court held that while the applicants' conviction amounted to interference with their right to freedom of peaceful assembly, this interference had a basis in domestic law and was neither arbitrary nor unpredictable. The interference had pursued the legitimate aims of 'prevention of disorder' and 'protection of the rights and freedoms of others' and was therefore not a violation.[24] In making this determination, the Court acknowledged that the authorities had not used physical force. The police had confined themselves to ordering the applicants to remove the roadblocks and to warning them about their possible legal liability. They had chosen not to disperse the gatherings even when the applicants refused to obey their lawful orders. When

20 Art. 11(1) provides that: 'Everyone has the right to freedom of peaceful assembly …' According to Art. 11(2), 'No restrictions shall be placed on the exercise of these rights other than such as are prescribed by law and are necessary in a democratic society in the interests of national security or public safety, for the prevention of disorder or crime, for the protection of health or morals or for the protection of the rights and freedoms of others …'

21 ECtHR, *Kudrevičius and Others* v. *Lithuania*, Judgment (Second Section), 26 November 2013, §67.

22 Ibid., §80.

23 ECtHR, *Kudrevičius and Others* v. *Lithuania*, Judgment (Grand Chamber), 15 October 2015, as reported in: Information Note on the Court's case-law 189, October 2015.

24 Ibid.

tensions had arisen between the farmers and truck drivers, the police had urged the parties to the conflict to calm down in order to avoid serious confrontations. Despite the serious disruptions caused by the applicants' conduct the authorities had showed considerable tolerance. They had attempted to balance the interests of the demonstrators with those of the users of the highways, in order to ensure the peaceful conduct of the gathering and the safety of the general public.[25]

Use of Force during Protests

As noted above, in addressing assemblies, the 1990 Basic Principles distinguish between three types of assembly: those that are lawful and peaceful; those that are unlawful but non-violent; and those that are violent. These three scenarios are discussed in turn.

Lawful and Peaceful Assemblies

According to Basic Principle 12, everyone is allowed to participate in lawful and peaceful assemblies. By 'lawful' the drafters of the 1990 Basic Principles meant under *domestic law* as opposed to international law. In such cases, where the authorities have granted permission for (or at least not opposed) an assembly, the task of law enforcement is to facilitate the assembly, including a peaceful protest. Thus, in February 2016, in their joint report to the Human Rights Council on peaceful protest, the UN Special Rapporteurs noted that the positive obligation of the state to 'ensure' rights requires that authorities facilitate the holding of assemblies.[26] This demands that law enforcement officials be trained in facilitating assemblies in accordance with human rights law,[27] and that such training 'include "soft skills" such as effective communication, negotiation, and mediation, allowing law enforcement officials to avoid escalation of violence and minimize conflict'.[28]

Law enforcement authorities should also 'as far as possible, protect and facilitate spontaneous assemblies, as they would any other assembly'.[29] In the 2007 *Bukta* case,[30] a chamber of the European Court of Human Rights held that Hungary had violated the ECHR because the police had

[25] Ibid. [26] 2016 Joint UN Report on Peaceful Protest, §37. [27] Ibid., §42.
[28] Ibid. [29] Ibid., §23.
[30] ECtHR, *Bukta and Others* v. *Hungary*, Judgment (Second Section), 17 July 2007 (as rendered final on 17 October 2007).

moved participants in a peaceful assembly away from the target of their protest, despite their having heard a 'loud noise' that they feared was a threat to the security of the Hungarian Prime Minister and the visiting Romanian Prime Minister.[31]

The police in this case were acting on the basis of domestic legislation, which required that they be informed of an assembly at least three days in advance and gave the police the authority to disperse any assembly that took place without such prior notification. But in the Court's view, in 'special circumstances' when an immediate response to a political event in the form of a demonstration might be justified, 'a decision to disband the ensuing, peaceful assembly solely because of the absence of the requisite prior notice, without any illegal conduct by the participants, amounts to a disproportionate restriction on freedom of peaceful assembly'.[32] The Court found 'no evidence to suggest that the applicants represented a danger to public order beyond the level of the minor disturbance which is inevitably caused by an assembly in a public place'. It reiterated its view, previously expressed in a case brought against Turkey,[33] that

> where demonstrators do not engage in acts of violence, it is important for the public authorities to show a certain degree of tolerance towards peaceful gatherings if the freedom of assembly guaranteed by Article 11 of the Convention is not to be deprived of all substance.[34]

In determining whether or not an assembly is 'peaceful', the UN Special Rapporteurs on freedom of assembly and on unlawful killings argue that the peacefulness of an assembly should be presumed and the term 'peaceful' should be interpreted broadly. 'Regard must be given to the manner in which the assembly is held and to the intentions of the participants.'[35] The 2010 Guidelines on Freedom of Peaceful Assembly, issued by the Organization for Security and Co-operation in Europe (OSCE)'s Office for Democratic Institutions and Human Rights (ODIHR), state that:

> An assembly should be deemed peaceful if its organizers have professed peaceful intentions and the conduct of the assembly is non-violent. The

[31] Ibid., §10. [32] Ibid., §36.

[33] ECtHR, *Oya Ataman* v. *Turkey*, Judgment (Second Section), 5 December 2006 (as rendered final on 5 March 2007).

[34] ECtHR, *Bukta and Others* v. *Hungary*, Judgment, §37, citing ibid., §42.

[35] 2016 Joint UN Report on Peaceful Protest, §18.

> term "peaceful" should be interpreted to include conduct that may annoy or give offence, and even conduct that temporarily hinders, impedes or obstructs the activities of third parties.[36]

Whether or not the fact that a substantial number of participants in a given protest carry weapons for self-defence (e.g. a stick or baton) precludes an assembly from being considered peaceful is not settled under international law. Arguably, if such weapons are not visible and do not include knives and, *a fortiori*, firearms, the assembly should still be considered peaceful, if no violent acts occur.[37]

Unlawful but Non-Violent Assemblies

Principle 13 of the 1990 Basic Principles governs the use of force in respect of unlawful but non-violent assemblies: 'In the dispersal of assemblies that are unlawful but non-violent, law enforcement officials shall avoid the use of force or, where that is not practicable, shall restrict such force to the minimum extent necessary.' This category is especially contentious given residual uncertainty as the precise scope and definition of the term 'unlawful'; it also suggests that the appropriate law enforcement response to such an assembly is its dispersal. Arguably, the evolution of international human rights law since 1990 renders dispersal of a non-violent assembly to be generally unlawful, unless there exist objective grounds for its dispersal (i.e. necessity) and the measures taken are also proportionate.

An 'Unlawful' Assembly

Some states make the organisation and holding of a 'lawful' assembly wholly dependent on authorisation by the government of the day. The UN Special Rapporteurs on freedom of assembly and on unlawful killings jointly assert that because international law recognises 'an inalienable right to take part in peaceful assemblies, it follows that there is a presumption in favour of holding peaceful assemblies'.[38] As a

[36] OSCE ODIHR, *Guidelines on Freedom of Peaceful Assembly*, 2010, §1.3.

[37] According to Italian law, a peaceful assembly is defined as one that does not 'disturb the public order' ('turbi l'ordine pubblico'). D. Figueroa, 'Italy', in T. Papademetriou, 'Right to Peaceful Assembly. European Court of Human Rights', Report, Law Library of Congress, p. 7, at: www.loc.gov/law/help/peaceful-assembly/right-to-peaceful-assembly.pdf.

[38] 2016 Joint UN Report on Peaceful Protest, §18.

consequence, assemblies should, in general, only be subject to the permissible limitations set out in ICCPR Article 21,[39] not to prior authorisation by the authorities:

> Freedom of peaceful assembly is a right and not a privilege and as such its exercise should not be subject to prior authorization by the authorities. State authorities may put in place a system of prior notification, where the objective is to allow State authorities an opportunity to facilitate the exercise of the right, to take measures to protect public safety and/or public order and to protect the rights and freedoms of others. Any notification procedure should not function as a de facto request for authorization or as a basis for content-based regulation. Notification should not be expected for assemblies which do not require prior preparation by State authorities, such as those where only a small number of participants is expected, or where the impact on the public is expected to be minimal.[40]

Although, in all likelihood, it was not intended to be so understood at the time of the adoption of the Basic Principles in 1990, today one should construe lawful as meaning 'in accordance with domestic law as constrained by international human rights law'. In many cases, this would narrow the discretion granted to national authorities to prevent an assembly from taking place or to put an end to an assembly that is already occurring. This implies that it would be lawful to prevent or disperse an assembly if there is a serious risk of violence that cannot reasonably be avoided or curtailed by the deployment of police or other law enforcement officials.

In addition, according to the two UN Special Rapporteurs, a peaceful assembly that incites discrimination, hostility, or violence, in contravention of ICCPR Article 20, 'may warrant dispersal' where less intrusive means of managing the situation have failed.[41] They argue further that while mere inconvenience to others[42] or temporary disruption to traffic 'are to be tolerated', where an assembly prevents access to essential services (such as blocking the entrance to a hospital's emergency department) or where interference with traffic or the economy 'is serious and sustained (for example, where a major highway is blocked for days), dispersal may be justified'. They assert that failure to notify the authorities of an assembly 'does not render an assembly unlawful, and consequently should not be used as a basis for dispersing the assembly'.[43] In

[39] Ibid. [40] Ibid., §21. [41] Ibid., §62.
[42] IACmnHR, *Report on Citizen Security and Human Rights*, §198.
[43] 2016 Joint UN Report on Peaceful Protest, §31.

any event, restrictions on any assembly must be both necessary and proportionate in the circumstances.

The fact that the authorities may not be entitled to disperse a given assembly does not, of course, preclude the police from lawfully arresting and detaining suspected criminals from among the participants and bystanders. As the UN Special Rapporteurs observe, 'The authority to arrest can play an important protective function in assemblies, by allowing law enforcement to remove from an assembly individuals who are acting violently.'[44] Of course, as they also recall:

> No one may be subject to arbitrary arrest or detention. In the context of assemblies this has particular import for the "criminalization" of assemblies and dissent. Arrest of protestors to prevent or punish the exercise of their right to freedom of peaceful assembly, for example, on charges which are spurious, unreasonable or lack proportionality, may violate these protections. Similarly, intrusive pre-emptive measures should not be used unless a clear and present danger of imminent violence actually exists. "Mass arrest" of assembly participants often amounts to indiscriminate and arbitrary arrests.[45]

The Special Rapporteurs recommend that participants on their way to an assembly 'not be stopped, searched or arrested unless there is a clear and present danger of imminent violence.'[46]

Given the option lawfully to arrest violent individuals, dispersal of an assembly should be considered a last resort, even when circumstances exist that might justify such a measure. 'Before countenancing dispersal, law enforcement agencies should seek to identify and isolate any violent individuals separately from the main assembly and, differentiate between violent individuals in an assembly and others. This may allow the assembly to continue.'[47] Dispersal risks violation of the rights to freedom of expression and peaceful assembly as well as to bodily integrity; it may also escalate tensions between participants and law enforcement.[48]

> For these reasons, it must be resorted to only when strictly unavoidable. For example, dispersal may be considered where violence is serious, widespread, and represents an imminent threat to bodily safety or property, and where law enforcement officials have taken all reasonable measures to facilitate and protect participants in the assembly from harm.[49]

[44] Ibid., §44. [45] Ibid., §45. [46] Ibid., §49(g). [47] Ibid., §61. [48] Ibid.
[49] Ibid.

The case of *Florentina Olmedo* v. *Paraguay* concerned an agricultural worker, Blanco Dominguez, who took part in a peaceful demonstration in Paraguay in favour of agrarian reform. The demonstrators came face to face with a police barrier and decided to blockade the road. The prosecutor ordered the leaders of the demonstration to unblock the road, and told them that if they failed to do so it would be cleared by force. While negotiations were underway, the prosecutor ordered the road to be cleared. The police attack was immediate and violent, and involved use of tear gas, firearms, and water cannon. The police beat many demonstrators, fired indiscriminately at those who were fleeing, and violently broke into and damaged various nearby houses, beating severely any persons they managed to catch. Both metal-jacketed and rubber bullets were used indiscriminately.

Mr Dominguez had been at the head of the demonstration and, along with other demonstrators, had peacefully surrendered to the police, kneeling down with his hands up. While he was in this position, an officer of the National Police shot him in the back at very close range. After he fell to the ground, he was hit on the head by the police. After two operations, Blanco Dominguez died on 5 June 2003.[50] In finding a violation of the right to life, the Human Rights Committee reiterated Paraguay's obligation to protect the life of the demonstrators.[51]

Violent Assemblies

According to Basic Principle 14, 'In the dispersal of violent assemblies, law enforcement officials may use firearms only when less dangerous means are not practicable and only to the minimum extent necessary. Law enforcement officials shall not use firearms in such cases, except under the conditions stipulated in principle 9.' As discussed in Chapters 3 and 4, Basic Principle 9 provides that:

> Law enforcement officials shall not use firearms against persons except in self-defence or defence of others against the imminent threat of death or serious injury, to prevent the perpetration of a particularly serious crime involving grave threat to life, to arrest a person presenting such a danger and resisting their authority, or to prevent his or her escape, and only when less extreme means are insufficient to achieve these objectives. In

[50] Human Rights Committee, *Florentina Olmedo* v. *Paraguay*, Views (Comm. No. 1828/2008), UN doc. CCPR/C/104/D/1828/2008, 2012, §§2.4–2.7.

[51] Ibid., §7.5.

> any event, intentional lethal use of firearms may only be made when strictly unavoidable in order to protect life.[52]

This suggests that the possibility of lawful recourse to firearms is an individualised and not a collective issue. In the *Giuliani and Gaggio* case before the European Court of Human Rights, a number of distinct demonstrations – some peaceful, others involving violence – were mounted against and during the G8 Summit in Italy in July 2001. Two jeeps of *carabinieri* (Italian military police) were travelling from an area of earlier contention during which one of the vehicles was suddenly surrounded by rioters and the police attacked by stones, sticks, and iron bars. One of the rioters, Carlo Giuliani, tried to throw a fire extinguisher despite a warning from one *carabiniere* not to do so. The officer stated that he perceived an imminent threat to his own life and bodily integrity and to that of his colleagues. He fired his weapon at Mr Giuliani, killing him.[53]

In this case, the Court's Grand Chamber concluded that the killing could be justified by ECHR Article 2(2)(a) on the basis that it was action that was no more than absolutely necessary in the circumstances in defence of a person from unlawful violence. This made it 'unnecessary' for the Court to consider whether the use of force was also unavoidable 'in action lawfully taken for the purpose of quelling a riot or insurrection' within the meaning of Article 2(2)(c).[54] In fact, today it is hard to conceive of a situation whereby use of a firearm against an individual that was unjustified in the particular circumstances would somehow become lawful merely because it took place against the backdrop of a riot. In this respect, Article 2(2)(c) of the ECHR, which was adopted in 1950, must be seen as a creature of its time. Thus, many of the approaches proposed in *Kill or Get Killed: Riot Control Techniques*, a US book published as recently as 1976, must be considered an anachronism, at least as far as riot control is concerned.[55]

But how is a 'violent' assembly to be defined? The question is not as foolish as might initially appear. Supporters of one football team may threaten the supporters of an opposing team with significant violence, for

[52] See Chapter 4 for detailed discussion of this provision.

[53] ECtHR, *Giuliani and Gaggio* v. *Italy*, Judgment (Grand Chamber), 24 March 2011, §§21–7.

[54] Ibid., §§194–96.

[55] R. Applegate, *Kill or Get Killed: Riot Control Techniques*, Paladin Press, Boulder, CO, 1976. Rex Applegate wrote the book during the 'turbulent' 1960s.

example in songs or gestures, and some of them may even engage in violent acts, but this does not mean that the crowd as a whole is violent and that automatically the assembly may be lawfully dispersed. (Otherwise, in many countries precious little football would be witnessed by fans in certain stadia.) In this regard, it is notable that the phrasing of Basic Principle 14 refers to a violent assembly as a whole, rather than to the acts of individual participants. This implies that individuals within an assembly may have recourse to violence without the assembly as a whole being deemed violent. Indeed, in its 2014 resolution on peaceful protest, the Human Rights Council '[r]ecall[ed] that isolated acts of violence committed by others in the course of a protest do not deprive peaceful individuals of their rights to freedom of peaceful assembly, of expression and of association'.[56]

Thus, the term 'violent assembly' should best be considered akin to that of major, widespread rioting. This is notwithstanding a lack of clarity as to the precise meaning of the term 'riot' under international law, despite its employment in three major treaties: the 1977 Additional Protocol II to the four 1949 Geneva Conventions,[57] the 1992 Chemical Weapons Convention,[58] and the ECHR.

Article 2(2) ECHR specifies the exceptional circumstances where deprivation of life by a state may be justified, one of which is use of force 'in action lawfully taken for the purpose of quelling a riot or insurrection'. In *Stewart* v. *UK*, the case before the erstwhile European Commission on Human Rights concerned the applicant's son who died after being struck on the head by a plastic bullet fired by a British soldier serving in Northern Ireland. The Commission acknowledged that the legal definitions of 'riot' differ among the law and practice of states parties to the ECHR and did not consider it necessary to define it precisely. The Commission asserted that 'an assembly of 150 people

[56] Human Rights Council Resolution 25/38: 'The Promotion and Protection of Human Rights in the Context of Peaceful Protests', adopted on 28 March 2014, 22nd preambular para.

[57] Art. 1(2) of 1977 Additional Protocol II explicitly mentions 'riots' as being instances of internal disturbances and tensions where the Protocol does not apply 'as not being armed conflicts'. The commentary on the provision published by the International Committee of the Red Cross describes 'riots' as 'demonstrations without a concerted plan from the outset'. *Commentary on the Additional Protocols of 8 June 1977 to the Geneva Conventions of 12 August 1949*, ICRC, Geneva, 1987, p. 1354.

[58] Art. II(9), 1992 Chemical Weapons Convention.

throwing missiles at a patrol of soldiers to the point that they risked serious injury' clearly constitutes a riot.[59]

The case of *Güleç* v. *Turkey* concerned spontaneous and unauthorised demonstrations, shop closures, and attacks on public buildings in the town of Idil. The applicant's son was hit and killed from a ricochet bullet fired by a gendarme to disperse the demonstrators. Evidenced by the damage to movable and immovable property and the injuries sustained by the gendarmes, the Court accepted the Commission's assessment, which described the demonstration as 'far from peaceful' and which could constitute a 'riot' within the meaning of the Convention.[60] But it held that the authorities should have provided their law enforcement officials with alternatives to firearms to disperse the assembly: the government had produced no evidence to support its assertion that terrorists were among the demonstrators, which might have justified recourse to live fire.

Dispersal

Firearms A number of less-lethal options exist to disperse a riot, such as police charges (whether mounted or on foot), use of tear gas, or use of water cannon. Each has potential dangers both for the user and the targets. If dispersal is truly necessary, 1990 Basic Principle 14 suggests that this might be facilitated by recourse to firearms. If this was the law in 1990, it is certainly not the law today. As the two UN Special Rapporteurs noted in their 2016 report on peaceful protest to the Human Rights Council, firearms may never be used simply to disperse an assembly

[59] European Commission of Human Rights, *Stewart* v. *UK*, Report of the Commission, 2 July 1985, §25.

[60] ECtHR, *Güleç* v. *Turkey*, Judgment (Chamber), 27 July 1998, §§68, 71. Sometimes police responses to protests are so excessive that they attract the epithet of 'police riots'. The phrase was coined in the Walker Report that followed rioting around the 1968 Democratic Convention in Chicago, and has since entered the law enforcement lexicon following the eponymous book by Rodney Stark in the early 1970s on US police actions in countering anti-government and anti-Vietnam War protests. 'Rights in Conflict: The Violent Confrontation of Demonstrators and Police in the Parks and Streets of Chicago during the Week of the Democratic National Convention of 1968', Report submitted by Daniel Walker, Director of the Chicago Study Team, to the National Commission on the Causes and Prevention of Violence, 1 December 1968. Stark defines a police riot as an 'event ... when roving bands of policemen set upon non-provocative persons and/or property in an excessively violent manner. When only one small group of policemen sets upon citizens and/or property in a single location it may be useful to call this a police attack. A police riot is any such event involving two or more attacks.' R. Stark, *Police Riots*, Wadsworth Publishing, Belmont, CA, 1972, p. 17.

and, of course, indiscriminate firing into a crowd is always unlawful.[61] Firing over the heads of protesters is also unacceptable as it risks killing or seriously injuring those standing behind, for a rifle bullet may kill or seriously injure someone a mile away or even further.

The UN Special Rapporteurs recommend that automatic firearms should not be used under any circumstances in the policing of assemblies.[62] In fact, this should be considered a statement of law, not merely a recommendation. The Marikana Commission of Inquiry followed very significant use of force by the South African Police Service (SAPS) against striking miners, some of whom were engaged or threatening violence. In the main volley of fire, the SAPS officers reportedly fired off 300 rounds in eight seconds, some using automatic rifles.[63] It was noted that:

> Several of the TRT [Tactical Response Team] members who fired at scene 1 admitted in the statements they made that their rifles were on automatic fire ... Lieutenant-Colonel Classen confirmed that in his view this was grossly negligent ... and Mr Cees de Rover, the policing expert called by the SAPS, said that in his view automatic rifle fire has no place in law enforcement. "You still at every pull of the trigger need to prove the existence of an imminent threat to life or serious injury".[64]

Police Crowd Control Units If done correctly, a steady move forward[65] by police officers equipped with suitable personal protective equipment

[61] 2016 Joint UN Report on Peaceful Protest, §60, citing 'Report of the Special Rapporteur on Extrajudicial, Summary or Arbitrary Executions, Christof Heyns', UN doc. A/HRC/26/36, 1 April 2014, §75.

[62] 2016 Joint UN Report on Peaceful Protest, §67(e).

[63] See, e.g., A. Saba, S. Cele, and M. Hussain, 'Marikana Countdown to Disaster', at: https://city_press.atavist.com/-marikana-countdown-to-disaster.

[64] Marikana Commission of Inquiry: Report on Matters of Public, National and International Concern arising out of the Tragic Incidents at the Lonmin Mine in Marikana, in the North West Province, 2015, §G41, p. 258 (footnotes omitted), at: www.sahrc.org.za/home/21/files/marikana-report-1.pdf.

[65] According to a security blog, 'tactics used to control riots in the past were very simple. The success was based on the fact that the police were almost always better armed than the rioters. The tactics they used basically consisted of forming a line and charging into the crowd. The police today are even better armed, but the techniques have advanced significantly and usually prevent the injuries that we have seen in the past'. 'Riot Control Tactics and Crowd Management Techniques', Staff Patrol, Self Defense and Security blog, at: https://staffpatrol.wordpress.com/2007/06/11/riot-control-tactics-and-crowd-management-techniques/.

(PPE), such as dedicated helmets, body armour, and large shields,[66] and using batons only when strictly necessary, can be effective in safely dispersing or channelling an assembly. The tactic demands training and discipline to be conducted effectively and lawfully. Lack of discipline may create panic or merely redistribute a problem.

In 2009, the Metropolitan Police Service (MPS) was accused of using batons against climate-camp protesters during the G20 protests in the City of London. The police had said they would ask the protesters, whom they acknowledged were peaceful, to move as night fell. Commander Simon O'Brien said officers would be 'politely and proportionately' asking campers to move on. But an eyewitness, Martin Horwood, the then Liberal Democrat MP for Cheltenham, said dogs were used on protesters near the camp. James Lloyd, a legal adviser in the camp, claimed that riot police had forcefully cleared the area using batons around midnight:

> There was no announcement, the riot police just started moving forward very quickly from the south. They were pushing everyone back, pushing forward quickly. They caused panic, people were screaming and shouting . . . There was a person in a wheelchair struggling to move, being pushed forcibly by them. It was totally disproportionate.[67]

Tear Gas Tear gas should normally be fired by police in front of protesters, for if it is fired behind them protesters may be constrained to move forward, increasing the likelihood of violent clashes that can cause injury both to citizens and to police officers. According to a former San Francisco police captain, Charlie Beene,

> When using tear gas, wind conditions must be accounted for. In cities with high-rise buildings, for example, the constantly whirling and changing wind is a major consideration when deciding whether or not to deploy tear gas. Years ago, before they were issued gas masks, officers in

[66] According to the UK College of Policing, for instance, a range of appropriate shield tactics can be used to protect officers, assist with the dispersal of crowds, and contain disorder. College of Policing, 'Public Order, Tactical Options: Shield Tactics', Last modified on 28 January 2016, at: www.app.college.police.uk/app-content/public-order/planning-and-deployment/tactical-options/#shield-tactics.

[67] Quoted in S. Laville and D. Campbell, 'Baton Charges and Kettling: Police's G20 Crowd Control Tactics under Fire', *The Guardian*, 3 April 2009, at: www.theguardian.com/world/2009/apr/03/g20-protests-police-tactics.

> San Francisco often gassed themselves or innocent bystanders more so than the violent crowd and, consequently, did not opt to use gas often.[68]

Even if correctly used, however, protesters may be prepared for – or even explicitly invite – tear gas. Beene, for example, records how in 1992 in Ann Arbor, Michigan, basketball fans clashed with police after the University of Michigan lost in the finals of a national competition. Some fans clapped and chanted: 'We want tear gas! We want tear gas!'[69] In 1999, the World Trade Organization (WTO) meeting in Seattle was ultimately cancelled after the police lost control of the streets and even ran out of tear gas, evidencing a failure to prepare adequately for the event. Certain protesters had come ready to engage in violence and, in anticipation of confrontation with the police, even brought gas masks with them as well as wrapping their faces with bandanas soaked in vinegar to neutralise the effects of tear gas.[70]

As discussed in Chapter 5, depending on the nature and context of their use most cases of tear gas exposure result in only temporary side-effects, though some cases can result in severe complications, including death. A journalist, Hunter Walker, who was affected by tear gas while covering 'Occupy Oakland' protests in 2011, describes being

> suddenly gripped by a pain so intense, I nearly fell to my knees. The most overwhelming aspect of the pain was an intense tightness in my chest. It felt like my heart might burst or collapse into itself and it was so bad I thought I might be having a serious medical issue.[71]

But dangers come not only from the gas itself but also from the canisters. If fired directly at protesters the impact of the canister, especially on a person's head or face, may be lethal. In July 2014, the European Court of Human Rights issued its judgment in the *Ataykaya* case.[72] In March 2006, as he was leaving his place of work, the applicant's son found himself in the middle of a demonstration and was struck in the head by one of several tear-gas canisters fired by the security forces. He died a few

[68] C. Beene, *Riot Prevention and Control*, Paladin Press, Boulder, CO, 2006, p. 84.

[69] Cited in ibid., p. 11.

[70] See, e.g., P. F. Gillham and G. T. Marx, 'Complexity & Irony in Policing and Protesting: The World Trade Organization in Seattle', *Social Justice*, Vol. 27, No. 2 (2000), pp. 212–36.

[71] Cited in B. Winsor, 'Tear Gas Can Cause Deaths, Amputations, and Miscarriages', *Business Insider*, 19 August 2014, at: www.businessinsider.com/side-effects-of-ferguson-tear-gas-can-kill-2014–8?IR=T.

[72] ECtHR, *Ataykaya* v. *Turkey*, Judgment (Second Section), 22 July 2014.

minutes later.[73] An eyewitness stated that the security force personnel were firing with one knee on the ground and taking aim. 'That means they were not firing in the air but towards people.'[74] On 30 March 2006, an autopsy carried out at Diyarbakir public hospital concluded that death had been caused by a haemorrhage and brain damage inflicted by a firearm projectile (tear-gas grenade). 'The characteristics of the projectile's point of entry show that it had not been fired from a short distance ...'[75]

An Iranian study of the use of tear gas during protests in 2008 and 2009 in Iran found that canister impacts had caused eighteen cases of severe bleeding and fractures, leading to at least three amputations.[76]

Water Cannon A water cannon is a machine that shoots a stream of water at high velocity, typically over a distance of several dozen metres. The device has been used in Belgium, Chile, Germany, and Turkey, among others. In 2013, water cannon reportedly killed a protester in Turkey while a report by the British government's Defence Science and Technology Laboratory found 'good evidence ... to indicate that serious injuries have been sustained by people subjected to the force of water cannon'.[77] The report noted that injuries sustained from water cannon output may be defined as primary, secondary or tertiary:

- Primary injuries are caused by the water jet impacting the body
- Secondary injuries are produced by impact on the body of street furniture or other debris
- Tertiary injuries are caused by impact of the body with other objects, such as may arise, for example, if the water jet causes people to fall over or to be thrown against rigid structures.

[73] ECtHR, Information Note on the Court's case-law No. 176, July 2014, p. 9, at: www.echr.coe.int/Documents/CLIN_2014_07_176_ENG.pdf.

[74] Reported in ECtHR, *Ataykaya* v. *Turkey*, Judgment, §9.

[75] Reported in ibid., §8. See also, with respect to the use of smoke bombs by the Spanish police which injured a youth during a violent assembly, ECtHR, *Iribarren Pinillos* v. *Spain*, Judgment (Third Section), 8 January 2009 (Rendered final on 8 April 2009).

[76] M. L. Wani *et al.*, 'Vascular Injuries Caused by Tear Gas Shells: Surgical Challenge and Outcome', *Iranian Journal of Medical Science*, Vol. 36, No. 1 (2011), pp. 14–17.

[77] Defence Science and Technology Laboratory, 'The Medical Implications of Vehicle-Mounted Water Cannon with Special Reference to the Ziegler Wasserwerfer 9000 (WaWe 9) System', 2013, p. i, at: www.gov.uk/government/uploads/system/uploads/attachment_data/file/445176/130719_DSTL_1_-_July_2013_-_TR74621_-_Ready_for_publication.pdf. The report also noted that a reporter was allegedly killed by water cannon fired at 'close range' in Tanzania in September 2012. Ibid., p. 25.

There is strong recent evidence for primary and tertiary injuries produced by water cannon in operational use.[78]

In the United Kingdom, water cannons have only been authorised for use by the Police Service of Northern Ireland. In the wake of the riots in cities across England during the summer of 2011, Sir Hugh Orde, the President of the Association of Chief Police Officers (ACPO), giving evidence to the London assembly, affirmed it 'buys you space' and would 'fill a gap in the armoury' of the MPS.[79] In June 2014, London's Deputy Mayor for Policing and Crime, Stephen Greenhalgh, authorised the MPS to buy three second-hand water cannon machines from the German Federal Police. The purchase was, though, authorised before Parliamentary approval had been secured for their use. In July 2015, after a study of their safety and effectiveness, Theresa May, the then Secretary of State for Home Affairs, told the British Parliament that she had decided not to licence them for use for three main reasons:

> Firstly, the medical and technical issues raised by the reviews do not give me the degree of confidence that I need to authorise less lethal weaponry.
>
> While evidence suggests that these water cannon are unlikely to result in serious or life-threatening injuries as currently built and used as envisaged, the assessment nonetheless poses a series of direct and indirect medical risks from their use. These include the possibility to cause primary, secondary and tertiary injuries, including musculoskeletal injuries such as spinal fracture, as well as other serious injuries such as concussion, eye injury and blunt trauma. International evidence supports this conclusion; in Stuttgart a 66-year old protestor was completely blinded during a protest by a similar model of water cannon to those under consideration . . .
>
> Secondly, my decision also takes into account the operational case for water cannon. The original police request argued that water cannon offered a flexible option to disperse crowds, protect premises and deter disruptive behaviour that might otherwise have to be dealt with by forcible means.
>
> However, it made clear that water cannon has limitations, especially in response to fast, agile disorder. This has been borne out by further discussion with chief constables, who raised the possibility that the vehicles may serve to attract crowds to a vulnerable location and noted

[78] Ibid., p. 22.

[79] R. Booth, 'Water Cannon: A Shocking Device that Could Transform British Policing', *The Guardian*, 4 April 2014, at: www.theguardian.com/uk-news/2014/apr/04/water-cannon-shocking-device-transform-british-policing.

> that evidence from Northern Ireland suggests that the deployment of water cannon usually requires significant advance notice – casting doubt on their utility in a riot scenario.
>
> Finally, I am acutely conscious of the potential impact of water cannon on public perceptions of police legitimacy. As a number of chief constables argued, in areas with a history of social unrest or mistrust of the police, the deployment of water cannon has the potential to be entirely counterproductive.[80]

Containment ('Kettling')

Another option used by certain law enforcement agencies is containment, sometimes called 'kettling',[81] where protesters (and often innocent bystanders) are contained within an encircling police cordon. Waddington and Wright assert that the strategy was first used in the United Kingdom during the Poll Tax riots in London's Trafalgar Square in March 1990.[82] Police strategists had realised that dispersing large disorderly assemblies could be ultimately ineffective, since it typically led to sporadic outbreaks of disorder over a wide area, which was even harder to control. Subsequently the strategy was developed whereby disorderly gatherings would be contained within 'tight, but essentially static cordons'.[83]

Protesters sometimes distinguish between a 'Kettle of First Resort' (holding people against their will and without intention to charge them); an 'Open Kettle' (a variant with porous police lines where the intention is to take control of the space from the protest while allowing individuals to move through the lines); and a 'Pressure Cooker' (an Open Kettle in which the police progressively move inwards, diminishing the space in which the protesters can move). With regard to the latter, it is observed

80 Rt. Hon. Theresa May MP, 'Home Secretary's Oral Statement on Water Cannon', 15 July 2015, at: www.gov.uk/government/speeches/home-secretarys-oral-statement-on-water-cannon.

81 The etymology of the term is unclear. According to one source, it is from the idea that steam is confined to one small area of a boiling kettle. 'What is Kettling', undated. According to another, the most plausible suggestion is that the word is from German, in which Kessel is the everyday word for a kettle, but has an older sense of a semi-circular ring of hunters driving game before them. The best-known example of the military sense is the Stalingrad Kessel of 1942, so called at the time by the German forces besieged in the Russian city. M. Quinion, 'Kettling', at: www.worldwidewords.org/turnsofphrase/tp-ket1.htm.

82 P. A. J. Waddington and M. Wright, 'Police Use of Force, Firearms and Riot-Control', in T. Newburn (ed.), *Handbook of Policing*, 2nd Edn, Routledge, London, 2011, p. 472.

83 Ibid.

that: 'Those who maintain this is not meant to be intimidating are welcome to stand inside one.'[84] As protesters can expect to be kettled for hours at a time, some come prepared for prolonged periods of time without access to toilets, for example by wearing nappies.

Use of kettling is normally traced back to the actions of the German police in Hamburg in 1986 during a protest against nuclear weapons. Waddington and Wright, however, claims its origins go back to the actions of Hannibal in his battle against the Roman legions at Cannae in 216 BC, when his relatively small force encircled a much larger force. The reason for using this technique is that only those at the outer rim of the circle have contact with the enemy; the remainder only have contact with each other. Transposed to the policing context, the advantage for the police is that, 'unlike dispersal, their use of force is essentially defensive: if members of the contained gathering attempt to break out of the containment then it is they who must attack, not the police'.[85]

The European Court of Human Rights has considered the legality of the technique. In *Austin* v. *UK*, decided in 2012, the Court's Grand Chamber adjudged that the cordon, which lasted for up to seven hours, did not constitute an arbitrary deprivation of liberty within Article 5 of the ECHR.[86] The case concerned a challenge to the decision by the Metropolitan Police Service to kettle a group of several thousand people at Oxford Circus in London during May Day protests in 2001. The police, perceiving a risk of violence and disorder (which did occur), imposed a cordon under the common-law power to 'keep the peace'. The applicants to the European Court – one protester and three innocent bystanders caught up in the containment – lost their case in the House of Lords in 2009. According to the European Court,

> the police must be afforded a degree of discretion in taking operational decisions. Such decisions are almost always complicated and the police, who have access to information and intelligence not available to the general public, will usually be in the best position to make them ... Police forces in the Contracting States face new challenges, perhaps unforeseen when the Convention was drafted, and have developed new policing

[84] 'A Dictionary of Terms for the Shafted: Political Policing', 10 November 2011, at: http://withtheresistance.com/a-dictionary-of-terms-for-the-shafted-political-policing/.

[85] Waddington and Wright, 'Police Use of Force, Firearms and Riot-Control', p. 472.

[86] ECtHR, *Austin and Others* v. *UK*, Judgment (Grand Chamber), 15 March 2012. See D. Mead, 'The Right to Protest Contained by Strasbourg: an Analysis of Austin v. UK & the Constitutional Pluralist Issues it Throws Up', UK Constitutional Law Group, 16 March 2012.

> techniques to deal with them, including containment or "kettling". Article 5 cannot be interpreted in such a way as to make it impracticable for the police to fulfil their duties of maintaining order and protecting the public, provided that they comply with the underlying principle of Article 5, which is to protect the individual from arbitrariness.[87]

The decision, and the reasoning that supported it, have justly been criticised. Indeed, as David Mead has observed, 'it is hard not to see how being held for up to seven hours without access to food or water, without shelter or perhaps suitable clothing on a wet, windy day was not depriving someone of their liberty. In common sense terms, what more was needed?'[88] In this regard, the Court noted that: 'There was space within the cordon for people to walk about and there was no crushing, but conditions were uncomfortable, with no shelter, food, water, or toilet facilities. Throughout the afternoon and evening attempts were made by the police to commence collective release, but the violent and uncooperative behaviour of a significant minority both within the cordon and in the surrounding area outside led the police repeatedly to suspend dispersal.'[89] The Court also underlined that

> measures of crowd control should not be used by the national authorities directly or indirectly to stifle or discourage protest, given the fundamental importance of freedom of expression and assembly in all democratic societies. Had it not remained necessary for the police to impose and maintain the cordon in order to prevent serious injury or damage, the "type" of the measure would have been different, and its coercive and restrictive nature might have been sufficient to bring it within Article 5.[90]

More sensible argumentation was put forward by the minority dissenting opinion in the Court. Judges Tulkens, Spielmann, and Garlicki, citing the 2010 case of *Gillan and Quinton* v. *UK* (which the Grand Chamber in its judgment in the *Austin* case did not),[91] affirmed that deprivation of liberty within the meaning of Article 5 ECHR had occurred and that the right had been violated:

> In the present case, the applicants were confined within a relatively small area, together with some 3,000 other people, and their freedom of movement was greatly reduced; they were only able to stand up or sit on the ground and had no access to toilet facilities, food or water. The cordon

[87] ECtHR, *Austin and Others* v. *UK*, Judgment, §56.
[88] Mead, 'The Right to Protest Contained By Strasbourg'.
[89] ECtHR, *Austin and Others* v. *UK*, Judgment, §62. [90] Ibid., §68.
[91] ECtHR, *Gillan and Quinton* v. *UK*, Judgment (Fourth Section), 12 January 2010.

> was maintained through the presence of hundreds of riot police officers and the applicants were entirely dependent on the police officers' decisions as to when they could leave. Furthermore, the police could use force to keep the cordon in place, and refusal to comply with their instructions and restrictions was punishable by a prison sentence and could lead to arrest. All the applicants were contained in those conditions for six to seven hours.[92]

This accords with the position of the US Supreme Court on what amounts to being in custody. The Court has interpreted the scope of the term as meaning not only a formal arrest, but also restraint on freedom of movement of the degree associated with a formal arrest.[93]

In his 2013 report on his mission to the United Kingdom, the Special Rapporteur on the rights to freedom of peaceful assembly and of association specifically criticised the use of kettling.[94] He was 'particularly troubled to hear alarming stories of peaceful protestors, as well as innocent bystanders, including tourists, held for long periods with no access to water or sanitary facilities'.[95] Acknowledging the European Court's judgment in the *Austin* case, he affirmed that this and other relevant decisions in domestic courts 'by no means constitute a blanket endorsement' of kettling and asserted that the tactic 'is intrinsically detrimental to the exercise of the right to freedom of peaceful assembly, due to its indiscriminate and disproportionate nature'.[96]

While the Special Rapporteur is absolutely right to raise concerns about the 'powerful chilling effect on the exercise of freedom of peaceful assembly', in decrying all and any use of kettling he goes too far. The police in England have undoubtedly abused the tactic of containment on several occasions, but if used appropriately and selectively it can successfully isolate violent individuals from other participants in an assembly and allow the assembly to proceed. In its response to the Special Rapporteur's report, the United Kingdom stated the following:

> The use of containment by police at demonstrations is an operational matter for Chief Officers of the Police. The Government believes that a

[92] Joint dissenting opinion of Judges Tulkens, Spielmann, and Garlicki, §§14 and 15.

[93] US Supreme Court, *Maryland* v. *Michael Blaine Shatzer*, Sr., Decision (Case No. 08–680), Writ of Certiorari to the Maryland Court of Appeals, 24 February 2010; see also L. A. Steverson, *Policing in America*, ABC CLIO, Santa Barbara, CA, 2008, p. 35.

[94] 'Report of the Special Rapporteur on the Rights to Freedom of Peaceful Assembly and of Association, Maina Kiai. Addendum: Mission to the UK', UN doc. A/HRC/23/39/Add.1, 17 June 2013, §§36–38.

[95] Ibid., §37. [96] Ibid.

> targeted and proportionate use of containment is in line with its commitments under international human rights. The Government works to ensure that containment is used by the police in a way that minimises the impact on those protesting peacefully.[97]

But the United Kingdom has some way to go in these efforts. As noted by the United Kingdom's Joint Committee on Human Rights, 'it would be a disproportionate and unlawful response to cordon a group of people and operate a blanket ban on individuals leaving the contained area, as this fails to consider whether individual circumstances require a different response'.[98]

The Right to Protest in the United States

The right to freedom of assembly, and specifically the right to protest, is incorporated in the national laws and even the constitutions of many states. In the United States (US), for example, the First Amendment to the Constitution guarantees the right of citizens to free speech, to assemble peaceably, and to petition the US government.[99] Any restrictions must be narrowly drawn, serve a legitimate public interest, and, in general, not be discriminatory in nature. In the late 1960s, a suit was brought against the Chicago Police Department by Earl Mosley, a federal postal employee, who for seven months prior to the enactment of a local ordinance had frequently picketed Jones Commercial High School in Chicago. During school hours and usually by himself, Mr Mosley would walk along the public sidewalk of the school, carrying a sign that read: 'Jones High School practices black discrimination. Jones High School has a black quota.' According to the US Supreme Court, 'His lonely crusade was always peaceful, orderly, and quiet, and was conceded to be so by the city of Chicago.'[100] The Court held that:

[97] 'Report of the Special Rapporteur on the Rights to Freedom of Peaceful Assembly and of Association, Maina Kiai. Addendum: Mission to the United Kingdom of Great Britain and Northern Ireland: Comments by the State on the Report of the Special Rapporteur', UN doc. A/HRC/23/39/Add.3, 28 May 2013, §15.

[98] Joint Committee on Human Rights, *Demonstrating Respect for Rights? Follow-up*, HMSO, HL Paper 141/ HC 522, London, 14 July 2009, §§28–29; see OSCE ODIHR, *Guidelines on Freedom of Peaceful Assembly*, 2010, p. 79.

[99] 'Congress shall make no law respecting an establishment of religion, or prohibiting the free exercise thereof; or abridging the freedom of speech, or of the press; or the right of the people peaceably to assemble, and to petition the government for a redress of grievances.'

[100] US Supreme Court, *Police Dept. of Chicago* v. *Mosley*, 408 US 92 (1972), p. 96.

> government may not grant the use of a forum to people whose views it finds acceptable, but deny use to those wishing to express less favored or more controversial views. And it may not select which issues are worth discussing or debating in public facilities. There is an 'equality of status in the field of ideas,'[101] and government must afford all points of view an equal opportunity to be heard. Once a forum is opened up to assembly or speaking by some groups, government may not prohibit others from assembling or speaking on the basis of what they intend to say. Selective exclusions from a public forum may not be based on content alone, and may not be justified by reference to content alone.[102]

In its 2014 judgment in *McCullen* v. *Coakley*, the US Supreme Court held that a 35-feet buffer zone outside abortion clinics in the state of Massachusetts was unconstitutional. The Court acknowledged that the buffer zones served 'legitimate interests in maintaining public safety on streets and sidewalks and in preserving access to adjacent reproductive healthcare facilities', but affirmed that

> they impose serious burdens on petitioners' speech, depriving them of their two primary methods of communicating with arriving patients: close, personal conversations and distribution of literature. Those forms of expression have historically been closely associated with the transmission of ideas. While the Act may allow petitioners to 'protest' outside the buffer zones, petitioners are not protestors; they seek not merely to express their opposition to abortion, but to engage in personal, caring, consensual conversations with women about various alternatives. It is thus no answer to say that petitioners can still be seen and heard by women within the buffer zones. If all that the women can see and hear are vociferous opponents of abortion, then the buffer zones have effectively stifled petitioners' message.[103]

The constitutional rights set out in the First Amendment are not, though, absolute, and restrictions may, in certain circumstances, even be discriminatory and not unlawful where issues of safety and security are involved. In *Wood* v. *Moss*,[104] in a judgment issued a month before its decision in the *McCullen* case, the Supreme Court held unanimously that two Secret

[101] A. Meiklejohn, *Political Freedom: The Constitutional Powers of the People*, Harper & Bros., New York, 1948, p. 27.

[102] US Supreme Court, *Police Dept. of Chicago* v. *Mosley*, 408 US 96.

[103] US Supreme Court, *McCullen and Others* v. *Coakley*, Judgment (Case No. 12–1168), 573 US___ (2014) 26 June 2014, p. 3, at: www.supremecourt.gov/opinions/13pdf/12-1168_6k47.pdf.

[104] US Supreme Court, *Wood* v. *Moss*, Judgment (Case No. No. 13–115), 27 May 2014, 572 US ___ (2014).

Service agents who ordered that individuals protesting against the policies of President George W. Bush be moved away from the outdoor area where the president was eating were entitled to qualified immunity on the basis of a legitimate security rationale. This is despite the fact that this placed the protesters further away from the president than the president's supporters. The protesters' lawsuit had alleged viewpoint discrimination in violation of the First Amendment.[105] According to the Court,

> It is uncontested and uncontestable that government officials may not exclude from public places persons engaged in peaceful expressive activity solely because the government actor fears, dislikes, or disagrees with the views those persons express. . . . It is equally plain that the fundamental right to speak secured by the First Amendment does not leave people at liberty to publicize their views "whenever and however and wherever they please."

2015: A Year of Protests against Excessive Use of Police Force in the United States

Demonstration are not infrequently organised specifically to protest against the actions of law enforcement officials and agencies. The year 2015, though, is particularly memorable for the widespread and angry protests against excessive and discriminatory police use of force in the United States, especially police action against African Americans.[106] Protests were organised, or erupted spontaneously, in Baltimore, Chicago, Ferguson, Los Angeles, New York, and Washington DC, among others.

New York

The year 2015 began with a 'die-in' in New York City's Times Square, a Black Lives Matter[107] demonstration against police brutality. The movement began in 2013 with use of the hashtag #BlackLivesMatter on social media, after George Zimmerman was acquitted of charges of

[105] See, e.g., SCOTUS blog, at: www.scotusblog.com/case-files/cases/wood-v-moss/.

[106] The following summary is adapted from RT, '2015: A Year of Protests in America', 30 December 2015 (edited on 31 December 2015), at: www.rt.com/usa/327455-protest-police-wages-year/.

[107] See: http://blacklivesmatter.com/. According to the website, Black Lives Matter 'is an ideological and political intervention in a world where Black lives are systematically and intentionally targeted for demise. It is an affirmation of Black folks' contributions to this society, our humanity, and our resilience in the face of deadly oppression'.

second-degree murder for the shooting to death of an unarmed African-American teenager, Trayvon Martin.

Chicago

On 28 February, activists in Chicago demanded a thorough investigation of a criminal detention centre at a warehouse in Homan Square in the city that they compared to a CIA black site.[108] The *Gitmo2Chicago* hashtag drew attention to allegations of detainees being tortured and having their constitutional rights being violated by police.[109]

Los Angeles

On 1 March 2015, members of the Los Angeles Police Department (LAPD) shot and killed an unarmed, homeless man with mental health issues, even though he was being restrained by three other officers. Smartphone footage of the incident released the following day triggered protests on social media and in front of the LAPD headquarters. Chanting 'You can't kill Africa' (the nickname of the deceased victim), people on Saturday marched from LAPD headquarters to skid row to protest the shooting during a struggle with officers. Cue Jn'Marie, a skid row preacher, said police should have sent a mental health team to handle Charly 'Africa' Leundeu Keunang, whose shooting was caught on video and viewed by millions of people. Mr Keunang, who was convicted of armed bank robbery in 2000, was committed to a psychiatric prison hospital three years into his 15-year federal prison term.[110]

South Carolina

On 4 April 2015, Walter Scott, a 50-year-old man, was fatally shot by white South Carolina police officer Michael Slager while trying to run from a traffic stop in North Charleston, having been pulled over for a faulty brake light. A bystander recorded the shooting with a mobile

[108] S. Ackerman, 'The Hidden: How Chicago Police Kept Thousands Isolated at Homan Square', *The Guardian*, 13 April 2016, at: www.theguardian.com/us-news/2016/apr/13/homan-square-chicago-police-records-secret-interrogation-facility-new-documents-lawsuit?CMP=Share_iOSApp_Other.

[109] See, e.g., Z. Stafford, '#Gitmo2Chicago: Protests Target Police "Black Site"', *The Guardian*, 28 February 2015, at: www.theguardian.com/us-news/2015/feb/28/chicago-protests-police-black-site-homan-square.

[110] G. Holland, 'Dozens Protest LAPD Shooting of Homeless Man on Skid Row', *Los Angeles Times*, 7 March 2015, at: www.latimes.com/local/california/la-me-0308-lapd-protest-20150308-story.html.

phone as Officer Slager shot Mr Scott, who was unarmed and running away from him, eight times in the back. Officer Slager, who lied about the circumstances of the shooting before the video was released, was sacked from the force after his arrest on a murder charge.[111] His trial on the charge of murder in state court was scheduled to begin at the end of October 2016, while his trial on a federal civil rights charge was pushed back until 2017.[112] Pre-trial testimony reported on 25 October 2016 focused on filling in the gaps between Mr Slager's official account of the shooting in North Charleston – he said Walter Scott grabbed his Taser and attacked him with it – when the video evidence taken from a bystander shows that never happened.[113]

At a rally held one month after the shooting, a coalition of neighbourhood organisations, religious leaders, labour organisers and activist groups voiced support for a common agenda, demanding equal access to education and other opportunities for all North Charleston residents, transparency in city government, an end to racial profiling and police brutality and 'independent, community-based oversight and accountability over the police department'. Muhiyidin d'Baha, an organiser with the Charleston Black Lives Matter chapter, said his group would continue to protest. 'All along, our strategy was to negotiate, demonstrate, and resist. That hasn't gone anywhere', he said. 'We have the same strategy. It's just that now we have more political and social capital behind it.'[114] Legislators agreed to equip every police officer in the city with body cameras to record interactions with citizens.[115]

Baltimore

On 19 April 2015, Freddie Gray, a 25-year-old black man died from spinal injuries sustained after his arrest a week earlier in Baltimore. It was reported in the press that he might have been the victim of what is

111 Associated Press, 'A Look at Police Use-of-Force Cases before Freddie Gray', *Forensic Magazine*, 19 April 2016, available at: www.forensicmag.com.

112 A. Knapp, 'Despite Defense Request, Judge Pushes Michael Slager's Federal Trial to 2017', The Post & Courier, 30 August 2016, at: www.postandcourier.com/20160830/160839974/despite-defense-request-judge-pushes-michael-slagers-federal-trial-to-2017.

113 J. Walsh, 'Walter Scott Trial Update: Did Officer Slager Lie about South Carolina Shooting?', *International Business Times*, 25 October 2016, at: www.ibtimes.com/.

114 P. Bowers, 'After Walter Scott Shooting, South Carolina Protesters Make Slow Progress', *Aljazeera America*, 19 May 2015, at: http://america.aljazeera.com/articles/2015/5/19/after-walter-scott-shooting-south-carolina-protesters-make-slow-progress.html.

115 Ibid.

euphemistically called a 'rough ride'. This is where a handcuffed detainee is placed in a police van without a seatbelt and then thrown about violently by the van being driven erratically. Police subsequently said that he should have received medical attention at the scene. It was also reported that, because the investigation did not start for several days, opportunities were missed to gather crucial evidence, such as a surveillance tape from a nearby shop that was taped over.[116]

On 21 April, police released the identities of the six officers involved, escalating protests that had been occurring for several days.[117] Despite Baltimore Mayor Stephanie Rawlings-Blake's call for 'peaceful and respectful' protests, violence broke out in downtown Baltimore, with demonstrators throwing bottles at police and smashing cars. Police in riot gear clashed with protesters, and a total of twelve people were arrested. The DOJ would report later that the unrest following the death of Freddie Gray in police custody had demonstrated the deep and enduring divide between police officers and parts of the Baltimore community.[118]

As tensions mounted, the day of the funeral of Mr Gray on 27 April also saw the declaration of a state of emergency in Baltimore by Governor Larry Hogan as a result of riots across the city. The National Guard was called in, and the following day, 2,000 troops arrived with armoured vehicles, leaving only on 3 May when the protests ended. But Freddie Gray protests spread to other cities, including a riot in Seattle. In response, police deployed flash-bang grenades, pepper spray, and tear gas in an attempt to get the crowd under control. Three officers were injured and fifteen protesters were arrested. The American Civil Liberties Union (ACLU) subsequently obtained records from the Federal Bureau of Investigation (FBI) showing that the agency had flown at least ten surveillance flights over Baltimore from 29 April to 3 May 2015, when

[116] D. A. Graham, '"Rough Rides" and the Challenges of Improving Police Culture. Freddie Gray Isn't the First Person to be Gravely Injured while Riding in a Police Van', *The Atlantic*, 27 April 2015, at: www.theatlantic.com/politics/archive/2015/04/the-rough-ride-and-police-culture/391538/.

[117] As of writing, no officer had been found responsible under criminal law for the death of Mr Gray. After the acquittal of three officers on serious charges, in July 2016 Baltimore's state attorney dropped all charges in the case. K. Rector, 'Charges Dropped, Freddie Gray Case Concludes with Zero Convictions against Officers', *Baltimore Sun*, 27 July 2016, at: www.baltimoresun.com/news/maryland/freddie-gray/bs-md-ci-miller-pretrial-motions-20160727-story.html.

[118] US DOJ, *Investigation of the Baltimore City Police Department*, 10 August 2016, p. 19.

the city streets were filled with protesters and mourners. The FBI's aircraft, which were registered to front companies to conceal their ownership, were said to have carried sophisticated camera systems on board, complete with night-vision capabilities.[119]

Wisconsin

On 13 May, protests erupted in Madison, Wisconsin, in response to a decision not to indict the police officer who had shot an unarmed 19-year-old black man. At least twenty-five protesters were arrested as a group linked arms to block traffic in the middle of the street in front of the city's courthouse. Madison police spokesman Joel DeSpain said the protesters were obstructing an intersection near the state Capitol building; almost all were released with a $124 misdemeanour fine.[120]

Texas

On 8 June, hundreds of people took to the streets in McKinney, Texas, following an incident in which a police officer pulled a gun on black teenagers at a private pool party that they had gate-crashed, resulting in violent arrests. The officer who drew his gun on the teenagers subsequently resigned from the police. About 800 protesters marched through McKinney to the swimming pool where the incident had occurred, demanding that the officer involved be dismissed. Many of the protesters accused the officers involved of being racially biased while some held up signs that said 'My skin color is not a crime' and 'Don't tread on our kids.'[121] McKinney Police Chief Greg Conley said that the officer's actions were 'indefensible' and that the officer was 'out of control' during the incident.[122]

[119] N. F. Wessler & N. Dwork, 'FBI Releases Secret Spy Plane Footage from Freddie Gray Protests', ACLU, 4 August 2016, at: www.aclu.org/blog/speak-freely/fbi-releases-secret-spy-plane-footage-freddie-gray-protests.

[120] Associated Press, 'The Latest in Madison: 25 Arrested during Protest of Decision not to Charge Cop in Man's Death', *US News*, 13 May 2015, at: www.usnews.com/news/us/articles/2015/05/13/the-latest-protesters-seek-walkout-over-wisconsin-shooting.

[121] R. Villeda, 'McKinney Rally Draws Hundreds of Protesters and Some Supporters', *NBC 5*, Dallas, 8 June 2015, at: www.nbcdfw.com/news/local/McKinney-Protest-Rally-Draws-Hundreds-306575061.html.

[122] B. Chappell, 'Chief Calls Actions of Officer From McKinney, Texas, Pool Party Video "Indefensible"', *NPR*, 9 June 2015, at: www.npr.org/sections/thetwo-way/2015/06/09/413153057/hundreds-march-in-mckinney-s-streets-to-protest-police-action.

New York

On 17 July, several thousand people gathered in New York at a protest marking the one-year anniversary of the death of Eric Garner from Staten Island (see Chapters 1 and 2). Mr Garner died after being placed in a chokehold by police; two New York Police Department (NYPD) officers had approached him on suspicion of selling 'loosies' (single cigarettes) from packs without tax stamps. A mobile phone camera held by a friend of Mr. Garner recorded the struggle, including the eleven pleas for breath. However, the NYPD's initial account did not mention any contact with Mr. Garner's neck. The autopsy report found that on the inside of Mr Garner's neck were tell-tale signs of choking: strap muscle haemorrhages in his neck and petechial haemorrhages in his eyes.[123]

Mr. Garner's final words – 'I can't breathe' – became a rallying cry for a protest movement. A grand jury in December 2015 had declined to bring any charges in relation to his death.[124] More than twenty people were arrested during the protests on the anniversary of Mr Garner's death.

Ferguson, Missouri

On 9 August, the anniversary of Michael Brown's shooting to death by a police officer in Ferguson, Missouri, there were protests across the city over the course of two days. Though demonstrations were initially peaceful, two groups of looters began firing at each other and a state of emergency was declared. Some 50 protesters were arrested at a rally in front of the federal courthouse on the anniversary of Mr Brown's death. In total, more than 100 protesters were arrested during the demonstrations.

New York

On 22 October, hundreds gathered in New York's Times Square to launch a three-day protest, 'Rise Up October', against police killings and brutality and mass incarceration.[125] At least a dozen people were arrested the following day after protesters gathered near Rikers' Island

123 A. Baker, J. D. Goodman and B. Mueller, 'Beyond the Chokehold: The Path to Eric Garner's Death', *New York Times*, 13 June 2015, at: www.nytimes.com/2015/06/14/nyregion/eric-garner-police-chokehold-staten-island.html?_r=0.

124 Ibid.

125 See, e.g., A. Lidgett, 'Rise Up October NYC Police Brutality Protest Results in Multiple Arrests: Report', *International Business Times*, 24 October 2015, at: www.ibtimes.com/rise-october-nyc-police-brutality-protest-results-multiple-arrests-report-2155195.

prison to call attention to brutality towards inmates. Film director Quentin Tarantino took part in the Rise Up October protests, leading to the NYPD police union to call for a boycott of his films.

On 24 October, the protest began in Washington Square Park then moved along 6th Avenue to the Midtown area; people with megaphones shouted stories of the men and women who have been killed by cops as others waved signs with their photos. While things were calm at the start of the event, things got heated as protesters got close to Bryant Park. One commentator alleged that: 'Despite the fact that the organizers of the protest jumped through the arduous hoops of obtaining a parade permit, the NYPD showed up for the event as if they were prepared for a riot, and deployed numerous questionable tactics, trampling on the demonstrators constitutional rights to free speech and to peaceably gather.'[126] Police said that eleven protesters were arrested, which included a woman in her seventies; charges included disorderly conduct, obstructing vehicular traffic, failing to disperse, and resisting arrest.[127]

Chicago

On 24 November, protests erupted after a video showed Laquan McDonald, a 17-year-old black youth armed with a knife, being shot sixteen times by a police officer in Chicago. Protests began in Chicago, but spread to other cities across the country. Three activists were arrested during the first night of demonstrations in Chicago. Protests continued throughout December, with protesters marching through downtown Chicago on 9 December, blocking traffic as they reiterated their demands for the mayor to resign.

On 7 December 2015, the DOJ opened a 'Pattern or Practice' Investigation into the Chicago Police Department.[128] In January 2016, the Cook County board of commissioners, which oversees the second largest county in the United States including the entirety of Chicago, called on the DOJ to expand its investigation 'to look into allegations of civil and

[126] B. Yakas, 'Videos: 11 People Arrested During "Rise Up October" Protest Against Police Brutality', *Gothamist*, 25 October 2015, at: http://gothamist.com/2015/10/25/video_11_people_arrested_during_ris.php.

[127] Ibid.

[128] DOJ, 'Justice Department Opens Pattern or Practice Investigation into the Chicago Police Department', 7 December 2015, at: www.justice.gov/opa/pr/justice-department-opens-pattern-or-practice-investigation-chicago-police-department.

human rights violations' at Homan Square.[129] The results of the DOJ investigation were announced in January 2017. The Department of Justice found reasonable cause to believe that the Chicago Police Department had engaged in a pattern or practice of using force, including deadly force, in violation of the Fourth Amendment of the US Constitution. The DOJ found that CPD officers' practices were unnecessarily endangering themselves and resulting in unnecessary and avoidable uses of force.[130]

On 27 December 2015, protests again broke out in Chicago this time in response to a Chicago police officer shooting and killed a 19-year-old student and his 55-year-old neighbour, a mother of five, after responding to a domestic disturbance call. The teenager's mother said she had been hoping to get help from police. Hundreds of people gathered in the streets of Chicago, claiming that police were killing civilians instead of protecting them.

Peaceful Protest in Repressive Regimes

Hong Kong

The exercise of the right to assembly, especially when it concerns criticism of the regime in power, is strictly controlled in authoritarian regimes. In Hong Kong, for instance, protests are often violently repressed. In 2014, the Umbrella Movement was so named after the means protesters used to defend themselves from teargas and pepper spray diffused by the police.[131] According to Chan Kin-man, co-founder of democracy group Occupy Central with Love and Peace (OCLP) and a professor of sociology at the Chinese University of Hong Kong, 'We are seriously upholding the principle of nonviolence ... We are fighting a non-democratic regime; we don't

[129] Z. Stafford, 'Homan Square: US Inquiry into Chicago police "Should Also Cover Facility"', *The Guardian*, 14 January 2016, at: www.theguardian.com/us-news/2016/jan/14/homan-square-justice-department-investigation-chicago-police-.

[130] Department of Justice, "Justice Department Announces Findings of Investigation into Chicago Police Department", Press release, Office of Public Affairs, Washington DC, 13 January 2017, at: www.justice.gov/opa/pr/justice-department-announces-findings-investigation-chicago-police-department.

[131] T. Phillips, 'Hong Kong "Umbrella Movement" Marks First Anniversary and Vows to Fight on', *The Guardian*, 28 September 2015, at: www.theguardian.com/world/2015/sep/28/hong-kong-umbrella-movement-first-anniversary-democracy.

have as many resources as them, we don't have weapons. The only thing we rely on is our spirit.'[132]

Venezuela

In 2014, with respect to the situation in Venezuela, the Inter-American Commission on Human Rights[133] declared itself to be 'profoundly disturbed' by complaints alleging violations of the demonstrators' rights to peaceful protest and their rights to life and humane treatment, liberty, freedom of association, and freedom of expression.[134] The Commission noted that several people had been injured and one was killed after being shot during demonstrations in the city of Valencia on 18 February 2014. In addition, according to figures provided by the Ministry of Interior, Justice and Peace, the following day four people suffered bullet wounds and another died in protests in the city of Puerto Ordaz. In respecting and ensuring the right to protest, a 'primary function of law enforcement, in addition to the obligation to facilitate, is protecting the safety and rights of those who participate in assemblies as well as monitors and bystanders'.[135]

Syria, before the War

In Syria, the origins of the brutal conflict that was continuing to rage in 2016 despite attempts to achieve a ceasefire sprang from violent repression of peaceful protests in 2011. As the BBC reported in 2013, the movement started with protests

[132] L. Westcott, 'Hong Kong's Protesters Say Peaceful Resistance is Key', *Newsweek*, 29 September 2014, at: http://europe.newsweek.com/peaceful-resistance-key-strategy-hong-kongs-pro-democracy-protesters-274110.

[133] The IACmnHR is an autonomous body of the Organization of American States (OAS) which derives its mandate from the OAS Charter and the 1969 American Convention on Human Rights. The Commission has a mandate to promote respect for human rights in the region and acts as a consultative body to the OAS. The Commission is composed of seven independent members who are elected in an individual capacity by the OAS General Assembly and who do not represent their countries of origin or residence.

[134] IACmnHR, 'IACHR Expresses Deep Concern over the Situation with Respect to the Right to Peaceful Protest, Freedom of Association and Freedom of Expression in Venezuela', Press release, Washington, DC, 21 February 2014, at: www.oas.org/en/iachr/media_center/PReleases/2014/017.asp.

[135] 2016 Joint UN Report, §41.

> calling for more freedom and dignity. The way the government handled the events since those first days drove more and more people to oppose President Bashar al-Assad. At first, no-one was calling for the regime to fall. Many people had hopes that the young president would respond to their calls and punish those of the security forces who killed innocent civilians. But the wave of killings and arrests, torture and humiliation targeting people who were not even involved in the demonstrations drove many who steered clear of politics to join the protest movement ... Today, government shelling has silenced the voices of peaceful protest.[136]

As the 1948 Universal Declaration of Human Rights recalls, 'it is essential, if man is not to be compelled to have recourse, as a last resort, to rebellion against tyranny and oppression, that human rights should be protected by the rule of law.'[137]

Policing and Crowd Safety at Major Sporting Events

Finally, the duty on the police under international human rights law to ensure crowd safety at major sporting events is considered. Here the authorities typically have plenty of notice (and a great deal of experience), so a high standard of care applies and should legitimately be expected. A case study of serious failure to meet that standard is the police action prior to, during, and following the 1989 Hillsborough disaster. This case concerned the deaths as a result of crushing of 96 Liverpool football fans at Sheffield Wednesday's Hillsborough stadium in northern England.

The Case of the 1989 Hillsborough Disaster

As a Panel set up to investigate recalled, the 1989 Hillsborough disaster remains the most serious tragedy in UK sporting history. In addition to those who perished, thousands suffered physical injury and/or long-term psychological harm.[138] The facts of the case are as follows.[139] On

[136] L. Sinjab, 'Syria Conflict: From Peaceful Protest to Civil War', *BBC*, 15 March 2013, at: www.bbc.com/news/world-middle-east-21797661.

[137] Third preambular para., 1948 Universal Declaration of Human Rights.

[138] Hillsborough Independent Panel website, at: http://hillsborough.independent.gov.uk/.

[139] Unless otherwise stated, this overview of the facts is derived from the summary of the Hillsborough Independent Panel at: http://hillsborough.independent.gov.uk/report/Section-1/summary/; and BBC, 'How the Hillsborough Disaster Happened', 14 April 2009, at: http://news.bbc.co.uk/2/hi/uk/7992845.stm.

15 April 1989, more than 50,000 men, women, and children travelled to Hillsborough Stadium to watch an FA Cup Semi-Final between Liverpool and Nottingham Forest that was kicking off at 3pm. Hillsborough was a neutral venue which, like so many stadia of that era, contained a mix of seated areas and modified standing terraces. As the match started, it became apparent that in the central area of the terraces on one end of the ground at Leppings Lane, already visibly overcrowded before the kick-off, Liverpool fans were in considerable distress.

The small area in which the crush occurred comprised two pens. Fans had entered down a tunnel under the West Stand into the central pens 3 and 4. Each pen was segregated by lateral fences and a high, overhanging fence between the terrace and the perimeter track around the pitch. There was a small locked gate at the front of each pen. At 14:52, police made the fateful decision to order a large exit gate to be opened to alleviate the crush outside the ground. Around 2,000 fans then made their way into the ground and headed straight for a tunnel leading directly to pens 3 and 4. It was later estimated that more than 3,000 supporters were admitted to the central pens: almost double what was considered the safe capacity. The crush became unbearable and fans collapsed underfoot. To the front of pen 3, a safety barrier broke, creating a pile of people struggling for breath.

Despite closed circuit television (CCTV) cameras transmitting images of distress in the crowd to the Ground Control Room and to the Police Control Box at the stadium, as well as the presence of officers on duty on the perimeter track, minutes went by before the seriousness of what was happening was realised and rescue attempts were made. At 15:06, a policeman finally ran on to the pitch and ordered the referee to stop the game. As fans were pulled from the terrace through the narrow gates onto the pitch, the scale of the tragedy became evident. Fans tore down advertising hoardings and used them to carry the dead and dying the full length of the pitch to the stadium gymnasium.

The authorities' response to the disaster was slow and badly coordinated. Firefighters with cutting gear had difficulty getting into the ground, and although dozens of ambulances were dispatched, access to the pitch was delayed because police were inaccurately reporting 'crowd trouble'. Of the 96 people who died, only 14 were ever admitted to hospital.

In the immediate aftermath there was a rush to judgement concerning the cause of the disaster and culpability. In a climate of allegation and counter-allegation, the Government appointed Lord Justice Taylor to lead a judicial inquiry. What followed, over an 11-year period, were various different modes and levels of scrutiny, including Lord Justice Taylor's interim and final reports, civil litigation, criminal and disciplinary investigations, inquests into the deaths of the victims (which originally returned a majority verdict of accidental death), judicial reviews, a judicial scrutiny of new evidence, and the private prosecution of the two most senior police officers in command on the day. One officer was acquitted while the jury were unable to reach a verdict in the second case.

Lord Justice Taylor stated in his report that the key element of police control at fault was the failure to close off the tunnel leading to pens 3 and 4 once the exit gate had been opened. He criticised police for their failure to handle the build-up of fans outside the ground properly, and their slow reaction to the unfolding disaster. Some of his strongest words were reserved for the police commander on the day, Chief Superintendent David Duckenfield, for 'failing to take effective control', and for South Yorkshire police, who attempted to blame supporters for the crush by arriving at the ground 'late and drunk'.[140]

Despite the range of inquiries and investigations, many bereaved families and survivors considered that the truth of the Hillsborough disaster had not been made public. In July 2009, the Hillsborough Family Support Group, supported by a group of Merseyside MPs, presented to the UK Secretary of State for Home Affairs a case for the truth to be revealed. In January 2010, the Hillsborough Independent Panel, chaired by James Jones, Bishop of Liverpool, was appointed.

Based on the Panel report and following an application by the UK Attorney-General, in December 2012 the High Court quashed the verdicts in the original inquests and ordered fresh inquests to be held; hearings started on 31 March 2014 in Warrington, Cheshire. After almost two years of sometimes harrowing evidence, the Coroner began his summing-up in late January 2016. Among other issues, Coroner Sir John Goldring told the jury they must consider whether they believed that former Chief Superintendent Duckenfield was responsible for gross negligence manslaughter of the 96 deceased fans.[141] On 26 April 2016, the inquest jury announced its verdict that the 96 football fans had been

[140] See also: http://hillsborough.independent.gov.uk/report/Section-1/summary/page-14/.

[141] See the transcript of the inquest at: http://hillsboroughinquests.independent.gov.uk/wp-content/uploads/2016/01/hill250116amjurypresentonly.txt; and see K. Pilling, 'Hillsborough Inquest Jury must Decide Whether Former Top Cop David Duckenfield Guilty of Unlawful Killing', *Daily Mirror*, 26 January 2016, at: www.mirror.co.uk/sport/football/news/hillsborough-inquest-jury-must-decide-7245967.

unlawfully killed. The jury also found Chief Superintendent Duckenfield responsible for manslaughter by gross negligence, due to a serious breach of his duty of care. Police errors, the jury concluded, had added to a dangerous situation at the FA Cup semi-final. The UK Prime Minister at the time, David Cameron, said the inquests had provided 'official confirmation' that Liverpool fans were 'utterly blameless'.[142]

A separate independent investigation into police actions in the aftermath of the disaster was announced by the Independent Police Complaints Commission (IPCC) on 12 October 2012 and remained underway as of writing. The Hillsborough investigation is the biggest criminal investigation into alleged police misconduct ever conducted in England and Wales.[143] Operation Resolve,[144] which was considering the following possible criminal offences as part of its investigation: gross negligence manslaughter, misconduct in public office, perverting the course of justice, the 1975 Safety at Sports Grounds Act (s. 12(1)(d)), and the Health and Safety at Work Act (ss. 3, 7, and 37).[145] In December 2016, Operation Resolve handed over files of evidence relating to 15 suspects to the Crown Prosecution Service, who were expected to make decisions whether or not to charge individuals in the Summer of 2017.[146]

[142] BBC, 'Hillsborough Inquests: Fans Unlawfully Killed, Jury Concludes', 26 April 2016, at: www.bbc.com/news/uk-england-36138337.

[143] www.ipcc.gov.uk/hillsborough. [144] http://operationresolve.co.uk/.

[145] 'Latest Update from Operation Resolve October 2016', Posted by Glenn Bowley, 21 October 2016, at: http://operationresolve.co.uk/news/.

[146] Operation Resolve, at: http://operationresolve.co.uk/.

7

Use of Force in Custodial Settings

> 'My husband had been taken into custody by the state – he was their responsibility. They are accomplices in his death', Ms. Pereira said. 'They took him from the security of our home and dumped him there ... They sentenced him to death – to decapitation, to be more precise.'[1]

Introduction

This chapter discusses the use of force against detainees, that is, persons deprived of their liberty by the state for whatever reason and in whichever circumstances. The Inter-American Commission of Human Rights has defined the concept 'deprivation of liberty' in broad terms, as follows:

> Any form of detention, imprisonment, institutionalization, or custody of a person in a public or private institution which that person is not permitted to leave at will, by order of or under de facto control of a judicial, administrative or any other authority, for reasons of humanitarian assistance, treatment, guardianship, protection, or because of crimes or legal offenses.[2]

The Commission clarifies that, as a category, detainees include those who are deprived of their liberty 'because of crimes or infringements or non-compliance with the law, whether they are accused or convicted'. Also encompassed are those under the custody and supervision of institutions, such as psychiatric hospitals and other establishments for persons with physical, mental, or sensory disabilities; institutions for children and the elderly; and centres for migrants, refugees, or asylum seekers.[3]

[1] S. Nolen, 'Brazil's Brutal Prison System in Crisis Proves a Tough Cage to Rattle', *Globe and Mail*, 4 October 2015, at: www.theglobeandmail.com/news/world/brazils-brutal-prison-system-in-crisis-proves-a-tough-cage-to-rattle/article26646883/.

[2] Inter-American Commission on Human Rights (IACmnHR), 'Revision of the United Nations Standard Minimum Rules for the Treatment of Prisoners', UN doc. UNODC/CCPCJ/EG.6/2014/INF/2, 8 October 2013, p. 3.

[3] Ibid.

All detainees are entitled to respect and protection of their fundamental human rights. As the 1990 Basic Principles for the Treatment of Prisoners provide: 'Except for those limitations that are demonstrably necessitated by the fact of incarceration, all prisoners shall retain the human rights and fundamental freedoms' set out in universal human rights treaties.[4]

Respecting and ensuring these rights, however, is a major challenge for many states. The following section of the chapter describes prison populations and conditions in selected states, including Brazil, China, England and Wales, South Africa, and the United States (US). The corresponding situation in women's prisons is also summarised. The second part of the chapter sets out the human rights framework for the treatment of detainees, including use of force by law enforcement officials. Respect for the rights to life and to humane treatment of detainees is accorded particular attention, with examples given of what amounts to inhumane treatment. This comprehends collective punishment, corporal punishment, forced feeding, and unnecessary or inappropriate restraints and use of pepper spray. The final subsection looks at the legality of use of force during interviews of criminal suspects.

[4] Principle 5, 1990 Basic Principles for the Treatment of Prisoners, adopted by United Nations (UN) General Assembly Resolution 45/111 of 14 December 1990. The term prisoner in this context is to be construed broadly, as it is in the 1955 Standard Minimum Rules for the Treatment of Prisoners (as revised). Thus, in the latest iteration of the Standard Minimum Rules, known as the 2015 Nelson Mandela Rules, in Preliminary observation 3(1) it is stipulated that: 'Part I of the rules covers the general management of prisons, and is applicable to all categories of prisoners, criminal or civil, untried or convicted, including prisoners subject to "security measures" or corrective measures ordered by the judge.' UN Standard Minimum Rules for the Treatment of Prisoners (the 'Nelson Mandela Rules'), adopted without a vote by UN General Assembly Resolution 70/175 of 17 December 2015. See also: Ch. 8 (International Legal Standards for the Protection of Persons Deprived of their Liberty), in Office of the UN High Commissioner for Human Rights (OHCHR), *Manual on Human Rights for Judges, Prosecutors and Lawyers*, Professional Training Series No. 9, UN, New York and Geneva, 2003, available at: www.ohchr.org/EN/PublicationsResources/Pages/TrainingEducationtwo.aspx. Even prisoners sentenced to death retain such rights and freedoms. In a 1998 case, the African Commission on Human and Peoples' Rights held that where the state held death-row prisoners in leg irons and handcuffs, and denied them access to legal counsel and necessary medicine, it violated their right to dignity (Article 5 of the 1981 African Charter on Human and Peoples' Rights). African Commission on Human and Peoples' Rights (ACHPR), *International Pen and Others* v. *Nigeria*, Decision (Comm. Nos. 137/94, 139/94, 154/96 and 161/97), 1998.

Prison Conditions in Selected States

Brazil

The situation in prisons around the world varies materially to the extent that the prison in which a detainee finds himself or herself may mean the difference between life and death. For instance, Brazil, which has the fourth-largest prison population in the world after the United States, China, and Russia, faces huge problems in complying with its duty to respect and protect the rights of those it detains. A more than 500 per cent increase in prisoner numbers between 1990 and 2013 has resulted in chronic and severe overcrowding in Brazil's jails. According to Amnesty International, degrading conditions, torture, and violence remained endemic in 2014.[5] In October 2015, Human Rights Watch issued a report on prisons in the north-eastern state of Pernambuco, saying that the conditions amounted to a 'human rights disaster':

> The prevalence of HIV infection in Pernambuco's prisons is 42 times that of the general population; the prevalence of tuberculosis is almost 100 times that of the general population. Prison clinics are understaffed, medication is scarce, and ill detainees are often not taken to hospitals for lack of police escort. . . . Extreme overcrowding also puts detainees at risk of sexual violence. Human Rights Watch interviewed two detainees who said they were gang raped and reported the attacks to guards who ignored them.[6]

Between April 2013 and April 2014, Brazil's courts sentenced 75 police officers for the killing of 111 prisoners in the 1992 Carandiru prison riots.[7] The officers lodged appeals and remained on active service at the end of 2014. The commander of the police operation had been convicted in 2001, although this was overturned;

[5] Amnesty International (AI), 'Prison Conditions, in Brazil Report: 2014', at: www.amnesty.org/en/countries/americas/brazil/report-brazil/.

[6] Human Rights Watch, 'The State Let Evil Take Over: The Prison Crisis in the Brazilian State of Pernambuco', 19 October 2015, at: www.hrw.org/report/2015/10/19/state-let-evil-take-over/prison-crisis-brazilian-state-pernambuco.

[7] The riot began on 2 October 1992 after an argument between two inmates (reportedly during a football match) quickly spread, with rival gangs facing off in what was at the time one of South America's largest prisons, housing 10,000 inmates. See, e.g., BBC, 'Brazil Carandiru Jail Massacre Police Guilty', 3 August 2013, at: www.bbc.com/news/world-latin-america-23560362; and J. Fortin, 'Twenty Years after Carandiru Massacre, Brazil's Prisons Still Deplorable', *International Business Times*, 4 October 2012, at: www.ibtimes.com/twenty-years-after-carandiru-massacre-brazils-prisons-still-deplorable-799697.

he was murdered by his girlfriend in 2006. The prison governor and the Minister of Public Security at the time of the riots were not charged in connection with the case.[8] A critical protection problem is that many prisons are largely in the control of gangs. In May 2015, riots broke out at the Feira da Santana jail in Bahia state, also in north-eastern Brazil. The violence, which started between rival gangs at the prison, resulted in two prisoners being decapitated and at least seven others killed.[9]

In one prison complex at Pedrinhas, 40km outside the capital of Maranhão, one of Brazil's least-developed states, prisoners have also been beheaded and there have even been reports of cannibalism. In 2013, 60 detainees were murdered in the prison while more than 18 were killed between January and October 2014. Videos of beheadings were broadcast in the media.[10] Victoria Pereira, aged 12, learnt that her father had been killed – decapitated – by watching the television news. Elson de Jesus Pereira had been taken to the jail in 2013 after his conviction for selling stolen tyres at his repair shop. Mr. Pereira was given a six-year prison sentence, despite having no prior record. Eleven days later, the day after he turned 44, he was killed, though prison authorities did not tell his wife until after they had first informed media about the riot.[11]

The state government admitted it had lost control of the interior of Pedrinhas prison and sent in a heavily-armed elite national police squad, who fought for more than two weeks to reclaim control. Prisoners were forced back into cells and gradually stripped of most weapons. The government shipped the leaders of the gangs to a federal maximum-security prison and divided up other inmates by affiliation, each gang with their own jail so they could no longer engage in 'warfare' within the prison. The murder rate dropped immediately.[12]

[8] AI, 'Prison Conditions'.

[9] 'Two Prisoners Decapitated and At least Six Others Dead after Riots at a Brazilian Prison', *news.com.au*, 26 May 2015, at: www.news.com.au/world/two-prisoners-decapitated-and-at-least-six-others-dead-after-riots-at-a-brazilian-prison/news-story/99ef327c5b7a2860116aaf1c55c5ef0c.

[10] AI, 'Prison Conditions'.

[11] Nolen, 'Brazil's Brutal Prison System in Crisis Proves a Tough Cage to Rattle'.

[12] Ibid.

The United States

The United States has less than one in twenty of the world's population yet nearly one in four of the world's prisoners.[13] Some 2.2 million are incarcerated in jails and prisons[14] (more than four times the population detained in 1980) and on average about a dozen inmates die each day, according to the Department of Justice.[15] The Bureau of Justice Statistics (BJS) reported that in 2013, the number of inmates who died in state prisons and local jails had increased for the third consecutive year. A total of 4,446 inmates died in 2013, an increase of 131 deaths from 2012. This was the highest number of deaths reported to the BJS Deaths in Custody Reporting Program since 2007.[16]

As in every year since 2000, suicide was the leading cause of death in local jails, accounting for more than a third (34 per cent) of all jail deaths in 2013. From 2012 to 2013, homicides rose from 22 to 28 deaths. Homicides or accidental deaths were less common than other causes of death, each accounting for 3 per cent or less of jail deaths in 2013.[17]

Recorded homicides included the death on 3 March 2012 of Eugene Gruber, a 51-year-old man and inmate of Lake County jail in Illinois. Mr Gruber died from pneumonia resulting from paraplegia, which followed spinal injuries suffered in an altercation with a corrections officer. Jail staff described Mr Gruber as drunk and combative when he was brought in on 31 October 2011 after being arrested for disorderly conduct and trespassing. Guards pepper-sprayed him and then used a neck-twisting

[13] See, e.g., C. Kubrin and C. Seron, 'The Prospects and Perils of Ending Mass Incarceration in the United States', *The Annals of the American Academy of Political and Social Science*, Vol. 664, No. 1 (March 2016), pp. 16–24, at: http://ann.sagepub.com/content/664/1/16.full, citing J. Travis, B. Western, S. Redburn (eds.), *The Growth of Incarceration in the United States: Exploring Causes and Consequences*, National Research Council, National Academies Press, Washington, DC, 2014.

[14] The main differences between jails and prisons in the United States is that jails are most often run by sheriffs and/or local governments and are designed to hold individuals awaiting trial or a serving short sentences. Prisons are operated by state governments and the Federal Bureau of Prisons and are designed to hold individuals convicted of crimes. There are approximately 3,600 jails in the United States. Sheriff Scott Israel, 'Frequently Asked Questions', Broward Sheriff's Office, Florida, accessed on 20 February 2016 at: http://sheriff.org/.

[15] M. Berman, 'How Often do Prisoners Die Behind Bars?', *Washington Post*, 23 July 2015, at: www.washingtonpost.com/news/post-nation/wp/2015/07/23/how-often-do-prisoners-die-behind-bars/. The figure does not include judicially-ordered executions.

[16] BJS, 'Deaths in Local Jails and State Prisons Increased for the Third Consecutive Year', Press release, 4 August 2015, at: www.bjs.gov/content/pub/press/mljsp0013stpr.cfm.

[17] Ibid.

'take-down' measure while struggling to change his clothes. Correctional officers did not initially document the physical struggle with Gruber in their daily reports, according to the state attorney.[18]

Over the next 24 hours, Mr Gruber complained of an inability to move his legs, and he was carried around, sometimes with his legs dragging, as guards tried to take his mug shot. He was not taken to the hospital until the next day, when his condition deteriorated. Once at hospital, doctors determined that Mr Gruber had suffered paralysis from a broken neck; they performed two surgical operations on him. He was undergoing rehabilitation and being weaned off a ventilator before he died.[19]

In January 2014, Lake County Board's financial and administrative committee approved a settlement of US$1.95 million to the family of Mr Gruber.[20] In October, three years after the incident at Lake County jail, two former correctional officers were indicted by a grand jury on official misconduct charges for their involvement. In December 2014, one died while awaiting trial.[21]

England and Wales

In 2014, in England and Wales, there were 242 deaths in prison (narrowly defined), two-thirds of which were not the result of suicide. This was the highest number since 1996, when detailed statistics began to be recorded by the Home Office.[22] The year 2015 saw a very small reduction: to 238. The number of homicides was, though, very low: eight in 2015, with a ninth due to restraint.[23] A further 18 people died in police custody in 2015, and 26 the year before.[24]

[18] L. Black, 'Death of Jail Inmate Ruled Homicide, State's Attorney Asks for Special Prosecutor', *Chicago Tribune*, 10 April 2012, at: http://articles.chicagotribune.com/2012-04-10/news/chi-lake-county-inmate-death-eugene-gruber_1_death-of-jail-inmate-homicide-ruling-special-prosecutor.

[19] Ibid.

[20] R. Lissau, 'Lake County Approves $1.95 Million Settlement in Lawsuit over Jail Inmate's Death', *Daily Herald*, 8 January 2014, at: www.dailyherald.com/article/20140108/news/701089811/.

[21] J. Newton, 'Former Lake County Jail Guard Dies Awaiting Trial in Inmate's Death', *Lake County News-Sun*, 17 December 2014, at: www.chicagotribune.com/suburbs/lake-county-news-sun/chi-former-lake-county-sheriffs-officer-dies-awaiting-trial-20141217-story.html.

[22] See Inquest, 'Deaths in Prison', Last updated 28 January 2016, at: www.inquest.org.uk/statistics/deaths-in-prison.

[23] Ibid.

[24] See Inquest, 'Deaths in Police Custody', Last updated 21 January 2016, at: www.inquest.org.uk/statistics/deaths-in-police-custody. Inquest defines police custody

As elsewhere, the United Kingdom faces a particular challenge when detaining individuals with severe mental health problems. In October 2016, the College of Policing issued new guidance on dealing with detainees with mental health issues. Officers are instructed that they should not use methods of restraint on those with mental ill health issues or vulnerabilities, unless absolutely necessary.[25] This is not a 'niche' concern, with the Association of Police and Crime Commissioners warning that 'responding to the needs of individuals with mental health needs can account for up to 20 per cent of police time when, in many cases, many of these individuals need help from health and social care agencies, not the police'.[26] One mental health group has estimated that one in four people are affected by mental illness in England at some stage in their life.[27]

South Africa

In South Africa, at least 57 unnatural deaths were reported in South African prisons between 1 April 2012 and 31 March 2013, according to information from the Department of Correctional Services.[28] Of the unnatural deaths recorded in prisons, 26 were as a result of suicide. In all but five cases, the victims hung themselves. Nine prisoners died at the hands of fellow inmates and two others were assaulted by prison officials. In 16 of the deaths reported, the cause was cited as unknown. The total number of deaths in prison in 2012–13 was higher than in 2011–12 when 46 incidents were recorded.[29]

deaths as deaths that take place while the individual is in contact with police, whether or not they have been arrested, or that happen shortly after that contact. The death may not necessarily have occurred inside a police station. It does not include self-inflicted deaths following contact with police or deaths as a result of domestic violence where the police have been involved. Ibid.

[25] College of Policing, 'Mental Health – Detention', at: www.app.college.police.uk/app-content/mental-health/mental-health-detention/#restraint.

[26] Association of Police and Crime Commissioners, 'Detainees and Victims of Crime with Mental Health Problems Need Better Support', at: www.apccs.police.uk/press_release/detainees-victims-crime-mental-health-problems-need-better-support/?cookie_dismiss=true.

[27] Rethink Mental Illness, 'Mental Health Act 1983', at: www.rethink.org/living-with-mental-illness/mental-health-laws/mental-health-act-1983.

[28] G. Raubenheimer, '57 Unnatural Deaths in SA Prisons', *Eye Witness News*, 5 September 2013, at: http://ewn.co.za/2013/09/05/57-unnatural-deaths-in-SA-prisons. South Africa has 243 correctional facilities around the country, which collectively house more than 150,000 inmates.

[29] Ibid.

In April 2016, the Human Rights Committee, the United Nations body that oversees implementation of the 1966 International Covenant on Civil and Political Rights (ICCPR), expressed its concern about 'the number of reported cases of violence, including sexual violence, excessive use of force, torture and other forms of ill-treatment against detainees, as well as deaths resulting from actions of police and prison officials'.[30] It further noted with concern overcrowding, dilapidated infrastructure, unsanitary conditions, inadequate food, lack of exercise, poor ventilation, and limited access to health services in some of the nation's prisons.[31]

The Situation in Women's Prisons

According to Prison Reform International, more than 700,000 women and girls are being held in prisons around the world. 'Women are always a small minority in national prison populations – only 2–9% on average. However, their numbers are growing every year, and at a faster rate than men.'[32] In 2012, women were estimated to account for about 9% of the prison population in the United States, while in China about 4–6% of inmates were women.[33] The number of women in Brazil's prisons grew 567% in 15 years, from 5,601 in 2000 to 37,380 in 2015, according to a report by the Ministry of Justice published in November 2015.[34] This growth rate pushed Brazil into fifth place internationally in terms of the number of women in prison, behind the United States (205,400); China (103,766); Russia (53,304); and Thailand (44,751). Most of the women in Brazil's prisons range in age from 18 to 29 and nearly two-thirds of them are of African descent. Of the female convicts 68% are serving time for drug offences, compared with 25% of their male counterparts.[35]

As in the United States, the female prison population has been on the rise in China, with a total 10% increase in the prison population in the past ten years, but a 46% increase in the female prison population over

[30] Human Rights Committee, 'Concluding Observations: South Africa', UN doc. CCPR/C/ZAF/CO/1, 27 April 2016, §28.

[31] Ibid., §29.

[32] Penal Reform International, 'Key Facts', undated but accessed on 6 February 2016 at: www.penalreform.org/priorities/women-in-the-criminal-justice-system/key-facts/.

[33] D. K. Tatlow, 'Women in Prison Fare Better in China', *New York Times*, 11 September 2012, at: www.nytimes.com/2012/09/12/world/asia/12iht-letter12.html?_r=2.

[34] 'Brazil's Female Prison Population Soars 567%', *Latin American Herald Tribune*, 6 November 2015, at: www.laht.com/article.asp?ArticleId=2399480&CategoryId=14090.

[35] Ibid.

the same period.[36] The head of the Institute of Sociology at the Zhejiang Academy of Social Sciences further estimated that about 70% of women in Chinese prisons were 'secondary criminals', individuals who had aided men in crimes such as trafficking in women and children or organising prostitution. In contrast, in the United States, as in Brazil, narcotics offences are said to be a leading cause of female imprisonment.[37]

According to Rule 31 of the 2010 Bangkok Rules, 'Clear policies and regulations on the conduct of prison staff aimed at providing maximum protection for women prisoners from any gender-based physical or verbal violence, abuse and sexual harassment shall be developed and implemented.'[38] A commentary on the provision drafted by the UN Office on Drugs and Crime (UNODC) noted that

> in some systems it has been reported that sexual services by prisoners may be required before they are accorded their most basis human rights, such as access to food and essential services. This Rule therefore explicitly prohibits sexual misconduct and abuse, which can amount to torture or ill treatment. Obviously such a prohibition is all the more vital in systems that have a policy of mixed gender staffing.[39]

As an example of the problems that can be faced in women's prisons, in March 2015, a report by the Corrections Institutions Inspection Committee found that sexual contact between staff and inmates at the Dayton Correctional Institution in Ohio appeared to be prevalent. The report termed 'concerning' the number of open sexual assault cases from 2014: of 89 allegations of sexual assault – including 22 against staff – 46 were still open at the end of the year. The report noted that several staff members had been fired or forced to resign, including the man in charge of investigating inappropriate staff-inmate relationships, due to allegations of inappropriate contact with inmates, including sexual contact in some cases. In addition, although the number of use of force reports was

[36] C. Hatton, 'Why is China's Female Prison Population Growing?', China Blog, BBC, 25 June 2015, at: www.bbc.com/news/blogs-china-blog-33268611.

[37] Tatlow, 'Women in Prison Fare Better in China'.

[38] Rule 31, UN Rules for the Treatment of Women Prisoners and Non-custodial Measures for Women Offenders (Bangkok Rules), adopted by UN General Assembly Resolution 65/229, 21 December 2010.

[39] Commentary on Rule 31 drafted by UNODC and approved by the Open-ended intergovernmental expert group meeting to develop supplementary rules specific to the treatment of women in detention and in custodial and non-custodial settings, Bangkok, 23–26 November 2009, p. 46, available at: www.penalreform.org/priorities/women-in-the-criminal-justice-system/international-standards/.

rising, video surveillance had not been preserved to help determine whether the force was justified. Dayton Correctional Institution has 900 inmates, 250 employees, and an annual budget of $23 million.[40]

In England (there are no women's prisons in Wales), the year 2016 through late October saw the highest number of women prisoner deaths for the period of public recording by the NGO Inquest began (in 1990): 22.[41] Women represent around 5 per cent of the overall prison population in the United Kingdom.[42] Writing in January 2014, Inquest stated that: 'Though the vulnerabilities and needs of women prisoners are well established, the criminal justice system continues to sentence them to custody in unsafe institutions that are ill equipped and under resourced to deal with their complex needs.'[43]

The Human Rights Framework

As the European Court of Human Rights has observed, and as is evident from the selected reports on prison conditions above, persons in custody are in an especially vulnerable position.[44] The authorities have a clear duty under international human rights law to protect them. Detainees are at particular risk of unlawful use of force, whether from law enforcement officials responsible for administering and running custodial settings or other detainees. The human rights most at risk of violation in custodial settings are the rights to life and to humane treatment, which includes the prohibition on torture or other forms of cruel, inhuman, or degrading treatment or punishment. The state has the duty both to respect those rights (i.e. not to commit violations itself, including through its agents) and to protect rights against infringement by third parties, whether these be other inmates or private security personnel.

[40] L. A. Bischoff, 'Sex, Drugs, Use of Force Problems Plague Women's Prison, Report Says', *Dayton Daily News*, 31 March 2015, at: www.daytondailynews.com/news/news/local/sex-drugs-use-of-force-problems-plague-womens-pris/nkjPT/.

[41] See: www.inquest.org.uk/statistics/deaths-of-women-in-prison.

[42] Women in Prison, 'Key Facts', accessed 27 October 2016 at: www.womeninprison.org.uk/research/key-facts.php.

[43] Inquest, *Preventing the Deaths of Women in Prison: The Need for an Alternative Approach*, Report, January 2014, p. 2, at: http://inquest.org.uk/pdf/briefings/Jan2014_updated_INQUEST_Preventing_deaths_of_women_in_prison.pdf.

[44] European Court of Human Rights (ECtHR), *Bouyid* v. *Belgium*, Judgment (Grand Chamber), 28 September 2015, §83.

Rule 1 of the Nelson Mandela Rules, a revised set of rules, originally adopted in 1955, on the minimum treatment of prisoners, which were endorsed by the United Nations (UN) General Assembly in December 2015, stipulates that:

> All prisoners shall be treated with the respect due to their inherent dignity and value as human beings. No prisoner shall be subjected to, and all prisoners shall be protected from, torture and other cruel, inhuman or degrading treatment or punishment, for which no circumstances whatsoever may be invoked as a justification. The safety and security of prisoners, staff, service providers and visitors shall be ensured at all times.[45]

According to the 1990 Basic Principles on the Use of Force and Firearms, 'Law enforcement officials, in their relations with persons in custody or detention, shall not use force, except when strictly necessary for the maintenance of security and order within the institution, or when personal safety is threatened.'[46] Similarly, the Nelson Mandela Rules stipulate that: 'Prison staff shall not, in their relations with the prisoners, use force except in self-defence or in cases of attempted escape, or active or passive physical resistance to an order based on law or regulations. Prison staff who have recourse to force must use no more than is strictly necessary and must report the incident immediately to the prison director.'[47]

Any use of force by custodial officials must respect the core law of law enforcement (LOLE) principles of necessity and proportionality. As discussed in Chapter 3, when it is necessary to use force, the force actually used must be no more than the minimum necessary in the circumstances (the principle of necessity). According to the European Court of Human Rights, with respect to any person deprived of liberty, any recourse to physical force not made strictly necessary by the detainee's own conduct 'diminishes human dignity and is, in principle, an infringement' of the prohibition on torture or inhuman and degrading treatment.[48] Second, all use of force must be proportionate to the threat

[45] The Standard Minimum Rules for the Treatment of Prisoners were originally adopted in 1955. Principle 1 of the 1990 Basic Principles for the Treatment of Prisoners similarly provides that 'All prisoners shall be treated with the respect due to their inherent dignity and value as human beings.'

[46] Basic Principle 15. The Basic Principles were adopted by the Eighth UN Congress on the Prevention of Crime and the Treatment of Offenders, Havana, Cuba, 27 August to 7 September 1990, and welcomed by the UN General Assembly in Resolution 45/166, adopted without a vote on 18 December 1990 (operative §4).

[47] Rule 82(1), 2015 Nelson Mandela Rules.

[48] ECtHR, *Bouyid* v. *Belgium*, Judgment (Grand Chamber), 28 September 2015, §88.

(the principle of proportionality). In principle, any force that does not meet both criteria will amount to inhumane treatment.

The Right to Life

The state is generally obliged under customary and treaty law to respect and protect the right to life of all persons under its jurisdiction.[49] This applies to all those it detains, including in private prisons. This means it must not only refrain from unlawfully killing a detainee it must also protect him or her against suicide and from violence by other detainees. Thus, Christopher Edwards, a prisoner in the United Kingdom with signs of serious mental illness, was stamped and kicked to death by another prisoner with a history of violence and also affected by mental illness. The European Court of Human Rights, which bore in mind 'the difficulties in policing modern societies, the unpredictability of human conduct and the operational choices which must be made in terms of priorities and resources', affirmed that 'the scope of the positive obligation must be interpreted in a way which does not impose an impossible or disproportionate burden on the authorities'.[50] Not every claimed risk to life, therefore, will entail for the authorities an ECHR requirement

> to take operational measures to prevent that risk from materialising. For a positive obligation to arise, it must be established that the authorities knew or ought to have known at the time of the existence of a real and immediate risk to the life of an identified individual from the criminal acts of a third party and that they failed to take measures within the scope of their powers which, judged reasonably, might have been expected to avoid that risk.[51]

In the case at hand, the Court considered it 'self-evident that the screening process of the new arrivals in a prison should serve to identify effectively those prisoners who require for their own welfare or the

[49] The duty to protect encompasses a positive duty on the state to take reasonable measures to prevent a detainee from committing suicide. In the *Isenc* case, a chamber of the European Court of Human Rights held that the French authorities had failed to comply with its positive obligation to protect the right to life with respect to an inmate who hung himself in prison. The case concerned the suicide of the applicant's son twelve days after he was admitted to prison. ECtHR, *Isenc* v. *France*, Judgment (Fifth Section), 4 February 2016.

[50] ECtHR, *Paul and Audrey Edwards* v. *UK*, Judgment (Third Section), 14 March 2002 (as rendered final on 14 June 2002), §55.

[51] Ibid.

welfare of other prisoners to be placed under medical supervision'.[52] It concluded that the failure of the agencies involved in the case (the medical profession, the police, the prosecution, and the court) to pass information about Mr Edwards's ultimate killer on to the prison authorities and the inadequate nature of the screening process on that man's arrival in prison 'disclose a breach of the State's obligation to protect the life of Christopher Edward'.[53]

In March 2016, also in the United Kingdom, two police officers and two members of police staff were found to have committed misconduct over the way they dealt with a 'very vulnerable' woman who was found dead in a police cell on 1 November 2014. The Independent Police Complaints Commission (IPCC) found systemic and individual failings in the care provided to Martine Brandon, 48, by Hampshire Constabulary. An inquest concluded that she killed herself.[54]

Ms Brandon was arrested in 2014 after she was seen in the street waving a large kitchen knife. She was overheard saying that an invisible demon and her sister were threatening to kill her. She was arrested on suspicion of a criminal offence rather than being detained under mental health laws and spent 18 hours in custody before being found dead in a cell. The IPCC investigation concluded that two custody detention officers had conducted 'unsatisfactory and inadequate' checks on Brandon. These included quick glances through the spy hole in the cell door, one check that was missed completely, and inaccurate entries on the custody logs.[55]

Furthermore, given the level of control the state has over a detainee, it holds a burden of responsibility to demonstrate that its agents are not responsible for any death in a custodial setting, whether directly or indirectly, through a failure to protect. According to the African Commission on Human and Peoples' Rights,

> Where a person dies in State custody, there is a presumption of State responsibility and the burden of proof rests upon the State to prove otherwise through a prompt, impartial, thorough and transparent investigation carried out by an independent body. This heightened responsibility

[52] Ibid., §62. [53] Ibid., §64.

[54] S. Morris, 'Police Guilty of Misconduct over Woman Who Died in Cell', *The Guardian*, 16 March 2016, at: www.theguardian.com/uk-news/2016/mar/18/police-guilty-misconduct-woman-found-dead-cell?CMP=Share_iOSApp_Other.

[55] Ibid.

> extends to persons detained in prisons, in other places of detention (official and otherwise), and to persons in other facilities where the State exercises heightened control over their lives.[56]

Deaths in Custody

In the *Zhumbaeva* case before the Human Rights Committee,[57] the authorities had claimed that Mr Zhumbaeva had committed suicide by hanging. The forensic evidence suggested otherwise. On 24 October 2004, the victim and his wife had been asked to follow police officers to Bazarkorgon police station in Kyrgyzstan after a quarrel that was qualified as a public disturbance. The victim was kept in custody, while his wife was released.

Testimony by an ambulance doctor indicated that the victim did not have strangulation marks but red finger marks on his neck. A forensic expert who examined the victim's body on 25 October 2004, in the presence of doctors and two of the victim's relatives, found scratches on the eyebrow, under the chin, on the neck and the right upper arm, as well as a bloody wound on the left side of the victim's neck. The expert stated that the wounds could appear from something hard such as fingernails or a wrist, and that histological examination of body tissues[58] indicated that the victim died of mechanical asphyxiation. The mechanical asphyxiation could have been caused by hanging from a soft fabric. When asked if manual strangulation could have been the cause of the victim's death, the forensic expert stated that no scratches were found on the cervical fabrics or skin but that the fracture of the horn of the thyroid could result from pressure by hands.[59]

On 21 September 2005, Suzak district court held that the victim had hanged himself on his sport trousers in the administrative detention cell. On appeal, however, Zhalalabad regional court concluded that the case should be retried based on a complete and objective study of all circumstances. Subsequently, the Supreme Court, in its judgment of

[56] ACHPR, 'General Comment No. 3 on the African Charter on Human and Peoples' Rights: The Right to Life (Article 4)', November 2015, §37. See similarly Human Rights Committee, *Sanjeevan* v. *Sri Lanka*, Views (Comm. No. 1436/05), 8 July 2008, §6.2

[57] Human Rights Committee, *Turdukan Zhumbaeva* v. *Kyrgyzstan*, Views (Comm. No. 1756/2008), UN doc. CCPR/C/102/D/1756/2008 (2011). The Committee oversees the implementation by states parties of the ICCPR.

[58] Histology is the study of the microscopic anatomy of cells and tissues of plants and animals.

[59] Human Rights Committee, *Zhumbaeva* v. *Kyrgyzstan*, Views, §8.3.

27 December 2006, found criminal negligence on the part of a police officer involved, but concluded that payment of compensation to the family of the victim had resolved the affair.[60]

Mr Zhumbaeva's mother applied to the Human Rights Committee, claiming that the victim died in police custody as a result of excessive and unnecessary use of force by police officers. The victim was in good physical and mental health before being taken into custody and, according to his wife, did not possess any sports trousers which he had allegedly used to hang himself. The trousers were never forensically examined and, due to the victim's high alcohol level, it was argued that he had neither the physical capacity nor the time to hang himself. Ms Zhumbaeva affirmed that accepting a small payment to assist with funeral costs had not waived her rights to establish the truth of how her son died and to hold the perpetrators accountable.[61]

The Human Rights Committee reiterated that any state party to the ICCPR that arrests and detains individuals, assumes the responsibility to care for their life. It stated further that criminal investigation and consequential prosecution are necessary remedies for violations of the right to life.[62] The Committee observed that Kyrgyzstan had not explained the basis on which it was concluded that the victim had committed suicide in police custody. The testimony by the forensic expert and the ambulance doctor allied to the fact that the concerned police officer had proffered three different versions of the victim's death while another police officer's testimony had not even been considered led the Committee to conclude that Kyrgyzstan was responsible for arbitrary deprivation of Mr Zhumbaeva's life.[63]

In the earlier *Burrell* case,[64] the Human Rights Committee were asked for their views on a communication concerning the death of a prisoner at the hands of the prison guards. Mr Rickly Burrell was a prisoner on death row in Jamaica who was killed by a warder following a disturbance at the prison in October 1993. Legal counsel for Mr Burrell submitted evidence that he had been shot in cold blood. Jamaica argued that Mr Burrell had

60 Ibid., §8.4. 61 Ibid., §8.5. 62 Ibid., §8.6.

63 Ibid., §8.8. Joseph and Castan assert that the decision probably manifests 'a more robust and confident approach to evidence' by the Committee than in earlier cases. S. Joseph and M. Castan, *International Covenant on Civil and Political Rights: Cases, Materials, and Commentary*, 3rd Edn, Oxford University Press, Oxford, 2014, p. 175.

64 Human Rights Committee, *Burrell* v. *Jamaica*, Views (Comm. No. 546/1993), UN doc. CCPR/C/53/D/546/1993 (1996).

been killed accidentally during the rescue of a number of warders who had been taken hostage by other prisoners.[65]

The Committee expressed its regret that Jamaica did make available the autopsy report or the results of the Coroner's inquest in the case. Counsel for Mr. Burrell alleged, on the basis of letters received from other inmates in St. Catherine Prison, that he was shot after the warders had already been released, and thus the need for force no longer existed. The Committee noted Jamaica's acknowledgement that Mr. Burrell's death was 'the unfortunate result of confusion' on the part of the warders, who panicked when seeing their colleagues being threatened by the inmates, and that the shooting had continued after the warders were rescued. In the circumstances, the Committee concluded that Jamaica had failed to take effective measures to protect Mr. Burrell's life.[66]

Joseph and Castan suggest that the Committee gave Jamaica the benefit of the doubt, accepting that the killing of Mr Burrell was not intentional. Instead, it found that the state in question had failed in its positive duty to protect Mr Burrell's life while he was in custody.[67] Whether it would be as accommodating to a state party if a case on the same facts came before the Human Rights Committee today is doubtful.

The Duty to Investigate

The duty to investigate alleged violations in a prompt, impartial, and effective manner is an integral element in the protection of the right to life. Thus, as the 2015 Nelson Mandela Rules provide:

> Notwithstanding the initiation of an internal investigation, the prison director shall report, without delay, any custodial death, disappearance or serious injury to a judicial or other competent authority that is independent of the prison administration and mandated to conduct prompt, impartial and effective investigations into the circumstances and causes of such cases. The prison administration shall fully cooperate with that authority and ensure that all evidence is preserved.[68]

Where there is evidence that the state or its agents, including of course its law enforcement officials, seeks to cover up the circumstances of a death in custody, invariably a violation of the right to life will have occurred. It is implicit in such cases that the death itself has been unlawful, while

[65] Joseph and Castan, *International Covenant on Civil and Political Rights*, p. 170.

[66] Human Rights Committee, *Burrell* v. *Jamaica*, Views, §9.5.

[67] Joseph and Castan, *International Covenant on Civil and Political Rights*, p. 170.

[68] Rule 71(1), 2015 Nelson Mandela Rules.

clearly the duty to investigate effectively any alleged unlawful killing has also been infringed. In the *Sanjeevan* case,[69] the authors' son, Sathasivam Sanjeevan, had been arrested by the Sri Lankan police without apparent reason.[70] When his parents visited him in police custody, he was in poor physical health and he alleged he had been tortured. Four days after his arrest, the parents found their son's body in the morgue; the night before, the police had told them to go to the hospital.

An inquest concluded that Mr Sanjeevan had died of gunshot wounds. The police claimed he had been injured in crossfire when the convoy transferring him to another police station had come under attack from Tamil Tiger rebels. The Sri Lankan authorities themselves did not believe the police officers' account but took only disciplinary measures against them. The Human Rights Committee found that the right to life under Article 6 of the ICCPR had been violated:

> As to the claim under article 6 that the death of the victim is directly attributable to the State party, the Committee recalls that according to the uncontested material the victim was in normal health before being taken into police custody, where he was shortly thereafter seen by eyewitnesses suffering substantial and severe injuries. The alleged reasons for his subsequent death, namely that he died during an LTTE [Tamil Tiger] attack, have been dismissed by the State party's own judicial and executive authorities. In these circumstances, the Committee must give due weight to the presumption that injury and, *a fortiori*, death suffered in custody must be held to be attributable to the State party itself.[71]

> In the instant case, the State party's own authorities dismissed the explanation for the victim's death advanced by the police in whose custody the victim died, and its judicial authorities directed criminal proceedings against the offending police officers. In the absence of any explanation by the State party and in view of the detailed evidence placed before it, the Committee must conclude that the Attorney-General's decision not to initiate criminal proceedings in favour of disciplinary proceedings was clearly arbitrary and amounted to a denial of justice. The State party must accordingly be held to be in breach of its obligations under articles 6 and 7 to properly investigate the death and torture of the victim and take appropriate action against those found guilty.[72]

[69] Human Rights Committee, *Sanjeevan* v. *Sri Lanka*, Views (Comm. No. 1436/05), 8 July 2008.

[70] See summary in Joseph and Castan, *International Covenant on Civil and Political Rights*, pp. 179–80.

[71] *Sanjeevan* v. *Sri Lanka*, Views, §6.2.

[72] Ibid., §6.4.

The Duty to Investigate during Armed Conflict According to the Grand Chamber of the European Court of Human Rights, the obligation to respect and protect the life of detainees and to investigate any death of a detainee persists during a situation of armed conflict, including when that death occurs extraterritorially. In the *al-Skeini* case, one of the applicants was a Colonel in the Basra police force in Iraq whose son, Baha Mousa, was twenty-six when he died while in the custody of the British army, three days after his arrest by British soldiers on 14 September 2003.[73] Mr Mousa was visited by a Royal Military Police unit who told him that his son had been killed in custody at a British military base in Basra. He was asked to identify the corpse. The body and face were covered in blood and bruises; his nose was broken and part of the skin of his face had been torn away.[74]

A pathologist flown in from the United Kingdom found that Baha Mousa had ninety-three identifiable injuries on his body and had died of asphyxiation. Eight other Iraqis had also been inhumanely treated, with two requiring hospital treatment.[75] On 19 July 2005, seven British soldiers were charged with criminal offences in connection with Mr Mousa's death. On 19 September 2006, at the start of the court martial, one of the soldiers pleaded guilty to the war crime of inhumane treatment but not guilty to manslaughter. On 14 February 2007, charges were dropped against four of the seven soldiers, and on 13 March 2007, the other two soldiers were acquitted. On 30 April 2007, the soldier convicted of inhumane treatment was sentenced to one year's imprisonment and dismissal from the army.[76]

On 26 March 2004, the UK Secretary of State for Defence decided, with respect to the deaths of thirteen Iraqi civilians, including the relatives of the six applicants in the *al-Skeini* case, not to conduct independent inquiries into the deaths, not to accept liability for the deaths, and not to pay compensation.[77] A divisional court in the United Kingdom held that the European Court's controversial decision in the *Banković* case[78] meant that jurisdiction under the 1950 European Convention on Human Rights (ECHR) was essentially territorial, but that an exception would apply where a state party had effective control of an area outside its own territory but on the territory of another state party. The

[73] ECtHR, *Al-Skeini and Others* v. *UK*, Judgment (Grand Chamber), 7 July 2011, §63.

[74] Ibid., §64. [75] Ibid., §66. [76] Ibid., §68. [77] Ibid., §72.

[78] ECtHR, *Banković and Others* v. *Belgium and Others*, Decision on Admissibility (Grand Chamber), 2001.

divisional court did accept that Mr Mousa's case fell within the jurisdiction of the United Kingdom's 1998 Human Rights Act, which incorporates the ECHR into domestic law, but essentially by analogy with the extraterritorial exception made for embassies. This holding was affirmed by the majority in the House of Lords.[79]

The European Court held, relying on both international humanitarian law (IHL) and international human rights law, and jurisprudence before the International Court of Justice on the interrelationship between the two bodies of international law, that jurisdiction was founded as the United Kingdom (together with the United States) had 'assumed in Iraq the exercise of some of the public powers normally to be exercised by a sovereign government'.[80] In addition, as the Court noted, it has found that, in certain circumstances, use of force by a state's agents operating outside its territory may bring the relevant individuals under the state's jurisdiction for the purpose of human rights.[81]

This principle applies where a person is taken into the custody of state agents abroad. For example, in the *Öcalan* case, the European Court held that

> directly after being handed over to the Turkish officials by the Kenyan officials, the applicant was effectively under Turkish authority and therefore within the "jurisdiction" of that State for the purposes of Article 1 of the Convention, even though in this instance Turkey exercised its authority outside its territory.[82]

Thus, in *Issa*, the Court indicated that, had it been established that Turkish soldiers had taken the applicants' relatives into custody in northern Iraq, taken them to a nearby cave and executed them, the deceased would have been within Turkish jurisdiction by virtue of the soldiers' authority and control over them.[83] In *Al-Saadoon*, the European Court held that two Iraqi nationals detained in British-controlled military prisons in Iraq fell within the jurisdiction of the United Kingdom, by virtue of its exercise of total and exclusive control over the prisons and the individuals detained in them.[84]

[79] ECtHR, *Al-Skeini and Others* v. *UK*, Judgment, §88.

[80] Ibid., §149.

[81] Ibid., §136.

[82] ECtHR, *Öcalan* v. *Turkey*, Judgment (Grand Chamber), 12 May 2005, §91.

[83] ECtHR, *Al-Skeini and Others* v. *UK*, Judgment, §136, citing *Issa* v. *Turkey*, Decision on Admissibility (Second Section).

[84] ECtHR, *Al-Skeini and Others* v. *UK*, Judgment, §136, citing *Al-Saadoon and Mufdhi* v. *UK*, Decision (Fourth Section), 30 June 2009, §§86–89.

The Right to Humane Treatment

The Inter-American Commission on Human Rights recalled in 2013 that the 'right of persons deprived of liberty to humane treatment while under the custody of the State is a universally accepted norm in international law'.[85] In the global human rights system, the ICCPR 'expressly enshrined the principle of humane treatment as the core of its Article 10, which establishes the fundamental norms applicable to persons deprived of liberty'.[86]

Article 10(1) provides that: 'All persons deprived of their liberty shall be treated with humanity and with respect for the inherent dignity of the human person.' The Human Rights Committee has affirmed that this provision exists as a positive obligation towards those who are particularly vulnerable because of their status as persons deprived of liberty. Application of this 'universally applicable rule' is not dependent on the material resources available in any state and must be applied without adverse distinction of any kind.[87] Standards also evolve as society evolves. In the famous words of Chief Justice Warren in the 1958 US Supreme Court decision in *Trop* v. *Dulles*, 'The basic concept underlying the Eighth Amendment [which prohibits cruel and inhuman punishment] is nothing less than the dignity of man . . . The Amendment must draw its meaning from the evolving standards of decency that mark the progress of a maturing society.'[88]

The Prohibition on Torture

According to Article 7 of the ICCPR, 'No one shall be subjected to torture or to cruel, inhuman or degrading treatment or punishment.' No derogation from this provision is possible at any time or in any circumstances. In early cases concerning Latin American states, the Human Rights Committee found combinations of the following acts to amount to torture: systematic beatings, electroshocks, burns, extended hanging from

[85] IACHR, Report on Terrorism and Human Rights, OEA/Ser.L/V/II.116. Doc. 5 rev. 1 corr., adopted on 22 October 2002, §147.

[86] Revision of the UN Nations Standard Minimum Rules for the Treatment of Prisoners, Prepared by the IACHR, 2013, p. 4.

[87] Human Rights Committee, 'General Comment No. 21: Article 10 (Humane Treatment of Persons Deprived of Their Liberty)', adopted on 10 April 1992, §§3, 4.

[88] *Trop* v. *Dulles*, 356 US 86 (1958), pp. 100–01.

hand and/or leg chains, repeated immersions in a mixture of blood, urine, vomit, and excrement ('submarino'), standing for great lengths of time, simulated executions, and amputations.[89]

The 1984 Convention against Torture (CAT) defines torture as encompassing the infliction of severe pain or suffering, whether mental or physical, on detainees, for the purpose of punishment, coercion, or intimidation, or for reasons of discrimination (among others).[90] Specifically excluded from the definition, though, is pain or suffering 'arising only from, inherent in or incidental to lawful sanctions'.[91] In 2004, the *Dragan Dimitrijevic* case represented the first time the UN Committee against Torture, which oversees the implementation of CAT by states parties, had found a violation of the specific prohibition on torture.[92] The case concerned abuse of a Serb citizen of Roma origin by the Serb police.

Mr Dimitrijevic was arrested on 27 October 1999 at his home in Kragujevac, Serbia, in connection with the investigation of a crime. He was taken to the local police station where he was handcuffed to a radiator and beaten by several police officers, some of whom he knew by name. The officers kicked and punched him all over his body while insulting his ethnic origins and cursing his 'gypsy mother'. One of the officers struck him with a large metal bar. Some time later, the officers unfastened the complainant from the radiator and handcuffed him to a bicycle. They then continued to punch and beat him with their nightsticks and the metal bar. At one point the complainant began bleeding from his ears, but despite this the beating continued until, about five hours after his original arrest, he was released.[93]

As a result of his ill-treatment Mr Dimitrijevic had to stay in bed for several days. He sustained injuries on both arms and legs, an open wound on the back of his head, and numerous injuries on his back. For several days following the incident he bled from his left ear and his eyes and lips remained swollen. Fearing reprisals by the police he did not go to hospital for treatment. Consequently, there is no official medical

[89] Joseph and Castan, *International Covenant on Civil and Political Rights*, p. 240.

[90] Art. 1(1), CAT, adopted by UN General Assembly Resolution 39/46 of 10 December 1984.

[91] Ibid.

[92] Committee against Torture, *Dragan Dimitrijevic* v. *Serbia and Montenegro*, Views (Comm. No. 207/2002, UN doc. CAT/C/33/D/207/2002 (2004). See Joseph and Castan, *International Covenant on Civil and Political Rights*, pp. 227–28.

[93] Committee against Torture, *Dimitrijevic* v. *Serbia and Montenegro*, Views, §2.1.

certificate documenting his injuries. He provided the Committee with written statements from his mother, sister, and a cousin indicating that he was in good health when he was arrested and severely injured at the time of his release.[94]

The Committee against Torture held that the treatment to which the complainant was subjected while in detention, 'which can be characterized as severe pain or suffering intentionally inflicted by public officials in the context of the investigation of a crime', amounted to torture. The Committee noted that Serbia and Montenegro had not contested the facts as presented by Mr Dimitrijevic.[95]

In the *Aydin* case before the European Court of Human Rights, the applicant, a 17-year-old Turkish woman of Kurdish origin,[96] was arrested and taken, along with two other members of her family, into custody. She was blindfolded, beaten, stripped naked, placed in a tyre, and hosed with pressurised water, before being raped by a member of the security forces, and then beaten for about an hour by several people. The applicant claimed that the family was subsequently intimidated and harassed by the authorities to try to coerce them into withdrawing their complaint before the European Court.[97]

The Court stressed that rape of a detainee by an official of the State must be considered to be an especially grave and abhorrent form of ill-treatment given the ease with which the offender can exploit the vulnerability and weakened resistance of his victim. Furthermore, rape leaves deep psychological scars on the victim. The Court found that both the accumulation of acts of physical and mental violence inflicted on the applicant while in custody, and the especially cruel act of rape to which she had been subjected, amounted to torture.[98] In order to determine whether any particular form of ill-treatment should be qualified as torture, the Court noted that the distinction in the ECHR between torture and inhuman treatment 'would appear to have been embodied in the Convention to

[94] Ibid., §2.2. [95] Ibid., §5.3.

[96] The 2001 European Code of Police Ethics, adopted by the Council of Europe's Committee of Ministers, requires police personnel to act with integrity and respect towards the public and with particular consideration for the situation of individuals belonging to especially vulnerable groups. Recommendation Rec(2001)10 of the Committee of Ministers, adopted on 19 September 2001, §44.

[97] ECtHR, *Aydın* v. *Turkey*, Judgment (Grand Chamber), 25 September 1997, *esp.* §§16–18, 20, 35.

[98] Ibid., §§82–84.

allow the special stigma of "torture" to attach only to deliberate inhuman treatment causing very serious and cruel suffering'.[99]

It is also unlawful for the police to threaten torture against a detainee. In 1983, in the *Estrella* case, the Human Rights Committee concluded that Mr Estrella, a concert pianist, had been 'subjected to severe physical and psychological torture, including the threat that . . . [his] hands would be cut off by an electric saw, in an effort to force him to admit subversive activities'.[100] The Committee found that Mr Estrella had been subjected to torture in violation of Article 7 of the ICCPR.[101] In 1992, the Committee noted in its General Comment on the provision that the prohibition 'relates not only to acts that cause physical pain but also to acts that cause mental suffering to the victim'.[102] In addition, according to the UN Special Rapporteur on torture, 'serious and credible threats, including death threats, to the physical integrity of the victim or a third person can amount to cruel, inhuman or degrading treatment or even to torture, especially when the victim remains in the hands of law enforcement officials'.[103]

In the 2003 *Maritza Urrutia* case, the Inter-American Court of Human Rights found that Ms Urrutia was subjected to very long interrogations during which she was shown photographs of individuals who had been tortured or killed in combat and threatened that she would be found by her family in the same way. Guatemalan state agents also threatened to torture her physically or to kill her or members of her family if she did not collaborate. Ms Urrutia was also constrained to appear in a video that was later broadcast by two Guatemalan television channels.[104] The Court held that:

> An international juridical regime of absolute prohibition of all forms of torture, both physical and psychological, has been developed and, with regard to the latter, it has been recognised that the threat or real danger of subjecting a person to physical harm produces, under determined

[99] Ibid., §82.

[100] Human Rights Committee, *Estrella* v. *Uruguay*, Views (Comm. No. 74/1980), 29 March 1983, §8.3.

[101] Ibid., §10. [102] Human Rights Committee, General Comment 20, Article 7, 1992, §5.

[103] Report of the UN Special Rapporteur on the question of torture and other cruel, inhuman, or degrading treatment or punishment to the UN General Assembly, UN doc. A/56/156, 3 July 2001, §8.

[104] IACtHR, *Maritza Urrutia* v. *Guatemala*, Judgment (Merits, Reparations, and Costs), 27 November 2003, §85.

> circumstances, such a degree of moral anguish that it may be considered "psychological torture".[105]

In the *Gäfgen* case, the applicant to the European Court of Human Rights, Magnus Gäfgen, had been arrested on suspicion of having abducted an 11-year-old boy.[106] Mr Gäfgen alleged that his treatment during police interrogation constituted torture.[107] On 1 October 2002, the deputy chief of the Frankfurt police ordered another officer to threaten Mr Gäfgen with great physical pain, and, if necessary, to subject him to such pain in order to make him reveal the boy's whereabouts. This officer subsequently threatened Mr Gäfgen that an expert in pain infliction would seriously hurt him. According to the applicant, the officer also threatened to lock him in a cell with two huge black men who would anally assault him. He further alleged that the officer hit him several times on the chest with his hand and shook him such that, on one occasion, his head hit the wall. The government denied that the applicant had been threatened with sexual abuse or had been physically assaulted during the questioning.[108] Out of fear, the applicant disclosed the whereabouts of the child's body (who he had in fact murdered) after ten minutes.[109]

The Frankfurt am Main regional court had adjudged that the method of investigation had not been justified. It rejected the two officers' defence of 'necessity' because the threats violated human dignity, as codified in German law. The protection of dignity was absolute, allowing no exceptions or balancing of interests.[110] The court convicted the two officers of coercion committed in the course of official duties and both were given small suspended fines.[111] The Frankfurt am Main court of appeal held that violating Mr Gäfgen's dignity by threat of torture did not warrant payment of compensation since he had obtained satisfaction by the exclusion of the incriminating statements he had made under duress as evidence and the criminal conviction of the police officers.[112]

In its judgment, the European Court's Grand Chamber held that to threaten an individual with torture may constitute at least inhuman treatment.[113] In the case at hand, the Court was unable to conclude that

[105] Ibid., §92.

[106] ECtHR, *Gäfgen* v. *Germany*, Judgment (Grand Chamber), 1 June 2010 (as rectified on 3 June 2010).

[107] Ibid., §2 and see §§10–14. [108] Ibid., §§15, 26. [109] Ibid., §16. [110] Ibid., §48.

[111] Ibid., §48. [112] Ibid., §57. [113] Ibid., §91.

Mr Gäfgen's complaints of physical assaults and injuries and the alleged threat of sexual abuse during interrogation were established beyond reasonable doubt.[114] It did conclude that threat of imminent and severe physical pain was proven, observing that the threat was not a spontaneous act but was premeditated and calculated in a deliberate and intentional manner.[115] The Court noted that

> the fear of physical torture may itself constitute mental torture. However, there appears to be broad agreement, and the Court likewise considers, that the classification of whether a given threat of physical torture amounted to psychological torture or to inhuman or degrading treatment depends upon all the circumstances of a given case, including, notably, the severity of the pressure exerted and the intensity of the mental suffering caused.[116]

Based on its own caselaw, the Court considered that the method of interrogation was sufficiently serious to amount to inhuman treatment, but that it did not reach the level of cruelty required to attain the threshold of torture.[117] It further determined that imposing 'almost token fines . . . and, furthermore, opting to suspend them, cannot be considered an adequate response' to a breach of the prohibition of inhumane treatment in the ECHR Article 3:

> Such punishment, which is manifestly disproportionate to a breach of one of the core rights of the Convention, does not have the necessary deterrent effect in order to prevent further violations of the prohibition of ill-treatment in future difficult situations.[118]

The Prohibition on Inhumane Treatment or Punishment

In its general comment on Article 7 of the ICCPR, which prohibits, in addition to torture, the infliction of other forms of cruel, inhuman, or degrading treatment or punishment, the Human Rights Committee has stated that: 'The Covenant does not contain any definition of the concepts covered by article 7, nor does the Committee consider it necessary to draw up a list of prohibited acts or to establish sharp distinctions between the different kinds of punishment or treatment; the distinctions depend on the nature, purpose and severity of the treatment applied.'[119] In general terms, however, cruel treatment refers to pain or suffering that is applied wantonly, gratuitously, or sadistically; inhuman treatment is the inflicting of

[114] Ibid., §98. [115] Ibid., §104. [116] Ibid., §108. [117] Ibid. [118] Ibid., §124.

[119] Human Rights Committee, 'General Comment 20, Article 7', Forty-fourth session, 1992, §4.

severe pain or suffering;[120] while degrading treatment is that which humiliates the victim or which is intended to do so.[121]

According to the European Court of Human Rights, 'Ill-treatment that attains a minimum level of severity usually involves actual bodily injury or intense physical or mental suffering.'[122] The Court has considered treatment to be 'inhuman' because it was premeditated, was applied for hours at a stretch, and caused either actual bodily injury or intense physical and mental suffering. Treatment has been held to be 'degrading' when it arouses in its victims feelings of fear, anguish, and inferiority capable of humiliating and debasing them and possibly breaking their physical or moral resistance, or when it was such as to drive the victim to act against his will or conscience.[123]

During his visit to Chile in 2008, at all of the prisons he visited, the Inter-American human rights system's Rapporteur on the Rights of Persons Deprived of Liberty witnessed excessive and gratuitous use of force and punishment, systematic physical abuse by members of the *Gendarmeria* (the correctional security force), and use of solitary confinement in subhuman conditions.[124] But while a violation of the

[120] In the *Polay Campos* case, the Human Rights Committee found that displaying the applicant publicly in a cage and isolating him for 23 hours a day in a small cell with only ten minutes of sunlight a day amounted to inhuman treatment. Human Rights Committee, *Polay Campos* v. *Peru*, Views (Comm. No. 577/1994), 1997. In *Bouyid* v. *Belgium*, the European Court of Human Rights emphasised that a slap by a law enforcement officer on an individual entirely under his control constitutes a serious attack on the individual's dignity. But given that the applicants referred only to minor bodily injuries and did not demonstrate they had undergone serious physical or mental suffering, the Court held that the treatment they allegedly received could not be described as inhuman or, *a fortiori*, torture. ECtHR, *Bouyid* v. *Belgium*, Judgment (Grand Chamber), 28 September 2015, §103.

[121] In the *Antti Vuolanne* case, the Human Rights Committee was asked to consider the solitary confinement of a Finnish soldier who was punished for abandoning his military service. The Committee determined that for punishment to be degrading, the humiliation involved must exceed a particular level and entail something more than the mere fact of deprivation of liberty. In determining the severity of the mistreatment alleged, it held that a court should consider all the circumstances, including the duration and manner of treatment, its physical and mental effects, and the sex, age, and health of the victim. Human Rights Committee, *Antti Vuolanne* v. *Finland*, Views (Comm. No. 265/1987), 1989, p. 311. According to the European Court, 'It . . . may well suffice that the victim is humiliated in his own eyes, even if not in the eyes of others.' ECtHR, *Bouyid* v. *Belgium*, §87, citing also *Tyrer* v. *UK*, 25 April 1978, §32. 103.

[122] ECtHR, *Bouyid* v. *Belgium*, §87.

[123] ECtHR, *Gäfgen* v. *Germany*, §89.

[124] IACHR, 'Rapporteurship on the Rights of Persons Deprived of Liberty Concludes Visit to Chile', Press Release 39/08, Santiago, 28 August 2008.

prohibition of inhumane treatment generally requires bodily injury or intense physical or mental suffering be caused, the European Court of Human Rights has held that, even in their absence, 'where treatment humiliates or debases an individual, showing a lack of respect for or diminishing his or her human dignity, or arouses feelings of fear, anguish or inferiority capable of breaking an individual's moral and physical resistance, it may be characterised as degrading'.[125]

The Duty to Investigate

There is a duty to investigate whenever there are 'reasonable grounds to believe' that an act of torture or other inhumane treatment or punishment has been committed in prison, 'irrespective of whether a formal complaint has been received'.[126] In addition, the prison director is obliged to 'report, without delay', any serious injury that occurs in custody to 'a judicial or other competent authority that is independent of the prison administration' and which is 'mandated to conduct prompt, impartial and effective investigations into the circumstances and causes of such cases'. The prison administration must cooperate 'fully' with that authority and 'ensure that all evidence is preserved'.[127]

Examples of Inhumane Treatment of Detainees

The 2015 Nelson Mandela Rules stipulate that in no circumstances may restrictions or disciplinary sanctions amount to torture or other inhumane treatment or punishment. It requires that the following practices 'in particular' be prohibited:

- indefinite solitary confinement
- prolonged solitary confinement
- placing a prisoner in a dark or constantly lit cell
- corporal punishment
- reduction of a prisoner's diet or drinking water
- collective punishment.[128]

The Rules further state that instruments of restraint must never be applied as a sanction for disciplinary offences.[129]

[125] ECtHR, *Bouyid* v. *Belgium*, §87. [126] Rule 71(2), 2015 Nelson Mandela Rules.
[127] Rule 71(1), 2015 Nelson Mandela Rules.
[128] Rule 43(1), 2015 Nelson Mandela Rules. [129] Rule 43(1), ibid.

The 2008 Principles and Best Practices of the Inter-American Commission on Human Rights called for prohibitions to be incorporated into the domestic laws of American states on the imposition of collective punishment,[130] the suspension or restriction of food and drinking water,[131] and the application of corporal punishment.[132]

Collective Punishment

Collective punishment is always prohibited. The *Miguel Castro-Castro Prison* case before the Inter-American Court of Human Rights concerned treatment of prisoners following a riot in the prison. Those suspected of involvement were subjected to the *callejón oscuro* ('dark alley'), a method of collective punishment which consisted of being forced 'to walk between a double file of agents who would beat them with blunt instruments such as sticks and metal or rubber batons, and whoever fell down on the ground received more beatings until they reached the other end of the alley'.[133] The prisoners were also subjected to beatings with metal rods on their soles (commonly known as 'falanga' beatings); electric shocks; beatings with sticks and kicking that included blows to the head, the hips, and other parts of the body; and a punishment known as the 'hole'.[134]

Corporal Punishment

Similarly, violence to the body of a detainee as an individual and targeted punishment is always prohibited. In the *Caesar* case, the Inter-American Court of Human Rights held that a state party to the 1969 American Convention on Human Rights (ACHR) 'has an obligation *erga omnes* to refrain from imposing corporal punishments, as well as to prevent their imposition inasmuch as they constitute, in any circumstance, cruel, inhuman or degrading treatment or punishment'.[135]

[130] Principle XXII.4, Principles and Best Practices on the Protection of Persons Deprived of Liberty in the Americas, adopted by the IACHR in Resolution No. 1/08, at: www.oas.org/en/iachr/mandate/Basics/principlesdeprived.asp.

[131] Principle XI, ibid. [132] Principle I, ibid.

[133] IACtHR, *Miguel Castro-Castro Prison* v. *Peru*, Judgment (Merits, Reparations and Costs), 25 November 2006, §297.

[134] Ibid., §320.

[135] Inter-American Court of Human Rights (IACtHR), *Caesar* v. *Trinidad and Tobago*, Judgment, 11 March 2005, §§57–70.

The same presumption of state responsibility with respect to deaths in custody applies to those injured during custody. According to the European Court of Human Rights' judgment in the *Getiren* case, 'where an individual is taken into custody in good health but is found to be injured by the time of release, it is incumbent on the State to provide a plausible explanation of how those injuries were caused and to produce evidence casting doubt on the veracity of the victim's allegations, particularly if those allegations are supported by medical reports. Failing this, a clear issue arises under Article 3 of the Convention'.[136]

Forced Feeding

According to the 2015 Nelson Mandela Rules, every prisoner must be provided with food 'of nutritional value adequate for health and strength, of wholesome quality and well prepared and served' and drinking water 'must be available to every prisoner whenever he or she needs it'.[137] As Sir Nigel Rodley observed, the 'controversial and emotive issue' of the forced feeding of detainees who are on hunger strike raises the difficult question whether giving potentially life-saving treatment may constitute prohibited inhumane treatment. 'In essence, the argument is between two principles: respect for the moral autonomy of the prisoner, against the responsibility of the state for the fate of those it has deprived of liberty.'[138]

The methods of force-feeding at the US detention facility in Guantánamo Bay, Cuba, have been described as follows:

> They are being force-fed through the nose. The force-feeding happens in an abusive fashion as the tubes are rammed up their noses, then taken out again and rammed in again until they bleed. For a while tubes were used that were thicker than a finger because the smaller tubes did not provide the detainees with enough food. The tubes caused the detainees to gag and often they would vomit blood. The force-feeding happens twice daily with the tubes inserted and removed every time. Not all of the detainees on hunger strike are in hospital but a number of them are in their cells, where a nurse comes and inserts the tubes there.[139]

[136] ECtHR, *Getiren* v. *Turkey*, Judgment, 22 July 2008 (as rendered final on 22 October 2008), §71.

[137] Rule 22, 2015 Nelson Mandela Rules.

[138] N. Rodley with M. Pollard, *The Treatment of Prisoners under International Law*, 3rd Edn, Oxford University Press, Oxford, 2011, p. 419.

[139] Accounts by Attorney Julia Tarver, 28 October 2005, note 73 in 'Situation of detainees at Guantánamo Bay Report of the Chairperson of the Working Group on Arbitrary Detention, Ms Leila Zerrougui; the Special Rapporteur on the independence of judges and lawyers,

In the *Nevmerzhitsky* case, the applicant to the European Court of Human Rights spent almost three years in pre-trial detention between 1997 and 2000. In the course of his detention, he went on hunger strike on a number of occasions and was subjected to forced feeding. The Court noted (controversially) its view that forced feeding could not be considered degrading treatment if it were necessary to save a person's life. However, the Government had not demonstrated that force-feeding had been medically necessary in the applicant's case. Moreover, the manner of forced feeding, involving handcuffs, a mouth-widener, and a special rubber tube inserted into the food channel, had amounted to torture.[140]

Restraints

According to the 2015 Nelson Mandela Rules, 'use of chains, irons, or other instruments of restraint which are inherently degrading or painful shall be prohibited'.[141] Other instruments of restraint may only be used when authorised by domestic law. These may not be unlawful under international law if applied as a precaution against escape during a transfer, 'provided that they are removed when the prisoner appears before a judicial or administrative authority'. Another potentially lawful scenario is when they are used to prevent prisoners from injuring themselves or others or from causing damage to property. In this case, restraint must be ordered by the prison director who in turn must 'immediately alert the physician or other qualified health-care professionals and report to the higher administrative authority'.[142]

In the United Kingdom, prison rules on use of force specify that control and restraint techniques 'are used as a last resort in order to bring a violent or refractory prisoner under control. The techniques are applied for as short a time as is possible'.[143] According to the rules,

Mr Leandro Despouy; the Special Rapporteur on torture and other cruel, inhuman, or degrading treatment or punishment, Mr Manfred Nowak; the Special Rapporteur on freedom of religion or belief, Ms Asma Jahangir and the Special Rapporteur on the right of everyone to the enjoyment of the highest attainable standard of physical and mental health, Mr Paul Hunt', UN doc. E/CN.4/2006/120, 15 February 2006, p. 48.

[140] ECtHR, *Nevmerzhitsky* v. *Ukraine*, Judgment (Second Section), 5 April 2005 (as rendered final on 12 October 2005).

[141] Rule 47(1), 2015 Nelson Mandela Rules.

[142] Rule 47(2), 2015 Nelson Mandela Rules.

[143] HM Prison Service, 'Use of Force', p. 9.

> Control and Restraint basic techniques are used by a team of three officers (with the option of having another person involved to control the legs) in order to manage a violent or refractory prisoner.
>
> The deployment of a Three Officer Team is the approved method of dealing with a violent or recalcitrant prisoner. It must only be used as a last resort after all other means of de-escalating (e.g. persuasion or negotiation) the incident, not involving the use of force, have been repeatedly tried and failed.[144]

In the *Tali* case, Andrei Tali was serving a life sentence in an Estonian prison following his conviction in 2001 for the murder of two people and attempted manslaughter of another.[145] On one occasion in 2009, after being pepper-sprayed he was strapped to a restraint bed based on the orders of a duty officer, as he was behaving aggressively and offering physical resistance to the prison officers.[146] According to a report on the use of the restraint bed, the applicant was strapped to the bed for almost four hours. His condition was monitored once an hour, when the need for continued use of the restraint was assessed on the basis of his behaviour.[147]

In a judgment of March 2010, Estonia's Tartu Administrative Court declared the use of the restraint unlawful. The court found that although the applicant's failure to comply with the orders given to him had undeniably constituted a threat to the general security of the prison, the use of handcuffs and his immobilisation had not been justified, as there was no evidence that Mr Tali had been armed or equipped with a dangerous item, or that he had intended to escape or attack anyone.[148]

The European Court noted that use of handcuffs or other instruments of restraint 'does not normally give rise to an issue' under the ECHR's prohibition of inhumane treatment 'where the measure has been imposed in connection with lawful detention and does not entail the use of force, or public exposure, exceeding what is reasonably considered necessary'.[149] The Court has accepted that 'on occasion' force may be needed to ensure prison security and to maintain order or prevent crime in detention facilities. 'Nevertheless, such force may be used only if indispensable and must not be excessive.'[150]

144 Ibid., §§4.23–4.24.

145 ECtHR, *Tali* v. *Estonia*, Judgment (First Section), 13 February 2014 (as rendered final on 13 May 2014), §§1, 6.

146 Ibid., §17. 147 Ibid., §19. 148 Ibid., §41. 149 Ibid., §58. 150 Ibid., §59.

In the circumstances of the case, the European Court did not consider use of the restraint bed to have been justified. While Mr Tali's behaviour was described as 'aggressive' after a physical confrontation with prison officers, the Court reiterated that means of restraint 'should never be used as a means of punishment, but rather in order to avoid self-harm or serious danger to other individuals or to prison security'.[151] After the end of the confrontation, Mr Tali was locked in a single-occupancy disciplinary cell and thus no longer posed a threat to himself or others that could have justified such a measure. The Court also found that the period during which he was strapped to the restraint bed was 'by no means negligible' and that his 'prolonged immobilisation must have caused him distress and physical discomfort'.[152]

Particular rules apply to use of restraints on female detainees, especially those who are pregnant. In the United Kingdom, rules on use of force in prisons dictate that in case of a planned use of force on a female prisoner who is known or suspected of being pregnant, a full risk assessment must be carried out and staff must be fully briefed before any control and restraint techniques are employed.[153] In 2012, only 16 US states had outlawed shackling of pregnant women: some US prisons chain a woman's hands and ankles, before, after, and sometimes even during childbirth on the grounds that a birthing inmate may try to flee.[154]

A similar situation exists in Turkmenistan. In northern Turkmenistan, for example, inmates at the Dashoguz Women's prison colony are said to be handcuffed to the bed from both sides while giving birth. The baby is then given away and the woman returns to forced labour a day or two later. More than 2,000 women are housed in the colony, which was built for 1,000. Fights break out when food is handed out: black bread, porridge, and a thin soup made of bones, cotton oil, and pumpkin make up the daily diet.[155]

151 Ibid., §81. 152 Ibid.

153 HM Prison Service, 'Use of Force', Prison Service Order 1600, §4.36, at: www.justice.gov.uk/downloads/offenders/psipso/.../pso-1600.doc.

154 Tatlow, 'Women in Prison Fare Better in China'.

155 M. Guinness, 'Force-fed and Beaten – Life for Women in Jail', *Independent*, 18 December 2011, at: www.independent.co.uk/news/world/politics/force-fed-and-beaten-life-for-women-in-jail-6278849.html.

Use of Pepper Spray

Pepper spray is commonly used in the detention facilities of many countries and its use is growing. In the United States, for example, most federal correctional officers started carrying pepper spray in March 2015. This represents a major policy shift for the Bureau of Prisons, which had long been opposed to arming its employees, on the basis that weapons could be taken by inmates and used against staff. Pressure for policy change increased after the murder of an officer, Eric Williams, who was equipped with only a radio and handcuffs when a prisoner at a Pennsylvania prison stabbed him to death in 2013.[156] Expansion in pepper spray availability was also taking place in state and local jails. In February 2016, New York State's corrections commissioner declared that prison officials wanted to introduce pepper spray to de-escalate confrontations between officers and inmates.[157]

A report by Human Rights Watch published in May 2015 affirmed that misuse of force on prisoners with mental illnesses such as schizophrenia and bipolar disorder was 'widespread and may be increasing'.[158] The report concluded that prisoners with mental health problems are more likely to have force used against them, including by means of pepper spray and Tasers (firearms are banned or restricted in most prisons and jails).

In 2014, a federal judge deemed California's use of pepper spray on prisoners suffering from mental illness a 'horrific violation' of their constitutional rights and ordered restrictions on its use. In one of the incidents presented to the federal court, a California prisoner who thought that officers executing a cell extraction had come to 'harvest his organs' was sprayed six times over the course of six-and-a-half minutes.[159] Arizona also settled a court case in 2014, and agreed to restrict use of chemical agents on those deemed 'seriously mentally ill' to incidents where an 'imminent threat' was present.[160]

[156] 'Adding Pepper Spray to the Prison Arsenal', Marshall Project, 5 December 2015, at: www.themarshallproject.org/2015/05/12/adding-pepper-spray-to-the-prison-arsenal#.CE7XX0yhP.

[157] Associated Press, 'NY Prison Officials Consider Introducing Pepper Spray', Albany, NY, 5 February 2016, at: www.northcountrypublicradio.org/news/story/30905/20160205/ny-prison-officials-consider-introducing-pepper-spray.

[158] Human Rights Watch, *Callous and Cruel: Use of Force against Inmates with Mental Disabilities in US Jails and Prisons*, 12 May 2015, at: www.hrw.org/report/2015/05/12/callous-and-cruel/use-force-against-inmates-mental-disabilities-us-jails-and.

[159] 'Adding Pepper Spray to the Prison Arsenal', Marshall Project, 5 December 2015.

[160] Ibid.

The European Committee for the Prevention of Torture (CPT) has expressed its concern about use of pepper spray in prisons and other centres of detention. For example, in its report on a visit to Bosnia and Herzegovina it noted:

> Pepper spray is a potentially dangerous substance and should not be used in confined spaces. Even when used in open spaces the CPT has serious reservations; if exceptionally it needs to be used, there should be clearly defined safeguards in place. For example, persons exposed to pepper spray should be granted immediate access to a medical doctor and be offered an antidote. Pepper spray should never be deployed against a prisoner who has already been brought under control. Further, it should not form part of the standard equipment of a prison officer.

The CPT recommended that Bosnia and Herzegovina draw up a clear directive governing the use of pepper spray, which should include, as a minimum:

- an explicit statement that pepper spray should not be used in a confined area
- the right of prisoners exposed to pepper spray to immediate access to a doctor and to an antidote
- the qualifications, training, and skills of staff members authorised to use pepper spray, and
- an adequate reporting and inspection mechanism with respect to use of pepper spray.[161]

In the *Tali* case referred to above, the European Court held that pepper spray should never be deployed against a prisoner who has already been brought under control. Given the potentially serious effects of pepper spray in a confined space and the alternative equipment at the disposal of the prison guards, such as flak jackets, helmets, and shields, the Court found that the circumstances did not justify the use of the spray.[162]

Use of Force in Interviews

Force must never be used to coerce a confession or obtain information during interviews with suspects or witnesses. In the *Maslova* case, the

[161] European Committee for the Prevention of Torture and Inhuman or Degrading Treatment or Punishment, Report on visit to Bosnia and Herzegovina, Doc. CPT/Inf (2009), §79.

[162] ECtHR, *Tali* v. *Estonia*, Judgment, §78.

applicant, who had been called in for questioning at her local police station in Russia, was coerced by police officers into confessing to involvement in a murder through the use of physical and sexual violence. One police officer put thumb cuffs on her, beat her, raped her, and then forced her to perform oral sex. Subsequently he and another officer repeatedly hit her in the stomach, put a gas mask over her face, blocking the air to suffocate her, and ran electricity through wires attached to her earrings. When allowed to go to the lavatory, she tried to cut the veins of her wrists. Three prosecution officers, after interrogating her at the police station, drank alcohol and continued to rape her.[163]

The applicant filed a complaint in a domestic court in Russia alleging that she had been raped and tortured. A used condom found in the station was determined to have a 99.99 per cent probability of having traces of her vaginal cells. Disposable wipes were found with traces of sperm and various items of clothing with traces of sperm and vaginal tissue of the same antigen group as the applicant. However, a court ruled that the evidence collected was inadmissible, as a special procedure for bringing proceedings against prosecution officers had not been followed. The case was finally discontinued for lack of evidence of a crime.[164]

The European Court noted the impressive and unambiguous body of evidence in support of the applicant's version of events. It further reiterated that rape of a detainee by an official of the state had to be considered an especially grave and abhorrent form of ill-treatment given the ease with which an offender could exploit the vulnerability and weakened resistance of his victim. It held that the physical violence to which the applicant had been subjected, especially the cruel acts of repeated rape, amounted to torture.[165]

In *Zyakun* v. *Ukraine*, the Court noted that the fact that the applicant confessed after held in unrecorded detention for at least two days, combined with medical evidence of unexplained injuries, 'creates an appearance that his confession may not have been given freely'.[166] The Court considered it 'sufficiently established' that Mr Zyakun was injured 'as a result of ill-treatment for which the Government must

[163] ECtHR, 'Violence against Women', Factsheet, January 2016, p. 5, summarising *Maslova and Nalbandov* v. *Russia*, Judgment (Chamber), 24 January 2008; see also Court press release at: http://hudoc.echr.coe.int/eng-press?i=003-2241782-2402590#{"itemid":["003-2241782-2402590"]}.

[164] Ibid. [165] Ibid.

[166] ECtHR, *Zyakun* v. *Ukraine*, Judgment (Fifth Section), 25 February 2016, §52.

bear Convention responsibility and which must be classified as inhuman and degrading'.[167]

'Truth Serums'

As Michael Crowley has observed,[168] for the purpose of interrogation law enforcement officials in a number of states are believed to have used psychoactive incapacitating chemical agents (e.g. sodium thiopental, sodium amytal, or scopolamine) as so-called truth drugs or truth serums against detainees without their consent. Malcolm Dando and Martin Furmanski[169] and Julian Perry Robinson[170] have documented attempts by the United States and the Soviet Union during the Cold War to develop such chemical aids to interrogation. More recently, such methods are reported to have been used in India,[171] Turkmenistan,[172] and in the US detention centre at Guantánamo Bay.[173]

167 Ibid., §54.

168 This section is based on M. Crowley, 'The Use of Incapacitants in Law Enforcement', in S. Casey-Maslen (ed.), *Weapons Under International Human Rights Law*, Cambridge University Press, 2014, pp. 371–73.

169 M. Dando and M. Furmanski, 'Midspectrum Incapacitant Programs', in M. Wheelis, L. Rózsa, and M. Dando (eds.), *Deadly Cultures: Biological Weapons Since 1945*, Harvard University Press, Cambridge, MA, 2006.

170 J. Perry Robinson, 'Disabling Chemical Weapons: A Documented Chronology of Events, 1945–2003', Unpublished monograph, 1 November 2003. On US research see also US Senate, Committee on Intelligence and Human Resources Subcommittee on Health and Scientific Research, Joint Hearing, Project MKULTRA, the CIA's Program of Research in Behavioral Modification, 3 August 1977.

171 S. Acharya, 'Is Narco Analysis a Reliable Science? – Present Legal Scenario in India', *Legal Service India*, 19 February 2008, available at: www.legalserviceindia.com/article/l176-Narco-Analysis.html; 'Mumbai Attacks: Militant Kept in Underwear to Prevent Suicide', *Daily Telegraph*, 8 December 2008.

172 Amnesty International, 'Turkmenistan: Individuals Continue to Be at Risk of Violations in Turkmenistan', AI Index: EUR 61/001/2009, 12 February 2009; Human Rights Watch, Turkmenistan: Open Letter from a Coalition of Human Rights Organizations, 17 July 2006.

173 J. Warrick, 'Detainees Allege Being Drugged, Questioned. US Denies Using Injections for Coercion', *Washington Post*, 22 April 2008. See also UN Commission on Human Rights, 'Situation of Detainees at Guantánamo Bay', 27 February 2006, UN doc. E/CN.4/2006/120. This report was prepared jointly by: the Chairperson-Rapporteur of the Working Group on Arbitrary Detention, the Special Rapporteur on the independence of judges and lawyers, the Special Rapporteur on torture and other cruel, inhuman or degrading treatment or punishment, the Special Rapporteur on freedom of religion or belief, and the Special Rapporteur on the right of everyone to the enjoyment of the highest attainable standard of physical and mental health.

Such practices are contrary to international human rights law.[174] The UN Principles for the Protection of Detainees, addressing the issue of interrogation, states that:

> It shall be prohibited to take undue advantage of the situation of a detained or imprisoned person for the purpose of compelling him to confess, to incriminate himself otherwise or to testify against any other person ... No detained person while being interrogated shall be subject to violence, threats or methods of interrogation which impair his capacity of decision or his judgement.[175]

In May 2010, India's Supreme Court ruled that the administration of incapacitants to detainees without their consent during interrogation, a practice known in India as 'narcoanalysis', violated the Indian Constitution and was illegal as it constituted cruel, inhuman, or degrading treatment.[176] The Court stated that:

> Even though "the right against cruel, inhuman and degrading punishment" cannot be asserted in an absolute sense, there is a sufficient basis to show that Article 21 [of the Indian Constitution which protects "personal liberty"] can be invoked to protect the "bodily integrity and dignity" of persons who are in custodial environments. This protection extends not only to prisoners who are convicts and under trials, but also to those persons who may be arrested or detained in the course of investigations in criminal cases.[177]

> It must be remembered that the law disapproves of involuntary testimony, irrespective of the nature and degree of coercion, threats, fraud or inducement used to elicit the same ... we must recognise that a forcible intrusion into a person's mental processes is ... an affront to human dignity and liberty, often with grave and long-lasting consequences.[178]

The Court left open the possibility of admitting into evidence information obtained under narcoanalysis when the suspect volunteered to receive the drug in question (potentially undermining the prohibition). And, despite the decision, it appears that narcoanalysis has continued in

[174] See also ECtHR, *Gäfgen* v. *Germany*, Judgment, §94.

[175] Principle 21, UN Body of Principles for the Protection of All Persons under Any Form of Detention or Imprisonment, 9 December 1988.

[176] Principle 21, UN Body of Principles for the Protection of All Persons under Any Form of Detention or Imprisonment.

[177] Supreme Court of India, Criminal Appellate Jurisdiction, *Selvi* v. *State of Karnataka & Anr.*, Criminal Appeal No. 1267 of 2004, 5 May 2010, §195, available at: www.indiankanoon.org/doc/338008/.

[178] Ibid., §205.

India. In 2014, an article analysing Indian jurisprudence noted the value that has been attached to the practice, particularly in suspected terrorist cases.[179] Thus, for example, in 2012 Mr V. H. Patel, deputy director at the Directorate of Forensic Sciences in Gujarat, western India, told *The Guardian* newspaper in the UK that he had personally conducted narcoanalysis in nearly 100 cases. He estimated that his laboratory received requests for narcoanalysis three to four times a month.

> There is no violence involved. It's a good methodology that helps the investigation. After all, there has to be justice for the victims. If we conduct narcoanalysis on a terror suspect, everyone kicks up a fuss, but what about the people who have suffered?[180]

[179] A. K. Barnwal and Dr S. N. Ambedkar, 'Narco-analysis Test: An Analysis of Various Judgements of Indian Judiciary', *Journal of Humanities and Social Science*, Vol. 19, No. 10 (October 2014), pp. 52–57, at: http://iosrjournals.org/iosr-jhss/papers/Vol19-issue10/Version-1/H0191015257.pdf; see also B. Panda, 'Narco-Analysis and its Evidentiary Value in India Narco-Analysis and its Evidentiary Value in India', *The Practical Lawyer*, July 2011, at: www.supremecourtcases.com/index2.php?option=com_content&itemid=5&do_pdf=1&id=21437.

[180] H. Pidd, 'Indian Police Still Using Truth Serum', *TheGuardian*, 5 July 2012, at: www.theguardian.com/uk/2012/jul/05/india-truth-serum.

8

Use of Force in Counterterrorism

'There will definitely be more November 13-type attacks planned against targets in France and Europe ... We have seen significant evolution since 2013 towards individuals acting under orders from the Islamic State group. These small groups are getting much more organised, and they are getting much more help in planning and preparation from Islamic State ...'[1]

Introduction

This chapter discusses police use of force in counterterrorism operations. Increasingly, specialist police units are being trained, equipped, and either deployed or held ready for rapid deployment to respond to terrorist attacks in public spaces. The introduction to the chapter summarises the definition of, and threat from, terrorism as well as some of the strategic frameworks that have been elaborated to respond to terrorism. A second section describes the human rights framework for police use of force in counterterrorism operations, in particular the rights to life and to humane treatment. The third section looks at the response of law enforcement to specific terrorist attacks, in Gibraltar in 1988; in Moscow in 2002; in London in 2005; in Nairobi in 2013; and in Paris in 2015.

While figures should be treated with caution (not least given the lack of an accepted definition of terrorism under international law, as discussed below) according to one statistical source, acts of terrorism killed more than 160,000 people worldwide between 2006 and the end of 2014. Records suggested that 32,727 people were killed by terrorists in

[1] Jean-Charles Brisard, Chair, Centre d'Analyse du Terrorisme (Centre for the Analysis of Terrorism) in France, cited in T. Todd, 'French 2015 Terror Attacks a "Dress Rehearsal" for 2016, Experts Say', *France 24*, 12 January 2016, at: www.france24.com/en/20160111-france-november-13-paris-attacks-terrorism-charlie-hebdo-intelligence-security.

2014 compared to 20,487 in 2006, with a low of 11,198 recorded in 2012.[2] In January 2015, a single attack in Baga, Nigeria, by Boko Haram may have killed as many as 2,000 people.[3] In 2015, one source recorded 11,774 recorded terrorist attacks in 92 countries, a decrease of 13 per cent compared with its 2014 total, largely as a result of fewer attacks in Iraq, Nigeria (despite the Baga attacks) and Pakistan.[4] In several other countries, including Afghanistan, Bangladesh, Egypt, Syria, and Turkey, the number of attacks and fatalities increased in 2015.[5]

As of writing, the greatest threat to security in both Arab and Western nations was perceived to come from those joining or supporting Islamic State (IS)[6] or similarly extreme Islamist ideologies. In December 2015, the United Nations (UN) Security Council adopted Resolution 2253 in which it expressed its 'gravest concern about the presence, violent extremist ideology and actions' of IS, al-Qaeda, 'and their affiliates in the Middle East and North Africa and beyond'. It further expressed concern at the scale of the flow of international recruits to those groups.[7]

At the end of May 2016, the UN Secretary-General said that IS was moving into 'a new phase', leading to 'increased risk that well-prepared and centrally directed attacks on international civilian targets may become a more frequent occurrence'.[8] He noted that in the past six months alone, IS had carried out, inspired, or claimed responsibility for, terrorist attacks in Bangladesh, Belgium, Egypt, France, Germany,

[2] Statista, 'Number of Fatalities Due to Terrorist Attacks Worldwide Between 2006 and 2014', undated but accessed 10 February 2016 at: www.statista.com/statistics/202871/number-of-fatalities-by-terrorist-attacks-worldwide/.

[3] P. Bump, '2015 Has Seen Six Terror Attacks Deadlier Than Paris', *Washington Post*, 18 November 2015, at: www.washingtonpost.com/news/the-fix/wp/2015/11/18/2015-has-seen-six-terror-attacks-deadlier-than-paris/.

[4] National Consortium for the Study of Terrorism and Responses to Terrorism (START), 2015. See: www.start.umd.edu/news/2015-gtd-data-informs-latest-statedepartment-country-reports-terrorism-release.

[5] UK Government, *CONTEST: The United Kingdom's Strategy for Countering Terrorism: Annual Report for 2015*, Doc. CM 9310, July 2016, §1.2, at: www.gov.uk/government/uploads/system/uploads/attachment_data/file/539683/55469_Cm_9310_Web_Accessible_v0.11.pdf.

[6] See, e.g., D. L. Byman, 'The Islamic State threat to the Middle East', Blog entry reposted on Brookings website, 1 August 2016, at: www.brookings.edu/blog/markaz/2016/08/01/the-islamic-state-threat-to-the-middle-east/.

[7] UN Security Council Resolution 2253, 17 December 2015, preambular paras. 4 and 27.

[8] 'Report of the Secretary-General on the Threat Posed by ISIL (Da'esh) to International Peace and Security and the Range of United Nations Efforts in Support of Member States in Countering the Threat', UN doc. S/2016/501, 31 May 2016, §5.

Indonesia, Lebanon, Pakistan, Russia, Turkey, and the United States (US); the attacks had killed more than 500 people and injured many hundreds more. Furthermore, the list did not include attacks and fighting in conflict zones inside Afghanistan, Iraq, Libya, Syria, or Yemen. The Secretary-General concluded that IS 'continues to pose a significant global terrorist threat'.[9]

The Definition of Terrorism

Although no universally accepted definition of either 'terrorism' or 'counterterrorism' exists under international law,[10] common elements are typically that they concern acts intended to kill or injure and which are committed with a view to either influencing government policy or creating terror among the general public. It is contested whether the definition of terrorism does or should extend to encompass attacks against members of the armed forces (which are not prohibited by international humanitarian law during armed conflict),[11] and whether acts committed in furtherance of the right of peoples to self-determination are excluded (which are considered legitimate by a significant minority of states).

In 2004, the UN High-level Panel on Threats, Challenges and Change suggested that terrorism should be defined as to encompass any action 'that is intended to cause death or serious bodily harm to civilians or non-combatants, when the purpose of such act, by its nature or context, is to intimidate a population, or to compel a Government or an international organization to do or to abstain from doing any act'.[12] As the High-level Panel explained: 'Attacks that specifically target innocent civilians and non-combatants must be condemned clearly and unequivocally by all.'[13]

[9] Ibid.

[10] See, e.g., N. Boister, *An Introduction to Transnational Criminal Law*, Oxford University Press, Oxford, 2012, pp. 62–63.

[11] In October 2016, the International Committee of the Red Cross (ICRC), for example, stated that 'in armed conflicts, the draft comprehensive convention [on terrorism] should not criminalize actions that are authorized or not prohibited under IHL, such as attacking military objectives or persons not entitled to protection against direct attacks'. 'Measures to Eliminate International Terrorism', ICRC statement to the 71st session of the UN General Assembly (Sixth Committee), New York, 5 October 2016, at: www.icrc.org/en/document/measures-eliminate-international-terrorism-icrc-statement-united-nations-2016?mc_cid=752eaf8017&mc_eid=572784c656.

[12] 'A More Secure World: Our Shared Responsibility, Report of the High-level Panel on Threats, Challenges and Change', UN, 2004, §164(d), p. 52.

[13] Ibid., p. 52.

In 2011, the Appeals Chamber of the Special Tribunal for Lebanon, an ad hoc mechanism set up in relation to the attack that killed former Lebanese Prime Minister Rafik Hariri on 14 February 2005, issued a decision in which it claimed that terrorism during peacetime was defined under customary international law and that it comprised the following three key elements:

(i) the perpetration of a criminal act (such as murder, kidnapping, hostage-taking, arson, and so on), or threatening such an act;
(ii) the intent to spread fear among the population (which would generally entail the creation of public danger) or directly or indirectly coerce a national or international authority to take some action, or to refrain from taking it;
(iii) when the act involves a transnational element.[14]

But as Marko Milanovic has observed, this definition is 'controversial to say the least'.[15] Rob Cryer disputes not only that the definition asserted by the Special Tribunal for Lebanon reflects customary international law, but also contests whether any such definition exists.[16]

The Focus of Counterterrorism

Despite the similar lack of an accepted definition of counterterrorism under international law, the focus of policies and strategies that use this nomenclature tends to be on ensuring a degree of normality to society against a terrorist threat while respecting human rights. For instance, the United Kingdom (UK)'s counterterrorism strategy, CONTEST, aims to 'reduce the risk to the UK and its interests overseas from terrorism, so that people can go about their lives freely and with confidence'.[17] The 2011 strategy asserts that 'four factors will continue to enable terrorist groups to grow and to survive: conflict and instability; aspects of modern

[14] Special Tribunal for Lebanon (STL), Interlocutory Decision on the Applicable Law: Terrorism, Conspiracy, Homicide, Perpetration, Cumulative Charging (Case No. STL-11-01/I), 16 February 2011, §85.

[15] M. Milanovic, 'Special Tribunal for Lebanon Delivers Interlocutory Decision on Applicable Law', *EJIL Talk!*, Published on 16 February 2011, at: www.ejiltalk.org/special-tribunal-for-lebanon-delivers-interlocutory-decision-on-applicable-law/.

[16] R. Cryer *et al.*, *An Introduction to International Criminal Law and Procedure*, Cambridge University Press, Cambridge, 2014, p. 314.

[17] CONTEST: The United Kingdom's Strategy for Countering Terrorism, July 2011, available at: www.gov.uk/government/publications/counter-terrorism-strategy-contest.

technology; a pervasive ideology; and radicalisation'.[18] CONTEST is claimed to reflect 'fundamental values' and not only to protect the people of the United Kingdom and its interests overseas, 'but to do so in a way that is consistent with and indeed advances our commitment to human rights and the rule of law'.[19]

At regional level, the European Union (EU)'s strategic commitment is 'to combat terrorism globally while respecting human rights, and make Europe safer, allowing its citizens to live in an area of freedom, security and justice'.[20] The EU organises its counterterrorism actions around four objectives (reflecting the UK model): prevention, protection, pursuit, and response. The Prevention pillar aims to combat radicalisation and recruitment of terrorists by identifying the methods, propaganda, and the instruments used by terrorists. The Protection pillar aims to reduce the vulnerability of targets to attack and to limit the resulting impact of attack. The aim of the third pillar is to pursue terrorists across borders, while respecting human rights and international law. But since the risk of terrorist attacks cannot be eliminated, the fourth pillar is of response. The strategy asserts that response systems to terrorist attacks will often be similar to those in place to manage natural, technological, or man made disasters.[21]

Globally, the UN adopted a global strategy to counter terrorism in September 2006. The Strategy proposed to address conditions conducive to the spread of terrorism; to prevent and combat terrorism; to take measures to build state capacity to fight terrorism; to strengthen the role

[18] Ibid., §1.04.

[19] Ibid., §1.14. The 'Prevent' component of the strategy has been widely criticised for being counterproductive. See, e.g., N. Magney, 'CONTEST, Prevent, and the Lessons of UK Counterterrorism Policy', *Georgetown Security Studies Review*, 16 May 2016, at: http://georgetownsecuritystudiesreview.org/2016/05/16/contest-prevent-and-the-lessons-of-uk-counterterrorism-policy/; and D. Casciani, 'Analysis: The Prevent Strategy and its Problems', *BBC*, 26 August 2014, at: www.bbc.com/news/uk-28939555. In February 2016, David Anderson QC, the independent reviewer of UK counterterrorism laws, called for an independent review of the anti-radicalisation strategy, claiming that the programme, particularly the duty it imposes on schools to spot and report signs of radicalisation in pupils, has become a 'significant source of grievance' among British Muslims, encouraging 'mistrust to spread and to fester'. Cited in D. Batty, 'Prevent Strategy "Sowing Mistrust and Fear in Muslim Communities"', *The Guardian*, 3 February 2016, at: www.theguardian.com/uk-news/2016/feb/03/prevent-strategy-sowing-mistrust-fear-muslim-communities.

[20] EU Counter-Terrorism Strategy, 2005, at: http://register.consilium.europa.eu/doc/srv?l=EN&f=ST%2014469%202005%20REV%204.

[21] See: http://eur-lex.europa.eu/legal-content/EN/TXT/?uri=URISERV%3Al33275.

of the UN in combating terrorism; and to ensure the respect of human rights while countering terrorism.[22]

The Human Rights Framework

In October 2016, the International Committee of the Red Cross (ICRC) delivered a speech to the UN General Assembly in which it opined that the international community 'must be clear and firm about the need for counterterrorism activities to be conducted with full respect for the protection afforded to all individuals by international law', in particular international humanitarian law (IHL, also known as the law of armed conflict) and international human rights law.[23] This, the organisation argued, is 'in the interest of the international community, as there is a growing recognition today that violations of these bodies of international law may exacerbate the very phenomenon that counterterrorism purports to fight'.[24]

With respect to use of force in counterterrorism action, the primary human rights at risk of violation are the rights to life and to freedom from torture. The right to humane treatment, which includes the prohibition on torture, is absolute and applies everywhere and in all circumstances, including throughout situations of armed conflict.[25] In contrast, while the protective content of the right to life similarly applies at all times, the determination of whether any given act amounts to arbitrary deprivation of life amid an ongoing armed conflict may depend on whether the act is one of law enforcement or is conducted as part of hostilities.

Hence, under international law, each use of force by agents of the state, including the police, falls to be judged under either the law of law enforcement (LOLE) or under *jus in bello*, in particular IHL/ the law of armed conflict (LOAC) rules that govern the conduct of hostilities.[26] In December 2013, the UN General Assembly adopted, by consensus,

[22] UN General Assembly Resolution 60/288 (The United Nations Global Counter-Terrorism Strategy) and annexed Plan of Action, 8 September 2006, at: http://daccess-dds-ny.un.org/doc/UNDOC/GEN/N05/504/88/PDF/N0550488.pdf?OpenElement; see also United Nations Action to Counter Terrorism, at: www.un.org/en/terrorism/.

[23] 'Measures to Eliminate International Terrorism', ICRC statement to the 71st session of the UN General Assembly (Sixth Committee), New York, 5 October 2016.

[24] Ibid.

[25] According to Art. 2(2) of the 1984 Convention against Torture, 'No exceptional circumstances whatsoever, whether a state of war or a threat of war, internal political instability or any other public emergency, may be invoked as a justification of torture.'

[26] Where one state uses forces on the territory of another, or against the armed forces of another state, these actions also fall to be considered under *jus ad bellum* rules (those that

Resolution 68/178, which urged states 'to ensure that any measures taken or means employed to counter terrorism, including the use of remotely piloted aircraft, comply with their obligations under international law, including the Charter of the United Nations, human rights law and international humanitarian law, in particular the principles of distinction and proportionality'.[27]

The default legal framework for adjudging any police use of force is law enforcement. Outside armed conflict, that framework cannot, by definition, be LOAC. Even in armed conflict, there is a presumption that the police are not combatants unless they have been integrated into the armed forces.[28] Accordingly, only exceptionally should the legality of any use of force be assessed under LOAC rules, which are far less restrictive with respect to use of deadly force than are law enforcement rules. The prerequisites for such exceptional application of LOAC rules are that:

- there is an ongoing armed conflict involving a state whose police or security forces are engaged in violent action
- the act in question is directly related to that armed conflict, and involves forcible action such as violence or the imminent threat of its use, and
- with respect to police use of force against a non-state armed group – as opposed to another state[29] – the act in question occurs in an area in which fighting between a state and the group is ongoing.

Thus, counterterrorism operations against individuals who align themselves with, or even be a member of, a terrorist group that is actively involved in hostilities in an armed conflict elsewhere in the country (and *a fortiori* elsewhere in the world) fall to be addressed under law enforcement rules. Moreover, demonstrators may actively protest in support of

govern inter-state use of force). These rules operate in parallel to, and are distinct from, the rules considered in this chapter.

27 UN General Assembly Resolution 68/178 'Protection of Human Rights and Fundamental Freedoms While Countering Terrorism', adopted by consensus on 18 December 2013, §6(s).

28 See, e.g., ICRC, Fourth Expert Meeting on the Notion of Direct Participation in Hostilities, Geneva, 27–28 November 2006, Summary Report, pp. 52–53. But see also ICRC, Fifth Expert Meeting on the Notion of Direct Participation in Hostilities, Geneva, 5–6 February 2008, Summary Report, pp. 54, 68.

29 A non-state actor may be considered 'an individual or entity not acting under the lawful authority of any state'. See UN Security Council Resolution 1540, adopted on 28 April 2004; and see also the summary at: www.un.org/press/en/2004/sc8076.doc.htm. In contrast to such operations in a non-international armed conflict, hostilities by the armed forces of one state against another state may occur anywhere in the world.

an armed group, or against the regime in power, without that protest justifying recourse to LOAC rules. For instance, in April 2016 in Mali, demonstrators stormed an airport runway in northern Mali on Monday to protest against arrests by French forces of people suspected of links to Islamist militants who operate in the region. According to press reports, security forces 'fired warning shots and teargas to deter the mostly female protesters in the town of Kidal who also ransacked and set fire to airport facilities'.[30]

The Right to Life

The state is generally obliged under customary and treaty law to respect and protect the right to life of all persons under its jurisdiction.[31] According to the Human Rights Committee, the right to life under Article 6 of the 1966 International Covenant on Civil and Political Rights (ICCPR) 'concerns the entitlement of individuals to be free from acts and omissions intended or expected to cause their unnatural or premature death, as well as their legitimate expectation to enjoy a dignified existence'.[32] Article 6 guarantees this right 'for all individuals, including persons suspected or convicted of serious crimes, such as terrorist crimes'.[33]

The Committee has reiterated its view that any state party to the ICCPR is obliged to respect and to ensure the rights under Article 6 of 'all persons who are found within their territory and all persons subject to their jurisdiction, power and effective control'.[34] Respect for the right to life also requires that states adopt measures that are protective. Thus, the Human Rights Committee has also recalled that states parties must take adequate measures to protect individuals against being murdered or

[30] 'Protests Against French Forces in Mali Turn Deadly', *France24*, 18 April 2016, at: www.france24.com/en/20160418-mali-kidal-deadly-protests-against-french-forces?ns_campaign=reseaux_sociaux&ns_source=FB&ns_mchannel=social&ns_linkname=editorial&aef_campaign_ref=partage_user&aef_campaign_date=2016-04-18.

[31] See, e.g., 'Report of the Special Rapporteur on Extrajudicial, Summary or Arbitrary Executions, Christof Heyns', UN doc. A/HRC/26/36, 1 April 2014, §42, citing D. Moeckli *et al.* (eds.), *International Human Rights Law*, Oxford University Press, New York, 2010, p. 221.

[32] Human Rights Committee, Draft General Comment No. 36 (Article 6: Right to life), Draft prepared by Yuval Shany and Nigel Rodley, Rapporteurs, UN doc. CCPR/C/GC/R.36/Rev.2, 7 September 2015, §3.

[33] Ibid. [34] Ibid., §62.

killed by criminals and organised crime or militant groups, including armed or terrorist groups.[35]

The prohibition on arbitrary deprivation of life means that, although 'it inheres in every human being by virtue of membership in the human family, the right to life is not absolute'.[36] By requiring that deprivation of life must not be arbitrary in nature, ICCPR Article 6(1) 'implicitly recognizes that some deprivations of life may be justified in some cases. For example, the use of lethal force against a person who poses an immediate threat to the lives of others when no other, less harmful, means of protection are or could have been available does not prima facie constitute an arbitrary deprivation of life'.[37]

Use of Firearms

In addition to the general principles of necessity and proportionality, which apply to any use of force, specific provisions of the 1979 Code of Conduct for Law Enforcement Officials and the 1990 Basic Principles on the Use of Force and Firearms by Law Enforcement Officials[38] cover use of firearms. As discussed in Chapters 3 and 4, the 1990 Basic Principles identify four scenarios may allow recourse to use of firearms, though in each such use is only lawful when less extreme means are insufficient:

1. Imminent threat of death or serious injury to a person
2. To prevent a particularly serious crime involving grave threat to life
3. To stop a person resisting arrest from committing a particularly serious crime that involves a grave threat to life
4. To prevent a person resisting arrest from escaping and committing a particularly serious crime that involves a grave threat to life.[39]

Intentional Killing

A distinct standard applies when law enforcement officials shoot 'to kill' rather than shoot to stop/incapacitate. Although there is an obvious reluctance on the part of authorities to embrace the concept of 'shoot to kill', it is clear that in certain instances death is the deliberate intention. An example would be to stop a suicide bomber or a hostage-taker from

[35] Ibid., §25. [36] Ibid., §16. [37] Ibid.

[38] The Basic Principles were adopted on 7 September 1990 by the Eighth UN Congress on the Prevention of Crime and the Treatment of Offenders and welcomed by the UN General Assembly in Resolution 45/166, adopted without a vote on 18 December 1990 (operative §4).

[39] Principle 9, 1990 Basic Principles.

killing others. Clearly, this may be particularly relevant in counterterrorism operations.

Thus, according to the final sentence of Basic Principle 9, 'In any event, intentional lethal use of firearms may only be made when strictly unavoidable in order to protect life.' The UN Special Rapporteur on extrajudicial, summary or arbitrary executions has termed this the 'protect life' principle, whereby 'a life may be taken intentionally only to save another life'.[40]

The Special Rapporteur has further affirmed that: 'A common sense understanding of the scope of application of Principle 9 suggests that all weapons that are designed and are likely to be lethal should be covered, including heavy weapons such as bombs and (drone) missiles, the use of which constitutes an intentional lethal use of force.'[41] Landmines should also be considered as such weapons according to jurisprudence from the European Court of Human Rights.[42]

On 15 February 2006, the German Constitutional Court controversially declared Germany's Aviation Security Act unconstitutional, insofar as it authorised the armed forces to shoot down, by direct use of armed force, aircraft that intended to be used as weapons in crimes against human lives.[43]

The Right to Humane Treatment

It is unlawful for the police to commit or threaten acts of torture against any detainee, including a suspected terrorist. Torture is defined as 'severe pain or suffering, whether physical or mental' that is intentionally inflicted, for example by a law enforcement official.[44] In cases

[40] 'Report of the Special Rapporteur on Extrajudicial, Summary or Arbitrary Executions, Christof Heyns', UN doc. A/HRC/26/36, 1 April 2014, §70.

[41] *Ibid.*, §71. See also, e.g., European Court of Human Rights (ECtHR), *Esmukhambetov and Others* v. *Russia*, Judgment (First Section), 29 March 2011 (as rendered final on 15 September 2011).

[42] In *Alkin* v. *Turkey*, the European Court affirmed that injury resulting from landmines is a violation of Art. 2 of the 1950 European Convention on Human Rights because the very nature of the weapon makes their use unlawful: "the Court considers that the laying of such indiscriminate and inhumane weapons as anti-personnel landmines, which affect the lives of a disproportionate number of civilians and children, amounts to intentional use of lethal force." ECtHR, *Alkin* v. *Turkey*, Judgment (Second Section), 13 October 2009, §30.

[43] ECtHR, *Finogenov and Others* v. *Russia*, Judgment (First Section), 20 December 2011 (rectified on 6 March 2012 and as rendered final on 4 June 2012), §164.

[44] According to the 1984 Convention against Torture, torture means: 'Any act by which severe pain or suffering, whether physical or mental, is intentionally inflicted on a person for such purposes as obtaining from him or a third person information or a confession,

concerning, especially, Latin American states, the Human Rights Committee found combinations of the following acts to amount to torture: systematic beatings, electroshocks, burns, extended hanging from hand and/or leg chains, repeated immersions in a mixture of blood, urine, vomit, and excrement ('submarino'), standing for great lengths of time, simulated executions, and amputations.[45] Waterboarding is another clear example of torture.[46]

With respect to threats of torture, in 1992, the Human Rights Committee noted in a General Comment that the prohibition of inhumane treatment in the ICCPR 'relates not only to acts that cause physical pain but also to acts that cause mental suffering to the victim'.[47] In addition, according to the UN Special Rapporteur on torture, 'serious and credible threats, including death threats, to the physical integrity of the victim or a third person' can amount to torture, 'especially when the victim remains in the hands of law enforcement officials'.[48]

In the 2003 *Maritza Urrutia* case, the Inter-American Court of Human Rights found that Ms Urrutia was subjected to torture by virtue of very long interrogations during which she was shown photographs of individuals who had been tortured or killed in combat and threatened that she would be found by her family in the same way. Guatemalan state agents also threatened to torture her physically or to kill her or members of her family if she did not collaborate with them.[49]

punishing him for an act he or a third person has committed or is suspected of having committed, or intimidating or coercing him or a third person, or for any reason based on discrimination of any kind, when such pain or suffering is inflicted by or at the instigation of or with the consent or acquiescence of a public official or other person acting in an official capacity.' Art. 1, 1984 UN Convention against Torture and Other Cruel, Inhuman or Degrading Treatment of Punishment.

45 S. Joseph and M. Castan, *International Covenant on Civil and Political Rights: Cases, Materials, and Commentary*, 3rd Edn, Oxford University Press, 2014, p. 240.

46 See, e.g., J. Bravin, 'Waterboarding is Torture, Says International Red Cross. Humanitarian Organization Declares That Interrogation Technique Violates Geneva Conventions' *Wall Street Journal*, 7 August 2014, at: www.wsj.com/articles/waterboarding-is-torture-says-international-red-cross-1407449858#.

47 Human Rights Committee, General Comment 20 (Article 7: the right to freedom from torture), 1992, §5.

48 'Report of the UN Special Rapporteur on the Question of Torture and Other Cruel, Inhuman or Degrading Treatment or Punishment to the UN General Assembly', UN doc. A/56/156, 3 July 2001, §8.

49 IACtHR, *Maritza Urrutia* v. *Guatemala*, Judgment (Merits, Reparations, and Costs), 27 November 2003, §85.

In the *Gäfgen* case before the European Court of Human Rights,[50] the applicant, who had been arrested on suspicion of having abducted an 11-year-old boy, was threatened with great physical pain by the police in order to make him reveal the boy's whereabouts. In its judgment, the Court's Grand Chamber held that to threaten an individual with torture may constitute at least inhuman treatment.[51] In the case at hand, the Court was unable to conclude that Mr Gäfgen's complaints of physical assaults and injuries and the alleged threat of sexual abuse during interrogation were established beyond reasonable doubt.[52] It did conclude that threat of imminent and severe physical pain was proven, observing that the threat was not a spontaneous act but was premeditated and calculated in a deliberate and intentional manner.[53] The Court noted that fear of physical torture may itself constitute mental torture.[54]

Examples of Use of Force in Counterterrorism Operations

This section discusses the legality of five high-profile counterterrorism operations around the world over the past 30 years that involved force that proved, or was intended to be, lethal. The first case reviewed is the counterterrorism operation by the United Kingdom against three Irish republicans planning a bombing attack on Gibraltar in 1988; the operation resulted in the shooting to death of all three suspected terrorists by British soldiers. The second case concerns the Moscow theatre siege in which up to 50 Chechen militants took hundreds of people hostage at the Dubrovka Theatre on 23 October 2002. Russian special forces forcibly ended the siege but hundreds of hostages died in the aftermath, many as a result of the effects of a gas that the authorities pumped into the theatre. The legality of the state responses in each of these two instances was later assessed by the European Court of Human Rights.

In July 2005, Islamist terrorists killed more than fifty Londoners in a series of bomb attacks across the UK capital. Thankfully, a second wave of attacks two weeks later did not inflict further casualties as the detonators failed to set off the main explosive charges. In hunting down the perpetrators, Metropolitan police officers shot to death a Brazilian electrician, mistaking him for one of the terrorists. The legality of the United Kingdom's actions, which are discussed below, was adjudged by the

[50] ECtHR, *Gäfgen* v. *Germany*, Judgment (Grand Chamber), 1 June 2010 (as rectified on 3 June 2010).

[51] Ibid., §91. [52] Ibid., §98. [53] Ibid., §104. [54] Ibid., §108.

European Court of Human Rights in 2016. The fourth case concerns the Kenyan government response to the killings by al-Shabaab-aligned militants at the Westgate shopping centre in Nairobi, Kenya, in October 2013. The fifth and final case describes the attacks in Paris by Islamic State militants in November 2015 and the response of the French police.

Death on the Rock, 1988

On 6 March 1988, members of a British Special Air Service (SAS) unit shot to death Provisional Irish Republican Army (IRA) members Mairead Farrell and Sean Savage on the Rock of Gibraltar.[55] A third IRA member, Daniel McCann, who was walking a hundred yards behind, was pursued and killed seconds later. All three deceased had been part of an IRA active service unit that was planning to bomb a parade of the Royal Anglian Regiment in the centre of Gibraltar two days later. Both British and Spanish security forces had been aware of the IRA operation for months and were working closely together in an attempt to thwart it. Operation Flavius, as the counterterrorism operation was code-named, had been weeks in the planning.

Nearly four months before, in November 1987, the IRA had killed eleven people in a bombing of a Remembrance Day service in Enniskillen, Northern Ireland. The bombing had provoked a significant loss of sympathy for Irish republicanism, and with it some of the IRA's supply lines for weapons and explosives. Sinn Féin's weekly newspaper, *An Phoblacht*, criticised the bombing, calling it a 'monumental error' that would strengthen the IRA's opponents, while the IRA itself disbanded the unit responsible.[56] In an attempt to regain the initiative, the IRA chose to target British military personnel overseas.

On the day of the shootings, the IRA unit in Gibraltar parked a rented Renault car close to the point at which the Regiment band was to assemble for the Changing of the Guard ceremony, a popular tourist attraction which took place every Tuesday. The Renault was intended to hold the parking space for a car bomb that was to be prepared elsewhere. Once the car was parked, the three IRA operatives (Ms Farrell, Mr Savage,

[55] Unless otherwise stated, the facts of the incident are from BBC, 'Three IRA Members Shot Dead in Gibraltar', undated but accessed on 8 February 2016 at: www.bbc.co.uk/history/events/three_ira_members_shot_dead_in_gibraltar.

[56] For details of the bombing and the reaction to it within Ireland and internationally, see, e.g., BBC, 'Enniskillen Bombing', at: www.bbc.co.uk/history/events/enniskillen_bombing.

and Mr McCann) were walking in the direction of the Spanish border when they were intercepted and killed by the SAS.

The British government initially said that a bomb had already been planted. Within 24 hours, however, Geoffrey Howe, the Secretary of State for Foreign Affairs, admitted that there had been no bomb in the car and that the three killed were unarmed. Shortly after the shootings, a car used by the IRA unit was found over the border in Spain. It contained a timing device, screwdrivers, false passports, and wire. Two days later, a second car rented by Ms Farrell was discovered by Spanish police in Marbella. It contained 132 pounds of Semtex plastic explosive and several rounds of ammunition for an assault rifle.

The Irish government, while acknowledging the necessity for British security forces to combat terrorism, declared itself 'gravely perturbed' by the killings. A book of condolence was opened outside the General Post Office in Dublin, scene of the nationalist Easter Rising in 1916. In Belfast, there were protests from students of all political persuasions outside Queen's University, where Ms Farrell was enrolled on a course in political science and economics. Investigations by an ITV documentary, *Death on the Rock*, and BBC Northern Ireland's *Spotlight* programme were subject to challenge by the UK government, which argued that the programmes might prejudice the outcome of the inquest into the deaths.

More deaths quickly followed. On 16 March 1988, at the funerals in Belfast's Milltown cemetery of the three IRA operatives killed in Gibraltar, mourners were attacked by Michael Stone, a man with links to loyalist paramilitaries. Mr Stone killed three and injured many more by firing shots and hurling grenades at the crowd. Three days later, two British Army corporals were dragged from their car, taken to waste ground, and shot dead after driving into the funeral cortège of Kevin Brady, one of the victims of Michael Stone's attack.

An inquest into the deaths of the three IRA operatives opened in Gibraltar on 6 September 1988. The families of the deceased were represented, as were the SAS soldiers and the UK Government. The inquest was presided over by Gibraltar's Coroner, who sat with a jury chosen from the local population.[57] The inquest lasted until 30 September and during the nineteen days it sat, evidence was heard from seventy-nine witnesses, including the soldiers, police officers, and surveillance personnel involved in the operation. Evidence was also heard from

[57] ECtHR, *McCann and Others* v. *UK*, Judgment, §103.

pathologists, forensic scientists, and experts in relation to the detonation of explosive devices.[58]

At the inquest, the two soldiers who shot and killed Mr Savage stated under cross-examination that once it became necessary to open fire they would continue shooting until the person 'was no longer a threat'. One of the two soldiers (each of whom was referred to only by letters during his testimony) agreed that the best way to ensure this result was to kill. The other stated that he was firing at Savage to kill him and that this was the way that all soldiers were trained. Both soldiers, however, denied that they had shot Savage while he was lying injured on the ground.

The tactical commander stated that the intention at the moment of opening fire was to kill since this was the most effective way to remove the threat. He added that this was the standard followed by any soldier in the army who opens fire.[59] In further evidence, the senior military commander and the tactical commander denied that a plan, express or tacit, existed to execute the suspects. The four soldiers who were directly engaged in the operation also denied that they had been sent out either expressly or on the basis of 'a nod or a wink' to kill the suspects.[60]

A post-mortem was conducted in respect of the three deceased on 7 March 1988. Professor Watson, a pathologist from the United Kingdom, had carried out the procedure. His report was later provided to a second pathologist, Professor Pounder, who was instructed by the applicants. Comment was later made at the inquest by both pathologists with regard to defects in the post-mortem procedures. In particular, the bodies had been stripped before Professor Watson saw them, depriving him of possible aid in establishing entry and exit wounds; there had been no X-ray facilities; and Professor Watson had not later been provided with either a full set of photographs for reference or the forensic and ballistics reports.[61]

The evidence concerning the shooting of Ms Farrell indicated that she had been shot three times in the back, from a distance of some three feet according to Professor Pounder. She had five wounds to the head and neck. The facial injuries suggested that either the entire body or at least the upper part of the body was turned towards the shooter. A reasonable scenario consistent with the wounds was that she received the shots to the face while facing the shooter, then fell away and received the shots to the back. Professor Watson agreed that the upward trajectory of the

[58] Ibid., §106. [59] Ibid., §80. [60] Ibid., §119. [61] Ibid., §102.

bullets that hit Farrell indicated that she was going down or was down when she received them. Altogether she was shot eight times.[62]

Mr McCann was shot in the back twice and had three bullet wounds in the head. The wound on the top of the head suggested that the chest wounds came before the head wound and that he was down, or very far down, when it was inflicted. The shots to the body were at about a 45-degree angle.[63]

Mr Savage was hit by a total of 16 bullets. He had seven wounds to the head and neck, five on the front of the chest, five on the back of the chest, one on the top of each shoulder, three in the abdomen, two in the left leg, two in the right arm, and two on the left hand. The position of the entry wounds suggested that some of the wounds were received facing the shooter. But the wounds in the chest had entered at the back of the chest. Professor Watson accepted the proposition that Savage was 'riddled with bullets' and that 'it was like a frenzied attack'. He agreed that it would be reasonable to suppose from the strike marks on the pavement that bullets were fired into Savage's head as he lay on the ground. Professor Pounder agreed that the evidence from strike marks on the ground, and the angle and state of wounds, indicated that Savage was struck by bullets when lying on his back on the ground by a person shooting standing towards his feet.[64]

Addressing the jury at the end of the inquest, the Coroner concluded from the evidence given by the soldiers that when they opened fire they shot intending to kill, and directed the jury as to the range of possible verdicts:

> If the soldiers set out that day with the express intent to kill that would be murder and it would be right to return a verdict of unlawfully killed. Example two: were you to find in the case of Savage (or any of the other two for that matter) that he was shot on the ground in the head after effectively being put out of action, that would be murder if you come to the conclusion that the soldiers continued to finish him off. In both cases they intended to kill not in self-defence or in the defence of others or in the course of arrest ... so it is murder and you will return a verdict of unlawfully killed.
>
> . . . If you accept the account that the soldiers' intention was genuinely to arrest . . . and that the execution of the arrest went wrong and resulted in the three deaths because either (a) force was used when it was not necessary or (b) the force that was used was more than was reasonably

[62] Ibid., §108. [63] Ibid., §109. [64] Ibid., §110.

> necessary, then that would not be murder ... and the verdict would be . . . unlawfully killed.
>
> . . . [I]f you are satisfied that the soldiers were acting properly but nevertheless the operation was mounted to encompass the deaths of the three suspects to the ignorance of the soldiers, then you would also bring in a verdict of unlawfully killed.
>
> . . . So there are only three verdicts reasonably open to you and these are:
>
> (a) Killed unlawfully, that is unlawful homicide.
> (b) Killed lawfully, that is justifiable, reasonable homicide.
> (c) Open verdict.[65]

The jury returned verdicts of lawful killing by a majority of nine to two.[66]

The families of the deceased took action for loss and damage to the respective estates in the High Court of Justice in Northern Ireland against the UK Ministry of Defence. The applicants' actions were struck off on 4 October 1991.[67] The families applied first to the European Commission of Human Rights,[68] complaining that the killings constituted a violation of Article 2 of the 1950 European Convention on Human Rights (ECHR). On 3 September 1993, the Commission declared the applicants' complaint admissible. In its report of 4 March 1994, it expressed the opinion that there had been no violation of Article 2. The decision was made by eleven votes to six.[69] In its submission to the subsequent case before the European Court of Human Rights, the United Kingdom argued that the deaths of the three IRA members resulted from use of force which was no more than absolutely necessary in defence of the people of Gibraltar from unlawful violence.[70]

In determining the legality of the shootings under international law, the Court referred to the 1990 Basic Principles on the Use of Force and Firearms by Law Enforcement Officials. As discussed briefly above, and in greater detail in Chapters 3 and 4, Basic Principle 9 provides, inter alia, that 'intentional lethal use of firearms may only be made when strictly unavoidable in order to protect life'.[71] In analysing domestic law applicable in Gibraltar, the Court noted that Article 2 of the Gibraltar Constitution was similar to ECHR Article 2, with the exception that the

[65] Ibid., §120. [66] Ibid., §121. [67] Ibid., §§123–24.

[68] The applicants lodged their application (No. 18984/91) with the European Commission on 14 August 1991.

[69] ECtHR, *McCann and Others* v. *UK*, Judgment, §§141–42. [70] Ibid., §143.

[71] Ibid., §§138–39.

standard of justification for use of force that resulted in the deprivation of life was that of 'reasonably justifiable' as opposed to 'absolutely necessary' in Article 2(2), ECHR.[72] In the Court's view, the difference between the two standards was 'not sufficiently great' such that a violation of Article 2 'could be found on this ground alone'.[73]

The Court accepted that the soldiers 'honestly believed', in light of the information they had been given by the authorities, that it was necessary to shoot the suspects to prevent them from detonating a bomb and causing serious loss of life. 'The actions which they took, in obedience to superior orders, were thus perceived by them as absolutely necessary in order to safeguard innocent lives.'[74] The Court held that use of force by agents of the state for legitimate law enforcement purposes may be justified

> where it is based on an honest belief which is perceived, for good reasons, to be valid at the time but which subsequently turns out to be mistaken. To hold otherwise would be to impose an unrealistic burden on the State and its law-enforcement personnel in the execution of their duty, perhaps to the detriment of their lives and those of others.[75]

The lack of a dedicated explosives expert among the British security forces teams was not discussed by the Court in any depth, though it was noted that removing the car's aerial might have prevented remote detonation of a car bomb (which itself was the central justification for shooting to death the three terrorist suspects).[76] It did consider 'disquieting' that the assessment made by one soldier, after a cursory external examination of the car parked in Gibraltar, that there was a 'suspect car bomb' was conveyed to the soldiers, according to their own testimony, as a definite identification that there was such a bomb. It recalled that while the soldier had some experience in car bombs, 'it transpired that he was not an expert in radio communications or explosives'.[77]

The Court discussed, but rejected, the proposition that the use of the SAS, 'in itself, amounted to evidence that the killing of the suspects was

[72] Ibid., §154. [73] Ibid., §155. [74] Ibid., §200.

[75] Ibid. See similarly *Bubbins* v. *UK*, Judgment (Third Section), 17 March 2005. The applicant's brother, Michael Fitzgerald, was shot dead by the police at his flat following a siege lasting almost two hours. As Mr Fitzgerald had appeared to aim a gun at one of the police officers and had not responded when ordered to drop it, a police officer had fired one shot, which had killed Mr Fitzgerald. Only on very close examination of his weapon was it revealed to be a replica.

[76] See ECtHR, *McCann and Others* v. *UK*, Judgment, *esp*. §§53, 114. [77] Ibid., §209.

intended'. The Court noted that the SAS 'is a special unit which has received specialist training in combating terrorism. It was only natural, therefore, that in light of the advance warning that the authorities received of an impending terrorist attack they would resort to the skill and experience of the SAS in order to deal with the threat in the safest and most informed manner possible'.[78]

The legality of using military personnel for law enforcement tasks is, though, being increasingly questioned. In October 2015, the African Commission on Human and Peoples' Rights issued a General Comment on the right to life under the 1981 African Charter in which it stated that: 'Members of the armed forces can only be used for law enforcement in exceptional circumstances and where strictly necessary.'[79] Where this does occur, the African Commission observed that 'all such personnel must receive appropriate instructions, equipment and thorough training on the human rights legal framework that applies in such circumstances.'[80]

Indeed, while the choice of the SAS for Operation Flavius was not criticised, the soldiers' training was questioned. Although detailed investigation at the inquest into their training was precluded by the UK government, 'it is not clear whether they had been trained or instructed to assess whether the use of firearms to wound their targets may have been warranted by the specific circumstances that confronted them at the moment of arrest'. The Court affirmed that the soldiers'

> reflex action in this vital respect lacks the degree of caution in the use of firearms to be expected from law enforcement personnel in a democratic society, even when dealing with dangerous terrorist suspects, and stands in marked contrast to the standard of care reflected in the instructions in the use of firearms by the police which had been drawn to their attention and which emphasised the legal responsibilities of the individual officer in the light of conditions prevailing at the moment of engagement.
>
> This failure by the authorities also suggests a lack of appropriate care in the control and organisation of the arrest operation.[81]

While European Court did not find a violation of the right to life on the basis of the immediate actions of the soldiers to shoot, it did hold

[78] Ibid., §183.

[79] African Commission on Human and Peoples' Rights (ACHPR), 'General Comment No. 3 on the African Charter on Human and Peoples' Rights: The Right to Life (Article 4)', adopted during the 57th Ordinary Session of the African Commission on Human and Peoples' Rights, 4–18 November 2015, Banjul, The Gambia, §29.

[80] Ibid.

[81] ECtHR, *McCann and Others* v. *UK*, Judgment, §212.

that the United Kingdom had failed in its duty to plan the operation in such a way as to minimise the risk of recourse to lethal force.[82] In addition to the issue of training, the Court asked why the three suspects had not been arrested at the border immediately on their arrival in Gibraltar and why the decision was taken not to prevent them from entering Gibraltar given that they were believed to be on a bombing mission:

> Having had advance warning of the terrorists' intentions it would certainly have been possible for the authorities to have mounted an arrest operation. Although surprised at the early arrival of the three suspects, they had a surveillance team at the border and an arrest group nearby . . . In addition, the Security Services and the Spanish authorities had photographs of the three suspects, knew their names as well as their aliases and would have known what passports to look for.[83]

The United Kingdom had argued that evidence to warrant the detention and trial of the suspected terrorists might have been insufficient and to release them would obviously increase the risks.[84] In assessing the validity of this assertion, the Court observed that the danger to the population of Gibraltar in not preventing the entry of the three suspects 'must be considered to outweigh the possible consequences of having insufficient evidence to warrant their detention and trial'. As a result, the Court noted, 'the scene was set in which the fatal shooting, given the intelligence assessments which had been made, was a foreseeable possibility if not a likelihood'.[85]

The European Court's judgment in the *McCann* case was its first manifest exposition of the duty of precaution under the right to life, a duty that certainly applies to all planned counterterrorism operations. As the UN Special Rapporteur on extrajudicial, summary or arbitrary executions has observed, 'Once a situation arises where the use of force is considered, it is often too late to rescue the situation. Instead, in order to save lives, all possible measures should be taken "upstream" to avoid situations where the decision on whether to pull the trigger arises, or to ensure that all the possible steps have been taken to ensure that if that happens, the damage is contained as much as is possible.'[86]

[82] Ibid., §§213–14. [83] Ibid., §203. [84] Ibid., §204. [85] Ibid., §205.

[86] 'Report of the Special Rapporteur on Extrajudicial, Summary or Arbitrary executions, Christof Heyns', UN doc. A/HRC/26/36, 1 April 2014, §62.

The Moscow Theatre Siege, 2002

The 2002 Moscow theatre siege also concerned a planned operation by the security forces of a state party to the ECHR. It differed, however, in that the authorities seemingly had no advance warning of the attacks. On the evening of 23 October 2002, more than forty terrorists armed with assault rifles and explosives (the exact number is not known), all belonging to the Chechen separatist movement, took hostages in Moscow's Dubrovka theatre. For three days, more than 900 people were held at gunpoint in the theatre's auditorium. The building was booby-trapped and eighteen suicide bombers were positioned in the hall among the hostages. Another group of terrorists occupied the theatre's administrative premises.[87] During the siege, several hostages who tried to escape or resist were reportedly shot and killed.[88]

The terrorists demanded the withdrawal of Russian troops from Chechnya and direct negotiations between federal authorities and the separatist movement. Following talks, the terrorists released several hostages and accepted food and drinking water for the remainder, while continuing to insist on their broader demands.[89] One may safely assume, though, that at least some among the group would have known from the outset that there was no reasonable prospect of the Russian government acceding to their demands.

In the early morning of 26 October, Russian security forces pumped a narcotic gas (believed to be a derivative of the opiate fentanyl)[90] into the main auditorium through the building's ventilation system. The applicants in the case to the European Court on Human Rights, which included survivors of the operation, insisted that both the terrorists and the hostages could both smell and see the gas. A few minutes later, when the terrorists controlling the explosive devices and the suicide bombers in the auditorium lost consciousness, a special forces' team stormed the building. Most of the suicide bombers were shot while unconscious; others actively resisted, but were killed in the ensuing gunfire.[91] It is clear from the witnesses' statements reviewed by the European Court that

[87] ECtHR, *Finogenov and Others* v. *Russia*, Judgment (First Section), 20 December 2011 (as rectified on 6 March 2012 and rendered final on 4 June 2012), §8.

[88] Ibid., §11. [89] Ibid., §9.

[90] See M. Crowley, *Chemical Control*, Palgrave Macmillan, London, 2015, pp. 15–16. Crowley cites a research paper that suggested, based on analysis of the clothing of some of the hostages, that the chemical was a mixture of carfentanil and remifentanil.

[91] ECtHR, *McCann and Others* v. *UK*, Judgment, §22.

most of the hostages took the terrorists' threats seriously. 'Some of them, however, noted that they feared storming by the security forces more than the terrorists themselves.'[92]

As a result of the operation, most of the hostages (more than 730 people) were released. The exact number is unknown since, following their release, not all reported to the authorities. However, many others were badly affected by the gas; according to official information (which is sometimes contradictory) by the end of 2002, a total of 129 hostages had died: 102 died on the spot, including 3 people who were shot; 21 died in the course of evacuation and transportation to hospital; and 6 died in the emergency rooms of various hospitals.[93] Many of those who died either choked on their own vomit, or perished because their tongues were blocking their airways.[94]

In 2007, one of the applicants to the European Court commissioned an expert examination of the lethality of the gas used by the Russian security forces. The examination was carried out by Dr Mark Wheelis, a microbiologist and professor at the University of California in Davis in the United States (US). In his report, Dr Wheelis concluded as follows:

> Significant numbers of fatalities among the hostages inside the Dubrovka theatre should have been anticipated. Fatalities were certain to occur from two distinct mechanisms. First, fatalities and permanent injury should have been anticipated from direct toxic effects of the chemical agent. Although the Russian Federation has not identified the agent, they have said it is a member of the phentanyl class of synthetic opioids. Several of these are in medical use as analgesics for severe chronic pain, and as anaesthetics, and it is known that the margin between the effective dose for unconsciousness and the lethal dose is very small. Death is usually by respiratory depression. Phentanyl is also known as a drug of abuse, and many fatalities have been recorded among recreational users. Since all known phentanyls have similar, and very narrow, safety margins, fatalities from respiratory depression should have been anticipated.
>
> Second, even if the chemical agent itself was safe, fatalities should have been anticipated as a result of asphyxiation from airway obstruction consequent upon sudden collapse from a seated or standing position. Some lethality or permanent injury should also have been anticipated as a result of aspiration of vomit, as vomiting is a common side effect of opioids.[95]

[92] Ibid., §43. [93] Ibid., §24. [94] Ibid., §25.
[95] Report dated 12 March 2007, cited in ibid., §109.

As also noted by the Court, according to evidence by Dr Martin Furmanski, a toxicologist practicing in the United States and a specialist on chemical weapons, the effects of the fentanyl family of drugs are well known. At moderate doses, those drugs suppress pain; at high doses they cause a sleep-like state; while at very high doses they cause a coma. All opiates also suppress the urge to breathe in a dose-dependent way. When someone is unconscious, breathing may slow below the point needed to maintain sufficient oxygen in the blood to sustain normal body functioning. Even if breathing continues at a reduced rate, the relaxation caused by opiates can cause the neck and tongue to become limp and result in an occlusion of the airway. This positional asphyxia is a particular risk if the recipient is sitting upright. In addition, when opiates (and particularly fentanyl-type drugs) are given rapidly, this causes muscular rigidity, which can stop breathing entirely.[96]

In criticising Russia's use of the gas prior to storming the theatre, the applicants to the European Court referred to the hostage-taking crisis in Peru in 1997. The Peruvian authorities reportedly requested an opinion from the United States on possible use of a fentanyl-based narcotic gas during the storming. The United States dissuaded them, arguing that use of such a gas would require simultaneous deployment of 1,000 doctors to provide rapid medical assistance to 400 hostages. Since it was impossible to organise such massive medical assistance, the Peruvian authorities decided not to use the gas.[97]

The Government recalled[98] that Russia is a state party to the 1979 International Convention against the Taking of Hostages, Article 3 of which provides that: 'The State Party in the territory of which the hostage is held by the offender shall take all measures it considers appropriate to ease the situation of the hostage, in particular, to secure his release'. According to Russia's 1998 Suppression of Terrorism Act, the consequences of a terrorist act should be minimised. The head of the crisis cell, whose establishment during a terrorist incident the Act demands, may authorise negotiations with the terrorists, but it is specifically prohibited to discuss possible exchange of hostages for other people, to provide guns or other dangerous items to the terrorists, or to enter into political negotiations.[99]

Russia further observed that the gas they used was not intended to kill the terrorists, but to send them to sleep, to avoid any need to use firearms

[96] Evidence cited in ibid., §113. [97] Ibid., §172. [98] Ibid., §186.
[99] S. 14, Law No. 130-FZ, 25 July 1998; see *Finogenov and Others* v. *Russia*, Judgment, §191.

during the storming. When assessing options for intervention, the authorities had considered possible losses among the hostages, but these had been unavoidable in the circumstances. It had also been impossible to calculate the dose of the gas more precisely because of differences in the physical condition of those in the theatre: young, physically fit terrorists, and the hostages, weakened by the siege, suffering from lack of food, fresh air, chronic diseases, some of them too old or too young to withstand the effects of the gas. As a result, the dose of the gas had been calculated on the basis of the 'average person's' resistance to it. Any other approach, the authorities argued, would have undermined the efficiency of the operation, and removed the 'surprise effect' of the storming. The authorities had simultaneously tried to avoid maximum damage, to neutralise the terrorists, and to minimise negative consequences. Consequently, the use of the gas had been 'absolutely necessary' in the circumstances.[100]

On several occasions, Russia had also sought to claim that the gas was 'harmless' in that there had been no 'direct causal link' between the death of the hostages and the gas.[101] The official explanation of the mass death of the hostages on 26 October 2002 was that all those who had died were weakened by the siege or seriously ill.[102] This the European Court found 'difficult to accept'. Indeed, the Court considered it 'unthinkable that 125 people of different ages and physical conditions died almost simultaneously and in the same place because of various pre-existing health problems. Equally, the mass death of hostages cannot be attributed to the conditions in which they had been held for three days, during which none of them had died, despite prolonged food and water deprivation, immobility, psychological stress, etc'. In addition, the Russian Government had itself admitted that it had been 'impossible to foresee the effects of the gas, and had considered that some losses had been unavoidable . . . This implies that the gas was not "harmless", because "harmless" means that it does not have important adverse effects'.[103]

The Court accepted that the gas was probably not intended to kill the terrorists much less the hostages. It remarked that it was closer to 'non-lethal incapacitating weapons' than to firearms as regulated in the 1990 Basic Principles.[104] The Court observed that it may occasionally depart from the standard of 'absolute necessity' in Article 2 ECHR (which identifies when loss of life may not violate the right to life).

[100] *Finogenov and Others* v. *Russia*, Judgment, §194. [101] Ibid., §198.
[102] Ibid., §201. [103] Ibid. [104] Ibid., §202.

In particular, applying the standard 'may be simply impossible where certain aspects of the situation lie far beyond the Court's expertise and where the authorities had to act under tremendous time pressure and where their control of the situation was minimal'.[105]

The hostage-taking in Moscow came as a surprise for the authorities (which the Court contrasted with another case it had judged involving Russian military action in Chechnya itself),[106] 'so the military preparations for the storming had to be made very quickly and in full secrecy'. It noted that the authorities were not in control of the situation inside the theatre. 'In such a situation the Court accepts that difficult and agonising decisions had to be made by the domestic authorities. It is prepared to grant them a margin of appreciation, at least in so far as the military and technical aspects of the situation are concerned, even if now, with hindsight, some of the decisions taken by the authorities may appear open to doubt.'[107]

While, in the circumstances, allowing a margin of appreciation may not have been wholly unreasonable (albeit of questionable standing under international law), the Court's analysis is certainly, in other respects, surprising. In particular, it did not even discuss whether, in using the gas, Russia had violated its obligations under the 1992 Chemical Weapons Convention.[108] According to the Convention, it is prohibited 'under any circumstances' to use chemical weapons.[109] Chemical weapons include toxic chemicals, which in turn are defined as: 'Any chemical which through its chemical action on life processes can cause death, temporary incapacitation or permanent harm to humans or animals.'[110] Excepted from the definition, however, are toxic chemicals

[105] Ibid., §211.

[106] *Isayeva* v. *Russia*, Judgment, 24 February 2005, §§180 et seq. The case concerned an aerial bombing in a village by Russian combat aircraft which resulted in considerable civilian loss of life.

[107] *Finogenov and Others* v. *Russia*, Judgment, §213. It has been questioned whether this margin of appreciation would have survived an appeal to the European Court's Grand Chamber. Remarks by speaker citing conversation with the Deputy Registrar of the European Court of Human Rights, Michael O'Boyle, at 'Lethal Force, Policing and the ECHR: *McCann and Others v UK* at Twenty', Event organised by the University of Exeter's Centre for European Legal Studies and Doughty Street Chambers, Doughty Street Chambers, London, 25 March 2015.

[108] Convention on the Prohibition of the Development, Production, Stockpiling and Use of Chemical Weapons and on Their Destruction, adopted in Paris on 3 September 1992. Russia adhered to the Chemical Weapons Convention on 5 November 1997.

[109] Art. I(1)(b), 1992 Chemical Weapons Convention.

[110] Art. II(2), ibid.

where they are intended for purposes not prohibited under the Convention, 'as long as the types and quantities are consistent with such purposes'.[111] One such purpose not prohibited is 'Law enforcement including domestic riot control purposes'.[112]

What the Court should have done is to discuss the application of the 1992 Chemical Weapons Convention to the case at hand. In practice, this would be a two-stage test. First, it would have required assessment of whether the use of the gas constituted an act of law enforcement or of hostilities. As noted above,[113] each use of force must be one or the other, and the decision on this issue will determine which body of international law applies. If, as some have argued privately, it was an act conducted as part of the hostilities within the non-international armed conflict ongoing in Chechnya at the time, this would be a clear violation of the general prohibition on the use of a chemical weapon (and indeed potentially a war crime).[114]

If, however, it was an act of law enforcement (as the present author would argue), it could be lawful if it respected the principles of precaution, necessity, and proportionality. Here views differ, and especially whether use of chemical incapacitants is good policy, as discussed by Dr Michael Crowley.[115] It has to be acknowledged that, given the options open to the authorities, none was attractive.[116] Had the medical response been better organised and informed (the inadequate response by the authorities was one of the grounds on which the European Court of Human Rights found that Russia had violated the right to life in the case),[117] a far greater number of hostages might have survived.

[111] Art. II(1), ibid. [112] Art. II(9), ibid.

[113] See above section, The Human Rights Framework.

[114] See ICRC 2005 Study of Customary International Humanitarian Law, Rule 74 (Chemical Weapons): 'The Use of Chemical Weapons is Prohibited.' At: www.icrc.org/customary-ihl/eng/docs/v1_rul_rule74. According to the ICRC, using prohibited weapons may amount to a war crime. Rule 156 (Definition of War Crimes): 'Serious Violations of International Humanitarian Law Constitute War Crimes.' See point iv (Other serious violations of international humanitarian law committed during a non-international armed conflict), (i), at: www.icrc.org/customary-ihl/eng/docs/v1_rul_rule156.

[115] Crowley, Chemical Control, pp. 126–29, 168–71.

[116] The high number of casualties in the 2004 Beslan school siege demonstrates the dangers of storming a building with firearms and explosive weapons. The incident, which started on 1 September 2004 and lasted three days, involved the taking hostage of more than 1,100 people, including 777 children, and ended in controversial circumstances with a storming during which at least 385 people were killed. The hostage-takers had previously smashed school windows to prevent the effective use of gas by the security services.

[117] *Finogenov and Others* v. *Russia*, Judgment, §§237–66.

The Killing of Jean Charles de Menezes, London, 2005

On 22 July 2005, Jean Charles de Menezes, a 27-year-old Brazilian electrician, was shot to death by Metropolitan Police Service (MPS) firearms officers, after being mistaken for a failed suicide bomber, Hussain Osman. His killing occurred two weeks after the 7 July ('7/7') suicide bombings in London, which killed fifty-six people and injured hundreds more. On 21 July, a second group of Islamist extremists triggered homemade rucksack bombs on London's transport system but the devices failed to explode.[118] As the Metropolitan Police Authority noted: 'The shooting dead of Jean Charles de Menezes was a tragedy that should never have happened, whatever the circumstances were at the time.'[119]

The basic facts of the case are as follows.[120] Mr de Menezes was living in the same building as Hussain Osman, a small block of flats with a communal entrance. The police had placed the building under surveillance from the early morning of 22 July.[121] While the surveillance was ongoing, armed police officers, who were supposed to be at the scene in order to arrest Mr Osman, were still being briefed at a police station two miles away. Several people left the building but none was stopped or questioned. At 9.33am, Mr de Menezes left the building. Although he resembled one of the suspects, according to one report he was never properly identified in part because one police officer was 'relieving himself' at the time.[122] Another officer with

[118] See, e.g., S. Laville and H. Siddique, 'Jean Charles de Menezes Inquest Records Open Verdict', *The Guardian*, 12 December 2008, at: www.theguardian.com/uk/2008/dec/12/de-menezes-verdict.

[119] Metropolitan Police Authority, 'MPA Stockwell Scrutiny', Final Report, July 2008, p. 2.

[120] P. Squires and P. Kennison, *Shooting to Kill? Policing, Firearms and Armed Response*, Wiley-Blackwell, London, 2010, pp. 38–51.

[121] Independent Police Complaints Commission (IPCC), *Stockwell One, Investigation into the Shooting of Jean Charles de Menezes at Stockwell Underground Station on 22 July 2005*, London, 2006, p. 24.

[122] R. Cowan, D. Campbell, and V. Dodd, 'New Claims Emerge over Menezes Death', *The Guardian*, 17 August 2005, at: www.theguardian.com/uk/2005/aug/17/july7.menezes. In addition, the surveillance team had not been shown a high-quality picture of Mr Osman. All they had seen was a faded passport photograph at briefing at Scotland Yard at 5am and not all of them had a copy at the scene. The inquest jury decided that the failure of the police to provide better photographs to the officers contributed to Mr de Menezes's death. M. Hughes, 'Seven Mistakes that Cost De Menezes his Life', *Independent*, 13 December 2008, at: www.independent.co.uk/news/uk/crime/seven-mistakes-that-cost-de-menezes-his-life-1064466.html.

potentially the best view had a radio malfunction that prevented him from communicating his opinion.

Six minutes after leaving his house, Mr de Menezes boarded a bus towards Brixton tube station. When he got off the bus, he realised that the tube station was closed (as a continuing result of the 7/7 attacks) and he joined a queue to get back on the bus. By now, despite the apparent absence of positive identification by any police officer, senior officers in the police control room were operating under the conviction that he was the suicide bomber they were looking for. Commander Cressida Dick, the Designated Senior Officer for the firearms aspect of the operation (now the Metropolitan Police Commissioner), recalled being informed that 'it is him, the man is off the bus. They think it is him and he is very, very jumpy'.[123]

Mr de Menezes got back on a bus and headed for Stockwell tube station. As firearms officers arrived at the station one claimed to have heard over the radio that he was definitely 'our man' and that he was nervous and twitchy. They were instructed to 'stop' him entering the tube system. Far from leaping a ticket barrier and fleeing from police, as was initially claimed by the authorities, de Menezes was filmed on closed-circuit television (CCTV) calmly entering the station and picking up a free newspaper before boarding the train. He was dressed in jeans, a T-shirt, and wore a denim jacket but was not carrying anything. He was thus not wearing a heavy padded jacket or belt, as reports at the time suggested.[124]

The details of the briefings to firearms officers were not recorded, but, based on testimony, the two officers who shot and killed de Menezes apparently believed that they were dealing with a suicide bomber and that if the subject was 'non-compliant' a 'critical shot could be taken'.[125] The officer giving the briefing accepted that he had referred to the possible need for 'unusual tactics'[126] but stated that 'no instruction was issued for a critical shot to be taken'.[127]

As Mr de Menezes was heading for Stockwell tube station, the instruction was transmitted over the radio 'to stop the subject getting on the

[123] 'Jean Charles de Menezes Inquest Timeline', *Daily Telegraph*, 22 September 2008, at: www.telegraph.co.uk/news/uknews/3061485/Jean-Charles-de-Menezes-inquest-timeline .html.

[124] Ibid.

[125] IPCC, *Stockwell One, Investigation into the Shooting of Jean Charles de Menezes at Stockwell Underground Station on 22 July 2005*, London, 2006, §11.9, p. 51.

[126] Ibid., §11.9. [127] Ibid., §18.85.

tube'.[128] The understanding of what 'stop' meant in practice was the subject of differing interpretation among the police officers engaged in the operation. Firearms officers, who entered the tube station 90 seconds after Mr de Menezes, shouted 'armed police' to clear the path. They claimed to have also shouted similar words when they entered the carriage where he was seated, though the inquest jury rejected this[129] (and, as has been observed, appears inconsistent with a perception that they were dealing with a suicide bomber).[130]

But perhaps the 'most uncomfortable revelation' for the police was that Mr de Menezes had already been restrained by a surveillance officer before being shot eight times.[131] The officer grabbed him 'by wrapping both his arms around his torso pinning his arms to his side, and pushing him back to the seat where he had been sitting'. The officer 'then heard gunshots as he was himself dragged away on the floor by armed officers'.[132] Of the nine hollow-point bullets[133] fired at Mr de Menezes, all discharged at between 1cm and 8cm away from him,[134] seven hit him in the head, one bullet missed, and another round misfired.[135] At the inquest into Mr de Menezes' death, Cressida Dick, who was promoted to Deputy Assistant Commissioner a year after the

128 At the inquest into the death of Mr de Menezes, Brian Paddick, who retired as Metropolitan Police Commissioner in 2007, argued that Ms Dick's order to 'arrest him, but whatever you do, don't let him get on the Tube' was open to critical misinterpretation. R. Edwards, 'De Menezes Inquest: Retired Police Chief Brian Paddick Attacks Cressida Dick', *Daily Telegraph*, 5 November 2008, at: www.telegraph.co.uk/news/uknews/law-and-order/3386293/De-Menezes-inquest-retired-police-chief-Brian-Paddick-attacks-Cressida-Dick.html.

129 BBC, 'Open Verdict at Menezes Inquest', 12 December 2008, at: http://news.bbc.co.uk/2/hi/uk/7764882.stm.

130 See Squires and P. Kennison, *Shooting to Kill?*

131 Cowan, Campbell, and Dodd, 'New Claims Emerge over Menezes Death'.

132 IPCC, *Stockwell One, Investigation into the Shooting of Jean Charles de Menezes at Stockwell Underground Station on 22 July 2005*, London, 2006, §20.59, p. 129. The officer had a gun pointed at him before he was able to identify himself. Ibid., §13.13.

133 In May 2011 it was announced that the MPS would issue all its firearms officers with expanding ammunition. The MPS said the rounds were less likely to splinter and harm bystanders. BBC, 'Met Police to Use Jean Charles De Menezes Death Bullets', 11 May 2011.

134 O. Bowcott, 'De Menezes Family Takes Case to European Court of Human Rights', *The Guardian*, 3 June 2015, at: www.theguardian.com/uk-news/2015/jun/03/de-menezes-family-take-case-to-european-court.

135 IPCC, *Stockwell One, Investigation into the Shooting of Jean Charles de Menezes at Stockwell Underground Station on 22 July 2005*, London, 2006, §16.11 p. 81; but see also Squires and Kennison, *Shooting to Kill?*, p. 14.

shooting, stated that: 'I am afraid that I do believe that this or something like this could happen again.'[136]

A few days after the killing, Lord Stevens, the former Metropolitan Police Commissioner, made public – in a British tabloid newspaper, now defunct – a policy, code-named Operation Kratos, that had been adopted when he was in charge in 2002.[137] He told the newspaper that, after the 11 September 2001 attacks in the United States, teams sent to Israel and other countries hit by suicide bombers (reportedly Russia and Sri Lanka) had learned a 'terrible truth': that the only way to stop a suicide bomber was to 'destroy his brain instantly, utterly'.[138] Previously, officers had fired at the offender's body, 'usually two shots, to disable and overwhelm'. Sir Ian Blair stated that there was 'no point' in shooting a suspect in the chest as that is where a bomb would most likely be and that it would detonate.[139]

In December 2008, an inquest jury returned an open verdict by eight votes to two after rejecting the claim by the MPS that the shooting was a lawful killing. The coroner had not allowed the jury to consider unlawful killing as a possible verdict,[140] a decision that is open to serious question under human rights law. The Met was convicted of criminal negligence under health and safety at work legislation, fined £175,000, and ordered to pay £385,000 costs. The

136 R. Edwards, 'Jean Charles de Menezes: Cressida Dick Admits an Innocent Man Could be Killed Again", *Daily Telegraph*, 7 October 2008.

137 See, e.g., 'De Menezes Police "Told to Shoot to Kill"', *Daily Telegraph*, 3 October 2007; Squires and Kennison, *Shooting to Kill?*, p. 32.

138 BBC, 'Debate Rages over "Shoot-to-Kill"', 24 July 2005. Lord Stevens said: 'We are living in unique times of unique evil, at war with an enemy of unspeakable brutality, and I have no doubt that now, more than ever, the principle is right despite the chance, tragically, of error . . . And it would be a huge mistake for anyone to even consider rescinding it.' This contrasts starkly with the September 2005 testimony by the then-Home Secretary Charles Clarke, who stated: 'I think shoot to kill is not an appropriate phrase or description to use . . . Where a firearm was actually discharged of course death may result and has resulted absolutely tragically, but that is not the objective.' Cited in Squires and Kennison, *Shooting to Kill?*, p. viii.

139 The use of 'less-lethal' weapons such as the Taser is also not recommended for fear it might detonate the explosives. See, e.g., Memorandum entitled 'Counter Suicide Terrorism' from the Clerk to the Metropolitan Police Authority to the Members of the MPA, London, 8 August 2005.

140 BBC, 'Open Verdict at Menezes Inquest', 12 December 2008, at: http://news.bbc.co.uk/2/hi/uk/7764882.stm. The coroner, Sir Michael Wright, told the jury they would not be allowed a verdict of unlawful killing because that would suggest the officers who shot the Brazilian 'had committed a very serious offence, murder or manslaughter'. Hughes, 'Seven Mistakes that Cost De Menezes his Life'.

same year, Patricia Armani da Silva, a cousin of Jean Charles de Menezes who was living with him in London at the time of his death, made an application to the European Court of Human Rights, complaining about the decision not to charge any officers in connection with the death. Ms da Silva said:

> For ten years our family has been campaigning for justice for Jean because we believe that police officers should have been held to account for his killing. Jean's death is a pain that never goes away for us ... Nothing can bring him back but we hope that this legal challenge will change the law so that no other family has to face what we did.[141]

In June 2015, at hearings at the Court in Strasbourg, Hugh Southey QC for the applicants challenged the adequacy of the United Kingdom's definition of self-defence since the officers who shot Mr De Menezes only had to show that they had an honest belief – as opposed to an honest and reasonable belief – that the use of force was absolutely necessary.[142] At the instant of firing, however, there was also a critical question of the necessity to shoot at Mr de Menezes's head once his arms had been pinned back by two police officers in the tube-train carriage. There is, a priori, a strong argument that the requisite necessity was lacking, although the Court's judgment reported claims by one witness that despite his arms being pinned 'his hand may have moved towards the left hand side of his trouser waistband'.[143]

In addition, the failure by police officers engaged in the surveillance operation to determine whether or not Mr de Menezes was one of the suspected terrorists was a key factor that led to his wrongful shooting.[144] Given the importance of the issue, better surveillance should have been ensured, consonant with the United Kingdom's duty of precaution under the right to life. This should have been a critical issue in determining whether the United Kingdom had violated Mr De Menezes' right to life but the application to the Court, and the Court's judgment of 30 March 2016, does not address this.[145]

[141] O. Bowcott, 'Jean Charles de Menezes Arguments Heard in Strasbourg', *The Guardian*, 10 June 2015, at: www.theguardian.com/uk-news/2015/jun/10/jean-charles-de-menezes-arguments-strasbourg.

[142] Ibid. [143] ECtHR, *da Silva* v. *UK*, Judgment (Grand Chamber), 30 March 2016, §37.

[144] This is despite the surprising finding by the inquest jury that this was not, in general terms, the case. BBC, 'Open Verdict at Menezes Inquest', 12 December 2008.

[145] ECtHR, *da Silva* v. *UK*, Judgment (Grand Chamber), 30 March 2016.

The Attack on the Westgate Shopping Centre, Nairobi, 2013

On 21 September 2013, at midday, four men allied to al-Shabaab,[146] an armed group engaged in the ongoing non-international armed conflict in Somalia, entered the Westgate shopping centre in Nairobi, the Kenyan capital, and started throwing grenades and shooting at fleeing shoppers.[147] According to an investigation by the New York Police Department (NYPD), a review of video footage and ballistics evidence indicates the terrorists were carrying assault rifles as well as grenades, the latter of which were only used on their entrance to the mall, after which the terrorists fired single shots to target fleeing shoppers. Although carrying hundreds of rounds of ammunition in magazines strapped to their bodies, the attackers were believed not to be wearing any form of body armour or carrying handguns.[148]

Around one hour into the attack, security forces entered the building and gun battles ensued between police and the attackers.[149] Gunfire and explosions continued overnight, although it is claimed that the actual attack lasted only six hours, after which the NYPD's report asserted that the terrorists hid in a storeroom where they prayed and tended to one of their wounded. Further, despite claims to the contrary, the NYPD believes no heavy explosions were caused by the attackers. Instead, it claimed that all of the heavy damage to the shopping mall's structure had been caused by anti-tank missiles being fired into the building by Kenyan military.[150]

According to the BBC, security sources suggested a breakdown in control of the counterterrorism operation occurred when the military took over the operation and soldiers launched an 'uncontrolled shooting spree'.[151] Several hours after the first shootings, the Kenyan government

[146] See Associated Press (Nairobi), 'FBI Says All Attackers Probably Died in Westgate Mall Siege in Nairobi', *The Guardian*, 11 January 2014, at: www.theguardian.com/world/2014/jan/11/fbi-westgate-mall-attack-nairobi.

[147] See S. Casey-Maslen (ed.), *War Report: Armed Conflict in 2013*, Oxford University Press, Oxford, 2014, pp. 23–24.

[148] 'NYPD Investigation into Kenya's Westgate Mall Terror Attacks Reveals the Truth Behind the Massacre of More Than 60 Civilians", *news.com.au*, 11 December 2013, at: www.news.com.au/world/nypd-investigation-into-kenyas-westgate-mall-terror-attacks-reveals-the-truth-behind-the-massacre-of-more-than-60-civilians/story-fndir2ev-1226780483902.

[149] BBC, 'Nairobi Siege: How the Attack Happened', 18 October 2013, at: www.bbc.com/news/worldafrica-24189116.

[150] 'NYPD Investigation into Kenya's Westgate Mall Terror Attacks Reveals the Truth Behind the Massacre of More Than 60 Civilians'.

[151] BBC, 'Nairobi Siege: How the Attack Happened'.

had sent in the military but rivalry between the army and the police started when a commander of the police's elite squad was killed in friendly fire by the military. The changeover angered the police and they left in protest. A military commander involved in the operation, who spoke to the BBC on condition of anonymity, said that is when things started to go wrong.

> We entered the mall blindly with no guide, with no concept of anything. Command and control was not there ... The police felt they were undermined. The military thought the police didn't want to give them enough information so everything went wrong.[152]

The attack resulted in confirmed deaths of 61 civilians and 6 security officers, with the Kenya Red Cross Society listing a further 23 people as missing.[153] More than 175 people were reported wounded.[154] Al-Shabaab claimed responsibility for the attack, which it characterised as 'retributive justice for crimes committed' by the Kenyan military in Somalia, against which it had been fighting since 2011.[155]

If the incident at the Westgate centre were considered to fall within the conduct of hostilities of the armed conflict in Somalia, use by Kenyan soldiers or police officers of tear gas 'to smoke out the terrorists' would be a serious violation of LOAC/IHL rules.[156] In contrast, use of rocket-propelled grenades inside the complex,[157] or mortar shells against the

[152] D. Okari, 'Kenya's Westgate Attack: Unanswered Questions One Year on', BBC, 22 September 2014, at: www.bbc.com/news/world-africa-29282045.

[153] Ibid. Officials initially claimed that 10 to 15 attackers were involved, but CCTV recordings show only four men. BBC, 'Westgate Siege: Four Charged over Nairobi Attack', 4 November 2013, at: www.bbc.com/news/world-africa-24804892.

[154] See, e.g., Dr F. C. Onuoha, 'Westgate Attack Al-Shabaab's Renewed Transnational Jihadism', *Aljazeera Center for Studies*, 11 November 2013, at: http://studies.aljazeera.net/en/reports/2013/11/20131111112818580417.htm.

[155] Kansas Intelligence Fusion Center, *Lessons Learned: Westgate Mall Attack*, p. 9. In March 2015, Adan Garaar, the alleged 'mastermind' of the Westgate stacks was fatally wounded in Somalia after the car he was traveling in was hit by Hellfire missiles fired from a US drone. C. Bucktin, 'Westgate Mall Attack: Alleged Mastermind of Kenyan Shopping Centre Massacre "Killed in US Drone Strike"', *Daily Mirror*, 13 March 2015, at: www.mirror.co.uk/news/world-news/westgate-mall-attack-alleged-mastermind-5330738.

[156] M. Pflanz and H. Alexander, 'Nairobi Shopping Mall Attacks: Britons among Those Caught up in Terrorist Assault', *Daily Telegraph*, 21 September 2013, at: www.telegraph.co.uk/news/worldnews/africaandindianocean/kenya/10325536/Nairobi-shopping-mall-attacks-Britons-among-those-caught-upin-terrorist-assault.html.

[157] S. Tomlinson, 'The Wreckage of Westgate: First Pictures Taken Inside Kenyan Massacre Mall Show Wasteland of Crumpled Cars and Twisted Metal', *Daily Mail*,

fighters, with the consequent risk to civilians, would not, per se, be unlawful. The better view, though, is that this was a law enforcement operation (albeit one involving military forces),[158] the legality of which falls to be judged by LOLE rules.[159]

As the African Commission on Human and Peoples' Rights has opined, 'Organised crime and terrorism can pose significant threats to the enjoyment of the right to life and require a robust State response, but one that at all times takes into account the requirements of international human rights law'.[160] This means use of minimum necessary force with the possibility of intentional lethal use of force, including through use of missiles and rockets, only when this is strictly unavoidable to protect life. It is highly questionable whether use of force by the Kenyan military in this case complied with international law of law enforcement rules. The African Commission has further noted that: 'Derogation from the right to life is not permissible in a time of emergency, including a situation of armed conflict, or in response to threats such as terrorism.'[161]

No case has been brought before the African Commission on Human Rights concerning the acts of the Kenyan state in suppressing the terrorist attack on the Westgate shopping centre.

The Paris Attacks, November 2015

In 2015, France was rocked by two major terrorist attacks. In January, an assault on the offices of satirical magazine *Charlie Hebdo* – which had angered many by publishing cartoons of the Prophet Mohammed in 2006 – was the first in three days of attacks in Paris that claimed a total of seventeen lives. Then on 13 November, coordinated attacks in Paris killed 130 people, the greatest loss of life in France since the Second World War.

26 September 2013, at: www.dailymail.co.uk/news/article-2432943/Kenya-Westgate-mall-attack-video-shows-gaping-chasm-3-storeys-collapsedsiege.html#ixzz2wnjcRH5o.

158 In accordance with the commentary to Art. 1 of the 1979 Code of Conduct for Law Enforcement Officials, the term 'law enforcement officials' includes all officers of the law, whether appointed or elected, who exercise police powers, especially the powers of arrest or detention. In countries where police powers are exercised by military authorities, whether uniformed or not, or by state security forces, the definition of law enforcement officials shall be regarded as including officers of such services.

159 Casey-Maslen, *War Report: Armed Conflict in 2013*, p. 24.

160 ACHPR, 'General Comment No. 3 on the African Charter on Human and Peoples' Rights: The Right to Life (Article 4)', §2.

161 Ibid., §7.

French authorities believe that IS in Syria decided to launch the attacks, and that the operation was planned in Belgium, probably in Molenbeek, a Brussels district known for high unemployment, social problems, and a mixed immigrant population. The alleged mastermind of the attacks, Abdelhamid Abaaoud, who was killed in a shootout with French police a few days afterwards, was living in that area, as was Salah Abdeslam, who has been charged by French prosecutors with 'participation in terrorist murders' in Paris.[162] IS said its militants had attacked Paris in order to punish 'crusader' France for its air strikes against 'Muslims in the lands of the Caliphate' (meaning Iraq and Syria). The attack 'targeted the capital of prostitution and obscenity, the carrier of the banner of the Cross in Europe: Paris'.[163]

The first of three explosions occurred outside the Stade de France stadium on the northern edge of Paris where France was playing Germany in an international football friendly. It appears that a man wearing a suicide belt was prevented from entering the stadium after a routine security check detected the explosives. According to a report in the media, the man backed away from security guards and detonated the explosives. The bomber and a passer-by were killed. The game, attended by President François Hollande, was being broadcast on TV. After a second man detonated his suicide vest outside a different stadium entrance at 21:30, the president was rushed to safety. A third suicide bomber blew himself up at a fast-food outlet near the stadium at 21:53. The attackers all wore identical explosive vests.[164]

Other attacks began nearer to the centre of Paris, around popular nightlife spots. The first took place at about 21:25 in the 10th *arrondissement* (district), not far from the Place de la République. Witnesses at *Le Carillon* bar came under fire from semi-automatic rifles. A man then crossed the road and turned his gun on a restaurant, *Le Petit Cambodge*.

[162] See, e.g., BBC, 'Paris Attacks: Who was Abdelhamid Abaaoud?', 19 November 2015, at: www.bbc.com/news/world-europe-34835046; B. Farmer, 'Who is Salah Abdeslam and Who Were the Paris Terrorists? Everything We Know about the Isil Attackers', *Daily Telegraph*, 18 March 2016, at: www.telegraph.co.uk/news/worldnews/europe/france/11996120/Paris-attack-what-we-know-about-the-suspects.html; S. Osborne, 'Paris Attacks Suspect Salah Abdeslam's Lawyers Say They will "No Longer Defend Him"', *Independent*, 12 October 2016, at: www.independent.co.uk/news/world/europe/salah-abdeslam-paris-attacks-november-130-dead-lawyers-no-longer-defend-a7357216.html.

[163] L. Peter, 'Paris Attacks: Key Questions after Abaaoud Killed', *BBC*, 24 November 2015, at: www.bbc.com/news/world-europe-34866144.

[164] BBC, 'Paris Attacks: What Happened on the Night', 9 December 2015, at: www.bbc.com/news/world-europe-34818994.

Fifteen people died in the attack on the bar and restaurant, with a further fifteen severely injured. More than 100 bullets were fired. Then came an attack on restaurants a few streets away, in front of the *Café Bonne Bière* and *La Casa Nostra* pizzeria, during which five people were killed and eight others severely injured.[165]

The next reports of shootings came to the south of the first restaurant attacks, at *La Belle Equipe* bar in the 11th district of the capital. Nineteen people died in the shooting, with a further nine left in a critical condition. A few minutes later, an attacker killed himself by detonating a suicide bomb at the restaurant *Le Comptoir Voltaire* on the Boulevard Voltaire. One other person was severely injured in this incident.[166]

The deadliest attack of the night came at a concert venue on Boulevard Voltaire, also in the 11th district, where Californian rock group Eagles of Death Metal was playing. The 1,500-seat Bataclan hall was sold out. The Paris chief prosecutor said three attackers wearing suicide belts were involved. Witnesses said they arrived in a car then stormed in through the main entrance and into the back of the concert hall. Eighty-nine people died as the men fired assault rifles into the crowd. At least ninety-nine others were taken to hospital in a critical condition.[167]

The order was given to send elite security forces into the concert hall. As the operation came to a head, at about 00:20, a police officer shot one of the gunmen, and his suicide belt detonated. The siege ended with the other two blowing themselves up. The three attackers were subsequently identified as Omar Ismail Mostefai, 29; Samy Animour, 28; and Foued Mohamed-Aggad, 23. Abdelhamid Abaaoud, the Moroccan-born organiser of the attacks, was killed in a police raid in the Paris suburb of Saint-Denis on November 18.

The UN Security Council '[u]nequivocally condemn[ed] in the strongest terms the horrifying terrorist attacks perpetrated by ISIL also known as Da'esh which took place . . . on 13 November 2015 in Paris.'[168] Yet, despite their severity, French anti-terrorism experts believe the two major attacks in Paris in 2015 were a 'dress rehearsal' for more professional and better-organised terror attacks on a much larger scale in 2016. According to Yves Trotignon, a former member of the French intelligence services, the January and November attacks, for all the bloodshed they achieved, were 'amateur':

[165] Ibid. [166] Ibid. [167] Ibid.

[168] UN Security Council Resolution 2249 (2015), adopted on 20 November 2015, Operative §1.

> The November 13 attacks, from the terrorists' point of view, involved a large number of tactical mistakes that they will learn from. For example, the death toll at the Bataclan was limited because the attackers ran out of ammunition.
>
> At the Stade de France the bombers were unable to get into the stadium. Three suicide bombers blew themselves up outside the arena, killing one person. And the suicide vests turned out to be less than lethal for bystanders, while at least one failed to detonate and was abandoned.[169]

After the initial period of mourning the dead, questions began to be asked as to why a specialised counterterrorist unit did not reach the Bataclan concert hall until half an hour after the attack had begun and why it took officers nearly three hours to secure the venue. It is, though, reported that individual police officers showed 'extraordinary courage, particularly the first officer to arrive at the concert hall 15 minutes into the attack. Armed with only a pistol, he managed to interrupt the murder of hostages by shooting one of the terrorists and forcing the other two gunmen to flee upstairs'.[170]

French commentators suggested the delayed response of the French police's Search and Intervention Brigade (BRI) reflected a highly centralised structure that might need to be changed. Some experts have argued that more police patrols in Paris might have helped to end the killing more quickly. According to Christian Mouhanna, a security expert at France's National Centre for Scientific Research, French police 'are not organised along local lines. Everything has to filter up to the central organisation. The beat officers are not highly trained and so you've got to

[169] Cited in T. Todd, 'French 2015 Terror Attacks a "Dress Rehearsal" for 2016, Experts Say', *France 24*, 12 January 2016, at: www.france24.com/en/20160111-france-november-13-paris-attacks-terrorism-charlie-hebdo-intelligence-security.

[170] 'French Police Admit Mistakes in Response to Paris Terror Attacks', *TrueBlueLine*, 3 January 2016, at: http://trueblueline.net/2016/01/french-police-admit-mistakes-in-response-to-paris-terror-attacks/. At the end of February 2016, French interior minister Bernard Cazeneuve announced that many of Paris's anti-criminal (BAC: 'brigades anticriminalité') police units, who most often operate in plain clothes, would be equipped with Heckler & Koch G36 assault rifles, bulletproof vests, and ballistic shields that offer protection against bullets fired from assault rifles. The new equipment also included Tasers. 'Paris Police to be Equipped with Assault Rifles and Kalashnikov-Resistant Shields', *Daily Telegraph*, 29 February 2016, at: www.telegraph.co.uk/news/worldnews/europe/france/12178589/Paris-police-to-be-equipped-with-assault-rifles-and-Kalashnikov-resistant-shields.html; see also 'A Paris, les policiers des BAC équipés de fusils d'assaut contre les "tueries de masse"', *Le Monde*, 29 February 2016, at: www.lemonde.fr/police-justice/article/2016/02/29/a-paris-les-policiers-des-bac-equipes-de-fusils-d-assaut-contre-les-tueries-de-masse_4873881_1653578.html.

wait for the specialists to arrive ... We have a police force that is disconnected from the field'.[171]

Another issue concerned the relationship between the police and the military, a key issue in the Westgate Centre attacks in Nairobi. In April 2016, Bernard Cazeneuve, the Minister of the Interior announced that France would 'guarantee' a 20-minute response of police and military anti-terrorism units to any future terrorist attacks. In addition to more security personnel, specialist units would be given new clearances to bypass the traditional carve-up of responsibilities between police and military forces that can hinder a timely armed response.[172]

A parliamentary committee in March 2016 was told that military units were close to the music venue at the time but did not intervene. Incidents within Paris typically fall within the competence of the specialist BRI police division, which arrived on the scene within about 40 minutes. Jean-Luc Taltavull, a senior police union official, told the committee that better-armed military personnel outside the Bataclan had refused to join police preparing to enter the building because they had not been ordered to do so.[173]

As of writing, law enforcement agencies around the world were seeking to learn the lessons of the Paris attacks. In the United States, much of the training of US law enforcement officers relies on lessons from the 1999 Columbine High School attack, which taught police to be aggressive in situations where shooting is continuing. Instead of waiting for tactical units, police are now instructed to enter as quickly as possible and try and disrupt the attack.[174] This appears to be what prevented far greater loss of life at the Bataclan.

In contrast, according to Mark Lomax, Executive Director of the National Tactical Officers Association, 'After Mumbai [the 2008 terrorist attack on Mumbai, India, where terrorists attacked several sites in a coordinated effort confused and confounded local police], there's the potential for more than one scene occurring simultaneously.' Lomax argues that Mumbai inspired a new training model ('Multiple Assault Counter-Terrorism Action Capabilities'), which emphasises the need to

[171] Ibid.

[172] Reuters, 'France Pledges Faster Response to Possible Terror Attacks after Paris Delays', *The Guardian*, 19 April 2016, at: www.theguardian.com/world/2016/apr/19/france-police-response-terror-attacks-paris.

[173] Ibid.

[174] M. Kaste, 'American Police Learn Conflicting Lessons of Terrorist Attacks', *NPR*, Updated 30 November 2015, at: www.npr.org/sections/thetwo-way/2015/11/16/456269321/american-police-learn-conflicting-lessons-of-terrorist-attacks.

get a global view of what is happening before a decision is taken to send all security force assets to a scenario.[175]

In this light, American police departments are looking at social media with a view to quickly appreciating the threat in a critical situation. Twitter and other platforms can draw a map of coordinated attacks; to avoid the information becoming overwhelming, several police departments have subscribed to data analysis services to filter the flood of social media that flows from an attack. It is also suggested that the Paris attacks may 'shift the debate' over the 'militarisation' of local police. Since the Ferguson, Missouri protests, American police departments have been criticised for stockpiling military-grade weapons and gear, which often end up being used for raids on low-threat targets, such as small-time drug dealers.[176]

In March 2016, it was reported that UK Special Forces and police had been put on standby to tackle up to ten simultaneous terror attacks on London following the Paris attacks.[177] On 3 August 2016, the Metropolitan Commissioner, Sir Bernard Hogan-Howe, and the Mayor of London, Sadiq Khan, announced the start of Operation Hercules in which 600 additional firearms officers will be deployed in visible roles in London. Sir Bernard Hogan-Howe, said:

> Anyone who's been following events in Europe over the past few weeks will understand why we want to show our determination to protect the public. We are deadly serious about the protection that we are offering the people of London and we will never be complacent. I want the public to know that we have substantial resources and a range of tactics that we can call on to protect them ... The reality of having to deal with armed and deadly attackers is that you need firearms officers who will use force to stop those attackers in their aim.[178]

Meanwhile, France has warned that IS might use a chemical or biological weapon in a future attack. French emergency teams are to be supplied with atropine sulfate, an antidote to nerve gas.[179]

175 Cited in Ibid. See also J. Dettmer, 'Fumbles, Mistakes Prompt Talk of Major French Intelligence Failure', *Voice of America*, 17 November 2015, at: www.voanews.com/content/fumbles-mistakes-prompt-talk-of-major-french-intelligence-failure/3061990.html.

176 Kaste, 'American Police Learn Conflicting Lessons of Terrorist Attacks'.

177 J. Curtis, 'Special Forces and Police are on Standby to Battle up to TEN Simultaneous Terror Attacks on London', *Daily Mail Online*, 20 March 2016, at: www.dailymail.co.uk/news/article-3501186/Special-forces-police-standby-battle-10-simultaneous-terror-attacks-London.html.

178 Met, 'Armed Officers Increased to Protect London', 3 August 2016, at: http://news.met.police.uk/news/armed-officers-increased-to-protect-london-177226.

179 L. Peter, 'Paris Attacks: Key Questions after Abaaoud Killed', *BBC*, 24 November 2015.

9

Private Security and Use of Force

'Even professional, bureaucratic policing was pioneered by private firms: Allan Pinkerton founded his detective company before the [American] Civil War, and well into the twentieth century he and his competitors provided America's only national law enforcement organizations.'

David Sklansky[1]

Introduction

The use of private security for policing[2] is anything but new. As Chapter 1 illustrated, while the state has long used its own security forces to enforce laws, often those forces have concentrated on guarding the sovereign or collecting taxes. This has effectively constrained individuals who wish to protect themselves against violence or their property against damage or theft, or who seek to secure justice for a prior wrong, to have recourse to private means.

Today, to save money amid widespread budgetary austerity, nation states are increasingly keen to contract out many of their own law enforcement duties and services, while implicitly encouraging private companies and citizens to engage and pay for a large measure of their own policing needs (see also Chapter 2). In 2007, an indicative list of law enforcement tasks already being conducted by private security service providers was said to encompass the following:

[1] D. Sklansky, 'The Private Police', *University of California Los Angeles Law Review*, Vol. 46 (1998), p. 1182, available at: http://scholarship.law.berkeley.edu/facpubs/1048. See also, with respect to France, D. Kalifa, *Naissance de la police privée. Détectives et agences de recherches en France 1832–1942*, Plon, Paris, 2000.

[2] This chapter does not address use of private military companies to conduct hostilities in a situation of armed conflict.

- Prevention or detection of vandalism or trespass on private property. This includes guarding private property, (nuclear) power plants, military installations, and airport security[3]
- Prevention or detection of theft, including, for example, protection of cash in transit
- Protection of individuals from bodily harm, e.g. bodyguards
- Maintaining public order at events (e.g. concerts, football matches)
- Reporting and apprehension of criminal suspects
- Transporting prisoners and guarding prisons
- Reporting on and responding to incidents and calls.[4]

This is a global phenomenon, even though much of the focus in literature has been on the United States (US) and other Western nations. Sklansky cited work from the late 1980s in observing that one of the most striking aspects of police privatisation is its 'pervasive, international character',[5] with the 'exponential' growth of private security in the United States mirrored in Australia, Canada, New Zealand, and the United Kingdom (UK), as well as, though 'to a lesser extent', the rest of the world.[6]

In India, the private security sector has been growing at a rate of 20 per cent annually, already employing some five million people in the country.[7] Chinese companies are estimated to have spent more than US$8 billion on private security in 2014; this is a potential market thus far under-explored by national private security service providers but which has been earmarked for rapid expansion.[8] In January 2016, Pakistan's

[3] For example, Berndtsson and Stern note that, since 2007, guards from Securitas have performed most of the security duties at Stockholm airport, the busiest of Sweden's airports. J. Berndtsson and M. Stern, 'Private Security Guards', ch. 5 in R. Abrahamsen and A. Leander (eds.), *Routledge Handbook of Private Security Studies*, Routledge, Abingdon, 2015, p. 55.

[4] H. Born, M. Caparini, and E. Cole, 'Regulating Private Security in Europe: Status and Prospects', Geneva Centre for the Democratic Control of Armed Forces (DCAF), Policy Paper No. 20, Geneva, 2007, pp. 2–3.

[5] C. D. Shearing and P. C. Stenning, 'Reframing Policing', in C. D. Shearing and P. C. Stenning (eds.), *Private Policing*, Sage, Berkeley, CA, 1987, p. 9.

[6] Sklansky, 'The Private Police', p. 1181.

[7] 'Calling security', *Business World*, 5 January 2016, at: http://businessworld.in/article/Calling-Security/05-01-2016-89925/.

[8] ECNS, 'Private Security Companies Struggle to go Abroad Due to Legal Restrictions', *Global Times*, 24 December 2015, at: www.ecns.cn/2015/12-24/193540.shtml.

Ministry of Interior had registered 679 private security companies as operating within the country.[9]

Although the figures are contested, a 2005 publication by the Geneva Centre for the Democratic Control of Armed Forces (DCAF) asserted that, in South Africa, ten times more people were engaged in private policing than were employed in the police force.[10] The largest security force in the Philippines was said to be neither the 102,000-strong national police nor the 120,000-strong army, but the 182,000 private security guards, who are said to be 'virtually armies for hire'.[11]

Change may even be coming in traditionally statist France. In early September 2015, former French President Nicolas Sarkozy called for the tasks allocated to the police, the gendarmerie, and 25,000 customs officers 'to be redefined', intimating that private companies could deal with speeding on the roads and that the police 'shouldn't have to transport people in custody'.[12] Indeed, in April 2016 it was announced that companies would be operating mobile speed radar units from January 2017, 'to free up police officers for other duties'. The public reaction was distinctly negative. One French newspaper, *Le Parisien*, said that a poll showed that 83 per cent of people were against the privatisation, while 76 per cent believed it was intended to 'increase the amount of fines collected by the state'.[13]

The United Kingdom has even been privatising some of its law enforcement operations across the channel in France. In July 2016, the Home Office advertised a tender for an estimated £80 million contract to provide forty

9 'Regulating Security Firms: No Security Company Unregistered', *Express Tribune*, 3 January 2016, at: http://tribune.com.pk/story/1020829/regulating-security-firms-no-security-company-unregistered/.

10 Such figures have been rebutted by an industry representative. In September 2015, affirmed that: 'We have also heard that the ratio of police to private security guards is astronomically high. This is also not correct — there are 2.25 private security guards for every police officer. This ratio isn't much different from the US (2.26) or Australia (2.19).' S. Conradie, 'Private Security Law will Harm Our Land', *Business Day*, 17 September 2015, at: www.bdlive.co.za/opinion/2015/09/17/private-security-law-will-harm-our-land.

11 F. Schreier and M. Caparini, 'Privatising Security: Law, Practice and Governance of Private Military and Security Companies', Occasional Paper No. 6, DCAF, Geneva, 2005, p. 26, note 89.

12 'Sarkozy réfléchit à la privatisation de certaines missions de sécurité', *Le Journal du Dimanche*, 2 September 2015, at: www.lejdd.fr/Politique/Nicolas-Sarkozy-reflechit-a-la-privatisation-de-certaines-missions-de-securite-749209. Author's translation.

13 'Mobile Speed Cams "To be Privatised"', *Connexion*, 7 April 2016, at: www.connexionfrance.com/france-police-speed-cameras-infra-red-radar-unmarked-cars-privatised-17918-view-article.html.

Authorised Search Officers, 24 hours per day throughout the year for the Eurotunnel, and for the ports of Calais and Dunkirk. Three of the staff on duty must also be trained as 'detainee custody officers', responsible for holding arrested migrants in the Home Office's detention facilities at the ports, before they are handed over to French border police.[14]

Thus, Weber's debatable assertion that the state is an entity that claims the 'monopoly of the legitimate use of physical force within a given territory',[15] if ever it were true, can be considered 'increasingly out of sync with reality'.[16] As Abrahamsen and Leander observe:

> Today, private security services are ubiquitous and the marketplace is truly global: private security companies guard shopping malls, residencies and public streets. They run prisons, detention centres, and even police receptions. They train armed forces and police, and perform intelligence assessments and risk analyses ... They escort convoys and ships, and provide personal security for diplomats ... The list could go on.[17]

The remainder of this chapter considers first in more detail the extent of use of private security and the policing tasks that are typically being contracted out in selected states (the United States and the United Kingdom, where more money has been expended than anywhere else and where most of the research has been conducted thus far). A second section describes the human rights framework for private 'policing', including the extent to which private actors can be held to violate international human rights law. Legislation in selected national legal frameworks (Mexico, South Africa, Thailand, the United Kingdom, and the United States) is then considered before attention turns to particular issues of use of force by private actors carrying out law enforcement tasks. These include employment of 'less-lethal' weapons, restraint techniques, and firearms. Finally, the chapter assesses the extent to which an accountability gap exists under international and national law for abuses committed by private security services.

[14] Calais Research Network, 'Home Office Quietly Advertises £80 Million Privatisation of Calais Border Security', Calais Migrant Solidarity, 10 September 2016, at: https://calaismigrantsolidarity.wordpress.com/2016/09/10/home-office-quietly-advertises-80-million-privatisation-of-calais-border-security/.

[15] M. Weber, *From Max Weber: Essays in Sociology*, Oxford University Press, New York, 1963, p. 78.

[16] Introduction in Abrahamsen and Leander, *Routledge Handbook of Private Security Studies*, p. 1.

[17] Ibid.

Private Policing in Selected States

Private Policing in the United States

Private security services operate widely in the United States. San Francisco is a rare, but longstanding example of institutionalised private policing. Since 1847, the San Francisco Patrol Special Police, a body composed of private citizens, has operated as a private neighbourhood police force. Its operation is specifically authorised in the city's Charter, but it is not part of the San Francisco Police Department.[18] Rates charged to clients vary according to the service requested, but the average hourly cost for an officer on normal duty ranges between $50 and $60,[19] which includes the costs of his or her patrol car and liability insurance.[20]

Although until recent times the situation in San Francisco might be considered exceptional, writing in 1998 David Sklansky was already arguing that, with respect to the situation in the United States:

> Legal scholars have largely neglected private policing, and the neglect is increasingly indefensible. The private security industry already employs more guards, patrol personnel, and detectives than the federal, state, and local governments combined, and the disparity is growing; to a striking extent, private firms now perform many of the beat-patrol tasks once thought central to the mission of the public police.[21]

Economist Simon Hakim, who directs Temple University's Center for Competitive Government, claims that in the 1970s, there were 40 per cent more police than private security guards. By 2009, those positions had 'flipped', with about 60 per cent more private guards than public officers.[22]

[18] Formed in 1847 by merchants to combat the insurgence of Barbary Coast outlaws, the Patrol Special Police was incorporated into the city's charter in 1856. See 'History of the San Francisco Patrol Special Police', 2010, at: http://sfpatrolspecpolice.com/history.html.

[19] This contrasts with a claimed budget for San Francisco Police Department officers of US $250,000 per officer annually, not including pension costs, which is roughly double the cost of the private force. See 'Police privée: ça existe et ça fonctionne!', *Police et armées*, Opinion published in *Contrepoints* on 28 September 2015, available at: www.contrepoints.org/2015/09/28/223289-police-privee-ca-existe-et-ca-fonctionne.

[20] 'Field Operations and Fees', 2010, at: http://sfpatrolspecpolice.com/fieldoperations.html.

[21] Sklansky, 'The Private Police', p. 1165.

[22] Yoder, 'Outsourcing the Police'. In 2005, however, a DCAF publication estimated the ratio of private security guards to police throughout the country at three to one. Schreier and Caparini, 'Privatising Security: Law, Practice and Governance of Private Military and Security Companies', p. 26, note 89.

Public policing functions have been shrinking in many parts of the United States. In Augusta, the capital of the state of Maine, a city-commissioned study recommended that police no longer respond in person to crimes involving property damage, petrol station drive-offs, stolen bicycles, and hit-and-run accidents (if no one is seriously injured). In Baltimore, since 2011 the police department has no longer provided security at fairs and festivals unless it is reimbursed by the organisers.[23] In Illinois' St. Clair County, the sheriff's department announced in January 2011 that it would stop responding to tripped business and residential burglar alarms and calls about property crimes that are not in progress. Such cuts in policing services 'have opened the doors for private companies to move in'. Thus, in St. Clair County, for an extra US$25 an alarm company was promising to send an armed guard to the homes of their customers whose alarms are triggered.[24]

Private Policing in the United Kingdom

In January 2015, the United Kingdom's first private police force opened for business, trialling in two areas of Stoke-on-Trent, a city in Staffordshire of some 470,000 people.[25] Homeowners in the scheme who pay the £1 weekly charge also get burglar and panic alarms linked to a rapid response unit.[26] Retired Metropolitan Police Officer Stewart Brown, who served with the Met for 33 years, said:

[23] S. Yoder, 'Outsourcing the Police', *The Crime Report*, 10 March 2011, at: www.thecrimereport.org/news/inside-criminal-justice/2011-03-outsourcing-the-police#.

[24] Yoder, 'Outsourcing the Police'.

[25] The 2002 Police Reform Act gives chief constables in England and Wales the ability to grant limited powers to civilians as part of a community safety accreditation scheme. C. Smyth, 'Former Staffordshire Police Officers Offer Families Private Police Officers – for £1 a Week', *The Sentinel*, 14 January 2015, at: www.stokesentinel.co.uk/Staffordshire-Police-officers-offer-families/story-25854938-detail/story.html.

[26] Home protection is a significant growth business for the private security sector. According to DCAF, in north-western Bulgaria, crime has been a protracted problem among the many small villages with ageing populations and very low incomes. The police were perceived to be ineffective in tackling frequent burglaries and thefts of agricultural produce, allegedly by members of the local Roma community. A small private company, Sova 7, set up a programme whereby households pay up to €5 per month for the provision of security services to the entire village. The permanent presence of guards often includes Roma guards. The crime rate in villages using the service is said to have decreased significantly. F. Klopfer and N. van Amstel, *A Force for Good?*, DCAF, Geneva, 2015, p. 55 (Box 4).

> It is not a rent-a-cop scheme. We are offering a contract between the homeowners and ourselves to protect their homes and patrol the streets. This is another level of policing. When I started as a policeman in 1977, the cops went to everything. Now you are lucky if you see one in a day.[27]

In January 2016, it was reported that a single police force, Lincolnshire, which covers the non-metropolitan county in the East Midlands of England, had paid G4S £67.5 million over five years for a total of 585 roles.[28] These roles are said to have encompassed the investigation of crimes.[29] In November 2015, G4S claimed that police forces in England and Wales could save £1bn a year by outsourcing backroom services to private companies.[30] But this claim was overshadowed the following May when five G4S Lincolnshire Police control room staff were suspended over allegations they were making hundreds of emergency calls at quiet times to improve their perceived performance. The suspended officers were all former Lincolnshire police employees who transferred to G4S in 2012 when the private security company took the £200m contract to run the force's back-office services. Two of the staff were later dismissed while two had resigned and the fifth person returned to work after being cleared of any wrongdoing.[31] G4S had claimed the contract saves the force £6m a year and hailed it as a potential model for the rest of British policing.[32]

Where is the trend in private security leading? In 2013, a political consultant writing for the Libertarian Alliance had even called for the total privatisation of the police in England, arguing that this would 'at a stroke raise the standard of criminal justice in this country. It would make us, the honest majority, safer about our daily business'.[33] While that assertion is

[27] A. Potter, 'Britain's First Private Police Force Charging £1 a Week to Protect Locals' Homes', *Metro*, 16 January 2015, at: http://metro.co.uk/2015/01/16/britains-first-private-police-force-charging-1-a-week-to-protect-locals-homes-5024070/.

[28] T. Harper and G. Greenwood, 'Security Firms are Paid £170m to do Police Job', *The Sunday Times*, 3 January 2016.

[29] Ibid.

[30] BBC, 'Police Cuts: G4S Says Private Firms Could Save Forces £1bn a Year', 19 November 2015, at: www.bbc.com/news/uk-34864781.

[31] BBC, 'Lincolnshire Police 999 Call Staff Sacked over Fake Calls', 17 August 2016, at: www.bbc.com/news/uk-england-lincolnshire-37107635.

[32] A. Travis, 'G4S Police Control Room Staff Suspended over Claims of Bogus 999 Calls', *The Guardian*, 23 May 2016, at: www.theguardian.com/uk-news/2016/may/23/g4s-police-control-room-staff-suspended-claims-bogus-999-calls-lincolnshire-force.

[33] S. Gabb, 'The Case for Privatising the Police', Libertarian Alliance, London, 2013, p. 1, at: www.libertarian.co.uk/lapubs/polin/polin058.pdf. But see also A. White, 'Five Reasons Why it's Difficult to Privatise the Police', Blog entry, London School of Economics, 2012, at: http://blogs.lse.ac.uk/politicsandpolicy/five-reasons-why-its-difficult-to-privatise-the-police/.

highly questionable, what is not open to dispute is that public policing in the United Kingdom, as in other countries, is under pressure as never before. Steve White, who chairs the Police Federation of England and Wales, claimed in May 2015 that the police service was 'on its knees'. He predicted the end of policing 'by consent' and a move towards a more violent, 'paramilitary' style of law enforcement, telling *The Guardian* newspaper that more cuts in funding would be devastating:

> You get a style of policing where the first options are tear gas, rubber bullets, and water cannon, which are the last options in the UK.[34]

Despite these concerns, private security may be seen as not only a significant element of the past, it is also likely to be the mainstay of law enforcement in many countries in the future.[35] Perhaps the greatest doubt is whether certain law enforcement tasks, particularly those linked to the protection of the executive and to counterterrorism operations, will be immune to being contracted out to the private sector.

The Human Rights Framework

Applicability of International Human Rights Law to Private Actors

Set against the backdrop of an ever-growing role for private policing, it is still widely argued that private security companies (in their capacity as 'non-state actors') do not have any legally binding human rights obligations.[36] Anton Katz, for example, asserts unequivocally that such

[34] V. Dodd, 'Police Warn Big Budget Cuts will Lead to "Paramilitary" Force', *The Guardian*, 17 May 2015, at: www.theguardian.com/uk-news/2015/may/17/police-warn-big-budget-cuts-will-lead-to-paramilitary-force.

[35] Corinna Seiberth affirms, though, that in states 'such as Germany, the use of private contractors for the provision of services [which are] part of the [state] monopoly on the use of force is seen as a weakness and they reject this practice'. C. Seiberth, *Private Military and Security Companies in International Law*, Intersentia, Cambridge, 2014, p. 73.

[36] For some of the background to the debate Andrew Clapham refers to P. Alston (ed.), *Non-State Actors and Human Rights*, Oxford University Press, Oxford, 2005; A. Clapham, *Human Rights Obligations of Non-State Actors*, Oxford University Press, Oxford, 2006; N. Rodley, 'Non-State Actors and Human Rights', in S. Sheeran and N. Rodley (eds.), *Routledge Handbook of International Human Rights Law*, Routledge, Abingdon, 2013, pp. 523–44; A. Clapham (ed.), *Human Rights and Non-State Actors*, Elgar, Cheltenham, 2013. Clapham's own summary of the issues in *The Arms Trade Treaty: A Commentary* is particularly helpful. See A. Clapham, 'Violations by Armed Non-State Actors' in S. Casey-Maslen, A. Clapham, G. Giacca, and S. Parker, *The Arms Trade Treaty: A Commentary*, Oxford University Press, Oxford, 2016, §§7.70ff.

companies 'are not directly bound by international human rights law'.[37] In a book chapter published in 2015, *The Extension of International Human Rights Law to Private Military and Security Companies*, he claims that: 'Unlike international humanitarian law, which encompasses all actors engaged in conflict areas and hostilities, international human rights law becomes binding for states through treaties and the emergence of customary international legal norms.'

This is, however, a conclusory argument. It is also legally incorrect, at least insofar as international humanitarian law (IHL) is concerned.[38] States become bound by IHL in exactly the same manner as they do with respect to human rights law: by adherence to treaties and through the emergence of customary international law (unless and to the extent that any given state can successfully claim persistent objector status).[39] They are then bound insofar as they are party to an armed conflict, not merely from their presence in a conflict area.

Moreover, the means by which non-state actors are bound by IHL – if bound directly they are – is more contested.[40] In 2004, the Appeals Chamber of the Special Court for Sierra Leone (SCSL) held, though without offering strong supporting evidence, that 'it is well settled that all parties to an armed conflict, whether states or non-state actors, are bound by international humanitarian law, even though only states may become parties to international treaties'.[41] A widely advanced argument to justify this conclusion is that Common Article 3 to the 1949 Geneva

[37] A. Katz with M. Maffai, 'The Extension of International Human Rights Law to Private Military and Security Companies', ch. 23 in Abrahamsen and Leander, *Routledge Handbook of Private Security Studies*, p. 228.

[38] As noted in Chapter 8, IHL and the law of armed conflict (LOAC) should be considered synonyms.

[39] M. D. Evans (ed.), *International Law*, 4th Edn, Oxford University Press, Oxford, 2014, p. 103.

[40] See, for more detail on this debate, S. Casey-Maslen, 'Armed Non-State Actors and "Nuclear Terrorism"', in G. Nystuen, S. Casey-Maslen, and A. Golden Bersagel (eds.), *Nuclear Weapons Under International Law*, Cambridge University Press, Cambridge, 2014, pp. 431–32; and A. Bellal *et al.*, 'International Law and Armed Non-State Actors in Afghanistan', *International Review of the Red Cross*, Vol. 93, No. 881 (March 2011), 47–79. Katz further asserts that IHL 'encompasses all actors engaged in conflict areas and hostilities'. These requirements are cumulative. Under IHL, to be a party to the conflict a non-state actor must possess a certain level of organisation within its military arm and its acts must have a sufficient nexus to sustained ('protracted') armed violence against a state that is also party to the conflict.

[41] SCSL, *Prosecutor* v. *Sam Hinga Norman*, Decision on Preliminary Motion Based on Lack of Jurisdiction (Appeals Chamber), 31 May 2004, §22.

Conventions explicitly states that the provision binds 'each Party to the conflict', a formulation widely understood to encompass non-state actors. A major drawback of this approach, though, is that it implies that where a treaty does not use such express language, as is the case with the 1977 Additional Protocol II to the Geneva Conventions, it would logically not bind a non-state actor that is party to the non-international armed conflicts governed by the instrument.

Another argument, known as the doctrine of legislative jurisdiction, asserts that the rules of IHL bind any private individuals, including armed groups, through domestic law, via implementation of these rules into national legislation or direct applicability of self-executing norms. This theory is also problematic, since what is questioned is not whether armed groups are subjects of domestic law (which they clearly are) but whether, and if so, how and to which extent, their acts are directly regulated under international law.[42]

More persuasive is the argument that non-state actors are bound by customary international law. Thus, with respect to Common Article 3 to the Geneva Conventions, the SCSL Appeals Chamber has asserted that 'there is now no doubt that this article is binding on states and insurgents alike, and that insurgents are subject to international humanitarian law'. A 'convincing theory' is that insurgents 'are bound as a matter of customary international law to observe the obligations declared by Common Article 3 which is aimed at the protection of humanity'.[43]

Andrew Clapham, a leading authority on the issue, believes that this theory also explains why international human rights law binds non-state actors, including private security companies.[44] He notes that within the United Nations (UN) 'the most recent statement (and perhaps the clearest)' has been made by a 2014 report on human rights in South Sudan:[45]

[42] Y. Sandoz, C. Swinarski, and B. Zimmermann (eds.), *Commentary on the Additional Protocols of 8 June 1977 to the Geneva Conventions of 12 August 1949*, International Committee of the Red Cross (ICRC)/Martinus Nijhoff, Geneva/Dordrecht, 1987, p. 1345; S. Sivakumaran, 'Binding Armed Opposition Groups', *International and Comparative Law Quarterly*, Vol. 55 (2006), 369–94, at 381.

[43] SCSL, *Prosecutor* v. *Morris Kallon and Brima Buzzy Kamara*, SCSL-2004-15-AR72(E) and SCSL-2004-16-AR72(E), Decision on Challenge to Jurisdiction: Lomé Accord Amnesty, Appeals Chamber, 13 March 2004, §§45–47.

[44] See A. Clapham, 'Focusing on Armed Non-State Actors', in A. Clapham and P. Gaeta (eds.), *The Oxford Handbook of International Law in Armed Conflict*, Oxford University Press, Oxford, 2014, pp. 766–810, esp. 793–99.

[45] In Casey-Maslen *et al.*, *The Arms Trade Treaty: A Commentary*, §7.73.

> The most basic human rights obligations, in particular those emanating from peremptory international law (*ius cogens*), bind both the State and armed opposition groups in times of peace and during armed conflict. In particular, international human rights law requires States, armed groups and others to respect the prohibitions of extrajudicial killing, maiming, torture, cruel, inhuman or degrading treatment or punishment, enforced disappearance, rape, other conflict related sexual violence, sexual and other forms of slavery, the recruitment and use of children in hostilities, arbitrary detention as well as of any violations that amount to war crimes, crimes against humanity, or genocide.[46]

The examples of unlawful use of force enumerated by the UN Mission in the Republic of South Sudan (UNMISS)'s 2014 report capture the most problematic instances of use of force by private security companies, some of which are illustrated in the following section. Ralph Steinhardt has argued that the correct analysis under international law is exemplified by a US court's decision in *Kadic* v. *Karadzic*,[47] in which the US Court of Appeals for the Second Circuit (covering Connecticut, New York, and Vermont) concluded that customary (and indeed also conventional) international law imposes human rights obligations on a variety of persons who are not 'state actors'. Specifically, the Court ruled that:

> the law of nations as understood in the modern era [does not] confine its reach to state action. Instead, certain forms of conduct violate the law of nations whether undertaken by those acting under the auspices of a state or only as private individuals.[48]

Steinhardt recalls that, in the *Karadzic* case the court

> articulated two separate circumstances under which a nominally private actor might bear international responsibility: the first was those instances when the individual commits one of a narrow class of wrongs identified by treaty and custom as not requiring state action to be considered wrongful and the second when the offensive conduct is

[46] UN Mission in the Republic of South Sudan (UNMISS), 'Conflict in South Sudan: A Human Rights Report', 8 May 2014, p. 12, §18, at: https://unmiss.unmissions.org/Portals/unmiss/Human%20Rights%20Reports/UNMISS%20Conflict%20in%20South%20Sudan%20-%20A%20Human%20Rights%20Report.pdf.

[47] *Kadic* v. *Karadzic*, 70 F.3d 232 (Second Circuit, 1995), cert. denied 518 US 1005 (1996), cited with approval in *Sosa* v. *Alvarez-Machain*, 542 US 692 (2004), p. 748.

[48] *Kadic* v. *Karadzic*, at 236.

> sufficiently infused with state action to engage international standards. In both cases, it is the nature of the conduct, not the nature of the actor, that matters.[49]

The Normative Framework

The International Code of Conduct for Private Security Service Providers (ICoC), a voluntary system of rules and accountability established in 2010 in Geneva, has important rules governing use of force. Although they seek to regulate the actions of signatory companies only when they are operating in 'complex environments' (see below), the rules set out in this soft-law instrument are of wider relevance. A provision on 'general conduct' obliges ICoC signatories to treat all persons 'humanely and with respect for their dignity and privacy'.[50] There is also a requirement that signatory companies adopt rules on the use of force that are 'consistent with applicable law and the minimum requirements contained in the section on Use of Force' in the ICoC.[51] These can be seen as minimum requirements for any corporate entity engaged in private security service provision.

Three paragraphs in the ICoC establish important principles with respect to the use of force. Paragraph 30 provides as follows:

> Signatory Companies will require their Personnel to take all reasonable steps to avoid the use of force. If force is used, it shall be in a manner consistent with applicable law. In no case shall the use of force exceed what is strictly necessary, and should be proportionate to the threat and appropriate to the situation.

In a commentary on this provision, the Geneva Academy of International Humanitarian Law and Human Rights asserts that in most national legal regimes, private security personnel may typically

> only use force in self-defence or to defend others. The force they use must also be "reasonable". The meaning given to "reasonable" varies from state to state, however, and in practice there is no precise agreement about how much force is appropriate or in which situations it is justified. Personnel using force beyond what is deemed lawful may be liable to criminal prosecution under national law.[52]

[49] R. Steinhardt, 'Weapons and the Human Rights Responsibilities of Multinational Corporations', ch. 17 in S. Casey-Maslen (ed.), *Weapons Under International Human Rights Law*, Cambridge University Press, 2014, p. 514.

[50] ICoC, §28. [51] ICoC, §29.

[52] 'The International Code of Conduct for Private Security Service Providers', Geneva Academy Briefing No. 4, Geneva Academy of International Humanitarian Law and

Paragraph 31 of the ICoC then states that:

> Signatory Companies will require that their Personnel not use firearms against persons except in self-defence or defence of others against the imminent threat of death or serious injury, or to prevent the perpetration of a particularly serious crime involving grave threat to life.

This means that, consonant with international law, as set out in Principle 9 of the 1990 Basic Principles on the Use of Force and Firearms by Law Enforcement Officials (1990 Basic Principles), private security force personnel will not be justified in using firearms to protect property from damage, even serious damage, unless the firearms are used to defend individuals against an imminent threat of death or serious injury or the danger also involves a grave threat to life.[53]

The third paragraph on use of force is potentially more limited in scope. It provides that signatory companies must ensure their use of force or weapons comply with all national and international obligations applicable to regular law enforcement officials of that state and, as a minimum, with the standards expressed in the 1990 Basic Principles, but limits the obligation to situations where personnel 'are formally authorized to assist in the exercise of a state's law enforcement authority'. As the Geneva Academy commentary observes, however, the Code applies in environments 'in which the capacity of the state authority to handle the situation is diminished, limited or non-existent'. Accordingly, it is not clear how such formal authorisation may be given where, for example, a host state's capacity is deemed to be non-existent. 'In such situations it is of course possible that the company is authorized by another state (or group of states) to exercise enforcement authority.'[54]

Of course, that private security companies may be bound directly by international human rights law does not in any way absolve the state or states concerned from their own human rights obligations in regard to the acts of private companies: the protection afforded is supplementary not substitutional. Thus, the state has a duty not only to respect anyone falling under its jurisdiction but also to protect them from the acts of third parties.

Human Rights, Geneva, August 2013, p. 36, at: www.geneva-academy.ch/docs/publications/briefing4_web_final.pdf.

[53] See ibid. [54] Ibid.

Selected National Legal Frameworks

The United Kingdom

In the United Kingdom, the 2001 Private Security Industry Act is the most significant piece of legislation governing private security providers.[55] The 2001 Act established the Security Industry Authority (SIA), which was launched in 2003, to license and regulate all 'contract' private security providers. The SIA, which is an independent body reporting to the Secretary of State for the Home Department, has two main duties. One is the compulsory licensing of individuals undertaking designated activities within the private security industry, while the other is to manage the voluntary Approved Contractor Scheme, which measures private security suppliers against independently assessed criteria.[56]

SIA licensing covers among others manned guarding and vehicle immobilising. Licensing ensures that private security operatives are 'fit and proper' persons who are properly trained and qualified to do their job. The Approved Contractor Scheme introduced a set of operational and performance standards for suppliers of private security services, with organisations that meet the standards awarded Approved Contractor status.[57] The SIA's enforcement powers are described below in the section on accountability.

The United Kingdom is host to the world's single largest private security service provider, G4S (an abbreviation for Group 4 Securicor).[58] The company's history dates back to 1901, when Marius Hogrefe started a company in Denmark that offered to guard premises. In 1906, Sophus Falck established Redningskorpset, an independent fire and rescue service; Falck became a nationwide operator in 1930. Night Watch Services

[55] See A. Crawford, 'Sowing the Seeds of Privatisation', *Police*, May 2013, at: www.policemag.co.uk/editions/sowing_seeds_for_privatisation.aspx. The Act was introduced to shift the industry into the mainstream of policing services by encouraging a higher degree of professionalism and to regulate unscrupulous operators.

[56] SIA, 'About Us', Undated but accessed on 5 December 2015 at: www.sia.homeoffice.gov.uk/Pages/about-us.aspx.

[57] Ibid.

[58] In contrast, Canadian firm GardaWorld claims to be the largest *privately-owned* security company in the world. The company's headquarters are in Montreal, and it employs some 45,000 people across North America, Europe, Africa, Asia, Latin America, and the Middle East. GardaWorld is said to protect 28 North American airports. '30 Most Powerful Private Security Companies in the World', *Security Degree Hub*, 11 January 2014, at: www.securitydegreehub.com/30-most-powerful-private-security-companies-in-the-world/.

started up with four guards on bicycles in 1935 and in 1951 it became Securicor. In 2004, the British company Securicor merged with Group 4 Falck's security businesses to form Group 4 Securicor and began trading on the London and Copenhagen Stock Exchange; roll-out of G4S as its new corporate identity began worldwide in 2006.

In 2011, G4S was appointed official security services provider for the London 2012 Olympic Games, a contract that it was notoriously unable to fulfil.[59] Today, G4S claims to have more than 623,000 employees worldwide.[60] The company states that its values are: safety first; customer focus; integrity; the best people; performance; teamwork and collaboration; and expertise.[61] Their law enforcement services include the following:

> **Juvenile and adult custody.** Management of all aspects of a facility and those held within the facility – similar centres are also used for the detention of asylum applicants.
>
> **Prisoner escorting.** Transportation of prisoners and asylum applicants between courts, police stations and custody and asylum centres.
>
> **Asylum services.** Management of housing provision and other services for asylum seekers.
>
> **Electronic monitoring.** Electronic tagging and monitoring of offenders at home or in the community.
>
> **Police services.** Back-office support functions for police forces, support for front-line policing, including provision of custody-suite services and forensic medical services.[62]

The United States

In the United States, Kevin Lanigan recalls that the government's hiring of armed private operatives from the Pinkerton Detective Agency and

59 G4S had a £284m contract to provide 10,400 staff for Olympic events but could not supply enough personnel, leaving some 4,700 members of the armed forces to stand in. The company, which described its failures as a 'humiliating shambles', was forced to apologise publicly. BBC, 'G4S Olympic Failure Prompts Ministers to "Think Again" over Outsourcing', 14 August 2012, at: www.bbc.co.uk/news/uk-19251772. Perhaps the saving grace is that the company did not attempt to meet the contract in name only by employing large numbers of staff who did not possess the requisite skills and training.

60 G4S, 'Our History', undated but accessed on 6 December 2015 at: www.g4s.com/en/Who%20we%20are/History/.

61 G4S, 'Our Values at Work, Corporate Social Responsibility Report 2014', p. 2, at: www.g4s.com/~/media/Files/CSR%20Reports/G4S%20CSR%20Report%202014.pdf.

62 G4S, 'Care and Justice Services', undated but accessed on 6 December 2015 at: www.g4s.com/en/What%20we%20do/Services/Care%20and%20Justice%20Services/.

other companies to break strikes led to Congress enacting the Anti-Pinkerton Act in 1893. This law prohibited the government from employing Pinkerton or similar private companies from performing such policing or other public security functions. Notwithstanding the fact this Act remains in force,[63] and even though private security companies do not have statutory 'police powers', as Lanigan notes for a long time companies have been deemed 'vital to the maintenance of public order and crime prevention – particularly in private spaces, but increasingly in public spaces as well'.[64]

There is, though, no comprehensive federal legal regime that regulates private security service providers and their activities, and their regulation as corporations tends to occur mainly under state and/or local law rather than federal law. Indeed, such companies may face both criminal and civil liability for violations of state criminal and tort law.[65] However, the 1789 Alien Tort Claims Act gives federal courts jurisdiction over any civil action by an alien for a tort (civil wrong), committed in violation of the 'law of nations' (i.e. international law) or a treaty to which the United States is party.[66] In 2009 in *Presbyterian Church* v. *Talisman*, the Court of Appeals for the Second Circuit assumed, 'without deciding, that corporations … may be held liable for the violations of customary international law'.[67]

In contrast, in September 2010 the Second Circuit's Court of Appeal ruled that corporations cannot be properly sued under the ATS for violations of customary international law: '[T]he principle of individual liability for violations of international law has been limited to natural persons – not "juridical" persons such as corporations.' The *Kiobel* case went up to the Supreme Court, which dodged the question in its judgment, justifying its decision to exclude liability on other grounds.[68]

[63] According to Title 5 of the US Code, Section 3108 ('Employment of detective agencies; restrictions'): 'An individual employed by the Pinkerton Detective Agency, or similar organization, may not be employed by the Government of the United States or the government of the District of Columbia.' Available at: http://uscode.house.gov/view.xhtml?req=granuleid:USC-prelim-title5-section3108&num=0&edition=prelim.

[64] K. Lanigan, 'Legal Regulation of PMSCs in the United States: The Gap between Law and Practice', p. 1, at: www.privatesecurityregulation.net/files/Microsoft%20Word%20-%20PMSC%20Article,%20US,%20Kevin%20Lanigan,%20Final.pdf.

[65] Ibid., p. 2. [66] Title 28 of the US Code, Section 1350.

[67] US Court of Appeals (Second Circuit), *The Presbyterian Church of Sudan and Others* v. *Talisman Energy, Inc.*, 582 F.3d 244 (2009), Judgment, Conclusion 12.

[68] US Court of Appeals (Second Circuit), *Kiobel* v. *Royal Dutch Petroleum*, Judgment, 17 September 2010, p. 7, available at: http://online.wsj.com/public/resources/documents/091710atsruling.pdf (accessed 9 April 2017).

Meanwhile, decisions in 2011, by the DC Circuit Court of Appeals in *Doe* v. *Exxon*[69] and by the Seventh Circuit Court of Appeals in *Flomo* v. *Firestone*,[70] explicitly rejected the Second Circuit's reasoning in *Kiobel*.

At an individual level, under US common law every citizen, including personnel of private security companies, has the right to make an arrest in certain circumstances. If an individual has committed a felony[71] in the presence of a private security company employee, no warrant is needed; this is also the case if the arrestor has reasonable cause to believe that a felony has been committed, even if he or she did not witness it. The scope of a citizen's arrest power is thus similar to that of a law enforcement officer in relation to a felony. There is, however, a caveat:

> The arrest power is valid only where the purpose of such arrest is to turn the subject over to proper authorities as soon as practicable. The arrest power does not allow for other purposes (such as to obtain a confession) and liability is imposed if there is unreasonable delay in turning the suspect over to the authorities.[72]

Moreover, many states do not authorise citizens' arrests for misdemeanours. Among those that do have such provisions, some limit misdemeanour arrests to 'public offences', such as disturbing the public peace or violating the public order. In most states, however, a private person may effect an arrest without a warrant of an individual who commits a misdemeanour in his or her presence. The amount of force that can lawfully be used in making an arrest depends on the type of offence and the status of the arresting person. The general rule is that force cannot exceed the extent of resistance offered.[73]

[69] Available at: http://hrp.law.harvard.edu/wp-content/uploads/2011/09/doe-v-exxonmobil-dc-cir-opinion-7-8-2011.pdf.

[70] Available at: http://hrp.law.harvard.edu/wp-content/uploads/2011/09/firestone-appeal-decision-7-11-2011.pdf.

[71] Under US federal law, a felony is a criminal offence that incurs a possible penalty of more than one year; offences for which the punishment is up to one year are termed misdemeanours. See: 18 US Code §3559 – Sentencing classification of offenses, available at: www.law.cornell.edu/uscode/text/18/3559.

[72] M. J. Palmiotto, *Policing: Concepts, Strategies, and Current Issues in American Police Forces*, 3rd Edn, 2013, p. 75, citing J. S. Kakalik and S. Wildhorn, *The Law and Private Police*, Vol. 6, Rand Corporation, Santa Monica, CA, 1971, p. 107.

[73] See 'Police: Private Police and Industrial Security – Legal Authority – Officer, Citizen, Law, and Arrest', *JRank*, at: http://law.jrank.org/pages/1687/Police-Private-Police-Industrial-Security-Legal-authority.html#ixzz3tSxZfsIx.

South Africa

South Africa is said by some to have the largest private security industry in the world, with nearly 9,000 registered companies as of 2012.[74] The Private Security Industry Regulatory Act (No. 56 of 2001)[75] established the Private Security Industry Regulatory Authority (PSIRA) 'to exercise effective control over the practice of the occupation of security service provider in the public and national interest and in the interest of the private security industry itself'.[76] On 30 October 2012, however, Minister of Police Nathi Mthethwa presented a Private Security Industry Regulation Amendment Bill to South Africa's Parliament, arguing that the industry's regulation needed to be revised. The Minister stated that:

> The South African private security industry is increasingly performing functions which used to be the sole preserve of the police. This has, and will continue to have, a serious influence on the functioning of the criminal justice system as a whole. While it is true that private security does and can fill certain vacuums, private security can never replace the public police.[77]

Parliament subsequently adopted the Bill, but as at December 2016 the resultant Act remained before South African President Jacob Zuma for his signature.[78] President Zuma was said to have claimed that the growth of private security companies in the country had led to the creation of a private force. In response, an industry representative argued for the removal of a clause in the Act requiring multinational private security companies such as ADT, Chubb, G4S, and Securitas to relinquish 51 per cent or more of their local shareholding.[79]

[74] Writing in September 2015, however, an industry representative argued that South Africa was in seventh place (although it was not explained how this ranking was arrived at, in particular whether it was in terms of market share at US$ value or in terms of number of personnel). Conradie, 'Private Security Law Will Harm Our Land'.

[75] Private Security Industry Regulatory Act 56 of 2001.

[76] PSIRA, 'Regulatory Mandate', 2013, at: http://www.psira.co.za/psira/index.php/about-us/mandate.

[77] Ministry of Police, 'South Africa has world's largest private security industry; needs regulation – Mthethwa', 30 October 2012, published on *DefenceWeb* at: http://www.defenceweb.co.za/index.php?option=com_content&task=view&id=28306&Itemid=116.

[78] 'Editorial: Paper Jam on Zuma's desk', *Business Day*, 12 December 2016, at: www.businesslive.co.za/bd/opinion/editorials/2016-12-12-editorial-paper-jam-on-zumas-desk/.

[79] Conradie, 'Private security law will harm our land'.

In September 2015, it was reported in the media that South Africa's Department of Correctional Services (DCS) had stated that G4S's record-keeping of deaths in custody was not up to standard and that it might be covering up deaths through torture.[80] The latest revelations came two years after evidence was uncovered that G4S might be giving forced injections and electric shock treatment to subdue unruly inmates. As a result of the alleged abuses, forty-three prisoners lodged legal claims against G4S through the UK law firm Leigh Day.

Around the same time, the government decided to take over the running of Bloemfontein's Mangaung prison from G4S, saying it had 'lost effective control' in the wake of a series of stabbings, riots, strikes, and a hostage taking.[81] An EST (Emergency Security Team), also known colloquially as the 'Ninjas', reportedly took inmates to the 'dark room', a windowless cell with thick walls ensuring that sound does not travel. This is where an EST member, interviewed by BBC television on 28 October 2013, admitted to taking inmates to torture them.

> Yeah we stripped them naked and we throw with water so the electricity can work nicely. I will shock him until he tells the truth that I want even if it's a lie.[82]

Later in November 2015, it was claimed that G4S had denied lawyers access to a prisoner who claimed to have been shot in the head with a rubber bullet by a warder.[83]

Thailand

In Thailand, already in April 2005 it was being reported that demand for private security services was likely to grow substantially in the wake of mounting unrest in the three southernmost provinces and bombings in Hat Yai, a city in southern Thailand near the Malaysian border. The private security services industry was expected to increase by at least 30 per cent over the course of 2005 compared with average growth of 15 per cent over the previous five years, according to the Kasikorn

[80] R. Hopkins, 'G4S accused of "torturing inmates to death" in South Africa', *Daily Telegraph*, 6 September 2015, at: www.telegraph.co.uk/news/worldnews/africaandindianocean/southafrica/10409477/G4S-tortured-inmates-at-South-African-prison-as-they-were-understaffed.html.

[81] Ibid. [82] Cited in ibid.

[83] R. Hopkins, 'Tortured Mangaung Prisoners Seek Justice', *Mail & Guardian* (South Africa), 27 November 2015, at: http://mg.co.za/article/2015-11-26-tortured-mangaung-prisoners-seek-justice.

Research Center. According to Kasikorn, increased demand for security services was expected to come particularly from commercial banks, financial institutions, hotels, embassies, and factories.[84]

A decade later, Thailand's National News Bureau reported that the Royal Thai Police was setting up a Security Service Check Centre to conduct background and profile checks on private security staff. The intention was to regulate the private security industry effectively, to reduce criminality within the industry, and to raise standards of service. Thailand's Deputy National Police Chief, Pol Gen Somyot Pumpunmuang, revealed that the centre was needed in light of private security guards being at the top of the list of crimes involving security personnel. The rape and murder of a young girl earlier in 2014 was said to be the impetus for immediate action.[85] In May 2016, the parliament adopted the Security Business Act, however, marking a 'reverse in the privatisation trend by granting the Royal Thai Police authority over security companies and security guards. This authority extends to licensing of security guards and companies, overseeing mandatory training, collection of licensing fees, and monitoring of daily security company records'.[86] As a local security expert notes, despite the new Act:

> The police authority to deputise private security personnel to assist in public law enforcement activities such as arrests, quelling disturbances, crime reporting, and preservation of crime scenes means that security guards are now entrusted with much greater responsibility, requiring higher standards of admittance and training.[87]

Mexico

In Mexico, private security firms have seen business surge during the last decade, 'overrunning regulations and legal means of control', and leaving at least 250,000 and possibly as many as 600,000 private security guards

[84] C. Kittikanya, 'Thailand: Private Security Booms with Insecurity', *Bangkok Post*, 18 April 2005, available at: www.corpwatch.org/article.php?id=12128.

[85] National News Bureau of Thailand, 'Police Set up Security Industry Check Center', Bangkok, 10 September 1014, available at: www.thaivisa.com/forum/topic/759224-thai-police-set-up-security-industry-check-center/.

[86] D. Lawrence, 'The Security Business Act 2016: Are You Good Men and True?', Tilleke & Gibbons, Bangkok, 13 May 2016, at: www.tilleke.com/sites/default/files/2016_May_Thailand_Security_Business_Act.pdf.

[87] Ibid.

(the overwhelming majority unregistered) 'with little accountability for their actions'.[88]

One former private security professional told *Al Jazeera* that the boom was an unintended 'by-product of the government offensive that caused the large drug cartels that specialised in transnational drug-trafficking to fragment into smaller gangs dedicated to more predatory crimes such as kidnapping, robbery and extortion ... With Mexico's middle and upper classes increasingly affected, the demand for private security skyrocketed'.[89]

In 2015, several people were reported to have been killed in incidents involving bodyguards in Mexico City. In most of these cases, bodyguards, known as *Guaruras*, shot and killed alleged robbers, 'though doubts over whether the show of force was excessive often remain'.[90] One Mexican political analyst, Alfonso Zárate, wrote that 'Politicians, businessmen and celebrities alike surround themselves with these arrogant types not just out of fear of being abducted, but also because they can exert power.' He claimed that the numbers of private security personnel 'are worrisome from any point of view. Especially when we see that we are facing a kind of irregular army — dispersed, fragmented, informal — exceeding the approximately 544,000 making up the national police force'.[91] Antoine Perret, a research fellow at Columbia Law School, argued in a 2013 paper that there is little oversight of their conduct because Mexico's laws are not designed to confront possible human rights violations by non-state actors such as private security firms.[92]

National legislation on private security companies precludes the companies from hiring anyone serving in any public institution or the armed forces, or anyone who has been dismissed by any such institution for disciplinary infractions or corruption, or who has been sentenced for a

[88] 'Security Firms are Big Business in Mexico. But Many are Unregulated and Those That Are Don't See Enforcement', *Mexico News Daily*, 23 February 2016, at: http://mexiconewsdaily.com/news/security-firms-are-big-business-in-mexico/.

[89] D. Tucker, 'Mexico Drug War Fuels Private Security Boom', *Aljazeera*, 7 September 2016, at: www.aljazeera.com/indepth/features/2016/08/mexico-drug-war-fuels-private-security-boom-160818091244131.html.

[90] J.-A. Hootsen, 'The Bodyguards of Mexico's Elite Are Getting Out of Control', *Vice News*, 9 March 2016, at: https://news.vice.com/article/the-bodyguards-of-mexicos-elite-are-getting-out-of-control.

[91] Cited in ibid.

[92] A. Perret, 'Privatization of the War on Drugs in Mexico and Colombia. Limiting the Application of Humanitarian Law and Endangering Human Rights', 2013, at: www.americanstudents.us/content/wp-content/uploads/2013/10/Perret_Proof_8_7_13.pdf.

premeditated crime.[93] But the law is said to be poorly enforced. In March 2016, one of Mexico's most powerful drug cartels even sought to attract new recruits by handing out flyers promising jobs with rapid career advancement, benefits, and a Christmas bonus in a fake private security firm fronted by a US citizen. The Jalisco New Generation Cartel set up a security firm called Segmex which it used for recruitment in Puerto Vallarta, a popular Pacific coast resort, and in Tlaquepaque, a working-class district within the state capital, Guadalajara. The flyer said that applicants should be able to handle firearms, have basic knowledge of self-defence, and show 'initiative and a desire to better themselves'. It said new recruits would receive an initial weekly salary of 3,000 pesos (approximately $170), plus benefits, though former soldiers or police officers would be offered a higher wage.[94]

The Mexican Association of Private Security Firms, along with other organisations, has been lobbying for four years for the creation of a federal law to replace the existing federal regulation and the thirty-two state laws. According to a study by the Chamber of Deputies, there are more than 100 discrepancies between the different private security regulatory laws.[95] In August 2016, change seemed to be on its way. On 29 August, Mexico City's mayor, Miguel Angel Mancera, announced new regulations to standardise the training, certification, registration, and insignia of every private bodyguard in the capital. The next day, National Security Commissioner Renato Sales proposed legislation to create new regulatory bodies and a database of all private security personnel in Mexico. In a subsequent press release, he said this would make the industry 'more effective and responsible'.[96]

Examples of Unlawful Use of Force by Private Security Actors

'Less-Lethal' Weapons and Restraint Techniques

The United States

Custodial facilities and situations managed by private security companies give rise to obvious human rights concerns (as they do, of course, also with state-run facilities). Lanigan estimated that, by 2007, private companies

[93] Art. 28(VI), Federal Law on Private Security, Mexico, 6 July 2006.

[94] D. Tucker, 'A Mexican Drug Cartel Posed as a Private Security Firm to Lure Recruits', *Vice Daily*, 11 March 2016, at: https://news.vice.com/article/a-mexican-drug-cartel-posed-as-a-private-security-firm-to-lure-recruits.

[95] 'Security Firms are Big Business in Mexico. But Many are Unregulated and Those That Are Don't See Enforcement', *Mexico News Daily*, 23 February 2016.

[96] Tucker, 'Mexico Drug War Fuels Private Security Boom', *Aljazeera*, 7 September 2016.

were operating more than 225 adult and juvenile correctional and (increasingly) immigration detention facilities across the United States, incarcerating more than 120,000 individuals, equating to 7 per cent of the total US prison population at that time.[97] According to *In the Public Interest*, a resource centre on privatisation and responsible contracting,

> Incarceration for profit has caused many problems, as private companies fail to make decisions in the best interest of the inmates or the communities in which the prisons are located. Private prison companies have employed unqualified guards, resorted to excessive violence and cruelty to control inmates, and provided substandard medical care, resulting in unnecessary deaths. Prison privatization has led to numerous lawsuits and litigation, fines, and increased need for federal oversight, at great cost to taxpayers, communities, inmates and their families.[98]

As an example of how seriously things can go wrong, in 2010 a class action was filed against a number of defendants, including Geo Group, the second largest private correctional company in the United States. The action concerned in particular Geo Group's responsibility for day-to-day operations at the Walnut Grove Correctional Facility (WGYCF) juvenile prison in Mississippi. The complaint alleged that a number of the youth were kicked and punched while handcuffed, and beaten all over, while others were stripped naked and placed in solitary confinement for weeks. Some WGYCF staff sprayed 'dangerous chemical restraints' for 'the sole purpose of inflicting excruciating pain'.[99]

An 18-month investigation by the US Department of Justice (DOJ) concluded that the state of Mississippi was 'deliberately indifferent to the constitutional rights of young men confined at WGYCF'. It uncovered evidence of 'systematic, egregious, and dangerous practices exacerbated by a lack of accountability and controls', with detailed findings including the following:

- WGYCF is deliberately indifferent to staff sexual misconduct and inappropriate behaviour with youth. Further, staff fails to report allegations of staff sexual abuse to supervisors and state officials, as required by law.

[97] Lanigan, 'Legal Regulation of PMSCs in the United States: The Gap between Law and Practice', p. 1.

[98] Reported in B. Fischer, 'Violence, Abuse, and Death at For-Profit Prisons: A GEO Group Rap Sheet', PR Watch, 26 September 2013, at: www.prwatch.org/news/2013/09/12255/violence-abuse-and-death-profit-prisons-geo-group-rap-sheet.

[99] US District Court for the Southern District, *C. B. and Others* v. *Walnut Grove Correctional Facility, Geo Group, and Others* Class Action, Filed 10 November 2010, pp. 2–3, available at: www.splcenter.org/sites/default/files/d6_legacy_files/downloads/case/cb_v_walnut_grove_complaint.pdf.

- WGYCF is engaged in a pattern or practice of using excessive force against youth. Staff often use excessive force as a first response, not as a last resort, including the use of pepper spray in excessive amounts. Further, staff fail to adequately report and investigate uses of force.[100]

With respect to use of chemical agents, the DOJ found that the facility used excessive amounts of chemical spray. In use-of-force reports, staff describe using only one to two short bursts of OC (pepper) spray during incidents. In one video, an officer used so much chemical spray on a youth that the surrounding staff, some as far as 20 feet away, are seen to be coughing and having difficulty breathing and seeing. Some of the youth interviewed described instances where entire spray cans were emptied into a cell, after which staff secured the door with the young detainee inside.[101]

According to the DOJ, WGYCF officers most commonly use a chemical agent known as the 'Fox Fogger'. The Fox units

> discharge as much of their formula as possible per one-shot burst, regardless of the size of the can. Inhalation of high doses of some of the chemicals found in OC spray can produce adverse cardiac, respiratory, and neurologic effects, including arrhythmias and sudden death. Exposure to OC spray may occur through skin or eye contact, or inhalation. With acute exposure, there is a rapid onset of symptoms including nausea, fear and disorientation. Respiratory responses to OC spray include burning of the throat, wheezing, dry cough, shortness of breath, gagging, gasping, and inability to breathe or speak.[102] When WGYCF officers deploy chemical agents in unnecessary and excessive quantities, this is a violation of the Eighth Amendment [to the US Constitution].[103]

In a subsequent settlement of the class action, it was agreed that juveniles incarcerated in Mississippi would no longer be housed in the privately run prison but housed at a stand-alone facility governed by juvenile justice rather than adult standards.[104]

[100] Letter from the US Department of Justice Civil Rights Division, Washington DC, to the Honourable Phil Bryant, Governor of the state of Mississippi, 20 March 2012, available at: www.splcenter.org/sites/default/files/d6_legacy_files/downloads/case/walnutgroveDOJ.pdf.

[101] DOJ, *Investigation of the Walnut Grove Youth Correctional Facility Walnut Grove, Mississippi*, 20 March 2012, p. 10.

[102] C. G. Smith and W. Stopford, 'Health Hazards of Pepper Spray', *North Carolina Medical Journal*, Vol. 60 (1999), 268, 274.

[103] DOJ, *Investigation of the Walnut Grove Youth Correctional Facility Walnut Grove, Mississippi*, pp. 10–11. The Eighth Amendment to the US Constitution prohibits cruel and unusual punishment.

[104] US District Court for the Southern District, *C. B. and Others* v. *Walnut Grove Correctional Facility, Geo Group, and Others*, Consent Decree, 26 March 2012, available at: www.splcenter.org/sites/default/files/d6_legacy_files/downloads/case/WalnutGrove_consentdecree.pdf.

The United Kingdom

In 2015, in the United Kingdom, undercover filming at a juvenile detention centre managed by G4S showed private security personnel improperly using force on several of the young inmates.[105] The footage showed how the guards tried to conceal their behaviour by ensuring that incidents took place in areas where surveillance equipment in the detention centre could not film them. This raises serious concerns about potential undocumented and under-reported violations of the same nature. Following the affair, Chief Inspector of Prisons Nick Hardwick said all prison officers dealing with children should wear cameras in order to monitor behaviour. In February 2016, it was reported that G4S had started a process to sell its UK children's services business, including the contracts to run two youth jails.[106] In fact, in December 2016 it was reported that G4S Children's Services had been renamed Homes2Inspire and was planning to open a new home in Mansfield for children and young people with social emotional and behavioural difficulties.[107]

The death in 2010 of Jimmy Mubenga, a failed asylum seeker, while being restrained on board an aircraft by three guards employed by G4S, continues to raise major concerns, not least about accountability for human rights violations. The Home Office and G4S initially said that Mr Mubenga, a 46-year-old being returned to Angola, had been taken ill on the flight on 12 October 2010. However, following an investigation by *The Guardian* newspaper, which tracked down witnesses who said the detainee had been complaining of difficulty breathing while being restrained by the guards, and shouting 'they are going to kill me', the guards were arrested and questioned on suspicion of manslaughter.[108]

[105] BBC, 'G4S Medway Young Offenders Centre Staff Suspended over Abusive claims", 8 January 2016, at: www.bbc.com/news/uk-england-kent-35260927.

[106] R. Bury, 'G4S to Sell Controversial Children's Services Business', *Daily Telegraph*, 26 February 2016, at: www.telegraph.co.uk/business/2016/02/26/g4s-to-sell-controversial-childrens-services-business/.

[107] N. Charity, 'G4S plans new children's home in Mansfield', *Chad*, 20 December 2016, at: www.chad.co.uk/news/breaking-g4s-plans-new-children-s-home-in-mansfield-1-8298602.

[108] P. Lewis and M. Taylor, 'Failure to Bring Charges in Jimmy Mubenga Case "Perverse", Says Peer', *The Guardian*, 20 July 2012, at: www.theguardian.com/uk/2012/jul/20/jimmy-mubenga-case-charges-perverse.

Initially, the Crown Prosecution Service (CPS) decided not to bring charges against the three G4S guards, in part, because it could not rule out that the death was caused by 'a combination of factors such as adrenaline, muscle exhaustion or isometric exercise'. Following the decision, a crossbench peer in the UK House of Lords, Lord Ramsbotham, said: 'I have to say that in the face of all the evidence that we have gathered during our inquiry, quite apart from all the other evidence that was available, I find that CPS decision, at kindest, perverse. Passengers reported hearing Mr Mubenga cry out that he could not breathe and that the guards were killing him. There had been Home Office warnings to G4S in 2006 about the dangers of using [restraint techniques that might lead to] positional asphyxia.'[109]

The peer said there were parallels to be drawn with another case in which G4S staff restrained a person in their custody who died. 'There had been stringent criticisms by the coroner in the case of Gareth Myatt, a 15-year-old who died in Rainsbrook secure training centre in Northamptonshire following the use of similar procedures for restraint by G4S guards', he said.[110] 'He, too, had called out that he could not breathe before he died.'[111]

[109] Ibid. Lord Ramsbotham was at the time chairing an independent inquiry into the use of restraint techniques.

[110] Gareth Myatt died after three officers placed him in a hold called the Seated Double Embrace. Two staff members held his upper body and pushed his torso forward towards his knees while one officer held his head. He complained he could not breathe but was told that 'if you can talk then you can breathe'. He then said he was going to defecate and was told: 'you are going to have to shit yourself', which he did, and the restraint continued. He then vomited and slumped forward. When the restraint stopped it was too late. Attempts to resuscitate him failed. The cause of death was recorded as asphyxia resulting from inhalation of gastric content and his body position during the period of physical restraint. The inquest, held in 2007, heard that one year before Gareth died, one of the guards, David Beadnall, had been investigated for using pain-inducing 'distraction techniques' too often. Mr Beadnall told the inquest he had no recollection of that. G4S training documents listed guards' nicknames, which included 'Clubber', 'Crusher', and 'Mauler'. The CPS said in January 2006 that it had found insufficient evidence to bring prosecutions over Gareth's death. The Coroner recorded a verdict of accidental death in June 2007. In 2013, Mr Beadnall was promoted to Safety, Health and Environmental Manager at G4S Children's Services. G4S spokesperson Nicola Savage stated that: 'His current role does not involve any direct contact with young people.' C. Sambrook, 'G4S Guard Fatally Restrains 15 Year Old – Gets Promoted', *Open Democracy*, 22 July 2013, at: www.opendemocracy.net/ourkingdom/clare-sambrook/g4s-guard-fatally-restrains-15-year-old-gets-promoted. See also BBC, 'Criticism over Youth Jail Death', 28 June 2007, at: http://news.bbc.co.uk/1/hi/england/6250406.stm.

[111] Lewis and Taylor, 'Failure to Bring Charges in Jimmy Mubenga Case "Perverse", Says Peer'.

An inquest was subsequently held into Mr Mubenga's death, which concluded in July 2013 with the jury ruling that he had been unlawfully killed. G4S issued a statement following the jury's decision:

> The death of anyone in our care is deeply felt by all of us and the death of Mr Mubenga was a very tragic event.
>
> The welfare of those in our care is always our top priority and we take great care to ensure that our employees on this contract, which has been carried out by another provider since November 2011, were made aware of their responsibilities in this respect. Our employees were also trained, screened and vetted to the standards defined by strict Home Office guidelines.
>
> We believe that at all times we acted appropriately and in full compliance with the terms of our contract with UKBA [UK Border Agency] and it should be noted that the Crown Prosecution Service found no basis on which to bring criminal charges against G4S in this case.[112]

David Wood, the then head of the Home Office's immigration enforcement, offered a qualified apology to the Mr Mubenga's family. He refused to accept, though, that the death was the responsibility of either the now-disbanded UK Border Agency or G4S. 'I am willing to apologise to the extent that it was our responsibility', said Wood. 'There are occasions when people who work directly or indirectly do not do what they are told or comply with their training. That was an awful and regrettable incident.

[112] G4S, 'Jimmy Mubenga Inquest – G4S Statement', 9 July 2013, at: www.g4s.uk.com/en-GB/Media%20Centre/Viewpoint/Press%20articles%20and%20statements/Jimmy%20Mubenga%20Inquest%20-%20G4S%20statement/.aspx. In an opinion piece on *The Guardian* website in December 2014, two journalists wrote that: 'It is tempting to believe that the Mubenga case is a one-off. The reality is very different. While G4S employs many guards who do a professional job and abide by the terms of their contracts, it has a disturbing record of employing people with a history of racism, violence and/or criminality. It has an equally disturbing history of employing individuals who kill while in their employ, or restrain people in a manner that results in death.' S. Hattenstone and E. Allison, 'G4S, the Company with No Convictions – but Does it Have Blood on its Hands?', *The Guardian*, 22 December 2014, at: www.theguardian.com/commentisfree/2014/dec/22/g4s-convictions-deaths-employees-racial-overtones. This included security guard Clive Carter who was jailed for life in October 2012 after killing a female conference delegate at a conference in Glasgow in 2011. He followed her into the ladies toilet and bludgeoned her to death with a fire extinguisher because she complained about him using her security pass. Every bone on the left side of her face and neck was broken and her skull was shattered. Carter had a record of getting in a rage with women who contradicted him. BBC, 'Clive Carter Jailed for Life for Khanokporn Satjawat SECC Murder', 29 October 2013, at: www.bbc.co.uk/news/uk-scotland-glasgow-west-24727644.

I am not saying that we had no responsibility for that tragic incident. We have to learn lessons from it and make sure that it never happens again.' Wood stressed that 'getting it right was important', as the Home Office immigration enforcement directorate carried out 5,500 escorted removals every year. He added that the operation had been undertaken by independent contractors for more than 20 years and had 'generally been an enormously successful operation'.[113]

The CPS reconsidered its original decision not to bring criminal charges in the light of the inquest jury's verdict. In mid-December 2014, after a six-week trial, a jury at the Old Bailey acquitted the three guards of the charge of manslaughter. The jury was not told of the inquest's verdict of unlawful killing nor of the fact that two of the guards had a string of racist 'jokes' on their phones.[114] A G4S spokesman said:

> Providing a safe and caring environment for those in our custody or care is a priority for G4S. The death of Mr Mubenga was a tragic incident and our thoughts and condolences remain with his family and friends. We note the criminal case which has been under way at the Old Bailey in relation to Mr Mubenga's death and three former employees. We respect the legal process and the findings of the court.[115]

In the aftermath of the trial, Amnesty International raised the following five questions:

- Are security guards still using restraint methods that impair breathing?
- Has the UK government introduced scenario-based training suitable for aircraft for security guards?
- Have they delivered on their promise made in 2011 to require private security companies to introduce new safer restraint methods?
- Are guards now required to undergo mandatory training in the safe use of handcuffs during deportations? As far as Amnesty knows it is still only an optional element to their accreditation.
- An inquest last year found that Jimmy Mubenga was unlawfully killed. Who will be held accountable for his death?[116]

[113] A. Travis, 'Jimmy Mubenga: Home Office Official Makes Qualified Apology to Family', *The Guardian*, 16 July 2013, at: www.theguardian.com/uk-news/2013/jul/16/jimmy-mubenga-home-office-apology.

[114] R. Booth and M. Taylor, 'Jimmy Mubenga's Widow Shocked as Security Guards Cleared of Manslaughter', *The Guardian*, 16 December 2014, at: www.theguardian.com/uk-news/2014/dec/16/jimmy-mubenga-security-guards-trial-death.

[115] Ibid. [116] Ibid.

Subsequently a former British Airways flight attendant sued G4S for more than £100,000 after witnessing the death of Mr Mubenga. At the end of September 2015, Louise Graham, a former BA purser, told Central London county court she was 'left in pieces' after watching the three G4S guards grapple with Mubenga as he let out 'harrowing howls' before he fell silent. G4S Care and Justice Services (United Kingdom) said she was too far removed from the tragic sequence of events to be entitled to sue.[117]

The following month, Judge Heather Baucher QC agreed with this assessment, ruling that she could not be viewed as a direct 'participant' or 'primary victim' of what happened, as the law in England and Wales requires. The judge concluded: 'I can understand this must come as a great disappointment. But I hope Ms Graham will be reconciled with the knowledge that nobody doubts the veracity of her claim, nor the impact that these events have had on her.' Speaking after the ruling, regional general counsel for G4S in the United Kingdom and Ireland, Gawie Nienaber, said: 'Anyone who saw the very distressing circumstances of Mr Mubenga's death couldn't fail to have been affected. However, the law makes clear the basis on which those present may claim damages.'[118]

Use of Firearms

The importance of strict regulation of possession and use of firearms is self-evident. This requires registration of weapons at the level of the company, and also with respect to the individual responsible. In Panama, for example, each security guard must be assigned a specific firearm; not to do so is an offence.[119] 'Moreover, there should be adequate regulations in place to ensure that firearms are stored in secure places and that they are well controlled by the company.' Within the European Union (EU), possession and use of firearms by private security company personnel varies significantly. In Denmark, France, Ireland, the

[117] J. Grierson and agency, 'Ex-BA Flight Attendant Sues G4S after Witnessing Death of Jimmy Mubenga', *The Guardian*, 30 September 2015, at: www.theguardian.com/uk-news/2015/sep/30/g4s-sued-by-ex-flight-attendant-who-witnessed-jimmy-mubengas-death.

[118] C. Goodman, '"Traumatised" Former Flight Attendant from Bucks has Compensation Claim Rejected', *GetBucks*, 16 October 2015, at: www.getbucks.co.uk/news/local-news/traumatised-former-flight-attendant-bucks-10268916.

[119] Art. 27(d), Executive Order No. 21 of 31 January 1992 governing the functioning of private security agencies.

Netherlands, and the United Kingdom, firearms are prohibited for private security personnel, but are permitted by all other EU countries.[120]

According to the UN Office on Drugs and Crime (UNODC), in a significant number of states worldwide civilian private security staff are armed with firearms or other weapons even though the number of armed workers usually represents a small proportion of the total civilian private security personnel.[121] The Small Arms Survey's annual report for 2011 found that for every 100 civilian private security staff, two would be armed in Croatia, India, and Sweden while six would be armed in Germany. States where the ratio was higher included Turkey (22 armed workers out of every 100), Russia (23 of 100), and Spain (24 of 100), with the highest rates found in Bulgaria (40 of 100), the Dominican Republic (80 of 100), and Colombia (85 of every 100).[122]

Though not directed towards private security providers, a Human Rights Council resolution from July 2015 on the regulation of civilian acquisition, possession, and use of firearms is nonetheless relevant. The resolution, which was adopted by forty-four votes to nil, with six abstentions, called on all states

> to do their utmost to take appropriate legislative, administrative and other measures, consistent with international human rights law and their constitutional frameworks, in order to ensure that the civilian acquisition, possession and use of firearms are effectively regulated with the aim of enhancing the protection of human rights, in particular the right to life and security of person, of all.[123]

[120] Born, Caparini, and Cole, 'Regulating Private Security in Europe: Status and Prospects', p. 27.

[121] UNODC, *State Regulation concerning Civilian Private Security Services and their Contribution to Crime Prevention and Community Safety*, New York, 2014, p. 43, at: www.unodc.org/documents/justice-and-prison-reform/crimeprevention/Ebook0.pdf.

[122] *Small Arms Survey 2011: States of Security*, Small Arms Survey, Geneva, 2011, ch. 4, cited by ibid.

[123] Human Rights Council Resolution 29/10: 'Human Rights and the Regulation of Civilian Acquisition, Possession and Use of Firearms', adopted on 2 July 2015. The six states abstaining were France, Japan, the Republic of Korea, the former Yugoslav Republic of Macedonia, the United Kingdom, and the United States. Following the adoption of the resolution the United States issued a statement explaining its vote, which included the following views: 'We do not believe that a State's regulation of the purely domestic acquisition, possession, and use of firearms is an appropriate topic for international attention generally or the Human Rights Council specifically. Further, we do not regard the domestic actions suggested by this resolution to be required by international human rights obligations. And we do not interpret this resolution as giving any international body or its representatives a voice in the domestic regulation of firearms ... We agree that domestic regulatory action can help deter the criminal misuse of firearms. We

This resolution should be taken to encompass possession and use of firearms by personnel working for security companies.

The use of firearms in the maritime environment, including by private security personnel, is addressed in Chapter 10 on counterpiracy. On land, perhaps the most notorious incident is the 2007 shooting and killing of multiple Iraqi civilians by Blackwater personnel in Nisour Square in Baghdad while operating a security detail for US diplomats travelling in a convoy. Blackwater was a US private security and military company founded in 1997, but following the notoriety it attained as a result of a number of incidents, especially this one, the company was renamed Xe Services in 2009, and then Academi in 2011.

Although the incident in Baghdad took place amid widespread violence in Iraq, this was not an instance of the conduct of hostilities governed by IHL, but a law enforcement operation. Under the firearms policy governing all US Department of State employees and contractors at the time, firearms could lawfully be discharged 'only in response to an imminent threat of deadly force or serious physical injury against the individual, those under the protection of the individual or other individuals'.[124] This is in line with (and arguably

regard firearms transfer or possession by private persons or non-state actors as falling within the sovereign responsibility that each government has toward its population. And we believe that it is the sovereign and exclusive right of any state to regulate and control conventional arms within its territory, pursuant to its own legal or constitutional system.' US Permanent Mission to the UN in Geneva, 'EOV [Explanation of vote] by the Delegation of the United States of America, Human Rights Council 29th Session', 2 July 2015, at: https://geneva.usmission.gov/2015/07/02/human-rights-and-the-regulation-of-civilian-acquisition-possession-and-use-of-firearms/.

124 Under the US Department of State Deadly Force and Firearms Policy, which became effective on 29 December 2011:

> A special agent of the Diplomatic Security Service (DSS) may use deadly force only when necessary, that is, when the special agent has a reasonable belief that the subject of such force poses an imminent danger of death or serious physical injury to the special agent or to another person.
>
> Deadly force may not be used solely to prevent the escape of a fleeing suspect.
>
> Firearms may not be fired solely to disable moving vehicles, vessels, or other conveyances.
>
> If feasible and if to do so would not increase the danger to the officer or others, a verbal warning to submit to the authority of the special agent shall be given prior to the use of deadly force.

stricter) than existing international law on the use of firearms for law enforcement purposes.[125]

Some of the facts of the case are still disputed, and have been, in particular, by Blackwater itself.[126] It appears, however, that a total of seventeen civilians were killed during the incident on 16 September 2007. Already by November of that year, federal agents investigating the shooting had concluded that at least fourteen of these killings were unjustified, violating the rules on use of firearms in effect for security contractors in Iraq.

US government officials said the shooting occurred when security guards fired in response to gunfire by other members of their unit in the mistaken belief that they were under attack. One official said, 'I wouldn't call it a massacre, but to say it was unwarranted is an understatement.' Investigators concluded that as many as five of the company's guards opened fire during the shootings, at least some with automatic weapons. Investigators found no evidence to support assertions by Blackwater employees that they were fired upon by Iraqi civilians. That finding sharply contradicted initial assertions by Blackwater officials, who said that company employees fired in self-defence and that three company vehicles were damaged by gunfire.

Among the seventeen killings, the FBI agents concluded that three might have been justified under rules that allow lethal force to be used in

> Warning shots are not permitted, except that they may be used by DSS special agents in exercising DSS's protective responsibilities.
>
> Special agents will be trained in alternative methods and tactics for handling resisting subjects, which must be used when the use of deadly force is not authorized by this policy.

US Department of State Deadly Force and Firearms Policy, 12 FAM Exhibit 023, available at: https://fam.state.gov/searchapps/viewer?format=html&query=use%20of%20force&links=US,FORC&url=/FAM/12FAM/12FAM0020.html#X023.

125 See also UNODC, *State Regulation concerning Civilian Private Security Services and their Contribution to Crime Prevention and Community Safety*, p. 44, which refers to the 1990 Basic Principles: 'In States where civilian private security staff are allowed to carry weapons, providers and operatives should work within these same broad principles and the regulations governing these areas should be guided by such standards and norms.'

126 Unless otherwise stated, the following account is based on a *New York Times* report, which in turn is informed by the investigation into the incident by the Federal Bureau of Investigation (FBI). D. Johnston and J. M. Broder, 'FBI Says Guards Killed 14 Iraqis without Cause', *New York Times*, 14 November 2007, at: www.nytimes.com/2007/11/14/world/middleeast/14blackwater.html?pagewanted=all.

response to an imminent threat.[127] They accepted that Blackwater guards might have perceived a threat when they opened fire on a white Kia sedan that moved toward Nisour Square after traffic had been stopped for a Blackwater convoy of four armoured vehicles. Two people were killed in the car: Ahmed Haithem Ahmed and his mother, Mohassin, a doctor. Relatives said they were on a family errand and posed no threat to the Blackwater convoy. Investigators said Blackwater guards might have felt endangered by a third, and unidentified, Iraqi who was killed nearby. But the investigators determined that the subsequent shootings of fourteen Iraqis, some of whom were shot while fleeing, were unprovoked.[128]

The subsequent criminal case against the Blackwater guards faced many obstacles, 'many of them of the government's own making. From the outset, there were indications that State Department officials tried to gather shell casings after the shooting in an effort to protect Blackwater. The State Department also gave the contractors limited immunity after the shooting, which made it significantly harder for the Justice Department to build its case ... A judge threw out all charges in 2009, citing "reckless" government behaviour'.[129] A new prosecution team resurrected the case but dropped charges against one guard because of a lack of evidence. Prosecutors then missed a deadline to re-charge one of the accused, Nicholas A. Slatten. That explains why he alone was charged with murder, which has no statute of limitations.[130]

After a series of abortive prosecutions, on 22 October 2014, seven years after the shootings, a jury in federal district court in Washington, DC, found that the deaths were 'not a battlefield tragedy, but the result of a criminal act'.[131] Mr Slatten, a sniper who the government said had fired the first shots, was convicted of murder while three others – Dustin L. Heard, Evan S. Liberty, and Paul A. Slough – were convicted of voluntary manslaughter and of using a machine gun to carry out a

[127] The *New York Times* reports, though, that a separate military review of the shootings concluded that all of the killings were unjustified and potentially criminal. One of the military investigators said the FBI was being 'generous' to Blackwater in characterising any of the killings as justifiable. Ibid.

[128] In 2010, it was reported that three private security guards working for Blackwater who witnessed the shootings had told a federal grand jury that they believed the shootings were unjustified. J. Risen, '3 Blackwater Guards Called Baghdad Shootings Unjustified', *New York Times*, 16 January 2010, at: www.nytimes.com/2010/01/17/world/middleeast/17blackwater.html.

[129] M. Apuzzo, 'Blackwater Guards Found Guilty in 2007 Iraq Killings', *New York Times*, 22 October 2014, at: www.nytimes.com/2014/10/23/us/blackwater-verdict.html?_r=0.

[130] Ibid. [131] Ibid.

violent crime. A fifth contractor, Jeremy Ridgeway, had previously pleaded guilty to manslaughter and cooperated with prosecutors, giving evidence against the defendants, his erstwhile colleagues.[132]

Welcoming the verdict, Ronald C. Machen Jr., US attorney in Washington, said:

> This verdict is a resounding affirmation of the commitment of the American people to the rule of law, even in times of war. Seven years ago, these Blackwater contractors unleashed powerful sniper fire, machine guns and grenade launchers on innocent men, women and children. Today, they were held accountable for that outrageous attack and its devastating consequences for so many Iraqi families.[133]

On 13 April 2015, federal district judge Royce C. Lamberth sentenced Mr Slatten to life in prison and the other three Blackwater guards to thirty years each.[134]

Blackwater is reported to have paid damages to the families of those killed, though the amount of compensation has not been made public.[135] In September 2007, in testimony before Congress, the Secretary of Defense, Robert Gates, affirmed that the Pentagon had sufficient legal authority to control its contractors, but said that commanders lacked sufficient 'means and resources' to exercise adequate oversight.[136]

An Accountability Gap?

Indeed, one of the most persistent charges levelled against private security companies is that they lack accountability. This should operate at a number of levels: internally, within the company itself; domestically within the national regulatory and civil and criminal law frameworks; and internationally. In Peru, for example, a 2015 decree regulating

132 Ibid. 133 Cited in ibid.

134 M. Apuzzo, 'Ex-Blackwater Guards Given Long Terms for Killing Iraqis', *New York Times*, 13 April 2015, at: www.nytimes.com/2015/04/14/us/ex-blackwater-guards-sentenced-to-prison-in-2007-killings-of-iraqi-civilians.html.

135 Apuzzo, 'Blackwater Guards Found Guilty in 2007 Iraq Killings'. See also M. Mazzetti and J. Risen, 'Blackwater Said to Pursue Bribes to Iraq after 17 Died', *New York Times*, 10 November 2009, at: www.nytimes.com/2009/11/11/world/middleeast/11blackwater.html?pagewanted=all.

136 Associated Press, '"Pentagon Dispatches Investigators to Iraq to Probe Private Security Contractors', Fox News, Published 26 September 2007 at: www.foxnews.com/story/2007/09/26/pentagon-dispatches-investigators-to-iraq-to-probe-private-security-contractors.html. See also P. Chatterjee, 'Blackwater USA', Crocodyl.org, at: www.corpwatch.org/section.php?id=210.

private security service stipulates that anyone who contracts a non-authorised company will be held responsible for any violation of the rights of third parties that could result from the contracted services.[137]

If it were true that such companies have no human rights obligations, this would be a first accountability gap, one that exists under international law. I have sought to argue that this is not the case, though even if private security companies do have binding obligations under international human rights law, securing an effective remedy for violations remains a major practical challenge. Of course, this may equally be the case with state violations of its human rights obligations. But it is generally agreed that, from an international legal perspective, states must at least exercise due diligence to protect persons under their jurisdiction, including from the acts of private security service providers.[138]

For signatory companies to the International Code of Conduct for Private Security Service Providers, there is an oversight mechanism in place. Founder members of the ICoC, which was finalised in 2010, include G4S and many other market-leading companies. The ICoC applies, though, only in 'complex environments', defined as 'any areas experiencing or recovering from unrest or instability, whether due to natural disasters or armed conflicts, where the rule of law has been substantially undermined, and in which the capacity of the state authority to handle the situation is diminished, limited or non-existent'.[139]

The ICoC Association[140] (ICoCA) receives complaints from individuals or their representatives on alleged violations of the ICoC and/or non-compliance of member companies' grievance mechanisms with the

[137] Art. 30(2), Decree No. 1213 regulating private security services, 24 September 2015.

[138] See, e.g., Amnesty International, 'Public Statement on the Montreux Document on Pertinent International Legal Obligations and Good Practices for States related to the Operations of Private Military and Security Companies during Armed Conflict', 14 October 2008, at: www.amnesty.org/ar/library/asset/IOR30/010/2008/en/5bca5962-99de-11dd-bf88-f59215f3db50/ior300102008en.pdf.

[139] Para. 13 and definition section, ICoC. See generally: 'The International Code of Conduct for Private Security Service Providers', Geneva Academy Briefing No. 4.

[140] See: http://icoca.ch/. According to the ICoC Association, membership consists of states or intergovernmental organisations, private security companies, and civil society organisations, also referred to as the three stakeholder groups. Member states of the ICoC Association are states that also support the Montreux Document, and include the main headquarter states of PSCs. PSC members come from all continents and range from smaller companies to some of the world market leaders. ICoC Association member companies provide both land-based and maritime-based security services. Civil society organisation members of the ICoC Association include international NGOs as well as local NGOs working in complex environments where PSCs operate.

Code. The ICoCA is to 'establish a process to support and oversee companies' responsibility to provide fair and accessible grievance procedures that offer effective remedies to address claims alleging violations of the Code.'[141] In 2016, procedures to process complaints with the ICoCA were being developed by the ICoCA. Members voted to adopt the procedures to process complaints at the Association's General Assembly in September 2016. There are three basic 'pathways' towards resolution of a complaint alleging violation of the Code of Conduct:

1. The complainant is directed to a fair and effective grievance mechanism, should the Member Company have one in place and should it be appropriate for the particular complaint;
2. If there is not an effective grievance mechanism, ICoCA shall offer guidance for its establishment, and, if necessary, shall seek an alternative mechanism (such as mediation or the use of the Association's good offices);
3. If the complaint involves allegations of criminal activity, and if it has taken place within a competent criminal jurisdiction, the matter will be reported to the relevant authority for follow up.[142]

Thus, in any event the task for addressing serious allegations of unlawful use of force shifts back to the domestic environment. In the United Kingdom, the SIA itself acknowledges that for its regulation to be 'effective and trusted it is vital that action is taken against those who no longer meet our criteria or who break the law'. The SIA affirms that it revokes licences where the licensing criteria are no longer met and it suspends licences if there is a threat to public safety. It concedes, though, that if the law is broken, 'prosecution is not our preferred option: we aim to encourage compliance with the law in the first instance and will do all we can to help organisations meet their obligations'. This does not suggest a robust system of regulation, even though it is also stipulated that 'in appropriate cases we have the will and capability to prosecute offenders, and to seek the confiscation of assets that have been obtained as a result of criminal activity.'[143]

[141] ICoCA, 'Complaints Process', undated but accessed on 7 December 2015 at: www.icoca.ch/en/complaints-process.

[142] The ICoCA announced that it planned to have implemented the procedures 'so as to be able to accept and treat complaints of alleged violations of the Code of Conduct from early 2017'. ICoCA, 'Complaints Process', undated but accessed 13 October 2016 at: www.icoca.ch/en/complaints-process.

[143] SIA, 'Enforcement', at: www.sia.homeoffice.gov.uk/Pages/enforcement.aspx.

In egregious cases, however, as we have described, criminal prosecutions have been undertaken against individual private security personnel for unlawful killing. Since 2007, the United Kingdom has also had an explicit corporate criminal liability statute in force, the Corporate Manslaughter and Corporate Homicide Act.[144] The Act sanctions 'organisational liability' according to which a company can be found guilty of corporate manslaughter 'if the way in which its activities are managed or organised . . . causes a person's death, and . . . amounts to a gross breach of a relevant duty of care owed by the organization to the deceased'. The Act further stipulates that 'senior management must play a substantial role in the breach'.[145] These 'dual requirements also anticipatorily rebut any argument that a corporate defendant might face criminal liability solely on the basis of a low-level employee's unauthorized acts'.[146] There is no individual liability available under the Act.[147]

With regard to remedies, the Act provides that an organisation or company found guilty will be liable to an unlimited fine, and allows courts to impose a publicity order, requiring the organisation to publicise details of its conviction and fine.[148] Courts may also require an organisation to take steps to address the failures behind the offence by means of a remedial order.[149] Notably, the Act applies to foreign companies and subsidiaries operating in the United Kingdom, as well as subcontractors.[150] In May 2015, Sherwood Rise, a care home company, was charged with corporate manslaughter, the first case of its kind in England and Wales. A woman in the company's care died after not being provided with adequate food and drink.[151]

[144] Corporate Manslaughter and Corporate Homicide Act, 2007, c. 19, at: www.legislation.gov.uk/ukpga/2007/19/pdfs/ukpga_20070019_en.pdf (hereafter Corporate Manslaughter Act). H. Stauffer, 'Corporate Liability for Drones and Fully Autonomous Weapons Systems: An Alternative Path to Accountability?', Unpublished monograph on file with the author.

[145] J. W. Harlow, 'Corporate Criminal Liability for Homicide: A Statutory Framework', *Duke Law Journal*, Vol. 61 (2011), pp. 150–51.

[146] Ibid. [147] 2007 Corporate Manslaughter Act, s. 17.

[148] 2007 Corporate Manslaughter Act, ss. 1(6) and 10.

[149] 2007 Corporate Manslaughter Act, s. 9.

[150] See generally: www.cps.gov.uk/legal/a_to_c/corporate_manslaughter/.

[151] CQMS, 'Corporate Manslaughter Prosecutions', undated but accessed on 7 December 2015 at: www.cqms-ltd.co.uk/news/landmark_corporate_manslaughter_case.html.

As Hilary Stauffer notes,[152] though, the United States has probably the most progressive regime of corporate criminal liability, developed through a century of case law. It follows the 'vicarious liability' model, and stems from a famous 1909 Supreme Court case, *New York Central & Hudson Railroad v. US*, where the Court 'upheld corporate punishment based on the *respondeat superior* theory of tort law, allowing a corporation to be held criminally liable for its agents' actions taken within the scope of their employment'.[153] According to this theory, there are three cumulative requirements for liability to be imposed on a company. First, a corporate agent must have committed an illegal act (actus reus) with the requisite state of mind (mens rea).[154] Second, the agent must have acted within his scope of employment. The scope of employment includes any act that 'occurred while the offending employee was carrying out a job-related activity'. Third, the agent must have intended to benefit the corporation. Under this standard, which is usually easily met, the employee need not act with the exclusive purpose of benefiting the corporation, and the corporation need not actually receive the benefit.[155]

The New York court adjudging the *New York Central & Hudson Railroad* case suggested that 'there are some crimes which in their nature cannot be committed by corporations',[156] but did not elaborate on what those might be. Over the next 100 years, corporate criminal liability in the United States has expanded to include 'almost all wrongs except rape, murder, bigamy, and other crimes of malicious intent'.[157] Notably, the list of crimes for which corporations have been held criminally liable in the United States includes manslaughter.[158]

[152] This section is also based on Stauffer, 'Corporate Liability for Drones and Fully Autonomous Weapons Systems: An Alternative Path to Accountability?'.

[153] E. Luna, 'The Curious Case of Corporate Criminality', *American Criminal Law Review*, Vol. 46 (2009), pp. 1507–08.

[154] Mens rea can also be shown on the basis of the 'collective knowledge' of the employees as a group, even though no single employee possessed sufficient information to know that the crime was being committed.

[155] V. S. Khanna, 'Corporate Criminal Liability, What Purpose Does It Serve?', *Harvard Law Review*, Vol. 109 (1996), pp. 1489–90 (citations omitted).

[156] *New York Central & Hudson. R. R. Co.* v. *United States*, at 494.

[157] Khanna, 'Corporate Criminal Liability, What Purpose Does It Serve?', p. 1484.

[158] To date, at least fifteen states plus the federal government have prosecuted corporations for manslaughter or criminally negligent homicide. See Harlow, 'Corporate Criminal Liability for Homicide: A Statutory Framework', p. 133.

Criminal penalties for corporate liability have evolved over time through a mix of case law and statute, but today are generally considered to include 'cash fines, probation, debarment, and loss of license',[159] among other remedies. A court can 'sanction the organization with forfeiture, restitution, or an order to notify victims; or it can combine any of these punishments'.[160] Fines can 'run into the hundreds of millions of dollars';[161] and if 'debarment' is imposed, 'any corporation convicted of a felony may be permanently barred from doing business with government agencies or participating in government programs'.[162] Imprisonment 'is not applicable in the corporate context',[163] unless of course individual liability is assessed. Alongside criminal penalties, civil and regulatory penalties are available to sanction corporations for their misdeeds, many of which are similar to the criminal remedies on offer.[164] However, many observers argue that the corresponding loss of reputation resulting from a criminal conviction provides an additional deterrent.[165]

In sum, US jurisprudence has evolved to include progressive and broad criminal liability for corporations, up to and including manslaughter. It is, though, unclear how successful a cause of action might be for violations occurring outside the United States, such as in the Blackwater case.

Of course, as the cliché reminds us, prevention is better than cure. The DOJ investigation into the Walnut Grove Correctional Facility (WGYCF) in Mississippi usefully addressed problems in the use of force policy for the WGYCF, which was contained in a section entitled 'Use of Force and Four-Point Restraint Policy'. While specific to that Facility, many of its detailed observations would be more broadly relevant to private security service providers. It offered the following as examples of the policy's deficiencies:

- While there was a requirement that photographs be taken of staff injuries following a use of force incident, there was no requirement to photograph injured youth.

[159] Khanna, 'Corporate Criminal Liability, What Purpose Does It Serve?', p. 1497.

[160] T. Johnson, 'Sentencing Organizations after Booker', *Yale Law Journal*, Vol. 116 (2006), pp. 632, 641–42.

[161] E. B. Diskant, 'Comparative Corporate Criminal Liability', *Yale Law Journal*, Vol. 118 (2008), pp. 140–41.

[162] *Ibid.*

[163] Khanna, 'Corporate Criminal Liability, What Purpose Does It Serve?', p. 1497.

[164] *Ibid.*, p. 1499.

[165] Harlow, 'Corporate Criminal Liability for Homicide: A Statutory Framework', pp. 142–43.

- No guidance was provided regarding the review process for determining whether or not force was justified and reasonable
- No guidance was provided to describe the type or amount of force. used. Staff used inadequate 'boiler-type descriptions' such as 'physical takedown' or 'took the inmate to the floor' to describe use of force actions.
- There was no explicit requirement that reviewing supervisors have prompt access to medical evidence such as nursing notes and anatomical drawings of the body that depict the specific areas where injuries are present following a use-of-force incident.[166]

The DOJ also criticised the WGYCF use of the state's Use of Force Training Policy (04-03), which sets out staff training requirements on use of force. The policy does not specify the number of hours that each employee should receive on use of force regulations not does it provide adequate guidance to staff on decontaminating procedures when chemical agents are deployed.[167]

Concluding Remarks

Private security providers are here in number, and they are here to stay, despite hiccoughs in several countries along the way. While the focus has been on what can go wrong, there is no reason why private security service providers cannot be a valuable complement to states law enforcement capabilities. Since rolling back the tide of contracting out of policing functions is hardly a realistic option in most scenarios, focus must be primarily on promoting the highest standards of conduct by private security providers and their staff, and on effective accountability for their compliance with those standards.

According to UNODC, challenges in some states have included 'little or no training for civilian private security guards, the abuse of authority and excessive use of force by security personnel, generally low professional standards, inadequate legal accountability mechanisms and non-compliance with the law'.[168] A variety of avenues for accountability do

[166] DOJ, *Investigation of the Walnut Grove Youth Correctional Facility Walnut Grove, Mississippi*, p. 12.

[167] Ibid.

[168] UNODC, *State Regulation concerning Civilian Private Security Services and their Contribution to Crime Prevention and Community Safety*, p. 21.

exist, though states may seek to avoid their human rights obligations by blaming the company, while the company contracted may seek to push responsibility onto the individual or individuals directly responsible for a human rights violation. This version of the 'hot potato' game will continue to be a major challenge to the ideology that the market can perform better than the state.

10

Counterpiracy at Sea

'Somalia is trying. But it's the problems ashore: the corruption, the conflict, the unemployment, that mean the threat of piracy resuming is going to be with us for a long time to come.'

Andrew Harding, BBC reporter, August 2015[1]

Introduction

This chapter discusses the use of force in counterpiracy operations. While the police per se are rarely involved in counterpiracy operations, acts to deter, arrest, and/or detain suspected pirates fall to be adjudged under the law of law enforcement (LOLE) rules. The chapter opens with a discussion of the definition of piracy under international law and describes the waxing and waning of the phenomenon over the past two decades. The following section addresses the human rights framework applicable to counterpiracy, including consideration of jurisdictional issues. Subsequent sections address the use of force against suspected pirates and pirate vessels, as well as the duty to rescue suspected pirates in distress on the high seas. The duty of the master of a vessel to protect his/her own crew and passengers remains paramount.

The Definition of Piracy

Under international law, particularly the 1982 United Nations Convention on the Law of the Sea (UNCLOS),[2] piracy is composed of five

[1] Report on piracy, available at: www.bbc.com/news/world-africa-34105277.

[2] According to Art. 101 of UNCLOS, piracy consists of any of the following acts:

(a) any illegal acts of violence or detention, or any act of depredation, committed for private ends by the crew or the passengers of a private ship or a private aircraft, and directed:

elements all of which must be present in a particular circumstance for the offence to be committed. First, there must be an act of unlawful violence[3] or robbery.[4] Second, the act must be committed against one or more passengers or member of crew of a ship, or against the vessel itself (i.e. it involves damage to the vessel, its hijacking, or theft from it).

Third, the ship must be sailing on the high seas,[5] or within a state's exclusive economic zone (EEZ) but outside the territorial waters.

(i) on the high seas, against another ship or aircraft, or against persons or property on board such ship or aircraft;
(ii) against a ship, aircraft, persons or property in a place outside the jurisdiction of any State;

(b) any act of voluntary participation in the operation of a ship or of an aircraft with knowledge of facts making it a pirate ship or aircraft;
(c) any act of inciting or of intentionally facilitating an act described in subparagraph (a) or (b).

As at 1 April 2017, there were 168 states parties to UNCLOS. See UN Treaty Section, at: https://treaties.un.org/Pages/ViewDetailsIII.aspx?src=TREATY&mtdsg_no=XXI-6&chapter=21&Temp=mtdsg3&clang=_en#1.

3 This would exclude reasonable force used in self-defence or defence of others.

4 Whether an unsuccessful attempt amounts to piracy, and whether piracy requires actual theft, has been controversial. The UNCLOS definition of piracy does not include either requirement, but there is old jurisprudence from the Privy Council that suggests an attempt might be sufficient. See the 1934 judgment of *In re Piracy Jure Gentium* in which the Council noted that 'a little common sense is a valuable quality in the interpretation of international law'. As a contrast, Douglas Guilfoyle refers to the case in the United States, *US* v. *Smith* 18 US 153 (1820), which held piracy to be 'robbery at sea'. D. Guilfoyle, 'Prosecuting Pirates in National Courts: US v Said and Piracy Under US Law', *EJIL Talk!*, 23 August 2010, at: www.ejiltalk.org/prosecuting-pirates-in-national-courts-us-v-said-and-piracy-under-us-law/. Guilfoyle criticised the decision of the US District Court in Norfolk, Virginia, in *US* v. *Said and Others* in which the six defendants are alleged to be Somali pirates who, on 10 April 2010, mistook the *USS Ashland* for a merchant vessel and attacked it using assault rifles. On appeal to the Fourth Circuit, the Court endorsed the UNCLOS definition of piracy as reflective of customary international law and seemingly endorsed at the same time the offence of attempted piracy. US Court of Appeals (for the Fourth Circuit), *US* v. *Said and Others*, Judgment (Case No. 14–4413), 13 August 2015.

5 The high seas are the open ocean outside a state's exclusive economic zone (EEZ), territorial waters, and internal waters. The exclusive economic zone (EEZ) is an area of water that extends 200 nautical miles seaward of the territorial baseline of a coastal state. In the EEZ, the coastal state has sovereign rights over natural resources in the waters, the seabed, and its subsoil. Art. 56(1)(a), UNCLOS. For the purposes of the definition of piracy under UNCLOS, the EEZ is treated in the same way as the high seas. Art. 58, UNCLOS. The territorial waters extend up to 12 nautical miles from the baseline, a baseline in the sea that follows the low-water line of a coastal state. Each coastal state has the right to establish the breadth of its territorial waters so long as they do not extend beyond 12 nautical miles. Art. 3, UNCLOS. Within its territorial waters, the coastal state exercises sovereignty, as an extension of territorial sovereignty. It enjoys sovereignty over the sea bed and subsoil, as well as the airspace over territorial waters. Art. 2, UNCLOS; and

(When piratical-type acts are committed not within a state's territorial waters, archipelagic waters,[6] or internal waters, this is referred to as 'armed robbery at sea'.[7]) Fourth, because the acts must be committed 'for private ends'[8], the perpetrators – i.e. the pirates – must be private individuals, not representatives of a state or state agents.[9] Fifth, the pirates must come on to the victim ship or use force from another ship or aircraft.[10]

Arts. 1–2, 1958 Geneva Convention on the Territorial Sea and Contiguous Zone. The 1958 High Seas Convention defines the high seas 'as all parts of the sea that are not included in the territorial sea or in the internal waters of a State'. Art. 1, 1958 High Seas Convention. UNCLOS effectively added the EEZ to the definition.

6 This comprises all waters within the baseline.

7 See, e.g., the International Maritime Organization (IMO)'s Code of Practice for the Investigation of the Crimes of Piracy and Armed Robbery Against Ships (IMO Code of Practice), which determines that armed robbery against ships consists of any of the following acts: '(a) any illegal act of violence or detention or any act of depredation, or threat thereof, other than an act of piracy, committed for private ends and directed against a ship or against persons or property on board such a ship, within a State's internal waters, archipelagic waters and territorial sea . . . (b) any act of inciting or of intentionally facilitating an act described above.' Annex, §2.2, IMO Code of Practice, Adopted on 2 December 2009 by IMO Resolution A.1025(26), at: www.imo.org/en/OurWork/Security/PiracyArmedRobbery/Guidance/Documents/A.1025.pdf. The IMO is the UN specialised agency responsible for improving maritime safety and preventing pollution from ships. www.imo.org.

8 The precise scope of this notion is debated. For a brief discussion see A. Priddy, 'The Use of Weapons in Counterpiracy Operations', ch. 5 in S. Casey-Maslen (ed.), *Weapons Under International Human Rights Law*, Cambridge University Press, Cambridge, 2014, p. 126. One approach is to require that the acts be conducted for pecuniary gain. This (narrow) interpretation would exclude acts committed for political purposes. Neil Boister argues that this is supported by practice (the 1985 *Achille Lauro* hijacking by Palestinian militants on board), even though this is better explained by the hijacking not meeting the two-ship criterion. He also refers to a 2011 opinion by the International Maritime Organisation (IMO)'s Legal Committee. IMO Legal Committee, 'IMO Piracy: Uniform and Consistent Application of the provisions of International Conventions Relating to Piracy', Leg 98/8, 18 February 2011, §9. See N. Boister, *An Introduction to Transnational Criminal Law*, Oxford University Press, Oxford, 2012, pp. 30–31. See also G. G. Ong-Webb, 'Introduction: Southeast Asian Piracy: Research and Developments', in G. G. Ong-Webb (ed.), *Piracy, Maritime Terrorism and Securing the Malacca Straits*, Institute of Southeast Asian Studies, Singapore, 2006, p. xiii.

9 Acts of a state agent were formally known as 'privateering' or acts under 'letters of marque'. For discussion of this practice, see e.g., R. Geiß and A. Petrig, *Piracy and Armed Robbery at Sea: The Legal Framework for Counter-Piracy Operations in Somalia and the Gulf of Aden*, Oxford University Press, Oxford, 2011, pp. 61–62. Privateering was abolished under the 1856 Paris Declaration Respecting Maritime Law. The Declaration was ratified by 55 states, though several of these are no longer states. See list at: www.icrc.org/applic/ihl/ihl.nsf/States.xsp?xp_viewStates=XPages_NORMStatesParties&xp_treaty Selected=105.

10 The two-ship requirement was reportedly adopted to ensure an international element in the definition of piracy by excluding offences that involved only ships and territory under the

The Phenomenon of Piracy

The location and prevalence of piracy have fluctuated significantly in recent years. After seeing rapid growth during the first decade of the twenty-first century, particularly off the coast of Somalia in the Indian Ocean (one of the busiest shipping routes in the world)[11] and increasingly also in the Gulf of Guinea, a stretch of water defined by Cape Palmas in Liberia to the west and Cape Lopez in Gabon to the south,[12] it has declined remarkably. The year 2011 may prove to be the high-water mark of piratical attacks off the east coast of Africa, especially in the Gulf of Aden, with 24 seafarers losing their lives at the hands of Somali pirates and 1,118 others taken hostage or continuing to be held.[13]

In 1992, the International Chamber of Commerce's International Maritime Bureau (IMB) established a Piracy Reporting Centre in Kuala Lumpur. It recorded a total of 246 actual and attempted piratical attacks (including armed robbery at sea) for 2015. Of these, almost half – 108 – occurred off the coast of Indonesia. None was recorded for the Gulf of Aden but 14 were reported off the coast of Nigeria.[14] The total for the year saw 203 vessels boarded and 15 hijacked; in 104 of the 246 instances the ship was anchored while in 91 it was steaming on the sea.[15] In only one instance was a member of the crew killed, and though 271 crew members were taken hostage during the year, this was the lowest number recorded over the previous five years.[16]

In late 2015, the UN Security Council adopted Resolution 2246 in which it noted that the joint counterpiracy efforts of states, regions, organisations, the maritime industry, the private sector, think tanks, and civil society had resulted in a steady decline since 2011 in pirate attacks as well as hijackings.[17] During 2015, there were said to have been no attacks on vessels in

ordinary jurisdiction of a single state. Stanley Morrison, writing in 1932, cited by P. Campbell, 'A Modern History of the International Definition of Piracy', in B. A. Elleman, A. Forbes, and D. Rosenberg (eds.), *Piracy and Maritime Crime: Historical and Modern Case Studies*, Newport Papers, No. 35, Naval War College Press, Newport, RI, 2011, p. 32.

11 It is the gateway in and out of the Suez Canal. North Atlantic Treaty Organization (NATO), 'Counter-Piracy Operations', Last updated on 12 July 2016, at: www.nato.int/cps/en/natohq/topics_48815.htm.

12 See Priddy, 'The Use of Weapons in Counterpiracy Operations', pp. 122–23.

13 One Earth Future Foundation (OEFF), *The Economic Cost of Somali Piracy 2012*, February 2013, p. 1; see Priddy, 'The Use of Weapons in Counterpiracy Operations', p. 123.

14 IMB, Annual Report 2015, February 2016, p. 5, available on request at: https://icc-ccs.org/piracy-reporting-centre.

15 Ibid., p. 7.

16 Ibid., p. 9.

17 UN Security Council Resolution 2246, adopted on 10 November 2015, fourth preambular para.

waters patrolled by the European Union Naval Force, known as EU NAVFOR,[18] compared with two in 2014[19] but 176 in 2011.[20]

In January 2016, however, IHS, a risk-management company headquartered in Colorado, cautioned against complacency, arguing that ships travelling through waters off the coast of Somalia faced an increased risk of piracy during the year, fostered by deteriorating political conditions in Somalia's Galmudug region in the centre of the country. IHS claimed that conditions that led regional politicians to provide safe havens between 2005 and 2012 for hijacked ships to be stored during lengthy ransom negotiations were being recreated:

> This means that Somali pirates, who still have the technical capabilities, manpower, weaponry and financing networks to organize deep-water hijacks, may soon regain the secure ship-storage locations required to resume operations.[21]

The North Atlantic Treaty Organization (NATO) was planning to maintain its counterpiracy efforts at sea and ashore, known as Operation Ocean Shield, by supporting countries in the region to build the capacity to fight piracy themselves until 15 December 2016. With no successful pirate attacks in the Gulf of Aden, off the Horn of Africa and in the Indian Ocean since May 2012, Operation Ocean Shield was only deploying vessels 'intermittently' by 2015.[22]

According to One Earth Future Foundation (OEFF)'s *Oceans Beyond Piracy* initiative, piracy and armed robbery at sea off the coast of West Africa remained a serious threat to shipping transiting the Gulf of Guinea in 2014.[23] 'Rates of violence against seafarers continue to be high, while protections for seafarer welfare remain minimal.'[24] In contrast, Dryad Maritime highlighted a reduction in offshore maritime crime in the Gulf

[18] In addition to Somalia's coastal territory, EU Navfor patrols cover the southern Red Sea, the Gulf of Aden, and areas of the Indian Ocean including Comoros, Mauritius, and the Seychelles.

[19] OEFF recorded no successful piratical attacks in 2014 off the coast of East Africa. OEFF, *Annual Report 2014*, 2015, p. 6, at: https://oneearthfuture.org/sites/oneearthfuture.org/files//images/content/annual_report_2014.pdf.

[20] P. Richardson, 'Piracy Threat Rises for Ships Off Somalia This Year, IHS Says', *Bloomberg Business*, 25 January 2016, at: www.bloomberg.com/news/articles/2016-01-25/piracy-threat-rises-for-ships-off-somalia-this-year-ihs-says.

[21] Richardson, 'Piracy Threat Rises for Ships off Somalia This Year, IHS Says'. See also the report by Andrew Harding of the BBC from Puntland in Somalia, at: 'Piracy: Outbreak Off Somalia Despite International Effort', 31 August 2015.

[22] NATO, 'Counter-Piracy Operations'.

[23] OEFF, *Annual Report 2014*, 2015, p. 6.

[24] Ibid.

of Guinea for 2014, which was followed in 2015 with the number of reported incidents dropping a further 29 per cent. This reduction in reported incidents for 2015 included an 'unprecedented' five-month break in piracy. Dryad noted, though, that the risk of kidnap remained a concern for crew of vessels operating off the coast of Nigeria, with the total number of crew kidnapped in 2015 surpassing that recorded for 2014.[25]

More generally, concern was increasing among insurance underwriters that the maritime market was 'letting its guard down' over piracy, as a result of the successes of efforts in the Gulf of Aden and off the coast of Somalia in reducing incidents of piracy. Elsewhere, in the view of one Singaporean underwriter reported in the media, 'We have seen a rise in the threat in South Asia and off the coast of Malaysia where the piracy gangs have become more organised and have been targeting high-value cargos.'[26]

There was also broader disquiet about the accuracy of statistical data. According to another broker, the IMB's Piracy Reporting Centre (IMB PRC) 'will admit that seeking to establish a true picture of the level of piracy across the world is difficult. There are owners who remain reluctant to publicly acknowledge they have fallen victim to piracy and therefore the true numbers are higher than those we see reported in the media'.[27]

NATO, though, remained upbeat. Writing in July 2016, the organisation affirmed that there had been no successful piracy attacks since May 2012 in the waters it patrolled. It accepted, though, that while Somalia-based piracy had been suppressed, it had not been eliminated, and acknowledged that pirates 'still seek, and have the capacity, to mount attacks'.[28] By October, Dryad Maritime was also expressing 'cautious optimism' regarding maritime crime and piracy, with third quarter numbers 'showing a significant reduction of activity in hotspot regions: the Gulf of Guinea, Southeast Asia and the high risk area off Somalia'.[29]

In south-east Asia, maritime crime was at its lowest levels in seven years, ascribed largely to the actions of law enforcement agencies in the Straits of Malacca and Singapore, while in the Gulf of Guinea, there had

[25] D. Rider, 'Dryad Issues 2015 Crime Report', *Maritime Security Review*, 26 January 2016, at: www.marsecreview.com/2016/01/dryad-issues-2015-crime-report/.

[26] J. Guy, 'Marine Insurers Wary of Increased Piracy Risk', *IHS*, 26 January 2016, at: http://fairplay.ihs.com/safety-regulation/article/4260986/marine-insurers-wary-of-increasing-piracy-risk.

[27] Ibid. [28] NATO, 'Counter-Piracy Operations'.

[29] MarEx, '"Cautious Optimism" as Piracy Numbers Decline', *The Maritime Executive*, 13 October 2016, at: www.maritime-executive.com/article/cautious-optimism-as-piracy-numbers-decline.

been only four attacks recorded in the third quarter of the year compared with thirty-five in the first half of the year. No attacks were reported off Somalia, the continuation of a two-year absence of pirate activity in the High Risk Area. Despite the global decline in reported maritime crime, however, Dryad warned that piracy remains a real threat to seafarers, noting that, in 2016 as at the end of September, 81 mariners have been kidnapped, 7 had been killed, and 61 remained in captivity.[30]

The Human Rights Framework

The human rights most at risk of being violated during counterpiracy operations are the rights to life, to humane treatment, and to liberty. The maritime environment, whose vast extent means that the prospect of independent monitoring of actions taken against piracy and individual pirates is scant, offers a heightened risk of unlawful conduct. At the same time, there is a duty to protect the right to life of the crew and passengers of ships, which implies that preventive and protective measures must be taken against piracy, both by states and by the shipping companies.

Jurisdictional Issues

It is a general principle of the law of the sea that ships must sail under the flag of one state only, and that each ship is generally subject to that flag state's exclusive jurisdiction on the high seas.[31] Further, every state is obliged to 'effectively exercise its jurisdiction and control in administrative, technical and social matters over ships flying its flag'.[32] That international human rights law is fully applicable is suggested, but not confirmed, by pertinent UN Security Council resolutions. Resolution 2246 of November 2015, for instance, calls upon all states:

> to criminalize piracy under their domestic law and to favourably consider the prosecution of suspected, and imprisonment of those convicted, pirates apprehended off the coast of Somalia, and their facilitators and financiers ashore, *consistent with applicable international law, including international human rights law*.[33]

Under Article 1 of the 1950 European Convention on Human Rights (ECHR), states parties are obliged to 'secure' to everyone within their

[30] Ibid. [31] Art. 92(1), UNCLOS. [32] Art. 94, UNCLOS.
[33] UN Security Council Resolution 2246, §19 (added emphasis).

'jurisdiction' the rights and freedoms set out in the Convention. As the Grand Chamber of the European Court of Human Rights stated in 2012, 'The exercise of jurisdiction is a necessary condition for a Contracting State to be able to be held responsible for acts or omissions imputable to it which give rise to an allegation of the infringement of rights and freedoms set forth in the Convention.'[34] While such jurisdiction is primarily territorial, the Court further observed that:

> by virtue of the relevant provisions of the law of the sea, a vessel sailing on the high seas is subject to the exclusive jurisdiction of the State of the flag it is flying. This principle of international law has led the Court to recognise, in cases concerning acts carried out on board vessels flying a State's flag, in the same way as registered aircraft, cases of extraterritorial exercise of the jurisdiction of that State ... Where there is control over another, this is *de jure* control exercised by the State in question over the individuals concerned.[35]

As discussed below, rescuing suspected pirates in distress at sea may also bring them within the jurisdiction of the flag state.

The Right to Life

That the right to life applies extraterritorially in certain circumstances, at least as guaranteed under Article 6 of the 1966 International Covenant on Civil and Political Rights (ICCPR), is generally contested by only two states: Israel and the United States (US). However, according to the 2015 draft General Comment on the right to life by the Human Rights Committee, states parties to the ICCPR are 'required to respect and protect the lives of all individuals located on marine vessels or aircrafts hoisting the State parties' flag or registered by them'.[36]

This is, though, quite a narrow interpretation, which ostensibly would not extend to action taken on a ship (e.g. firing a weapon) that resulted in the death of a suspected pirate on another vessel. Seemingly, only when a suspected pirate had successfully clambered aboard the flagged vessel would he enjoy the protection of his right to life. This is not correct. By analogy, in its 2007 decision on admissibility in *Mansur Pad* v. *Turkey*,

[34] European Court of Human Rights (ECtHR), *Hirsi Jamaa and Others* v. *Italy*, Judgment (Grand Chamber), 23 February 2012, §70.

[35] Ibid., §77.

[36] Human Rights Committee, 'Draft General Comment No. 36 (Article 6: Right to Life), Draft Prepared by Yuval Shany and Nigel Rodley, Rapporteurs', UN doc. CCPR/C/GC/R.36/Rev.2, 7 September 2015, §62.

the European Court of Human Rights held that in a case involving the shooting and killing of Iranian citizens by Turkish border patrol officers from a helicopter, the question of the exact location of the Iranians at the time of their death was irrelevant:

> The Court considers that it is not required to determine the exact location of the impugned events, given that the [Turkish] Government has already admitted that the fire discharged from the helicopters had caused the killing of the applicants' relatives.[37]

Furthermore, under US domestic law, while the US Constitution does not apply in Mexico it has been declared possible to indict an agent of the US Border Patrol on charges of murder for shooting and killing a Mexican boy across the international border.[38] The decision of the Arizona district court is on appeal, however, and whether US law would extend to protecting suspected pirates is more debatable.[39]

[37] European Court of Human Rights (ECtHR), *Mansur Pad and Others* v. *Turkey*, Decision as to Admissibility (Third Section), 28 June 2007, §54.

[38] J. Burnett, 'In a First, Border Agent Indicted for Killing Mexican Teen Across Fence', *NPR*, Updated 9 October 2015, at: www.npr.org/2015/10/09/446866267/in-a-first-border-agent-indicted-for-killing-mexican-teen-across-fence; R. O'Dell, 'Border Agent's Trial in Shooting Death of Mexican Teen Delayed, US Has at least 2 Videos of Incident', *The Republic*, 6 November 2015, at: www.azcentral.com/story/news/politics/immigration/2015/11/06/border-patrol-agent-murder-trial-delayed/75254244/; American Civil Liberties Union (ACLU), 'Rodriguez v. Swartz', Updated 9 July 2015, at: www.aclu.org/cases/rodriguez-v-swartz. See also the decision in the civil suit in US District Court for the District of Arizona, *Araceli Rodriguez* v. *Lonnie Swartz*, Order (Case No. 4:14-CV-02251-RCC), 9 July 2015, at: www.npr.org/documents/2015/oct/RodriguezSwartz.pdf. This decision is the subject of an appeal. In February 2016, the US Department of Justice filed an *amicus* brief objecting to the district court's finding and arguing that the Fourth Amendment 'does not extend extraterritorially to aliens without significant voluntary connections to the United States'. US Court of Appeals (Ninth Circuit), *Araceli Rodriguez* v. *Lonnie Swartz* (Case No. 15–16410), Amicus Curiae Brief of the United States in Support of Reversal, 29 February 2016, at: http://15ycf92lfvue3pm0as2w6tec-wpengine.netdna-ssl.com/wp-content/uploads/2016/05/US-amicus-brief.pdf.

[39] In *Araceli Rodriguez* v. *Lonnie Swartz*, the Arizona District Court paid particular attention to the activities of the victim of the shooting: 'J.A.'s status was that of a civilian foreign national engaged in a peaceful activity in another country, but within the U.S.'s small-arms power to seize.' The Court found that 'while J.A.'s nationality weighs against granting him protection pursuant to the Fourth Amendment ["The right of the people to be secure in their persons, houses, papers, and effects, against unreasonable searches and seizures"], his status as a civilian engaged in peaceful activity weighs in favour of granting him protection despite the fact that J.A. was in the territory of another country when he was seized'. This would suggest that an individual mistaken for a pirate could be protected under the US constitution but that a suspected or convicted pirate would

The Right to Freedom from Torture

There is less room for doubt as to the extraterritorial application of the 1984 Convention against Torture (CAT). According to Article 2(1), 'Each State Party shall take effective legislative, administrative, judicial or other measures to prevent acts of torture in any territory under its jurisdiction.' But Article 5(1)(a) also requires each state party to establish jurisdiction over torture '[w]hen the offences are committed in any territory under its jurisdiction or on board a ship or aircraft registered in that State'.[40] In 2014, the Committee against Torture, which oversees the application and implementation of CAT, welcomed the United States' 'unequivocal commitment to abide by the universal prohibition of torture and ill-treatment everywhere'.[41] The Committee noted the United States' review of its position concerning CAT's extraterritorial application, and its acceptance that the Convention applies to 'all places that the State party controls as a governmental authority', noting that it currently exercises such control 'with respect to U.S.-registered ships and aircraft'.[42]

In 2014, the Committee against Torture was asked to give its views on a complaint by the family of a Senegalese asylum seeker, Lauding Sonko, who along with three other swimmers was intercepted by a Spanish Civil Guard vessel and brought on board alive. He was returned to the water, in circumstances that are disputed, and upon reaching the shore, Mr. Sonko was manifestly extremely unwell. Despite efforts to revive him, he died.[43]

The government reported to the Committee[44] that in September 2007, a court in Ceuta had opened an inquiry to ascertain the facts. The very same day, the judge decided to dismiss the proceedings and close the case because the events in question did not occur on Spanish territory and the acts in question were not defined as offences in the Criminal Code. In January 2008, the Office of the Attorney General requested that the

not. A further obstacle to overcome is the jurisprudential requirement for 'substantial voluntary connections' to the United States. Ibid., pp. 13, 16.

40 See, e.g., C. Hall, 'The Duty of States Parties to the Convention against Torture to Provide Procedures Permitting Victims to Recover Reparations for Torture Committed Abroad', *European Journal of International Law*, Vol. 18, No. 5 (2007), pp. 921–37, at: http://ejil.oxfordjournals.org/content/18/5/921.full.

41 Committee against Torture, Concluding observations on the third to fifth periodic reports of the United States, UN doc. CAT/C/USA/CO/3–5, 19 December 2014, §10.

42 Ibid.

43 Committee against Torture, *Sonko* v. *Spain*, Decision (Comm. No. 368/2008), UN doc. CAT/C/47/D/368/2008, 20 February 2012, esp. §§2.1, 2.2, 2.5, 3.2, 3.3, 4.3, 10.2, at: http://daccess-dds-ny.un.org/doc/UNDOC/GEN/G12/408/69/PDF/G1240869.pdf?OpenElement.

44 See ibid., §6.3.

Ceuta court reopen the case in light of information that the events in question had taken place on board a vessel flying the Spanish flag, which would render the Spanish courts competent to hear the case. The Attorney General found that the preliminary inquiry had uncovered signs that a criminal offence had been committed, since Mr. Sonko's death occurred while he was in the custody of the Civil Guard, which meant that the Civil Guard officers were responsible for protecting his life and ensuring his safety. The case was subsequently dismissed.[45]

Spain argued that an unfortunate accident had occurred, that the events took place in Moroccan waters, that the persons picked up by the vessel were left in an area very close to the shore, that the Civil Guard officers did not puncture the dinghies of Mr. Sonko and his companions (as alleged by the complainant), and that Mr. Sonko was assisted by the Civil Guard officers, who used resuscitation techniques on him.[46]

The Committee recalled that, under CAT,

> the prohibition of ill-treatment is absolute and that its prevention is an effective and non-derogable measure.[47] The Committee considers that it falls to the State party to explain the circumstances surrounding Mr. Sonko's death, considering that he was alive when he was pulled out of the water. The Committee further considers that, regardless of whether or not the Civil Guard officers punctured Mr. Sonko's dinghy or at what distance from the shore he was expelled from the boat, he was placed in a situation that caused his death. As for the legal classification of the way in which Mr. Sonko was treated on 26 September 2007, the Committee considers that while the subjection of Mr. Sonko to physical and mental suffering prior to his death, aggravated by his particular vulnerability as a migrant, does not constitute a violation of article 1 of the Convention [the prohibition of torture], it does exceed the threshold of cruel, inhuman or degrading treatment or punishment, under the terms of article 16 of the Convention.[48]

Applying Law of Law Enforcement Rules to Use of Force against Suspected Pirates and Pirate Vessels

In determining the legality of any use of force against suspected pirates, a distinction should be made between, on the one hand, counterpiracy operations by states, including those forming part of the work of

[45] Ibid., §9.2. [46] Ibid., §6.4.

[47] Committee against Torture, General Comment No. 2 on Implementation of Article 2, UN doc. A/63/44, Annex VI, §16.

[48] Ibid., §10.4.

intergovernmental organisations (e.g. EU NAVFOR's Operation Atalanta)[49] and NATO's Operation Ocean Shield),[50] and, on the other, purely protective contingents for commercial shipping, such as vessel protection detachments (VPDs)[51] and private security personnel, whether on board or on separate vessels sailing alongside.

This distinction is important because typically only counterpiracy operations by states may exercise full law enforcement powers, including to arrest and detain suspected pirates. These powers, which cannot be contracted out to the private sector, allow states to pursue suspects in a manner that would, in all likelihood, be unlawful for other actors. Only state law enforcement officials who are engaged in such pursuit in accordance with the international law of the sea are entitled to use necessary and proportionate force in their efforts to repress piracy.

Use of Force by Government Vessels and Law Enforcement Officials

UNCLOS, which repeats Article 19 of the 1958 High Seas Convention, requires states parties to cooperate in suppressing piracy on the high seas and in any other place outside the jurisdiction of any state to the 'fullest possible extent'.[52] As an exception to the general principle that a flagged ship is entitled to enjoy the 'freedom of the high seas',[53] a warship or military aircraft or other duly marked government vessel (but only a

[49] EU NAVFOR launched its counterpiracy operation entitled Operation Atalanta off the coast of Somalia on 8 December 2008. Under EU Council Joint Action 851, Operation Atalanta: protects vessels of the World Food Programme (WFP), the African Union Mission in Somalia (AMISOM), and other vulnerable shipping; deters and disrupts piracy and armed robbery at sea; monitors fishing activities off the coast of Somalia; and supports other EU missions and international organisations working to strengthen maritime security and capacity in the region. On 21 November 2014, the EU Council extended the mandate of Operation Atalanta until December 2016. Information at: www.mschoa.org/on-shore/about-us/eu-operation-atalanta.

[50] According to NATO, its role is to provide naval escorts and deterrence, while increasing cooperation with other counterpiracy operations in the area in order to optimise efforts and tackle the evolving pirate trends and tactics. In June 2014, the North Atlantic Council extended Operation Ocean Shield until the end of 2016. Information at: www.mc.nato.int/ops/Pages/OOS.aspx.

[51] See A. Priddy and S. Casey-Maslen, *Counterpiracy under International Law*, Academy Briefing No. 1, Geneva Academy of International Humanitarian Law and Human Rights, Geneva, August 2012, p. 17.

[52] Art. 100, UNCLOS.

[53] According to Art. 87 of UNCLOS, 'The High Seas are Open to all States, Whether Coastal or Land-Locked.'

government vessel) is authorised to board and seize a pirate ship[54] or any ship taken over by pirates, and to arrest persons on board.[55] Thus, according to Article 105 of UNCLOS,

> On the high seas, or in any other place outside the jurisdiction of any State, every State may seize a pirate ship or aircraft, or a ship or aircraft taken by piracy and under the control of pirates, and arrest the persons and seize the property on board. The courts of the State which carried out the seizure may decide upon the penalties to be imposed, and may also determine the action to be taken with regard to the ships, aircraft or property, subject to the rights of third parties acting in good faith.

Any use of force by states on the high seas will only be lawful if it is in accordance with authority granted under the international law of the sea, is explicitly authorised under Chapter VII of the 1945 UN Charter, or is a lawful act of individual self-defence against an attack by pirates (or is conducted for the defence of others).[56] If a seizure of a ship or aircraft on suspicion of piracy has been effected without adequate grounds, the state making the seizure is liable to the flag state for any loss or damage caused by the seizure.[57]

Although UNCLOS does not expressly authorise the use of force, it is accepted that the authority Article 105 gives states to seize pirate vessels and arrest suspected pirates must include a derived authority to use force when necessary and reasonable, because otherwise the power of seizure would be largely ineffective.[58] In implicitly endorsing this position, the International Tribunal for the Law of the Sea (ITLOS), which oversees the application and implementation of UNCLOS, examined how much force may lawfully be used by states when they conduct law enforcement operations under the law of the sea. In the *M/V Saiga (No. 2)* case (*Saint Vincent and the Grenadines* v. *Guinea*), it stated:

> Although the Convention [UNCLOS] does not contain express provisions on the use of force in the arrest of ships, international law, which is

[54] Under Art. 103 of UNCLOS, a pirate ship or aircraft is one that the persons who are in control of it intend to use for the purpose of committing acts referred to in Art. 101 of the Convention, or have already used to commit such acts, for so long as the vessel or aircraft remains under the control of the pirates.

[55] Arts. 105 and 107, UNCLOS.

[56] See Priddy and Casey-Maslen, *Counterpiracy under International Law*, pp. 24*ff.*

[57] Art. 106, UNCLOS.

[58] T. Treves, 'Piracy, Law of the Sea, and Use of Force: Developments off the Coast of Somalia', *European Journal of International Law*, Vol. 20, No. 2 (2009), p. 412; and D. Guilfoyle, 'The Laws of War and the Fight against Somali Piracy: Combats or Criminals?', *Melbourne Journal of International Law*, Vol. 11, No. 1 (2010), p. 10.

> applicable by virtue of article 293 of the Convention,[59] requires that the use of force must be avoided as far as possible and, where force is unavoidable, it must not go beyond what is reasonable and necessary in the circumstances. Considerations of humanity must apply in the law of the sea, as they do in other areas of international law.[60]

As discussed in Chapter 3, central to the international law of law enforcement (LOLE) are the general principles of necessity and proportionality. First, when it is necessary to use force (which implies that the decision must be objectively reasonable based on the duty of precaution), the force actually used must be no more than the minimum necessary in the circumstances (the principle of necessity). Second, that force must be proportionate to the threat (the principle of proportionality). ITLOS asserted that the principles it enunciated on use of force in the *Saiga* case – necessity and reasonableness[61] – have been followed 'over the years in law enforcement operations at sea'.[62] Similarly, the 2005 Protocol to the 1988 Suppression of Unlawful Acts at Sea Convention lays down rules on use of force when attempting to seize a vessel for law enforcement purposes that reflect LOLE principles. Although directly applicable only to situations in which one state party to the Protocol boards a vessel flagged to another, its standards are potentially of broader relevance. The Protocol states:

> [T]he use of force shall be avoided except when necessary to ensure the safety of its [government] officials and persons on board, or where the officials are obstructed in the execution of the authorized actions. Any use of force pursuant to this article shall not exceed the minimum degree of force which is necessary and reasonable in the circumstances.[63]

[59] According to Art. 293(1) of UNCLOS, 'A court or tribunal having jurisdiction under this section shall apply this Convention and other rules of international law not incompatible with this Convention.'

[60] International Tribunal for the Law of the Sea (ITLOS), *M/V 'Saiga' (No. 2)* case (*Saint Vincent and the Grenadines* v. *Guinea*), Judgment, 1 July 1999, §155. Although ITLOS made this point with regard to a case where piracy was not the reason why force was used to seize and arrest the crew of a ship, its findings are considered to articulate customary international law on use of force on the high seas. The Permanent Court of Arbitration (PCA) also 'accepts the argument that in international law force may be used in law enforcement activities provided that such force is unavoidable, reasonable and necessary'. PCA, *Guyana*, Award of 17 September 2007, §445.

[61] Reasonableness should here be equated with proportionality.

[62] ITLOS, *M/V 'Saiga' (No. 2)* case, Judgment, §156.

[63] Art. 8bis(9), 1988 Convention for the Suppression of Unlawful Acts Against the Safety of Maritime Navigation, as amended by the 2005 Protocol.

In the *Saiga* case, ITLOS recalled that the 'basic principle concerning the use of force in the arrest of a ship at sea has been reaffirmed' in the 1982 Agreement for the Implementation of UNCLOS on Straddling and Highly Migratory Fish Stocks.[64] Article 22(1)(f) of the Agreement stipulates that the inspecting state must ensure that its 'duly authorized inspectors ... avoid the use of force except when and to the degree necessary to ensure the safety of the inspectors and where the inspectors are obstructed in the execution of their duties. The degree of force used shall not exceed that reasonably required in the circumstances'.[65] ITLOS noted that the *Saiga*

> was almost fully laden and was low in the water at the time it was approached by the patrol vessel. Its maximum speed was 10 knots. Therefore it could be boarded without much difficulty by the Guinean officers. At one stage in the proceedings Guinea sought to justify the use of gunfire with the claim that the Saiga had attempted to sink the patrol boat. During the hearing, the allegation was modified to the effect that the danger of sinking to the patrol boat was from the wake of the Saiga and not the result of a deliberate attempt by the ship. But whatever the circumstances, there is no excuse for the fact that the officers fired at the ship itself with live ammunition from a fast-moving patrol boat without issuing any of the signals and warnings required by international law and practice.[66]

ITLOS further held that Guinean officers had used excessive force once on board the *Saiga*:

> Having boarded the ship without resistance, and although there is no evidence of the use or threat of force from the crew, they fired indiscriminately while on the deck and used gunfire to stop the engine of the ship. In using firearms in this way, the Guinean officers appeared to have attached little or no importance to the safety of the ship and the persons on board. In the process, considerable damage was done to the ship and to vital equipment in the engine and radio rooms. And, more seriously, the indiscriminate use of gunfire caused severe injuries to two of the persons on board.[67]

This case was easy to judge, at least from a LOLE perspective, based on the apparent absence of any necessity for use of force, let alone for firearms. But more difficult scenarios may occur in the maritime

[64] Agreement for the Implementation of the Provisions of the United Nations Convention on the Law of the Sea of 10 December 1982 Relating to the Conservation and Management of Straddling Fish Stocks and Highly Migratory Fish Stocks.

[65] ITLOS, *M/V 'Saiga' (No. 2)* case, Judgment, §156. [66] Ibid., §157. [67] Ibid, §158.

environment, especially with respect to the legality of the use of firearms. Consonant with the duty to respect and protect life, and international law enforcement standards, force short of firearms should be privileged whenever it is necessary to use force.

ITLOS affirmed that normal practice to stop a ship at sea 'is first to give an auditory or visual signal to stop, using internationally recognized signals. Where this does not succeed, a variety of actions may be taken, including the firing of shots across the bows of the ship'.[68] Only if such actions failed may a pursuing vessel 'as a last resort' use force. But even then, appropriate warning must be issued to the ship to be targeted with force and all efforts made to ensure that life is not endangered.[69]

Some states have detailed legislation setting out the actions to be taken when force is used on the high seas. France, for example, has a 1995 decree governing 'recourse to coercion and use of force at sea'.[70] The decree specifies that warning shots comprise a single shot followed by three shots across the bow. This sequence is preceded by warnings to the ship to stop or reroute that are transmitted by any visual, radio, or acoustic means.[71] In the event the Master of the target vessel fails to comply with the challenges, which may be followed by warning shots, live firing may be ordered. The use of force may lead to taking control of the other vessel. A report is to be made immediately to the Prime Minister, the Minister responsible for the resources and staff used, and other relevant ministers.[72]

In the event the warning shots and, if conducted, live firing, have no effect, the Prime Minister may be requested to authorise live firing against the vessel. This authorisation is given after reasonable efforts have been made to obtain the views of the Minister for Foreign Affairs. Live firing is preceded by renewed challenges. This is reported in the ship's logbook. In no case may it be directed against individuals. Explosive projectiles may not

[68] In the case of hot pursuit (from the internal waters, the archipelagic waters, the territorial sea, or the contiguous zone of the pursuing state), Art. 111(4) of UNCLOS requires that the pursuit 'may only be commenced after a visual or auditory signal to stop has been given at a distance which enables it to be seen or heard by the foreign ship'.

[69] ITLOS, *M/V 'Saiga' (No. 2)* case, Judgment, §156.

[70] Decree No. 95-411 of 19 April 1995 governing recourse to coercion and use of force at sea, at: www.legifrance.gouv.fr/affichTexte.do?cidTexte=JORFTEXT000000187811&categorieLien=cid. See also Law No. 94-589 of 15 July 1994 governing the exercise by the state of its enforcement powers at sea. Unofficial translations.

[71] Art. 2, Decree No. 95-411. Article 2 was modified by Decree No. 2005-1514 of 6 December 2005.

[72] Art. 3, Decree No. 95-411.

be used. A report is made in the same manner as above.[73] The provisions of the decree are without prejudice to the exercise of self-defence.[74]

Use of Force by Vessel Protection Detachments or Private Security Personnel

When force is being used by VPDs or private security personnel, that force should be both necessary and proportionate. Force may only be used in self-defence or in defence of others. As Gian Maria Farnelli explains, the fact that VPDs may be composed of state military or law enforcement personnel does not confer on them additional powers to use force beyond this:

> international law does not seem to recognise an active counter-piracy role on the part of VPDs, namely interception measures, or the power to carry out police enforcement operations against piracy suspects.[75]

Nonetheless, as he notes, VPDs may retain a counterpiracy role with regard to the detention of pirates captured during self-defence operations.[76]

It is expected that all merchant vessels have appropriate active and passive security measures to deter and impede unauthorised boarding. If they do not, the risk of unlawful use of force may be heightened. Thus, the IMO's 2011 *Best Management Practices for Protection against Somalia Based Piracy*[77] call for the following preventive measures to be taken:

- Increased vigilance (lookouts) when entering a high-risk area[78]
- Reinforced protection on the bridge, which is often the focus of pirate attacks[79]
- Proper securing of doors and hatches providing access to the bridge, accommodation, and machinery spaces[80]
- Physical barriers (e.g. razor wire) to make it as difficult as possible to gain access to vessels by increasing the height and difficulty of any climb for an attacking pirate[81]

[73] Art. 4, Decree No. 95-411. [74] Art. 5, Decree No. 95-411.

[75] G. M. Farnelli, 'Vessel Protection Detachments and Maritime Security: An Evaluation of Four Years of Italian Practice', *Maritime Safety and Security Journal*, No. 1, 2015, p. 27.

[76] Ibid., citing N. Ronzitti, 'The Use of Private Contractors in the Fight against Piracy: Policy Options', in F. Francioni and N. Ronzitti (eds.), *War by Contract. Human Rights, Humanitarian Law and Private Contractors*, Oxford University Press, 2011.

[77] IMO, *BMP4: Best Management Practices for Protection against Somalia Based Piracy*, Version 4 (August 2011), at: www.imo.org/en/MediaCentre/HotTopics/piracy/Documents/1339.pdf.

[78] Ibid., §8.2. [79] Ibid., §8.3. [80] Ibid., §8.4. [81] Ibid., §8.5.

- Water cannon and foam[82]
- Alarms (to inform the crew that a piracy attack has commenced and to demonstrate to a potential attacker that the ship is aware of the attack and is reacting to it)[83]
- Safe muster points[84] or a citadel[85]
- Unarmed or armed private maritime security contractors.[86]

A failure to install at least basic security measures and to take reasonable precautions to prevent piratical acts being successful could bring into question the necessity for use of force under international human rights law, especially where potentially lethal force is concerned. There is a duty of precaution under the right to life to minimise the risk of recourse to firearms and other potentially lethal weapons, as discussed in Chapter 3.

Use of Firearms

Under Principle 9 of the 1990 Basic Principles on the Use of Force and Firearms by Law Enforcement Officials,[87] the default position for use of firearms is that use must be necessary and must be 'in self-defence or defence of others against the imminent threat of death or serious injury'. Thus, under 1990 Basic Principle 9, it is not lawful to use a firearm purely to protect property. A threat to the integrity of the hull of a ship, though,

[82] Ibid., §8.6. [83] Ibid., §8.7.

[84] A Safe Muster Point is a designated area chosen to provide maximum physical protection to the crew, preferably low down within the vessel. Ibid., §8.13.

[85] A citadel is a designated pre-planned area purpose built into the ship where, in the event of imminent boarding by pirates, all crew will seek protection. As the BMP note, '**The establishing of a Citadel may be beyond the capability of ship's staff alone, and may well require external technical advice and support.**' Ibid. [original emphasis].

[86] Ibid., §§8.14, 8.15. In 2013, an article suggested a range of weapons that could be used for counterpiracy. Raunek, '18 Anti-Piracy Weapons for Ships to Fight Pirates', *Marine Insight*, 18 January 2013, at: www.marineinsight.com/marine-piracy-marine/18-anti-piracy-weapons-for-ships-to-fight-pirates/. The article suggests that this could include Molotov cocktails, which it claimed had already been used by the crew of several merchant ships that had not been provided with anti-piracy weapons or armed guards. 'Molotov cocktail [*sic*] can be made on ships using empty glass bottles, flammable substance such as gasoline, and source of ignition such as burning cloth wick. It can be thrown on an approaching pirate boat to set it ablaze and disturb their manoeuvrability.' See also B. Farmer, 'Repelling Pirate Attacks: The Measures to Protect a Ship', *Daily Telegraph*, 10 February 2014, at: www.telegraph.co.uk/sponsored/culture/captain-phillips-film/10367534/security-against-pirate-attacks.html.

[87] Adopted by the Eighth UN Congress on the Prevention of Crime and the Treatment of Offenders in Havana, 27 August to 7 September 1990, and welcomed by UN General Assembly Resolution 45/121 of 18 December 1990.

is clearly a threat to the safety of the ship and all its crew and passengers. This means that a threat from a rocket-propelled grenade would potentially allow use of firearms at a distance of up to a kilometre or more.

The position under international law is generally reflected in the US Coast Guard and the Department of Homeland Security's joint 'Guidance on Self-defence and Defence of Others by U.S. Flagged Commercial Vessels Operating in High Risk Waters'.[88] The Guidance is provided to all personnel on board US-flagged vessels, including contracted security personnel, and sets out the current US rules for defence against piracy. Use of lethal force is permitted in self-defence or to defend others where there is reason to believe that there is imminent danger of death or great bodily harm. Non-deadly use of force is permitted in self-defence or defence of others as well as in defence of the vessel and its cargo from theft or damage. With regard to protection of property, force may only be used to defend the vessel and its cargo when authorised by the vessel's master.

In any event, as Principle 9 further stipulates, intentional lethal use of firearms may only be made when strictly unavoidable in order to protect life. This would apply, for example, where pirates had taken a hostage, that hostage's life was in imminent danger, and no other means would be effective to prevent the hostage being executed. An instance of intentional lethal use of firearms occurred in the denouement of the *Maersk Alabama* hijacking, an incident dramatised in the Hollywood film, *Captain Phillips.* Commander Frank Castellano, the captain of the USS Bainbridge, authorised the shooting after determining that Phillips' life was in immediate danger, on the basis that a pirate was pointing an AK-47 assault rifle at him.[89] It is questionable, though, whether the initial description of events given to the media was what in fact transpired.[90]

The decision to use force is, in any event, an individual one. The United Kingdom (UK) Department for Transport released interim

[88] US Coast Guard and the Department of Homeland Security, 'Guidance on Self-Defense or Defense of Others by U.S. Flagged Commercial Vessels Operating in High Risk Waters', Port Security Advisory (3-09), 18 June 2009, at: www.marad.dot.gov/wp-content/uploads/pdf/Port_Security_Advisory_3-09_Self_Defense.pdf.

[89] See, e.g., D. Gardner, '"Flawless": U.S. Navy Snipers Killed Three Somali Pirates with Just Three Shots... in the Dark, from the Deck of a Rolling Ship', *Daily Mail Online*, 14 April 2009, at: www.dailymail.co.uk/news/article-1169712/Flawless-How-U-S-Navy-snipers-killed-Somali-pirates-just-shots–dark-deck-rolling-ship.html#ixzz3ykZYQrqj.

[90] See: Associated Press, 'The SEALs Rescue Depicted in "Captain Phillips" Wasn't So Tidy in Real Life', 11 October 2013, available at: www.moviefone.com/2013/10/11/seals-rescue-captain-phillips/.

guidance in 2011 to help clarify the use of force by private security company personnel. It advised that:

> The decision to use force must lie with the person using force . . . Neither the Master nor the security team leader can command a member of the security team against that person's own judgement to use force or to not use force.[91]

The Need for Greater Clarity on Use of Force in Counterpiracy Operations

Despite the existence of valuable guidance on use of force in counterpiracy operations, it is widely agreed that greater clarity and detail is warranted. In May 2012, the IMO's Maritime Security Committee issued Interim Guidance for privately contracted armed security personnel. It stated that private maritime security companies should ensure that its personnel 'have a complete understanding of, and fully comply with, the applicable laws governing the use of force'. In particular, it should ensure that personnel understand that:

- they should act according to applicable laws 'in the knowledge that their role in regard to the above is exclusively for the protection of life of persons on board and the ship from armed pirate attacks'
- 'all reasonable steps should be taken to avoid the use of force and, if force is used, that force should be used as part of a graduated response plan, in particular including the strict implementation of the latest version of BMP' [IMO's Best Management Practices]
- 'the use of force should not exceed what is strictly necessary and reasonable in the circumstances and that care should be taken to minimize damage and injury and to respect and preserve human life'

[91] Department for Transport, *Interim Guidance to UK Flagged Shipping on the Use of Armed Guards to Defend Against the Threat of Piracy in Exceptional Circumstances*, United Kingdom, November 2011 (last updated December 2015), §5.6, at: www.gov.uk/government/uploads/system/uploads/attachment_data/file/480863/use-of-armed-guards-to-defend-against-piracy.pdf. The latest text differs from the original 2011 version, which stated as follows: 'Lethal force can generally only be used in the context of self-defence or defence of others. The decision to use lethal force must lie with the person using force where they believe there to be a risk to human life. Neither the Master nor the security team leader can command a member of the security team against that person's own judgement to use lethal force or to not use lethal force.'

- Private security personnel should only use firearms against persons in self-defence or in defence of others.[92]

The lack of detailed guidance on the lawful use of force in warding off piratical attacks was, though, criticised by the United Kingdom's House of Commons' Foreign Affairs Committee in 2012:

> Guidance over the use of potentially lethal force should not be left to private companies to agree upon. We recommend that the change of policy be accompanied by clear, detailed and unambiguous guidance on the legal use of force for private armed guards defending a vessel under attack. This guidance should be consistent with the rules that would govern the use of force by members of the UK armed forces in similar circumstances, and should include:
>
> - the circumstances in which private armed security guards faced with a clear threat of violence may respond with force, including lethal force, where proportionate and necessary, and
> - examples of a 'graduated response' to an attack, including confirmation that nothing in UK law or the CPS [Crown Prosecution Service] guidance requires a victim of pirate attack to await an aggressor's first blow before acting in self-defence.[93]

The Committee's chairman, Richard Ottaway, illustrated these concerns:

> There is a question to which everyone needs an answer, however. If a skiff is approaching a ship at high speed carrying pirates with rifles or rocket-propelled grenade launchers, can the armed guards on board the ship open fire?[94]

In 2012, based on general principles of criminal law – despite differences between national legal systems – as well as applicable human rights law and good shipping industry practice, a Briefing Paper published by the Geneva Academy of International Humanitarian Law and Human Rights (Geneva Academy) suggested the following guidelines on use of force by

[92] IMO, *Interim Guidance to Private Maritime Security Companies Providing Privately Contracted Armed Security Personnel on Board Ships in the High Risk Area*, MSC.1/Circ.1443, 25 May 2012, §5.15.

[93] House of Commons Foreign Affairs Committee, *Piracy off the Coast of Somalia: Tenth Report of Session 2010–12*, HC 1318 2010–12, 5 January 2012, §37, at: www.publications.parliament.uk/pa/cm201012/cmselect/cmfaff/1318/1318.pdf.

[94] House of Commons Hansard Debates, 9 February 2012, col. 525, at: www.publications.parliament.uk/pa/cm201212/cmhansrd/cm120209/debtext/120209-0002.htm.

vessel crews and private security personnel confronting a suspected piratical attack.[95]

> When a suspected pirate vessel (SPV) is spotted coming towards the ship, an auditory or visual signal should be given to the SPV to stop or change course away from the ship, using internationally recognized signals. Flares may be employed. An acoustic warning may also be given, for example using the Long Range Acoustic Device (LRAD).[96] A ship's master should be fully informed of these actions, and wherever possible should be the person to authorize them.
>
> Sounding the ship's alarms/whistle serves to inform the ship's crew that the ship is under attack from pirates and, importantly, demonstrates to any potential attacker that the ship is aware of the attack and is reacting to it. In addition to the emergency alarms and announcements for the benefit of the vessel's crew the ship's whistle/foghorn should be sounded continuously to demonstrate to any potential attacker that the ship is aware of the attack and is reacting to it. (The piracy alarm must be distinctive in order to avoid confusion with other alarms, potentially leading to the crew mustering at the wrong location.)
>
> Should the SPV continue on a course towards the ship, attempts should be made to shake off the SPV, for example by increasing the ship's speed and directing a course away from the SPV. Should these attempts fail, a variety of actions may be taken, such as firing tracer rounds as warning shots across the bows of the oncoming SPV.[97] These should be aimed no closer than 50 metres and no further than 100 metres from the SPV when the SPV is at a distance of about one kilometre from the

[95] Priddy and Casey-Maslen, *Counterpiracy under International Law*, p. 22. The guidelines also drew on a piece by K. C. Doherty, the President of Nexus Consulting Group entitled 'Nexus Consulting Analysis on Use of Force Video', dated 9 May 2012, at: https://maritimerisk.files.wordpress.com/2012/05/nexus-consulting-analysis-on-use-of-force-video.pdf.

[96] The LRAD can be used to deter pirates by issuing a warning or as a weapon, by producing an intolerable level of sound. LRADs have been credited with successfully repelling a number of piracy attacks, including one against the cruise liner *Spirit of Adventure* in 2011. Priddy, 'The Use of Weapons in Counterpiracy Operations', citing LRAD Corporation, 'Anti-Piracy', at: www.lradx.com/site/content/view/286/110; and 'Protecting Yourself Before, During and After a Pirate Attack', *gCaptain*, 28 March 2012, at: http://gcaptain.com/2012/03/28/protecting-before-during-pirate/. See also www.lradx.com/video/cnn-lrad-thwarts-pirates-in-cruise-liner-attack/.

[97] A warning shot 'means a signal to a vessel to stop. The term does not include shots fired as a signal that the use of deadly force is imminent, a technique that should not be employed'. US Coast Guard and the Department of Homeland Security, Guidance on Self-Defense or Defense of Others by U.S. Flagged Commercial Vessels Operating In High Risk Waters', Port Security Advisory (3-09), 18 June 2009, §2(i), p. 2.

> ship.[98] A distress signal and report of piratical attack should already have been made by now.
>
> It is only after these actions fail that the ship may, as a last resort, use force against the SPV or its personnel. The primary function of the PMSC [private maritime security company] security team must be to prevent illegal boarding of the ship and to protect the lives of those on board, using the minimum force necessary to do so. By now, the crew should be safely locked into the ship's citadel. Wherever possible, "less-lethal" weapons and tactics should first be employed, such as the use of acoustic weapons or dazzling lasers or, at closer range, water hoses.[99]
>
> If these actions are unsuccessful, firing into the SPV's engine block or hull may be considered. It is suggested that this should be countenanced when an SPV is some 500 metres away from the ship[100] (and only if it is still on a course towards the ship). If all the above efforts have failed to stop the SPV and its intent remains clearly hostile, the use of firearms may now be countenanced. Intentional lethal force may only be used in self-defence or defence of others on board the ship and where such force is strictly unavoidable in order to protect life. Offensive use of firearms or a rocket-propelled grenade (RPG) launcher within the weapon's operating range[101] by persons on the SPV, against the ship or its crew, may thus give rise to the right to use such lethal force. The decision to use firearms must rest with the person using force and must only be taken where he or she believes there is an imminent risk to human life. Only armed individuals with clearly hostile intent may be targeted. Firearms with optical enhancements (not only iron sights) should be used.[102]

Possession of Firearms

Finally, there is also a legal issue under domestic law with respect to possession of firearms. As soon as a vessel enters the territorial waters of a state it will fall within its jurisdiction. The thirty-five crew and guards (from Estonia, India, Ukraine, and the United Kingdom) of the *Seaman Guard Ohio*, a floating armoury, were given five-year prison sentences in

[98] Ibid., p. 12.

[99] According to BMP 4, 'Improved water coverage may be achieved by using fire hoses in jet mode but by using baffle plates fixed a short distance in front of the nozzle . . . Hot water, or using a diffuser nozzle to produce steam to deter pirates has also been found to be very effective in deterring attacks.'

[100] Ibid., p. 13.

[101] According to Doherty, an RPG has almost 100 per cent accuracy from 300 metres and closer. Ibid., p. 18.

[102] Ibid., p. 27.

south India on illegal weapons charges. They were first arrested by Indian coastguard officials in 2013 in contested circumstances. India has tightened up on arms carriage, especially since the terrorist attack on Mumbai by ten Pakistan-based Lashker-e-Taiba terrorists, who came by sea from Karachi to carry out the attacks in November 2008. In addition, illegal arms are reportedly used in more than 85 per cent of reported serious crimes in India.[103]

Protection and Rescue

Duty to Rescue Suspected Pirates

International law imposes a general obligation on the master of a vessel to rescue[104] any person (including a suspected pirate) who is in danger of being lost at sea.[105] This applies whether or not force has been used. At the same time, the master holds ultimate responsibility for the safety of his vessel and its crew. Thus, the duty to rescue those in danger is not absolute but qualified by the condition that providing assistance will not pose a serious danger to the vessel, or its crew and passengers. According to Article 98(1) of UNCLOS, for example, every state is obliged to require the master of a ship flying its flag, insofar as (s)he can do so 'without serious danger to the ship, the crew or the passengers' to 'render assistance to any person found at sea in danger of being lost' and 'to proceed with all possible speed to the rescue of persons in distress, if informed of their need of assistance', at least insofar as this 'may reasonably be expected' of the master.

Thus, according to the Geneva Academy's Briefing, *Counterpiracy under International Law*, if a pirate is in a sinking skiff but continues

[103] G. Shettar, 'Why Seaman Guard Ohio Case Touches an Indian Nerve', *IHS Fairplay*, 14 March 2016, at: http://fairplay.ihs.com/safety-regulation/why-seaman-guard-ohio-case-touches-an-indian-nerve_20160314.html?utm_source=email&utm_medium=newsletter&utm_campaign=dailynewswire&mgs1=ff06mqTQnT.

[104] The 1979 International Convention on Search and Rescue defines rescue as 'an operation to retrieve persons in distress, provide for their initial medical treatment or other needs, and deliver them to a place of safety'. Ch. 1, §1.3.2. There is an obligation to ensure that assistance is provided 'to any person in distress at sea' and this obligation is to assist 'regardless of the nationality or status of such a person or the circumstances in which the person is found'. Ch. 2, 2.1.10.

[105] The obligation of ship masters to rescue individuals in danger at sea stems from five international treaties: the 1958 High Seas Convention, UNCLOS, the 1974 International Convention for the Safety of Life at Sea (SOLAS), the 1979 International Convention on Maritime Search and Rescue, and the 1989 International Convention on Salvage.

to shoot at the crew of a ship that attempts to rescue him, the ship is not obliged to rescue that individual. However, if the pirate begins to drown and falls unconscious, and therefore ceases to pose a danger, the master has a duty to rescue him.[106] The Academy Briefing notes that flag states may adopt domestic laws deepening the international law obligation. It cites Canada's national legislation, which makes it a criminal offence for a master not to render assistance to a distress call, unless this would pose a danger to the master's vessel.[107]

The rescue of individuals, including suspected pirates, may bring them under the jurisdiction of a state for the purpose of human rights protection. In the *Hirsi Jamaa* case before the European Court of Human Rights, Italy, the respondent state, had argued that the obligation to save human lives on the high seas, as required under UNCLOS, did not in itself create a link between Italy and the applicants.[108] As regards the applicants' 'rescue', which lasted no more than ten hours in total, Italy stated that the authorities had provided the necessary humanitarian and medical assistance and had not used violence, had not boarded the boats, and had not used weapons.[109]

In contrast, the applicants submitted 'that there was no question, in the instant case, but that Italy had jurisdiction. As soon as they had boarded the Italian ships, they had been under the exclusive control of Italy, which had therefore been bound to fulfil all the obligations arising out of the Convention'.[110] In addition, 'third-party interveners' who provided *amicus curiae* briefs to the Court 'stressed the importance of avoiding double standards in the field of safeguarding human rights and ensuring that a State was not authorised to commit acts outside its territory which would never be accepted within that territory'.[111]

In its judgment in 2012, the European Court's Grand Chamber observed that, 'by virtue of the relevant provisions of the law of the sea, a vessel sailing on the high seas is subject to the exclusive jurisdiction of the State of the flag it is flying. This principle of international law has led the Court to recognise, in cases concerning acts carried out on board vessels flying a State's flag, in the same way as registered aircraft, cases of extraterritorial exercise of the jurisdiction of that State . . . Where there is control over another, this is *de jure* control exercised by the State in

[106] Priddy and Casey-Maslen, *Counterpiracy under International Law*, pp. 37–38.
[107] Art. 131(1), read with Art. 137(1)(a), Canada Shipping Act 2001.
[108] ECtHR, *Hirsi Jamaa and Others* v. *Italy*, Judgment (Grand Chamber), 23 February 2012, §65.
[109] Ibid., §66. [110] Ibid., §67. [111] Ibid., §69.

question over the individuals concerned'.[112] The Court concluded that the case did indeed amount to extraterritorial exercise of jurisdiction by Italy.[113] It further held that Italy could not

> circumvent its 'jurisdiction' under the Convention by describing the events in issue as rescue operations on the high seas. In particular, the Court cannot subscribe to the Government's argument that Italy was not responsible for the fate of the applicants on account of the allegedly minimal control exercised by the authorities over the parties concerned at the material time.[114]

Detention of Suspected Pirates

Once captured, a suspected pirate may be detained in order to take him to the state territory of the seizing vessel, or deliver him to another state (with that state's approval), for prosecution. The European Court of Human Rights has noted that the difference between deprivation and restriction of liberty is 'merely one of degree or intensity, and not one of nature or substance'.[115] Deprivation of liberty includes arrest and detention, as well as other forms of detention such as house arrest.[116] The arbitrary deprivation of liberty is prohibited by numerous international human rights treaties.[117]

The grounds for depriving a person of his or her liberty must be both established by law and in conformity with law. With regard to the principle of legality, the Human Rights Committee has stated that 'it is violated if an individual is arrested or detained on grounds which are not clearly established in domestic legislation'.[118]

In 2010, in its judgment in the *Medvedyev* case the European Court of Human Rights laid down a two-stage test that must be satisfied before a detention at sea is compliant with Article 5(1) of the ECHR. First, a state's domestic law must clearly authorise detention, to ensure that the detention is lawful. A state party to the ECHR that wishes to detain

[112] Ibid., §77. [113] Ibid., §78. [114] Ibid., §79.

[115] See ECtHR, *Guzzardi* v. *Italy*, Judgment, 6 November 1980, §93.

[116] See, e.g., Human Rights Committee, *Mandani* v. *Algeria*, Views (Comm. No. 1172/2003), 2007.

[117] See, e.g., Art. 9, ICCPR; Art. 5, ECHR; Art. 6, 1981 African Charter on Human and Peoples' Rights; Art. 7, 1969 American Convention on Human Rights; and Art. 14, 2004 Arab Charter of Human Rights.

[118] Human Rights Committee, *McLawrence* v. *Jamaica*, Views (Comm. No. 702/1996), 1997, §5.5.

suspected pirates must have legislative authority to do so. Second, there needs to be express textual authority in public international law that authorises the boarding of vessels at sea and detaining persons on board and subsequently prosecuting them. Article 105 of UNCLOS would satisfy the second limb of this test.[119]

In the *Medvedyev* case, the applicants had alleged that they had been arbitrarily deprived of their liberty following the boarding of their ship by the French authorities and complained that they had not been brought 'promptly' before a judge or other officer authorised by law to exercise judicial power.[120] The applicants were crew members of a cargo vessel registered in Cambodia. As the French authorities suspected the vessel was carrying significant quantities of narcotics for distribution in Europe, the French Navy apprehended it off the shores of Cape Verde and confined the crew to their quarters on board under French military guard.[121]

The Court held that France had exercised full and exclusive control over the Cambodian vessel and its crew, at least de facto, from the time of its interception, in a continuous and uninterrupted manner. Besides the interception of the vessel, its rerouting had been ordered by the French authorities, and the crew had remained under the control of the French military throughout the voyage to Brest in France. Accordingly, the applicants had been effectively within France's jurisdiction.[122]

The case involved a French warship, the frigate *Lieutenant de vaisseau Le Hénaff*, which was specially instructed by the French naval authorities to intercept the *Winner*, had on board a Special Forces team specialised in boarding vessels at sea. 'When the *Winner* was spotted off Cape Verde on 13 June 2002, the frigate issued several warnings and fired warning shots, before firing directly at the merchant ship, under orders from France's maritime prefect for the Atlantic.'[123] After the French Special Forces team boarded the *Winner*, they were 'obliged to use their weapons to defend themselves, and subsequently kept the crew members under their exclusive guard and confined them to their cabins during the journey to France, where they arrived on 26 June 2002'.[124]

[119] Priddy and Casey-Maslen, *Counterpiracy under International Law*, p. 34; see ECtHR, *Medvedyev and Others* v. *France*, Judgment (Grand Chamber), 29 March 2010, *esp.* §§79–80.

[120] ECtHR, *Medvedyev and Others* v. *France*, Judgment (Grand Chamber), 29 March 2010, §3.

[121] ECtHR, 'Extra-Territorial Jurisdiction of States Parties to the European Convention on Human Rights', July 2015, p. 10.

[122] Ibid. [123] ECtHR, *Medvedyev and Others* v. *France*, §66. [124] Ibid.

The French government had argued that since the applicants' movements prior to the boarding of the *Winner* were already confined to the physical boundaries of the ship, so that there was a *de facto* restriction on their freedom to come and go, the measures taken after the ship was boarded merely placed a further restriction on their freedom of movement.[125] The Court rejected the argument, noting that the crew members were placed under the control of the French Special Forces and confined to their cabins during the voyage.[126] This, it determined, 'because of the restrictions endured, amounted in practice to a deprivation of liberty', and the Court thus held that Article 5(1) of the ECHR did apply.[127]

The Duty to Treat Humanely and with Dignity

In any event, states are generally required to treat detainees under their jurisdiction humanely and with dignity, as discussed in detail in Chapter 7. Article 10(1) of the ICCPR provides that 'All persons deprived of their liberty shall be treated with humanity and with respect for the inherent dignity of the human person.' This language is reproduced verbatim in the 2004 Arab Charter of Human Rights.[128] The 1969 American Convention on Human Rights (ACHR) uses very similar language but does not include the reference to humanity.[129]

Sir Nigel Rodley noted that the 'juridical status of this principle is more difficult to assess than is the prohibition of torture and other ill-treatment'. He noted that derogation under the ICCPR appears possible whereas with respect to the rule in the ACHR it is not.[130] However, based on customary and conventional law of armed conflict and on the views of the Human Rights Committee he concluded that the principle set out in Article 10 of the ICCPR enunciates a rule of general international law.[131] According to the Human Rights Committee's General Comment on states of emergency,

> All persons deprived of their liberty shall be treated with humanity and with respect for the inherent dignity of the human person. Although this right, prescribed in article 10 of the Covenant, is not separately mentioned in the list of non-derogable rights in article 4, paragraph 2, the Committee believes that here the Covenant expresses a norm of general international

[125] See ibid., §74. [126] Ibid. [127] Ibid., §75. [128] Art. 20(1). [129] Art. 5.

[130] N. Rodley with M. Pollard, *The Treatment of Prisoners under International Law*, 3rd Edn, Oxford University Press, Oxford, 2011, pp. 380–81.

[131] Ibid., pp. 381–82.

> law not subject to derogation. This is supported by the reference to the inherent dignity of the human person in the preamble to the Covenant and by the close connection between articles 7 [the prohibition of torture and inhumane treatment] and 10.[132]

The Standard Minimum Rules for the Treatment of Prisoners were first adopted in 1955, and in 2015 were revised and adopted by the UN General Assembly as the Nelson Mandela Rules.[133] According to Rule 1,

> All prisoners shall be treated with the respect due to their inherent dignity and value as human beings. No prisoner shall be subjected to, and all prisoners shall be protected from, torture and other cruel, inhuman or degrading treatment or punishment, for which no circumstances whatsoever may be invoked as a justification. The safety and security of prisoners, staff, service providers and visitors shall be ensured at all times.[134]

While on board a vessel, suspected pirates may not be able to benefit from full application of all the Nelson Mandela Rules (which are primarily intended for penal institutions), but many of the principles set out in the 2015 Rules are nonetheless relevant. Notably, this includes by analogy those detailed to guard suspected pirate detainees. Thus, Rule 82(1) stipulates that:

> Prison staff shall not, in their relations with the prisoners, use force except in self-defence or in cases of attempted escape, or active or passive physical resistance to an order based on law or regulations. Prison staff who have recourse to force must use no more than is strictly necessary and must report the incident immediately to the prison director.

The Master of the vessel may serve as the prison director in this analogy.

Consonant with the Rules,[135] each detainee must have clean bathroom facilities in the interests of dignity and hygiene. Access to water, toilet items, adequate clothing, and bedding must also be provided.[136] Prisoners must be provided with nutritious food of wholesome quality and also

132 Human Rights Committee, General Comment No. 29: States of Emergency (article 4), 2001, §13(a), at: http://tbinternet.ohchr.org/_layouts/treatybodyexternal/Download.aspx?symbolno=CCPR%2fC%2f21%2fRev.1%2fAdd.11&Lang=en.

133 The revised Standard Minimum Rules were adopted unanimously by the UN General Assembly in Resolution 70/175 on 17 December 2015.

134 Rule 1, 2015 Nelson Mandela Rules.

135 See Penal Reform International, *The Revised United Nations Standard Minimum Rules for the Treatment of Prisoners (Nelson Mandela Rules): Short Guide*, January 2016, at: www.penalreform.org/wp-content/uploads/2016/01/PRI_Nelson_Mandela_Rules_Short_Guide_WEB.pdf.

136 Rules 15, 16, 18–21, 2015 Nelson Mandela Rules.

drinking water whenever they need it. Food and water cannot be restricted as a disciplinary sanction and must be provided without exception.[137]

Given its 'devastating effect on physical and mental health', the Rules stipulate that solitary confinement should only be used in exceptional cases, as a last resort, for as short a time as possible, after authorisation by a competent authority, and subject to independent review. Indefinite and prolonged solitary confinement (of more than fifteen days) is prohibited entirely.[138] Instruments of restraint that are inherently degrading or painful are prohibited. The use of any other instrument is subject to strict conditions: their use is only legitimate if no lesser form of controlling an actual risk is available and they must be removed as soon as possible.[139]

Duty to Protect Crew and Passengers of Vessels

Last but not least, there is a duty on states under the rights to life and humane treatment to protect persons under its jurisdiction. A legal duty to ensure a safe environment for work applies to shipping companies. In June 2012, two seafarers sued two companies, Heidmar and Marida Tankers, for failing to place armed guards on a ship that fell into pirate hands. In the autumn of 2010, Somali pirates commandeered the *MT Marida*, in the Gulf of Aden, off the coast of Yemen. The *MT Marida* was a German-owned and operated vessel, flagged in the Marshall Islands, and staffed by Indian crew members. The vessel was sailing from India to Belgium at the time of its capture and remained under the control of Somali pirates for eight months. The pirates tortured the crew in hopes of receiving ransom monies. The plaintiffs, Chirag and Sandeep, were two of the Indian crew members that were held hostage aboard the *MT Marida*.

The two assistant engineers from the *Marida Marguerite* filed their complaint in the United States, arguing that taking the ship through pirate-infested waters violated 1920 Jones Act rules.[140] Under the Act,

[137] Rules 22, 35, 42, and 43, 2015 Nelson Mandela Rules.

[138] Rules 43–46, 2015 Nelson Mandela Rules. The Rules define solitary confinement as confinement for more than 22 hours per day without meaningful human contact. Interpretation of 'meaningful human contact' should recognise the suffering that any person will experience if isolated from and deprived of contact with other human beings.

[139] Rules 43, 47–49, 2015 Nelson Mandela Rules.

[140] See Merchant Marine Act of 1920, Title 46 of the US Code; and especially Section 33 of the Jones Act, Recovery for Injury to or Death of Seaman (46 App. US Code 688 (2002)).

which governs the relationship between employer and crew on US-flagged vessels, an employee has a right to a 'safe place to work'. Employers are liable for 'any injury' arising in whole or in part from the negligence of any of their officers, agents, or employees, or from any defect or insufficiency of equipment attributable to their negligence. The employee must prove negligence. The act that is negligent is not required to be the sole proximate cause of an injury.[141]

According to court documents, Bahri Chirag and Dangwal Sandeep claimed the vessel was unseaworthy because it lacked 'adequate security, including but not limited to, weapons and non-lethal methods of resisting intruders'. They suggested the vessel did not have an adequate security system, the crew did not have an adequate security plan, and the owners did not complete negotiations with the pirates in a timely manner. With their colleagues, Chirag and Sandeep were held for eight months.[142]

In *Chirag* v. *MT Marida Marguerite*, the US Court of Appeals for the Second Circuit (covering Connecticut, New York, and Vermont) affirmed the Connecticut District Court's dismissal of the case on the grounds of *forum non conveniens* and for lack of personal jurisdiction over the primary defendants.[143] First, the Second Circuit held that the District Court had not abused its discretion in denying jurisdictional discovery, as the plaintiffs had not established a *prima facie* case for jurisdiction over the *MT Marida* and held that there was no American interest in the case. The Second Circuit also held there was 'no plausible allegation that the *MT Marida* had sufficient continuous and systematic contacts with Connecticut that invoked the protections and benefits of Connecticut's laws' and therefore the District Court did not err in dismissing the complaint against *MT Marida*.[144] The Second Circuit further concluded that the plaintiff's choice of forum should receive less deference because the plaintiffs were nationals and residents of India and noted that an adequate and alternative forum existed in Germany.

[141] Maritime Law Center, 'The Jones Act', undated, at: www.maritimelawcenter.com/html/the_jones_act.html.

[142] 'Arms Suit Hits Heidmar', *Tradewinds*, 21 June 2012, at: www.tradewindsnews.com/piracy/278663/arms-suit-hits-heidmar.

[143] US Court of Appeals (for the Second Circuit), *Chirag* v. *MT Marida Marguerite*, Summary Order, 11 March 2015.

[144] Chalos, 'No Jurisdiction for Foreign Seafarers to Pursue Negligence Claims Resulting from Foreign Pirate Attack', undated but accessed on 28 January 2016 at: www.chaloslaw.com/no-jurisdiction-for-foreign-seafarers.html.

Moreover, documents, exhibits, and witnesses were all located in foreign countries and there were no public factors in favour of maintaining the case in the United States.[145]

Seemingly more successful lawsuits were initiated in the aftermath of the resolution of the hijacking of the *Maersk Alabama*, which was dramatised in the Hollywood film, *Captain Phillips*. The suit was brought by nine of the crew members aboard the *Alabama* that was attacked by pirates on 9 April 2009.[146] The crew were not permitted to have weapons on board (a common safety regulation among merchant vessels worldwide), and the ship lacked any defensive technology or hardware to protect them from pirates. The journey was on the basis of a contract secured by Maersk Lines to deliver humanitarian aid and cargo to Kenya. The crew, which was contracted by Waterman Steamship, was American (ensuring the link with the United States as jurisdiction for the subsequent lawsuit).

According to the attorneys for the plaintiffs, Captain Phillips, after discussing the route with Maersk, had decided that traveling outside the 600 nautical mile safety zone would take too much time and be too expensive. He decided instead to take the ship within 250 nautical miles of the coast in an area where thirty-nine pirate attacks had occurred the previous week. Captain Phillips did not conduct any pirate attack safety drills. The attack on the *Maersk Alabama* was the first time an American ship had been hijacked by pirates since 1821.[147]

In response to the lawsuits against them,[148] Maersk Lines and Waterman Steamship argued that the ship was maintained to industry standards. In 2009, the industry standards in place were 'essentially to keep the doors locked, to keep a lookout for pirates, and to have a safe room'.[149] Maersk denied claims about the ship's proximity to the coast, asserting that the Somali pirates were criminals who were responsible for any harm to the crew members. In December 2013, it was reported that Mobile County Circuit Judge Michael A. Youngpeter had postponed the case

[145] Ibid.

[146] The description of facts is based on the online report by the attorney for the plaintiffs. See B. Beckcom, 'Maersk Settles Lawsuit Brought by Victims of Somali Piracy', VB Attorneys, undated but accessed on 30 January 2016 at: www.vbattorneys.com/case_results/maersk-settles-lawsuit-brought-by-victims-of-somali-piracy.cfm.

[147] Ibid.

[148] Case No. 02-CV-2012–900747-90, filed in Circuit Court of Mobile County, Alabama; and Case No. 2009–64336, filed in 164th Harris County District Court, Texas.

[149] Beckcom, 'Maersk Settles Lawsuit Brought by Victims of Somali Piracy'.

because attorneys for crew members of the *Maersk Alabama* were entering mediation talks with lawyers for the shipping companies.[150] A confidential settlement was subsequently reached in the case against Maersk.[151]

[150] 'Trial Delayed in Ala. Lawsuit over Pirate Drama off Somalia Portrayed in "Captain Phillips"', *Star Tribune*, 3 December 2013, at: http://hiiraan.com/news4/2013/Dec/52326/trial_delayed_in_ala_lawsuit_over_pirate_drama_off_somalia_portrayed_in_captain_phillips.aspx.

[151] Beckcom, 'Maersk Settles Lawsuit Brought by Victims of Somali Piracy'.

11

Accountability

'Law enforcement officials worldwide play an important role in protecting society from violence, enforcing justice, and securing the rights of people . . . They often do so under difficult and dangerous circumstances, and in some cases they cannot fulfil their functions without resorting to force . . . The extensive powers vested in the police are easily abused in any society, and it is in everyone's interests for it to be the subject of constant vigilance. To function properly, the police need proper guidelines on the use of force and appropriate mechanisms for accountability to be in place.'

Christof Heyns, United Nations Special Rapporteur on extrajudicial, summary or arbitrary executions[1]

Introduction

The fear of the power of the police, whether actual or potential, explains and suffuses the history of law enforcement, as Chapter 1 illustrated. In the absence of effective accountability, the core principles governing use of force by law enforcement officials – necessity and proportionality, and the principle of precaution that underpins them– are effectively dead letter.

To see what can happen to policing where accountability is lacking, one only has to look at policing in Brazil. At least 2,212 people were killed by the police in Brazil in 2013, according to the Brazilian Public Security Forum, an independent research group, though the true number is likely to be much higher because some states do not report killings by their police forces.[2] Indeed, Amnesty International documented 8,466 cases of registered police

[1] 'Report of the Special Rapporteur on Extrajudicial, Summary or Arbitrary Executions, Christof Heyns', UN doc. A/HRC/26/36, 1 April 2014, pp. 4–5.

[2] S. Romero and T. Barnes, 'Despair, and Grim Acceptance, Over Killings by Brazil's Police', *New York Times*, 21 May 2015, at: www.nytimes.com/2015/05/22/world/americas/police-killings-brazil-rio.html?_r=0.

killings in the state of Rio de Janeiro alone between 2005 and 2014. Of this total, 5,132 (60 per cent) occurred in the city of Rio de Janeiro itself: these amounted to nearly 1 in 6 of all homicides in 2014.[3]

The victims of police shootings in Brazil are generally recorded as having been 'killed while resisting arrest'. In this, while Brazil is an egregious example of policing out of control, it is not unique. One officer involved in an infamous case in 2014 was recorded as having been involved in 57 separate incidents leading to 62 deaths that were recorded as *autos de resistência* (resisting arrest), said to be 'the phrase used in Rio for homicide by police in the line of duty'.[4] This officer was one of three who were involved in a shootout with suspected members of a drug gang in which a 38-year-old mother of four, Cláudia da Silva Ferreira, was caught in the crossfire. The officers dumped her into the boot of their police car, allegedly to take her to hospital, but her body fell out and she was dragged for 300 metres behind the car before they stopped and put her back in. The incident, which was filmed by a bystander, caused outrage across Brazil, a country otherwise seemingly resigned to police brutality, and even elicited comment from the Brazilian President.[5]

In January 2013, in an extraordinary step, the state security secretary covering São Paulo introduced a new policy that sought to protect life: he prohibited police officers from providing first aid at the scene of shootings.[6] Ostensibly a violation of international law, the intent of the policy was to prevent such 'first aid' being used by police officers to cover up a murder they had committed by interfering with the scene, or even to commit murder on the way to the hospital, where the police would routinely hand over a dead body and lie about the circumstances. In the following months, the rate at which the state's police killed in the line of duty fell by two-fifths.[7]

[3] See Amnesty International (AI), *You Killed My Son: Homicides by Military Police in the City of Rio de Janeiro*, 2015; see also M. Lohmuller, 'Amnesty International Criticizes Brazil Police Violence', *Insight Crime*, 4 August 2015, at: www.insightcrime.org/news-briefs/amnesty-international-criticizes-brazil-police-violence.

[4] H. J., 'Police Violence in Brazil: Serial Killing', *Economist*, 20 March 2014, at: www.economist.com/blogs/americasview/2014/03/police-violence-brazil.

[5] See ibid.; BBC, 'Police Car Death Shocks Brazil, Says President Rousseff', 18 March 2014, at: www.bbc.com/news/world-latin-america-26638995; and M. L. Canineu, 'False Police Rescues and the Case of Cláudia da Silva Ferreira', *Folha de São Paulo*, 22 March 2014, at: www.hrw.org/news/2014/03/22/false-police-rescues-and-case-claudia-da-silva-ferreira.

[6] L. Jordan, 'SP Police Banned from First Aid', *Rio Times*, 10 January 2013, at: http://riotimesonline.com/brazil-news/rio-politics/sp-police-banned-from-first-aid-victims/#.

[7] H. J., 'Police Violence in Brazil: Serial Killing'.

The reduction in police killings was not sustained, however. In January 2016, data released by São Paulo's State Secretariat of Public Security revealed that 532 deaths were caused by 'police intervention' in the state between January and November 2015. What is more, it appears that the figures do not include deaths caused by off-duty military police officers or cases involving intentional killings by officers.[8] One explanation offered for the increase in lethal police action was a brutal training regime of recruits to the military police. A study of an unnamed state reported in the BBC found that recruits were subjected to sleep deprivation and regular beatings, given tasks in rooms filled with tear gas and pepper spray, and the victims of ritualised humiliation and bullying by superiors.[9]

In October 2015, an article by a journalist and assistant professor of anthropology at the College of Staten Island argued, despondently, that there seemed to be no hope of changing the Brazilian police force:

> Contrary to many other countries, public safety is a responsibility of each state in Brazil. There is no coordinated effort between the federal and state government to train and control the police ... Meanwhile, the police continue to hold extraordinary discretionary power — far beyond anything one would consider outrageous. Even more troublesome is that wrongdoings by officers are investigated by the police itself in a predictable corporativist culture that almost always results in no formal charges.[10]

Perhaps he was too gloomy in his assessment. At the beginning of December 2015, four military police officers in Rio de Janeiro were arrested following allegations that they killed five black and mixed-race youths from a favela and then doctored the crime scene to make it appear like self-defence. The five victims aged 16 to 25, from Morro da Lagartixa, were said to be out celebrating a first pay-cheque when the police peppered their car with bullets. Márcia Ferreira told local reporters that her son Wilton Domingos Jr was still alive when she arrived at the scene, but police refused to take him to a nearby hospital emergency unit and then threatened her and her daughter with a rifle when they tried to

8 Insight Crime, 'Tracking São Paulo Police Killings in 2015', 7 January 2016, at: www.insightcrime.org/news-briefs/tracking-sao-paulo-police-killings-in-2015.

9 Thiago Guimarães, '"Rituais de sofrimento" em treinamento alimentam violência policial, diz capitão da PM', BBC Brazil, 5 January 2016, at: www.bbc.com/portuguese/noticias/2016/01/151231_treinamento_policia_tg.

10 J. A. Alves, 'Police Terror in Brazil', *Open Democracy*, 10 October 2015, at: www.opendemocracy.net/jaime-alves/police-terror-in-brazil.

approach. Locals claimed police tried to make the killing look like self-defence by placing a gun inside the car.[11]

Investigators charged three officers with homicide and a fourth was arrested for fabricating evidence. Their commander, Lieutenant-Colonel Marcos Netto, was also dismissed. It was the second recent controversy surrounding his unit following a shooting in November of two men on a motorbike by a police sergeant who mistook their hydraulic jack for a rifle. Rio security authorities said the punishments were the result of stricter discipline to try to stem the violence.[12]

This final chapter looks at ways and means to hold the police to account for their actions, but without making individual officers feel persecuted or even just undervalued. Accountability for use and misuse of force by police and other law enforcement officials can be seen to operate at three levels: the individual (both the officer using force and his or her superiors in the hierarchy), the police force (or company providing law enforcement functions), and of course the state, which is responsible for the actions of its agents. Good policing rests on accountability, but the line between responsibility and scapegoating can be a fine one to draw. And as with any profession, competitive pay and conditions, scenario-based training, and the prospect of career development based on merit are essential to attract and sustain the brightest and the best. This gold standard for police services is rarely met in practice.

The Human Rights Framework

The Duty to Investigate

A critical element in the protection of both the right to life and the right to humane treatment (specifically the right to freedom from torture and other cruel or degrading treatment) is the duty to investigate alleged or suspected violations. International law requires that investigations be effective and thorough, independent, and prompt, and that they evidence a certain level of transparency.[13]

[11] J. Watts, 'Rio de Janeiro Police Officers Arrested for Killings of Black and Mixed-Race Youths', *The Guardian*, 1 December 2015, at: www.theguardian.com/world/2015/dec/01/rio-de-janeiro-military-police-killings-youths?CMP=Share_iOSApp_Other.

[12] Ibid.

[13] See Human Rights Committee, General Comment No. 31: 'Nature of the General Legal Obligation on States Parties to the Covenant', UN doc. CCPR/C/21/Rev.1/Add.13, 2004, §15; Report of the UN Fact-Finding Mission on the Gaza Conflict, UN doc. A/HRC/12/

The Human Rights Committee, which oversees implementation of the 1966 International Covenant on Civil and Political Rights (ICCPR), has asserted that although certain rights under the Covenant may be subject to derogation, 'the duty to take all feasible measures to investigate, prosecute, punish and remedy violations of the right to life, must not be diminished by measures of derogation'.[14] According to the African Commission on Human and Peoples' Rights, 'States must take steps both to prevent arbitrary deprivations of life and to conduct prompt, impartial, thorough and transparent investigations into any such deprivations that may have occurred, holding those responsible to account and providing for an effective remedy and reparation for the victim or victims.'[15] For, as the Grand Chamber of the European Court of Human Rights observed in its 1995 judgment in the *McCann* case, 'a general legal prohibition of arbitrary killing by the agents of the State would be ineffective, in practice, if there existed no procedure for reviewing the lawfulness of the use of lethal force by State authorities'.[16]

In 1998, in the *Aksoy* case, a Chamber of the European Court stated that: 'Given the fundamental importance of the prohibition of torture ... and the especially vulnerable position of torture victims', the right to an effective remedy under Article 13 of the 1950 European Convention on Human Rights (ECHR) 'imposes, without prejudice to any other remedy available under the domestic system, an obligation on States to carry out a thorough and effective investigation of incidents of

48, 25 September 2009, §1814; see also 1990 Basic Principles on the Use of Force and Firearms by Law Enforcement Officials, Principles 22 and 23; IACtHR, *Gómez Palomino* v. *Peru*, §79ff; *Landaeta Mejías Brothers and Others* v. *Venezuela*; African Commission on Human and Peoples' Rights, *Amnesty International and Others* v. *Sudan*, 15 November 1999, §51.l; African Commission on Human and Peoples' Rights, General Comment No. 3 on the Right to Life, November 2015, §7; International Convention on the Prevention of Enforced Disappearance, Art. 12(1). With respect to transparency, see, e.g., N. Rodley with M. Pollard, *The Treatment of Prisoners under International Law*, 3rd Edn, Oxford University Press, Oxford, 2011, p.149, citing, inter alia, the judgment by the European Court of Human Rights (ECtHR) in *Maslova and Nalbandov* v. *Russia*, Judgment (First Section), 24 January 2008.

[14] Human Rights Committee, 'Draft General Comment No. 36 (Article 6: Right to Life), Draft prepared by Yuval Shany and Nigel Rodley, Rapporteurs, UN doc. CCPR/C/GC/R.36/Rev.2', 7 September 2015, §64.

[15] ACHPR, General Comment No. 3 on the African Charter on Human and Peoples' Rights: The Right to Life (Article 4), adopted during the 57th Ordinary Session of the ACHPR, held on 4–18 November 2015 in Banjul, The Gambia, §7.

[16] ECtHR, *McCann and Others* v. UK, Judgment (Grand Chamber), 27 September 1995, §161.

torture'.[17] In the specific context of detention facilities, allegations of torture or inhumane treatment or punishment of prisoners must be dealt with 'immediately' and 'must result in a prompt and impartial investigation conducted by an independent national authority'.[18]

An Effective Investigation

To fulfil the 'procedural' aspect of the right to life, an investigation must first and foremost be effective. According to the European Court, the obligation to protect the right to life, read in conjunction with the state's general duty to secure to everyone within its jurisdiction the rights and freedoms set out in the ECHR, 'requires by implication that there should be some form of effective official investigation when individuals have been killed as a result of the use of force by, inter alios, agents of the State'.[19] Similarly, with respect to alleged inhumane treatment, the Human Rights Committee has affirmed that '[c]omplaints about ill-treatment must be investigated effectively by competent authorities'.[20]

To be effective means that an investigation into an alleged violation of the right to life must evidence due diligence of effort[21] to identify the immediate and broader causes of the loss of life; determine whether that loss of life was unlawful; and, if so, ascertain where responsibility lies. In its draft General Comment on the right to life of September 2015, the Human Rights Committee affirmed that: 'Investigations and prosecutions of alleged deprivations of life should be aimed at ensuring that those responsible are brought to justice, at promoting accountability and preventing impunity, at avoiding denial of justice and at drawing

[17] ECtHR, *Aksoy* v. *Turkey*, Judgment (Chamber), 18 December 1996, §98. More recently, the Court has tended to base the duty to investigate alleged torture under the prohibition in the ECHR (Article 3) read in conjunction with the State's general duty under Article 1 of the Convention to 'secure to everyone within their jurisdiction the rights and freedoms defined in ... [the] Convention'. See, e.g., ECtHR, *Labita* v. *Italy*, Judgment (Grand Chamber), 6 April 2000, §131. This reading 'requires by implication that there should be an effective official investigation'.

[18] Rule 57(3), UN Standard Minimum Rules for the Treatment of Prisoners, adopted by General Assembly Resolution 70/175 on 17 December 2015 (hereafter, 2015 Nelson Mandela Rules).

[19] ECtHR, *McCann and Others* v. *UK*, Judgment (Grand Chamber), 27 September 1995, §161.

[20] Human Rights Committee, 'General Comment No. 7: Article 7 (Prohibition of Torture or Cruel, Inhuman or Degrading Treatment or Punishment)', Sixteenth session (1982), §1.

[21] See, e.g., S. Joseph and M. Castan, *International Covenant on Civil and Political Rights: Cases, Materials, and Commentary*, 3rd Edn, Oxford University Press, Oxford, 2014, §25.11 and also §§8.16ff and 9.16ff.

necessary lessons for revising practices and policies with a view to avoiding repeated violations.'[22]

The Human Rights Committee also stresses that an effective investigation is one that explores 'the legal responsibility of superior officials for violations of the right to life committed by their subordinates'.[23] Similarly, in this regard, as the UN Committee against Torture has observed with respect to the corresponding duty to investigate under the 1984 Convention against Torture: 'It is essential to investigate and establish the responsibility of persons in the chain of command as well as that of the direct perpetrator(s).'[24] Thus, an investigation that scapegoats low-ranking officials or throws a rank-and-file law enforcement official to the wolves is not an effective investigation under international human rights law.

At the same time, the duty to investigate applies to all suspicious deaths or alleged ill-treatment, whether or not the direct involvement of the state is either suspected or alleged. Thus, as the African Commission has noted, states 'must hold to account private individuals and corporations, including private military and security companies, that are responsible for causing or contributing to arbitrary deprivations of life in the State's territory or jurisdiction'.[25] Likewise, with respect to inhumane treatment, the Committee against Torture 'has made clear that where State authorities or others acting in official capacity or under colour of law, know or have reasonable grounds to believe that acts of torture or ill-treatment are being committed by non-State officials or private actors and they fail to exercise due diligence to prevent, investigate, prosecute and punish such non-State officials or private actors consistently with the Convention, the State bears responsibility . . .'[26]

An Independent Investigation

To be effective, an investigation should normally be independent (and perceived as such). History is replete with examples of where internal investigations have covered up the truth rather than elucidating it. The

[22] Human Rights Committee, Draft General Comment No. 36 (Article 6: Right to Life), §29.

[23] Ibid.

[24] Committee against Torture, 'General Comment No. 2: Implementation of Article 2 by States Parties', UN doc. CAT/C/GC/2, 24 January 2008, §11.

[25] ACHPR, General Comment No. 3 on the African Charter on Human and Peoples' Rights: The Right to Life (Article 4), §18.

[26] Committee against Torture, 'General Comment No. 2: Implementation of Article 2 by States Parties', §18.

Human Rights Committee has referred to a 'general obligation to investigate allegations of violations promptly, thoroughly and effectively through independent and impartial bodies'.[27] A particular obligation for independent investigation exists in relation to deaths in custody. According to the 2015 Nelson Mandela Rules,

> Notwithstanding the initiation of an internal investigation, the prison director shall report, without delay, any custodial death, disappearance or serious injury to a judicial or other competent authority that is independent of the prison administration and mandated to conduct prompt, impartial and effective investigations into the circumstances and causes of such cases. The prison administration shall fully cooperate with that authority and ensure that all evidence is preserved.[28]

A Prompt Investigation

An unreasonably delayed investigation calls into question whether the state is exercising the requisite due diligence for an effective investigation. A failure to open an investigation when allegations or suspicions of foul play exist and therefore to secure relevant evidence may taint the investigation and even make it impossible to identify the causes and any culprit(s).

On 18 April 2002, the author of a subsequent complaint to the Human Rights Committee, Mr Sundara Arachchige Lalith Rajapakse, a 19-year-old Sri Lankan citizen, was arrested by police officers at a friend's house. He alleged that he was beaten and dragged into a jeep outside the house, before being taken to a police station where he was formally detained and charged with two counts of robbery. During his detention he was tortured for the purpose of obtaining a confession, which caused serious injuries: he was forced to lie on a bench and beaten with a pole; held under water for prolonged periods; beaten on the soles of his feet with blunt instruments; and had books placed on his head which were then hit with blunt instruments.[29]

Mr Rajapakse attested that no criminal investigation was initiated for more than three months after the torture, despite the severity of

[27] Human Rights Committee, 'General Comment No. 31: The Nature of the General Legal Obligation Imposed on States Parties to the Covenant', adopted on 29 March 2004, UN doc. CCPR/C/21/Rev.1/Add. 13, 26 May 2004, §15.

[28] Rule 71(1), 2015 Nelson Mandela Rules.

[29] Human Rights Committee, *Rajapakse* v. *Sri Lanka*, Views (Comm. No. 1250/2004), UN doc. CCPR/C/87/D/1250/2004 (2006), §§1, 2.1.

his injuries and the necessity to hospitalise him for over a period of one month; that the alleged perpetrators were neither suspended from their duties nor taken into custody, enabling them to place pressure on and threaten the author; and that, as of submitting his communication to the Human Rights Committee, investigations were at a standstill.[30]

The Committee expressed its views on the complaint in 2006, considering that each state party to the ICCPR 'is under a duty to investigate thoroughly alleged violations of human rights, and to prosecute and punish those held responsible for such violations'.[31] It observed that a criminal investigation was not initiated by Sri Lanka's Attorney General until more than three months after the incident, 'despite the fact that the author had to be hospitalised, was unconscious for 15 days, and had a medical report describing his injuries . . .'[32]

The Committee recalled the obligation on each state party to the ICCPR to ensure that remedies for violations of human rights are effective,[33] asserting that: 'Expedition and effectiveness are particularly important in the adjudication of cases involving torture.'[34] It explicitly rejected Sri Lanka's argument that its High Court had a large workload constituted a legitimate excuse from compliance with its international legal obligations.[35] Since it found a violation of the right to a remedy had occurred, the Committee did not consider it necessary to determine whether the right to freedom from torture had also been infringed.[36]

Although the obligation of promptness implies speed, 'the authorities must always make a serious attempt to find out what happened and should not rely on hasty or ill-founded conclusions to close their investigation or as the basis for their decisions'.[37] A precipitate investigation is also unlikely to be an effective one. Thus, in the *Pomilyayko* case, the European Court found that: 'Overall, it appears that the manner in which the authorities approached the investigation of the applicant's complaints was largely aimed at exonerating the suspected officers, rather than establishing the actual circumstances in which her injuries had been sustained.'[38]

[30] Ibid., §3.5. [31] Ibid., §9.3. [32] Ibid., §9.4. [33] Art. 2(3), ICCPR.
[34] Human Rights Committee, *Rajapakse* v. *Sri Lanka*, Views, §9.5. [35] Ibid., §§9.4, 7.5.
[36] Ibid.
[37] ECtHR, *Pomilyayko* v. *Ukraine*, Judgment (Fifth Section), 11 February 2016, §53.
[38] Ibid., §56.

The Form of the Investigation

Regional courts have tended not to comment on the form that any given investigation should take as long as it respects the principles enunciated above. Thus, in its 1995 decision in the *McCann* case, while the European Court concluded that 'by implication' there should be 'some form of effective official investigation when individuals have been killed as a result of the use of force by, inter alios, agents of the State', it determined that in the case at hand it was not necessary for the Court 'to decide what form such an investigation should take and under what conditions it should be conducted'.[39]

Some detail on the form of investigations, and considerable detail on their process and nature, is provided in the Minnesota Protocol on the Investigation of Potentially Unlawful Deaths (revised in 2016 under the auspices of the UN Special Rapporteur on extrajudicial, summary, or arbitrary executions and the Office of the High Commissioner for Human Rights) and the 1999 Istanbul Protocol on the Investigation of Torture.[40]

The Duty to Prosecute

According to the ACHPR, 'accountability in relation to the right to life requires investigation and, "where appropriate", criminal prosecution'.[41] The Human Rights Committee observes that the obligation to 'prosecute allegations of deprivation of life by State authorities or by private individuals and entities, including allegations of excessive use of lethal force' is an 'important element' of the protection of the right to life under the ICCPR.[42] The aims of prosecution should be to ensure that 'those responsible are brought to justice, at promoting accountability and preventing impunity, at avoiding denial of justice' with a view to 'avoiding repeated violations'.[43]

39 ECtHR, *McCann and Others* v. *UK*, Judgment, §§161–62.

40 *Manual on the Effective Investigation and Documentation of Torture and Other Cruel, Inhuman or Degrading Treatment or Punishment*, available at: www.ohchr.org/Documents/Publications/training8Rev1en.pdf.

41 ACHPR, General Comment No. 3 on the African Charter on Human and Peoples' Rights: The Right to Life (Article 4), §17.

42 Human Rights Committee, Draft General Comment No. 36 (Article 6: Right to Life), §29.

43 Ibid.

The Committee further affirms that:

> Given the importance of the right to life, States parties should refrain from addressing possible violations of article 6 [the right to life in the ICCPR] merely through administrative or disciplinary measures, and a criminal investigation, which should lead if enough incriminating evidence is gathered to a criminal prosecution, is normally required. Immunities and amnesties provided to perpetrators of intentional killings and to their superiors, leading to de facto impunity, are, as a rule, incompatible with the duty to respect and ensure the right to life, and to provide victims with an effective remedy.

In its 1992 General Comment on the prohibition on torture and other inhumane treatment as set out in ICCPR Article 7, the Human Rights Committee has called on states parties to 'indicate when presenting their reports the provisions of their criminal law which penalize torture and cruel, inhuman and degrading treatment or punishment, specifying the penalties applicable to such acts, whether committed by public officials or other persons acting on behalf of the State, or by private persons'.[44] It affirmed that those who violate the prohibition, 'whether by encouraging, ordering, tolerating or perpetrating prohibited acts, must be held responsible'.[45] Clearly, as Sir Nigel Rodley has observed, if torture and other inhumane treatment are criminal, 'the obligation to bring perpetrators of such violations to justice presumably entails criminal prosecution in such cases'.[46]

The case of *Benitez* v. *Paraguay* before the Human Rights Committee concerned a complaint of torture by the author who, after participating in a protest, was beaten with batons, kicked, and stamped on and then shot, probably with a rubber bullet.[47] After being beaten, the complainant and the other detainees were taken to a police station where they were beaten again. The author, who had previously sought to call a radio station to describe what was occurring, was taken separately to a room

> where police officers and military personnel kicked him and beat him with batons on the back, feet, stomach and head while he was handcuffed

44 Human Rights Committee, 'General Comment No. 20: Article 7 (Prohibition of Torture, or Other Cruel, Inhuman or Degrading Treatment or Punishment)', 44th Session (1992), §13. At the same time, the Human Rights Committee stated that those 'who have refused to obey orders must not be punished or subjected to any adverse treatment'. Ibid.

45 Ibid.

46 Rodley and Pollard, *The Treatment of Prisoners under International Law*, p. 151.

47 Human Rights Committee, *Ernesto Benitez Gamarra* v. *Paraguay*, Views (Comm. No. 1829/2008), UN doc. CCPR/C/104/D/1829/2008 (2012), §§2.7, 2.8.

> with his hands behind his back. While beating him, they threatened him, saying that he had been the cause of the problems in the area and that the only solution was for them to kill him. They also sprayed an irritant gas in his face. When they saw he was crying, the police officers made fun of him, painted his face with lipstick and cut locks of his hair which they said they would "take as a trophy to their chief". This treatment went on for several hours and stopped only when journalists who were covering the demonstration arrived at the police station.[48]

Mr Benitez made a complaint of torture in Paraguay but asserted that the complaint was not dealt with promptly and was processed 'slowly and incompetently'. Two officials 'whose possible individual criminal liability was self-evident' were only charged more than a year after the alleged events had occurred. He noted that the Public Prosecution Service did not request the temporary suspension of those officials (or of any others) from their duties as a precautionary measure to prevent them from obstructing the investigation and influencing the course of the public prosecution. Later on, the prosecutor assigned to the case appealed an order dismissing the case two months after the deadline for submitting a challenge.[49]

In giving its views on the case, the Committee recalled its 1992 General Comment (referred to above) as well as its 'settled jurisprudence',[50] according to which complaints alleging a violation of the prohibition on inhumane treatment 'must be investigated promptly, thoroughly and impartially by the competent authorities and appropriate action must be taken against those found guilty'. On the facts of the case, the Committee found that the author did not have access to an effective remedy and that they amounted to a violation of the right to a remedy, read in conjunction with Article 7 of the Covenant.[51]

Policies on Use of Force and the Duty of Precaution

As the UN Special Rapporteur on extrajudicial, summary or arbitrary executions has observed, 'Once a situation arises where the use of force is considered, it is often too late to rescue the situation. Instead, in order to save lives, all possible measures should be taken "upstream" to avoid

48 Ibid., §2.9. 49 Ibid., §3.6.

50 *Sathasivam/Saraswathi* v. *Sri Lanka*, Views (Comm. No. 1436/2005), 8 July 2008, §§6.3 and 6.4; and *MacCallum* v. *South Africa*, Views (Comm. No. 1818/2008), 25 October 2010, §6.7.

51 Human Rights Committee, *Ernesto Benitez Gamarra* v. *Paraguay*, Views, §7.5.

situations where the decision on whether to pull the trigger arises, or to ensure that all the possible steps have been taken to ensure that if that happens, the damage is contained as much as is possible.'[52]

In respecting the duty of precaution, setting clear policies (and making it clear that law enforcement officials will be held accountable for failure to respect them) is a key element in restraining use of force, especially when combined with scenario-based training and skills development for operational planning. Investigations into either specific incidents or a particular law enforcement agency may contribute positively to this process.

'Pattern or Practice' Investigations by the US Department of Justice

An excellent example of such an approach is the work of the US Department of Justice (DOJ)'s Civil Rights Division,[53] which conducts an investigation where a particular police department reveals a pattern or practice of unlawful conduct under the US Constitution and federal statutory law. It then seeks to negotiate a settled, court-enforceable agreement to implement the recommendations of the investigation. The DOJ has investigated more than twenty law enforcement agencies for systemic violations in the last six years.[54]

On 4 March 2015, the DOJ announced the results of its investigation of the Ferguson Police Department (FPD), finding that FPD's police and municipal court practices systematically violate the First, Fourth, and Fourteenth Amendments of the US Constitution.[55] The DOJ determined that the FPD's law enforcement practices both

[52] 'Report of the Special Rapporteur on Extrajudicial, Summary or Arbitrary Executions, Christof Heyns', UN doc. A/HRC/26/36, 1 April 2014, §63.

[53] The DOJ's Civil Rights Division was created in 1957 under the 1957 Civil Rights Act to 'uphold the civil and constitutional rights of all Americans, particularly some of the most vulnerable members of our society. The Division enforces federal statutes prohibiting discrimination on the basis of race, color, sex, disability, religion, familial status and national origin'. See: www.justice.gov/crt/about-division.

[54] 'Justice Department Enters Civil Rights Suit against Ferguson in Strong Position', *Chicago Tribune*, 11 February 2016, at: www.chicagotribune.com/news/nationworld/ct-justice-department-ferguson-case-20160211-story.html.

[55] The First Amendment to the Constitution guarantees the right of citizens to free speech, to assemble peaceably, and to petition the US government. The Fourth Amendment prohibits unreasonable searches and arbitrary arrests. The Fourteenth Amendment protects the right to life.

reflected and exacerbated existing race bias.[56] In particular, the report found that the FPD had engaged in a pattern of excessive force during unreasonable searches and arbitrary arrests. 'Many officers are quick to escalate encounters with subjects they perceive to be disobeying their orders or resisting arrest.' They have come to rely on Tasers® 'where less force — or no force at all — would do. They also release canines on unarmed subjects unreasonably and before attempting to use force less likely to cause injury'.

In addition, FPD records suggested that police officers tended to use unnecessary force against vulnerable groups such as people with mental health issues or cognitive disabilities. 'Ferguson's pattern of using excessive force disproportionately harms African-American members of the community. The overwhelming majority of force — almost 90% — is used against African Americans.'[57] US Attorney General Eric Holder said the Department's investigation revealed racially discriminatory practices that have 'severely undermined the public trust' and used law enforcement 'not as a means for protecting public safety, but as a way to generate revenue'.[58] Following the publication of the report, the FPD Police Chief, Thomas Jackson, resigned. The police force had only three black officers, despite the fact that the city of 21,000 people was predominately black.[59]

Following the publication of the report, the City of Ferguson and the DOJ entered into discussions about an agreement to remedy the situation. At the end of January, the DOJ put forward a plan to the City that it initially accepted. With respect to use of force, the negotiated consent decree required that action be taken to ensure that all FPD officers, including civilian correctional officers, would:

- use force only when necessary to accomplish a legitimate public safety objective
- use de-escalation techniques and tactics to minimise the need to use force

[56] DOJ Civil Rights Division, *Investigation of the Ferguson Police Department*, 4 March 2015, at: www.justice.gov/sites/default/files/crt/legacy/2015/03/04/ferguson_findings_3-4-15.pdf.

[57] Ibid., p. 28.

[58] 'U.S. Justice Department Finds Ferguson Police and Courts Targeted African Americans', Equal Justice Initiative, 9 March 2015, at: www.eji.org/node/1048.

[59] 'Ferguson Police Chief Tom Jackson Quits', BBC, 11 March 2015, at: www.bbc.co.uk/news/world-us-canada-31843626.

- use force in a manner that avoids unnecessary injury or risk of injury to both officers and civilians and is proportional to the level of resistance or threat encountered
- intervene to stop any officer from using unreasonable or unnecessary force
- immediately provide necessary emergency medical assistance after using force and summon additional medical assistance as necessary
- accurately and completely report all reportable force used or observed by officers
- be disciplined when they use unnecessary or objectively unreasonable force.[60]

The FPD would further undertake to specify 'all weapons and force techniques' officers are authorised to use, and which officers must carry while on duty. In addition, FPD policies would 'clearly define and describe each force option and the circumstances under which use of such force is appropriate'. If FPD were to make any additional weapons available to its officers in the future, it would create a policy for the weapon/equipment.[61] The decree also required that the City would equip FPD officers with body-worn and in-car cameras, and would ensure that the devices were used consistent with law and policy.[62]

Despite apparent agreement with the City of Ferguson in late January 2016,[63] ultimately the City voted to request a series of amendments, seeking to renegotiate the deal because of cost concerns. According to the US Attorney General Loretta Lynch, this left the Department of Justice with no option other than to file a civil-rights lawsuit to force change:

> From the outset, we made clear that our goal was to reach an agreement to avoid litigation. But we also made clear that if there was no agreement, we would be forced to go to court to protect the rights of Ferguson residents. Painstaking negotiations lasted more than 26 weeks as we sought to remedy literally years of systematic deficiencies. A few weeks ago, the Department of Justice and Ferguson's own negotiators came to an

[60] US District Court for the Eastern District of Missouri, *US* v. *City of Ferguson*, Consent Decree, §128, available at: https://assets.documentcloud.org/documents/2699153/Negotiated-Ferguson-Draft-Consent-Decree.pdf.

[61] Ibid., §132. [62] Ibid., §§228–39.

[63] See, e.g., E. Peralta, 'Ferguson, Justice Unveil Draft of Negotiated Consent Decree', *NPR*, Updated 27 January 2016, at: www.npr.org/sections/thetwo-way/2016/01/27/464610005/ferguson-justice-unveil-draft-of-negotiated-consent-decree.

> agreement that was both fair and cost-effective – and that would provide all the residents of Ferguson the constitutional and effective policing and court practices guaranteed to all Americans. As agreed, it was presented to the Ferguson City Council for approval or rejection. And last night, the city council rejected the consent decree approved by their own negotiators. Their decision leaves us no further choice.[64]

The DOJ had more success in 2015 with its discussions with another police department. In May, the DOJ announced that the Department and the City of Cleveland had entered into a court-enforceable agreement to address the DOJ's findings that the Cleveland Division of Police (CDP) was engaging in a pattern or practice of using excessive force in violation of the Fourth Amendment to the US Constitution. The agreement was expected to lead to widespread reforms and changes within the CDP, including greater efforts to build community trust, create a culture of community and problem-oriented policing, and promote officer accountability.

A DOJ investigation published in December 2014 had found 'reasonable cause to believe' that Cleveland police officers had been engaging in 'a pattern or practice of unreasonable and in some cases unnecessary force'. This included unnecessary and excessive use of deadly force, including shootings and head strikes with impact weapons; unnecessary, excessive, or retaliatory use of less-lethal force, including Tasers, chemical spray, and fists; excessive force against persons with mental health problems or in crisis; and poor and dangerous tactics that put officers in situations where force became inevitable.[65]

The 2015 agreement called, among other things, for the CDP to reform its use-of-force policies, 'including requirements for the use of de-escalation techniques whenever possible and appropriate, a prohibition on retaliatory force, mandatory reporting and investigation standards following use of force, and medical care for the subjects of force'. The CDP was also obliged to set up a Mental Health Response Advisory Committee and to provide its officers with sufficient training to identify

[64] 'Attorney General Loretta E. Lynch Delivers Remarks at Press Conference Announcing Lawsuit to Bring Constitutional Policing to Ferguson, Missouri', Washington, DC, 10 February 2016, at: www.justice.gov/opa/speech/attorney-general-loretta-e-lynch-delivers-remarks-press-conference-announcing-lawsuit.

[65] DOJ, 'Justice Department Reaches Agreement with City of Cleveland to Reform Cleveland Division of Police Following the Finding of a Pattern or Practice of Excessive Force', 26 May 2015, at: www.justice.gov/opa/pr/justice-department-reaches-agreement-city-cleveland-reform-cleveland-division-police.

and appropriately respond to situations involving individuals in crisis. Under the agreement, the DOJ and the City of Cleveland are to jointly select an independent monitor to assess and report whether the requirements of the agreement have been implemented for a term of at least five years.[66]

As at April 2017, there was concern that the Trump administration would seek to roll back years of progress by scrapping or scaling down consent decrees agreed with the US Department of Justice following a 'Pattern or Practice' investigation and potentially preventing the Department from engaging in further such investigations.[67]

Peer-to-Peer Learning

Peer-to-peer learning may also help to shape effective use-of-force policies and promote accountability. Thus, with the mounting criticism of US law enforcement in many quarters in 2014 and 2015, in particular regarding excessive use of force against blacks, representatives of US law enforcement travelled to Scotland to find ways for American police officers to improve the way they handle encounters with people who are armed, though not with guns.[68] The group of US leaders learned how the Scottish police equip officers with batons, handcuffs, and pepper spray – but no guns – and how the department's elite armed response teams have shot civilians only twice in the last decade.[69]

As the *New York Times* reported, in Scotland, as elsewhere in the United Kingdom (UK), officers who retreat are not considered 'cowards', as they could be in the United States. Rather, the Scots define backward steps as 'tactical withdrawal', to slow the pace of a street confrontation. In fact, they have taken the American model of hostage negotiation, developed decades ago, and infused it into everyday patrols. A Scottish constable's measure of success is whether everyone involved – not just the police officers – survives the confrontation.[70]

[66] Ibid.

[67] J. Swaine and L. Beckett, 'Jeff Sessions Orders Review of Police Reforms Prompted by High-Profile Shootings, *The Guardian*, 4 April 2017, at: www.theguardian.com/us-news/2017/apr/04/jeff-sessions-review-police-reforms-high-profile-shootings.

[68] A. Baker, 'U.S. Police Leaders, Visiting Scotland, Get Lessons on Avoiding Deadly Force', *New York Times*, 11 December 2015, at: www.nytimes.com/2015/12/12/nyregion/us-police-leaders-visiting-scotland-get-lessons-on-avoiding-deadly-force.html.

[69] Ibid. [70] Ibid.

Technology

Much is being made of the potential contribution of technology, particularly body-worn cameras, to better and more accountable policing. In March 2016, for example, the Independent Police Complaints Commission (IPCC) in the United Kingdom (in an otherwise rather disappointing study of police use of force) opined that body-worn video 'can assist with the investigation of complaints or allegations of misconduct' and recommended that 'all police forces that currently use body-worn video keep footage if a complaint has been made, or a referral has been sent to the IPCC, or if the footage relates to a death or serious injury'.[71] As the IPCC observed, clear standards for retention of footage would help to ensure that important footage is not lost. 'This in turn will help to make sure that the use of force can be scrutinised properly.'

In his April 2015 report on use of information and communications technologies to secure the right to life,[72] the UN Special Rapporteur on extrajudicial, summary or arbitrary executions, Christof Heyns, noted that a 2014 study of the use of this technology in California found that officers' use of force dropped by 59 per cent on the introduction of the cameras, and complaints concerning excessive force dropped by nearly 90 per cent.[73] He cautioned, though, that concerns exist

> around possible violations of the right to privacy that body-worn cameras may generate, leading to suggestions that they be turned off upon entering a home or when speaking with victims. Others consider that individual officers should not have control over their cameras, so as to reduce opportunities for selective documentation.[74] Concerns also exist with respect to access to and secure storage of the footage. Although questions remain to be answered, many feel that the deterrent effect of police body-worn cameras warrants further deployment.[75]

[71] IPCC, *Police Use of Force: Evidence from Complaints, Investigations and Public Perception*, London, March 2016, p. 18.

[72] 'Use of Information and Communications Technologies to Secure the Light to Life, Report on the Special Rapporteur on Extrajudicial, Summary or Arbitrary Executions, Christof Heyns', UN doc. A/HRC/29/37, 24 April 2015.

[73] B. Ariel, W. A. Farrar, and A. Sutherland, 'The Effect of Police Body-Worn Cameras on Use of Force and Citizens' Complaints against the Police: A Randomized Controlled Trial', *Journal of Quantitative Criminology*, November 2014, cited by ibid., §57.

[74] B. Stockley 'Public Support for Police Body Cameras – but Who Controls On/Off Switch?', *The Justice Gap*, March 2014, http://thejusticegap.com/2014/03/body-worn-video-cameras-scrutiny/.

[75] R. Muggah, 'Why Police Body Cameras are Taking Off, even after Eric Garner's Death', *IPI Global Observatory*, 11 December 2014, at: http://theglobalobservatory.org/2014/12/

In his recommendations, the Special Rapporteur called on states to 'consider measures that may be taken innovatively to use ICTs [information and communication technologies] to prevent violations of the right to life by its agents, particularly the excessive use of force by law enforcement officers, or in custodial settings. That could include, but is not limited to, innovations such as body-worn cameras, with due consideration given to the necessary safeguards of the right to privacy'.[76]

Violence as a Catalyst for Reform

The modern era has seen many efforts to enhance accountability in law enforcement agencies; too often, however, they have occurred belatedly and only as the result of an explosion of violence as frustration within a particular community has boiled over. Thus, reform of policing in South Africa, the United Kingdom, and the United States has often been prompted by outbreaks of public violence prompted, or in reaction to, excessive police use of force where accountability was visibly absent. India, the example that ends this section, can be seen as a case in which root and branch reform is desperately needed, the nation's police force a legacy of the harsh colonial policing bequeathed by the British (see Chapter 1). One can but hope that an Indian government in a very near future takes on the challenge of this enterprise of police reform for otherwise citizens might turn to violence to force change through.

The Case of the United Kingdom

On the weekend of 10–12 April 1981, hundreds of mostly black youths rioted in Brixton, an area of South London. Police were attacked with stones, bricks, iron bars, and petrol bombs; this was the first time that petrol bombs had been used on mainland Britain. The worst of the violence occurred on the evening of 11 April when 279 policemen and at least 45 members of the public were injured. Widespread looting took

police-body-cameras-eric-garner/; see also A. Mateescu, A. Rosenblat and D. Boyd, 'Police Body-Worn Cameras', Data & Society Research Institute Working Paper, February 2015, at: www.datasociety.net/pubs/dcr/PoliceBodyWornCameras.pdf. 'Use of Information and Communications Technologies to Secure the Right to Life, Report on the Special Rapporteur on Extrajudicial, Summary or Arbitrary Executions, Christof Heyns', §59.

[76] Ibid., §119.

place and twenty-eight buildings were damaged or destroyed by fire as were numerous police cars and other vehicles.[77]

According to one report, a catalyst in the days before the riot was the decision of the Metropolitan Police Force (later renamed the Metropolitan Police Service, MPS, to reflect better its duty to 'serve and protect') to launch the ill-conceived and tactlessly named Operation Swamp. Operation Swamp saw hundreds of police officers sent in to stop and search local (mostly Black) youth, with no legal requirement at that time of 'reasonable cause to suspect' that the targets of the operation were either committing a crime or were about to do so.[78] It is difficult to see how police officers can be held accountable for abuse of their constabulary powers when there is no legal standard for the officer to meet. The onus is thereby shifted to the victim to prove that power was exercised in a discriminatory manner.

> On the first day of the Brixton riots, officers attempted to arrest youths who had stabbed a young man, without success. The victim ran away, not wanting the police's help, and the officers followed. When they caught up with him he was bleeding profusely. The crowd thought the police had injured him. In the aftermath of Operation Swamp and those years of mutual suspicion, they were seen as the enemy. What the crowd mistakenly thought had occurred was enough to start battles between them and the police.[79]

Lord Scarman was appointed by the Secretary of State for Home Affairs, William Whitelaw, to 'inquire urgently' into the violence and 'to report, with the power to make recommendations'. Lord Scarman concluded that 'complex political, social and economic factors' had created a 'disposition towards violent protest'. He believed that the violence was not planned, but a spontaneous outburst of built-up resentment sparked by particular incidents. In particular, he found loss of confidence and mistrust in the police and their methods of policing. Liaison arrangements between police, community, and local authority had already collapsed before the disturbances.[80]

The Scarman Report recommended concerted efforts to recruit more ethnic minorities into the police force and changes in training and law

[77] BBC, 'Q&A: The Scarman Report', 27 April 2004, at: http://news.bbc.co.uk/2/hi/programmes/bbc_parliament/3631579.stm.

[78] 'The Scarman Report – 30 Years On', Nothing Like the Sun (blog), 1 September 2011, at: https://ffgqc.wordpress.com/2011/09/01/the-scarman-report-30-years-on/.

[79] Ibid. [80] Ibid.

enforcement rules and procedures. One of the indirect results of the report was the 1984 Police and Criminal Evidence Act, which set out how police officers were to carry out their duties. It required specific codes of practice for police procedures and established the rights of suspects detained by the police.[81]

Today, policing in the United Kingdom needs to take another step forward in robust, independent oversight with concerns about the fitness for purpose of the Independent Police Complaints Commission (IPCC) widely expressed. Whether its renaming will be sufficient to restore confidence in the mechanism remains to be seen.

The Case of the United States

A decade later, the 1991 report of the Christopher Commission that followed the videotaped beating of black motorist Rodney King detailed a culture of racism and abuse within the Los Angeles Police Department (LAPD), where excessive force was not only tolerated but often also covered up by fellow officers in a code of silence.[82] The riots in Los Angeles that erupted on 29 April 1992 after four white police officers were acquitted of criminal charges over the assault on Mr King led to fifty-four deaths, days of looting and burning, and US$1 billion of damage to the city. A state of emergency was declared in South Central Los Angeles.[83]

Change, particularly the move to a more multicultural LAPD, was slow to come. When the Commission released its report and recommended ways to reduce racism, sexism, and use of excessive force, some officers reportedly held a bonfire party to show what they thought of the findings.[84] In 1992, some LAPD officers reporting on disturbances in the black communities of South Los Angeles were said to use code to describe disturbances in their areas: NHI – 'No Humans Involved'.[85]

Five years after the Christopher Commission published its findings, a follow-up report called for a 'new standard of accountability', recommending that all personnel within the LAPD 'explicitly be held responsible for their personal acts and omissions, and, when reasonable and

[81] Ibid.
[82] Independent Commission on the Los Angeles Police Department, 9 July 1991.
[83] R. Morris, 'LA Riots: How 1992 Changed the Police', *BBC*, 28 April 2012, at: www.bbc.com/news/world-us-canada-17878180.
[84] Ibid. [85] Ibid.

appropriate, the acts and omissions of their direct and indirect subordinates'.[86] The report concluded that:

> Ugly incidents will not diminish until ranking officers know they will be held responsible for what happens in their sector, whether or not they personally participate.[87]

The LAPD's strategic plan through to 2020 sets as one of its ten strategic goals to 'Drive Accountability and Reward Creativity'.[88] Notable by its absence is any reference to holding individual officers more accountable for their actions, beyond the deployment of body-worn cameras with all LAPD officers. That much delayed measure was finally voted through in June 2016, with the Los Angeles City Council's unanimous approval of a $69.6 million plan to place body-worn cameras on 7,000 Los Angeles patrol officers by the end of 2017.[89]

The LAPD's strategic plan claimed that by 2020 Los Angeles would be the safest big city in the United States; one measure would be the lowest overall use of force by the police.[90] In September 2015, however, activists claimed that the LAPD had killed more people that year than any other law enforcement agency in the United States. In November, *The Guardian* newspaper was reporting official statistics that so far that year, there had been 45 officer-involved shootings, 19 of which were fatal, compared to 23 shootings through the same period in 2014.[91] Matthew Johnson, the president of the Los Angeles Police Commission, said his plan to lower the number of officer-involved shootings in the city would include increasing relationship-based policing and wider use of Tasers and beanbag shotguns. He has also proposed an analysis of the department's use of force over the past decade with a comparison to large agencies across

86 M. J. Bobb *et al.*, *Five Years Later: A Report to the Los Angeles Police Commission on the Los Angeles Police's Implementation of the Independent Commission Recommendations*, Report, Los Angeles, May 1996, p. 62.

87 Ibid., p. ii.

88 LAPD, 'LAPD in 2020', at: http://assets.lapdonline.org/assets/pdf/LAPD%20Strategic%20Plan.pdf.

89 F. Stoltze, 'LA City Council Approves $69.6 Million Body Camera Program for LAPD', *KPCC* (radio), 22 June 2016, at: www.scpr.org/news/2016/06/22/61881/la-city-council-approves-69-6-million-body-camera/.

90 'LAPD in 2020', p. 1.

91 Associated Press, 'Shootings Involving Los Angeles Police Officers have Doubled this Year', *The Guardian*, 11 November 2015, at: www.theguardian.com/us-news/2015/nov/11/los-angeles-police-shootings-double-this-year.

the country.[92] A man wearing a Black Lives Matter T-shirt was quoted as remarking at a Police Commission meeting, though: 'We come here every day on behalf of people who have died, on behalf of the families of people who have died in Los Angeles, by the police department, and you laugh in our faces. You won't listen to us.'[93]

Elsewhere in California, in October 2016 the DOJ released a highly critical report on the San Francisco Police Department (SFPD), finding that, from May 2013 to May 2016, nine out of eleven individuals fatally shot by police were people of colour. Investigations into all but one of those cases remained ongoing. San Francisco is one of the only cities in the United States not to allow police officers to carry Tasers. The DOJ has recommended that the SFPD implement 272 reforms following the six-month investigation that found 'numerous indicators of implicit and institutionalized bias against minority groups'.[94] One of these involved enhancing investigations of officer use of force. According to the DOJ,

> There is minimal documentation of witnesses, no separate or summarized interview of witnesses, no routine collection of photographic evidence, and minimal analysis of the event from an evidentiary standpoint. If a supervisor does not respond, then it falls to the officer who used force to complete the investigation, which is unacceptable.[95]

The Case of South Africa

In South Africa, the Marikana Commission of Inquiry was appointed by the South African President, Jacob Zuma, on 23 August 2012 'to investigate matters of public, national and international concern' arising from events at the Lonmin mine in Marikana, some 100km north-west of Johannesburg, in the North West Province on 11–16 August 2012, which

[92] Ibid.

[93] P. M. Beers, 'As LAPD Killings Soar, Police Commission Trying to Remove Last Shred of Accountability', *Anti Media*, 14 September 2015, at: http://theantimedia.org/as-lapd-killings-soar-police-commission-trying-to-remove-last-shred-of-accountablility/.

[94] J. C. Wong, 'DoJ Review of San Francisco Police Finds "Institutional Bias" against Minorities', *The Guardian*, 13 October 2016, at: www.theguardian.com/us-news/2016/oct/12/san-francisco-police-justice-department-report-bias.

[95] Office of Community Oriented Policing Services, *Collaborative Reform Initiative: An Assessment of the San Francisco Police Department*, Washington, DC, October 2016, Finding 18, p. 47, available at: https://info.publicintelligence.net/DoJ-SFPD-Reform.pdf.

led to the deaths of 'approximately' 44 people, injuries to more than 70 others, and the arrest of some 250 people.[96]

The worst of the violence occurred on 16 August 2012, when the South African Police Service (SAPS) opened fire on striking mineworkers at Marikana, killing thirty-four. In the main volley of fire, SAPS officers reportedly fired off 300 rounds in eight seconds, several using automatic rifles.[97] The protesting mineworkers were demanding a wage increase at the Lonmin platinum mine.[98] The Marikana massacre, as it has been referred to in the media, was the single most lethal use of force by South African security forces against civilians since 1960.

The report of the Marikana Commission,[99] a summary of which was delivered publicly by the South African President in June 2015, found that the police operation should not have taken place on 16 August because of the defects in the planning. The plan was to encircle – effectively kettle – a relatively small group of strikers and then disarm them. The strategy entailed encircling the strikers with barbed wire, and offering them an exit point through which they would need to move while handing over their weapons. The operation needed to be conducted in the morning when relatively few striking miners were present. After delaying the operation and changing tactics, the SAPS leadership did not 'initially' disclose to the Commission the fact that the original plan was not capable of being implemented as planned and that it had been abandoned.[100]

The Commission also found that the operation should have been stopped after the shooting at the first scene of bloodshed and that command and control at the second was completely lacking. There was a delay of about an hour in getting medical assistance to injured strikers

[96] The Marikana Commission of Inquiry, 'About the Commission', undated but accessed on 13 February 2016 at: www.marikanacomm.org.za/.

[97] See, e.g., A. Saba, S. Cele, and M. Hussain, 'Marikana Countdown to Disaster', at: https://city_press.atavist.com/-marikana-countdown-to-disaster.

[98] South African History Online, 'Marikana Massacre 16 August 2012', at: www.sahistory.org.za/article/marikana-massacre-16-august-2012.

[99] *Marikana Commission of Inquiry: Report on Matters of Public, National and International Concern arising out of the Tragic Incidents at the Lonmin Mine in Marikana, in the North West Province*, 2015, at: www.sahrc.org.za/home/21/files/marikana-report-1.pdf.

[100] 'Release by President Jacob Zuma of the Report of the Judicial Commission of Inquiry into the events at the Marikana Mine in Rustenburg, Union Buildings, Pretoria', Marikana Commission of Inquiry, 25 June 2015, at: www.thepresidency.gov.za/pebble.asp?relid=19997.

at the first scene and at least one striker might have survived if he had been treated in a timely manner.[101]

The Commission recommended that plans to demilitarise and professionalise the SAPS should be implemented as a matter of priority. It called on the SAPS and its members to 'accept that they have a duty of public accountability and truth-telling because they exercise force on behalf of all South Africans'. In implying that the Independent Police Investigations Directorate (IPID) was not fit for the purpose of oversight of the SAPS it called for the IPID's staffing and resourcing to be reviewed 'to ensure that it is able to carry out its functions effectively'. The Commission also noted that, in operations with a high likelihood that force will be used, the policing plan should include the provision of adequate and speedy first aid to the injured. Specialist firearm officers should receive additional training in basic first-aid skills needed to deal with gunshot wounds.[102]

In October 2015, President Zuma suspended SAPS Police Commissioner, General Riah Phiyega, while allegations of misconduct in relation to her role in the killing of the miners were examined. General Phiyega had disputed the findings of the Commission of Inquiry and defended police handling of the strike.[103] At the beginning of February 2016, it was announced that criminal cases had been opened against General Phiyega for allegedly obstructing the work of the Marikana Commission of Inquiry.[104]

No one in power had otherwise been charged or held responsible for the killings. In January 2016, though, Police Minister Nathi Nhleko announced that a panel of experts was being established to study and help implement the Commission of Inquiry's recommendations.[105]

The Case of India

In India, the world's largest democracy, some 1.5 million officers police a population that numbers more than 1.25 billion. Yet the federal statute

[101] Ibid. [102] Ibid.

[103] BBC, 'Marikana Inquiry: South Africa Police Chief Suspended', 14 October 2015, at: www.bbc.com/news/world-africa-34532893.

[104] T. Gqirana, 'Criminal Cases Opened against Phiyega, Mbombo', *News24*, 2 February 2016, at: www.news24.com/SouthAfrica/News/criminal-cases-opened-against-phiyega-mbombo-20160202.

[105] B. Bateman, 'Panel of Experts to Study, Implement Marikana Commission of Inquiry Recommendations', *EyeWitness News*, 24 January 2016, at: http://ewn.co.za/2016/01/24/Panel-of-experts-to-study-and-implement-Marikana-Commission-of-Inquirys-recommendations.

that governs the police remains the 1861 Police Act that was enacted by a British colonial government. The law was passed in the wake of the Indian Sepoy Mutiny in 1857, when Indian soldiers in the colonial army revolted against their British commanders. Though the mutiny, which developed into a rebellion against British rule in India, was forcibly put down, it spurred the British into taking steps to consolidate their rule in India, including through the establishment of an authoritarian police force to support the colonial government.[106]

The problems of a police force that is subservient to the executive and which in turn the executive protects from accountability persist to this day. Thus, in August 2009 Human Rights Watch published a report entitled *Broken System: Dysfunction, Abuse, and Impunity in the Indian Police*, in which the organisation stated that:

> While India rightly touts itself as an emerging economic powerhouse that is also the world's largest democracy, its police forces — the most visible arm of the Indian state — are widely regarded within India as lawless, abusive and ineffective.
>
> A dangerous anachronism, the police have largely failed to evolve from the ruler-supportive, repressive forces they were designed to be under Britain's colonial rule. While sixty years later much of India is in the process of rapid modernization, the police continue to use their old methods. Instead of policing through public consent and participation, the police use abuse and threats as a primary crime investigation and law enforcement tactic. The institutional culture of police practically discourages officers from acting otherwise, failing to give them the resources, training, ethical environment, and encouragement to develop professional police tactics. Many officers even told Human Rights Watch that they were ordered or expected to commit abuses.[107]

In 1968, the Khosla Commission had famously declared that: 'Independent India must choose whether we will have a people's police or a ruler appointed police, or in other words whether the people should rule or whether the parties should rule. The Constitution has laid down that the people should rule, so the police must also be the people's police.'[108]

[106] G. P. Joshi, 'Police Accountability in India', *Human Rights Initiative*, pp. 1–2, at: www.humanrightsinitiative.org/programs/aj/police/papers/gpj/police_accountability_in_india.pdf.

[107] Human Rights Watch, *Broken System: Dysfunction, Abuse, and Impunity in the Indian Police*, 4 August 2009, at: www.hrw.org/report/2009/08/04/broken-system/dysfunction-abuse-and-impunity-indian-police.

[108] See, e.g., U. Baxi, *The Crisis of the Indian Legal System. Alternatives in Development: Law*, Vikas Publishing House, India, December 1982, ch. 4

In November 1977, a National Police Commission was appointed to examine the role and performance of the police both as a law enforcing agency and as an institution to protect the rights of the citizens enshrined in the Constitution. The Commission called for a new statute to replace the 1861 Police Act, a call repeated by India's Supreme Court in 2006 in its judgment in the landmark case, *Prakash Singh* v. *Union of India.*[109] Among many other recommendations, the Court also called for a Police Complaints Authority to be set up to oversee the work of the police.

According to one commentator, 'where the police are needed by government to deal with serious or significant law and order problems of political significance such as terrorism, police excesses get state implicit or even explicit approval, if not encouragement and support. In some cases, the assurance of impunity is granted in advance'.[110] The example is cited of an address to state police officers on 30 April 1998 by the Chief Minister of the state of Uttar Pradesh, Mr Kalyan Singh:

> I want performance results. I want you to take a vow that you will create a dhamaka [explosion] in the state. If noted criminals can be liquidated in encounters, do it. If you take the life of one person who has taken the lives of 10 others, then people will praise you. And I am here to protect you.[111]

As was observed, 'When the assurance of impunity comes from the highest quarter in the State, police officers become emboldened to misuse their powers or to become silent spectators to incidents involving major violations of law.'[112]

To improve accountability in the police force, the 1977 Commission had argued that a judicial inquiry should be made mandatory where a complaint against the police concerned the alleged rape of a woman in police custody; death or grievous harm caused to a detainee while in police custody; and the death of two or more persons resulting from police firing during dispersal of an unlawful assembly.[113] These recommendations have never been implemented.

The 1993 Protection of Human Rights Act is a potential means by which the police may be held accountable for misuse of force. The Act

[109] Supreme Court of India, *Prakash Singh* v. *Union of India*, Judgment (Writ Petition No. 310 of 1996), 22 September 2006, available at: http://indiankanoon.org/doc/1090328/.

[110] Joshi, 'Police Accountability in India', p. 8.

[111] Cited in G. P. Joshi, *Police Brutality in India, A Media Scan*, Commonwealth Human Rights Initiative, New Delhi, November 2000, p. 12.

[112] Joshi, 'Police Accountability in India', p. 8. [113] Ibid.

established the National Human Rights Commission (NHRC), which receives more complaints about the police than on any other subject. However, the Commission has no power to enforce its decisions, is dependent on government for human and financial resources, and is not authorised to enquire into complaints of violations of human rights committed by the members of the armed forces and certain federal armed police bodies such as the Border Security Force.[114]

Given the major lacunae in ensuring police services that are answerable for their excesses, in 2014 a paper on the legal accountability of the police in India published by the Centre for Law and Policy Research argued that criminal, public, and private law-based remedies (e.g. through tort law) would be worth pursuing, despite the problems experienced in pursuing claims under each body of law.[115]

In the 1990 division bench judgment in *Saheli* v. *Commissioner of Police, Delhi*, a nine-year-old child was beaten up by the police so severely that he later died. The Delhi Administration was ordered to pay compensation of 75,000 rupees (US$4,500 at the time) to the mother of the deceased child on the basis that the state was responsible for the tortious acts of its employees.[116] But in *Sube Singh* v. *State of Haryana*,[117] the Supreme Court held that compensation for violation of constitutional rights would only be ordered if the violation involving custody death or torture is 'established or is incontrovertible' and is gross and of a magnitude to shock the conscience of the court.

Criminal law sanctions for excessive use of police force are also restrained in India. The 1973 Code of Criminal Procedure affords procedural safeguards to government servants performing a public function. Sanction must first be imposed by the national or state government before any criminal proceedings are instituted against a police officer alleged to have committed a criminal offence 'while acting or purporting to act within the discharge of his official duty'.[118]

In certain instances, though, courts have narrowed the scope and nature of acts that fall the purview of within this statutory protection.

[114] Ibid., pp. 13, 14.

[115] 'Legal Accountability of the Police in India', Centre for Law and Policy Research, 2014, at: http://clpr.org.in/wp-content/uploads/2014/02/140214-Police-Accountability-website.pdf.

[116] *All India Reporter* 1990, SC 513.

[117] Supreme Court of India, *Sube Singh* v. *State of Haryana* (2006) 3 SCC 178; see 'Legal Accountability of the Police in India', Centre for Law and Policy Research, p. 7.

[118] S. 132, 1973 Code of Criminal Procedure.

In *Uttarakhand Sangharsh Samiti* v. *State of Uttar Pradesh*,[119] a division bench of the High Court of Allahabad held that 'it is not every act done by a public servant while on duty' that falls within the purview of the 1973 Code, but 'only those acts which have direct nexus to the discharge of official duty'.

The case concerned alleged very widespread human rights violations, including firing by the police and paramilitary forces on an assembly of protestors, which killed twenty-four and mass sexual assaults (including rape), illegal detention, and incarceration. The Court held that acts of wrongful restraint and detention, planting weapons, intentional shooting of unarmed protesters, tampering with or falsifying records, and the commission of rape and sexual assault were not acts done or purported to be done in the discharge of official duties.[120]

[119] High Court of Allahabad, *Uttarakhand Sangharsh Samiti* v. *State of Uttar Pradesh*, *Uttar Pradesh Local Bodies & Educational Cases*, Vol. 31 (1996), p. 461.

[120] 'Legal Accountability of the Police in India', Centre for Law and Policy Research, p. 9.

INDEX